THE PUBLICATIONS

OF THE

𝕾𝖊𝖑𝖉𝖊𝖓 𝕾𝖔𝖈𝖎𝖊𝖙𝖞

περὶ παντὸς τὴν ἐλευθερίαν

VOLUME CXXI

FOR THE YEAR 2004

REPORTS OF CASES

FROM THE TIME OF

KING HENRY VIII

VOLUME II

EDITED

FOR THE SELDEN SOCIETY

BY

J. H. BAKER, Q.C., LL.D., F.B.A.

Downing Professor of the Laws of England, Cambridge;
Honorary Bencher of the Inner Temple

LONDON

SELDEN SOCIETY

2004

Printed on acid-free paper

ISBN 085423 175 7

Typeset and printed in Europe
by the Alden Group, Oxford

CONTENTS

Note that tables of the statutes and cases in both volumes are printed in Volume I.

THE REPORTS

CONTINUED

6. CASES FROM THE NOTEBOOK OF RICHARD POLLARD
(*c.* 1515–1534)[1]

[1]

Abilitie et disabilitie. 23 H. 8. [Fo. 62v.]

En det, dit fuit per tout le court que un alien navera ascun action reall si non que il soit fait deinzin pur ceo que il nest pas able de aver avantage per le ley dengleterre. Et mesme le ley est en trnz de baterie, pur ceo que cel action serra ajuge come le person est. Mez en det quere. Mez Litleton dit que est bon ple en toutz manerz de actions portez per un alien que nest my ney en Engleterre adire que il est alien et nee hors de allegeans le roy, jugement si serra responde etc. Et en toutz ceux casez il avera son remedie devaunt le counsell per bill et nemi auterment: et ceo 13 E. 4, etc. <Pollarde>

[2]

Accessorie al felonie. P. 22 H. 8. [Fo. 53v.]

Nota que si un home est indite come principal et un auter come accessorie, et si eux ii. sont presentz al barre, donques primez serra demande del principal que il voile dire al felonie, et si il plede De rien culpable donques serra demande del accessorie que il voile dire al felony, quel plede auxi De rien culpable, en ceo

---

[1] Extracted from BL MS. Hargrave 388, ff. 13–95, 149–150. These, together with Spelman's reports, were rearranged by or for Christopher Yelverton in a chronological sequence, with undated cases at the end. They are here rearranged under their alphabetical titles as given in the margin. The dates are also written in the margin, above the titles.

6. CASES FROM THE NOTEBOOK OF RICHARD POLLARD
(c. 1515–1534)

Ability and disability

1. ANON.

1531/32.

In debt, it was said by the whole court that an alien shall not have any real action unless he is made a denizen, because he is unable to take advantage by the law of England. The law is the same in trespass for battery, because that action shall be adjudged as the person is. But query in debt. However, Littleton says it is a good plea in all kinds of action brought by an alien who is not born in England to say that he is an alien and born outside the king's allegiance, and pray judgment whether he shall be answered etc.[1] And in all these cases he shall have his remedy before the Council by bill and not otherwise: see this in 13 Edw. IV,[2] etc.

Accessory to felony

2. ANON.

King's Bench, Pas.1530.

Note that if one man is indicted as principal and another as accessory, and both of them are present at the bar, the principal shall be asked first what he will say to the felony; and if he pleads Not guilty the accessory shall then be asked what he will say to the felony, and, if he also pleads Not guilty, in that case one inquest shall be sworn upon them both. And the inquest must first find

---

[1] Littleton, *Tenures*, s. 198.
[2] *The Carrier's Case* (1473) YB Pas. 13 Edw. IV, fo. 9, pl. 5; 64 Selden Soc. 30.

case un enquest serra jure sur eux ii. Et primez il covient que lenquest chaunt del principal, et si il soit trove culpable donques ilz enqueront del accessorie. Mez si[1] ilz trovont le principal de rienz culpable, donques ilz ne parler[ont] pluis de accessorie etc. Et ceo nota per *Fitzjames*, Chiefe Justice etc. <Pollarde>

[3]

Accessorie al felonye. Anno 22 H. 8. [Fo. 53v.]

Nota que si home procure [et commaunde un auter][2] de occiser un auter et puis il luy occist, en ceo case cesti que procure et commaunde de faire le murdre nest auxi principal come cesti que fist le murdre mez il est un accessorie et nemi principal. Et issint vide que home poet estre accessorie devaunt le felonie come puis. Et issint fuit ajuge per un John Bracier, clerke, al Exeter etc. <Pollarde>

[4]

Action populer et barre de ceo. H. 21 H. 8. [Fo. 50.]

Si jeo soy seisi de terre et un auter fait trnz sur le terre et puis jeo alien le terre a un auter, uncore jeo avera bon brefe de trnz del trnz fait devaunt, et ceo per agard etc. <Pollarde>

[5]

Apportionment de rentz et auterz servicez. M. 22 H. 8. [Fo. 53.]

En det fuit dit pur ley per *Fitzjames*, Chiefe Justice de Banke le Roy, que si home ad un acre de terre per bon title et auter acre de terre per disseisin et face lease a terme danz de lez ii. acrez, rendant certen rent, et le disseisie que ad droit a un dez acrez entre en lun de lez ii. acres, ore le rent serra apportion pur ceo que[i] parcel del rent est determine per lact del estraunger et nemi per le acte del lessour: quod nota. <Pollarde>

---

[1] *Interlined.*   [2] *Altered from* un auter et commaunde.

a verdict in respect of the principal, and if he is found guilty they shall enquire into the accessory. But if they find the principal not guilty, they shall say no more concerning the accessory etc. Note this, by FITZJAMES, Chief Justice etc.

3. R. v. BRACIER

Exeter assizes, 1530/31.

Note that if a man procures and commands another to kill someone, and afterwards he kills him, in this case the person who procured and commanded the murder to be done is not also a principal, like him who committed the murder, but is an accessory and not a principal. Observe, therefore, that a man may be accessory before the felony as well as after. So it was adjudged in respect of one John Bracier, clerk, at Exeter etc.

Action popular

4. ANON.

Hil 1530.

If I am seised of land and someone else commits a trespass upon the land, and afterwards I alien the land to another, I may still have a good writ of trespass for the earlier trespass; and this [was adjudged] by award etc.

Apportionment

5. RYSHTON v. CRIPCE[1]

Exchequer Chamber, *c.* 1531.

In debt it was said for law by FITZJAMES, Chief Justice of the King's Bench, that if someone has an acre of land by good title and another acre of land by disseisin, and makes a lease for a term of years of the two acres, rendering certain rent, and the disseisee who has right to one of the acres enters in one of the two acres, the rent shall now be apportioned, because part of the rent is determined by the act of the stranger and not by the act of the lessor: note that.

---

[1] Probably: cf. next case.

[6]

Apportionment de rentz et servicez. M. 23 H. 8. [Ff. 62–63.]

Nota que dit fuit per *Spilman, Ingelfeilde* et *Fitzherbert*, Justicez, que si home fait lease a terme danz de ii. acrez de terre rendant x. li. de rent, et le lesse graunt tout son estate que il ad en un de lez ii. acrez a un auter, que donques chescun de eux tiendra pro particula et serra apportion per le comen ley et nemi per lestatut, quar lestatut parle ou feffement en fee est fait, per que ceo est per le comen ley et nemi per lestatut. Et issint est si le revercion discende a ii. homez, scilicet a lun come heire a son pier et a lauter come heire a sa mier, en cest case serra apportion. Et issint est sur un surrendre, mez nemi sur un entre per tout en parte etc. En lescheker chambre. Et auxi si le lessour recover parte de terrez lessez per brefe de wast, que en ceo case le rent serra auxi apportion. Et auxi dit fuit que rent fuit apportionable al comen ley devaunt lestatut per le act de tenant, come si le tenant enfeffe le seignior de parcel de tenancie, que donques le rent serra apportion et chescun tiendra pro particula sua. Et ore per lestatut est done que si un estraunger purchase parte del tenancie donques le tenant tiendra pro particula sua. Et sic nota diversitatem etc.<Pollarde>

[7]

Avouson. [Fo. 149.]

Nota que sont vii. voiez a faire avouson voide. Inprimis un resignation, et ceo est lou le parson ou vicar desglise voile resigner en lez mainz le ordinarie. Privation est lou lencumbent est deprive de son benefice pur cause spirituall, et ceo fait lesglie voide. Creation est lou un parson ou vicar est create evesque, toutz cez beneficez sont voide per le creation et nemi adevaunt. Cession est lou home ad ii. beneficez ove cure, ou deux dignities en un esglise, sanz dispensation ou pluralitie, si il eux teigne ii. moiz ambideux sont voide. Et ceo appert 14 E. 3, f. 6. Mez de ii. dignitiez ou ii. prebentz en un esglise,

6. RYSHTON v. CRIPCE

Exchequer Chamber, Mich. 1531. Also reported in Dyer, fo. 4; Spelman, pp. 16–17, 93-95; Yorke, above, p. 193, no. 267; and Yelverton, below, p. 290, no. 1. Record: KB 27/1076, m. 33 (Trin. 1530; pr. 94 Selden Soc. 290).

Note that it was said by SPELMAN, ENGLEFIELD and FITZHERBERT, Justices, that if someone makes a lease for a term of years of two acres of land, rendering £10 rent, and the lessee grants to another all his estate which he has in one of the two acres, then each of them shall hold *pro particula* and it shall be apportioned by the common law and not by the statute;[1] for the statute speaks of the case where a feoffment is made in fee, and so this is by the common law and not by the statute. So it is if a reversion descends to two men, namely to one of them as heir to his father and to the other as heir to his mother: in this case it shall be apportioned. So it is upon a surrender; but not upon an entry by all in part etc. (In the Exchequer Chamber.) Also, if the lessor recovers part of the lands leased by a writ of waste, in this case also the rent shall be apportioned. It was also said that rent was apportionable at common law, before the statute, by the act of the tenant: as where the tenant enfeoffs the lord of part of the tenancy, the rent shall be apportioned and each of them shall hold *pro particula sua*. And now by the statute it is enacted that if a stranger purchases part of the tenancy the tenant shall hold *pro particula sua*. Thus note the distinction etc.

Advowson

7. NOTE

Undated.

Note that there are seven ways to make an advowson vacant:[2] [1] resignation, and that is where the parson or vicar of a church will resign into the ordinary's hands; [2] deprivation is where the incumbent is deprived of his benefice for a spiritual cause, and that makes the church vacant; [3] creation is where a parson or vicar is created bishop: all his benefices are vacant by the creation and not before; [4] cession is where someone has two benefices with cure, or two dignities in one church, without dispensation or plurality: if he keeps them for two months, both become vacant—and this appears in 14 Edw.

---

[1] 18 Edw. I, *Quia emptores* (*SR* i. 106).

[2] There are really only five listed here, since nos. 5 and 6 did not result in a vacancy. Cf. the medieval form of the mnemonic, which listed four kinds of avoidance: *Catalogue of English Legal MSS. in Cambridge University Library*, p. xxvii.

ambideux ne sont my voide mez il perdra le primer per le prisel del darrein. Consolidation est lou sont ii. beneficez que sont cy pover que ambideux ne purront my estre serve per ii. priestes, ore per agrement de patron et ordinarie ilz ferront eux ii. destre un benefice, et pur ceo lun est void, de quel avoidanz nul avera avauntage. Appropriation est lou esglise est appropriate al patron, come a un abbe etc., et ceo ne fait le esglise voide. Provision fait le esglise voide. <Pollarde>

[8]

Avowre. Anno 21 H. 8. [Fo. 50.]

Nota que un estatut fuit fait que le seignior poet faire [avowre][1] pur rent service ou auter service sur le terre issint tenus de luy as in landes within his fee et seignorie, et sur nul person certen, et ceo est assetz bon etc.<Pollarde>

[9]

Barre per jugement sanz execution pleder. M. 23 H. 8. [Fo. 63.]

Vide que fuit dit per *Fitzherbert*, Justice, pur ley que en det vers executourz quex pledont Pleinement administre forsque x. li. et pur lez x. li. il dit que un auter pendant cel brefe suist tiel brefe de det vers luy et avoit jugement de recover lez x. li. etc., que ceo est bon ple en barre de lez x. li. nient obstant que il ne dit ouster, scilicet que il ad auxi execution de mesme lez x. li. Et la cause est pur ceo que lez x. li. sont liez per cest jugement en cez mainz, per que etc. 9 E. 4. <Pollarde>

[1] avoir'.

III, fo. 6[1]—though where there are two dignities or two prebends in one church both are not vacated, but he shall lose the former by taking the latter; [5] consolidation is where there are two benefices which are so poor that both cannot be served by two priests, and so by agreement of the patron and ordinary they make these two into one benefice, thereby one of them is vacated, though no one shall take advantage of this vacancy; [6] appropriation is where a church is appropriated to the patron, as to an abbot etc., but that does not make the church vacant; [7] provision makes the church vacant.

Avowry

8. ANON.

Probably Common Pleas, 1529/30.

Note that a statute was made[2] that the lord may make avowry for rent-service or other service upon the land so held of him 'as in lands within his fee and lordship', and not upon any person certain, and this is good enough etc.

Bar

9. GRYSLYNG v. BOROUGH

Common Pleas, Mich. 1531. Record: CP 40/1071, m. 548.

Observe that it was stated as law by FITZHERBERT, Justice, that in debt against executors, who plead Fully administered except for £10, and for the £10 they say that someone else pending this writ sued a writ of debt against them and had judgment to recover the £10 etc., this is a good plea in bar of the £10 even though they did not go on to say that he also had execution for the same £10. The reason is because the £10 in their hands is bound by this judgment, and so etc. 9 Edw. IV.[3]

---

[1] YB Mich. 14 Edw. III (Rolls Ser.), p. 36, pl. 12.
[2] 21 Hen. VIII, c. 19 (*SR* iii. 303).   [3] YB Trin. 9 Edw. IV, fo. 12, pl. 4.

Note from the record

CP 40/1071, m. 548, Conyngesby.

William Gryslyng, citizen and mercer of London, brings debt against Katherine Borough, widow and executrix of Henry Borough, gentleman of the cardinal's household, otherwise called Katherine, Lady Stryklond, for £180 on a bond made on 4 Nov. [1527], 19 Hen. VIII, in the ward of St Stephen Walbrook, payable on 1 May 1528. The defendant pleads that she has fully administered save for £30 which Ralph Waren, citizen and alderman of London, has recovered against her, as executrix, in a

[10]

Brefe al evesque. M. 21 H. 8. [Fo. 50.]

En quare impedit port vers le patron et lencumbent deinz le vi. moiz, et devaunt que le pleintife ad son jugement lez vi. moiz passa, uncore le pleintife avera brefe al evesque per agarde etc. <Pollarde>

[11]

Colour en trnz. M. 25 H. 8. [Fo. 83v.]

En trnz le defendant justifie pur ceo que un J. S. fuit seisie de [acre de terre dont]¹ le lue ou le trnz est suppose destre fait et issint seisie fist lease a un R. P. a terme danz, et le defendant come servaunt al dit R. P. et per son comaundement entra et fist le trnz etc. Et agarde fuit en lescheker pur nul ple, pur ceo que il ne done al pleintife un colour. Et est un diversitie quaunt home justifie en auter droit, come servauntz et fait title a son master, come le case est adevaunt, et quaunt il ne fait ascun title a son master, come le defendant dit que le liewe ou etc. est le fraunctenement dun A. B. et come servaunt a luy et per son commaundement il entra come bien a luy list, ceo est bon ple sanz

¹ *Corrected by Y from* de le lue ou.

Note from the record

De Banco roll, Mich. 1531.

[continued from opposite page]

writ of debt on a bond; and she sets out the record of Waren's action, commencing with a writ purchased on 6 April 1531. The plaintiff replies that she had sufficient other goods in her hands on the day when his writ was purchased, and issue is joined thereon.

Writ to the bishop ('Brefe')

10. ANON.

Common Pleas, Mich. 1529. Also reported below, p. 257, no. 26.

In *quare impedit* brought against the patron and the incumbent within the six months, the six months elapsed before the plaintiff had his judgment; nevertheless the plaintiff shall have a writ to the bishop, by award of the court etc.

Colour in trespass

11. ANON.

Exchequer, Mich. 1533.

In trespass the defendant justified because one John Style was seised of an acre of land whereof the place where the trespass is supposed to have been committed is part, and being so seised made a lease to one R. P. for a term of years, and the defendant as servant to the said R. P. and by his command entered and committed the trespass etc. And it was awarded in the Exchequer to be no plea, because he did not give the plaintiff a colour. There is a distinction when someone justifies in right of another, as where he is a servant and makes title to his master—as the case is above—and when he does not make any title to his master, as where the defendant says that the place where etc. is the freehold of one A. B., and as his servant and by his command he

colour pur ceo que il ne fait ascun title a son master, come le primer case est: quod nota. <Pollarde>

[12]

[Conclusion]. *Ou home serra conclude per acceptans de servicez etc.*
M. 25 H. 8. [Fo. 83v.]

Si enfant fait lease a terme danz rendant certen rent et quant il vient a son pleine age il accepte le rent, dit fuit que il ne avoidra en apres cest lease etc.<Pollarde>

[13]

Condition, ou serra voide et ou nemy. T. 21 H. 8. [Fo. 50.]

Vide si home done terre a un auter en le taile sur condition que si il aliena a ascun person que donques le donour et cez heirez bein poient entrer ceo est bon condition, et le donour et cez heirez bein enteront: quod nota. 10 H. 7, f. 11. <Pollarde>

entered, as well he might, this is a good plea without colour, because he does not make any title to his master as in the former case: note that.[1]

Conclusion[2]

12. NOTE

Mich. 1533.

If an infant makes a lease for a term of years, rendering certain rent, and when he reaches his full age he accepts the rent, it was said that he may not afterwards avoid this lease etc.

Condition

13. NOTE

Trin. 1529.

Observe that if someone gives land to another in tail upon condition that if he aliens to any person the donor and his heirs may well enter, this is a good condition and the donor and his heirs may well enter: note that. 10 Hen. VII, fo. 11.[3]

---

[1] There are marginal references to YB Pas. 2 Edw. IV, fo. 8, pl. 18; Mich. 12 Edw. IV, fo. 15, pl. 17; Hil. 10 Hen. VII, fo. 14, pl. 10; Hil. 5 Hen. VII, fo. 11, pl. 3.

[2] I.e. estoppel (in pais). But there is also a heading *Estoppel* at p. 258, below.

[3] YB Mich. 10 Hen. VII, fo. 11, pl. 28. This is identifiable as *Hulcote* v. *Ingleton* (1493) CP 40/924, m. 156; YB Mich. 11 Hen. VII, fo. 6, pl. 25; Port, p. 87; Caryll's reports, 115 Selden Soc. 138.

[14]

Conspiracie. P. 26 H. 8. [Fo. 94v.]

Nota que est dit per ascunz de le court que si home soit jury et don evidenz vers un home pur luy enditer, que donques il ne serra punis de ceo en apres del conspiracie, pur ceo que il est jurye. Et est auxi agre pur bon ley per tout le court que si home vient a lez justicez et dit a eux que il savoit bien que un J. S. fist tiel murdre ou tiel felony, per que lez justicez luy commaund de doner ceo en evidens, et sur ceo est jurye, il ceo pledra en conspiracye. Et bon ple de justification, pur ceo que il est comaunde de doner le evidenz et auxi pur ceo que il est jurye. Issint quant home est jurye il serra intende que il ne ceo fait del malis mez sur le verite que il savoit. Mez nota que conspiracie serra proprement lou ii. ou plus voilent conspirer de inditer un auter et ilz ne sont mye jurez sur ceo mez ilz font privement [de]¹ luy inditer, donques ceo est conspiracie et en nul auter maner etc.<Pollarde>

[15]

Contracte. 14 H. 8. [Fo. 30v.]

En second deliveranz dit fuit per *Fitzherbert* que si jeo vende mon chival a un auter pur x. li. en ceo case est bon contracte, mez il navera le chival si non que il

---

¹ *Interlined after* luy.

Conspiracy

14. WALKER v. COLLYNS[1]

Common Pleas, Pas. 1534. Record: CP 40/1081, m. 444 (*Walker v. Collyns*), or ibid., m. 449 (*Melley v. Stafford*). Perhaps the case reported in Yorke, above, p. 216, no. 340 (dated Mich. 1535). Cf. Yelverton, below, p. 317, no. 12 (1528/29), which is a different case, as is YB Pas. 27 Hen. VIII, fo. 2, pl. 6 (Pas. 1535).

Note that it is said by some members of the court that if a man is sworn and gives evidence against someone to indict him,[2] he shall not be punished for this afterwards as a conspiracy, because he was sworn. It is also agreed as good law by the whole court that if someone comes to the justices and says to them that he knows well that one John Style committed such and such a murder or felony, as a result of which the justices command him to give this in evidence, whereupon he is sworn, he may plead this in an action of conspiracy and it is a good plea of justification, because he was commanded to give the evidence and also because he was sworn. Thus when someone is sworn it shall be presumed that he did not do it of malice but upon the truth that he knows. But note that a conspiracy is properly where two or more conspire to indict another, and they are not sworn to do it but act secretly to indict him: that is a conspiracy, and not in any other way etc.

Contract

15. SOUTHWALL v. HUDDELSTON

Common Pleas, 1522. Also reported in YB Hil. 14 Hen. VIII, fo. 17, pl. 6 (119 Selden Soc. 150); Spelman, pp. 136, 137. Record: CP 40/1030, m. 731 (judgment for plaintiff, Mich. 1522); printed, 102 Selden Soc. 90–94. A writ of error was sued on 20 May 1523, and judgment affirmed Pas. 1524; the King's Bench proceedings are reported in Port, p. 90.

In second deliverance it was said by FITZHERBERT that if I sell my horse to another for £10, in this case it is a good contract but he shall not have the horse

---

[1] Or *Melley v. Stafford*: see headnote. Both have almost identical pleadings, though they are unrelated: Thomas Walker was acquitted at Northampton assizes, John Melley at Worcester. In the former case the jury was discharged by consent at the assizes (summer 1534) and a *venire de novo* awarded; in the second case there is no *postea*.

[2] I.e. before the grand jury. Each defendant pleaded that, since the plaintiff was suspected by the common voice and fame of stealing his goods, he so informed the justices at the sessions, and they gave him an oath to say the truth according to his conscience, and then commanded him upon this oath to inform the grand jurors ('juratores sessionis illius qui pro domino rege adtunc ibidem jurati et onerati fuerunt') of the truth concerning the felony ('de perfecta noticia et veritate quam ipse tunc habuit de perpetratione felonie predicte'), which he did, and concluded by traversing the conspiracy with an *absque hoc*.

paia lez x. li. maintenaunt. Mez auterment est si jeo don a luy un jour de paiement, quar la il avera le chival maintenaunt saunz paier lez denerz etc. Et *Pollard* fuit de mesme loppinion etc. <Pollarde>

[16]

Contracte. 14 H. 8. [Fo. 30v.]

Nota que est dit per toutz lez justicez que si jeo vende a vous mon terre pur certen denerz destre paiez <a un>[i] jour, que non obstaunt que nest pas ascun dener paie maintenaunt uncore le bargaine est bon et ceo change le use maintenaunt, et le vendour avera action de det a son jour de paiement. Et mesme le ley est mis per *Fitzherbert*: si jeo vende a vous mon terre pur certen some dargent destre paie quant le maior de Londres vient al Westm', ceo est bon bargain et contract maintenaunt, et si il ne unques vient a Westm' il avera unques sez denerz etc. <Pollarde>

[17]

Contracte. 14 H. 8. [Fo. 31.]

Nota que dit fuit per *Norwich*, Chiefe Justice de Comen Banke, que si home vende a moy son terre pur x. li. destre paie a certen jour que donques le use est change maintenaunt sanz ascun dener paie, pur ceo que est son folie de limiter tiel jour de paiement. Mez auterment est si home vende a moy terre pur certen some dargent et nul jour limitte quant ceo serra paie ne nul dener est paie en poigne, mez issint ilz departe: en ceo case ceo nest mye ascun bargaine ne per ceo ascun use change pur que nest ascun dener paie ne ascun jour limit quant lez denerz serront paiez: quod nota. <Pollarde>

unless he pays the £10 at once. It is otherwise if I give him a day of payment, for there he shall have the horse at once without paying the money etc. POLLARD was of the same opinion etc.

16. SOUTHWALL v. HUDDELSTON

Common Pleas, 1522. See no. 15.

Note that it is said by all the justices that if I sell you my land for certain money to be paid at a specified day, the bargain is good even though no money is paid at once, and it changes the use forthwith; and the vendor shall have an action of debt at his day of payment. The same law is stated by FITZHERBERT: if I sell you my land for a certain sum of money to be paid when the mayor of London comes to Westminster, this is a good bargain and contract at once, and if he never comes to Westminster [I] shall never have [my] money etc.

17. SOUTHWALL v. HUDDELSTON[1]

Common Pleas, 1522 (or perhaps another case after 1530). See no. 15.

Note that it was said by NORWICH, Chief Justice of the Common Bench,[2] that if someone sells me his land for £10 to be paid at a certain day, the use is changed at once without any money paid, because it is his foolishness to appoint such a day of payment. It is otherwise, however, if someone sells me land for a certain sum of money and no day is appointed when it shall be paid, and no cash is paid in hand, but they leave it at that: in that case it is no bargain, and no use is changed by it, because no money is paid and no day is appointed when the money shall be paid: note that.

---

[1] The text is dated 14 Hen. VIII, and presumably belongs with nos. 15–16, but Norwich C.J. was not appointed until 1530.
[2] I.e. 1530–35. This does not square with the date given: last note.

[18]

Conusaunz. [Fo. 149.]

Si conusanz soit graunt, donques le record serra maunde del Comen Place en le court ou le fraunches est. Mez si le conusanz soit demande forsque de parcel del demande, donques issera un transcript de le Comen Place de le record en le court ou conusanz est graunt. Mez auterment est lou ancien demesne est plede a parcel ou a tout, quar la le record ne serra maunde etc. mez il serra mis de suer la per brefe de droit. Et en lauter case il ne poit auterment suer forsque en le Comen Place, et sic quere diversitatem etc. <Pollarde>

[19]

Count. M. 22 H. 8. [Fo. 53v.]

En annuitie, le annuitie fuit graunt a un home pur lez servicez que il ad fait et[i] que il ferra en apres. Et ceo fuit per fait. Et il port brefe de annuitie generalment, et le count fuit challenge pur ceo que il nad allege en son count coment le annuitie fuit graunt pur lez servicez faitz et a faire, et que il ad fait cez servicez al defendant. Et ceo non obstant le count fuit tenuz assetz bon per tout le court. Et lauter [avera][1] avauntage de ceo per pleding, come a reherser tout le fait et que il nad my fait sez servicez etc.<Pollarde>

[1] *Altered from* m[onst]re.

Cognizance

18. NOTE

Undated.

If cognizance is granted, the record shall be sent from the Common Place into the court where the franchise is. But if cognizance is demanded only for part of the claim, then a transcript of the record shall issue from the Common Place into the court where cognizance is granted. But it is otherwise where ancient demesne is pleaded, whether as to part or the whole, for there the record shall not be sent etc. but he shall be driven to sue there by writ of right. And in the other case he cannot sue otherwise than in the Common Place, so query the distinction etc.

Count

19. ANON.[1]

Common Pleas, Mich. 1530.

In annuity, the annuity was granted to someone for the services which he had done and which he should do thereafter; and this was by deed. He brought a writ of annuity generally, and the count was challenged because he had not alleged in his count that the annuity was granted for services done and to be done and that he had performed these services for the defendant. But, despite this, the count was held good enough by the whole court. The other may take advantage of this in pleading, for instance by reciting the whole of the deed and saying that he has not performed the services etc.

---

[1] Cf. *Fitzherbert v. Viscount Fitzwater*, CP 40/1061, m. 527. In annuity, Humphrey Fitzherbert counts that he was appointed auditor to the defendant in 1510 for life and discharged in 1513, and claimed arrears for the period when he was auditor (without averring that he did anything); the defendant pleads that in 1511 he requested the plaintiff to hear an account and he was not ready; the plaintiff demurs, and the court takes advisement until Trin. 1530.

[20]

Cui in vita ante divorcium. P. 22 H. 8. [Fo. 53v.]

Nota si terre soit don al baron et sa feme et puis divorce est sue perentre eux, <per que>[1] le baron avera lun moitie et la feme lauter moitie. Mez si le baron ad terre en droit sa feme, donques si devorce soit sue perenter eux en ceo case le feme avera le terre et le baron nemi etc. <Pollarde>

[21]

Doble ple. M. 23 H. 8. [Fo. 63.]

En det le pleintife counte que il lessa ii. acrez de terre a un J. T. rendant certen rent a terme de vi. anz et counte auxi que le dit J. T. avoit lessa tout son estate al defendant, et pur tant aderere puis le grant il port ceo action etc. Et le defendant dit que le dit J. T. graunt a luy tout son estate en un acre de terre, et puis cesti ore defendant fist feoffement en fee a un J. B., devaunt quel feoffement rien aderere, sanz ceo que le dit J. T. graunt tout son estate en lez ii. acrez al defendant come le pleintife avoit allege etc. Et ceo ple fuit tenuz assetz single et nemi doble, pur ceo que nient obstant que le ple est doble pur ceo que il ad allege ii. materz, scilicet lun que il graunt son estate forsque en parcel, un auter que il avoit fait feoffement, [uncore][2] entant que il avoit pris travers per quel toutz lez pleez sont weives et relinquishe, come si home voile plede en trnz le reles del [pleintife][3] ou auter ple et conclude ouster, scilicet absque hoc que il est culpable, ore il ad pris le general issue et toutz lez pleez adevaunt sont weives et void etc.: per *Spilman* et *Inglefelde*. <Pollarde>

[1] *Deleted.*
[2] *Altered from* mez.
[3] *Altered from* def.

Cui ante divorcium

20. ANON.

Common Pleas, Pas. 1530.

Note that if land is given to a husband and wife, and afterwards a divorce is sued between them, the husband shall thereby have one moiety and the wife the other moiety. But if the husband has land in right of his wife, and a divorce is sued between them, in that case the wife shall have [all] the land and not the husband etc.

Double plea

21. ANON.

Perhaps Exchequer Chamber, Mich. 1531. Cf. below, p. 277, no. 75 (Mich. 1530).

In debt the plaintiff counted that he leased two acres of land to one J. T., rendering a certain rent, for a term of six years, and counted also that the said J. T. had leased the whole of his estate to the defendant, and for so much in arrear since the grant he brought this action etc. The defendant said that the said J. T. granted to him the whole of his estate in one acre of land, and afterwards the present defendant made a feoffment in fee to one J. B., before which feoffment nothing was in arrear, without this that the said J. T. granted the whole of his estate in the two acres to the defendant as the plaintiff has alleged etc. And this plea was held single enough, and not double, because even though the pleading is double—forasmuch as he alleges two matters, namely one that he granted his estate only in part, and another that he has made a feoffment—nevertheless, since he has taken a traverse, all the [other] pleas are thereby waived and relinquished. Similarly if in trespass someone pleads a release from the plaintiff or some other plea, and concludes over 'without this that he is guilty', now he has taken the general issue and the previous pleas are waived and void etc.: by SPELMAN[1] and ENGLEFIELD [J.C.P.].

[1] Appointed J.K.B. this term.

[22]

Dower. [Fo. 149v.]

Nota, si le tenant en brefe de dower vouche le heire del baron deinz mesme le countie ou le brefe est porte, le quel ne purra my barrer le demandant, per que jugement fuit don que le demandant recover vers le vouche et le tenant tiendra en paiz, et puis le terre que le feme ad pur son dower est recover vers le tenant en dower per un estraunge sur un eigne title, en cest case la feme serra novelment indowe vers le heire etc. <Pollarde>

[23]

Droit, et ou jugement final serra don. M. 23 H. 8. [Fo. 63.]

Nota si home purchase un advouson dun auter home et puis le esglise se void et un auter home present sanz ascun title, et son clerke est einz per vi. moiz, en ceo case[i] cesti que purchase le advouson est sanz remedie quar il navera brefe de droit pur ceo que il ne poit alleger le presentement en luy mesme ou en cez auncestourz, per que etc. <Pollarde>

[24]

Ejectione firme. M. 22 H. 8. [Fo. 54.]

Nota que fuit tenus per tout la court que le lesse a terme danz recovera son terme per brefe de ejectione firme vers estraunger auxibien come il fra per brefe <dentre ad terminum qui preteriit>[1] vers le lessor etc. Et auxi nota que cest brefe nest forsque brefe de trnz en son nature, et le brefe serra vi et armis etc. Et auxi nota que home navera cest brefe si non que avoit possession en fait. <Pollarde>

---

[1] *Y suggests* de quare ejecit infra terminum.

Dower

22.

Note, undated.

Note that if the tenant in a writ of dower vouches the husband's heir within the same county where the writ is brought, and the vouchee cannot bar the demandant, so that judgment is given that the demandant recover against the vouchee and that the tenant shall hold in peace; and then the land which the woman has for her dower is recovered against the tenant in dower by a stranger upon an older title: in this case the woman shall be freshly endowed as against the heir etc.

Right ('Droit')

23. NOTE

Mich. 1531. Cf. Yorke, above, p. 166, no. 202, which may be the same case.

Note that if someone purchases an advowson from another, and afterwards the church becomes vacant, and someone else presents without any title, and his clerk is in for six months, in this case the person who purchased the advowson is without remedy. He shall not have a writ of right, forasmuch as he cannot allege a presentment by himself or his ancestors. And so, etc.

Ejectment

24. ANON.

Probably Common Pleas, Mich. 1530.

Note that it was held by the whole court that a lessee for term of years may recover his term by writ *de ejectione firmae* against a stranger as well as he may by writ of entry *ad terminum qui praeteriit*[1] against the lessor etc. Note also that this writ is only a writ of trespass in its nature; and the writ shall be *vi et armis* etc. Note also that one shall not have this writ unless he had possession in fact.

---

[1] Yelverton suggested emending this to *quare ejecit infra terminum*.

[25]

Emparlanz. M. 22 H. 8. [Fo. 54.]

En annuitie fuit tenus per tout la court pur ley que si le defendant prist un general emparlanz il ne serra receu en apres a demaunder oier del fait pur ceo que il ad estoppe luy mesme per le general emparlanz. Mez auterment serra si il avoit pris un especial emparlanz, scilicet salvis advantagiis, quar donques il avera oier del fait etc. <Pollarde>

[26]

[Encumbent.] *Ou encumbent serra remove.* T. 21 H. 8. [Fo. 50.]

En quare impedit fuit move al barre per *Willoughby*: si home port quare impedit et apres le vi. moiz passe il recover vers le defendant, si lencumbent serra remove[1] ou nemi, entant que il fuit einz per vi. moiz? Et non obstant dit fuit per tout le court que il serra remove si il port son quare impedit deinz lez vi. moiz, et si il recover xx. anz apres uncore le clerke serra remove etc. <Pollarde>

[27]

Entre congeable. [Fo. 149v.]

Nota, si le roy seisit certen terre dun home que est atteint de felony daver annum, diem et vastum, en ceo case le seignior de que le terre est tenuz ne poit entrer sur le possession le roy mez il suera un ouster le maine etc. <Pollarde>

---

[1] *Altered from* move.

Imparlance ('Emparlanz')

25. ANON

Common Pleas, Mich. 1530. Also noted below, p. 258, no. 29.

In annuity it was held as law by the whole court that if the defendant takes a general imparlance he shall not be received afterwards to demand oyer of the deed, because he has estopped himself by the general imparlance. It would be otherwise, however, if he took a special imparlance (that is, *salvis advantagiis*); for then he may have oyer of the deed etc.

Incumbent ('Encumbent')

26. ANON.

Common Pleas, Trin. 1529. Also reported above, p. 250, no. 10.

In *quare impedit* it was moved at the bar by *Willoughby*: if someone brings *quare impedit*, and recovers against the defendant after the six months have passed, shall the incumbent be removed or not, inasmuch as he was in for six months? Notwithstanding this, it was said by the whole court that he shall be removed if the plaintiff brought his *quare impedit* within the six months; and even if he recovers twenty years later the clerk shall still be removed etc.

Entry

27. NOTE

Undated, but evidently from the reading on Prerogativa Regis, below, p. 270, no. 56.

Note that if the king seizes certain land of a man who is attainted of felony, so as to have year, day and waste (*annum, diem et vastum*), in this case the lord of whom the land is held may not enter upon the king's possession but shall sue an ousterlemain etc.

[28]

Error. T. 25 H. 8. [Fo. 84.]

Apres le recorde maunde en Banke le Roy per brefe de errour le pleintife en le brefe de errour vient al barre et fait suggestion al court que cesti que apparust come atturney pur cesti ore pleintife en le primer action navoit unques garrante datturney, et pria brefe as justicez de Comen Banke et auter brefe al custos brevium si ascun garrante datturney fuit la avaunt eux, et le brefe fuit graunt pur ceo que nest my ascun auter voie pur le court de saver si soit ascun garrante de atturney ou nemie, quar le garrante datturny nest mie ascun parte de le recorde que est maunde en Banke le Roy. Mez nota que ceo doit estre prie del court avant que le brefe de scire facias soit agarde vers le defendant ad audiendum errores, et apres lez errourz assigne: quod nota. <Pollarde>

Note from the record

KB 27/1088, m. 30, Rooper.

A writ of error tested 1 May [1533], 25 Hen. VIII, is directed to Norwich C.J.C.P. to send the record of the suit between Richard Palmer and Thomas Swayne, executors of Jane Takell, widow, and Humphrey Loveys of Bockington, Devon, for a debt of £20. The records certified are Mich. 23 Hen. VIII, m. 683; Trin. 24 Hen. VIII, mm. 107 and 701. The principal entry records that the defendant appeared by Thomas Burgeyne his attorney and said nothing in answer, so that judgment was given for the plaintiff to recover the debt and 20 s. damages. The final entry records a *capias ad satisfaciendum* and subsequent outlawry of Loveys at Stone Cross, Middlesex, on 7 Nov. [1532], 24

[29]

[Estoppel.] *Ou home serra estoppe per pleding*. M. 22 H. 8. [Fo. 54.]

Nota que fuit tenuz per tout la court que si le defendant prist un general emparlanz en brefe de annuitie il ne serra resceive de demaunder <oier de>[i] le fait. Mez si soit un especial emparlanz auterment est etc. <Pollarde>

Error

28. PALMER v. LOVEYS[1]

Common Pleas, Trin. 1533. Record: KB 27/1088, m. 30 (noted below).

After the record was sent into the King's Bench by writ of error, the plaintiff in the writ of error came to the bar and made suggestion to the court that the person who appeared as attorney for the present plaintiff in the former action never had a warrant of attorney; and he prayed a writ to the justices of the Common Bench and another writ to the *custos brevium* [to certify] whether any warrant of attorney was there before them; and the writ was granted, because there is no other way for the court to know whether there was any warrant of attorney or not, for the warrant of attorney is no part of the record which is sent into the King's Bench. But note that this ought to be prayed from the court before the writ of *scire facias ad audiendum errores* is awarded against the defendant, but after the errors assigned: note that.

Note from the record

Coram rege roll, Trin. 25 Hen. VIII (1533).

[continued from opposite page]

Hen. VIII. Now, on 4 July 1533, Loveys comes and assigns three errors, the third of which is that Thomas Burgeyne had no warrant of record to appear for him. A *certiorari* is directed to Norwich C.J. and the custos brevium, who both certify that they cannot find any warrant for Burgeyn in the rolls and remembrances for the relevant terms. Loveys prays a writ to warn the executors to appear and hear the record in Michaelmas term, when they do not appear and the outlawry is reversed.

Estoppel

29. ANON.

Common Pleas, Mich. 1530. Also noted above, p. 257, no. 25.

Note that it was held by the whole court that if the defendant takes a general imparlance in a writ of annuity he shall not be received to demand oyer of the deed. But if it is a special imparlance it is otherwise etc.

---

[1] Cf. two similar precedents the previous year: *Lomnor* v. *Byrde* (1532) Spelman, p. 115; KB 27/1071, m. 22 (94 Selden Soc. 307); *Botiller* v. *Garlonde* (1532) Spelman, p. 116; KB 27/1084, m. 73 (94 Selden Soc. 313).

[30]

[Estoppel.] *Ou home serra estoppe per son fait demesne.*
M. 25 H. 8. [Fo. 84.]

En det sur obligation le defendant dit que le condition del obligation est tiel, scilicet que sil deliver al pleintife toutz lez chartrez et escriptz quex il ad concerninge le maner de Dale avant tiel jour que donques lobligation etc. Et il dit auxi que il navoit al temps del obligation fait ne unques puis ascun chartrez ou escriptz concerninge le maner de D. etc. Et le opinion de tout le court forsque *Fitzherbert* que le defendant ne serra estoppe daver cest ple pur ceo que sil navoit ascun chartrez donques il ad deliver toutz que il avoit, et auxi pur ceo que lentent del fesanz del obligation nest auter mez que il delivera toutz lez chartrez que il ad, et donques sil nad my ascun <donques>[1] ceo ple est assetz bon etc. Et auxi agarde fuit que [si jeo][2] graunt un rent horz de le maner de D. et puis jeo purchase le maner, que donques jeo ne serra receu adire que jeo navoy riens[1] en le maner al temps de graunt fait: quod nota. <Pollarde>

[31]

Execution. P. 23 H. 8. [Fo. 63v.]

En det, dit fuit pur ley que si home port action de det vers executourz, quex pledont Rienz enter mainz, et trove est que ilz nount rienz en lour mainz, et puis assetz vient a lour mainz, donques le pleintife en ceo case avera execution de ceo sur son primer action: quod fuit concessum. Mez dit fuit que execution ne serra my agarde si non que soit trove que lez executourz ount parcel del demande en lour mainz etc. <Pollarde>

[1] *Deleted.*
[2] *Altered from* il.

30. SAYNTPOLL v. CONYERS

Common Pleas, Mich. 1533. Also reported in BL MS Harley 1691, ff. 123v–124; below, p. 423, no. 4. Record: CP 40/1079, m. 612 (declaration, Mich. 1533; imparlance to Trin. 1534).[1]

In debt on a bond the defendant said that the condition of the bond is this: that if he should deliver to the plaintiff all the charters and writings which he had concerning the manor of Dale, before such and such a day, the bond [would be void] etc. He also said that he did not, at the time of making the deed or ever thereafter, have any charters or writings concerning the manor of Dale etc. And the opinion of the whole court except FITZHERBERT was that the defendant shall not be estopped from having this plea, because if he has no charters then he has delivered all that he had, and also because the intention in making the bond is no other than that he should deliver all the charters that he has, and so if he does not have any the plea is good enough etc. It was also awarded that if I grant a rent out of the manor of Dale, and afterwards I purchase the manor, I shall not then be received to say that I had nothing in the manor at the time when the grant was made: note that.

Execution

31. ANON.

Common Pleas, Pas. 1531. Cf. below, p. 273, no. 65.

In debt, it was stated as law that if someone brings an action of debt against executors, who plead 'Nothing in their hands', and it is found that they have nothing in their hands, and afterwards assets come into their hands, the plaintiff in this case shall have execution thereof upon his former action: which was granted. But it was said that execution shall not be awarded unless it is found that the executors have part of the demand in their hands etc.

---

[1] Debt by John Sayntpoll (St Paul) of Snarford, Lincs., against Simon Conyers of Danby on Ure, Yorks., on an indenture of sale of the manors of Aylesby and Swallow, Lincs., with covenant to deliver all evidences, muniments, charters and other writings concerning the manors, and counts that he did not do so.

[32]

Executours.[1] M. 26 H. 8. [Fo. 95v.]

Notá que executourz ne serront charge de lour bienz propers si non pur le insufficiency dez bienz le testatour en nul case: quod tota curia concessit etc. <Pollarde>

[33]

Executourz. 17 H. 8. [Fo. 39.]

En lescheker chambre agarde fuit que executourz de executourz ne poient faire vende de terre. Come en case si home devise que cez executourz vendront le terre et lez executourz fount lour executourz et murront, en ceo case lez executourz de executourz ne poient faire vende de[2] terre pur ceo que nest chose testamentall, et auxi le primer testatour ne mist lez executourz dexecutourz en confidenz, per que agarde fuit que ilz ne poient vendre le terre etc. Et en mesme le case concessum fuit que si jeo voile que mez executourz vendront mon terre et si lun de eux le vende ceo est voide, et si toutz murront forsque lun de eux donques cesti poet bien vendre le terre per reson de survivour: quod nota. Et auxi nota que est don per lestatut anno 21 H. 8. que si jeo voile que mez executourz vendront mon terre et ascun de eux refuse le administration et lauterz quex ne refuse le administration vendront ma terre sanz nosmer de eux quex refuse, ceo est assez bon, mez si nul de eux ne refuse le administration donques le vende de terre covient estre fait per eux toutz etc. <Pollarde>

[34]

Executourz. P. 23 H. 8. [Fo. 63v.]

En det port vers executourz, quex pledont un ple que ne vaut rienz pur mispledre, et sur ceo demurrer, et le ple agarde pur nul ple, per que agarde fuit

---

[1] *Copied out of alphabetical sequence.*   [2] *Altered from* le.

Executors

32. NOTE

Mich. 1534.

Note that executors shall not be charged in respect of their own goods in any case except for insufficiency of their testator's goods: which the whole court granted etc.

33. ANON.

Exchequer Chamber, '17 Hen. VIII' (1525/26), but more likely 1527. Also reported in YB Trin. 19 Hen. VIII, fo. 9, pl. 4; anon. reports, above, p. 60, no. 49 (also dated Trin. 1527); Yelverton, below, p. 361, no. 103 (also dated 19 Hen. VIII).

In the Exchequer Chamber it was awarded that the executors of executors may not make a sale of land. For instance, if someone devises that his executors should sell the land, and the executors appoint their executors and die, in this case the executors of the executors may not make sale of the land because it is not a testamentary thing; and also the first testator did not place his trust in the executors' executors. And so it was awarded that they could not sell the land etc. And in the same case it was granted that if I will that my executors should sell my land, and only one of them sells it, this is void; but if they all die except one, he may well sell the land by reason of survivorship: note that. Note also that it is enacted by the statute of 21 Hen. VIII[1] that if I will that my executors should sell my land, and some of them refuse the administration, and the others who do not refuse the administration sell my land without naming those who refuse, this is good enough; but if none of them refuse the administration then the sale of land must be done by them all etc.

34. ANON.

Probably Common Pleas, Pas. 1531.

In debt brought against executors, who plead a plea which is invalid by reason of mispleading, and there is a demurrer thereon and the plea is awarded to be no plea, it is thereby awarded that the plaintiff recover his debt and his

---

[1] 21 Hen. VIII, c. 4 (SR iii. 285).

que le pleintife recovera son det et cez damagez et costages de bienz le mort. Mez si ilz ussent plede Pleinement administre, et ceo trove encounter eux, ilz serront chargez de costages et damagez de lour bienz proprez: quod vide. <Pollarde>

[35]

Executourz. P. 23 H. 8. [Fo. 63v.]

Nota, si executour plede un reles fait a lour testatour ou que le obligation nest my le fait son testatour, que en ceux casez ilz serront my chargez de lour bienz propers. Mez si il voile plede un reles fait a luy mesme, donques ilz serront chargez dez bienz properz pur defaut de bienz le mort: quod fuit concessum. Et auxi dit fuit que si executour plede un ple que nest my sufficient en le ley, et sur ceo le pleintife demurre en ley, et est ajuge pur la pleintife, en ceo case il ne serra charge de cez bienz properz pur ceo que nest ascun defaut en luy, per que etc. Et auxi nota que fuit dit pur ley que si lexecutour plede Pleinement administre et issint rienz entre mainez, et trove est que ilz ount forsque x. li., parcel del demande, en ceo case il ne serra charge forsque pur lez x. li. et rienz de cez bienz properz pur ceo que le ple ne vaut en barre a toutz foitz, forsque pur un temps, quar si il nad assetz apres donques il ne suera execution: quod fuit concessum, per que etc. <Pollarde>

[36]

Fee taile. M. 26 H. 8. [Ff. 94v–95.]

Nota, si terre soit done a un home per le roy et a cez heirez malez, agarde fuit que ceo serra bon estate taile, pur ceo que lentent de roy apperust que le done avera estat a luy et a cez heirez malez de son corps engendrez, et le graunt le roy ne serra prise pur voide lou poet estre fait bon. Et icy lentent et volunte le roy apperust que il avera plus que[i] a terme de vie [quar il][1] avoit nosme cez heirez malez, per que lez heirez malez de son corps avera le terre, mez ceo ne poet estre dit fee simple, quar donques le roy serra desceive en son graunt, quel nest

---

[1] *Altered from* que.

damages and costs from the goods of the deceased. But if they had pleaded 'Fully administered', and this was found against them, they would be charged with costs and damages out of their own goods: observe that.

35. ANON.

Probably Common Pleas, Pas. 1531.

Note that if executors plead a release made to their testator, or that the bond is not the deed of their testator, in these cases they shall not be charged in respect of their own goods. But if they plead a release made to themselves, they shall be charged from their own goods for want of goods of the deceased: which was granted. It was also said that if an executor pleads a plea which is insufficient in law, and thereupon the plaintiff demurs in law, and it is adjudged for the plaintiff, in this case he shall not be charged in respect of his own goods because there is no fault in him; and so etc. Note also that it was stated for law that if executors plead 'Fully administered, and so nothing in their hands', and it is found that they have only £10, part of the demand, in this case case they shall only be charged for the £10 and nothing from their own goods, because the plea does not avail in bar for ever, but only for a time, for if they have no assets thereafter he shall not sue execution: which was granted; and so etc.

Fee tail

36. ANON.

Common Pleas, Mich. 1534. Also reported in BL MS Harley 1691, ff. 142–143; below, p. 431, no. 6.

Note that if land is given by the king to someone and his heirs male, it was awarded that this shall be a good estate tail, because the king's intention appears to be that the donee should have an estate to him and to his heirs male of his body begotten, and the king's grant shall not be taken as void where it may be made good. And here the king's intention appears that he should have more than for term of life, for he has named his heirs male, and so the heirs male of his body shall have the land; but it cannot be called fee simple, for then the king would be deceived in his grant, which is not right. But it is otherwise if land is given by a

my reson. Mez auterment est[i] si terre soit don per un comen person a un auter et a cez heirez malez, ceo est fee simple et cez heirez femalez avera la terre. Mez auterment est si le done ust estre fait per volunte, quar donques nest que un estate taile, pur ceo que lentent de donour issint apperust. Et sic nota diversitatem. Et auxi dit fuit pur ley que si terre soit don a un home et sanguine sue, carne sue, ou semini suo, ceo est estate taile.<Pollarde>

[37]

Feffementz. H. 24 H. 8. [Fo. 75v.]

Nota que est dit pur ley per chiefe justice que si home soit seisi dun maner a que avouson est appendant, et fait feffement del moitie del maner cum pertinenciis, que en ceo case il avera chescun second presentement. Et issint est ou feffement est fait de ii. partez, iii. parte ou xx. parte del maner cum pertinenciis. Mez si feffement soit fait de un acre ou ii. acrez ou x. acrez, parcel del maner, cum pertinenciis, donques rienz passa del avouson pur ceo que le feffement est fait de cy petit chose del maner: quod nota. 33 H. 6. 18 E. 3. <Pollarde>

[38]

Fine al roy. M. 25 H. 8. [Fo. 84.]

Nota que sur un recoverie en brefe dentre en le post nul fine serra fait, ne sur fine sur release etc. <Pollarde>

common person to another and his heirs male: this is fee simple, and his heirs female shall have the land. It would be otherwise, however, if the gift had been made by will, for then it would be but an estate tail, because that appears to be the donor's intention. Thus note the distinction. It was also said to be law that if land is given to a man 'and his blood' (*et sanguini suae*), 'his flesh' (*carne suae*)[1] or 'his seed' (*semini suo*), this is an estate tail.[2]

Feoffments

37. ANON.

Common Pleas, Hil. 1533. Cf. Yelverton, below, p. 321, no. 19, where the same point is attributed to all the justices of the Common Pleas in 21 Hen. VIII.

Note that it is stated as law by [NORWICH] C.J. that if someone is seised of a manor to which an advowson is appendant, and makes a feoffment of a moiety of the manor 'with the appurtenances' (*cum pertinenciis*), in this case he shall have every second presentation. So it is where a feoffment is made of two parts, three parts or a twentieth part of a manor *cum pertinenciis*. But if a feoffment is made of one acre, or two acres, or ten acres, part of the manor [of Dale], *cum pertinenciis*, then nothing of the advowson passes because the feoffment is made of such a small part of the manor: note that. 33 Hen. VI;[3] 18 Edw. III.[4]

Fine to the king

38. ANON.

Common Pleas, Mich. 1533.

Note that upon a [common] recovery in a writ of entry in the *post* no fine shall be made, nor on a fine upon release etc.

---

[1] YB 37 Edw. III, Lib. Ass., pl. 15.
[2] These cases were discussed at readings: see J. H. Baker, *The Common Law Tradition*, pp. 40–43. Cf. *Anon.* (1549) in Yelverton, below, p. 347, no. 73.
[3] *Dame Alice Ogard's Case* (1455) YB Hil. 33 Hen. VI, fo. 4, pl. 14.
[4] YB Mich. 18 Edw. III, fo. 43, pl. 49.

[39]

Forcible entre et restitution sur ceo.
Lectura de Saunderz. [Fo. 149v.]

Nota que tenant a terme danz si il soit ouste poit bien aver avantage del estatut fait anno 8 H. 6, et auxi il avera restitution per lez justicez de paiz: quod nota. 19 H. 7, f. 14, contra. <Pollarde>

[40]

Forfeture. M. 22 H. 8. [Fo. 54.]

Nota que fuit tenuz per toutz lez justicez que si home soit arrain de felony et trove culpable et puis morust avant jugement render, en ceo case il ne forfet cez bienz, pur ceo que nul jugement est don. Mez dun utlagarie auterment est etc., quar maintenaunt per lexigent agarde il forfetra cez bienz, et ceo est destre intende ou lexigent est agarde pur felonie, murdre ou treson: mez auterment nemi, quar en action personal ou proces de utlagarie gist le defendant ne forfetra cez bienz per lexigent agarde tanque il soit utlage, ceo est quant lexigent est returne et nemi adevaunt, quar si il voile se render al court avant lexigent returne et sue supersedeas il ne forfet nul bienz. Mez si home soit utlage en action personal et sua son chartre de pardon, uncore il ne serra restore a sez bienz. Mez auterment est si il sue brefe derrour et revers mesme le utlagaric, donques il serra restore a sez bienz et ne forfet ascun de cez bienz. Et issint est lou home est utlage en auter countie que ou[i] il est demurrant, sanz brefe de proclamation, en ceo case ne forfetra cez bienz pur ceo que le utlagarie est voide per estatute etc. <Pollarde>

Forcible entry

39. WILLIAM SAUNDERS' READING

Middle Temple, probably Lent 1533. His first reading was in Lent 1525. There are further extracts below, p. 267, no. 49, and p. 273, no. 64.

Note that if a tenant for term of years is ousted he may well take advantage of the statute made in 8 Hen. VI,[1] and shall also have restitution through the justices of the peace: note that. 19 Hen. VII, fo. 14, contra.[2]

Forfeiture

40. ANON.

Perhaps Exchequer Chamber, Mich. 1530.

Note that it was held by all the justices that if someone is arraigned of felony and found guilty, and then dies before judgment is given, in this case he shall not forfeit his goods, because no judgment has been given. But it is otherwise in respect of an outlawry, for immediately by the exigent awarded he shall forfeit his goods. This is to be understood where the exigent is awarded for felony, murder or treason: otherwise not, for in a personal action where process of outlawry lies the defendant shall not forfeit his goods by the exigent awarded until he is outlawed—that is, when the exigent is returned, and not before then—for if he will surrender himself to the court before the exigent returned and sue a *supersedeas* he shall not forfeit any goods. However, if someone is outlawed in a personal action and sues his charter of pardon, he shall nevertheless not be restored to his goods. But it is otherwise if he sues a writ of error and reverses the same outlawry: then he shall be restored to his goods and shall not forfeit any of his goods. So it is where someone is outlawed in a county other than that where he lives, without a writ of proclamation, in this case he shall not forfeit his goods, because the outlawry is void by statute etc.[3]

---

[1] Statute of forcible entry, 8 Hen. VI, c. 9 (*SR* ii. 244).
[2] Cf. YB Hil. 1 Hen. VII, fo. 12, pl. 21; F.N.B. 248E.
[3] 6 Hen. VIII, c. 4 (*SR* iii. 126). There is a marginal reference to YB Mich. 9 Hen. V, fo. 14, pl. 24.

[41]

Gager de ley. 6 H. 8. [Fo. 13.]

En det nota que si action de det soit port vers un prior et counte dun contract fait per son predecessour ove le pleintife et conveia lez bienz al ops del meason, et le defendant tender son ley que rien a luy doit, et ne purra estre receu a faire son ley pur ceo que il est estraunge al contract, per que il ne serra receu de faire son ley de auterfoitz etc. <Pollarde>

[42]

Gard' en chivalre. M. 26 H. 8. [Fo. 95; also on fo. 84 but struck out.]

Nota, si terre soit don a un home et sa feme et as heirez del corps le baron engendrez a tener de luy per service de chivalrie, et le baron morust, son issue deinz age, en ceo case le issue ne serra en garde durant le vie del mere que ad estate a terme de vie, pur ceo que el est tenant al donour, quar el avoit un jointe estate ove son baron. Mez quant le feme est mort, donques le heire et le terre serront en garde. Et issint est si lease soit fait a terme devie, le remainder en taile a un auter, et cesti en le remainder morust, son issue deinz age[i], vivant le tenant a terme devie, le issue en le taile ne serra mye en garde pur ceo que le tenant a terme de vie est tenant al donour, mez apres son mort auterment est etc. <Pollarde>

[43]

Inditement. P. 22 H. 8. [Fo. 54v.]

Nota que si home soit indite de ceo que il felonice furatus fuit unum equum etc., ceo est assetz bon inditement: per opinionem *Fitzjames*, Chiefe Justice etc. <Pollarde>

Wager of law ('Gager')

41. COWPLOND v. ABBOT OF WYMONDHAM

Common Pleas, *c.* 1514/15. Also reported by Caryll senior, 116 Selden Soc. 679–681. Record: CP 40/1010, m. 404 (judgment for plaintiff).

Debt. Note that if an action of debt is brought against a prior, and the plaintiff counts of a contract made by his predecessor with the plaintiff, and traces the goods to the use of the house, and the defendant tenders his law that he owes him nothing, he cannot be received to do his law, inasmuch as he is a stranger to the contract and shall not be received to do his law in respect of another time etc.

Guardian in chivalry

42. ANON.

Common Pleas, Mich. 1534. Also noted below, p. 271, no. 59.

Note that if land is given to a man and his wife and to the heirs begotten of the husband's body, to hold of the donor by knight-service, and the husband dies, his issue under age, in this case the issue shall not be in ward during the lifetime of the mother, who has an estate for term of life, because she is tenant to the donor; for she had a joint estate with her husband. But once the woman is dead, then the heir and the land shall be in ward. So it is if a lease is made for term of life, the remainder in tail to someone else, and the remainderman dies, his issue under age, while the tenant for term of life is alive, the issue in tail shall not be in ward, because the tenant for term of life is tenant to the donor; but after his death it is otherwise etc.

Indictment

43. NOTE

Probably King's Bench or Serjeants' Inn, Pas. 1530.

Note that if someone is indicted for that he feloniously stole one horse etc. (*felonice furatus fuit unum equum etc.*), this is a good enough indictment: by the opinion of FITZJAMES, Chief Justice etc.

[44]

Infant. H. 21 H. 8. [Fo. 50v.]

En det sur obligation port vers un auter per un enfant deinz [age] come executour, et le defendant plede le release del pleintife que est executour, et le pleintife dit que il fuit deinz age al temps del reles fait, [est][1] nul ple pur le pleintife: per opinionem curie etc. Et si lenfant fait lease a terme danz rendant certen rent que ceo lease nest my voide mez voidable, pur ceo que il ad reserve un rent. Et issint est dun feffement fait per infant. Mez si il fait un garrante datturney a un auter de faire livere et seisin, ceo est voide. Et si latturney [ceo][2] fait ceo est disseisin etc. <Pollarde>

[45]

Jefaile. M. 24 H. 8. [Fo. 75v.]

Nota que fuit dit en le Comen Banke pur ley que si un plede en arrest de jugement per reson dun jefaile, que donques tout le recorde est voide et le pleintife ou demandant covient de comenser novel original et plede tout de novel. Et ceo est toutz foitz ou le issue est male joine, quar nest mye jefaile sinon ou le issue est male joine. Mez contrarie ley est dun repleder, quar si home plede un misple et puis plede ceo en arrest de jugement, donques en ceo case il repledera et le pleintife ou demandant ne doit comenser novel original: et sic nota diversitatem etc. <Pollarde>

---

[1] et.
[2] se *deleted*.

Infant

44. ANON.

Common Pleas, Hil. 1530. Also reported in Spelman, p. 133, pl. 5; Yelverton, below, p. 323, no. 24; BL MS Harley 1691, fo. 141v, and BL MS. Hargrave 5, fo. 106; below, p. 417, no. 1.

In debt on a bond brought against another by an infant under age as executor, the defendant pleaded a release from the plaintiff executor, and the plaintiff said that he was under age at the time of making the release. This is no plea for plaintiff, by opinion of the court etc. And if an infant makes a lease for a term of years, rendering certain rent, this lease is not void but voidable, because he has reserved a rent. So it is of a feoffment made by an infant. But if he makes a warrant of attorney to another to make livery of seisin, that is void; and, if the attorney does it, it is a disseisin etc.

Jeofail

45. ANON.

Common Pleas, Mich. 1532.

Note that it was stated as law in the Common Bench that if someone pleads in arrest of judgment by reason of a jeofail, the whole record is void and the plaintiff or demandant must commence a new original writ and plead everything afresh. But this is always where the issue is badly joined, for it is not a jeofail except where the issue is badly joined. The law is contrary in the case of a repleader, for if someone pleads a bad plea and afterwards pleads this in arrest of judgment, in this case he shall replead and the plaintiff or demandant ought not to commence a new original: thus note the distinction etc.

[46]

Joinder en action. T. 24 H. 8. [Fo. 75v.]

En errour, dit fuit per *Fitzjames*, Chiefe Justice, que si faux jugement soit don vers ii. ou plusourz, donques ilz covient que ilz joindront en brefe de errour nient obstant que soit en brefe de trnz. Mez en atteint auterment est, quar si soit en trnz que est several en son nature ilz purront aver several atteintz, issint ilz purront aver several atteintz mez nemi several brefes de errour: et sic nota diversitatem etc. <Pollarde>

[47]

Journez accomptz. 21 H. 8. [Fo. 50v.]

En errour vide lou brefe de dower est porte vers iii., lun de eux morust pendant le brefe, et ceo non obstant le demandant avera jugement de recover. Et puis lez tenantz en le brefe de dower sueront brefe de errour et allegont pur errour que un dez tenantz morust pendant le brefe et le demandant en le brefe de [dower]¹ confesse le errour, per que le jugement fuit revers. Et le demandant en le brefe de dower pria novel brefe per journez accomptz, et non potuit habere pur ceo que il avoit un foitz jugement de recover. Mez si le primer brefe ust estre abate et nul jugement done, donques il avera son prier. Issint nota que apres un jugement home navera auter brefe per journez accomptz agarde etc. <Pollarde>

[48]

Jurour. T. 23 H. 8. [Fo. 64.]

Nota, si un juror soit present avant lez justicez quaunt il est demande et ne voile my appere et parle, donques le partie pleintife ou defendant purra prier

¹ *Corrected from* errour.

Joinder in action

46. WOLLEY v. LECHE AND ANDREWE

King's Bench, Trin. 1532. Also reported in Spelman, pp. 91, 111, 114. Record: KB 27/1073, m. 63 (abstracted in 94 Selden Soc. 305).

In [a writ of] error, it was said by FITZJAMES, Chief Justice, that if a false judgment is given against two or more, they must join in a writ of error, even if it is in a writ of trespass. But it is otherwise in attaint, for if it is in trespass—which is several in its nature—they may have several attaints. And so they may have several attaints but not several writs of error: thus note the distinction etc.

Journeys accounts

47. ANON.

King's Bench, 1529/30.

Error. See where a writ of dower is brought against three, and one of them dies while the writ is pending, and despite this the demandant [had] judgment to recover. And afterwards the tenants in the writ of dower sued a writ of error and alleged for error that one of the tenants died while the writ was pending; and the demandant in the writ of dower confessed the error, and so the judgment was reversed. And the demandant in the writ of dower prayed a new writ by journeys accounts, but could not have it, because he had already had a judgment to recover. However, if the first writ had been abated and no judgment given, he would have had his prayer. Thus note that after a judgment one shall not have another writ awarded by journeys accounts etc.

Juror

48. ANON.

Trin. 1531.

Note that if a juror is present before the justices when he is demanded, and will not appear and speak, the party (plaintiff or defendant) may then pray from the justices a *voire dire*, and thereupon the justices shall cause two of the

dez justicez un voier dire, et sur ceo lez justicez ferront deux de lez jurrourz estre jure de enquerer si cesti que ne voile apperer ne parle fuit present ou nemi, et si trove soit que il fuit present et ne voile my parle donques il serra amercie per le discretion dez justicez: et nota. <Pollarde>

[49]

Justice de peace. Lectura Saunders. [Fo. 149v.]

Nota, dit fuit que lez justicez de paiz nont my power denquirer dun comen nusaunz, pur ceo que ilz nount my power si non per lour comission, et en le comission nest ascun tiel parol mez de feloniis et transgressionibus. Issint si home leve un nusaunz en le haut chimin lez justicez de paiz ne purront my enquerer de ceo per cest parol transgressionibus, pur ceo que nest my trnz a ascun home, pur ceo que le fraunctenement del chimin nest mye en ascun person certen, per que etc. Quere tamen. <Pollarde>

[50]

Livere hors de main le roy. H. 24 H. 8. [Ff. 75v–76.]

Nota, si le tenant le roy que tient in capite morust seisi, son heire de pleine age, et le heire entre en le terre et le roy luy pardon de toutz manerz de intrusionz, et puis un office est trove pur le roy, scilicet que le tenant le roy morust seisi de terre tenuz de roy in capite, son heire de pleine age, en ceo case le heire ne suera livere horz de main le roy. Mez auterment est si le roy luy pardon apres office trove: et sic nota diversitatem. <Pollarde>

jurors to be sworn to enquire whether the one who would not appear or speak was present or not; and if it is found that he was present and would not speak he shall be amerced by the discretion of the justices: note [that].

Justice of the peace

49. WILLIAM SAUNDERS' READING

Middle Temple, probably Lent 1533. His first reading was in Lent 1525. See above, p. 263, no. 39.

Note that it was said that justices of the peace have no power to enquire into a common nuisance,[1] because they have no powers except by their commission, and there is no such word in the commission, but only 'concerning felonies and trespasses' (*de feloniis et transgressionibus*). Thus if someone raises a nuisance in the highway the justices of the peace may not enquire into this by virtue of the word 'trespasses', because it is not a trespass to anyone, forasmuch as the freehold of the highway is not in any certain person; and so etc. Query nevertheless.

Livery out of the king's hand

50. NOTE

Hil. 1533.

Note that if the king's tenant who holds in chief dies seised, his heir being of full age, and the heir enters in the land, and the king pardons him for all kinds of intrusions, and afterwards an office is found for the king to the effect that the king's tenant died seised of land held of the king in chief, his heir being of full age: in this case the heir shall not sue livery out of the king's hand. But it is otherwise if the king pardons him after the office is found: and so note a distinction.

---

[1] Cf. *Anon.* (1526), above, vol. I, p. 57, no. 43; and Yorke, above, vol. I, p. 159, no. 184.

[51]

Monstranz de faitz et auterz chosez. [Fo. 149v.]

Si home suist execution sur estatut merchant, il covient de monstre lestatut al court de Chauncerie et sur ceo il avera capias, et le capias serra returnable avant lez justicez de Comen Banke, et si le vicont returne Non est inventus donques issera un alias capias horz de Comen Banke, mez il covient de monstre lestatut en le Comen Banke pur ceo que ne fuit unques la monstre, nient contriteant que ceo fuit monstre en le Chauncerie: et sic nota. <Pollarde>

[52]

Peremtorie. M. 24 H. 8. [Fo. 76.]

Nota, dit fuit pur clere ley que si le tenant en precipe quod reddat pria aide dun estraunge, et le demandant demurre en ley si il avera le aide ou nemie, et puis agarde fuit que il navera le aide, per que agarde fuit que le tenant respondra ouster, et seisin de terre ne serra mye agarde. Et mesme le ley est lou le tenant vouche ou demande le vewe ou plede ascun auter ple que est dilatorye, come jointenancie ou mort ou tielz semblablez, et sur ceo demurre en ley, et ajuge enconter le tenant, que donques nul seisin de terre serra agarde mez que le tenant serra mis a respondre oustre. Et issint est en toutz actionz personelz lou le defendant plede ascun ple que est dilatorie. Mez si lez pleez que sont dilatoriez sont [trie]¹ per verdit et nemie per demurrer en ley, donques est peremptorie et le demandant ou pleintife avera jugement sur ceo verdit: quod nota. Et sic nota diversitatem etc. Mez sil soit adjourne a auter jour, semble autrement. 11 H. 4, f. 18 et 22. <Pollarde>

¹ *Altered from* pled.

Monstrance

51. NOTE

Undated.

If someone sues execution upon a statute merchant, he must show the statute to the Court of Chancery and thereupon he shall have a *capias*, and the *capias* shall be returnable before the justices of the Common Bench, and if the sheriff returns 'He has not been found' (*Non est inventus*) an *alias capias* shall issue out of the Common Bench; but he must show the statute in the Common Bench, because it was never shown there, even though it was shown in the Chancery: and so take note [of that].

Peremptory

52. ANON.

Probably Common Pleas, Mich. 1532.

Note that it was stated as clear law that if the tenant in a *praecipe quod reddat* prays aid of a stranger, and the demandant demurs in law as to whether he should have the aid or not, and afterwards it is awarded that he shall not have the aid, [it shall be awarded] that the tenant answer over, and seisin of the land shall not be awarded. The law is the same where the tenant vouches, or demands the view, or pleads any other plea which is dilatory, such as joint tenancy or death or such like, and thereupon there is a demurrer in law, and it is adjudged against the tenant, no seisin of the land shall be awarded, but the tenant shall be driven to answer over. So it is in all personal actions where the defendant pleads any plea which is dilatory. But if the pleas which are dilatory are tried by verdict and not by demurrer in law, then it is peremptory and the demandant or plaintiff shall have judgment upon this verdict: note that. And thus note a distinction etc. However, if it adjourned to another day it seems to be otherwise. 11 Hen. IV, ff. 18 and 22.[1]

---

[1] *Mortimer's Case* (1409) YB Mich. 11 Hen. IV, fo. 18, pl. 42; *Anon.*, ibid., fo. 19, pl. 44, at fo. 22.

[53]

Pledinge, et forme de ceo. T. 21 H. 8. [Fo. 51.]

Nota que ou^i home justifie ou face title a luy en ascun action per reason dun lease pur terme dauter vie, la il doit alleger que cesti que vie est uncore en pleine vie: per opinionem curie etc. <Pollarde>

[54]

Prerogativa regis. T. 21 H. 8. [Fo. 51.]

Nota que si le tenant le roy que tient en chiefe aliena sanz licenz le roy que donques il ferra fine al roy, scilicet le value de terre per un an. Mez le roy ne poet estre entitle avant que un office de ceo fuit trove, et donques le roy avera lez profitz del terre en le mesne temps apres le office trove et devant que gree soit fait ove le roy pur le fin, mez il navera ascun avantage del terre avant que le alienation soit trove per office etc. <Pollarde>

[55]

Prerogativa regis. T. 22 H. 8. [Fo. 54v.]

Vide quod dit fuit pur ley que si le tenant le roy que tient in capite morust, son heire deinz age^i, et le roy happa le garde del terre et del heire, et puis auter terre que est tenus de auter home discende a mesme lenfant per le mort dun auter auncestour, le roy navera le garde de mesme cel terre per son prerogative pur ceo que est discende al heire per auter auncestour etc. <Pollarde>

Pleading, and the form thereof

53. ANON.

Trin. 1529.

Note that where someone justifies or makes title to himself in any action by reason of a lease *pur terme d'auter vie*, he ought to allege that *cestuy que vie* is still alive: by the opinion of the court etc.

Prerogativa Regis

54. ANON.

Trin. 1529.

Note that if the king's tenant who holds in chief aliens without the king's licence, he shall make fine to the king, namely the value of the land for one year. But the king cannot be entitled before an office is found concerning this, and then the king shall have the profits of the land in the mean time after the office is found and before agreement is made with the king for the fine; but he shall not have any advantage from the land before the alienation is found by office etc.

55. ANON.

Trin. 1530.

Observe that it was stated as law that if the king's tenant, who holds in chief, dies, his heir being under age, and the king obtains the wardship of the land and of the heir, and afterwards other land which is held of someone else descends to the same infant through the death of another ancestor, the king shall not have the wardship of this same land by his prerogative because it has descended to the heir through another ancestor etc.[1]

---

[1] There are marginal references to *Skrene*'s *Case* (1474) YB Pas. 14 Edw. IV, fo. 4, pl. 4; Mich. 15 Edw. IV, fo. 10, pl. 16; Pas. 16 Edw. IV, fo. 4, pl. 8; *Anon.* (1496) Pas. 11 Hen. VII, fo. 18, pl. 2.

[56]

[Prerogativa regis.] *In lectura de prerogativa regis.* [Fo. 149v.]

Nota, si [home]¹ soit atteint de felony, que donques le roy avera le terre per annum, diem et vastum, et donques le seignior de que le terre est tenuz. Mez le roy ne avera ceo avant office trove. Et auxi il avera ceo a son plesure quant il voile, et apres ceo que le roy ad annum, diem et vastum, donques le seignior suera oustre le main: quod nota. Et auxi le seignior de que le terre est tenuz bien poet enter en le terre avant le temps que un office soit trove, et auxi avant que proces soit fait horz del Escheker al eschetour de seisier le terre pur le roy per annum, diem et vastum, et ceo le roy poit aver a son plesure quant il voile: quod nota. <Pollarde>

[57]

Proprietate probanda. T. 22 H. 8. [Fo. 54v.]

Nota si jeo baile certen bienz a un home a rebaile oustre a un auter, ceo ne change le propertie mez jeo ben purra prendre lez bienz a toutz foitz. Et issint est lou jeo baile certen bienz a un auter sanz pluz parler, ceo ne change le propertie. Mez auterment est lou jeo baile certen bienz a un auter home al use dun auter, [quar]² en ceo case le propertie est change maintenaunt pur ceo que le limitation del use change le propertie: quod nota pur bon ley etc. <Pollarde>

---

¹ *Altered from* mon t[enant].   ² q[ue].

56. FROM A READING ON PREROGATIVA REGIS

The statute was commonly chosen for a serjeant's reading, and this may have been the Middle Temple reading by Edward Mountague, serjeant-elect, in 1531: see *Readers and Readings*, p. 341. Also noted above, p. 257, no. 27.

Note that if someone is attainted of felony the king shall have the land for year, day and waste (*annum, diem et vastum*),[1] and then the lord of whom the land is held; but the king shall not have it before office found. Moreover he shall have it at his pleasure, when he will, and once the king has had year, day and waste the lord shall sue an ousterlemain: note that. Also, the lord of whom the land is held may well enter in the land at any time before an office is found, and before process is made out of the Exchequer to the escheator to seize the land for the king for year, day and waste; and the king may have that at his pleasure, when he wills: note that.

Proprietate probanda

57. ANON.

Probably Common Pleas, Trin. 1530.

Note that if I bail certain goods to someone to rebail over to someone else, this does not change the property, but I may well take the goods back at any time. So it is where I bail certain goods to someone else without saying more, that does not change the property. But it is otherwise where I bail certain goods to another man to the use of someone else, for in that case the property is changed immediately, because the limitation of the use changes the property: note that for good law etc.

---

[1] Prerogativa Regis, c. 16 (*SR* i. 226).

[58]

Relation. T. 22 H. 8. [Fo. 54v.]

Nota si home fait felonie et puis il vende sez bienz ou eux dona a un auter, et puis est atteint per verdit ou per utlagarie ou per ascun auter voie, que donques le roy navera lez bienz issint vendez ou donez quar le attaindre navera relation quant as chatellz al temps de felonie fait. Mez de terre auterment est etc. <Pollarde>

[59]

Reliefe. T. 26 H. 8. [Fo. 95.]

Nota, si seignior et tenant sont, et le tenant fait feffement en fee al use de luy mesme et E. sa feme et lez heirez del baron, le baron devie, son heire de pleine age, le feme esteant en vie, le heire ne paiera reliefe durant le vie del feme pur ceo que el est tenant del use, et serra del use come serra del terre, et donques le heire ne paiera reliefe durant le vie le feme. Come en case si terre soit don a ii. et as heires lun de eux, cesti que ad fe morust, son heire ne paiera reliefe vivant lauter, que ad estate forsque pur terme de vie, pur ceo que il est tenant al seignior. Et issint est en le case adevant, per que etc. <Pollarde>

[60]

Remainder et fee executed. [Fo. 150.]

Si lease soit fait a un home pur terme de vie dun J. T., le remainder a un A. B. in forma predicta, ceo semble bon remainder, et en ceo case il avera estate

Relation

58. NOTE

Trin. 1530.

Note that if someone commits felony and afterwards sells his goods or gives them to someone else, and he is afterwards attainted by verdict or by outlawry, or in any other way, the king shall not have the goods so sold or given, for with respect to chattels the attainder does not relate back to the time when the felony was committed. But it is otherwise of land etc.[1]

Relief

59. ANON.

Probably Common Pleas, Trin. 1534. Also noted above, p. 264, no. 42.

Note that if there are a lord and a tenant, and the tenant makes a feoffment in fee to the use of himself and E. his wife, and the heirs of the husband, the husband dies, his heir being of full age and the woman being alive, the heir shall not pay relief during the woman's lifetime because she is tenant of the use, and it shall be concerning the use as it shall concerning the land, and so the heir shall no pay relief during the woman's lifetime. Likewise if land is given to two and to the heirs of one of them, and the one who has fee dies, his heir shall not pay relief while the other is alive, even though he has an estate only for term of life, because he is tenant to the lord. So it is in the former case; and so etc.

Remainder

60. NOTE

Undated. Cf. Caryll's reports, below, p. 392, no. 53, and p. 396, no. 62.

If a lease is made to someone for term of the life of one J. T., the remainder to one A. B. 'in the form aforesaid' (*in forma praedicta*), this seems a good

---

[1] The following citations occur in the margin, in the same hand as the text: 15 Edw. IV, fo. 10; 12 Edw. IV, fo. 11; 11 Hen. VII, fo. 18. None of them are correct, so far as the printed YB are concerned. Cf. YB Pas. 8 Edw. IV, fo. 4, pl. 8.

pur terme de son vie demesne pur ceo que il ne purra aver estate durant le vie del dit J. T. pur ceo que il est mort, per que il avera terme de son vie demesne. Et si lease soit fait a terme de vie, le remainder in forma predicta, cesti en le remainder avera tiel estate come lauter avoit adevaunt etc. <Pollarde>

[61]

Remainder et fee executed. Anno 22 H. 8. [Ff. 54v–55.]

En trnz vide si home devise un greil a un home pur terme de sa vie, et apres son decease le remainder a un auter a terme de vie, le remainder oustre al lez gardenz del esglis de D.: et ceo tenus bon remainder. Tamen quere, quar fuit dit pur ley 22 H. 8. que home ne poet faier un remainder dun chatel en possession. Come si home que ad un lease [a terme dans]¹ ceo done a un auter per fait ou per volunte <un lease a terme danz>¹ durant le vie dun auter, et apres son decease le remainder a un auter, est voide causa qua supra. Mez autrement est si home done le occupation dun chatell pur terme de vie ou de anz, le remainder ouster: donques le remainder serra bon, pur ceo que le done nad ascun propertie forsque le occupation, per que etc. <Pollarde>

[62]

Resorter de terrez et hereditamentz. T. 24 H. 8. [Fo. 76.]

Nota, si home prist un feme seisi de terre et ad issue fitz et puis le baron morust, et <ad issue>² le feme prist auter baron et ount issue un auter fitz, et le baron et feme devie, et le primer fitz per le primer baron enter et morust sanz issue, en ceo case le second fitz per le second baron ne poet mye enter ne aver le terre pur ceo que il ne poet estre heire a primer fitz, pur ceo que il est de demie sanke. Mez en ceo case¹ le terre resortera al prochin heire de parte le mier. Et si ne soit ascun tiel heire, donques le terre resortera al seignior per eschete. Mez nota si soit dun don en le taile, donques le ii. fitz avera le terre nient obstant que il est de demie sanke: quod nota. <Pollarde>

---

¹ *Deleted.*
² *Deleted.*

remainder, and in this case he shall have an estate for term of his own life, because he cannot have an estate during the life of the said J. T., inasmuch as he is dead, and so he shall have a term of his own life. And if a lease is made for term of life, the remainder *in forma praedicta*, the remainderman shall have such estate as the other had before etc.

61. NOTE

1530/31.

In trespass, observe that someone devised a grail[1] to a man for term of his life, remainder after his decease to another for term of life, remainder over to the churchwardens of Dale, and this was held a good remainder.[2] Query nevertheless, for it was stated as law in 22 Hen. VIII that one may not make a remainder of a chattel in possession. Thus if someone who has a lease for a term of years gives it to another by deed, or by will, during the life of someone else, a remainder to another after his decease is void, for the above reason. But it is otherwise if someone gives the occupation of a chattel for a term of life or years, the remainder over: then the remainder shall be good, because the donee has no property but only the occupation; and so etc.

Resorter

62. NOTE

Trin. 1532.

Note that if a man marries a woman seised of land and has issue a son, and then the husband dies, and the woman marries another husband and they have issue another son, and the husband and wife die, and the first son (by the first husband) enters and dies without issue, in this case the second son (by the second husband) may not enter or have the land, because he cannot be heir to the first son inasmuch as he is of the half-blood. But in this case the land shall resort to the next heir on the mother's side; and if there is no such heir, then the land shall resort to the lord by escheat. But note that if there is a gift in tail, the second son shall have the land even though he is of the half-blood: note that.

---

[1] Or gradual, i.e. a service-book containing that part of the mass which was sung between the epistle and the gospel: *NED* grail.

[2] This is a reference to *Glover and Broun* v. *Forden* (1459) YB Trin. 37 Hen. VI, fo. 30, pl. 11; CP 40/794, m. 291; Dyer, fo. 359; 94 Selden Soc., intro., p. *219*.

[63]

[Reversion.] *Vide de feffementz et contractes et en title de reversion.*
T. 24 H. 8. [*Fo. 76v*]

Nota que le opinion de tout le court forsque *Inglefelde* que si jeo ad feffeez a mon use en fee et ilz font done en le taile de mesme le terre a un auter home sanz ascun bargaine et sale, donques le tenant en taile serra seisi a son use demesne et nemi a mon use, pur ceo que le done en taile fait un seignorie que serra dit auxi fort come si il avoit paie denerz pur le terre: quod nota. \<Pollarde\>

[64]

Riottez et rowtz. Lectura Saunderz. [Fo. 150.]

Nota que un riott est lou ii. homes ou plus eux assemble pur faire un tort, et ceo face, ceo est riot nient obstant que nest ascun person la enconter eux. Mez si ilz ne face ascun chose mez eux assemble, donques nest riott, forsque unlawfull assemble. Rowtz est lou un cominaltie eux assembleront pur faire un tort ou chose en tout lour nosmez, et ceo face, ceo est rowte: quod nota. \<Pollarde\>

[65]

Scire facias. P. 23 H. 8. [Fo. 64.]

Nota que dit fuit per tout le court que si un executour plede Pleinement administre, et trove est que il ad parcel del demande dez bienz le mort en son possession, per que il ad jugement de recover tout ceo que il ad en son possession, et puis auterz bienz viendront en son possession que fueront lez bienz le mort, \<per que\>[1] il avera un scire facias toutz foitz apres horz de mesme le jugement. Mez si trove soit adeprimez que il navoit rienz dez bienz

---

[1] *Deleted.*

Reversion

63. ANON.

Common Pleas, Trin. 1532.

Note the opinion of the whole court except ENGLEFIELD that if I have feoffees to my use in fee and they make a gift in tail of the same land to another man, without any bargain and sale, the tenant in tail shall be seised to his own use and not to my use, because the gift in tail makes a seignory which shall be deemed as strong as if he had paid money for the land: note that.

Riots and routs

64. WILLIAM SAUNDERS' READING

Middle Temple, probably Lent 1533. His first reading was in Lent 1525. See above, p. 263, no. 39.

Note that a riot is where two or more men assemble to commit a wrong, and do it; this is riot even though there is no one there to oppose them. But if they do not do anything but assemble themselves, it is not riot but only unlawful assembly. Rout is where a community assemble to commit a wrong or something in all their names, and do it, this is rout: note that.

Scire facias

65. ANON.

Probably Common Pleas, Pas. 1531. Cf. above, p. 259, no. 31.

Note that it was said by the whole court that if an executor pleads 'Fully administered', and it is found that he [can meet] part of the demand from the goods of the deceased in his possession, and so the plaintiff has judgment to recover everything that he has in his possession, and afterwards other goods which belonged to the deceased come into his possession, he shall have a *scire facias* out of the same judgment at all times afterwards. But if it is found at the outset that he had nothing from the goods of the deceased, in that case he shall never have a *scire facias* afterwards, even if goods belonging to the deceased

le mort, donques en ceo case il navera unques scire facias apres, nient obstant que lez bienz le mort viendront en son possession apres: et sic nota diversitatem etc. 4 H. 6, f. 4, sic. Vide 33 H. 6, f. 26, que il avera en le darren case. <Pollarde>

[66]

[Seisin.] *Que serra dit bon seisin.* T. 22 H. 8. [Fo. 55.]

Si le pier fait lease a terme danz et devie deinz le terme, et puis un estraunge enter sur le lesse a terme de anz, le heire en ceo case avera assise sanz ascun entre ou auter possession, pur ceo que le possession del lesse a terme de anz est le possession del heire: quod fuit concessum. Quere tamen etc. <Pollarde>

[67]

Statut merchant. [Fo. 150v.]

Nota que statut merchant serra pris avant le maior de chescun ville que ad auctoritie de prendre tiel statut, et nemi devaunt le meier de staple, quar le meier de staple ne poit prendre tiel estatut. Et ceo apperust per statutum de Acton Burnell etc. <Pollarde>

[68]

Tenaunt per copie. T. 21 H. 8. [Fo. 51.]

En le Comen Banke dit fuit per *Fitzherbert* que si le seigniour ousta le termour per copie de court rolle deinz le terme que donques il avera bon brefe

should come into his possession afterwards: so note the distinction etc. Thus is 4 Hen. VI, fo. 4.[1] See 33 Hen. VI, fo. 26,[2] as to what he shall have in the latter case.

Seisin

66. ANON.

Probably Common Pleas, Trin. 1530.

If a father makes a lease for a term of years and dies within the term, and afterwards a stranger enters upon the lessee for term of years, the heir in this case shall have an assize without any entry or other possession, because the possession of the lessee for a term of years is the heir's possession. This was conceded: query nevertheless etc.

Statute merchant

67. NOTE

Undated.

Note that a statute merchant may be taken before the mayor of every town which has authority to take such statutes, but not before the mayor of the staple, for the mayor of the staple may not take such a statute. This appears by the statute of Acton Burnel[3] etc.

Tenant by copy[hold]

68. ANON.

Common Pleas, Trin. 1529. Translated in Baker & Milsom, p. 202.

In the Common Bench it was said by FITZHERBERT that if the lord ousts the termor by copy of court roll within the term he shall have a good writ

[1] YB Mich. 4 Hen. VI, fo. 4, pl. 8.
[2] YB Trin. 33 Hen. VI, fo. 23, pl. 1, at fo. 24.
[3] 11 Edw. I, *De mercatoribus* (*SR* i. 53).

de trnz vers le seigniour etc. Quere tamen. Vide bon case de tenant per copie en 14 H. 4, f. 2. 7 E. 4, f. 19. 21 E. 4, f. 96. <Pollarde>

[69]

Travers. 23 H. 8. [Fo. 64.]

Nota que si le vicont returne un rescous que ceo ne serra mye travers, mez que il ferra son fine. <Pollarde>

[70]

Triall. [Fo. 150v.]

Nota que London ne Bristowe ne purront mye joindre ove jururz de auter countie. Mez lez jururz de ii. auterz countiez purront joindre: quod nota. <Pollarde>

[71]

Triall. [Fo. 150v.]

Nota que si assise soit port de rent issant hors de terre en ii. countiez, donques lassise serra tenuz en confinio comitatus. Et issint est lou home demaunde comen appendant a un maner en un countie issant horz de terre en auter countie: quod nota. <Pollarde>

of trespass against the lord etc. Query nevertheless. See a good case of tenant by copy in 14 Hen. IV, fo. 2;[1] [and also] 7 Edw. IV, fo. 19;[2] 21 Edw. IV, fo. 96.[3]

Traverse

69. NOTE

1531/32. Cf. above, p. 227, no. 375 (1534); below, p. 393, no. 55.

Note that if the sheriff returns a rescue this shall not be traversed, but he shall make his fine.

Trial

70. NOTE

Undated.

Note that neither London nor Bristol may join with jurors of another county. But the jurors of any two other counties may join. Note that.[4]

71. NOTE

Undated.

Note that if an assize is brought for rent issuing out of land in two counties, the assize shall be held at the edge of the county (*in confinio comitatus*).[5] So it is where someone demands common appendant to a manor in one county issuing out of land in another county: note that.

---

[1] YB Mich. 14 Hen. IV, ff. 2–9, pl. 6.
[2] YB Mich. 7 Edw. IV, ff. 18-19, pl. 16.
[3] YB Hil. 21 Edw. IV, fo. 80, pl. 27.
[4] There is a marginal reference to the statute 7 Ric. II, c. 10 (*SR* ii. 34).
[5] 7 Ric. II, c. 10 (*SR* ii. 34).

[72]

Usez. Anno 24 H. 8. [Fo. 76v.]

Si home fait covenaunt ove[i] un auter en consideration dun marriage que lez terrez discendront a son issue apres son mort, ceo ne change mye ascun use mez est tantsolement en covenaunt. Mez si il dit que il et toutz auterz personz quex serront seisiez de mesme le terre serront enapres seisiez a mesme cel use, donques auterment serra etc.[1]

[73]

Uses. Anno 24 H. 8. [Ff. 76v–77.]

Nota que est dit per plusourz dez justicez de Comen Banke que si cesti que use en taile fait feffement ou lease apres que il ad issue, que cest lease ou feffement liera le issue en taile pur ceo que tenant en taile en use serra pris come tenant en taile fuit devaunt lestatut de donis conditionalibus, W. second, capitulo primo, devaunt quel estatut chescun tenant en taile apres ceo que il ad issue poet bien alien le terre a son plesure, et donques per lestatut de donis conditionalibus est purveu que ou terrez ou tenementz est don en le taile que donquez il ne barrera son heire mez que le volunte del donour serra observe. Et icy est un use en le taile, le quel est a ore come fuit devaunt lestatut fait de donis conditionalibus, quel est come un fee simple apres ceo que il ad issue, quar lestatut de donis conditionalibus ne parle si non lou terre ou tenement est don en le taile que donques le volunte del donour serra observe, et icy nest ascun terre ou tenement don en le taile, ne est ascun donour en le taile, per que nest my deinz le compas del dit estatut de donis conditionalibus. Et pur ceo serra come fuit a comen lawe[2] devaunt cel estatut de donis conditionalibus fait, quel est que il ad fee simple apres que il ad issue. Et auxi lestatut de Ric. que done que toutz leasez fait ou a faire per cesti que use serront bon, per cel estatut

---

[1] *This is not marked* Pollarde, *but it is in the midst of a selection of his cases.*
[2] *Sic.*

Uses

72. ANON.

1532/33. Perhaps from the following case (no. 73).

If someone makes a covenant with another, in consideration of a marriage, that his lands will descend to his issue after his death, this does not change any use but is solely in covenant. However, if he says that he and all other persons who are seised of the same land shall thereafter be seised to this same use, then it will be otherwise etc.[1]

73. ANON.

Common Pleas, 1532/33. Perhaps the same as YB Trin. 19 Hen. VIII, fo. 13, pl. 11 (in Serjeants' Inn), which appears to be misdated.[2]

Note that it is said by several of the justices of the Common Bench that if cestuy que use in tail makes a feoffment or lease after he has had issue, this lease or feoffment shall bind the issue in tail, because tenant in tail in use shall be understood as tenant in tail was before the statute *De donis conditionalibus*, Westminster II, c. 1,[3] before which statute every tenant in tail after he had had issue could well alien the land at his pleasure; and then by the statute *De donis conditionalibus* it is provided that where lands or tenements are given in tail the donee shall not bar his heir, but the will of the donor shall be observed. And here there is a use in tail, which is nowadays as it was before the statute *De donis conditionalibus*, which is like a fee simple after he has had issue, for the statute *De donis conditionalibus* only says that where land or tenement is given in tail the will of the donor shall be observed, and here there is no land or tenement given in tail, nor is there any donor in tail, and so it is not within the compass of the said statute *De donis conditionalibus*. Therefore it shall be as it was at common law before this statute *De donis conditionalibus* was made, which is that he has fee simple after he has had issue. Moreover the statute of Richard[4] provides that all leases made or to be made by cestuy que use shall be

---

[1] There is a marginal note: '20 H. 7. f. 10. contra': i.e. *The Duke of Buckingham's Case* (1504) YB Mich. 20 Hen. VII, fo. 10, pl. 20.

[2] There is a marginal note: '19 H. 8. fo. 7 contra'. This presumably refers to YB Pas. 19 Hen. VIII, ff. 6–7, pl. 5; Dyer, fo. 3a; but that is a different case (as to the effect of a fine levied by tenant in tail at law).

[3] 13 Edw. I, Westminster II, c. 1, *De donis* (*SR* i. 71).

[4] 1 Ric. III, c. 1 (*SR* ii. 477).

tenant en taile en possession est save et excepte et nemi tenant en taile en use, pur ceo que lestatut est sil ait droit, scilicet ceux que ount ascun droit per reson de ascun done en le taile, issint sur le matter monstre semble que cesti que use en taile apres que il ad issue ad fee simple come fuit devaunt lestatut de donis conditionalibus fait, pur ceo que nest ascun done de terre ne de tenement, per que etc. <Pollarde>

[74]

Verdit. H. 21 H. 8. [Fo. 51.]

En det vers executourz en le com. de M. quex pledont Pleinement administre etc. et le pleintife averra que ilz ount assez de bienz le mort, et sur ceo a issue, et sur ceo trove fuit per nisi prius devaunt *Inglefelde,* justice de assize, que lez executourz ount assetz en lour mainz dez bienz le mort en auter countie que ou le brefe fuit port, et ceo verdit fuit tenus assetz bon etc. <Pollarde>

[75]

Weiver de suite et de ple. M. 22 H. 8. [Fo. 55.]

Nota que dit fuit per *Fitzjames,* Chiefe Justice, que si le defendant en det sur obligation voile dire que il est un [laie]¹ home et nemi letterd et que le obligation fuit lie a luy sur certen condition, issint ceo obligation sanz condition nest pas son fait, ore per cest conclusion al issue tout le residue del ple fuit [weive].² Et issint est si le defendant en trnz plede un reles en barre [ou]³ le lieu ou etc. le fraunctenement dun J. T. et il come servaunt a luy enter en le terre etc. et auxi dit que il nest pas culpable. Et issint est en formedon si le tenant plede un feffement ove garrante et assetz discende, [ou]⁴ un collaterall garrante, et puis dit auxi que le donour ne [dona]⁵ paz, prist etc., ore per le conclusion de son ple, que est all general issue, tout le residue de son ple est weve: quod nota. <Pollarde>

---

¹ lee.   ² viewe.   ³ *Altered from* en que.   ⁴ *Altered from* et auxi.   ⁵ *Altered from* dont

good, and by that statute tenant in tail in possession is saved and excepted, but not tenant in tail in use, because the statute is 'if he has right', namely those who have any right by reason of any gift in tail; and so, upon the matter shown, it seems that cestuy que use in tail, after he has had issue, has fee simple—as before the statute *De donis conditionalibus* was made—because there is no gift of land or tenement; and so etc.

Verdict

74. ANON.

Common Pleas, Hil. 1530.

In debt against executors in the county of M., they pleaded 'Fully administered' etc., and the plaintiff averred that they have assets of the goods of the deceased; and thereupon they were at issue, and it was found by nisi prius before ENGLEFIELD, justice of assize,[1] that the executors have assets in their hands from the goods of the deceased in another county than that where the writ was brought; and this verdict was held good enough etc.

Waiver of suit and of plea

75. ANON.

King's Bench or Serjeants' Inn, Mich. 1530. Cf. above, p. 255, no. 21.

Note that it was said by FITZJAMES, Chief Justice, that if the defendant in debt on a bond says that he is a layman and illiterate and that the bond was read to him upon certain condition, so that this bond without condition is not his deed, now by this conclusion to the issue all the residue of the plea is waived. And so it is if the defendant in trespass pleads a release in bar, or that the place in question is the freehold of one J. T., and that he as his servant entered in the land etc., and also says that he is not guilty.[2] So it is in formedon if the tenant pleads a feoffment with warranty and assets descended, or a collateral warranty, and then further also that the donor did not make the gift (*Ne dona pas*), ready etc.: now by the conclusion of his plea, which is to the general issue, all the rest of his plea is waived: note that.

---

[1] Englefield was justice of assize on the Home Circuit from 1527 until his death.
[2] Above, p. 255, no. 21, *per* Spelman and Englefield J. (Mich. 1531).

7. Reports by Robert Chaloner (*c.* 1515–1519)[1]

[1]

[*Fo. 19v*] Dominus *Fenex* dit en Bank le Roy termino Trinitatis anno viii H. 8. en brefe derrour sur jugement done en Comen Banke en brefe de dower pro uxore Christofori Gerth melitis quondam uxore Johannis Risley militis versus Dominum Zouch que chescun home que voiet construe un estatut covient aver iii chosez, scilicet de ceo construe accordant all parolx et nemi contra a eux, quar il confounde le text et nemi expound, et si lez parolx sunt defecult dunquez covient vier le mynde deux que ceo fist, et dunquez le 3. est de construer ceo accordant come avoit este construe devant per auterz sages homez. Et lez iii ensemblement combynes ove bon reason fra bon construction. Et pur ceo que lez justices de Comen Banke ad construe devant que el sera endowe il done mult credens[2] a ceo. Et auxi dit que exception et proviso en un estatut est tout un, et pur ceo si lact soit generall un proviso ou exception puit saver pur parcell, mez si lact soit especiall come lez nosmez de x. homez except un, ou providid pur un, cest voide. Mez cest paroll *voit*[3] paraventure puit faire novell act et dunquez ceo perfite un graunt que ne fuit bon devant. Mez proviso ne perfitt ascun graunt que est voide devaunt etc.

[2]

En Banke le Roy un fuit trove culpable et prie son liver, et latturney le roy dit que auterfoitz convict a Neugat, et en brefe al maire de Lond. fuit issint certifie, a que jour il dit que fuit prest et monstre lettrez dordinar., et brefe issist al ordinare et il certifie quun de mesme le nosme prist lorder de pristhod la, et il

---

[1] Extracted from Gray's Inn MS. 25. *Written in some of the blank pages in a collection of readings.*
[2] crededs.
[3] *Underlined.*

7. REPORTS BY ROBERT CHALONER (*c.* 1515–19)

1. GARTH v. LORD ZOUCHE

King's Bench, Trin. 1516. Cf. Yorke, above, p. 114, no. 73.

The lord FYNEUX said in the King's Bench in Trinity term 8 Hen. VIII, in a writ of error upon a judgment given in the Common Bench in a writ of dower for the wife of Christopher Garth,[1] knight, formerly the wife of John Risley, knight,[2] against the Lord Zouche,[3] that anyone who wishes to construe a statute must have [in mind] three things: that is, [1] to construe it according to the words and not against them, for otherwise he confounds the text and does not expound it; [2] and if the words are difficult he must look to the mind of those who made the statute; [3] and then the third is to construe it according to how it has been construed before by other wise men. These three together, combined with good reason, will make a good construction. And because the justices of the Common Bench have formerly construed that she should be endowed, he gave much credence to that. He also said that an exception and a proviso in a statute are all one; and therefore, if the act is general, a proviso or exception may save as to part, whereas if the act is special—for instance, naming ten men except one, or with a proviso for one—it is void. But this word 'wills' (*voit*) may perhaps make a new act, and then it perfects a grant which was not good before, whereas a proviso does not perfect any grant which is void before etc.

2. ANON.

In the King's Bench someone was found guilty and prayed his book, and the king's attorney said that he was previously convicted at Newgate, and in a writ to the mayor of London it was so certified; and at the day he said that he was a priest, and showed letters of ordination, and a writ issued to the ordinary, who

---

[1] Unidentified: perhaps the name has ben garbled.
[2] Of Eltham, Kent, died 1512: P.C.C. 8 Fetiplace; C142/79/174, 190, 191, 223.
[3] John le Zouche, Lord Zouche, died 1526.

dit que il fuit mesme le person, et latturney le roy averrera al contrarie, et enquest del counte ou il fuit pris fuit charge denquerir si mesme le person que fuit prist ou nemi, et nemi lenquest dell count ou il prist lorders.

[3]

Estatut de articuli super cartas, capitulo vii, est que un somons et atachment in ple de terre conteigne le somons ou latachement per space de xv jourz al meyns solonque le comen ley si ne soit in atachement dassises prendre in presens le roy ou dez plees devaunt justices en eire. 9 E. 4, f. 19. 13 E. 4, f. 14. Litt.

[4]

[*Fo. 172*] En atteint le brefe fuit varient del record, quar le record fuit inter J. S. et J. D. et le brefe fuit inter J. S., J. B. et J. D. Et si ceo soit misprision? Quar il avoit le record devaunt luy, come obligation. Et fuit dit que misprision en judiciall sera amende, et en ascun case en original: come det sur obligation, si varians il sera amende. Mez si loriginal bon et proces varie, le record sera amende et nemi le proces. Et fuit dit si home soit nonsuit il navera unquez atteint apres, mez discont. ou retraxit ou abatement de brefe pur fourme per jugement del court, uncore il avera auter brefe etc.

[5]

En trespas pur entrer en v acres de terre, [le] defendant [dit] que J. S. fuit seisi et luy enfeoffe etc. et done colour, et le pleintife dit que ceo est auter v acres, ceo nest ple, quar icy il maint[iendra] son brefe. Mez si le defendant avoit dit que le lieu est v acres apelle G. dunquez le pleintife puit dire que est auter v acres. Et issint diversitie quaunt le defendant done nosme et quaunt nemi: quod nota, per oppinionem justiciariorum.

certified that someone of the same name took the order of priesthood there; and the defendant said that he was the same person, and the king's attorney averred the contrary, and an inquest from the county where he was arrested was charged to enquire whether or not he was the same person who was priest, and not an inquest from the county where the priest took the orders.

3. NOTE

The statute of *Articuli super cartas*, chapter [15],[1] says that a summons and attachment in a plea of land shall contain a period of fifteen days at least, according to the common law, unless it is in an attachment of assizes to be taken in the king's presence or pleas before justices in eyre. 9 Edw. IV, fo. 19;[2] 13 Edw. IV, fo. 14, [*per*] Littleton.[3]

4. ANON.

In attaint the writ was variant from the record, for the record was 'between J. S. and J. D.' and the writ was 'between J. S., J. B. and J. D.'. Is this misprision? For [the clerk] had the record before him, as in the case of a bond. And it was said that misprision in a judicial writ shall be amended, and in some cases in an original: for instance, in debt on a bond, if there is a variance [from the bond] it shall be amended. But if the original is good and the process varies, the record shall be amended and not the process. And it was said that if someone is nonsuited he shall never have attaint afterwards, but in the case of a discontinuance, or a *retraxit*, or abatement of the writ for form, by judgment of the court, he shall have nevertheless another writ etc.

5. ANON.

In trespass for entering in five acres of land, the defendant said that John Style was seised and enfeoffed him etc., and gave colour, and the plaintiff said that it is another five acres: this is no plea, for he should maintain his writ. But if the defendant had said that the place is five acres called G., the plaintiff could say that it is another five acres. So there is a distinction when the defendant gives a name and when he does not: note that, by the opinion of the justices.

---

[1] 28 Edw. I, Articuli super cartas, c. 15 (*SR* i. 140).
[2] YB Trin. 9 Edw. IV, fo. 18, pl. 21.
[3] Unidentified. Cf. YB Mich. 12 Edw. IV, fo. 11, pl. 1.

[6][1]

Si le seignour oustera le tenant a terme danz fait [per] le pere leire fuit argue.

Et *Conisby* semble que nemi, quar auxi bien quil puit faire feoffment [ou] leez a terme de vie et le seignour ne oustera luy, per mesme le reson il ne oustera le tenant a terme danz, quar il puit charge le terre ove rent charge pur terme danz et le seignour tiendra charge: quod fuit concessum per omnes justiciarios. Et nest semble a tenant per estatute merchant etc., quar la il tient le terre forsque durant le temps que lez deners sount levez et nemi pur ascun temps certen. Et pur ceo si soit extente pur xx li. et apres le terre est wast, ou auter casuelte vient per que est empere, dunquez il ceo tiendra ouster cest terme extient. Et fuit concessum per omnes justiciarios. Dunquez icy il est seignour et il clame al jour de morant de le tenant et nemi devaunt, quar le brefe est morust en son homage, et donquez son title de leez est devaunt son title de garde, et donquez il ne luy oustera.

Burnell a mesme lentent. Et icy nest a arguer de priorite ne posteriorite[2] quar ceo est toutz foitz perenter ii seignours. Mez icy cest leez est un chose que est vestu et pur ceo ne puit estre devestu. Come home tient terrez de moy per service de chivaler et morust, et jeo seise le garde, et apres auterz terrez que sont del roy discendent a mesme le garde, uncore le roy navera le garde de leire quar fuit un foitz devestu en moy. Et icy sil soit ouste il ne puit aver mesme le chose que fuit graunt, quar le graunt fuit pur v anz prochyn ensuantes, le quell v anz ne poient estre quant leire est a son pleine age. Auxi icy semble que est seignour, mesne et tenant, quar tenant pur terme danz ferra fealte come est agre 5 H. 7. Dunquez est seignour, mesne et tenant, et dunquez le seignour navera auter chose del mesne forsque leire et service que sont reserves, quar si le mesne avoit reles al tenant a tener per un dener, le seignour navera pluys que cest dener. Come home fait leez a terme de vie ou danz, remainder en fee, si cesti en le remainder en fee morust, son heire deinz age, le seignour navera le garde durant le terme, quar ambideux ne sount forque un tenant. Issint icy, cest tenant est tenant al mesne, et dunquez le seignour avera lez services.

Fenex a mesme lentent. Et home puit faier[3] colour dambideux voiez. Mez quant est a estre determine et ajuge dunquez covient de faire ceo come home ad en son conceit. Donquez icy cest tenant pur terme danz clame ouster le title le seignour, quar le seignour le clame forque puis le mort. Mez tenant en

---

[1] *Over this is written:* Esk' tient diversite ou lesse puit aver action de covenant et ou nemi.
[2] pˢteriote.
[3] *Reading unclear.*

6. ANON.[1]

King's Bench. Extract in Baker & Milsom, p. 183.

It was argued whether the lord may oust a tenant for term of years made by the heir's father.

CONYNGESBY thought not, for just as he may make a feoffment or a lease for term of life and the lord may not oust the tenant, by the same reason he may not oust the tenant for term of years; for he may charge the land with a rent-charge for a term of years and the lord shall hold charged: which was granted by all the justices. It is not like tenant by statute merchant etc., for there he holds the land only while the money is being raised and not for any certain time; and therefore if it is valued for £20 and afterwards the land is wasted, or some other accident occurs whereby it is impaired, he shall then hold it beyond the term of the valuation: and that was granted by all the justices. Here, then, he is lord and he claims on the day when the tenant dies and not before, for the writ says 'died in his homage', and so the lessee's title to the lease is before the lord's title to the wardship, and therefore he shall not oust him.

BRUDENELL to the same intent. We need not argue here about priority or posteriority, for that is always between two lords. Here, however, this lease is something which is vested, and therefore it cannot be divested. Similarly if someone holds lands of me by knight-service and dies, and I seize the wardship, and afterwards other lands held of the king descend to the same ward, the king shall nevertheless not have the wardship of the heir, for it was already vested in me. If he is ousted here he cannot have the same thing which was granted, for the grant was 'for the five years next following', which five years cannot be when the heir comes of age. Also it seems that here there is a lord, mesne and tenant: for a tenant for term of years shall do fealty, as is agreed in 5 Hen. VII.[2] Now, when there is a lord, mesne and tenant, the lord shall have nothing from the mesne other than the heir and the services which are reserved; for if the mesne had released to the tenant to hold by one penny, the lord would not have more than this penny. Similarly if someone makes a lease for term of life or years, remainder in fee, and the remainderman in fee dies, his heir under age, the lord shall not have the wardship during the term, for both are but one tenant. Likewise here, this tenant is tenant to the mesne, and therefore the lord shall have the services.

FYNEUX [C.J.] to the same intent. One may colour it both ways; but when it is to be determined and adjudged it must be done as one has in one's mind.[3] Here, then, this tenant for term of years claims above the title of the lord, for

---

[1] Over this case is written: 'Hesketh makes a distinction where the lessee may have an action of covenant and where not.' Richard Hesketh was a bencher of Gray's Inn.

[2] *Anon.* (1490) YB Hil. 5 Hen. VII, fo. 10, pl. 2, at fo. 11, *per* Fairfax J. (queried by the reporter); Spelman, p. 26, pl. 1.

[3] Meaning obscure.

dower clame puis le coverture et pur ceo el avoidra toutz chargez apres, mez de chargez devaunt auterment est. Et icy est semble[1] si home ad title a un maner que jeo ay en possession per brefe dentre en le per et cui, et apres auterz terrez vient per eschet a le dit maner, dunquez covient que ad demande ceo per brefe dentre en le post, quar ceo est un chose venu de puisne temps. Issint icy, cest title le seignour est [de][2] puisne temps. Et semble que[3] le tenant per estatut merchant etc. et ceo est tout un, quar la est matter de recorde et le title le seignour . . .[4] en fait, et pur ceo est reson que le matter de recorde soit prove etc.

Et issint opinio curie que ne oustera le tenant . . .[5] Et fuit dit que coment que un home prist leez a terme de vie per fait endente de son terre demesne, unquore le seignour ne serra conclude . . .[6]

[7]

En dett vers executourz sur contract, ils pledront ne detinet, et trove encontre eux, et uncore oppinion . . .[7] navera jugement quar cest action ne gist verz executourz: quod nota bene.

[8][8]

En leschequer chambre le case fuit tiel. Home fuit oblige en single obligation et puis loblige vient en . . . apres port action de dett de ceo, et lauter demande oier del fait, et habuit, et dit que son obligation fuit simple: si ceo soit bone ple ou nemi?

Et *Dominus Fenex* semble bon ple, quar nest mesme lobligation que fuit deliver . . . et est en mesme le case si come il ust enrase le condition. Issint si ascun matter que est effectuall en lobligation . . . erase ou alterate en auter maner que fuit . . . aver mesme le fait . . . nest materiall sicome soit de nosme, some ou date, nest materiall . . . que ne alter ceo. Come si home escrie son . . .

---

[1] *Written twice.*
[2] *Word lost through fading.*
[3] *Perhaps for a.*
[4] *Word lost through fading.*
[5] *Word lost through fading.*
[6] *Word lost through fading.*
[7] *Word or two lost through fading.*
[8] *Badly affected by fading through damp, with the loss of numerous words in the lower part of the leaf.*

the lord claims it only since the death. But a tenant in dower claims since the coverture and therefore, although she may avoid all charges made after the marriage, it is otherwise as to charges before. Here it is like the case where someone has title to [recover] a manor which I have in possession, by a writ of entry in the *per* and *cui*, and afterwards other lands come to the said manor by escheat: it is then necessary to demand it by writ of entry in the *post*, for it is something which has come later. Likewise here, this title of the lord is of later time. And it seems that the case of tenant by statute merchant etc. and this case are all one, for there it is a matter of record and the lord's title [sounds] in fact, and therefore it is right that the matter of record be proved etc.

Thus the opinion of the court was that the lord should not oust the tenant . . . And it was said that if someone takes a lease for term of life of his own land by deed intended, the lord shall not be estopped . . .[1]

7. ANON.

In debt against executors upon a contract, they pleaded *Non detinent*, and it was found against them; and yet the opinion was that the plaintiff should not have judgment, for this action does not lie against executors: note that well.

8. MILLYS v. GULDEFORD[2]

Exchequer Chamber. Also mentioned by Yorke, above, p. 205, no. 307; Serjeant Caryll, 116 Selden Soc. 616; YB Hil. 26 Hen. VIII, fo. 10, pl. 4, *ad finem*. Record: KB 27/1005, m. 26 (printed in 94 Selden Soc. 244).

In the Exchequer Chamber the case was as follows. Someone was bound in a single bond, and then the obligee came . . .[3] and afterwards brought an action of debt upon it, and the other demanded oyer of the deed, and had it, and said that his bond was simple. Is this a good plea, or not?

And the lord FYNEUX thought it a good plea, for it is not the same bond which was delivered . . . and it is in the same case as if he had erased the condition. Likewise if any matter which is effectual in the bond [is] erased or altered in another way than it was . . . [it is not] the same deed . . . is not material, as where it is in the name, sum or date, it is not material . . . does not alter it. For instance, if someone writes his . . .

---

[1] This paragraph is too badly faded to be fully legible.

[2] Conjectural identification. The text of this case is badly affected by fading through damp, with the loss of numerous words.

[3] Text lost; but evidently he added a condition. In *Millys* v. *Guldeford*, of which this seems to be a report, the obligee added a condition to enfeoff him of a manor before a certain day.

Et nest dout mez le condition . . .
ou il covient dire sur . . .
il ne conclude en cest case . . .   come enfant,
feme covert etc. Mez il ne . . .
uncore est . . .
le quel matter il voille . . .
navera respons a ceo . . .
respons il ne ceo averre . . . Et fuit ajuge si jeo soy oblige de feoffer homez dun
maner in . . .schire
etc. en dett . . . moy . . . tiel schire . . .
                                   . . . cheiff justice le . . .
        . . . auterz jugez fueront ove defendant et iii jugez encontre eux etc.

[9]

[*Fo. 288v*] Quo warranto issist vers le clerke de marketes, et il vient et monstre lettres patentes le roy de ceo.

Et *Conysby* dit que il est justice per commission et pur ceo ne gist vers luy, nient pluys que vers justice de Comen Banke, justice de pees, ou coroner, ou tiel sembable, quar ills sount justices del cause, come viconte etc.

Et *Fenex* dit al contrarie, quar gist vers chescun que clame office que appent al corone. Come un home clame de faire justice de pees ou coroners ou tiel semblable per election, proces issera vers luy a monstre quo warranto il clame de faire justices de pees ou coroners etc. Mez ceo ne prove que issera[1] vers le justice. Mez loffice fuit seisi et comandement done a viconte de occupier ceo.

---

[1] issisera.

And there is no doubt but that the condition . . .
or he must say upon . . .
he shall not conclude in this case . . .   as an infant,
married woman etc. But he shall not . . .
still is . . .
which matter he will [aver] . . .
shall not have an answer to that . . .
answer he does not aver it . . .
And it was adjudged that if I am bound to enfeoff men of a manor in . . . shire
etc. in debt . . . me . . . such shire . . .

. . . chief justice . . .

. . . other judges were with the defendant and three judges against them etc.

9. ATT.-GEN. v. CLERK OF THE MARKETS

King's Bench. Presumably from the Middlesex *quo warranto* proceedings of
1519–20: cf. the five following cases (nos. 10–14).

Quo warranto issued against the clerk of the markets, and he came and
showed the king's letters patent for it.

CONYNGESBY said that he is a justice by commission and therefore it does
not lie against him, any more than against a justice of the Common Bench,
justice of the peace, coroner, or such like; for they are justices of the cause, like
a sheriff etc.

FYNEUX [C.J.] said to the contrary, for it lies against everyone who claims
an office which belongs to the crown. For instance, if someone claims to
appoint justices of the peace or coroners or such like, by election, process shall
issue against him to show by what warrant he claims to make justices of the
peace or coroners etc. [1](But this does not prove that it shall issue against
the justice. Nevertheless the office was seized and a command given to the
sheriff to occupy it.)

---

[1] This seems to be the reporter's own comment.

[10]

Nutigat clame lete, infangtheif etc.

Et lattorney le roy dit que il nad pillore, tumberelle ne furcas.

Et il dit que avoit eux mez ore soient eschue, mez il voille estre content del faire de novelle.

Et ascuns diount que cest nonuser est forfetour a toutz jours. Et ascuns al contrarie: quar sil ad excuse tanque per un an etc., et dunquez quo warranto est graunt, que nest resonable que sera forfette a toutz jourz. Ascuns diount que sil prist fyne de baker outer iii s. que ceo est abuser, que est forfetour a toutz jours. Tamen quere etc.r

[11]

Le priorese de Clerkynwell clame vue de frankplege, waift, etc. Et fuit demande a maintainer son title. Et la fuit dit que si un a cest jour clame ascun chose que gist per un prescription, si ascun aire ad estre in le counte ou il est clame puis temps dc memore quil covient monstre que il la mist einz son clame, et si ne fuit la allowe ne disalowe uncore il ceo avera, mez ex necessite covient pleder quil mist einz son clame, et [sur] ceo de monstre le lieu, jour, devaunt queux justices, quel fyne se prist, et tielx chosez semblable auxi certen come recorde. Et si soit de chose que ne gist en prescription, dunquez covient monstre allowance de ceo, et ceo exemplefy sous[1] le graunde sealle. Et fuit dit [que] per le quo warranto toutz libertez et fraunchez soient in le mayne le roy, et la demurrer[ont] a toutz jourz si ne soit replevin de ceo. Et pur ceo il covient monstre coment il eux ad hors de mayne le roy.

Mez *Conyngsby* dit que covient estre enquere quaunt fraunchez soient deinz le conte.

Mez *Fenex* dit que non, pur ceo que toutz soient en le mayne le roy al comencement etc. Et issint semble que si tiel chose que gist in graunt ne ad estre allowe in eire que il navera eux a cest jour: quod nota. Et fuit diversite quaunt un mist einz clame saunz title, et quaunt clame et title, et quaunt [face][2] clame ne title. Et uncore in toutz lez casez ils demurreront in le mayne le roy: quere etc.

---

[1] *Seemingly written* s[r].
[2] *Seemingly reads fee.*

10. ATT.-GEN. v. NEWDEGATE

King's Bench, 1519. The writ of *quo warranto* was tested on 1 July 1519.[1] Record of appearance noted in BL MS. Add. 25168, fo. 560. See also no. 12.

Newdegate[2] claimed a leet, infangthief etc.

And the king's attorney said that he did not have pillory, tumbrel or gallows.[3]

He said that he had had them, but they have fallen down, though he would be content to make them anew.

Some say that this non-user is a forfeiture for ever. And some say the contrary: for if they have [fallen down] only for one year etc., and then a *quo warranto* is granted, it is unreasonable that the leet should be forfeited for ever. Some say that if he took a fine above 3s. for baking that is an abuse, which is a forfeiture for ever. Query nevertheless etc.

11. ATT.-GEN. v. PRIORESS OF CLERKENWELL

King's Bench, 1519. The writ of *quo warranto* was tested on 1 July 1519. Record of appearance noted in BL MS. Add. 25168, fo. 560v.

The prioress of Clerkenwell claimed a view of frankpledge, waif etc. And she was asked to maintain her title. It was said there that if someone at the present day claims anything by a prescription, and there has been any eyre within time of memory in the county where it is claimed, he must show that he put in his claim, and even if it was neither allowed or disallowed there he shall still have it, but he must of necessity plead that he put in his claim, and thereupon show the place, the day, and before what justices, what fine was taken, and such like things, with as much certainty as a record. If it is of something which does not lie in prescription, then he must show an allowance thereof, exemplified under the great seal. And it was said that by the *quo warranto* all liberties and franchises are in the king's hand, and they remain there for ever unless they are replevied: therefore he must show how he has them out of the king's hand.

CONYNGESBY said that it must be enquired what franchises there are within the county.

But FYNEUX [C.J.] said that was not so, because all are in the king's hand at the commencement etc. (Therefore it seems that if such a thing as lies in grant has not been allowed in eyre he shall not have it at the present day: note that. A distinction was made between when someone puts in a claim without making title, and when he makes claim and title, and when he makes neither claim nor title. Nevertheless in all these cases the franchises remain in the king's hand: query etc.)

[1] BL MS. Add. 25168, fo. 559. For another case from these sessions, dated Mich. 1520, see above, Vol. I, p. 43, no. 27.

[2] John Newdegate, serjeant at law: BL MS. Add. 25168, fo. 560 (note of his appearance).

[3] This was a cause of forfeiture: see Spelman's reading the same year, 113 Selden Soc. 111.

[12]

Tumberell et cokkyngstolle.

Nutigat clame infangtheif et owtfangtheiff et assisa panis et service, et avoit allowans. Et lattorney le roy monstre que il nonuse et auxi misuse ceo, quar il nad furcas ne tumbrelle, et auxi il nad use de prender fyne de pistour contempt[1] et issint abuse etc.

Roo dit que nonuser nest forfetour ne finable pur ceo que est liberte graunt a luy quill puit user sil voille, et est a son avantage, et sil ne voille ceo use et prender lez profettes uncore serra punische come fuit devaunt le graunt, come le turne de viconte ceo punischera. Come si home ad faire et non use, semble que nest forfetour. Come conusance de plee nest demande, uncore il puit ly demaunde quant il voille. Tamen[2] pur misuser home ferra petit fyne. Et misuser de parcelle ne forfetra tout le lette einz forque cest parcelle etc.

Fenex. Cest lete est graunt auxibien pur le comen welth come pur lavantage le partie, et ceo covient estre use ou auterment est forfete. Et quaunt est in mayne le roy poy estre tielx considerations quil ne voille suffer ceo destre pleyne. Et in ascun case abuser de parcelle est forfetour pur tout.

Quere deux, quar Nutigat dit que cez furches fueront decoup per le vent. Et pur ceo il prie le court de prendre plegges pur luy <scilicet son fyne>[i] et que puit ceo aver hors de mayne le roy. Et issint fuit: quod nota. Quere que fuit le fyne.

[13]

Le priour de Towrhill monstre quun tiel fuit seisi dun maner in temps E. 1. et avoit vue de frankplegge, et monstre coment fuit allowe, quelle estate labbe ore avoit. Et fuit dit que [de][3] nul chose ingrose[4] per voy de title home ne conveyera luy per que estate, et coment que le roy port un quo warranto uncore le defendant est actor in maner pur ceo quil fist title vers le roy, come in quo jure.

---

[1] *Reading unclear.*
[2] *Reading unclear.*
[3] dd.
[4] *Reading unclear.*

12. ATT.-GEN. v. NEWDEGATE

King's Bench, 1519. See also no. 10, above.

Tumbrel and cucking-stool.

Newdegate claimed infangthief and outfangthief, and the assize of bread and ale, and had allowance. And the king's attorney showed that he had not used it, and had also misused it; for he did not have a gallows or tumbrel, and also he has not been accustomed to take fines from bakers for contempt; and so there is abuse etc.

Roo said that non-user is neither a forfeiture nor finable because this is a liberty granted to him which he may use if he wishes, and it is for his own advantage, and if he does not wish to use it and take the profits the offences may still be punished as they could before the grant—for instance, the sheriff's tourn shall punish them. Similarly if someone has a fair and does not use it, it seems that it is no forfeiture. Likewise if cognizance of plea is not demanded, he may still demand it when he will. Nevertheless, for misuse one shall make a small fine. And misuse of part shall not forfeit the whole leet but only that part etc.

FYNEUX [C.J.]. This leet is granted for the common wealth as well as for the benefit of the party, and it must be used or else it is forfeit. When it is in the king's hand there may be such considerations that he will not allow it to be filled. In any case, abuse of part is a forfeiture of the whole.

Query this, for Newdegate said that his gallows were blown down by the wind. And therefore he prayed the court to take pledges for him—namely for his fine—and that he might have it out of the king's hand. And so it was: note that. Query what the fine was.

13. ATT.-GEN. v. ABBOT ST MARY GRACES

King's Bench, 1519. The writ of *quo warranto* was tested on 1 July 1519. Record of appearance noted in BL MS. Add. 25168, fo. 560.

The prior of Tower Hill[1] showed that someone was seised of a manor in the time of Edward I and had a view of frankpledge, and showed how it was allowed [in eyre], which estate the abbot now has. And it was said that one could not convey title to oneself by *que estate* in respect of anything in gross[2] by way of title, and even if the king brings a *quo warranto* the defendant is still in a way *actor* because he makes out title against the king, as in *quo jure*.

---

[1] The Cistercian abbey of St Mary Graces by the Tower of London: VCH, *London*, i. 461; 102 Selden Soc. 46; BL MS. Add. 25168, fo. 560.
[2] Reading unclear.

Mez *Conyngby* dit que intant que est allege destre appendant al maner, sil convey a luy all maner per que estate que ceo est assetz bon pur ceo que ne convey a luy al chose, scilicet le liberte. Come in assise de comen sil fait title come appendant a un maner, suffist de luy de conveyer al maner per que estate. Et le que estate icy nest materiall einz le prescription est leffect.

Mez le case myse fuit deny pur ceo per *Fenex*, quar per voy de title et especiallement encontre le roy, in que toutz libertez est, un ne puit conveyer luy per que estate. Come si un voille dire que le roy graunt a tiel vue de frankplegge deinz son maner, que estate in le maner etc., ceo nest bon. Mez la semble que le graunt est severalle. Mez si disseisour ad manor semble quil avera lez libertez, mez semble que covient monstre coment, et dunquez quere si le conveyens est traversable ou nemi.

[14]

[*fo. 289*] En quo warranto vers le gardein del Fleit il vient einz et fist son clame a un mese, un gerdyn et certen rent, et loffice a custoder lez prisonerz committe in le Flet etc., per le reson quun J. S. fuit seisi de tout ceo et tout ceo tenoit de roy per graund serjantie, scilicet a gerder lez prisonerz la et le palace de Westm' etc., ratione de quell il doit aver x li. per lez maynes lez vicontes de Londres pur le temps, dount ils ount estre allow[ans] sur lour accompt, et auxi returne de toutz preceptes judicials issant deinz le palace, seaunt lez justices, et executiones eorundem etc. Fuit move que son clame ne fuit bone entre en ii, scilicet lun est pur ceo quil clame le meese, terre et loffice destre tenuz per le custodie del office. Et pur ceo, coment que nest bone title, uncore entaunt que est mater de title, scilicet le terres etc. et auxi loffice destre tenuz, ceo est ii chosez suppose destre tenuz etc. et pur ceo est [double].[1] Auxi est double pur ceo quil allege daver eux ratione le mease, terre et office, ou il avera ceo sil ad ascun [deux][2] et pur ceo dalleger ceo et daver ceo per reson de ii chosez ou il ad ceo per reson de chescun [de] eux ii est double. Come ii collaterall warranties, chescun deux est bare etc. Auxi si home clame voy al esglise per reson de deux manerz dount il est seisi, *Fitzherbert* dit que est double quar sil ad ascun [deux][3] il avera le voy: mez ascuns ceo deny pur ceo que puit aver graunt pur luy quaunt il demurt a chescun deux ou pur sez tenantes de chescun deux. Ideo quere.

[1] ii *(and similarly below)*.
[2] ii.
[3] ii.

But CONYNGESBY said that, since it is alleged to be appendant to the manor, if he traces the manor to himself by *que estate* this is good enough, because he does not trace the thing—namely the liberty—to himself. Likewise in an assize of common, if he makes title as appendant to a manor, it is sufficient to trace to himself a title to the manor by *que estate*. And the *que estate* here is not material, but the prescription is the effective matter.

However, the case which was put was denied (as to this point) by FYNEUX [C.J.], for one may not trace title to oneself by *que estate*, especially against the king, in whom all liberties are. For instance, if one wishes to say that the king granted so and so a view of frankpledge within his manor, whose estate in the manor [he has], this is not good. But it seems there that the grant is separate [from the manor]. However, if a disseisor has a manor, it seems he shall have the liberties, though it seems he must show how; and then query whether the tracing of title is traversable or not.

14. ATT.-GEN. v. BABINGTON

The writ of *quo warranto* was tested on 1 July 1519. Record of appearance (both as William Babington and as 'custos palacii domini regis apud Westmonasterium') noted in BL MS. Add. 25168, fo. 560v.

In *quo warranto* against the warden of the Fleet he came in and made his claim to a house, a garden and certain rent, and the office of keeping the prisoners committed to the Fleet etc., by reason that one John Style was seised of all this, and held it all of the king by grand serjeanty, namely keeping the prisoners there and keeping the palace of Westminster etc., by reason whereof he ought to have £10 by the hands of the sheriffs of London for the time being, of which they have had an allowance upon their account, and also the return of all judicial precepts issuing within the palace, while the justices are sitting, and executions of the same etc. It was moved that his claim was not well entered in two respects. The first is because he claims the house, land and office to be held by the custody of the office. Therefore, even if it is not a good title, nevertheless since there is a matter of title, namely the lands etc. and also the office to be held, these are two things supposed to be held etc. and therefore it is double. It is also double because he alleges to have them by reason of the house, land and office, whereas he shall have it if he has any of them; and therefore to allege that he has it by reason of two things, where he has it by reason of each of the two, is double. Likewise where there are two collateral warranties, each of them is a bar etc. Also if someone claims a church-way by reason of two manors of which he is seised, *Fitzherbert* said that it is double: for if he has either of them he shall have the way: but some denied this, because he might have a grant for himself when he lives at each of them, or for his tenants of each of them. Therefore query.

Dunquez aliquat[enus][1] fuit dit quun ne puit tener office a garder mesme loffice, pur ceo que per reson que il ad loffice il est tenuz de ceo gerder, et pur ceo a ceo tener per tielx chosez de queux est lie de faire est voide tenour. Et auxi est empertenaunt de tener un chose per mesme le chose, quar le tenour et chosez tenuz est ii chosez, scilicet lun al seignour et lauter al tenant, et pur ceo a tener rent per mesme le rent est voide, ou a tener mease de ceo repareler, ou faire chose[2] a luy mesme ou a demurrer in ceo est voide. Issint icy a tener loffice de gerder lez prisonerz est voide tenour. Mez un puit tener un office de garder auter office etc.

A cest point al contrarie quar ceo entier chose fuit done alle commencement a estre tenuz per tielx servicez, et coment que loffice per luy mesme ne puit estre issint tenuz uncore entaunt que est joine ove le mease etc. que puit estre tenuz per tielx servicez coment est entire chose tout sera tenuz per cest service. Come terre est done a home a tener per lez services destre parker de tiel forest etc. et daver chescun dame icy occist le schulder et de chescun arbour succide un dener, cest bone tenour. Auxi de repareler le paile et daver le olde paile etc. Icy per mesne il puit faire service a luy mesme, mez pur ceo que le premissez et le sequele nest que un entier chose est bone. Come maner ove emplementes de houshold poit estre lese ou done en taile et prise. Issint semble que puit estre done devaunt lestatut a estre tenuz per service et bone entaunt que est ajoine ove auter chose. Et amesnez[3] si fuit tiel done devaunt temps etc. si ne puit estre tenuz come est reherce, uncore serra construe accordaunt al reservation et le tener doffice a custoder etc. destre voide et le terre destre tenuz per tielx services, et donques coment que ore est allege destre tenuz nest que surplusage et pur ceo laleger de surplusage ne prejudicera son claime: come un voille claime certen terre et estoverz en comen destre tenuz etc.

Dunquez < si un puit prescribe >[4] daver rent ratione del meese et garde et auxi daver ceo per lez mayns dun viconte.

Et ascuns que nemi, quar rent ne puit estre appurtenaunt a un meese come puit a un maner etc., ne comen appendaunt a un meese etc. Auxi ne puit prescripe daver rent del roy, pur ceo que le chose que est in son coffer puit estre devest de ceo saunz graunt ou petition, quar sil voille graunt rent hors de sez coffers a cest jour cest voide quar jeo ne poy aver action de dette vers luy et sez coffers nest certen. Mez il puit graunt a estre paye per lez mayns son rescevour, customer, etc., et cest bone. Dunquez chescun viconte est baile le roy et chescun chose dont il est accomptaunt est ajuge in le possession le roy, quar il ne puit pair ascun chose graunt per le roy einz covient prier destre discharge de son petition. Uncore un coroner que see sur vie dun home occise doit aver vi s. vi d. dez bienz cestui que luy occist, mez le viconte ne puit ceo payer a luy einz le

---

[1] *Reading uncertain. Perhaps*: allegat[um].
[2] *Written twice.*
[3] *Reading unclear.*
[4] *Written twice.*

Then it was said that one may not hold office [by the service] of keeping the same office, because by reason that he has the office he is bound to keep it, and therefore to hold it by such things as he is bound to do is a void tenure. It is also absurd (*empertenaunt*) to hold a thing by the same thing; for the tenure and the thing held are two things, one of them to the lord and one to the tenant. Therefore to hold a rent by the same rent is void; or to hold a house by the service of repairing it, or doing something for his benefit, or living in it, is void. Likewise here, to hold the office by the service of keeping the prisoners is a void tenure. But one may hold one office by the service of keeping another office etc.

On this point [it was argued] to the contrary, for this entire thing was given at the outset to be held by such services, and although the office by itself cannot be so held, nevertheless since it is joined with the house etc., which may be held by such services, and it is an entire thing, everything shall be held by this service. Likewise if land is given to a man to hold by the services of being parker of such and such forest etc. and having the shoulder of every deer slain there, and a penny for every tree felled, this is a good tenure. Also repairing the fence and having the old fence etc. Here by a means he could do service to himself, but because the premises and the sequel are but one entire thing, it is good. Likewise a manor with household implements may be leased or given in tail and taken. Thus it seems that it could have been given before the statute[1] to be held by service and good will joined with something else. At least, if there was such a gift before time immemorial etc., and it cannot be held as recited above, nevertheless it shall be construed according to the reservation, so that the tenure of the office in keeping etc. shall be void, but the land is to be held by such services, and therefore even if it is now alleged to be held that is merely surplusage and the alleging of surplusage shall not prejudice his claim: as where someone wishes to claim certain land and estovers in a common to be held etc.

Next, may one prescribe to have rent by reason of the house and custody, and also to have it by the hands of a sheriff?

Some thought not, for rent cannot be appurtenant to a house as it may to a manor etc. Nor may common be appendant to a house etc. Also one may not prescribe to have a rent from the king, because the thing which is in his coffer may be divested therefrom without grant or petition, for if he will grant a rent out of his coffers at the present day it is void, in that I may not have an action of debt against him and his coffers are uncertain. But he may grant it to be paid by the hands of his receiver, customer, etc., and it is good. Now, then, every sheriff is the king's bailiff and everything for which he is an accountant is adjudged to be in the king's possession, for he may not pay anything granted by the king but must pray to be discharged of his petition. Nevertheless, a coroner who sits upon the view of a slain man ought to have 6s. 6d. from the goods of the person who slew him, though the sheriff may not pay him, but

---

[1] 20 Edw. I, *Quia emptores terrarum* (*SR* i. 106).

coroner viendra in lexchequer et la serra allowe etc. Auxi chescun chose per que le viconte est charge est mater de recorde in lexchequer, come terrez, eschettes et tielx semblables, queux chosez ne poient estre hors de roy per prescription come wrek etc.

Ascuns al contrarie, quar ceux chosez dont le viconte est accomptaunt nest certen a chescun purpos, quar sont plusourz casueltez queux ne sont in lez coffers le roy devaunt que soient payez, et pur ceo le viconte est toutes foitz charge al roy de ceo. Et sunt diverz chosez queux le viconte pay et ount allowans a lexchequer per petition. Quere de dette pay al master dez bukhoundes etc. Auxi cest mater ad estre allowe anuelment la, que est auxi haut mater de recorde come le charge le viconte, et per comen entendement ils ne voillent ceo payer al comencement et issint continuer sils naveront sufficient garrante, et coment que ceo est ore perde, uncore cest allowans de recorde luy eidera etc.

Dunquez al returne dez brefez.

Ascuns diont que sont cy haut chosez que ne purront estre graunte a cest jour: come le roy voille graunt returna brevium a cest jour uncore le court ne escriera a luy, quar le viconte est officer al court de roy et ils nescrieront a auter, quar il est officer de comen droit que ne puit estre chaunge. Mez il fra son precept al grantee et issint le graunt ne serra voide etc.

Al contrarie: il clame forque returne de judicialle brefez et son title commence per entendement quaunt lez vicontes commence, pur ceo que est deinz le palace le roy ou nul officer [fo. 289v] forque eux que serront contenualment in le meason le roy ferra rienz deinz le palace, come marescalle et stwerde sount a cest jour, que en son auncient palace est entende destre graunte a un dez servantes, come plusourz office de viconte sount grauntes in fee. Et auxi il ad estre allowe icy et chescun court le roy de temps etc., que est auxi fort come allowans in heir pur ceo que cest court est pluys haut de ceo. Et auxi cest mater que charge est parcell de son office etc., de quell il nad avauntage. Come si parkerschip soit graunt de lopper tres etc. pur lavantage le seignour, cest nul parcell de son office dont il puit aver avantage, et pur ceo ne besoigne monstre fait de ceo. Quere si le roy puit faire auter office. Et semble que si cest chose ne soit parcell del tenour il puit, mez si issint nemi etc.

More dit que rienz puit estre appurtenaunt a meason, et que le ple nest sufficient pur ceo que allege prescription in ceo come appurtenaunt, ne que il ceo tient per lez services etc. Et auxi lauterz prescriptions et ove lalowance allege est assetz bone.

Conyngysby que nest bone pur ceo que ne [prescribe][1] in ceo in gros ne monstre que fuit office de temps [etc.] come besoigne ex necessitate, quar ne puit estre appendaunt al mease. Et dit que loffice est a cesti que clame et lez services al roy, scilicet le garde del prisonerz, mez il covient prescribe in tout etc.

---

[1] prescripē.

the coroner must come into the Exchequer and it will be allowed there etc. Also everything whereby the sheriff is charged is a matter of record in the Exchequer—for instance, lands, escheats, and such like, which things cannot be out of the king by prescription (like wreck etc.).

Some thought the contrary, inasmuch as the things for which the sheriff accounts are not certain for every purpose; for there are various casual receipts which are not in the king's coffers before they are paid, and therefore the sheriff is always charged to the king with them, and there are various things which the sheriff pays and for which he has allowance at the Exchequer by petition. (Query of a debt paid to the master of the buckhounds etc.) Also this matter has been allowed annually there, which is as high a matter of record as the sheriff's charge, and by common presumption they will not pay it at the outset, and so they will continue it if they do not have sufficient warrant, and even if it is now lost nevertheless this allowance of record shall help him etc.

Then as to the return of the writs.

Some say that they are such high things that they cannot be granted at the present day. Thus if the king will grant *returna brevium* at the present day, the court will still not write to the grantee, for the sheriff is officer to the king's court and they will not write to anyone else; for he is an officer of common right, who cannot be changed. But he shall make his precept to the grantee, and so the grant shall not be void etc.

To the contrary. He claims only the return of judicial writs, and by presumption his title commenced when sheriffs commenced, because it is within the king's palace where no officer shall do anything within the palace except those who are continually in the king's household, as the marshal and steward are at the present day, which in his ancient palace is presumed to be granted to one of his servants, just as various offices of sheriff are granted in fee. Also it has been allowed here and in every one of the king's courts since time immemorial etc., which is as strong as an allowance in eyre, because this court is higher than that. Also this matter which charges is part of his office etc. whereof he does not have advantage. Similarly, if a parkership is granted to lop trees etc. for the advantage of the lord, this is no part of his office whereof he can have advantage, and therefore there is no need to show a deed thereof. Query whether the king may make another office? It seems that if this thing is not part of the tenure he may, but if it is he may not etc.

MORE said that nothing can be appurtenant to a house, and that the plea is insufficient because it alleges prescription in it as appurtenant, not that he holds it by the services etc. Also the other prescription with the allowance alleged is good enough.

CONYNGYSBY said it is not good, because he does not prescribe in it in gross or show that it was an office from time immemorial, as he needs must, for it may not be appendant to the house. And he said that the office belongs to the person who claims and the services belong to the king, namely the keeping of the prisoners, but he must prescribe in everything etc.

Fenex. Semble que al comencement le terre et office et tout ensemble fuit done al home que puit escrier, et auxi daver largent pur ceo, mez nemi daver de chescun person vii s. viii d. que est arest, ceo nest bone. Et le returna brevium fuit reserve quaunt viconte comence adeprimes. Et dit que quo warranto nest de terrez, quar le roy avera auter remedie de ceo, come office in nature de quo warranto. Mez uncore sil ad office et maner que est tenuz il covient monstre lentier mater et clame loffice et per cest voy daver ceo del roy, et uncore il ne r[espondra?] del tenour. Et cest court est pluys haut que justices en eire. Et dit que home puit aver tener per que a son avantage, come de garder parke et aver x li. pur ceo, et est bone. Et de returna brevium fuit reserve al roy al comencement. Mez il covient monstre allowance a que et per que, et monstre lour nosmez, et coment ne fait son office come un auter doccupier office etc. Et dit que in temps H. vii. fuit dobt si[1] le mease del Flet fuit appendaunt al office ou loffice all mease, ou tout done a un temps ils ne sav.[2]

Et pur cest consideration il avoit jour damender tout son mater, per lassent lattorne le roy etc.

Et 11 H. 6. f. 1, un in trespas dit quil fuit seisi dun meese et xx. acres de terre et quil et sez auncestors et toutz ceux que estate [etc.] ount use de temps [etc.] de garder un bois appelle B. et ad este use de tout temps que chescun que ad bestes la trovera messour in harvest ou pay x. s. et auxi chescun que ad voy deinz ceo pay i. d., et si soit nient trove et rent nest pay quil distreinera toutz lez bestez trove in le boys etc. et eux deteynera tanquez le rent soit pay etc. Quere si ceo soit bone?

[15][3]

(A)

Sig. K2v.

En Banke le Roy anno 7° H. 8. termino Michaelis un fuit endit qil procure un en Midd. de occider un home en Essex, et si fuit accessore ou nemi fuit debat. Et ascuns que nemi, quar poit enquere de ceo en auter counte. Et la agre que ressetment en auter counte nest felonie. Et fuit dit si bat en un counte et

---

[1] *Written twice.*
[2] *Meaning unclear.*
[3] Marginalia in HLS Beale R.400 (Y.B. 1–8 Hen. VII).

FYNEUX [C.J.]. It seems that in the beginning the land and the office and everything together were given to someone who could write, and also to have money for it, but not to have 7s. 8d. from every person who is arrested: that is not good. And the return of writs was reserved when sheriffs first began. And he said that *quo warranto* is not for lands, for the king shall have another remedy for them, such as an office in the nature of *quo warranto*. Nevertheless, if he has an office and a manor which is held, he must show the whole matter and claim the office, and in that way have it from the king, and yet he shall not answer for the tenure. This court is higher than justices in eyre. And he said that one may have a tenure for one's own advantage, such as keeping a park and having £10 for it, and it is good. And return of writs was reserved to the king in the beginning. But he must show an allowance—to whom, and by whom, and show their names—and how he does not perform his office since someone else occupies the office etc.[1] And he said that in the time of Henry VII it was doubted whether the house of the Fleet was appendant to the office or the office to the house, or all given at one time.[2]

For this reason he had a day to amend all his matter, by consent of the king's attorney etc.

And in 11 Hen. VI, fo. 1,[3] someone in trespass said that he was seised of a house and twenty acres of land and that he and his ancestors, and all those whose estate he had etc., had used since time immemorial to have the custody of a wood called B., and that it has always been used that whoever has beasts there should find a reaper in harvest or pay 10s., and also everyone who has a way therein should pay 1d., and if the reaper is not found and the rent is not paid he should distrain all the beasts found in the wood etc. and detain them until the rent be paid etc. Is this good?

15. ANON.[4]

King's Bench, Mich. 1515.

(A)

In the King's Bench in Michaelmas term 7 Hen. VIII someone was indicted that he procured someone in Middlesex to slay someone in Essex; and it was debated whether he was an accessory or not. Some said not, for [they cannot][5] enquire into this in another county. And it was there agreed that receiving in another county is not felony. It was said that if someone is beaten in one

---

[1] Reading uncertain.
[2] The case referred to may be *Lord Dynham* v. *Carvenell* (1489) CP 40/910, m. 608.
[3] YB Mich. 11 Hen. VI, fo. 2, pl. 4.
[4] From Chaloner's autograph marginal notes in a printed year book of Hen. VII.
[5] There is no negative in the manuscript, but this seems to be the sense.

morust en auter, super visum corporis il poit estre endict, mez nemi devant justices de pees.

Fenex. Est bon reson qil serra puny.

(B)

Sig. M1v.

Fitzherber demande cest question en Bank le Roy et dit que est ajuge 23 H. 6. qil nest accessore. Et *Brudnell* agre a luy.

Et *Dominus Fenex* que est reson que serra punisshe.

county and dies in another, [the offender] may be indicted *super visum corporis*, but not before justices of the peace.

FYNEUX [C.J.]. It is good reason that he should be punished.[1]

(B)

Fitzherbert asked this question in the King's Bench, and said that it is adjudged in 23 Hen. VI[2] that he is not an accessory. BRUDENELL agreed with him.

And my lord FYNEUX said, it is right that he should be punished.

---

[1] Cf. *R.* v. *Cressede* (1505) Caryll's reports, 116 Selden Soc. 462, *per* Fyneux C.J.
[2] Not in print.

8. CASES FROM THE NOTEBOOK OF WILLIAM YELVERTON (1526–1550)[1]

[1]

Casus.

[*Fo. 4*] Rusheton et sa feme port brefe de dett verz Henry Cryppis sur un lez pur terme danz supposant que il avoit lesse certen terre a un W. que avoit graunt son estate en le terre al dit H. C. Le defendant dit que il lessa que parcell de terre a luy et que il enfeffe Baron Halez et auterz, devaunt quell feffment riens arere, saunz ceo que il lessa tout le terme a luy.

Spilman, Justice. Primez est move, si le tenant pur terme danz lesse parcel de son terre a un estraunge, si le lesse tyendra pro particula?

Toutz lez justicez forsque *Fitzherbert* disont que non, quar nient obstant que est rent service (come ilz toutes agreont, pur ceo que il avera fealte etc.) uncore il ne serra apportion et tenuez pro particula per lact del tenant en nul case mez per acte del ley. Come si jeo face lez de ii. acrez dount lun discend a moy per mon pere, lauter per ma mere, reservant rent, et devie, ore cel rent alera per parcelx accordant al revercion. Issint est de devyse, et similia. Mez ycy, nient obstant le lez de parcel, le primer lesse dentier terre est chargeable pur tout le rent. Contrarie est sil avoit graunt tout son estate. Et, sir, devaunt lestatut Quia emptores terrarum si jeo avoy fait feffment de ii. acrez rendant rent, dont lun acre fuit a moy per disseisin, uncore si le disseisi avoit reentre en tiel acre uncore le rent serra apportion. Mez ceo fuit toutz distz per lacte del ley. Mez all mater, si ple soyt duble ou nemi, cel apportionment neque auget neque minuit.

[1] Extracted from BL MS. Hargrave 253.

8. CASES FROM THE NOTEBOOK OF WILLIAM YELVERTON (1526–1550)[1]

1. RYSHTON v. CRIPCE

Exchequer Chamber, c. 1531/32. Also reported in Spelman, pp. 16, 93 (Mich. 1531); Dyer, fo. 4 (Trin. 1532); Yorke, above, p. 193, no. 267; Pollard, above, p. 248, no. 6. Record: KB 27/1076, m. 33 (printed in 94 Selden Soc. 290).

Ryshton and his wife brought a writ of debt against Henry Cripce upon a lease for a term of years supposing that he had leased certain land to one W., who had granted his estate in the land to the said Henry Cripce. The defendant said that he only leased part of the land to him, and that he enfeoffed Baron Hales and others, before which feoffment nothing was in arrear, without this that he leased the whole term to him.

SPELMAN J.[2] first moved: if a tenant for term of years leases part of his land to a stranger, shall the lessee hold *pro particula*[3]?

All the justices except FITZHERBERT said that he shall not, for although it is rent-service—as they all agreed, because he shall have fealty etc.—nevertheless it shall in no case be apportioned and held *pro particula* by the act of the tenant, but only by the act of the law. For instance, if I make a lease of two acres, one of which descended to me through my father and the other through my mother, reserving rent, and die, this rent shall now go by parcels according to the reversion. So it is of a devise, and the like. Here, however, notwithstanding the lease of part, the first lessee of the whole land is chargeable for all the rent. It would be contrary if he had granted over all of his estate. Sir, if before the statute *Quia emptores terrarum*[4] I had made a feoffment of two acres, rendering rent, one of which acres was mine by disseisin, and the disseissee re-entered in that acre, the rent would still be apportioned. But that was always by the act of the law. As to the matter, however, whether the plea is double or not, this apportionment is neither here nor there (*neque auget nec diminuit*).

---

[1] This is primarily a collection of Gray's Inn readings and moots: see *Moots*, pp. lxxxiv–lxxxv, no. 47; *Readers and Readings*, pp. 335–337. The cases selected here are printed in the order in which they occur in the manuscript.

[2] Apparently stating the case as secondary justice of the King's Bench: cf. Spelman, p. 94.

[3] For this expression see 18 Edw. I, *Quia emptores terrarum* (*SR* i. 106).

[4] 18 Edw. I, *Quia emptores terrarum* (*SR* i. 106).

S., I., F., et *Fitzjames,* cheff justice, sembleront que nest duble, quar cel feffment nest traversable, mez le plaintife covient a fyne force meyntenir que son lesse lessa tout le terre a luy, et [sic][1] nest traversable mez il covient meyntnenir ut supra. Donques il ne serra forsque un issue ycy. Issint le court ne serra en dowght ove que ilz doneront jugement. Come payment et acquitans in action de dett sur obligation nest duble. Et sil serra duble ycy donques home in nul ple purra fayre un tytle in son barre et prender travers auxi mez que serra duble, que nest reson: quar in ascun actions, come in ravyshement de garde, il covient surmitter en le barre lespeciall mater devaunt et travers. Et, sir, in 3° H. vi.[i] in action pur necligent garder de son fewe, le defendant dit que necligement enconter son volonte entront dedeinz et la prist un chamber et fieront few, issint fuit arce per lour necligens, ore il covient prender travers absque hoc quill fuit arce per son necligens: et agree nient obstant, quar autrement il ne respondra all plaintife forsque per un argument. Et le plaintife de necessite covient mayntenir son brefe que il lessa tout etc. Et est agree si issue fuit prise sur un poynt que nest duble, et ycy est tout un, quar il covient responder cest saunz ceo, que est lissue tender, per que [etc.]. Et, sir, ou il devoyt concluder Et de ceo il mitte luy sur le payes? Semble que non, intant que son ple est en laffirmatyff, et nient obstant quill prist un saunz ceo, ceo ne fayt mater, per que il covient averrer ceo, scilicet Le quel mater. Mez si home plede De ryen culpable ou Ryenz entermaynz, ore il covient dire Et de ceo il mitt luy sur le pays. Et, sir, lez pregnotaryez diont que lour course est issint, per que [etc.].

S. et *C.,* le cheff baron, et le cheff justice del Comen Banke, all contrarie. Primez, le rent ne serra tenuez pro particula, pur le reson avaundit, et auxi il est un entyre contracte et graunde mischeffe ensueroyt all disavauntage del seignior, per que [etc.]. Semble que est duble, quar est mater del ple. Come in assise, feffment launcestor ove garrante, et ne relye sur le garrante, quar le court serra envegle per ceo. Et in brefe deschet le tenant dit que il que est suppose que morust saunz heyre avoit issue un J., que luy enfeffa, le demandant dit que il fuit bastard, saunz ceo que il luy enfeoffa, ceo est duble, quar coment que le chose mys en le ple nest materiall uncore le court serra envegle per ceo. Per [que] le court ne voyle suffer luy daver ceo enter, per que [etc.]. Donques le travers ne wayve le dublenes, quar le travers nextend all poynt del brefe mez a un contrarianz. Come en trnz. le defendant plede feffment et issint De ryen culpable, ore le dublenes est wayve et ryen serra entre mez Ryen culpable. Mez ycy il nest issue, per que le travers ne wayve ceo.

Fuit move ou cel feffment amounte all graunt de son estate.

---

[1] ss.

[SPELMAN],[1] FITZHERBERT, ENGLEFIELD, and FITZJAMES C.J., thought it was not double; for this feoffment is not traversable, but the plaintiff must of necessity maintain that his lessee leased all the land to him, and so it is not traversable but he must maintain [his writ] as above. Therefore there shall only be one issue here, and so the court shall not be in doubt for whom they should give judgment. Likewise, payment and acquittance in an action of debt on a bond is not double. If it were double here, then one could not in any plea make a title in one's bar and take a traverse also, but it would be double, which is not right: for in some actions, as in ravishment of ward, one must first put the special matter in the bar and then traverse. Sir, in 3 Hen. VI,[2] in an action for negligent keeping of his fire, the defendant said that negligently and against his will the plaintiffs entered in and took a room there and made a fire, so that it was burned by their own negligence, and it was agreed that he must now traverse 'without this, that it was burned by the defendant's negligence', for otherwise he would only answer the plaintiff by an argument. And the plaintiff here must needs maintain his writ that he leased the whole etc. This is agreed if issue is taken on a point which is not double; and here it is just the same, for he must answer this traverse, which is the issue tendered, and so etc. Now, sir, ought he to conclude 'And thereof he puts himself upon the country'? It seems not, inasmuch as his plea is in the affirmative; and although he took a traverse, that makes no difference. So he must aver it, that is, 'which matter [he is ready to aver]'. If, however, someone pleads Not guilty, or Nothing in hand, he must then say 'And thereof he puts himself upon the country'. And, sir, the prothonotaries say that this is their course; and so etc.

[SHELLEY] and [CONYNGESBY], [LYSTER] C.B., and [NORWICH] C.J. of the Common Bench, to the contrary. First, the rent shall not be held *pro particula*, for the reason aforesaid; also it is an entire contract, and great mischief would follow, to the disadvantage of the lord; and so etc. And it seems that it is double, for it is a material part of the plea. Likewise in an assize, a feoffment of the ancestor with warranty, if he does not rely on the warranty; for the court would be misled by that. And in a writ of escheat if the tenant says that he who is supposed to have died without heir had issue one J., who enfeoffed him, and the demandant says that he was a bastard, 'without this, that he enfeoffed him', this is double; for even though the thing put in the plea is immaterial, still the court would be misled by it. Therefore the court will not allow him to have it entered; and so etc. Now, then, the traverse does not waive the doubleness, for the traverse does not extend to the point of the writ but to a matter in dispute. Similarly if in trespass the defendant pleads a feoffment 'and so Not guilty', the doubleness is now waived and nothing shall be entered except Not guilty. But here it is not an issue, and so the traverse does not waive it.

It was moved whether this feoffment amounted to a grant of his estate.

---

[1] S. could also represent Shelley J.C.P., but Spelman, p. 94, shows that Spelman is intended.
[2] Not traced in YB.

F.-H. et *N.* sembleront que cy. Mez auterz econtra, quar est un disseisin fayt per le tenant, que est un tort et son acte.

S.[1] Issint est un lyver ajuge que si home plede un mater un fayt et un mater en ley, come il fayt ycy, et le mater en fayt est travers, ore le mater en ley est wayve.

Nota que fuit agre supra que apportionment fuit all comen ley devant lestatut Quia emptores, scilicet lou le seignior avoit parcel per purchas, car fuit lacte dambideux, ou per lact del tenant tantum, scilicet si le tenant ust enfeffe estraunge de parcel a tener del seignior, ou si le seignior ust venuez a parcell per lacte del ley: mez sil ust venuez a parcel de tort demesne, donques tout le rent est extincte.

[2]

Ou un protection serra allowe pur un feme ou nemi?

[*Fo. 4v*] Primez *Shelley* semble que cy, quar cest protection est done per le comen ley et ceo appert per lez plusourz auncienz registers que sont. Et, sir, coment que icy [n]ad ascun case de ceo devaunt cez howerz, uncore comen reson ceo provera. Quar Bracton en son lyver dit que est requisite in un prinsse arma et leges, et chescun besoygne deyde lauter, quar armez compellera home destre justefye per lez leyz, et est en defens del realme. Donquez pur tielx homez darmez pur defens del realme protection fuit ordeine, all intent que ilz ne encourgent ascun damage dascun suiste ew verz eux. Donquez [mesme] le reson fuit de granter protection pur eux que vytallont et ayedount tyelx homez darmez, queux actes fueront auxi profitable all comen weal come mesmez lez homez que portont armez. Donquez une feme per son provision et pollicye poit prender vitallx auxibien come un home, et peraventure meux que dyverz homez. Et le roy que ad le poletyke governans del comen welth ad per son discrescion espye in cest feme tiel qualite per que ne list a nous de arguer ceo, intant que il ad luy inable in ceo et son counsell. Et si home ad protection que est decrepite ou blynde, nous ne covient arguer sil soyt able ou nemi, per que est en nostre lyverz que infant get un protection et fuit allowe en le temps le E. le ii., per que [etc.].

Ingyllfeld a mesme lentent. Et, sir, coment que le roy avera cy graunde necessite del armez dun home deinz le realme, uncore protection ne serra allowe: come si fuit pur garder dun castell in Walys ou in auter lew deinz le realme. Et le reson est pur ceo que il poit resorter ycy tout temps pur enformer

---

[1] *Reading unclear.*

FITZHERBERT and NORWICH thought so. But others thought the contrary, for it is a disseisin done by the tenant, which is a wrong, and it is his act.

[SPELMAN].[1] There is a book adjudged to the effect that if someone pleads a matter in fact and a matter in law, as he does here, and the matter in fact is traversed, the matter in law is thereby waived.

Note that it was agreed above that apportionment was at common law, before the statute *Quia emptores*, namely where the lord had part by purchase, which was the act of them both, or by the act of the tenant alone—that is, if the tenant had enfeoffed a stranger of part to hold of the lord—or if the lord had come to part by the act of the law: but if he came to part by his own wrong, then the whole rent was extinguished.

2. Re LADY E. S.[2]

Common Pleas, *c.* 1530/35. Noted briefly in Spelman, p. 189, pl. 2.

May a protection be allowed for a woman, or not?

First, SHELLEY thought it could; for this protection is given by the common law, and that appears from the oldest registers there are. And, sir, even if there has been no case of it before the present time, nevertheless common reason will prove it. For Bracton in his book says that it is requisite in a prince to rule both by arms and by laws (*arma et leges*), and each needs the help of the other, for arms compel man to be justified by the laws and they are in defence of the realm.[3] Therefore protection was ordained for such men of arms, for defence of the realm, to the intent that they should not incur any damage from any suit against them. There was the like reason for granting protection for those who victualled and assisted such men of arms, for their acts were just as profitable to the common weal as the men who actually bore arms. Now, then, a woman by her providence and policy may get victuals as well as a man, and perhaps better than some men. And the king, who has the politic governance of the common weal, has by his discretion espied such a quality in this woman, and so it is not right for us to dispute it, inasmuch as he and his council have enabled her in this. If a man who is decrepit or blind has a protection, we must not dispute whether he is able or not; and so it says in our books that an infant cast a protection and it was allowed, in the time of Edward II;[4] and so etc.

ENGLEFIELD to the same purpose. Sir, even if the king shall have the like great need of a man's arms within the realm, a protection shall nevertheless not be allowed here: for instance, for guarding a castle in Wales, or in some other place within the realm. The reason is because he may always resort here to

---

[1] Reading and identification unclear.
[2] So named in Spelman. The protection was for a knight and his wife for victualling Berwick. Sir Thomas Strangways was appointed marshal of Berwick in 1528.
[3] The opening words of *Bracton*, fo. 1a (ii. 19): *Quae sunt regi necessaria*.
[4] Mich. 15 Edw. II, Fitz. Abr., *Protection*, pl. 110.

son consell. Mez si soyt pur necessarie defens dun castell hors del royalme, la il serra allowe. Et tamen si le roy graunt protection a un home all intent que il mariera feme a Calise, ceo ne serra allowe quar nest pur le necessarie defens del royalme. Mez ycy est, per que [etc.]. Et coment que il nad este myse en ure, ceo ne fayt mater. Quar le ley est, si home all barre estoist muet quant il est arret de felonie il serra presse, issint come jeo intende si feme estoist mute, et tamen jeo ne veyera unquez ascun case de ceo. Et feme avera cy graunt avauntage et serra eyd per le ley come un home serra, per que [etc.].

Fitzherbert all contrarie. Et primez, si cest protection fuit gett pur home et feme, come est, uncore il ne serra allowe, quar est quia profectura in comitiva de tyel home, et tamen moratura etc. nest bon, quar est graunt a tyel intent que el serra attendant hors del realme et ceo el nest quant el est uncore a aller: et protection ne serra graunt, come avaunt est dit, pur ascun chose fayt deinz le realme, per que il ne vaut clerement pur ceo. Et coment que le roy ad graunt le protection, uncore gist en le ley, scilicet in nostre discresionz, si nous voylomus allower ceo ou nemi, scilicet si le person soyt able pur prender ceo, ou pur quell cause il graunta ceo, quar sil graunt protection et ne nosme ascun cause il ne serra allowe. Et, sir, sont iii. protectionz per le comen ley, scilicet quia profecturus, quia moraturus, et quia etc., et auter protection per lestatut. Et, sir, nest ascun de ceux, per que [etc.]. Donques all mater: moy semble que il ne serra allowe pur un feme, quar ceo serra inconveniencye, et meux serroyt a suffer un mischeff quun inconveniencye, come nostre lernynge est. Et est inconvenient que feme portera armez, et pur ceo si home tient per castell garde et ad issue fyle, cest fyle ne unquez ferra ceo mez son baron. Mesme le ley est si cestui que est le champion del roy ad issue que fyle, et devie, le fyle ne serra arme et ferra le service, quar serra inconvenient et graund dishonour a roy: quar le roy ne poit intend luy able a ceo fayer, quar son fesaunz nest cy requisite mez que serront homez assez deinz le royalme a ceo fayre, quar est determine per le provision de Dew que serra tauntz dez homez come dez femez usque ad novissimum diem, et de chescun fowle et best tantz dez malez come dez femalez, per que [etc.]. Et, sir, le ley purra cybien[1] entender que feme ferra faytz darmez come de porter arkes [et] setes a tirer et getter stonez que vitalx <coment un uste donez>[2] come le protection est, quar le ley ne presumera tyel discretion en luy. Et, sir, ou cestui que ad protection soyt blynde ou lame ne poit vener in issue ycy, per que [etc.].

Norwiche, cheff justice, all contrarie. Et primez le protection est assez bon, quar coment que el doyt estre la murrant uncore el poit resorter deinz le royalme a carier vitalle et demander vitalle, quar el ne poit aver le vitalle la. Et

---

[1] *Interlined.*
[2] *Reading unclear.* coment (co^t) *could be read* tout; donez *could be* domez.

inform his council. But if it is for necessary defence of a castle outside the realm, it shall be allowed. However, if the king grants a protection to a man so that he can marry a woman at Calais, this shall not be allowed, since it is not for the necessary defence of the realm. But here it is; and so etc. Even if it has not been put in practice, that is immaterial. For example, it is the law that if a man stands mute at the bar when he is accused of felony, he shall be pressed; and it is the same (I think) if a woman stands mute, and yet I have never seen any case of it. A woman shall have as much advantage as a man, and shall be helped by the law as much as a man shall be; and so etc.

FITZHERBERT to the contrary. First, if this protection was cast for a man and woman (as it is), it shall nevertheless not be allowed, for it is *quia profectura* in the company of such a man, and yet she still remains (*moratura*) etc., which is not good, for it is granted with the intention that she should be attendant outside the realm, and she is not so when she has still to go: and a protection shall not be granted, as is said above, for anything done within the realm; and so, for this reason, it is clearly invalid. Even though the king has granted the protection, it still lies in the law—that is, in our discretions—whether we will allow it or not, namely whether the person is able to take it, or for what cause he granted it, for if he grants a protection and does not name any cause it shall not be allowed. Sir, there are three protections by the common law: *quia profecturus, quia moraturus,* and *quia [indebitatus nobis],*[1] and another protection by statute. And, sir, this is none of those; and so etc. Now to the matter. It seems to me that it shall not be allowed for a woman, for that would be unfitting; and—as our learning says—it is better to suffer a mischief than something unfitting. It is unfitting that a woman should bear arms, and therefore if a man holds by castle-guard and has issue a daughter, this daughter shall never do the service, but her husband shall. The law is the same if the person who is the king's champion has issue a daughter only, and dies, the daughter shall not be armed and perform the service, for it would be unfitting and a great dishonour to the king. For the king cannot suppose her able to perform it, inasmuch as her performance is not so requisite but that there shall be enough men within the realm to do it; for it has been determined by the providence of God that there shall be as many men as women until the end of time (*usque ad novissimum diem*), and for every fowl and beast as many males as females; and so etc. And, sir, the law may as well presume that a woman can perform feats of arms, such as bearing bows and arrows to fire and throwing stones, as [bearing] victuals . . .,[2] as the protection is, for the law shall not presume such discretion in her. And, sir, whether someone who has a protection is blind or lame cannot come in issue here; and so etc.

NORWICH C.J. to the contrary. First, the protection is good enough; for although she ought to stay abroad she may nevertheless resort within the realm to carry victuals and seek victuals, for she cannot have the victuals there.

---

[1] See F.N.B. 28B; 109 Selden Soc. lxxxiv.
[2] Some unintelligible words follow. The sense of the remark seems to be ironical.

coment que in un protection sont plusourz parolx que nount use estre in auterz uncore ceo ne fayt ceo vicious. Et, sir, est allowable pur un feme assez bien, quar feme est auxibien enable in le ley de fayre chosez etc. divers in ley come un home, et especialment pur le comen weale come est icy, come avaunt est dit, per que [etc.]. Mez si avoyt este ajuge all contrarie devaunt ceux heurez, donquez auterment seroyt, ou sil fuit ouste per ascun estatut, donquez le reson de ceo serra invincible. Mez issint nest ycy, per que [etc.].

[3]¹

[I]²

Le serjeants case anno 23 H. 8. termino Michaelis.

Repl., le defendant avowa pur ceo que le lew ou etc. sont x. acrez de terre parcell del manor de B. dount le Seignior Braye fuit seisi in fee, et que il ad use de temps dont etc. de lesser le dit terre en fee, fee tayle, ou pur terme de vie, ou pur terme danez, ad voluntatem domini secundum consuetudinem manerii, et dit que un J. at S. surrender ceo in manibus domini tyel jour etc. all use dun B., que surrender all use lavowant in fee, et puis il trove le pl[aintifes] bestes la damage fesant, per que etc. Le plaintife confesse que est parcel del maner et le tenure ut supra, et dit que le dit J. at S. <que>³ surrender all use de B. et sa feme et pur ceo que nad ryens que en droit sa feme surrender all avowant, et aprez le surrender et devaunt ascun entre del avowant le baron devie et le seignior entra et graunt ceo all plaintife, per que il mitta einz cez bestez etc.

Yorke. Primez semble que le barre all avowere nest bon, quar in son avowere il suppose que le baron fuit sole seisi et surrender, et in le barre il dit que le baron et feme fueront seisi, issint il doyt prender travers absque hoc que il fuit sole seisi. Quar lou un chose que est matter in fayt est allege in le ple il covient estre confesse et avoyde ou travers. Come in assise, le defendant plede morant seisi son pere, le plaintife dit que il mesme fuit joyntenant ove le pere le

---

¹ From BL MS. Harley 5103, ff. 65v–69v (*B*); collated with MS. Hargrave 253, ff. 12–15 (*A*). The two texts begin differently, but after Yorke's argument they are substantially the same. The *A* text is generally better, though *B* has been used as the prime text because *A* is in places difficult to decipher. However, *A* omits the passage in the penultimate paragraph and so both texts must have an independent source.
² *From A.*
³ *Sic but seemingly otiose.*

And even if there are various words in a protection which have not been accustomed to be used in others, this still does not make it defective. And, sir, a protection is perfectly allowable for a woman, for a woman is just as able in the law to do various things in law as a man, especially for the common weal, as here (as was said before); and so etc. If it had been adjudged to the contrary before these times, then it would be otherwise; or if it was forbidden by any statute, then the reason thereof would be invincible. But it is not so here; and so etc.

3. THE SERJEANTS' CASE[1]

Common Pleas, Mich. 1531. This is the first fully reported new serjeants' case.[2]

[I]

The serjeants' case in Michaelmas term 23 Hen. VIII.

In replevin the defendant avowed because the place where etc. is ten acres of land, parcel of the manor of B., whereof the Lord Bray[3] is seised in fee, and he has been accustomed since time immemorial to lease the said land in fee, in fee tail, or for term of life, or for term of years, at the will of the lord according to the custom of the manor (*ad voluntatem domini secundum consuetudinem manerii*); and he said that one John at Style surrendered it into the lord's hands on such and such a day etc. to the use of one B., who surrendered to the use of the avowant in fee, and afterwards he found the plaintiff's beasts there damage feasant, and so [he distrained] etc. The plaintiff confessed that it is parcel of the manor, and confessed the tenure as above, and said that the said John at Style surrendered to the use of B. and his wife, and because he had nothing but in right of his wife he surrendered to the avowant, and after the surrender and before any entry by the avowant the husband died, and the lord entered and granted it to the plaintiff, and so he put in his beasts etc.

Yorke.[4] First, it seems that the bar to the avowry is not good, for in his avowry he supposes that the husband was sole seised and surrendered, and in the bar he says that the husband and wife were seised, and therefore he ought to traverse 'without this, that he was sole seised'. For where something which is a matter in fact is alleged in the plea it must be confessed and avoided or traversed. As in an assize, if the defendant pleads the dying seised of his father,

---

[1] The two texts begin differently, but after Yorke's argument they are substantially the same.

[2] See Baker, *Serjeants at Law*, pp. 104, 168. About half of the previous serjeants' case is reported in YB Trin. 13 Hen. VIII, fo. 15, pl. 1 (119 Selden Soc. 81).

[3] Edmund Bray, created Lord Bray in 1529, died 1539.

[4] Roger Yorke, the puisne serjeant: below, p. 296. For the order of seniority at this call see Baker, *Serjeants at Law*, p. 168.

defendant, que morust, et le plaintife soye tyent eynz per le survyvour, ore il covient travers absque hoc que il fuit sole seisi. Mez in assise de mortdancestor et tyelz brefez lou il nest que supposell il ne traversera le sole morant seisi. Auterment est lou le matter in le declaration allege est matter in fayt. Come le lyver v. H. vii, in brefe dentre in le per, supposant que il avoit son entre per un tyel, et le tenant dit que il ad son entre per un auter, ore il covient prender travers, et ceo pur le mischeff de son voucher et voucher hors de lyne, per que [etc.]. Auxi semble que le barre est doble: lun est le joynt estate que il avoyt in droit sa feme, quell ust estre ple per luy mesme, lauter ou le seigniour poit entre ou nemi, quell est auter matter. Quar lou home plede ii. materz et chescun de [eux] [*fo. 12v*] issuable, et poit aver lun sanz lauter, ceo est doble. Come en assise, le defendant plede divers morants seisiez de fee simple, ceo est doble quar chescun est issuable. Auterment est in un formedon et il pled divers morants seisiez, il nest doble quar Ne dona pas fayt fyne de tout. Et in case home plede ii. materz et chescun issuable, et uncore nest doble, come in assise un plede feffment et si trove ne soyt nul tort ceo nest doble, quar coment que il navoyt parle de nul tort unquore il serra inquirable per mesme lassise. Issint est en brefe de droyt, le tenant travers lespleez, et si trove ne soyt que il ad melyour droit a tenyr etc. ceo nest doble, causa qua supra. Quere en cest case, per que etc. Donques all mater: ou tiel surrender per le baron soyt discontinuans ou nemi? Semble que cy, quar un discontinuans poit estre coment que il ny ad ascun lyvere: come le baron fayt feffment per fyne et le partie entre, ceo est discontinuans. Issint est si tenant en taylle soyt dun rent et ill graunt ceo ove garrante, ceo est discontinuans. Donquez, entant que il nentra si serra impediment pur que il ne serra discontinuans? Semble que non, quar il tient per le surrender et le graunt del seignior arere mayntenant et nest semble lou le tenant en tayle dona le terre per fyne, quar la lissue poit averrer un continuanz dell possession et donques nest discontinuans, mez auterment est ycy. Donquez ou le seignior poit ouster son tenant per copie de court roll? Semble que non, pur ceo que il ad fee simple per le custome, et coment que le seignior ad fee simple auxi uncore ceo nest impertinent mez que poit estre ii. fee simples dun mesme terre. Come lou jeo preigne leez de ma terre demesne pur terme dez anz, mez in fayt le veraye fee simple est en moy. Issint in fayt le veray fee simple est en le seignior et pur ceo le prescription serra allege in le seignior, come appert 9. H. 6. Mez quant le seignior ad entre le tenant ne poit aver action de recontinuer le seisin, quar le veraye franktenement et le fee simple est en le seignior. Mez pur le possession et lenheritauns que le tenant ad per le custome il avera action

and the plaintiff says that he was joint tenant with the defendant's father, who died, and the plaintiff held himself in by survivorship, he must now traverse 'without this, that he was sole seised'. However, in an assize of mort d'ancestor and such writs where it is but a supposal, he shall not traverse the dying sole seised. It is otherwise where the matter alleged in the declaration is a matter in fact. For instance, the book 5 Hen. VII,[1] in a writ of entry in the *per*, supposing that he had his entry though such and such a person, and the tenant says that he had his entry through another, now he must take a traverse, and that is on account of the mischief of his voucher and vouching out of line; and so etc. Also it seems that the bar is double: one of the matters is the joint estate which he had in right of his wife, which would have been a plea by itself, and the other is whether the lord may enter or not, which is another matter. For where someone pleads two matters and each of them is issuable, and he could have the one without the other, it is double. As in an assize, if the defendant pleads various dyings seised of fee simple, this is double, for each of them is issuable. It is otherwise in a formedon, if he pleads various dyings seised, it is not double, for *Ne dona pas* makes an end of all. And in some cases one may plead two matters, each of which is issuable, and yet it is not double: as in an assize, where he pleads a feoffment and, if that is not found, 'No wrong', this is not double, for even if he had not said 'No wrong' it would still be enquirable by the same assize. So it is in a writ of right, if the tenant traverses the esplees and, if it is not found, that he has a better right to hold etc., this is not double, for the above reason. (Query in that case.) And so etc. Now to the matter: is such a surrender by the husband a discontinuance, or not? It seems that it is, for there may be a discontinuance even though there is no livery: as where the husband makes a feoffment by fine and the party enters, that is a discontinuance. So it is if there is tenant in tail of a rent and he grants it with warranty, that is a discontinuance. Now, inasmuch as he did not enter, shall this be an impediment to its being a discontinuance? It seems not, for he holds by the surrender and the grant back again from the lord, and it is not like the case where the tenant in tail gives the land away by fine, for there the issue may aver a continuance of the possession and therefore it is not a discontinuance; but it is otherwise here. Now, then, may the lord oust his tenant by copy of court roll? It seems not, because he has fee simple by the custom, and even though the lord has fee simple also, it is nevertheless not impossible that there may be two fee simples of one same land. For instance, where I take a lease of my own land for a term of years, but in fact the true fee simple is in me. Thus in fact the true fee simple is in the lord, and therefore the prescription shall be alleged in the lord, as appears in 9 Hen. VI.[2] But once the lord has entered the tenant cannot have an action to recontinue the seisin, for the true freehold and the fee simple is in the lord. However, for the possession and the inheritance which

---

[1] Probably YB Mich. 5 Hen. VII, fo. 6, pl. 13, though it was an action of forcible entry. The reference in the parallel text is to 3 Hen. VII.

[2] *Chaworth's Case* (1431) YB Hil. 9 Hen. VI, fo. 62, pl. 16.

de trns. vers le seignior, come le tenant pur terme danz aver. Mez quant le
seignior ad graunt ceo ouster, il poit entrer vers son graunte. Come lou le roy
enter sur moy jeo nay remedy que mon petition, uncore sil graunt ceo ouster
jeo puis entrer sur son patente. Issint ycy, per que [etc.].[1]

[II][2]

Casus en le Comen Banke M. xxiii H. 8. en le quel
lez serjantes argew pur lour forme.

En un replevyn le defendant avowe pur le reson que le lew ou etc. fuit xx
acrez de terre, parcelle dell maner de B., de quel le maner le Seignior Bray fuit
seisi en fee et il ad use de temps etc. de faire lessez en fee, fee taile, pur terme de
vie, et pur terme dans, ou auterment, et que un J. S. fuit seisi de les dites maner
[et] xx acrez et le primer jour, an, etc., il surrendre le dit terre al seignior, et puis
le seignior graunta al avowant, et puis il entra et lez avers le plaintife vient sur
le terre et le avowant eux distreigne damage fesaunt etc. Le plaintife confesse
que lez xx acrez fueront parcelle dell maner de B. et que le Seignior Bray fuit
seisi etc., mez il dit que le dit J. S. fuit seisi forsque en droit sa feme < et que le
baron apres >[3] le surrendre et devaunt entre morust, et puis el prist le plaintife
all baron, et puis il mit eins sez avers etc.

York, le puisne serjant, prist exceptions al barre dell avowre, downt le primer
fuit que low il plede que low il avoit joint estat ovesque sa feme et >[4] pur ceo
que ladvowant [dit] que J. S. fuit seisi et le plaintife dit que il fuit jointment seisi
ovesque sa feme, en le quel cas il duist aver travers, quar chescun matter de fait
covient estre confesse et avoid ou travers. Come si le defendant en assise plede
le moraunt seisi son pere, le plaintife dit que il et le pere le tenaunt fueront
jointenantz, et le pere morust et il luy tient eins per le survivor etc., ceo nest bon
sauns prendre travers, ratio patet devaunt. Mez auterment est de maner de
supposell, come en assise de mortdancestor le moraunt seisi est forsque un
supposell si soit alege per voie de declaration. Mez auterment est en brefe
dentre en le per, come apert en 3 H. 7, quare est le title le demandant et un
matter en fait le quell covient estre travers. Donques ouster, quaunt il dit en
son barre que il avoit joint estat en droit sa feme, et ouster que le seignior entra,
le quel est le dowght ou il poit entre ou nemi, ceo est double ple, quar checun de
eux est issuable. Come si deus moraunt seisis plede en assise est double, quar
checun deux est issuable. Auterment est en formdon, quar la est forsque un
respons all ambideux, scilicet ne dona pas. Mez ascun foitz il pledra deux pleez

[1] *Continues as in B.*
[2] *From B.*   [3] *Interlined.*   [4] *Deleted.*

the tenant has by the custom, the tenant may have an action of trespass against the lord, just as the tenant for term of years may. But when the lord has granted it over, he may enter against his grantee. Likewise where the king enters upon me I have no remedy other than my petition, and yet if he grants it over I may enter upon his patentee. Likewise here; and so etc.[1]

[II]

A case in the Common Bench, Michaelmas 23 Hen. VIII, in which the serjeants argued for their form.

In a replevin the defendant avowed by reason that the place where etc. was twenty acres of land, parcel of the manor of B., of which manor the Lord Bray was seised in fee, and he has used since time immemorial to make leases in fee, in fee tail, for term of life, and for term of years, or otherwise, and that one John Style was seised of the said manor and twenty acres and on the first day [of etc. in the] year etc., he surrendered the said land to the lord, and afterwards the lord granted to the avowant, and afterwards he entered, and the plaintiff's beasts came onto the land, and the avowant distrained them damage feasant etc. The plaintiff confessed that the twenty acres were parcel of the manor of B. and that Lord Bray was seised etc., but he said that the said John Style was seised only in right of his wife, and that the husband died after the surrender and before entry, and afterwards she married the plaintiff, and afterwards he put in his beasts etc.

Yorke, the puisne serjeant, took exceptions to the bar of the avowry. The first was because the avowant said that John Style was seised and the plaintiff said that he was jointly seised with his wife, in which case he ought to have traversed, for every matter of fact must be confessed and avoided or traversed. For instance, if the defendant in an assize pleads the dying seised of his father, and the plaintiff says that he and the tenant's father were joint tenants, and the father died, and he held himself in by survivorship etc., this is not good without taking a traverse. The reason appears above. But it is otherwise of a matter of supposal, as in an assize of mort d'ancestor where the dying seised is only a supposal if alleged by way of declaration. But it is otherwise in a writ of entry in the *per*, as appears in 3 Hen. VII,[2] for it is the demandant's title and a matter in fact, which must be traversed. To move on, then: when he says in his bar that he had a joint estate in right of his wife, and further that the lord entered, which is the doubt (i.e. whether he could enter or not), that is a double plea, for each of them is issuable. Likewise if two dyings seised are pleaded in an assize it is double, for each of them is issuable. It is otherwise in formedon, for there it is only an answer to both, namely *Ne dona pas*. But sometimes one may plead

[1] The rest of the text continues as in (II), from the beginning of Serjeant Mountague's argument.
[2] See p. 295, above, note 1.

et ambideux isuable et unquore nest double, et ceo est lou le jure troveroit un de eux non obstante que le parte navoit ceo alege: come en assise un fefment et null tort, le jure trovera null tort etc. Issint en brefe de droit, le tenant travers lespleez et dit ouster que il avoit pluis droit a tener que il demande que lauter etc. Donques a le matter, si ceo soit [*fo. 66*] discontinuans? Et il semble que est discontinuans, quar discontinuans poit estre assez bien de[1] sauns livere, come si tenaunt en taile dun rent ceo graunt en fee ovesque garrante. Issint est dun comen, et auxi dun office. Et si terre soit appendant all office, la terre per le discontinuans dell office serra discontinue auxi, et unquore dell terre home poit faire livere. Issint icy etc. Donques al principall matter: si le seignior poit expulse son coppyholder? Et semble non, quar cest custome luy liera et est conditio tacita que le tenaunt avera la terre issint quil observe le custome. Et nest impertinent mez que deux fee simplez poient estre dun mesme terre. Come si un voile faire lez pur anns a moy de mon terre demesne: et issint est en 9 H. 6.

[2]*Montagu* all contrary, ex cujus argumento vix unius aut aulter' quicquam percipiebat adeo ima voce loquebatur.

Cholmeley all contrary. Et il doyt prendre traverz ou auterment il nest encontre ove luy. Come en trns, jeo plede agarde, lauter dit quil agard cest chose et diverz auterz chosez, ore il doit prendre traverz. Issint sur alienation en mortmayne le seigniour covient alegger qil entra deinz lan et jour, quar auterment poit estre a deux ententes. Issint icy, poit [estre][3] prise quun surrender per le barron tantum, auter per le barron et feme, per que etc. Auxi semble que est duble pur ceo que sont diverz materz deinz,[4] scilicet lun que debates et discordes fuit perenter lez tenauntz, auter le jointenancie, auter que le seignior poit enter, et ne serra suffre pur inveigling et incumbrance dell court. Come feffement ove garrante in assise sil ne relia sur le garrante ceo est [doble, et][5] le feffement aperluy nest ple, quar namownt forsque a null tort, per que [etc.]. Donques ou ceo soit discontinuans? Et semble que cy, quar auxi bien que le barron poit discontinue le droit sa feme per le comen ley auxi bien poit il per le custome, et tout un, quar el avera sa pleint < in nature de >[6] cui in vita et in nature de formedon et auters actions a son plesure. Et si ceo ne serra discontinuans, pur que furent ceux remediez purvews en [le][7] court le seignior? Et, sir, il ne besoigne ascun entre icy mez il est tenaunt en fait et [quant][8] al action user meintenaunt. Et nest semble low home recover terre et serra misse en possession per habere facias seisinam, mez icy il nad auter possession que per livere per le virge. Et est semblable a un devise low home devise terre a un, est en luy maintenaunt. Issint est de fyne de conusans de droit que est execute. Auterment est de fyne de graunt et rendre, quar ceo est executory, per que [etc.]. Donques ou le seignior poit ouster son tenant ou nemi? Semble que non,

---

[1] *Sic.*   [2] *From this point the text is the same in A and B.*
[3] *A. Indistinctly written in B.*
[4] dedeinz *A.*   [5] *A.* deblam etc. *B.*   [6] *Interlined.*
[7] *A.*   [8] q̄t *A.* q[ue] *B.*

two pleas, and both are issuable, and still it is not double; and that is where the jury find one of the things even though the party has not alleged it: for instance, in an assize [if the tenant pleads] a feoffment and No wrong, the jury may find no wrong etc. Likewise in a writ of right, the tenant traverses the esplees and says further that he has more right to hold what he demands than the other etc. Then as to the matter: is this a discontinuance? He thought that it is a discontinuance, for there may perfectly well be a discontinuance without livery, as where tenant in tail of a rent grants it in fee with warranty. So it is of a common, and also of an office. If land is appendant to the office, by the discontinuance of the office the land shall be discontinued also, and yet one may make livery of the land. Likewise here etc. Now, then, as to the principal matter: may the lord expel his copyholder? It seems not, for this custom shall bind him, and it is an implied condition (*conditio tacita*) that the tenant shall have the land provided he observes the custom. It is not impossible that there may be two fee simples of one same land. For instance, if someone makes a lease for years to me of my own land. So it is in 9 Hen. VI.[1]

[2]*Mountague* to the contrary; from whose argument nothing much could be gathered because he spoke in such a quiet voice.

Cholmeley to the contrary. He ought to take a traverse or else he is not in controversy with him. Thus in trespass, if I plead an award, and the other says that he awarded that thing and various others, he ought now to traverse. Likewise upon an alienation in mortmain, the lord must allege that he entered within the year and day, for otherwise it might be taken in two ways. Likewise here, it could be taken as a surrender by the husband alone, or by the husband and wife; and so etc. Also it seems that it is double because there are several matters in it, namely (1) that there were debates and disagreements among the tenants, (2) the joint tenancy, (3) that the lord could enter; and this shall not be allowed, because of the inveigling and incumbrance of the court. Thus a feoffment with warranty in an assize, if he does not rely on the warranty, is double; and the feoffment by itself is no plea, for it amounts only to 'No wrong'; and so etc. Then, is this a discontinuance? It seems it is, for just as the husband may discontinue the right of his wife by the common law so may he by the custom; and it is all one, for she shall have her plaint in the nature of a *cui in vita*, or in the nature of formedon and other actions, at her pleasure. If this were not a discontinuance, why were these remedies provided in the lord's court? And, sir, there is no need for any entry here, but he is tenant in fact for the purpose of using an action at once. It is not like the case where someone recovers land and shall be put in possession by *habere facias seisinam*; but here he has no other possession than by livery by the virge. It is like a devise: where a man devises land to someone, it is in him at once. So it is of a fine *sur conusance de droit* which is executed. It is otherwise of a fine *sur grant et render*, for that is executory. And so etc. Now, then, may the lord oust his tenant, or

---

[1] *Chaworth's Case* (1431) YB Hil. 9 Hen. VI, fo. 62, pl. 16.
[2] From this point the text is the same in *A* and *B*.

quar il ad enheritaunce in le custome auxibien come le seignior avoit en le seigniorie, et ad este continue de temps dont memorie pesablement, sauns ouster. Mez sil enfreint custome, jeo voie[1] que il serra ouste. Et, sir, le seignior nad la terre per le surrendre mez come un instrument de faire ceo vester en lauter: come le tenant pur vie [ferra][2] le revercion de passer per attornement, [*fo. 66v*] quar il ne observe son enheritance accordant all custome. Et il est inheritable per force dell custome, et sil serroit ouste il serroit in pier condytyon que tenaunt a volunt all comen ley: quar sil soit ouste uncore il avera temps de emporter son croppe et sez utensylez[3] dell meason, mez issint naveroit il icy quar nest cy allege per pleder ne appert mez generalment sil poit luy ouster. Et, sir, sont dyverz partyculer customez en Engleterre, come gavelkynd et borowynglysshe, [et ceux][4] sont allowablez et tamen sont encontre le comen ley. Mez cest custome extende a tout un comenalte, per que nest reson que soit disprove. Et, sir, le tenant que tient per homage auncestrell vouchera son seignior, et ceo est per le privyte de tenure que ad continue en lour sank de temps dont memorie. Et tamen il nest ascun tenure,[5] et jeo voile graunt que il avera ad voluntatem domini secundum consuetudinem manerii, issint que sil ne paie sez customez il serra oust, issint que son estate est a volunt dependant sur condition in ley. Come si jeo graunt a un destre mon parker et il occist mez damez, ore son offyce est determen quar fuit sur condition en ley. Issint icy. Auxi serroit encontre bon reson que le seignior reentroit,[6] quar est un grounde: si jeo done terre a un reservaunt un acre ou parcell dez profyttes, ceo est voyde, eo que [est][7] parcell dell chose done. Issint icy, si le seignior reentroit il averoit le terre arere enconter son done demesne, que ne soit resonable, per que [etc.].

Knytley[8] all contrarie. Et primez le avowre nest[9] bon, quar il dit que le Seignior Bray est seisi dell maner et que il ad este use, et ne dit que le Seignior Bray et toutes sez auncestors ou ceux que estate il ad ount use, per que nest bon, quia ad proximum antecedens fiat relatio, et ceo [est] all Seignior Bray lou [il][10] ne parle de sez awncestors. Awxi il nest bon pur ceo que un prescription covient daver son limytation dell temps le Roy E. le 1^e. come en brefe de droit. Et il ad prescrybe de faire [devise][11] de lez terrez en le taile, quell estate est fait per lestatut de W. ii., que est puis temps de memorie, per que [etc.]. Donsque all traveres: il ne besoigne de prendre traverz pur ceo que il confesse ly et pluz. Come en det sur un leez per J. S., le deffendant dit que il fuit fait per le dit J. S. et J. N., ore il ne prendra travers. Mez moy semble que la le cause est pur ceo

---

[1] voyle *A.*
[2] ferr' *A.* farra *B.*
[3] utenselz *A.*
[4] etc. *in both mss.*
[5] garr' *A.*
[6] entr' *A.*
[7] *A.*   [8] Knyghtley *A.*
[9] *A. Altered in B from* est.
[10] *A.*   [11] devyse *A.* deinz *B.*

not? It seems not, for he has an inheritance in the custom just as the lord has in the lordship, and it has continued peaceably since time immemorial without ouster. However, if the tenant breaks the custom, I concede that he may be ousted, for he has not observed his inheritance according to the custom.[1] And, sir, the lord does not have the land by the surrender but is like an instrument to cause it to vest in the other: just as the tenant for life shall cause the reversion to pass by attornment. The tenant is inheritable by virtue of the custom, and if he should be ousted he would be in a worse condition than tenant at will at the common law: for if the latter is ousted he shall still have an opportunity to carry away his crop and his household utensils; but he shall not here, for it is not so alleged in the pleading and it does not appear other than that he may oust him generally. And, sir, there are various particular customs in England, such as gavelkind and borough English, and these are allowable even though they are against the common law. But this custom extends to the whole of a community, and so it is not right that it should be disproved. And, sir, the tenant who holds by homage ancestral may vouch his lord, and that is by reason of the privity of tenure which has continued in their blood since time immemorial. Nevertheless it is no tenure,[2] and I concede that he shall have it *ad voluntatem domini secundum consuetudinem manerii*, so that if he does not pay his customs he shall be ousted, and therefore his estate is at will dependent upon a condition in law. Similarly if I grant someone to be my parker and he kills my deer, his office is now determined, because it was upon a condition in law. Likewise here. Also it would be contrary to good reason if the lord should re-enter, for it is a maxim (*grounde*) that if I give land to someone, reserving one acre, or part of the profits, this is void, inasmuch as it is part of the thing given. Likewise here, if the lord re-entered he would have the land back contrary to his own gift, which would not be reasonable; and so etc.

Knightley to the contrary. First, the avowry is not good, for he says that Lord Bray is seised of the manor and that it has been accustomed etc., and does not say that Lord Bray and all his ancestors, or those whose estate he has, have been accustomed, and so it is not good: for words relate back to the next antecedent (*quia ad proximum antecedens fiat relatio*),[3] and that is to Lord Bray—where there is no mention of his ancestors. It is also not good because a prescription must have its limitation from the time of King [Richard] I, as in a writ of right. But he has prescribed to make devises of the lands in tail, which is an estate created by the Statute of Westminster II,[4] which is since time of memory; and so etc. Now to the traverse. He need not take a traverse, because he has confessed him and more. Similarly in debt upon a lease by John Style, if the defendant says that it was made by the said John Style and John Noke, he

---

[1] This last clause is written after the next sentence, but clearly belongs here.

[2] *A* says 'warranty'.

[3] For this principle see YB Trin. 9 Hen. VI, fo. 28, pl. 30; *Bolde* v. *Molyneux* (1536) Dyer, fo. 14b; S. E. Thorne ed., *A Discourse upon the Exposicion & Understandinge of Statutes* (1942), p. 130.

[4] Statute of Westminster II, c. 1, *De donis* (*SR* ii. 71).

que est [per][1] voy de supposell. Et all [case][2] que fuit miz per Yorke dell moraunt seisi plede in assise, ceo est voer intaunt que quaunt il medle ove le moraunt seisi il [covient][3] confesse ceo et avoide ou travers a toutes intentes. Et in det sur leez dun acre, il dit que il lessa ceo et un auter, ore il covient prendre travers: come appert 35 H. 6. Donsque all dublenez: il nest duble, quar tout cest matter nest que un conveyance de cawser le seignior denter, quar le stryfe et debate conveia le seignior a son entre, per que [etc.]. Donsque ou le seignior poit ouster son tenant per copy de court rolle? Semble que cy, quar est expresse mentyon fait en mesme[4] le coppyez que il avera ad voluntatem domini, issint ne poit il aver mie melior estate que il mesme accept. Et, sir, tenaunt a volunte all comen ley est tenaunt tantsolement all volunte le lessor, et sil ne [unques][5] occupia unquore il payera le seignior son rent. Et, sir, le fee simple est en le seignior, quar le copy est ad usum un tiell. Come lou jeo enfeoffe homez a mon use, le fee symple est en eux et jeo nay que un use. Issint le tenaunt nad que un use. Mez, sir, cesti a que use per le comen ley, si lez feffez executount auter estate que il voille eux aver, action sur son caz gist verz eux pur ceo que il avoit mis confidenz et trust in eux a ceo faire et pur le disceit laction sur le caz gist. Mez issint nest de tenaunt per copy de court rolle, quar il nad mist tiell confidenz in son seignior mez fuit content de prendre ceo a son volunte, per que [etc.]. Et sub pena ne poit il aver verz le seignior ea de causa, et il ne poit aver action sur son caz, per que [etc.]. Et, sir, action de trnz ne gist, quar il fra fealte, quell prova que il est seignior, et si sic il ne serra punysshe, quar lestatut de Marlebryge prohybyt ceo, per que il nad auter remedie que petytyon. Tamen credo que petityon nest remedie, quar [gist][6] in le electyon le seignior de luy restorer ou non.[7] Et, sir, sil ne ousteroit son tenaunt il perderoit son rent, quar a [cest][8] jour home ne poit doner terre a tener de luy per copy de court rolle. Auxi a cest jour home ne poit doner terre en fee rendant rent, quar lestatut Quia emptores [terrarum][9] ceo prohibit. Issint vous volez que le seignior perderoit son rent, quell nest resonable que il perderoit son rent que est son enheritance, per que [etc.].

Marvyn al contrarie. Et a lexceptyon al avowre, que est a [toto][10] tempore predicto, quell navera relation mez all seigniorie et nemi sez auncestors: ceo nest issint, mez avera relatyon a tout le matter, scilicet all temps de prescriptyon. Come lou jeo recyte que lou jay un chivall, un vache [et] un toge, jeo done a vous omnia bona mea predicta, et ceo navera relatyon a un deux [*fo. 67*] mez a toutes. Donsque intaunt que le done in taile est fait puis le limitation et pur ceo il ne poit prescribe daver ceo, ceo nest issint. Quar il fuit

---

[1] *A.* p[u]r *B.*   [2] *A.* cacez *B.*
[3] *A.*   [4] *Om. A.*
[5] *A.* unc' *B.*
[6] *A.* list *B.*
[7] nemi *A.*   [8] *A.* ceo *B.*
[9] *A.*   [10] *A.* totuo *B.*

shall not traverse. But it seems to me that the reason there is because it is by way of supposal. As to the case put by Yorke of the dying seised in an assize, this is true, inasmuch as when he meddles with the dying seised he must confess and avoid it or traverse to all intents. And in debt upon a lease of one acre, if he says that he leased it and another acre, he must take a traverse: as appears in 35 Hen. VI.[1] Now to the doubleness. It is not double, for this whole matter is nothing but an introductory recital to cause the lord to enter, for the strife and debate connects the lord with his right of entry; and so etc. Now, then, may the lord oust his tenant by copy of court roll? It seems so, for there is express mention made in the copies themselves that the tenant shall have it *ad voluntatem domini*, and he cannot have a better estate than he himself accepted. And, sir, tenant at will at the common law is tenant only at the will of the lessor, and even if he never occupies he shall still pay the lord his rent. And, sir, the fee simple is in the lord, for the copy is to the use (*ad usum*) of such and such. Similarly, where I enfeoff men to my use, the fee simple is in them and I have but a use. Thus the tenant has only a use. But, sir, [as to] cestuy que use by the common law, if the feoffees execute some other estate than he wishes them to have, an action upon his case lies against them, because he put his confidence and trust in them to do it, and the action on the case lies for the deceit. But that is not so of tenant by copy of court roll, for he has not put such a confidence in his lord, but was content to take it at his will; and so etc. And he may not have a subpoena against the lord, for the same reason, and he may not have an action on his case; and so etc. And, sir, an action of trespass does not lie, for he shall do fealty, which proves that he is lord, and if so he shall not be punished, for the Statute of Marlborough prohibits it,[2] and so he has no other remedy than a petition. Nevertheless I believe that a petition is no remedy, for it lies in the election of the lord whether to restore him or not. And, sir, if he could not oust his tenant he would lose his rent, for one cannot at the present day give land to hold of oneself by copy of court roll. Also at the present day one cannot give land in fee rendering rent, for the statute *Quia emptores terrarum* prohibits it.[3] Therefore you want the lord to lose his rent, and it is not reasonable that he should lose his rent which is his inheritance; and so etc.

Marvyn to the contrary. As to the exception to the avowry, that it is 'for the whole time aforesaid' (*a toto tempore praedicto*), which refers only to Lord Bray and not to his ancestors: that is not so, but it shall refer to the whole matter, namely the time of prescription. Similarly where I recite that, whereas I have a horse, a cow, and a gown, I give you 'all my aforesaid goods' (*omnia bona mea praedicta*), this shall not relate only to one of them[4] but to all of them. Now, then, [as to the point] that a gift in tail was created since the limitation and therefore he cannot prescribe to have it, that is not so. For

[1] *Abbot of Bermondsey's Case* (1456) YB Mich. 35 Hen. VI, fo. 38, pl. 47.
[2] Statute of Marlborough, c. 3 (*SR* i. 20).
[3] 18 Edw. I, *Quia emptores terrarum* (*SR* i. 106).
[4] I.e. the last antecedent.

done en taille all comen ley et pur ceo home avoit formdon in reverter al comen ley. Et auxi pur ceo que cest estate taile est derive hors dell fee simple terre que est tenus per copy, pur ceo il serra de mesme le nature: come rent graunt a cest jour hors dell gavelkynd ou boroghenglisshe. Et, sir, coment que ne serroit bon pur estate taile, uncore il serra bon pur fee simple. Et le caz est icy de fee simple, issint est hors dargument. Come lou [jeo]¹ prescribe de distrener bestes damage fesantes per mon baile et a emparker eux et de prendre fyne pur le delyverance a mon plesure, ore le prender del fyn a mon plesure est voyde et le custome bon pur le remenant, per que [etc.]. Donsque all barre: moy semble que il doit prendre travers, quar auterment il [responde]² luy per un argument. Et, sir, est in nostre liverz que lou je port dett et declare dell vende dun chivall all defendant et il dit que je vende ceo a luy et a un auter, ore ceo nest plee entaunt que il [purra]³ gager sa ley eo que il ne poit estre entende un mesme contract. Issint est in le caz darbitrement, ou il dit que il agarda cell chose et diverz auterz, il doit prender travers. Donsque al dublenez: il semble duble pur ceo que sont ii matterz et chescun issuable, come avaunt est dit etc. Donsque ou ceo est discontinuance ou nemi? Semble que est, quar auxiforte est ceo pur determiner son estate come est dun fyne all comen ley, et tout un. Donsque lentre neque auget nec minuit, quar il ad fait tout ceo que in luy est de devester ceo hors de luy, et sil ne fuit hors de luy per cest surrender donsque le seignior ne purroit le done ouster, per que [etc.]. Donsque, ou le seignior poit enter ou nemi? Semble que non, quar le seignior ad done cest terre a performer le custome,⁴ [quell il]⁵ ne poit reprender de luy, quar [il]⁶ serroit contrariant. Come all comen ley home done terre in fee simple a tener a son volunte, ore il ne poit luy ouster quant il luy pleist, quar est contrariant: issint icy.

*Densill*⁷ all contrarie. Et primez, ceo navera relatyon mez ad proximum [antecedens]⁸ come avaunt est dit. Auxi a prescriber a doner in taile est voyd, quar devaunt lestatute il ny ad estate taile mez toutes estates fueront fee symple condytyonell issint que post prolem suscitatam habuit potestatem alienandi. Et in [auncient]⁹ yerez, come in lez anez E. ii., lyssu maintenoit assise de mortdancestor, per que [etc.]. Auxi a prescriber a doner in fee, fee taile etc. uncore ceo nest assez, mez il doit dire ouster et que le tenant enjoyeroit ceo enverz son seignior, quar ceo feroit per luy, per que pur cest cause son avowre nest bon. Sir, all traverz, ill ne doit prendre traverz, <et sir icy est dount>¹⁰ quar quant il confesse luy et plus ou confesse luy per matter en ley il ne prendra travers. Et, sir, icy est doubte in ley az xii. homez lou le surrender a [lun]¹¹ et le surrender a ii. sont tout un. Et icy le surrender nest le substanz¹² de son title, mez le conveiance, et in maner nient materiall pur son title mez solement le

¹ *A.* est *B.*   ² *A.* rñe *B.*   ³ *A.* p[ur]re *B.*
⁴ co[n]d[ition] *del. in B.*   ⁵ *A.* q̄ll *B.*
⁶ *A.*   ⁷ Densyll *A.*   ⁸ antecedenez.
⁹ *A.* aunca¹ *B.*   ¹⁰ *B, but del. as haplography.*
¹¹ *A.* lie *B.*   ¹² obstanz.

there was a gift in tail at common law, and therefore one could have formedon in the reverter at common law. Also, because this estate tail is derived out of fee simple land, which is held by copy, it shall therefore be of the same nature: as with rent granted at the present day out of gavelkind or borough English. And, sir, even if [the prescription] cannot be good for estate tail, still it shall be good for fee simple. And the case here is one of fee simple, and so the argument is irrelevant. Similarly where I prescribe to distrain beasts damage feasant through my bailiff, and to impound them, and to take a fine for their deliverance at my pleasure, the taking of the fine at my pleasure is void and yet the custom is good for the residue; and so etc. Now for the bar. It seems to me that he ought to traverse, for otherwise he answers him by an argument. And, sir, it says in our books that where I bring debt and declare of the sale of a horse to the defendant, and he says that I sold it to him and to someone else, this is no plea, inasmuch as he may wage his law, since it cannot be understood to be the same contract. So it is in the case of an arbitration, when he says that he awarded the thing mentioned and various other things, he ought to traverse. Next to the doubleness. It seems to be double, because there are two matters and each of them is issuable, as is said above etc. Next, is this a discontinuance or not? It seems that it is, for it is just as strong to determine his estate as a fine at common law, and all one. Therefore the entry makes no difference (*neque auget nec minuit*), for he has done everything in his power to divest it out of him, and if it was not out of him by this surrender then the lord could not have given it over; and so etc. Now, then, may the lord enter, or not? It seems not, for the lord has given this land to perform the custom, and he may not take it back from him, for it would be self-contradictory. Likewise at common law if someone gives land in fee simple to hold at his will, he may not oust him when he pleases, for it would be contradictory: likewise here.

Densell to the contrary. First, this can only relate back to the next antecedent (*ad proximum antecedens*), as is said above. Also, to prescribe to give in tail is void; for before the statute there was no estate tail, but all estates were fee simple conditional, so that once issue were born he had the power of alienation (*post prolem suscitatam habuit potestatem alienandi*).[1] In old year books, as in the years of Edward II, the issue could maintain an assize of mort d'ancestor; and so etc. Also, prescribing to give in fee, in fee tail, and so forth, is still not enough, but he ought to say further that the tenant should enjoy it against his lord, for that works for him;[2] and so, for this reason, his avowry is not good. Sir, as to the traverse, he ought not to take a traverse; for when he confesses him and more, or confesses him by matter in law, he shall not take a traverse. And, sir, there is a doubt in law here for the twelve men as to whether a surrender to one and a surrender to two are the same thing. And here the surrender is not the substance of his title, but an introductory recital, and in a way immaterial for his title,

---

[1] A quotation from the Statute of Westminster II, c. 1, *De donis* (*SR* ii. 71).
[2] Uncertain: the text appears to say *feroit per luy*.

done le seignior. Donsque il nest duble, quar tout son matter forsque lentre le seignior fait pur son title. Come in trns., le deffendant plede leez del terre et arbres, ceo nest duble, quar lez dell terre est sufficyent mez pur ceo que lauter et tout est emply in le lez dell terre, scilicet le leez dell terre et arbrez, pur ceo nest duble. Issint icy. Et, sir, a ceo que ad este dit que coment que le custome serroit voyde in parcell que il availera pur le remenant, ceo nest issint: quar est intier, et covient pleder ceo certen[ment] come un record <et sur ceo il serra trise>[1] quar sil faila parcell il pledera Nul tiell custome ou Nul tiel record, et sur ceo il serra trise. Et auxi le custome serra priz stricte, per que [etc.]. Donsque ou ceo est discontinewance ou nemi? Semble que non, quar cest surrender est in nature de surrender al comen ley, que ne done estate mez determyne estate. Et auxi cest surrender covient estre per lentier tenant del terre, et ceo nest le barron solement mez le barron et feme et elle nest parte a cest surrender, per que elle ne serra conclude. Et coment que le seignior ad done ceo ouster, ceo ne fait discontinewance eo que il ne fuit seisi de lestate que fuit in la feme: come tenant en taile ne poit discontinuer sinon que il soit seisi per force de taile, per que [etc.]. Donsque, ou le seignior poit luy ouster? Semble que cy, quar ne poit estre ii. fee simplez dune mesme terre. Mez poit estre un fee simple dell terre et auter dez profittes dell terre. Come home poit aver le fe simple in le terre et lauter le fee in le feyne, ou lun poit aver le terre et lauter poit aver le comen hors de ceo, ou rent. Mez dell [*fo. 67v*] terre tantum ii. fee simplez ne poient estre, quar est enconter tout lernyng et tout reson. Donsque, coment que ceo ad este custome de temps dont memorie uncore ceo ne servera a ore, quar ad este custome in Londrez que home gardera gagez enverz le verey onour, uncore il ne poit enverz le roy, come appert 35. H. 6. quar ne poit aver comensment sur ascun reson. Issint icy, ne poit comenser per ascun reson que serroit ii. fee simplez dun mesme terre. Et coment que ad este continue de temps dont memorie per le suffrance dez seigniorz, uncore ceo ne fera un ley, mez le seignior quant il voit[2] poit ceo rumper. Donsque, quant il graunt ceo ouster, uncore lauter ne poit enter. Et nest semble ou le roy enter sur moy et graunt ouster, je puis reenter: mes issint ne puis je icy, quar la demurrust un droit in moy verz le roy, mez issint nay je icy, per que [etc.].

Jenney al contrarie. Et ceux parolx a toto tempore predicto ad relation a tout le matter et all temps de prescription, pur ceo que le temps de prescriptyon fuit parle devaunt, per que predicto avera relation a ceo: come in le caz que Marvyn mist supra. Et all auter exception, eo que il dirroit que il auxi enjoieroit: ceo ne doit il, quar est implie in ceux parolz, scilicet que il poit demiser in fee ou fee taile, quar il ne purroit demiser si lauter ne purroit enjoier, per que sil dirroit et que il ne purroit enjoyer ceo serroit duble. Et donsque all prescriptyon destate

[1] *B, but del. as haplography.*
[2] luy pleast *A.*

which is simply the lord's gift. Therefore it is not double, for all his matter except the lord's entry makes for his title. Similarly in trespass, if the defendant pleads a lease of the land and trees, that is not double, inasmuch as a lease of the land is sufficient, because the other fact—namely the lease of the trees—is implied in a lease of the land, and therefore it is not double. Likewise here. And, sir, as to what has been said that even if the custom is void in part it should avail for the residue, that is not so. It is entire, and he must plead it as certainly as a record; for if he fails in part he may plead 'No such custom' or 'No such record', and thereupon he will be stumped. Also the custom shall be taken strictly; and so etc. Next, is this a discontinuance or not? It seems not, for this surrender is in the nature of a surrender at common law, which does not give an estate but determines an estate. Also, this surrender must be by the entire tenant of the land, and that is not the husband only but the husband and wife, and she is not party to this surrender, and so she shall not be estopped. Even though the lord has given it over, that does not make a discontinuance, since he was not seised of the estate which was in the wife; similarly, tenant in tail cannot discontinue unless he is seised by virtue of the tail; and so etc. Now, then, may the lord oust him? It seems so, for there cannot be two fee simples of one same land, though there may be a fee simple of the land and another of the profits of the land. For instance, one may have the fee simple in the land and another the fee in the hay, or one may have the land and another may have the common out of it, or rent. But of the land alone two fee simples cannot be, for it would be against all learning and all reason. Now, then, even though this has been the custom since time immemorial, still this shall not serve now; for it has been a custom in London that one may keep gages as against the true owner, and yet he cannot do so against the king— as appears in 35 Hen. VI[1]—for it cannot have had a reasonable beginning. Likewise here, it could not have begun upon any reason that there should be two fee simples of one same land. And even if it has continued since time immemorial by the sufferance of the lords, that shall still not make a law; but the lord may break it when he wishes. Then, when he grants it over, still the other may not enter. It is not like the case where the king enters upon me and grants over: there I may re-enter, for there remains a right in me as against the king; but I may not do so here, because I do not have such a thing here; and so etc.

Jenney to the contrary. These words 'for the whole time aforesaid' (*a toto tempore praedicto*) relate to all the matter, and to the time of prescription, because the time of prescription was mentioned before, so that 'aforesaid' (*praedicto*) relates to that: as in the case which Marvyn put above. As to the other exception, that he ought to have said that he also enjoyed it [against the lord], he need not do so: for that is implied in the words that he may demise in fee or fee tail; for he could not demise if the other could not enjoy; and so if he had said 'and that he [could]² enjoy' it would have been double. Next, as to

---

[1] *Simpkin Eyre*'s *Case* (1456) YB Mich. 35 Hen. VI, fo. 25, pl. 33; 51 Selden Soc. 114.
[2] Text reads 'could not'; but cf. the last paragraph of the report, below, p. 309.

tayll: appert per le rehersall de lestatut [de]¹ W. ii. que il fuit estate taile all comen ley, que voiet quod [post prolem suscitatam]² etc., mez ore son estate est abbryge. Donsque all traverz: il covient prender traverz, quar autrement il ne mete ove luy: come in assise le tenant plede que il fuit seisi et enfeoffe N., que estate le deffendant ad, le plaintife dit que il enfeoffe luy devaunt et puis contrarie a son feoffment enter sur luy et enfeoffe le dit N., ore il doit prender traverz, silicet sanz ceo que il ad lestate le dit N. Auxi il mitta le caz dell entre suppose in le [auter]³ in brefe dentre in le per. Donsque all dublenez <dell ple>:⁴ il est duble, quar il ad mit matter einz pur enveigler le court, per que quant lauter ad demurre sur ceo, ceo serra ajuge duble. Come in formdon, le tenant plede un lineall garrante in barre et auxi un collaterall garrante, ceo est duble et tamen lineall garrante saunz assez nest barre. Mesme [le]⁵ ley est agre in nostre liverz sil plede ii. lineall garrantes in barre, ceo est duble, et tamen chescun deux nest ple [aperluy].⁶ Issint icy. Donsque ou ceo soit un discontinuance ou non? Semble que est: et fist le reson que pur ceo que il ad fait tout que in ly est et per cest surrender le possession vest in le seignior, come surrender al comen ley per tenant a⁷ terme de vie a cesti en le revercyon. Ore per son agrement il est tenant maintenaunt in possessyon, et precipe quod reddat serra port verz luy, per que [etc.]. Donsque ou le seignior poit ouster son tenant per copy? Semble que non, quar il ad enheritance per le custome, et le custome est ceo que fait son enheritance et nemi parolz heyrez: come in diverz lewys Dengleterre lou terre est done per copy a un home et to hys, il ad fee simple. Mesme le ley in certen lieux Dengliterre lou il⁸ dona ceo a luy pur terme de vie. Et a ceo que est dit que ne poit estre ii. fee simplez dun mesme terre, in casez il poit. Et al meinz il poit estre un fee simple que remainera⁹ in privite enter le seignior et tenant et auter fee simple verz estrangez: come si sount seignior, mene et tenant, ore le meane ad le fee simple dell terre enverz le seignior et le tenant ad le fee simple enverz toutes estraungez. Et, sir, le seignior avera cessavit verz le meane et recovera le fee simple del terre verz luy. Issint icy, le tenant per copy ad le fee simple enter luy et le seignior, et enverz estraungez et a lour actyonez le seignior est very tenaunt, per que [etc.]. Et, sir, est use in diverz placez que de terre all comen ley quant home voiel faire feoffment il surrendra ceo et donsque le baylyffe donera ceo a lauter a que etc., et tamen le terre e[st]¹⁰ franktenement et nemi copy terre. Et ceo caz il mitte pur prover que discontinuance purroit estre saunce liverey. Et, sir, a ceo que ad este dit que le tenant covient prescriber en le nosme le seignior, ceo est verey¹¹ quant ill est pur lavauntage le seignior, mez quant il est pur lavauntage le tenant il poit prescriber in son nosme demesne, quar ceo est un custome que va all terre de que chescun avera avauntage, come est le custome de gavylkynde et similia, per que [etc.].

---

¹ A.   ² A. prolem B.   ³ gt' in both mss.   ⁴ B, but del.   ⁵ A only.   ⁶ A only.
⁷ pur A.   ⁸ terre est del.   ⁹ remaynd' A.   ¹⁰ A. et B.   ¹¹ voyer A.

the prescription for estate tail, it appears from the recital in the Statute of Westminster II that there was estate tail at common law—since it says *quod post prolem suscitatam etc.*—but now his estate is abridged. Now to the traverse. He must traverse, for otherwise he does not meet with him. Similarly in an assize, if the tenant pleads that he was seised and enfeoffed N., whose estate the defendant has, and the plaintiff says that he enfeoffed him earlier and then, contrary to his feoffment, entered upon him and enfeoffed the said N., he ought now to take a traverse 'without this, that he has the estate of the said N.'. (He also put the case of the entry supposed in the writ of entry in the *per*.) Next to the doubleness of the plea. It is double, for he has put in facts to inveigle the court, and so, when the other has demurred upon it, it shall be adjudged double. Similarly in formedon, if the tenant pleads a lineal warranty in bar and also a collateral warranty, this is double, and yet a lineal warranty without assets is no bar. The same law is agreed in our books if he pleads two lineal warranties in bar: that is double, and yet each of them is no plea by itself. Likewise here. Now, then, is this a discontinuance or not? It seems that it is. (And he made the argument that, because he has done everything in his power, by this surrender the possession vests in the lord, like a surrender at common law by tenant for term of life to the reversioner.) Now, by his agreement, he is forthwith tenant in possession, and a *praecipe quod reddat* may be brought against him; and so etc. Now, then, may the lord oust his tenant by copy? It seems not, for he has an inheritance by the custom, and the custom is what makes his inheritance, not the words 'heirs'. Thus in various places in England, where land is given by copy to a man 'and to his', he has fee simple. The law is the same in certain places in England where he gives it to him for term of life. As to what has been said that there cannot be two fee simples of one same land, in some cases there can. At the least there can be a fee simple which will remain in privity between the lord and tenant and another fee simple as against strangers. For instance, if there are a lord, a mesne and a tenant, the mesne now has the fee simple of the land as against the lord and the tenant has the fee simple as against all strangers. And, sir, the lord shall have *cessavit* against the mesne and recover the fee simple of the land against him. Likewise here, the tenant by copy has the fee simple as between him and the lord, while against strangers and their actions the lord is very tenant; and so etc. And, sir, it is the custom in various places, in respect of land at common law, that if anyone wishes to make a feoffment he shall surrender it and then the bailiff shall give it to the other to whom etc., and yet the land is freehold and not copy land. (He put these cases to prove that there may be discontinuance without livery.) And, sir, as to what has been said that the tenant must prescribe in the lord's name, that is true when it is for the lord's advantage, but when it is for the tenant's advantage he may prescribe in his own name, for it is a custom which goes with the land, of which everyone shall take advantage, like the custom of gavelkind and such like; and so etc.

Hynde all contrarie. Et quant a toto tempore predicto il semble que il navera relation mez ad proximum antecedenz, que est le seignior tantum, et donsque nest bon, quar un prescriptyon doit aver plus long contineance que le vie dun home, per que [etc.]. Et al traverz, semble que il ne besoigne, quar il ad confesse luy et plus, et auxi ad avoyde, per que il ne prendra traverz: come in assise, le tenant plede feoffment [etc. et le plaintife dit que il fuit fayt sur condition et ore il ne prendra travers. Issint in 3. E. 4. il plede feffment][1] az iiii. homez et lauter dit que il enfeoffa ceux iiii. et iiii. pluis, ore il ne prendra traverz. Donsque icy il confesse le surrender et avoide ceo per lentre le seigniour, que est tout leffect de son title. Donsque all dublenez, il est assetz sengle, quar tout ceo nest que conveiance: come si plede diverz feoffmentes in <brefe de >[2] tns. ceo nest duble, per que [etc.]. Donsque outer ceo nest discontinuance, quar per le surrender [*fo. 68*] le possession ne vest in lauter devaunt un entre. Come in Vampage caz, lou il fra leez pur anz a comenser a Michelmaz, et devaunt le feast il release all lesse, ceo fuit agre voyd eo que il navoit possession del terre devaunt le fest: nient pluiz ad il icy. Et, sir, je denie que sur un surrender a cesti in le revercion il nest[3] tenant devaunt un entre. Nient pluz est lou feme est indowe ad ostium[4] ecclesie, tout temps apres le mort son baron devaunt ascun entre el poit refuser cell dowre et prendre son dower all comen ley. Issint est de feoffment deinz le vew, il nest tenant devaunt ascun entre. Per que icy il nest ascun discontinuance. Donsque ouster, semble que le seignior poit ouster son tenant, quar il nest que tenant a son volunte: et est agre xl.[5] E. 3. que il navera monstraverunt envers le seignior ne injuste vexes. Nient pluz avera il remedie [de][6] recoverer le terre, quar si le seignior ne voile garder sa court ou accepter surrender les tenauntes [nount][7] remedie. Et, sir, ceux customez que surdunt dell usage dell court, come ceo est, illz ne sont allowablez in auter court que ou etc. Come custome est in Londres que action de dett girra verz executours sur un taille, et que home ne gagera sa ley pur son taille, et tamen all comen ley action sur cestes customez ne sont maintenable. Issint icy, intaunt que ceo est un privat custome que est deinz mesme le maner, il ne poit prender avauntage de ceo in auter lewe que in le maner, per que [etc.].

Badwhyn[8] al contrarie. Et primez ceux parollez a toto tempore predicto ne poient per reson estre referre que al tout le tempz. Et al prescription del estate taile, il est bon in cest court ou le copy terre est, quar il prescribe a doner terre in fee, fee taile, [etc.] et ceo est bon coment que est puis le tempz dell limitatyon, quar le limitatyon in brefe de droit ne serve mez pur prescription al comen ley et nemi pur prescription sur[9] customez, per que [etc.]. Et, sir, il doit prender traverz (et mit[ta] le diversitie ou est per voy de supposell come in assise de

[1] *A only, om. by haplography in B.*
[2] *Om. A.*
[3] *Sic in both mss.*   [4] hostium *A.*   [5] xliº *A.*   [6] *A.* dell *B.*
[7] *A.* nad *B.*   [8] Bawedwyn *A.*   [9] *Altered from* dell.

Hynde to the contrary. As to 'all the time aforesaid' (*a toto tempore praedicto*) he thought it related only to the next antecedent (*ad proximum antecedens*), which is the [present] lord alone, and therefore it is not good; for a prescription ought to have a longer continuance than a man's life; and so etc. As to the traverse, he thought it was not needed; for he has confessed him and more, and also avoided, and so he shall not traverse. Similarly in an assize, if the tenant pleads a feoffment etc. and the plaintiff says that it was made upon condition, he shall not take a traverse. Likewise in 3 Edw. IV,[1] he pleaded a feoffment to four men, and the other said that he enfeoffed these four and four more, and did not take a traverse. Here, then, he confesses the surrender and avoids it by the lord's entry, which is the whole effect of his title. Then as to the doubleness: it is sufficiently single, for all of it is only a recital. Similarly if one pleads various feoffments in a writ of trespass this is not double; and so etc. To move on, then, this is not a discontinuance, for by the surrender the possession does not vest in the other before an entry. Similarly in Vampage's case,[2] where he made a lease for years to begin at Michaelmas, and before the feast he released to the lessee, this was agreed to be void since he had no possession of the land before the feast: no more has he here. And, sir, I deny that upon a surrender to the reversioner he is tenant before an entry, any more than where a woman is endowed at the church door (*ad hostium ecclesiae*): at all times after her husband's death, before any entry, she may refuse this dower and take her dower at common law. So it is of a feoffment within the view: he is not tenant before any entry. And so there is no discontinuance. Moving on, then, it seems that the lord may oust his tenant, for he is but tenant at his will: and it is agreed in 40 Edw. III,[3] that he shall not have *monstraverunt* or *ne injuste vexes* against the lord. No more shall he have a remedy to recover the land; for if the lord will not keep his court, or accept a surrender, the tenants have no remedy. And, sir, these customs which arise from the usage of the court, as this is, are not allowable in any court other than the one where etc. For example, there is a custom in London that an action of debt shall lie against executors upon a tally, and that one shall not wage his law for his tally, and yet actions upon these customs are not maintainable at common law. Likewise here, inasmuch as this is a private custom within the same manor, he cannot take advantage of it in another place than in the manor; and so etc.

Baldwin to the contrary. First, these words 'all the time aforesaid' (*a toto tempore praedicto*) cannot by reason refer to anything but the whole time. As to the prescription for the estate tail, it is good in this court where the copy land is; for he prescribes to give land in fee, in fee tail, and so forth, and this is good even though it is since the time of the limitation, for the limitation in a writ of right serves only for prescription at common law and not for prescription upon customs; and so etc. And, sir, he ought to take a traverse. (And he put the

---

[1] *Hill's Case* (1463) YB Mich. 3 Edw. IV, fo. 17, pl. 11.
[2] *Vampage's Case* (temp. Edw. IV) cited in YB Mich. 15 Hen. VII, fo. 7, pl. 13.
[3] YB Mich. 40 Edw. III, fo. 45, pl. 30.

mortdancestor etc. et ou il est allege per matter in fait. Et auxi pur le dublenez il
mitta lez bonez groundes que fueront misez per Yorke que low il est conveiance
a son matter, come in assise de mortdancestor il plede le feoffment le
demandant, et similia.) Donsque il semble ceo discontinuance, quar il ad fait
tout que in luy est, et auter deliverance de possession nest il mez per surrender:
come si le roy <fait a moy >[1] sez letters patentes il est in moy maintenaunt,
quar auter liverey de cell terre per auter [forme][2] il nest. Et per mesme le reson
que home poit prendre estate per feoffment et discontinuer ceo per feoffment, le
feme nient parte, issint poit il per surrender, quar il nest auter mene a faire ceo
passer. Donsque semble que le seignior ne poit ouster son tenant, quar all
comensment il ne fuit ascun maner mez le terre fuit in le maine le seignior[3] et
donsque le seignior purroit ceo doner a tener de ly per [quecunque][4] services
que il voilest,[5] come per service de chivaler ou in socage ou per basse service,
donsque quant il ad exprese quell servicez il voiell pur ceo al comensment il ne
purroit changer sa volunte a ore. Et cest service fuit de faire diverz customez,
issint il ne poit enter ore et dire que il voile aver auterz servicez. Et coment que
ny ad ascun reson a [porter][6] ceo, ceo ne fait matter: quar petit reson [porta][7]
que leigne[8] fitz enheritera pluz que le puisne (quasi diceret nihil) mez que le
institution dell ley fuit issint al comensment. Issint fuit le institutyon de cest
tenure. Mesme ley de custome de gavylkynd et similia: petit reson eux [porta][9]
et allowa mez [solonque][10] linstitution deux.[11] Et a ceo que Hynde dit, que le
seignior esliera[12] sil voiell garder son court ou nemi, ceo est voier, uncore ceo
ne tolle lenheritance le tenant, quar si le roy ne voile garder ascun de sez courtes
uncore ceo ne tolle le comen ley: mez de comen droit et justice il est tenus deux
garder, issint est le seignior. Et coment que il navera action verz son seignior sil
est ouste, uncore nient obstant ceo son droit remayne issint que le seignior luy
fait tort. Quar si home est disseisi et releez toutes actyonez il ne poit aver action
et tamen il ad droit. Issint si home purchace avowsyon et suffre un usurpatyon
il est saunce remedie et tamen il ad droit. Issint est in brefe de droit sil ne poit
lier sez esplez, uncore il poit enter. Issint icy. Et action de trnz. avera il verz le
seignior pur lez profitez nient obstant lestatut de Marlebryge entant que il ne
fait ceo come dominus. Et nient obstant que le seignior poit eslier quant est
surrender in sez mainez a graunter ceo ouster, issint poit le roy eslier quant son
patente surrender cez letterz ea intentione que il doit graunter ouster a un S.,[13]
mez uncore le roy de droit est oblige a ceo faire accordant al surrender, issint
[est][14] le seignior, per que [etc.].

Luke al contrarie. Et primez all prescriptyon destate taile: sir, le prescriptyon
all comen ley fuit de tempore cujus <contrarii memoria hominum non
existit >,[15] et ore le prescriptyon est lymit per [lestatut][16] et le jure serra compelle

---

[1] *Written twice.*   [2] p[ur]m'.   [3] *Altered from roy.*   [4] *A.* conq' *B.*
[5] voyloyt *A.*   [6] p[or]t' *A.* p[ro]t' *B. Perhaps a misreading of* prover.
[7] *A.* p[ro]ta *B.*   [8] leysne *A.*   [9] *A.* p[ro]ta *B.*   [10] *A. Blank in B.*
[11] etc. *B.*   [12] poit eslier *A.* eslier' *B.*   [13] m[esme] *A.*
[14] *A only.*   [15] etc. *B.*   [16] *A.* lestate *B.*

distinction where it is by way of supposal, as in an assize of mort d'ancestor etc., and where it is alleged by matter in fact. Also, with respect to the doubleness, he put the good principles (*groundes*) which were put by Yorke as to where it is introductory to his matter: as where in an assize of mort d'ancestor he pleads a feoffment by the demandant, and such like.) Then he thought this a discontinuance, for he has done all in his power, and there is no other delivery of possession but by surrender. Similarly, if the king makes out his letters patent to me, it is in me at once, for there is no other delivery of this land in any other form. And for the same reason that one may take an estate by feoffment and discontinue it by feoffment, the wife not being party, so may he by surrender, for there is no other means to cause it to pass. Next, it seems that the lord may not oust his tenant. In the beginning there was no manor, but the land was in the lord's hand, and then the lord could give the land to be held of him by whatever services he wished, as by knight-service, or in socage, or by base service; and therefore, when he has expressed at the outset what services he wanted for it he cannot change his will now. And this service was to perform various customs; and so he may not enter now and say that he would like to have other services. And even if there is no reason to [prove] this, it does not matter: for there is not much reason to [prove] that the eldest son should inherit rather than the younger (meaning that there was none), but only that the institution of the law was such at the beginning. So was the institution of this tenure. The law is the same concerning the custom of gavelkind and such like: there is little reason to [prove] them except the institution thereof. As to what Hynde has said, that the lord may choose whether he will keep his court or not, that is true, and yet that does not take away the tenant's inheritance. For if the king will not keep any of his courts that does not take away the common law; but by common right and justice he is bound to keep them, and so is the lord. And even though he shall not have an action against his lord if he is ousted, his right nevertheless still remains, so that the lord does him a wrong. If someone is disseised, and releases all actions, he cannot have an action, and yet he has right. Likewise if someone purchases an advowson and permits a usurpation, he is without remedy and yet he has right. So it is in a writ of right if he cannot lay his esplees: he may still enter. Likewise here. And he may have an action of trespass against the lord for the profits, despite the Statute of Marlborough, since he does not do it as lord (*dominus*).[1] And notwithstanding that the lord may choose, when land is surrendered in his hand, whether to grant it over, so may the king choose when his patentee surrenders his letters patent with the intention that he should grant it over to one S., and yet by right he is bound to do it in accordance with the surrender. So is the lord; and so etc.

Luke to the contrary. First, as to the prescription for estate tail: sir, prescription at common law was 'from time whereof the memory of man does not exist' (*de tempore cujus contrarii memoria hominum non existit*), and now

---

[1] Probably referring to the Statute of Marlborough, c. 3 (*SR* i. 20). However, the provisions of the statute relating to misconduct by lords (cc. 1–4) deal with wrongful distress rather than eviction.

denquirer de ceo, et ceo est de tempore R. primi. Et lestatut de W. ii. fuit fait in tempz E. le primer, que est puis ceo, quar lestate taile est fait per cest estatut de W. ii. et formedon in discender est done per ceo et ore le volunte le donor serra observe et issint ne purroit il all comen ley, per que le prescriptyon nest bon. Donsque a toto tempore predicto: ceux ne sount parolz de prescriptyon ne impliont ascun prescriptyon mez [lavowre][1] est que il poit demiser in fee, fee taile ou pur terme de vie a toto tempore predicto et ceo nest bon sauns allegger prescriptyon, et ceux parolz ne fount prescriptyon ne illes purront aver relatyon que ad proximum antecedens. Mez [sil][2] ust interlesse ceux parolz donsque ust este assetz bon, intant que parolz de [*fo. 68v*] prescriptyon fueront avaunt in lavowre. Donsque al barre: ou il doit prender travers ou nemi? Semble que non, quar il ad confesse luy et pluz: come in brefe dentre sur disseisin de disseisin fait a son aille et il dit que laiel navoit rienz que in jointenure ove sa feme que survesquist, que estate le deffendant ad, ceo est bon saunce traverz. Issint est in wast supposant que il lessa a luy pur terme de vie, et le defendant dit que il lesse pur terme [de vie][3] et un an pluz, ceo est bon saunce traverz. Issint est in trnz. [si] le defendant dit que le trnz. fuit fait per luy et un estrange, a que le plaintife ad release, ore il ne prendra traverz. Issint icy, per que [etc.]. Donsque al dublenez: semble assetz sengle, quar cest matter, scilicet que le surrender fait all barron et feme nest que a faire nous prive a pleder cest ple. Et, sir, si ussomus plede lauter matter que le seigniour entra ceo nust estre ple aperluy eo que il serroit barre alarge, et home ne poit pleder barre alarge forsque in assise, per que nest duble. Come in dett verz executourz et illes pledont Pleynment [administer][4] et issint rienz enter maynez, ceo nest duble. Mesme ley in dett porte sur leez pur terme danez et il plede Leve per distres et issint rien arere, ceo nest duble. Nient plus icy, per que [etc.]. Donsque ou ceo est discontinuance? Semble que non, quar un surrender nest que render suy[5] un estate et ne done estate et ceo ne fait discontinuance. Come si precipe quod reddat est port verz le barron et il disclame, ceo nest discontinuance, quar nest que un surrender dell action le[6] demandant. Et entant que il ne entra per force [del][7] surrender ceo ne fait discontinuance, quar si tenant a terme de vie surrrender a cesti en le revercion il nest in luy devaunt un entre in fait. Et posito que home devie seisi dez terrez tenus per copy <de court >[8] role et son issu fait son fine et est admitt tenant all seignior, est il tenant dell terre devaunt ascun entre? Non certez, per que [etc.]. Donsque ou le seignior poit ouster son tenant per copy? Semble que cy, quar il [ne][9] tient que a volunte le seignior. Et pur ceo est un liver que lou le seignior avoit per escheat terrez queux fueront tenus in villenage et puis il done eux a tener per copy etc. et devie, que le seignior poit eux ouster a son pleasure,

---

[1] lavower' *A.* lawre *B.*   [2] *A.* sill[es] *B.*   [3] *A.* danez *B.*
[4] *A.* admynistat *B.*   [5] suiz *A.*   [6] del *A.*
[7] *A.* de *B.*   [8] *Written twice.*   [9] *A only.*

the prescription is appointed by the statute, and the jury shall be compelled to enquire into it, and that is from the time of Richard I. And the Statute of Westminster II was made in the time of Edward I, which is later than that; and estate tail is created by this Statute of Westminster II, and formedon in the descender is given thereby. And now the will of the donor shall be observed, which could not be so at common law; and so the prescription is not good. Then as to 'all the time aforesaid' (*a toto tempore praedicto*): those are not words of prescription and do not imply any prescription, but the avowry is that he may demise in fee, in fee tail, or for term of life, *a toto tempore praedicto*, and that is not good without alleging a prescription; but these words do not make a prescription, and relate only to the next antecedent (*ad proximum antecedens*). However, if he had left out these words it would have been good enough, since there were words of prescription before in the avowry. Now for the bar. Ought he to take a traverse, or not? It seems not, for he has confessed him and more: as in a writ of entry sur disseisin for a disseisin done to his grandfather, and he says that the grandfather had nothing save in joint tenure with his wife, who survived, whose estate the defendant has, this is good without a traverse. So it is in waste, supposing that he leased to him for term of life, and the defendant says that he leased for term of life and one year more: this is good without a traverse. So it is in trespass if the defendant says that the trespass was committed by him and a stranger, to whom the plaintiff has released, he shall not take a traverse. Likewise here; and so etc. As to the doubleness, it seems single enough, for this matter—namely the surrender made to the husband and wife—is only to make us privy for the purpose of pleading this plea. And, sir, if we had pleaded the other matter, that the lord entered, that would not have been a plea by itself, inasmuch as it would be a bar at large, and one may not plead a bar at large except in an assize; and so it is not double. Similarly in debt against executors, if they plead 'Fully administered and therefore nothing in hand', that is not double. The law is the same in debt brought upon a lease for term of years, and they plead 'Levied by distress and therefore nothing in arrears', that is not double. No more is it here; and so etc. Now, then, is this a discontinuance? It seems not, for a surrender is nothing other than a rendering up of an estate, not giving an estate, and it does not make a discontinuance. Similarly if a *praecipe quod reddat* is brought against a husband, and he disclaims, this is not a discontinuance; it is only a surrender of the demandant's action. And since he did not enter by virtue of the surrender it does not make a discontinuance; for if a tenant for term of life surrrenders to the reversioner it is not in him before an entry in fact. Suppose someone dies seised of lands held by copy of court roll, and his issue makes his fine and is admitted tenant to the lord, is he tenant of the land before any entry? Surely not; and so etc. Now, then, may the lord oust his tenant by copy? It seems so; for he holds only at the will of the lord. Therefore there is a book which says that where the lord had lands by escheat which were held in villeinage, and afterwards gave them to be held by copy etc., and died, the lord

quar tenant a volunte a le comen ley est lou il est a lour ii. voluntez mez issint
nest il icy forsque solement all volunte le seignior, quar issint est expresse in le
copy et priz sur cest condition. Et, sir, in le Auncyent Tenurez est appelle tenure
per base tenure, quar est baz eo que il est tenus a volunt le seignior. Et, sir, est
agre xli. E. 3. que pur le terre il nad remedie verz le seignior, mez il avera
resonable temps a carier sez utensylez[1] et crop come tenant a volunte per le
comen ley, come est agre in mesme le liver. Et, sir, il ne poit prescriber forsque in
droit et in nosme dell seignior. Auterment est de tenant all volunte le roy, come
chauncell[er][2] et hujusmodi, ilz poient prescriber pur ceo que ills fount ceo in
[le][3] droit le roy, mez tenant a volunte sil prescriberoit il ferroit ceo in son droit
demesne, per que [etc.].

Audeley[4] al contrarie. Et primez ceux paroles a toto tempore predicto
averont relation a tout le matter precydent, quar in cest paroll totum est
contenus omne, que est un generall paroll que avera relation a tout le matter.
Come in dett sur obligation a payer meindre somme a tiel leu, je veigne a
<mesme le >[5] lew devaunt dyner et apres dyner et issint suiz je la per totum
tempus predictum, ceo navera relation tantsolement all temps apres dyner mez
all temps devaunt dyner auxi. Issint est si je suy oblige de performer dyverz
condytyonez comprisez in un indenture, et in le fyne de indenture est ad
[omnes][6] predictas conventiones perimplendas etc., ceo navera relation
tantsolement a lez conditionz prochein all [omnes][7] mez a toutes [lez][8]
condytyonez comprisez in lendenture. Donsque ou [le][9] presciptyon est bon pur
lestate taile? Semble que cy, quar il fuit un[10] estate taile al comen ley: quar nient
obstant que devaunt lestatut de W. ii. il fuit appel in le vulger speche un fee
simple conditionell uncore lestate fuit fait come un taile a cest jour, et formdon
in le remainder et [formedon][11] in le reverter fueront all comen ley, et le done all
comen ley fuit per paroles a ly et a sez heyrez de son corps ou a ly et a sa feme et
a lez heyrez de lour ii. corps ingenderez etc. Et admit que le prescriptyon serroit
voyde pur ceo, uncore il serra bon pur le remenant. Come si je prescribe in
brefe de trns. dun chivall daver wayffe et strayffe et catalla felonum et
fugitivorum et conusanz de plez, coment que est voyd pur catalla felonum et
conusaunz dez plez uncore est bon pur le remenant, per que [etc.]. Et, sir,
coment que lestatut done ceux estates novel nosme, come lou illz fueront all
comen ley appelle fee simple condytionell et lestatut fait eux estate taile, uncore
le prescriptyon estoiera bon. Come lou le roy graunt a moy que je [alera][12]
discharge dascun tolle in le ville de Dalle, et puis le roy incorporate eux per le
nosme de ville de Sale, uncore ceo ne tollera mon graunt [de][13] discharge de tole
etc. Auxi si un priore ad este fonduz puis [temps] de memorie et le priore voil

---

[1] utenselx *A*.   [2] le chaunceller *A*.   [3] *A only.*
[4] Audley *A*.   [5] tiell *del.*
[6] oēz *A*. om̄e *B*.   [7] oēz *A*. cle *B*.   [8] *A*. le *B*.
[9] *A only.*   [10] *Om. A.*   [11] *A only.*
[12] aler' *A*. alala *B*.   [13] *A only.*

could oust them at his pleasure; for tenant at will at common law is where it is at their two wills, whereas here it is only at the will of the lord, for it is so expressed in the copy and it is taken upon that condition. And, sir, in the *Old Tenures* it is called tenure by base tenure; for it is base inasmuch as it is held at the will of the lord. And, sir, it is agreed in 41 Edw. III,[1] that he has no remedy against the lord for the land, though he shall have a reasonable opportunity to carry away his utensils and crop, like a tenant at will by the common law, as is agreed in the same book. And, sir, he may not prescribe except in the right of and in the name of the lord. It is otherwise of tenants at the will of the king, like the lord chancellor and such like; they may prescribe, because they act in the right of the king, whereas if a tenant at will were to prescribe he would do it in his own right; and so etc.

Audley[2] to the contrary. First, these words 'all the time aforesaid' (*a toto tempore praedicto*) relate to all the preceding matter, for in this word *totum* is contained *omne*, which is a general word and relates to the whole matter. For instance, in debt upon a bond to pay a lesser sum at such and such a place, if I [plead that I] came to the same place before dinner and after dinner, and so was there *per totum tempus praedictum*, this does not relate only to the time after dinner but to the time before dinner also. So it is if I am bound to perform various conditions comprised in an indenture, and at the end of the indenture it says 'for the performance of all the aforesaid covenants etc.' (*ad omnes praedictas conventiones perimplendas etc.*), this does not relate only to the conditions next to the word *omnes* but to all the conditions comprised in the indenture. Now, then, is the presciption good for the estate tail? It seems so, for there was an estate tail at common law. Even though, before the Statute of Westminster II, it was called in the vulgar speech a fee simple conditional, nevertheless the estate was made as a tail at the present day, and formedon in the remainder and formedon in the reverter were at common law, and the gift at common law was by the words 'to him and his heirs of his body', or 'to him and his wife and the heirs of their two bodies begotten' etc. But even if we admit that the prescription is void as to that, it shall nevertheless be good for the rest. Similarly if I prescribe, in a writ of trespass for taking a horse, to have waif and stray and *catalla felonum et fugitivorum* and cognizance of pleas, even though it is void for *catalla felonum* and cognizance of pleas, it is still good for the rest; and so etc. And, sir, even though the statute gives these estates a new name, in that whereas at common law they were called fee simple conditional and the statute makes them estate tail, still the prescription shall stand as good. Similarly where the king grants me that I may go discharged of any toll in the vill of Dale, and afterwards the king incorporates them by the name of the vill of Sale, this shall nevertheless not take away my grant of discharge from toll etc. Also, if a priory has been founded since time immemorial, and the prior

---

[1] YB Mich. 42 Edw. III, fo. 25, pl. 9.
[2] Thomas Audley argued last as senior of the call by reason of being king's serjeant designate: Baker, *Serjeants at Law*, p. 168, n. 2.

prescriber daver annuite, ceo est voyde, eo que il est puis temps de memorie: mez si un priore que fuit founduz devaunt temps de memorie ad estre seisi tout temps de memorie et puis est fait abbe, uncore cell novel corporation ne tollera son droit de prescriptyon [*fo. 69*] que il avoit devaunt. Nient pluz icy cel novel nosme done a ceux estates ne changera lestate, per que [etc.]. Donsque all traverz: semble que il doit prendre traverz, quar lou le chose est allege per matter in fait ceo covient estre confesse et avoyde ou travers per matter in fait. Contrarie est lou il est allege per voy de supposell (et mit[ta] lez comen caz sur ceo): come in precipe quod reddat verz un, il <poit pleder>[1] jointenancy ove un auter eo que brefe est que supposell. Issint[2] est si un fitz port assise de mortdancestor, est bon ple adire que il [ad][3] auter en vie nient nosme in le brefe saunce [prender][4] traverse. Mez contrarie est ou est allege per matter in fait, come le caz ou il plede moraunt seisi en barre et lauter dit que il fuit jointenant ove un auter que survive etc. Issint in le caz que ad este mis in 35. H. 6. Mez in ascun caz coment que soit matter in fait uncore il ne doit luy traverz pur le mischief que poit venir a luy: come in droit de garde supposant que il morust in son homage, le defendant dit que il tient jointement ove ly et ly tient einz per le survivour, ore il ne traversera saunce ceo que il morust in son homage,[5] quar serroit mischief a luy eo que il ad confesse ceo, et tamen est allege per matter in fait in le declaration. Auxi il ne traversera lou il nest a mischief: come in dett sur acchet[6] [dun][7] chivall et il dit que acchet[8] ceo et un auter, ore il ne prendra traverz quar il poit gager son ley. Auxi il ne traversera le matter allege ou son traverz ne serroit materiall: come in le caz que fuit daren[ment] [myse][9] de wast [ou le tenant dit que il tient cest acre pur terme de vie et une anne pluiz etc., quar sil tient per un dez estates et fayt wast][10] il serra punisshe. Mesme ley est in repl. de ii. chivalles priz et il avowa pur iiii., il ne prendra traverz, causa qua supra. Mez auterment est icy. Et, sir, son barre a nostre avowre est un title, per que covient estre certen a chescun entent et nemi per voy dargument come est icy. Auxi auter ground est lou ills conveiont dell mesme person il covient prendre traverz, come in trnz. le defendant plede feoffement de J. S. et le plaintife conveia ly de mesme le person, ore il covient prendre traverz. Mesme <ley est>[11] lou ylls conveiont dun mesme person de le possession: come in quare impedit le defendant claime le avowson come heyre a son auncestor per reson que il est appendant a un maner et le plaintife conveia de mesme launcestor mesme lavowson per graunt, ore il covient traverz lappendance. Issint icy, ambideux conveiont dell seignior, per que il doit prender traverz. Donsque al dublenez: il semble duble, quar [lun][12] nest conveiance a lauter, come si home plede que il discend a un tyel que ly enfeoffa, mez icy chescun title est estraunge al auter et chescun [deux][13] ust este sufficient

---

[1] pled' *A.*   [2] *Written twice.*   [3] *A only.*   [4] *A only.*
[5] le defendant dit que il tient jointement ove ly *B but del. as a haplography.*
[6] achate *A.*   [7] en.   [8] il achate *A.*   [9] *A only.*
[10] *A only; om. by haplography in B.*   [11] le ley *A.*   [12] lou.
[13] duex.

wishes to prescribe to have an annuity, this is void, in that it is since time immemorial: but if a priory which was founded before time immemorial has been seised at all times of memory and is afterwards made an abbey, this new incorporation shall nevertheless not take away the right of prescription which it had before. No more here shall this new name given to these estates change the estate; and so etc. As to the traverse: it seems that he ought to take a traverse, for where a thing is alleged by matter in fact it must be confessed and avoided or traversed by matter in fact. It is different where it is alleged by way of supposal (and he put the common cases upon that): as in *praecipe quod reddat* against one, he may plead joint tenancy with another, since the writ is merely a supposal. So it is if a son brings an assize of mort d'ancestor, it is a good plea to say that there is someone else alive not named in the writ, without taking a traverse. But it is different where it is alleged by matter in fact, as in the case where he pleads a dying seised in bar and the other says that he was joint tenant with another who survives etc. Likewise in the case which has been put in 35 Hen. VI.[1] But in some cases, even if it is a matter in fact, he still ought not to traverse him, on account of the mischief which might come to him: as in right of ward, supposing that he died in his homage, the defendant says that he held jointly with him and held himself in by survivorship, he shall not traverse 'without this, that he died in his homage', for it would be a mischief to him, in that he has confessed it, and yet it is alleged by matter in fact in the declaration. Also he shall not traverse where he is not at mischief: as in debt upon the purchase of a horse, where he says that he bought it and another, he shall not traverse here because he can wage his law. Also he shall not traverse the matter alleged where his traverse would not be material: as in the case which was last put of waste, where the tenant says that he holds this acre for term of life and one year more etc.; for if he holds by one of the estates and commits waste he shall be punished. The law is the same in replevin for two horses taken, and he avows for four, he shall not take a traverse, for the above reason. But it is otherwise here. And, sir, his bar to our avowry is a title, and therefore it must be certain to every intent and not by way of argument as here. Also, there is another principle (*ground*) that where they trace title from the same person it is necessary to traverse: as in trespass, if the defendant pleads a feoffment from John Style, and the plaintiff traces himself from the same person, he must take a traverse. The law is the same where they trace the possession from the same person: as in *quare impedit* where the defendant claims the advowson as heir to his ancestor by reason that it is appendant to a manor, and the plaintiff traces the same advowson from the same ancestor by grant, he must traverse the appendancy. Likewise here, both trace title from the lord, and so he ought to take a traverse. As to the doubleness: it seems double, for the one is not merely introductory to the other—as where someone pleads that it descended to such and such, who enfeoffed him—but here every title is different from the other

---

[1] *Abbot of Bermondsey's Case* (1456) YB Mich. 35 Hen. VI, fo. 38, pl. 47; above, p. 299.

plee aperly, et pur ceo in trns. port verz executourz [dexecutours][1] ils pledont
que lez bienz fueront devisez a lour testatour per le primer testatour, et que le
primer testatour fist lour testatour et le plaintife cez executourz, et le plaintife
delivera lez bienz a lour testatour, ceo est duble: [scilicet,][2] le devise et
[fesaunz][3] dexecutourz, et le deliverey. Mesme ley est de pleder dyverz
moraunts seisi in assise. Et icy un responz ne poit faire fyn de tout, per que
[etc.]. Donsque ou le seignior poit ouster son tenant per copy de court rolle?
Semble que non, quar il ad bon fee symple solonsque le custome, quar un fee
simple poit passer per custome saunce lyverey et seisin: come si je devisa terrez,
ore il ad fee simple saunce livere, et tamen cest device est contrarie al comen
ley, mez pur ceo que est per custome que est allowable eo que il est de temps
dount memorie allow per mesme le reson icy et nosment come est allege icy in
lavowre, scilicet que il poit deviser in fee, fee taile ou pur terme de vie ad
voluntatem domini secundum consuetudinem[4] etc. issint que ceux parolez ad
voluntatem refront que il poit deviser et demitter le terre per ascun de ceux iii.
estatez que il voit, scilicet il poit eslier a demitter in fee, fee taile ou pur terme de
vie. Mez a auter purpoz ceux parolz ad voluntatem sount voydez, quar est
contrariant a son estate: come si home per le comen ley infeoffe un auter a tener
a son volunte ceo est voyde, ou a tener pur terme de sa vie ceo est voyde. Mez si
le seignior lessa pur [terme de vie][5] sur condition que si face wast que il reavera
le terre ceo est bon, quar le ley estoit ove ceo que sil face wast que il reavera
la terre per action de wast. Mez auterment est icy. Et a ceo que est [dit][6]
que ceux parolz secundum consuetudinem serront prisez voyde,[7] ceo nest issint,
quar donsque chescun graunt serront prisez pluz forte verz le graunte et
plus beneficyall pur le grauntor: cujus contrarium est lex, quar il ne poit
prender ceo que est le melior pur luy et relinquiser ceo que est[8] enverz luy, mez
il covient prender lentier copie come il est. Quar come Bawdhyn[9] disoit, al
comensment tout le terre fuit in lez maines dun home ou certen personez queux
ne purront [manurer][10] tout lour terre ne order ceo eux mesmez saunz eide et
servauntes ne voil ceo faire crediblement pur ceo que ceo que ills fieront fuit
per cohercion, donsque quant lez seigniorz donont parcel de cell terre az
auterz homez et a lour heyrez a faire service a eux, come de plogher[11] lour terre
come est le tenure de[12] socage, ou auterz [villenes][13] servicez, et ceux personez
voilent ceo faire crediblement eo que illz avoient enheritance a ceo faire,
donsque nest reson, ills eiant enheritance in ceo, que le seignior per son absolut
volunte eux oustera, quar le custome dell maner ne suffre ceo et est done solonc
le custome dell maner. Et seignior ad enheritance en le rent auxibien come ills
ount in la terre, et si je done terre a tener solonc le ley Dengliterre, mittera je ly
hors per mon absolut volunte? Non, mez il enjoiera ceo come la ley voiet. Issint
icy, il injoiera ceo solonc le custome etc. A ceo que est dit que cest custome ne
poit aver resonable comensment, ceo nest issint, quar poit estre que il fuit done
a tener per mesme lez servicez al comensment. Auxi poit estre que cest order et

---

[1] *Interlined in B.*　　[2] *A only.*　　[3] *A.* feoffmt *B.*　　[4] *Om. A.*
[5] *A.* ten[er] *B.*　　[6] *A only.*　　[7] *Om. A.*　　[8] fayt *A.*　　[9] Bawedwyn *A.*
[10] manur' *A.* manar *B.*　　[11] plower *A.*　　[12] in *A.*　　[13] villen *A.* vilerez *B.*

and each of them would have been a sufficient plea by itself. Thus in trespass brought against executors of executors, if they plead that the goods were devised to their testator by the first testator, and that the first testator made their testator and the plaintiff his executors, and the plaintiff delivered the goods to their testator, this is double: namely, the devise and the appointment of executors, and the delivery. The law is the same in an assize, if one pleads various dyings seised. And here one answer cannot make an end of everything; and so etc. Now, then, may the lord oust his tenant by copy of court roll? It seems not, for he has a good fee simple according to the custom; for a fee simple may pass by custom without livery and seisin. Similarly if I devise lands, he has fee simple without livery; and yet this devise is contrary to the common law, but it is allowable because it is by custom, inasmuch as it has been allowed from time immemorial. The same reasoning applies here, and especially when it is alleged here in the avowry that he may devise in fee, in fee tail, or for term of life, *ad voluntatem domini secundum consuetudinem etc.*, so that these words *ad voluntatem* refer to the assertion that he may devise and let the land for any of these three estates that he wishes—that is, he may choose whether to demise in fee, in fee tail, or for term of life. But for any other purpose these words *ad voluntatem* are void, for they are contrary to his estate. Similarly if someone at common law enfeoffed another to hold at his will, that was void; or to hold for term of his life, that was void. However, if the lord leases for term of life upon condition that if the tenant commits waste the lord shall have the land back, that is good, for the law is consistent with this, that if he commits waste he shall have the land back by an action of waste. But it is otherwise here. As to what has been said that these words *secundum consuetudinem* should be taken as void, that is not so; for then every grant should be taken more strongly against the grantee and more beneficially for the grantor: the contrary of which is law (*cujus contrarium est lex*), for he may not take that which is best for him and leave aside that which is against him, but he must take the whole copy as it is. As Baldwin said, in the beginning all the land was in the hands of one man or certain persons who could not till all their land or order it themselves without help, and servants could not be relied upon to do it because what they did was by coercion, and therefore lords gave out part of the land to other men and their heirs to do service to them, as by ploughing their land (as is the tenure of socage), or other lowly services, and these persons could be relied upon to do it since they had an inheritance to do it. Therefore it is not right, inasmuch as they have an inheritance therein, that the lord should by his absolute will put them out; for the custom of the manor does not allow it, and the land is given in accordance with the custom of the manor. And the lord has an inheritance in the rent just as they have in the land. If I give land to hold according to the law of England, may I put him out according to my absolute will? No, but he shall enjoy it as the law wills. Likewise here, he shall enjoy it in accordance with the custom etc. As to what has been said that this custom cannot have a reasonable beginning, it is not so; for it may be that it was given to hold by the same

tenure fuit fait al temps que le comen ley fuit fait, quar nul home poit dire sur quell cause et reson le comen [*fo. 69v*] ley fuit fait, mez per usage tout temps puis est bon conuz a nous que ceo fuit le institutyon dell ley etc. A ceo que est dit per Knytley[1] que le seignior navera remedie pur son rent eo que lestatut Quia emptores terrarum ouste tiell reservation, ceo nest issint quar lestatut de Quia emptores [terrarum][2] fuit fait pur le mischefe del change del seigniors avowrye paramount. Mez icy il ne serra change, quar le franktenement demurt in le seignior, et pur ceo nient obstaunt alterationz de possessionz per surrender uncore ceo ne changera le seigniors avowre paramount. Auxi [cest][3] inheritance in le rent del seignior ad continue de temps dont memorie ne court, per que [etc.]. A ceo que est dit que ne poit estre ii. fee simplez dun mesme terre, je graunt bien, mez un poit aver fee simple in le terre et lauter in lez profitz, come appert in plusourz caz. Issint icy le franketnement est in le seignior et chescun precipe quod reddat serra port verz ly, et tamen dez profytez le tenant per copy ad le very fee simple et il ad droit de detieyner eux verz le seignior et avera brefe de trns. verz le seignior [sil][4] entra pur lez profytz, et le tenant prescribera daver eux nient [nosmant][5] le seignior, causa qua supra. Auxi quant il surrender all seignior al [use dun][6] auter le seignior ne[7] poit detiegner, quar il nest que un instrument de faire ceo passer et sil detiegne javera action sur mon caz verz ly nient obstant que il est un seignior que ad ladministration de justice, quar le roy que est le teste de justice il ly punissha et viera redresse in cest matter. Et, sir, [a][8] ceo que est dit que intant que il ne dit in le copye ad voluntatem domini et sez heirs que per le mort le seignior son estate [determinera],[9] ceo nest issint, mez sil ust dist ad voluntatem domini Johannis at S. ou nosme son nosme donsque determineroit ut supra. Mez celle nosme seignior continuera si longment que il y ad [le][10] maner la. Per que pur toutes ceux causez le seignior ne oustera son tenant. Donsque ou ceo est discontinue ou nemi? Ceo depende tout sur mon argument devaunt, que il est, quar il ad fait tout ceo que in luy est et nient obstant que il nentra ceo ne fait matter, come feoffment deinz le vew et similia, per que [etc.].

< His dictis cepit dominus Norwich capitalis justiciarius de Communi Banco mirum in modum collaudere omnes gratulabaturque eis insignam istam legis peritiam. >[11]

Quaunt all prescription que il poit deteigner enverz le seignior, ceo ne besoigne il, quar est imply que il poit deteigner quant il prescribe de deviser in fee, fee taile ou pur terme de vie, per que si il allege ceo serroit duble: come si home clame comen appendant et voit auxi prescriber, ceo serroit duble. Mez ou il nest implie il nest duble: come home prescribe daver un rent charge et ouster prescribe que ill poit distreigner pur ceo, ore ceo nest duble, quar lun nest implie in lauter. Mez auterment est icy, < per que [etc.] > .[12]

---

[1] Knyghtley *A.*   [2] *A only.*   [3] *A.* e[st] *B.*   [4] *A.* si *B.*
[5] nosme *in both mss.*   [6] *A.* un *B.*   [7] *Interlined in B.*   [8] *A only.*
[9] determiner' *A.* det'man' *B.*   [10] *A only.*   [11] *Om. A.*
[12] *Om. A.*

services at the outset. Also it may be that this order and tenure was made at the time when the common law was made, and no one can say for what cause and reason the common law was made, but by usage ever since it is well known to us that this was the institution of the law etc. As to what was said by Knightley that the lord shall not have a remedy for his rent, since the statute *Quia emptores terrarum* ousts such a reservation, that is not so; for the statute of *Quia emptores terrarum* was made on account of the mischief of the change of the lord's avowry paramount. But here the avowry shall not be changed, for the freehold remains in the lord, and therefore despite alterations of possession by surrender this shall not change the lord's avowry paramount. Also this inheritance of the lord's in the rent has continued from time immemorial; and so etc. As to what has been said that there cannot be two fee simples of one same land, I fully concede that; but one may have a fee simple in the land and another in the profits, as appears in many cases. Likewise here, the freehold is in the lord, and every *praecipe quod reddat* shall be brought against him, and nevertheless in respect of the profits the tenant by copy has the true fee simple, and has a right to withhold them as against the lord, and shall have a writ of trespass against the lord if he enters for the profits, and the tenant may prescribe to have them without naming the lord, for the reason given above. Also when he surrenders to the lord to the use of someone else, the lord may not withhold it, for he is only an instrument to cause it to pass, and if he withholds it I shall have an action upon my case against him, notwithstanding that he is a lord who has the administration of justice; for the king, who is the head of justice, will punish him and see that redress is provided in this matter. And, sir, as to what has been said that, since it does not say in the copy 'at the will of the lord (*ad voluntatem domini*) and his heirs', by the lord's death his estate should determine, that is not so: though if he had said *ad voluntatem domini Johannis at Style*, naming his name, it would have determined as above. But this name 'lord' continues as long as there is a manor there. And so, for all these reasons, the lord shall not oust his tenant. Now, then, is it discontinued or not? This depends altogether on my previous argument, that it is, for he has done all he can, and it is immaterial that he did not enter, as in the case of a feoffment within the view and such like; and so etc.

These things having been said, the lord NORWICH, Chief Justice of the Common Bench, praised them all with admiration and congratulated them on their accomplished legal learning.

(As to the prescription that he may withhold as against the lord, he need not say that, for it is implied that he may withhold when he prescribes [for the lord] to devise in fee, in fee tail, or for term of life; and so, if he had alleged it, it would have been double: as where someone claims a common appendant and also prescribes, that would be double. But where it is not implied it is not double: as where someone prescribes to have a rent-charge and goes on to prescribe that he may distrain for it, that is not double, for the one thing is not implied in the other. However, it is otherwise here; and so etc.)

[4]

[*Fo. 15*] Home chivacha[nt] sur son shyvall perde un de cez solyerz et il veigne a prochen vylle et require le smythe a shoer et offer luy ii. denerz, et pur malise il refuse, et ne sont plusorz smythes in mesme le vylle, m. reder dit que il avera action sur son case verz le smythe quar il est artificer pur le comen welthe et in ceo que il ad emprent sur luy office del smythe il ad emprent sur luy de fayer toutes chosez que apperteyne a son office. Sicome fuit agree in Streetes case, si jeo lesse a vous un meason pur anz et vous promitt de fayer un barn la deinz le terme, ore si ne faytez javera action sur mon case verz vous quar in ceo que intrastez in le meson vous empristez de fayer tout ceo que est dependant sur cest les, sed tamen laction gist merement pur non fesanz. Mesme le ley si vous empristez de garder mez beastez et sufferez eux de peresher in vostre necligens. Et ne suiz je damage ycy pur cest non suer? Et si vous ussez demurt in mesme le vylle un auter voyel occupier le rome la que il voyle ceo fayer. Et nest semble lou un hostler ne voyle herberge moy, quar per lestatut de Wynton. il nest tenuez a prender auterz que il voyle responder pur eux in le mattyn, auxi pur le herbergynge dun necligent persone le meson poit estre arse, per que il respondra pur lez bienz de toutz auterz deinz le meason.

[5][1]

[*Fo. 17v*] Un case fuit move a le Comen Place barre que fuit tyel: home recover en brefe dannuite, si il avera brefe de dett pur larrerages lannuite uncore continuant? Et semble al *Fitzherbert* J. que il avera, nient obstant [que] lannuite continue. Et issint mesme le ley est en un pluis fort case que ceo est, si un assise soyt port dun rent service et recover son rent et damages, il avera brefe de dett pur cest rent que est recovere et pur lez damages recovere en lassise, et eux joyndra en un mesme brefe et ne serront devidez ou severez. Mez il poit eux demander ut supra, et le reson appert destre pur ceo que per le jugment transfertur in rem judicatam. Quere ouster.

---

[1] This case is followed on fo. 18 by a case argued in Gray's Inn hall in Easter term 1538. Fitzherbert J. died in May 1538.

4. NOTE FROM JAMES HALES'S READING

Gray's Inn, August 1532.[1] Cf. another version of this passage in Baker & Milsom, pp. 346–347. The note is included in this volume because of the reference to *Strete*'s *Case* (1528), which is reported below, p. 313, no. 8.

A man riding on his horse lost one of its shoes, and came to the next vill and asked the smith to shoe it, and offered him twopence, and out of malice he refused; and there were no other smiths in the same vill. *Master Reader* said that he should have an action on his case against the smith, for he is a workman for the common wealth and in taking upon himself the office of a smith he has taken upon himself to do all things which belong to his office. Similarly it was agreed in Strete's case[2] that, if I lease a house to you for years and you promise to make a barn there within the term, and you do not do it, I shall have an action upon my case against you, for in entering in the house you took upon yourself to do everything which is dependent upon this lease. And yet the action lies here purely for nonfeasance. The law is the same if you have undertaken to look after my beasts and allow them to perish through your neglect.[3] And am I not damaged here by this non-shoeing? If you had dwelt in the same vill someone else would occupy the position and would do this.[4] It is not like the case where an innkeeper will not lodge me, for by the Statute of Winchester[5] he is not bound to take any but those he will answer for in the morning; and moreover by lodging a negligent person the house might be burned down, and so he shall answer for the goods of all others within the house.

5. ANON.

Common Pleas, perhaps *c.* 1538.

A case was moved at the Common Place bar, which was this: if someone recovers in a writ of annuity, shall he have a writ of debt for the arrears of the annuity while it is still continuing?

It seemed to FITZHERBERT J. that he shall, notwithstanding that the annuity continues. The law is the same in a stronger case than this: if an assize is brought for a rent-service, and he recovers his rent and damages, he shall have a writ of debt for this rent which is recovered and for the damages recovered in the assize, and join them in one same writ, and they shall not be divided or severed. But he may demand them as above, and the reason appears to be because by the judgment [the dept] is translated into *res judicata* (*transfertur in rem judicatam*). Query further.

---

[1] Hales read on 23 Hen. VIII, c. 15 (costs): BL MS. Hargrave 92, ff. 21–40. It must be Hales's first reading, because it is mentioned in Moyle's reading of 1533: ibid., fo. 47. In *Readers and Readings* (and in Baker & Milsom) the reading was tentatively but incorrectly dated 1537.

[2] *Strete* v. *Yardley* (1528), below, p. 313, no. 8.

[3] YB Hil. 2 Hen. VII, fo. 11, pl. 9; Baker & Milsom, p. 398.

[4] Sentence seemingly garbled.

[5] Statute of Winchester 1285, c. 6 (*SR* i. 97 at p. 98).

[6]

Casus xxi° H. viii.

[*Fo. 19v*] En un repl. le defendant avowa pur ceo que il est seisi dun maner deinz quell il ad un lete, et que all lete tenuez tiell jour present fuit per lez cheff plegges que le plaintife [a] tiel lew deinz le jurisdiction del dit lete fist affraie sur un J. at S. que sanke dispend, pur quell il fuit amercie all xii. d., et pur lez ditz xii. d. il distreina deinz le jurisdiction del dit lete lez ditz averz, et issint avowa. Et le plaintife dit que le dit lew est hors dell jurisdiction del dit lete, jugement, et pria cez damagez.

Et fuit agree per toutz lez justicez que ceo ne fuit my ple, quar son travers est ycy a le presentment, le quell nest traversable lou le presentment ne charge dascun enheritans, quar le presentment ycy est que a tiell lew etc. deinz le jurisdiction de cest courte etc. et le travers est que le lew est horse del jurisdiction de cest court, issint le travers est directment a le presentment. Et le ley done cy hawet credens a le verdit dez plegges que ceo que ilz ount present est voyer que null avera travers a cestui presentment sinon que il touche lenheritans.

Record

CP 40/1061, m. 693, Jenour.

Warr' Thomas Tydnam summonitus fuit ad respondendum Ricardo Burbury de placito quare cepit averia ipsius Ricardi et ea injuste detinet contra vadium et plegios etc. Et unde idem Ricardus, per Willelmum Faunt attornatum suum, queritur quod predictus Thomas, vicesimo tercio die Octobris anno regni domini regis nunc decimo nono apud Gaydon in quodam loco vocato Gaydon Grene cepit averia, videlicet duos equos, ipsius Ricardi et ea injuste detinet contra vadium et plegios quousque etc. Unde dicit quod deterioratus est et dampnum habet ad valenciam decem librarum. Et inde producit sectam etc.

Et predictus Thomas, per Thomam Sprotte attornatum suum, venit. Et defendit vim et injuriam quando etc. Et quo ad captionem unus equi de predictis duobus equis idem Thomas dicit quod ipse non cepit equum illum prout predictus Ricardus superius versus eum queritur. Et de hoc ponit se super patriam. Et predictus Thomas similiter. Et quo ad captionem alterius equi de predictis duobus equis residui idem Thomas ut ballivus Galfridi, Cov' et Lich' episcopi, bene cognoscit captionem alterius equi illius in predicto loco in quo etc. Et juste etc. quia dicit quod ante predictum tempus quo supponitur captionem averiorum predictorum fieri predictus episcopus fuit seisitus de quodam visu franciplegii annuatim in manerio suo de Tachebroke in comitatu predicto tenendo in

6. BURBURY v. TYDNAM

Common Pleas, 1529. Record: CP 40/1061, m. 693 (issue, Pas. 21 Hen. VIII; printed below). Cf. Dyer, fo. 13b, pl. 64, which is a similar but later case (Trin. 28 Hen. VIII).

In a replevin the defendant avowed because he is seised of a manor within which he has a leet, and at the leet held on such and such a day it was presented by the chief pledges that the plaintiff at such and such a place within the jurisdiction of the said leet made affray upon one John at Style, who shed blood, for which he was amerced at 12d., and for the said 12d. he distrained the said beasts within the jurisdiction of the said leet; and so he avowed. And the plaintiff said that the said place is outside the jurisdiction of the said leet, and prayed judgment, and his damages.

It was agreed by all the justices that this was no plea, for his traverse here is to the presentment, which is not traversable (when the presentment does not charge any inheritance); for the presentment here is that at such and such a place etc. within the jurisdiction of this court etc., and the traverse is that the place is outside the jurisdiction of this court, and so the traverse is directly contrary to the presentment. And the law gives such high credence to the verdict of the pledges, that what they have presented is true, that no one shall traverse this presentment unless it touches the inheritance.

Translation of the record

De Banco roll, Pas. 21 Hen. VIII (1529).

Warwickshire. Thomas Tydnam was summoned to answer Richard Burbury concerning a plea why he took the beasts of him the said Richard and unjustly withheld them against gage and pledges etc. And thereupon the same Richard, by William Faunt his attorney, complains that the aforesaid Thomas, on the twenty-third day of October [1527] in the nineteenth year of the reign of the present lord king at Gaydon, in a certain place called Gaydon Green, took the beasts, namely two horses, of the selfsame Richard, and unjustly withheld them against gage and pledges until etc. Whereby he says he is the worse and has damage to the extent of ten pounds. And thereof he produces suit etc.

And the aforesaid Thomas comes by Thomas Sprotte his attorney; and he denies the force and wrong when etc. And, as to the taking of one of the aforesaid two horses, the same Thomas says that he did not take the horse as the aforesaid Richard above complains against him. And of this he puts himself upon the country; and the aforesaid Thomas likewise. And as to the taking of the other of the two horses the same Thomas, as bailiff of Geoffrey, bishop of Coventry and Lichfield, fully acknowledges the taking of the other horse in the aforesaid place in which etc. And rightfully etc., because he says that before the aforesaid time when the taking of the aforesaid beasts is supposed to have occurred the aforesaid bishop was seised of a certain view of frankpledge held annually in his manor of Tachbrook[1] in the aforesaid county in his demesne as of fee in right of his

[1] Now Bishops Tachbrook.

dominico suo ut de feodo in jure ecclesie sue cathedralis Coventrie et Lich', quodque idem episcopus et omnes predecessores sui episcopi ecclesie illius a tempore cujus contrarii memoria hominum non existit habuerunt et tenuerunt ac habere et tenere consueverunt predictum visum franciplegii infra precinctum manerii predicti de omnibus tenentibus et residentibus infra precinctum manerii illius bis per annum tenendum, quodque ad predictum visum franciplegii tentum apud Nether Ichyngton infra precinctum manerii predicti die Jovis proxime ante festum Appostolorum Philippi et Jacobi anno regni domini regis nunc decimo octavo per sacramentum xii etc. presentatum fuit quod predictus Ricardus Burburey apud Gaydon predictam infra precinctum visus franciplegii predicti in quendam Johannem Saunders insultum et affraiam fecit contra pacem domini regis nunc, et quod idem Ricardus amerciatus fuit, quod quidem amerciamentum adtunc ibidem afforabatur per totum homagium visus franciplegii illius ad duos solidos, et quia predicti duo solidi de amerciamento predicto eodem tempore quo etc. eidem episcopo aretro fuerunt non soluti idem Thomas ut ballivus predicti episcopi pro eisdem duobus solidis eidem episcopo de amerciamento illo in forma predicta aretro existentibus bene cognoscit captionem predicti alterius equi in predicto loco in quo etc. Et juste etc. et infra feodum suum etc.

Et predictus Ricardus dicit quod predictus Thomas ratione preallegata captionem alterius equi predicti in predicto loco in quo etc. justam cognoscere non debet, quia dicit quod insultus et affraia predicti facti fuerunt apud manerium de Darsett in comitatu predicto, quod quidem manerium de Darsett est et predicto tempore quo supponuntur insultum et affraiam predictos fieri fuit extra precinctum visus franciplegii predicti, absque hoc quod insultus et affraia predicti facti fuerunt apud Gaydon predictam prout predictus Thomas superius allegavit. Et hoc paratus est verificare. Unde ex quo predictus Thomas captionem alterius equis predicti in predicto loco in quo etc. superius cognovit, idem Ricardus petit judicium et dampna sua occasione captionis et injuste detentionis alterius equi illius sibi adjudicari etc.

Et predictus Thomas ut prius dicit quod insultum et affraia predicti facti fuerunt apud Gaydon predictam infra precinctum visus franciplegii predicti episcopi prout ipse superius allegavit. Et de hoc ponit se super patriam. Et predictus Ricardus similiter. Ideo preceptum fuit vicecomiti quod venire faceret hic in crastino Ascensionis Domini xii etc. per quos etc. et qui nec etc. ad recognoscendum etc. quia tam etc. Ad quem diem hic veniunt partes etc. Et vicecomes non misit breve. Ideo sicut prius preceptum est vicecomiti quod venire faciat hic in octabis Sancte Trinitatis xii etc. ad recognoscendum in forma predicta etc.

[7]

Casus xviii° H. viii.

[*Fo. 19v*] Nota tenuez per *Fitzherbert*, I., et auterz justicez, que si lez averz le defendant sount deliverez all plaintife en wythernam que le plaintife eux usera et occupiera sicome cez proprez averz, quar ilz sount delyverez a luy en lew de cez proper[1] [averz]. Mes si lavowant ad lez averz le plaintife en wythernam, il

---

[1] proprer.

cathedral church of Coventry and Lichfield, and that the same bishop and all his predecessors as bishops of that church since time immemorial have had and held and have been accustomed to have and to hold the aforesaid view of frankpledge twice a year within the precinct of the aforesaid manor for all the tenants and residents within the precinct of the manor, and that at the aforesaid view of frankpledge held at Nether Itchington[1] within the precinct of the aforesaid manor on the Thursday [27 April 1526] next before the feast of the Apostles Philip and James in the eighteenth year of the reign of the present lord king it was presented by the oath of twelve etc. that the aforesaid Richard Burbury at Gaydon aforesaid, within the precinct of the view of frankpledge aforesaid, assaulted and made affray upon a certain John Saunders against the peace of the present lord king, and that the same Richard was amerced, which amercement was then and there affeered by the whole homage of the view of frankpledge at two shillings, and because the aforesaid two shillings of the aforesaid amercement at the same time when etc. were in arrear and unpaid to the same bishop, the same Thomas as bailiff of the aforesaid bishop full acknowledges the taking of the aforesaid other horse in the aforesaid place in which etc. for the same two shillings of that amercement being then in arrear to the same bishop in form aforesaid etc. And rightfully etc. and within his fee etc.

And the aforesaid Richard says that the aforesaid Thomas ought not rightfully to acknowledge the taking of the aforesaid other horse in the aforesaid place in which etc. for the reason previously alleged, because he says that the aforesaid assault and affray were committed at the manor of 'Darsett' in the county aforesaid, which manor of 'Darsett' is, and at the aforesaid time when the aforesaid assault and affray are supposed to have been committed was, outside the precinct of the aforesaid view of frankpledge, without this that the aforesaid assault and affray were committed at Gaydon aforesaid, as the aforesaid Thomas has above alleged. And this he is ready to aver. Whereupon, inasmuch as the aforesaid Thomas has above acknowledged the taking of the aforesaid other horse in the aforesaid place in which etc, the same Richard prays judgment and that his damages by reason of the taking and unlawful withholding of the other horse be awarded to him etc.

And the aforesaid Thomas, as before, says that the aforesaid assault and affray were committed at Gaydon aforesaid within the precinct of the aforesaid bishop's view of frankpledge, as he has above alleged. And of this he puts himself upon the country; and the aforesaid Richard likewise. Therefore the sheriff is commanded that he cause to come here on the morrow of the Ascension of Our Lord twelve etc. by whom etc. and who neither etc. to make recognition etc. because both etc. At which day the parties come here etc.; but the sheriff has not sent the writ. Therefore, as before, the sheriff is commanded that he cause to come here in the octaves of the Holy Trinity twelve etc. to make recognition in form aforesaid etc.

7. ANON.

Common Pleas, 1526/27.

Note that it was held by FITZHERBERT, ENGLEFIELD,[2] and other justices, that if the defendant's beasts are delivered to the plaintiff in withernam the plaintiff may use and occupy them as his own beasts, for they are delivered to him in place of his own beasts. But if the avowant has the plaintiff's beasts in

---

[1] Now Bishops Itchington.   [2] Assuming that I. (or J.) stands for Inglefield.

ne poet use ne occupier eux auterment que il poyet occupier le primer distres, quar ilz sount a luy deliverez en lew del primer distres.

[8]

Casus xx° H. viii.

[*Fo. 19v*] Un Williem Strete de Greysse Inne port action sur son case verz un B. et counte coment il avoyt les un mese a le dit B. pur iii. annez et fuit covenaunt et agreed enter eux que le lese doyt fayre un chemney deinz le mese et diverz auterz chosez, et monstre en certen, et que un peyre dez indentures de lez ditz covenauntz serront faytz et delyver a chescun deux accordant, et le plaintife monstre coment il escria et enseale son parte de lendenture et ceo proferra a le lesse accordant, et il refusa, et counta lou le defendant ad assume sur luy de fayre ceo parte de lendenture et delyver accordant, et de fayer lez auterz covenauntez, et il monstre coment il nad eux fayt, mez tout ousterment refusa, et le defendant plede quod non assumpsit. Et fuit dit per les justices a lenquest que silz troveront que le defendant assumpsit super se, donquez vous doyez enquirerer quant denerz le chymney et lez auterz chosez doyent coster [le]¹ defendant et taxer tout ceo en damagez.

Record

CP 40/1059, m. 415, Stubbe.

Midd'. Johannes Yardley nuper de Iseldon in comitatu predicto, yoman, attachiatus fuit ad respondendum Willelmo Strete de placito quare, cum idem Willelmus ultimo die Februarii anno regni domini regis nunc quintodecimo...² Et unde idem Willelmus in propria persona sua queritur quod, cum idem Willelmus ultimo die Februarii anno regni domini regis nunc quintodecimo quoddam mesuagium cum pertinenciis in Iseldon predicta vocatum Fynches tenement prefato Johanni a festo Annunciationis Beate Marie tunc proximo sequenti usque finem termini triginta et unius annorum tunc proximo sequentium et plenarie complendorum apud Iseldon predictam dimisisset, idemque Johannes quandam indenturam sigillo ipsius Johannis sigillatam pro secura performatione quarundam conventionum super dimissione predicta inter ipsum Willelmum et prefatum Johannem perimplendarum et custodiendarum concordatarum apud Iseldon predictam sigillare et ut factum ipsius Johannis eodem Willelmo apud Iseldon predictam deliberare promisisset et super se assumpsisset, predictusque

---

¹ de.
² *The substance of the writ is repeated in the count.*

withernam, he may not use or occupy them otherwise than he could the first distress, for they are delivered to him in place of the first distress.

8. STRETE v. YARDLEY

Common Pleas, 1528. Record: CP 40/1059, m. 415 (printed below). Cf. the reference to this case in Hales's reading, above, p. 310, no. 4.

One William Strete[1] of Gray's Inn brought an action on his case against one B. and counted that he had leased a house to the said B. for three years, and it was covenanted and agreed between them that the lessee should make a chimney within the house and various other things, and showed what they were with certainty, and that a pair of indentures of the said covenants should be made and delivered to each of them accordingly; and the plaintiff showed how he wrote and sealed his part of the indenture and proffered it to the lessee accordingly, and he refused [to deliver it]; and counted that, whereas the defendant had taken upon himself to make and deliver his part of the indenture accordingly, and to perform the other covenants, he had not performed them, but utterly refused. The defendant pleaded that he did not undertake (*Non assumpsit*). And it was said by the justices to the inquest that, should they find that the defendant did undertake, 'then you ought to enquire how much money the chimney and the other things ought to cost the defendant, and assess it all in damages'.

Translation of the record

De Banco roll, Mich. 20 Hen. VIII (1528).

Middlesex. John Yardley, late of Islington in the aforesaid county, yeoman, was attached to answer William Strete concerning a plea why, whereas the same William on the last day of February [1524] in the fifteenth year of the reign of the present lord king . . .[2] And thereupon the same William, in his own person, complains that, whereas the same William on the last day of February in the fifteenth year of the reign of the present lord king, at Islington aforesaid demised a certain messuage with the appurtenances in Islington aforesaid called Finch's Tenement to the said John from the feast of the Annunciation of the Blessed Mary then next following until the end of the term of thirty-one years then next following and fully to be completed, and the same John at Islington aforesaid promised and took upon himself to seal a certain indenture with the seal of the selfsame John for the sure performance of certain covenants agreed to be performed and kept upon the aforesaid demise between the selfsame William and the selfsame John and to deliver it to the same William as the deed of the selfsame John,

---

[1] Formerly of Barnard's Inn (sued for dues 1526); filazer of the Common Pleas 1522-37; attorney of the same court; M.P. Leominster 1553; died *c.* 1554/57.

[2] The substance of the writ is repeated in the count.

Johannes aliquem indenturam pro performatione conventium predictarum licet ipse ad hoc per ipsum Willelmum sepius requisitus fuit juxta promissionem et assumpsionem sua predicta hucusque non sigillavit, ad dampnum ipsius Willelmi viginti librarum etc. Et inde producit sectam etc.

Et predictus Johannes, per Hugonem Ratclyff attornatum suum, venit. Et defendit vim et injuriam quando etc. Et, protestando quod predictus Willelmus non dimisit eidem < Johanni mesuagium predictum cum pertinenciis prout idem Willelmus superius supponit, pro placito tamen idem Johannes dicit quod ipse non promisit nec super se assumpsit ad sigillandum {neque deliberandum prefato Willelmo}¹ aliquam indenturam concernentem mesuagium predictum cum pertinenciis >¹ in forma qua idem Willelmus per breve et narrationem sua predicta superius supponit. Et de hoc ponit se super patriam. Et predictus Willelmus similiter. Ideo preceptum est vicecomiti quod venire faciat hic < a die Sancti Martini in xv dies >² xii etc. per quos etc. et qui nec etc. ad recognoscendum etc. quia tam etc.

[9]

Casus xxiiº H. viii.

[*Fo. 20v*] En atteynt le graund jure apparust, et quant eux venirent destre jurez le defendant prist son chalenge as powelx dez diverz de lenquest, et quant ilz ount peruse le panell ceux del tales fueront demandez destre jurez, et le defendant chalenge larray del tales pur ceo que il fuit favorablement fayt all denomination del plaintife per T. H., viconte, et cez ministrez. Et le chalenge fuit admytt pur ceo que il ne poit aver son chalenge a lez tales tanque cez ount peruse le principall panell.

Et fuit dit per lez justicez a ceux del principall pannell queux fueront jurez que ilz doyent enquirerer si cest arraye del tales fuit favorablement fayt per [le] viconte, scilicet si le viconte avoyt un avauntage et un intent all temps del fesaunz del tales que ilz doyent plus tost passer pur le plaintife que pur le defendant, et sil avoyet empannell ascun home all denomination del plaintife, en ceux casez ilz doyent trove larraye favorablement fayt per le viconte.

Et puis larraye fuit afferme, et le defendant chalenge un des tales, et fuit compelle de monstre son cause meyntenant, quar fuit dit que est un rule quant larraye del principall ou tales est chalenge, le quell est afferme, si aprez il prist son chalenge all powels il covient monstre son cause mayntenant.

Et issint fuit ajuge en cest case lou home fait chalenge all powelx lou il doyt monstre son cause meyntenaunt et lou nemi.

---

¹ *Written over an erasure.*
² *Added in a window.*

and the aforesaid John has not yet sealed any indenture for performance of the aforesaid covenants, according to his aforesaid promise and undertaking, although he has often been asked to do this by the selfsame William, to the damage of him the said William twenty pounds etc. And thereof he produces suit etc.

And the aforesaid John comes by Hugh Ratclyff his attorney; and he denies the force and wrong when etc. And, making protestation that the aforesaid William did not demise the aforesaid messuage with the appurtenances to the same John as the same William has above supposed, nevertheless the same John says for a plea that he did not promise or take upon himself to seal, nor to deliver to the said William, any indenture concerning the aforesaid messuage with the appurtenances in the manner in which the same William above supposes by his aforesaid writ and count. And of this he puts himself upon the country; and the aforesaid William likewise. Therefore the sheriff is commanded that he cause to come here in fifteen days from Martinmas twelve etc. by whom etc. and who neither etc. to make recognition etc. because both etc.

9. ANON.

1530/31.

In attaint the grand jury appeared, and when they came to be sworn the defendant took his challenge to the polls of several of the inquest, and when they had used up the panel those of the *tales* were demanded in order to be sworn, and the defendant challenged the array of the *tales* on the grounds that it was made favourably at the nomination of the plaintiff by T. H., sheriff, and his ministers. And the challenge was admitted, because he cannot have his challenge to the *tales* until they have used up the principal panel.

It was said by the justices to those of the principal panel who were sworn that they ought to enquire whether this array of the *tales* was made favourably by the sheriff, namely whether the sheriff had an advantage and an intention at the time of making the *tales* that they ought rather to find for the plaintiff than for the defendant, and whether anyone had been impanelled at the nomination of the plaintiff, for in those cases they ought to find the array favourably made by the sheriff.

Afterwards the array was affirmed, and the defendant challenged one of the *tales*, and he was compelled to show his cause at once; for it was said that it is a rule when the array of the principal or *tales* is challenged, and it is affirmed, and he afterwards takes his challenge to the polls, that he must show his cause at once.

So it was adjudged in this case, where someone made a challenge to the polls, where he ought to show his cause at once and where not.

[10]

Casus xxi° H. viii.

[*Fo. 20v*] Sur un issue joyne perenter ii. le jure apparust all barre et le defendant prist son chalenge a lez powelx, scilicet all chescun juror quant il venir' destre jure il luy chalenge pur ceo que il ad prist manger et boyer, scilicet un supper et dyner ovesque le plaintife all costes et charges le plaintife. Et fuit adjuge un principall chalenge, et fueront traytes hors.

[11]

Casus xxii° H. viii.

[*Fo. 20v*] Si un enfant deinz age de xii. annez fayt covenaunt ove un auter destre son apprentice, cest covenaunt est voyde et non ligat, neque per le custome ne per le comen ley.

Record

CP 40/1065, m. 532, Jenour.

Lond' Johannes Fokes nuper de Wotton in comitatu Bedfordie, yoman, summonitus fuit ad respondendum Ricardo Hasilherst, civi et wireseller Lond', de placito quod teneat ei conventionem de eo quod idem Johannes posuit seipsum apprenticium prefato Ricardo ad artem ipsius Ricardi erudiendam et secum more apprenticii sui commoraturum et desserviturum a festo Sancti Laurencii Martiris anno regni domini regis nunc septimo usque finem septem annorum extunc proxime sequentium et plenarie complendorum juxta vim, formam et effectum quarundam indenturarum inde inter eos confectarum etc. Et unde idem Ricardus, per Ricardum Hert attornatum suum, dicit quod cum per quandam indenturam factam apud Lond' in parochia Sancti Martini Epsicopi in warda de Corduaner Strete nono die Augusti anno regni domini regis nunc septimo, quam idem Ricardus sigillo predicti Johannis signatam hic in curia profert, cujus data est die et anno supradictis[1] testatum sit quod predictus Johannes posuisset seipsum apprenticium prefato Ricardo ad artem suam erudiendam et cum ipso Ricardo more apprenticii commorandum a festo Sancti Laurencii Martiris proxime sequenti datam ejusdem indenture usque ad finem septem annorum extunc proxime sequentium et plenarie complendorum, per quem quidem terminum predictus apprenticius prefato

10. ANON.[1]

Common Pleas, Trin. 1529. Also reported in Spelman, p. 36, pl. 6 (Trin. 21 Hen. VIII).

Upon an issue joined between two parties the jury appeared at the bar, and the defendant took his challenge to the polls, that is, as each juror came to be sworn he challenged him because he had taken food and drink—namely a supper and dinner with the plaintiff—at the costs and charges of the plaintiff. And it was adjudged a principal challenge, and they were withdrawn.

11. HASILHERST v. FOKES

Common Pleas, Pas. or Trin. 1530. Record: CP 40/1065, m. 531 (printed below).

If an infant under the age of twelve years makes a covenant with another to be his apprentice, this covenant is void and does not bind, either by custom or by common law.

Translation of the record

De Banco roll, Pas. 22 Hen. VIII (1530).

London. John Fokes, late of Wotton in the county of Bedford, yeoman, was summoned to answer Richard Hasilherst, citizen and wireseller of London, concerning a plea that he keep with him the covenant that the same John placed himself as apprentice with the said Richard to learn the trade of the selfsame Richard and to live with and serve him as his apprentice from the feast of St Lawrence the Martyr [10 August 1515] in the seventh year of the reign of the present lord king until the end of seven years then next following and fully to be completed, in accordance with the force, form and effect of certain indentures thereof made between them etc. And thereupon the same Richard, by Richard Hert his attorney, says that, whereas by a certain indenture made at London in the parish of St Martin the Bishop in the ward of Cordwainer Street on the ninth day of August [1515] in the seventh year of the reign of the present lord king—which the same Richard proffers here in court, sealed with the seal of the aforesaid John, the date whereof is the day and year mentioned above—it is witnessed that the aforesaid John had placed himself as apprentice with the said Richard to learn his trade and to live with the selfsame Richard as his apprentice from the feast of St Lawrence the Martyr next following the date of the same indenture until the end of seven years then next following and fully to be completed, during which term the aforesaid apprentice would serve

[1] Cf. *Linney* v. *Hawte* (1529) CP 40/1060, m. 335 (debt on a bond tried at bar in Trin. 21 Hen. VIII), where it was discovered upon examination that five of the jurors had drunk one draught from a pot of ale and were fined 2s. each, the remaining seven being fined 12d. each even though they had not drunk anything. There is no suggestion in the record of food being consumed, or of the drink being provided before trial at the costs of the plaintiff, and the jurors were not withdrawn. This can hardly, therefore, be the same case.

Ricardo tanquam magistro suo die ac nocte bene et fideliter pro posse suo deserviret, preceptaque sua licita ubique libenter faceret, secreta sua celaret, dampnum ei non faceret nec fieri videret ad valorem duodecim denariorum nec amplius per annum quin illud impediret si potuisset aut statim predictum magistrum suum premuniret, ad talos non luderet unde predictus magister dampnum contraheret, cum bonis suis propriis nec alicujus durante termino predicto sine licencia predicti magistri sui non mercandizaret, a servicio predicti magistri sui die nec nocte illicite non recederet nec se elongaret, set in omnibus tanquam bonus apprenticius erga predictum magistrum suum et suos benigne se gereret et haberet per totum terminum predictum, et predictus Ricardus predictum apprenticium suum artem suam quam idem Ricardus uteretur meliori modo quo sciret aut posset doceret, tractaret et informaret seu informari faceret, debito modo castigando, inveniendoque eidem apprenticio suo esculenta, poculenta, vestitura, linea, calciamenta et lectum per totum terminum predictum, et ad omnes et singulas conventiones supradictas ex parte predicti apprenticii per totum terminum predictum fideliter tenendas et perimplendas idem apprenticius obligasset se, heredes et executores suos ac omnia bona sua prefato magistro suo, prout per eandem indenturam plenius apparet. Et idem Ricardus dicit quod predictus Johannes Fokes post confectionem indenture predicte, scilicet vicesimo die Octobris anno regni domini regis nunc octavo, apud Lond' in parochia et warda predictis, ante finem termini predicti, a servicio ipsius Ricardi illicite recessit et se elongavit contra formam et effectum indenture predicte, sicque predictus Johannes conventionem predictam eidem Ricardo non tenuit set infregit. Unde dicit quod deterioratus est et dampnum habet ad valenciam centum librarum. Et inde producit sectam etc.

Et predictus Johannes, per Thomam Ingler attornatum suum, venit. Et defendit vim et injuriam quando etc. Et dicit quod predictus Ricardus actionem suam predictam versus eum habere non debet, quia dicit quod per quendam actum in parliamento domini Ricardi nuper Regis Anglie secundi post conquestum apud Cantebrigiam anno regni sui duodecimo inter cetera ordinatum fuit quod ipse qui usus fuerit laborare ad carucam et carectam aut alium laborem seu servicium iconomie quousque ad etatem duodecim annorum pervenerit quod extunc ad hujusmodi laborem moretur absque positione ad artem seu misteriam, et si aliqua conventio vel obligatio apprenticietatis incontrarium extunc facta fuerit pro nullo teneatur. Et idem Johannes dicit quod ipse ab etate sua quatuor annorum quousque ad etatem duodecim annorum pervenisset idem Johannes apud Wotton predictam ad carucam et carectam ac aliud servicium iconomie cum quodam Johanne Fokes seniore laboravit, posteaque, scilicet predicto nono die Augusti anno septimo supradicto, idem Johannes Fokes jam defendens etatis tresdecim annorum et amplius tunc existens apud Lond' in parochia et warda predictis per indenturam predictam posuit seipsum apprenticium prefato Ricardo ad artem suam erudiendam et cum eodem Ricardo more apprenticii commorandum a predicto festo Sancti Laurencii usque finem septem annorum extunc proxime sequentium et plenarie complendorum prout idem Ricardus per narrationem suam predictam superius supponit, que quidem indentura ac conventio predicta in eadem indentura superius specificata virtute et auctoritate statuti predicti irrite et vacue ac nullius vigoris neque effectus in lege existunt. Et hoc paratus est[i] verificare. Unde petit judicium si predictus Ricardus actionem suam predictam versus eum debeat etc.

Et predictus Ricardus dicit quod predictum placitum predicti Johannis jam defendentis superius placitatum minus sufficiens in lege existit ad ipsum Ricardum ab actione sua predicta versus prefatum Johannem jam defendentem habenda precludendum, quodque ipse ad placitum illud modo et forma predictis placitatum necesse non habet nec per legem terre tenetur respondere. Et hoc paratus est verificare. Unde pro defectu sufficientis responsionis in hac parte idem Ricardus petit judicium et

the said Richard as his master day and night well and faithfully to the best of his ability, willingly perform his lawful commands, keep his secrets, not cause him damage or see damage caused to the value of twelve pence or more a year, but prevent it if possible or immediately warn his aforesaid master, nor play cards whereby his aforesaid master should contract any damage, nor trade with his own goods or those of anyone else during the aforesaid term without the leave of his aforesaid master, nor leave or eloign himself unlawfully from the service of his aforesaid master by day or by night, but in all things behave well and conduct himself as a good apprentice with respect to his aforesaid master and his family throughout the aforesaid term; and the aforesaid Richard would teach, treat and inform his aforesaid apprentice or cause him to be informed in his trade, which the same Richard used, in the best way he knew or could, duly chastising him, finding his same apprentice food, drink, clothing, linen, shoes and bedding throughout the aforesaid term; and the same apprentice bound himself, his heirs and executors, and all his goods, to his said master faithfully to hold and keep on his side all and singular the covenants above mentioned throughout the aforesaid term, as fully appears by the same indenture. And the same Richard says that the aforesaid John Fokes, after making the aforesaid indenture, namely on the twentieth day of October [1516] in the eighth year of the reign of the present lord king, at London in the parish and ward aforesaid, before the end of the aforesaid term, unlawfully left and eloigned himself from the service of the selfsame Richard contrary to the form and effect of the aforesaid indenture, and so the aforesaid John has not kept the aforesaid covenant with the same Richard but has broken it. Whereby he says he is the worse and has suffered damage to the extent of one hundred pounds. And thereof he produces suit etc.

And the aforesaid John comes, by Thomas Ingler his attorney; and he denies the force and wrong when etc. And he says that the aforesaid Richard ought not to have his aforesaid action against him, because he says that by a certain act in the parliament of the lord Richard the second after the conquest, lately king of England, at Cambridge in the twelfth year of his reign,[1] it was ordained amongst other things that whoever was accustomed to work at plough or cart or other work or service of husbandry (*iconomie*) until he reached the age of twelve years should remain thereafter at such work without being put to any trade or mystery, and if any covenant or bond of apprenticeship should thereafter be made to the contrary it should be held a nullity. And the same John says that from the age of four years until he reached the age of twelve years the same John at Wotton aforesaid worked at plough and cart and other service of husbandry for a certain John Fokes the elder, and afterwards, namely on the aforesaid ninth day of August in the above-mentioned seventh year, the same John Fokes (now defendant), then being of the age of thirteen years and more, at London in the parish and ward aforesaid, by the aforesaid indenture placed himself as apprentice with the said Richard to learn his trade and to live with the same Richard in the manner of an apprentice from the aforesaid feast of St Lawrence until the end of seven years then next following and fully to be completed, as the same Richard has above supposed by his aforesaid count, which same indenture and covenant aforesaid, in the same indenture above specified, were null and void by virtue and authority of the aforesaid statute, and of no force or effect in law. And this he is ready to aver. Whereupon he prays judgment whether the aforesaid Richard ought to have his aforesaid action against him etc.

And the aforesaid Richard says that the aforesaid plea of the aforesaid John (now defendant) as pleaded above is insufficient in law to prevent him the said Richard from having his aforesaid action against the said John (now defendant), and that he has no need and is not bound by the law of the land to answer that plea as pleaded in manner and form aforesaid. And this he is ready to aver. Whereupon, for want of a sufficient

---

[1] Statute of Cambridge, 12 Ric. II, c. 5 (*SR* ii. 57).

dampna sua occasione premissa sibi adjudicari etc.

Et predictus Johannes, ex quo ipse sufficientem materiam in lege in barram actionis predicti Ricardi predicte superius allegavit, quam ipse paratus est verificare, quamquidem materiam predictus Ricardus non dedicit nec ad eam aliqualiter respondet set verificationem illam admittere omnino recusat, petit judicium et quod predictus Ricardus ab actione sua predicta versus eum habenda precludatur etc. Et quia justiciarii hic se avisare volunt de et super premissis priusquam judicium inde reddant, dies datus est partibus predictis hic in octabis Sancte Trinitatis de audiendo inde judicio suo eo quod justiciarii hic inde non dum etc.

[12]

Casus xx° H. viii.

[*Fo. 20v*] Un brefe de conspiracy fuit port verz iii. homez et declare coment ilz conspyre enter eux le Lundy etc. de luy endyter, per reson de quell conspiracie a les cessions etc. il fuit endyte et puis il fuit sur ceo acquitte. Et le defendant disoyt que pur ceo [que] un chyvall dez byenz dun J. at S. fuit feloniousment emblye et le dit J. at S. vient a lez defendantz et monstre a eux coment le plaintife avoyt feloniousment embleye le dit chyvall, per force de quell aprez a lez cessionz tenuez etc. lez defendantz venoyent overtment en courte et don evydens all jure de mesme le felony enconter le plaintife, le quell est mesme le conspiracye dount le plaintife counte.

Et fuit move per *S.* que le ple ne fuit bon, pur ceo que lez defendantz ne traversont le plaintife entaunt que ilz ount justefye per reson dun conspiracye fayt apres, et auxi ilz ount dit Le quell est mesme le conspiracye, et ceo ne poit estre. Et auxi ilz nount monstre coment ilz fueront jurez, quar nest semble lou home conspire et puis est un de cez enditourz, mez per cest clerement il est excuse dez toutz conspiracies ewez devaunt.

Et toutz lez justicez tient le ple bon, et que il ne doyt prender travers, quar quant le conspiracye que est fayt all temps del enditement est justefiable il est excuse dez toutz conspiracies faytez devaunt. Donquez il ne devoyt prender travers. Si ii. conspire denditer un auter et puis cez sont jurez pur enquierer pur le roy et luy endiste, ore sont excusez dez toutz conspiracies devaunt: xx° H. vi. Et si un justice de pees deliver un byll del endytment en lez cessionz a le jure et eux enforme, ceo est justefiable et per ceo il est excuse de toutz

answer in that behalf, the same Richard prays judgment and that his damages by reason of the foregoing may be awarded to him etc.

And the aforesaid John, since he has above alleged sufficient matter in law in bar of the aforesaid action of the aforesaid Richard, which he is ready to aver, which matter the aforesaid Richard does not deny or in any way answer, but he utterly refuses to admit the averment, prays judgment and that the aforesaid Richard may be barred from having his aforesaid action against him etc. And because the justices here wish to advise themselves upon and concerning the foregoing before they give judgment therein, a day is given to the aforesaid parties here in the octaves of the Holy Trinity for hearing their judgment therein, forasmuch as the justices here are not yet therein etc.

12. ANON.

Probably Common Pleas, 1528/29.[1]

A writ of conspiracy was brought against three men, and the plaintiff declared that they conspired among themselves on the Monday etc. to indict him, by reason of which conspiracy he was indicted at the sessions etc. and afterwards thereupon acquitted. The defendant said that a horse had been stolen from the goods of one John at Style, and the said John at Style came to the defendants and showed them how the plaintiff had feloniously stolen the said horse, by virtue of which afterwards, at the sessions held on etc., the defendants came openly into court and gave evidence against the plaintiff to the jury concerning the same felony, which is the same conspiracy whereof the plaintiff counts.

It was moved by *S[pelman]*[2] that the plea was not good, because the defendants do not traverse the plaintiff, inasmuch as they have justified by reason of a conspiracy made afterwards; also they have said 'which is the same conspiracy', and that cannot be. Moreover they have not shown that they were sworn, for it is not like the case where someone conspires and is afterwards one of the indictors, for by that one is clearly excused of all earlier conspiracies.

And all the justices held the plea good, and that he ought not to take a traverse, for when the conspiracy which is committed at the time of the indictment is justifiable he is excused of all conspiracies committed earlier. Therefore he ought not to take a traverse. If two conspire to indict another, and afterwards they are sworn to enquire for the king and they indict him, they are excused of all earlier conspiracies: 20 Hen. VI.[3] And if a justice of the peace delivers a bill of indictment to the [grand] jury in the sessions and informs them, this is justifiable and he is thereby excused of all earlier conspiracies:

---

[1] The facts are slightly different from *Walker* v. *Collyns* (1534) as reported by Pollard, above, p. 252, no. 14, which is dated Pas. 26 Hen. VIII.
[2] Shelley was by this time a judge.
[3] YB Mich. 20 Hen. VI, fo. 5, pl. 15.

conspiracies devaunt: xii° E. 4^{ti}. Et quant a lauter poynt, Le quell est mesme le conspiracye: ceo est assetz bon, quar si home conspire un jour et puis un auter jour, uncore ceo nest forsque un conspiracye, pur ceo que le conspiracye tout temps continue. Et a ceo que il dit que il ne monstre que il fuit jure, ceo ne fayt mater, quar il ne poit estre jure si lez justices ne volount doner luy son serement. Et chescun conspiracye est un faux et prive conspirement enter eux, mez tiel entendment ne poit estre ycy quant il vient overtment en le courte et done cest evydens a lenquest. Et issint loppinion dez toutez lez justices que le ple fuit bon.

[13]

Casus xix° H. viii.

[*Fo. 21*][1] En brefe de dett si le defendant dit que lobligation est endoce sur tiel condition que si le defendant perfourme toutz lez conditions [...] en mesme lobligation ou toutz lez covenauntz comprise en un paire dendentures que donquez etc., ore est bon ple pur le defendant [...] reherser toutz lez conditionz ou covenauntz et adire que il ad perfourme generalment, et ne monstre coment il ad eux perfourme, nient obstant [...] condition vient[2] en le affirmatiff, et issint fuit ajuge.

Mez en auterz liverz un diversite ad este prise lou le condition extende [...] le affirmatiff et lou en le negatyff. Et semble cest darren jugement destre le meliour jugement, pur ceo que le court ne serra troble ove un tedyous bouke.[3] Un auter reson est que il serra frustrate de compeller le defendant pur monstre le certente coment il ad performe chescun condition quaunt lissue ne serra prise forsque sur lun, quar il nest ple pur le plaintife adire que il nad performe lez conditionz mez covient de monstre un a son perell. Issint pluis resonable est que le certente viendra del monstranz le plaintife que lissue serra prise sur son monstranz.

[14]

Casus xxi° H. viii.

[*Fo. 21*] En un quare clausum fregit le defendant dit que un J. at S. fuit seisi en son demesne come de fee del lew etc., et per protestation morust seisi, aprez

---

[1] *Damaged in top right corner.*   [2] *Reading unclear.*   [3] *Reading unclear.*

12 Edw. IV.[1] As to the other point, 'which is the same conspiracy' is good enough, for if someone conspires one day and afterwards on another day, this is still but one conspiracy, because the conspiracy continues throughout. As to the argument that he does not show that he was sworn, that does not matter, for he cannot be sworn if the justices will not give him his oath. Every conspiracy is a false and secret conspiring between them, but that cannot be presumed here when he comes openly into the court and gives this evidence to the inquest. Therefore the opinion of all the justices was that the plea was good.

13. ANON.

Common Pleas, 1527/28. Perhaps *Wellys* v. *Mompesson* (1528–29) CP 40/1058A, m. 455; reported by Yorke, above, vol. I, p. 244, no. 426.

In a writ of debt, where the defendant says that the bond is endorsed with a condition that if the defendant should perform all the conditions mentioned in the same bond, or all the covenants comprised in a pair of indentures, that then etc., it is a good plea for the defendant to recite all the conditions or covenants and say that he has performed generally, and not show how he has performed them, notwithstanding that the condition is in the affirmative; and so it was adjudged.

However, in other books a distinction has been taken as to whether the condition extends to the affirmative and where it is in the negative.[2] But this latest judgment seems to be the better judgment, because the court will not be troubled with a tedious book.[3] Another reason is that it would be pointless to compel the defendant to set out with certainty how he has performed every condition when the issue will only be taken on one of them; for it is no plea for the plaintiff to say that he has not performed the conditions, but he must show one at his peril. Therefore it is more reasonable that the certainty should come from the plaintiff's showing than that the issue should be taken on his showing.

14. GULDEFORD v. FRANKWELL

Common Pleas, 1529. Record: CP 40/1063, m. 313 (noted below). Cf. Yorke, above, vol. I. p. 212, no. 329 (Trin. 21 Hen. VIII; said to be in an assize).

In a *quare clausum fregit* the defendant said that one John at Style was seised in his demesne as of fee of the place etc., and by protestation died seised, after

---

[1] *John Jenney's Case* (1472) YB Mich. 12 Edw. IV, fo. 18, pl. 23.   [2] Cf. below, p. 337, no. 53 (1540s).   [3] If correctly interpreted, this refers to the 'paper book' (draft pleadings). Cf. next note.

que mort W. a S. come fytz et heyre entra, que estate le defendant[ad, et done colour all plaintife per W. a S. Et fuit tenuez que le colour done per W. a S. nest bon quar per ceo il ad distroye son barre: quar il covient que son mater aprez le colour soyt bon barre, quar tout le monstranz devaunt le colour serra misse horse del lyver. Come si le defendant dit que J. a S. fuit seisi et enfeffe J. a D., et J. a D. enfeffe le defendant, et done colour per J. a D., ore le feffement J. a S. serra myse horse del lyver, et le remenaunt serra son ple. Donquez le case ycy nest ple pur ceo que null chose est allege en le barre le quell est traversable. Mez si le defendant dit quun J. a S. fuit seisi et infeffe J. a D., le quell enfeffe le defendant, et done colour per J. a D., ceo est bon barre, quar nient obstant que le feffment J. a S. ne serra entre en le lyver uncore le feffment per J. a D. all defendant est bon barre. Et sic nota le divercite.

Note from the record

CP 40/1063, m. 313, Stubbe.

George Guldeford, esquire, George Congherst and John Carpenter bring trespass against Richard Frankwell of Waldron, Sussex, yeoman, and Richard Hunt of Hailsham, Sussex, husbandman, for breaking their close at Hailsham and depasturing cattle. The defendants plead that the close is twenty-four acres of arable land in Hailsham whereof Robert Twytt was seised in his demesne as of fee, and died (*protestando*) seised, after whose death they descended to Edward Twytt as his son and heir, who entered and was seised and on 2 October [1526] 18 Hen. VIII leased them to Richard Hunt for one year and thus from year to year at the parties' pleasure (*et sic de anno in annum quamdiu ambabus partibus placeret*), and Hunt was thereby possessed;

[15]

Casus xxi° H. viii.

En brefe dentre en le post sur un comen recovere, immediat[ment] sur le declaration et le voucher et lentre en le garrante del vouche, sur tout le mater plede all barre per lez serjauntz, et devaunt ascun entre de ceo fayt en lez rowelx le preignotaries, un vient et monstre all courte que le terre fuit lesse a luy pur annez per indenture, et pria que il poit estre resceyve pur saver son terme.

whose death William at Style entered as son and heir, whose estate the defendant has, and gave colour to the plaintiff through William at Style. And it was held that the colour given through William at Style is not good, for he has thereby destroyed his bar: for it behoves that his matter after the colour should be a good bar, inasmuch as all that is set out before the colour shall be put out of the book.[1] Similarly, if the defendant says that John at Style was seised and enfeoffed John at Down, and John at Down enfeoffed the defendant, and gives colour through John at Down, the feoffment of John at Style shall be put out of the book, and the remainder shall be his plea. Therefore in the case here it is no plea, because nothing is alleged in the bar which is traversable. But if the defendant said that one John at Style was seised and enfeoffed John at Down, who enfeoffed the defendant, and gave colour through John at Down, that would be a good bar, for although the feoffment by John at Style shall not be entered in the book, still the feoffment by John at Down to the defendant is a good bar. Thus note the distinction.

Note from the record

De Banco roll, Mich. 21 Hen. VIII (1529).

[continued from opposite page]

and the plaintiffs entered—claiming through a charter of demise for life made by Robert Twytt—and Richard Hunt, and the co-defendant as his servant, re-entered as well they might. The plaintiffs reply that they were seised until the defendants disseised them and enfeoffed Robert Twytt, who died (*protestando*) seised, and the land descended to Edward as his son and heir, and he leased them to Hunt on 2 October 1526, who was possessed, and they re-entered and were seised until the defendants committed the trespass. The defendants maintain their bar and traverse the disseisin. The record ends with the joinder of issue.

15. ANON.[2]

Common Pleas, 1529/30.

In a writ of entry in the *post* upon a common recovery, immediately upon the declaration and the voucher and the vouchee's entry into the warranty, all the matter having been pleaded at the bar by the serjeants, and before any entry made thereof in the prothonotaries' rolls, someone came and showed the court that the land was leased to him for years by indenture, and prayed that he

---

[1] For the 'book' (paper pleadings), see last note.
[2] Cf. *Wentworth* v. *Amyas* (Hil. 1529) CP 40/1060, m. 158 (John Mathewman received to save his term in a common recovery).

Et pur ceo que il navoyt son indenture, le courte dona a luy jour de porter einz son indenture, quar tout le court disoyt que il ne serra receu saunz indenture, quar lestatut de Glouc' est Et le tenant eyt querelle, issint que il poit aver brefe de covenant.

Et all jour le termour port eins son indenture, et un lettre dattourney per quell lettre le tenant en cest actyon avoyt done licens et power a un J. de fayer lez de mesme le terre en le nosme del tenant, all profyst et avauntage del tenant, et le dit J. fist lez per endenture resitaunt en lendenture lautorite a luy comyse per le letter del attourney a celui que pria destre receu, pur terme dez annez, et fist le lez en son nosme demesne et nemi en le nosme del tenant accordant a le lettre dattourney.

Brudnell. Il ne serra receu ycy, quar celui que fist le lez navoyt autorite de fayre le lez pur annez, quar le lettre dattourney que done a luy autorite expresse que il poit fayer lez pur le profytt le lessour et ne parle pur annez. Donquez il serra intend a volunte. Et auxi le lez ycy est fayt en le nosme del J. et nemi le nosme del tenant, le quell est voide lez. Et son garrant fuit de fayer lez en le nosme del tenant, et issint lendenture voyde, et saunz indenture ne poit estre receu, per que soyez ouste del rescayt. Et sil eyt terme il serroit eyd per le comen ley per fauxifier, mez sil ne pria destre receu quant le mater est monstre all barre per lez serjantez mez il vient aprez que le vouche ad fayt defaut ou render laction, ore il ne serra receu. Et ove ceo concordat xiiii° mesme le roy: et per ceo appert clere que le tenant per estatut merchaunt ou elegit ne serra receu, quar de cest resceyt pur le lessour nad fayt defaut ne reddition et sur feynt pleder il ne serra receu.

[16]

Casus xxii° H. viii.

Nota tenuez per toutz lez justicez del Comen Banke que un quare impedit est mayntenable verz lordinarie solment come distourber ou verz un distourber solement, quar il nest ple pur eux adire que null patron est nosme en le brefe, quar cesti ple ne gist forsque en le bouche de lencumbent, et il navera tiel general ple adire que null patron est nosme en le brefe, mez il covient dirre que il est eynz del present[ment] un tiel, le quell est en pleyne vie, nient nosme en le brefe, jugement del brefe.

might be received to save his term. And because he did not have his indenture, the court gave him a day to bring in his indenture, for the whole court said that he shall not be received without an indenture; for the Statute of Gloucester says 'And the [demandant]¹ have [his] suit, so that he may have a writ of covenant'.²

At the day the termor brought in his indenture, and a letter of attorney, by which letter the tenant in this action gave leave and power to one J. to make a lease of the same land in the tenant's name, for the profit and advantage of the tenant, and the said J., reciting in the indenture the authority committed to him by the letter of attorney, made the lease by indenture to the person who prayed to be received, for a term of years, and made the lease in his own name and not in the name of the tenant according to the letter of attorney.

BRUDENELL [C.J.]. He shall not be received here, for the person who made the lease had no authority to make the lease for years. The letter of attorney which gave him authority states that he may make a lease for the profit of the lessor, and does not say 'for years': therefore it shall be intended a lease at will. Also the lease here is made in the name of J. and not in the name of the tenant, which is a void lease. His warrant was to make a lease in the tenant's name, and so the indenture is void; and without an indenture he cannot be received. So, you are ousted from the receipt. If he had a term he would have been helped by the common law, by falsifying; but if he does not pray to be received when the matter is shown at the bar by the serjeants, but comes after the vouchee has made default or surrendered the action, he shall not be received. With this agrees [a case in the] fourteenth year of the same king:³ whereby it appears clear that the tenant by statute merchant or *elegit* shall not be received, for the lessor has not made default or surrender, and he shall not be received upon feint pleading.

16. ANON.

Common Pleas, 1530/31.

Note that it was held by all the justices of the Common Bench that a *quare impedit* is maintainable against the ordinary alone as disturber or against a disturber alone, for it is no plea for them to say that no patron is named in the writ; for that plea only lies in the mouth of the incumbent, and he shall not have such a general plea saying that no patron is named in the writ, but he must say that he is in by the presentation of such and such, who is alive and not named in the writ, and pray judgment of the writ.

---

¹ The text says 'tenant', as in the early printed editions. Corrected in Rastell and in the old translations.

² Statute of Gloucester, c. 11 (*SR* i. 49).

³ *Ferrour* v. *Rodley* (1522) YB Mich. 14 Hen. VIII, fo. 4, pl. 4; 119 Selden Soc. 105 (receipt allowed).

[17]

Casus xxi° H. viii.

Nota tenuez per toutz lez justicez del Comen Banke lou le plaintife declare de son close debruse iiii^{to} die Augusti et le defendant dit que le v. jour de August un J. a D. fuit seisi et luy enfeffe etc., saunz ceo que il est culpable devaunt le v. jour, ore poet le plaintife traverser le feffment ou mayntaine son brefe que il [est] culpable come le brefe suppose.

[18]

Bawedwyn. Lou le tenant per copye secundum consuetudinem manerii morust seisi, son heyre ne poit entrer devaunt que il soyt present, trove et [admit]¹ come prochein heyre a son pere devaunt le darrein tenant le seignior que darreinment morust seisi, si ne soyt que le custom voet war[anter] que il poit entrer meyntenant aprez le mort son per devaunt ascun presentment ou admission. Et il dit que nest le payment del fyne que fait luy tenant mez solement ladmission del seigniour daver luy pur son tenant.

[19]

Casus xxi° H. viii.

[*fo. 21v*]² [Fuit] tenuez per toutz lez justicez del Comen Banke [que] si home [est] seisi dun maner a que un avowson est appendant et fayt feffment [de] parcel del maner ou de toutz lez demesnez del maner et ne parle del avowson, ore lavowson ne passera. Mez sil fayt feffment del 3^e ou iiii^{te} parte del maner et ne parle del avowson, uncore le 3^e ou le iiii^{te} parte del avowson passera accordant all [. . .] del maner que est graunt, et serra appendant a cest parcell. Et sic nota le divercite lou le feffment est fayt per nosme del parte [del] maner et lou per nosme de terrez.

---

¹ *Word missing at foot of page.*
² *Damaged in top left corner, with loss of some words.*

17. ANON.

Common Pleas, 1529/30.

Note that it was held by all the justices of the Common Bench that where the plaintiff declares of his close broken on the fourth day of August, and the defendant says that on the fifth day of August one John at Down was seised and enfeoffed him etc., without this that he is guilty before the fifth day, the plaintiff may now traverse the feoffment or maintain his writ that he is guilty as the writ supposes.

18. ANON.

Common Pleas, c. 1530. Cf. Yorke, above, vol. I, p. 158, no. 181, per Broke and Fitzherbert.

Baldwin.[1] Where a tenant by copy according to the custom of the manor (*secundum consuetudinem manerii*) dies seised, his heir may not enter before he has been presented, found and admitted as next heir to his father before the last tenant of the lord who last died seised,[2] unless the custom will warrant that he may enter immediately after his father's death before any presentment or admission. And he said that it is not the payment of the fine which makes him tenant but solely the admission by the lord to have him for his tenant.

19. ANON.

Common Pleas, 1529/30. Cf. Pollard, above, p. 262, no. 37, where the same point is attributed to Norwich C.J. in 1533.

It was held by all the justices of the Common Bench that if someone is seised of a manor to which an advowson is appendant and makes a feoffment of part of the manor, or of all the demesnes of the manor, and does not speak of the advowson, the advowson will not pass. But if he makes a feoffment of the third or fourth part of the manor and does not speak of the advowson, a third or fourth part of the advowson will pass according to the fraction of the manor which is granted, and it shall be appendant to that part. Thus note the distinction as to where the feoffment is made by name of the part of the manor and where by the name of lands.

---

[1] Serjeant at law 1531-35, then C.J.C.P.
[2] Meaning not clear.

[20]

Casus xx° H. viii.

En brefe de dower le tenant plede en barre coment il mesme[1] auterfoitz porta brefe dentre sur disseisin verz le baron de mesme le terre, en quell action le baron apperust et vouche un B. a garranter, le quell B. entra en le garrante et aprez fist defaut, sur quell il avoyt jugement de recover etc., jugement si action. A que le feme dit que le recovere fuit per covyn de causer le feme de perder son dower, et travers le disseisin. Et le tenant demurre sur le ple. Et fuit agree per toutz lez justices que le feme poit fauxifier le recovere per le comen ley, et auxi le feme serra ayde per lez expresse parolx del [statut] de W. 2de ca° v°, In casu quo vir. Mez sil fuit per action trie, le feme ne poit fauxifier en mesme le poynt trie, pur ceo que le feme est privie all ple le baron et son title est per le baron, et quant el est endowe el serra adjuge einz en le per per le baron.

[21]

Casus xxi° H. viii.

Fuit tenuez per *Fitzherbert* et *Shelley* que lou un pleynt fuit en le court dadmirall dun chose de quell le court navoyt power de tener ple, le defendant en un action de trespas justefye per reson dun precept direct a luy horse del dit courte et fuit tenuz per eux, entant que ilz nount power de tener ple del dit mater, que ceo fuit coram non judice et donquez lez justicez sont trespasourz en agarder tiel proces: et per mesme le reson serra lour servaunt, quar il ne serra in meliour condition que son master. Et ilz teigne divercite lou lez juges sont jugez de mesme le mater et lou nemi: quar silz sont jugez de mesme le mater et ilz agardont proces saunz originall ou un proces en lew del auter, la le juge ou le viconte ne[2] serra punishe, quar le juge ne serra unquez punishe de tiel chose que il fayt come juge. Mes si le juge del Banke le Roy voylle agarder un graund cape en ple de terre, et le viconte prist le terre en le mayne le roy, la le juge et le viconte sont disseisourz. Et mesme le ley si lez jugez del Comen Banke voylent agarder execution del mort sur un condempnation de felony etc.

---

[1] *Seemingly del.*
[2] *Interlined.*

20. FOWLER v. LYNDESELL

Common Pleas, 1528/29. Also reported by Yorke, above, vol. I, p. 200, no. 292 (Hil. 1529). Record: CP 40/1059, mm. 828, 830 (judgment on demurrer, Hil. 1529).

In a writ of dower the tenant pleaded in bar that he had himself previously brought a writ of entry sur disseisin for the same land against the husband, in which action the husband appeared and vouched one B. to warrant, which B. entered into the warranty and afterwards made default, whereupon he had judgment to recover etc.; and he prayed judgment whether the plaintiff ought to have an action. To this the woman said that the recovery was by covin to cause her to lose her dower, and traversed the disseisin. The tenant demurred upon the plea. And it was agreed by all the justices that the woman could falsify the recovery by the common law, and also that she shall be helped by the express words of the Statute of Westminster II, c. 5, *In casu quo vir*.[1] But if it had been by action tried, the woman could not falsify in the same point which had been tried, because the wife is privy to the husband's plea and her title is through the husband, and when she is endowed she shall be adjudged to be in through the husband in the *per*.

21. ANON.

Common Pleas, 1529/30.

It was held by FITZHERBERT and SHELLEY that where there was a plaint in the admiralty court for a thing whereof the court had no power to hold plea, and the defendant in an action of trespass justified by reason of a precept directed to him out of the said court,[2] this was *coram non judice*, inasmuch as they have no power to hold plea of the said matter, and therefore the justices were trespassers in awarding such process: and so by the same reason was their servant, for he shall not be in a better condition than his master. And they held it a distinction where the judges are judges of the same matter and where not. For if they are judges of the same matter and they award process without original, or one process instead of another, there the judge or the sheriff shall not be punished, for the judge shall never be punished for something which he does as judge. But if a judge of the King's Bench awards a grand *cape* in a plea of land, and the sheriff takes the land into the king's hand, there the judge and the sheriff are disseisors. The law is the same if the judges of the Common Bench award execution of death upon a condemnation for felony etc.[3]

---

[1] Westminster II, c. 5 (*SR* i. 75).
[2] The words 'and it was held by them' are repeated unnecessarily in the text.
[3] Cf. Yorke, above, vol. I, p. 187, no. 258; Caryll, below, p. 390, no. 47.

[22]

Casus xix° H. viii.

Nota que fuit tenuez per toutz lez justicez del Comen Banke que si home soyt condempne en trns. all suyt le plaintife et aprez en execution pur le fyne le roy, ore le fyne le roy ne serra assesse ne paye tanque le plaintife soyt satisfie de son dett ou damage, pur ceo que le tytle et interest le roy comence per le plaintife et pur ceo le plaintife serra preferre etc.

[23]

Casus xxi° H. viii.

Nota quant home voyle jetter un essoigne il covient que lessoyne soyt jett le primer jour <del terme>[1] que le partie ad per le retourne ou auterment lessoigne ne serra allowe si lauter partie prist exception a ceo. Mez si null exception soit prise ne entre sur le roll de essoynez, il poit ceo jetter le iiii^te jour.

Et *Joynour*, le cheff preignotarie, disoyt que le comen course del place est en toutz brefez originallx de jetter son essoyne le iiii^te jour, quar devaunt cesti jour null brefe est retourne issint que le parte ne poit aver conusanz devaunt le retourne de ascun suyte, et pur ceo il poit ceo jetter le iiii^te jour. Mez en toutz judicialx brefez il ne serra allowe si exception soyt prise ut supra. Nota le divercite.

[24]

Casus xxi° H. viii.

Dett port per executourz, le defendant plede un relez del plaintife de toutz actions le quell le plaintife avoyt come executour, et le plaintife dit que all temps del reles fayt il fuit deinz age de xxi. anz etc., et sur ceo le defendant demurre en ley.

S., I. et *B.*, Justicez. Il serra barre per son reles. Et ilz preignont divercite lou un enfant fayt ascun chose en son nosme et droyt demesne et lou il face come attourney ou servaunt en droyt per auctorite et comaundement del terce person. Quar toutz chosez que il fayt en son droyt demesne est voyd ou voydable sil ne soyt pur le benefyte ou avauntage del enfant. Mez sil face en

---

[1] *Underlined with dots to indicate deletion.*

22. ANON.

Common Pleas, 1527/28.

Note that it was held by all the justices of the Common Bench that if someone is condemned in trespass at the suit of the plaintiff and is afterwards in execution for the fine to the king, the fine to the king shall not be assessed or paid until the plaintiff is satisfied in respect of his debt or damages, because the king's title and interest commences through the plaintiff and therefore the plaintiff shall be preferred etc.

23. ANON.

Common Pleas, 1529/30.

Note that when someone wishes to cast an essoin the essoin must be cast on the first day of the term which the party has by the return or else the essoin will not be allowed—if the other party takes exception to it. But if no exception is taken or entered on the roll of essoins, he may cast it on the fourth day.

Jenour, the chief prothonotary,[1] said that the common course of the Place in all original writs is to cast one's essoin on the fourth day, since before that day no writ is returned and so the party cannot know of any suit before the return; therefore he may cast it on the fourth day. But in all judicial writs it shall not be allowed, if exception is taken as above. Note the distinction.

24. ANON.

Common Pleas, 1529/30. Also reported in Spelman, p. 133, pl. 5 (Mich. 1529); Pollard, above, p. 265, no. 44 (Hil. 1530); and in BL MS Harley 1691, fo. 141v; BL MS. Hargrave 5, fo. 106, below, p. 417, no. 1. Cf. also below, p. 327, no. 32.

Debt was brought by executors, the defendant pleaded a release from the plaintiff of all actions which the plaintiff had as executor, and the plaintiff said that at the time when the release was made he was under the age of twenty-one years etc.; and thereupon the defendant demurred in law.

S[HELLEY], [ENGLEFIELD] and B[RUDENELL], Justices. He shall be barred by his release. And they took a distinction where an infant does something in his own name and right and where he does it as an attorney or servant, in right of a third person, by his authority and commandment. For everything that he does in his own right is void or voidable unless it is for the benefit or advantage of

---

[1] John Jenour was second prothonotary, though he is called 'one of the chief prothonotaries' in 119 Selden Soc. 177. The adjective 'chief' is therefore probably designed to distinguish the prothonotaries proper from their secondaries.

auter droyt, si il que done a luy lautorite fuit un person ablle en le ley, donquez toutz actez fayt per lenfant serra cy bien fayt per lenfant come per celuy que done a luy le autorite: quar si home face lettre dattourney a un enfant a deliver estate et il ceo face, ceo est bon, et mesme le ley est si un devyse que son terra serra vende per un tiel que est deinz age, et il esteant deinz age vende le terre, ceo est bon. Donquez, quant un enfant est fayt executour le [ley] luy permitt destre un executour, quar il serra entend que celuy que luy fayt son executour avoyt perfitt notice de son discretion de governer et administer cez bienz accordant a son volunte. Donquez, quant le testatour ad luy enablle et le [ley] luy admitt, ore il ad tout le autorite et power que appertient all office de un executour, et a cel office appertient de payer dettes et legacyes, de vender et doner lez bienz pro salute anime, et a demander lez dettes le testatour et de fayer relez et acquittauncez de eux. Et sil done lez bienz il ne poit eux repeler, et sil paye lez legacyes et le simple contractes le testatour devaunt lez especialtez sont payez, et nad quoy de payer lez especialtez, il serra charge de cez bienz proprez pur tiel dissipation. Et sil eux waste all dyce et cardes il serra charge de cez bienz proprez. Et lez dettes et byenz queux fueront all testatour ne sont lez byenz ou dettez lexecutour, mez ilz ount le governaunz, ladministration et disposition de eux all use le testatour. Quar silz sont utlagez lez bienz le testatour ne serront forfettes. Et si le executour port action il nest ple adire quil est utlage, pur ceo que il demande a auter use. Si un enfant soyt abbe ou moyne ou deane, toutz tielx chosez que lenfant fayt en droyt de son corporation ne serra avoyde per son nonage, pur ceo que il ceo face en droyt del corporation et nemi en son droyt demesne. Issint il semble, entaunt que le fesaunz de cest relez est un chose que appertient all office del executour, il est bon nient obstant que il soyt deinz age.

F.-H. all contrarie. Et jeo voylle agree a lez groundes que [*fo. 22*] [ont][1] este myse quun enfant, feme covert ou moigne poent estre faytz executourz. Et jeo voyle agree que toutz tielx chosez queux appertient merment all office del un executour, toutz tielx actez faytz per un enfant executour est bon. Et quant home est fayt executour, ore a son office appertient de payer dettes [et] legacies, et a demander dettes, et pur distributer lez bienz pro salute anime. Mez de fayer acquittaunz ou relez, ceo ne appertient a son office, quar sil ad cause [de] demander det sur especialte, quant le dett est paye il doyt redelyver lespecialte, et ceo est son office, et nemi de fayer acquittaunz ou reles. Et a ceo que est dit que [si] un enfant executour done lez bienz le testatour que il ne poit repeler son done, ceo nest issint, quar loffice del executour est de payer legacyes [et] dettes et pur administer le bienz pro salute anime et sil face auterment il serra compelle per lordinari daccompter devaunt luy. Donquez, quant il done lez bienz, ceo nest administration pro salute anime, et si nemi donquez il excede son office, et donquez il ceo fayt en son auctorite demesne, et donquez le relez nest barre.

---

[1] *Word lost in top corner.*

the infant. But if he does it in another's right, and the person who gave him the authority was a person able in the law, then all acts done by the infant shall be as well done by the infant as by the person who gave him the authority. Thus if someone makes a letter of attorney to an infant to deliver an estate, and he does it, this is good. And the law is the same if someone devises that his land shall be sold by such and such, who is under age, and he sells the land while he is under age: this is good. Therefore, when an infant is made executor the law permits him to be an executor, for it shall be presumed that the person who made him his executor had perfect notice of his discretion to govern and administer his goods according to his will. Therefore, when the testator has enabled him and the law admitted him, he has all the authority and power which belong to the office of an executor, and to that office it belongs to pay debts and legacies, to sell and give goods for the good of the testator's soul (*pro salute animae*), and to demand the testator's debts, and to make releases and acquittances for them. And if he gives away the goods he may not claim them back; and if he pays the legacies and the simple contracts of the testator before the specialties are paid, and does not have enough to pay the specialties, he shall be charged out of his own goods for such dissipation. And if he wastes them at dice and cards he shall be charged out of his own goods. The debts and goods which belonged to the testator are not the executors' goods or debts, but they have the governance, administration and disposition of them to the use of the testator. Therefore, if they are outlawed, the testator's goods shall not be forfeited. And if the executor brings an action it is no plea to say that he is outlawed, because he demands to another's use. If an infant is an abbot or monk or dean, all such things as the infant does in right of his corporation shall not be avoided by his infancy, because he does them in right of the corporation and not in his own right. Therefore it seems, since the making of this release is something which belongs to the office of an executor, that it is good notwithstanding that he is under age.

FITZHERBERT to the contrary. I will agree with the principles (*groundes*) which have been put that an infant, married woman or monk may be made executors. And I will agree that, in respect of everything that belongs absolutely to the office of an executor, all such acts done by an infant executor are good. Now, when someone is made an executor, it belongs to his office to pay debts and legacies, and to demand debts, and to distribute the goods *pro salute animae*. But making acquittances or releases does not belong to his office, for if he has cause to demand a debt upon specialty, he ought to redeliver the specialty when the debt has been paid, and that is his office, not to make an acquittance or release. As to what has been said that if an infant executor gives away the testator's goods he may not recall his gift, that is not so, for the office of an executor is to pay legacies and debts and to administer the goods *pro salute animae*, and if he does otherwise he shall be compelled by the ordinary to account before him. Therefore, when he gives away the goods, that is not an administration *pro salute animae*; and, if not, he exceeds his office and does it of his own authority, and therefore the release is no bar.

[25]

Casus xx° H. viii.

Nota fuit tenuez per *F.-H.* en le Comen Banke que lenquest est tenuez sur payne dattaynt de prender notyce sur eux de chescun feffment ou lez pur terme de vie, nient obstant que ne soyt don a eux en evydence. Mez auterment est dez matterz en escripte ou auterz privat materz, pur ceo que ilz sont privatz materz perenter partie et partie.

[26]

Casus en le Comen Banke.

Nota que dun parsonage approprie issint que labbe est person emparsone, ore cest parsonage jamez devient voyde, si labbe ore en cest case graunt le nomination del esglise si cest bon graunt ou nemi?

Et semble al *S. J.*[1] que est bon graunt, quar si serra voyd donquez le comen ground ne tiendra lew, scilicet que lacte del chescun home serra prise pluis fort etc. Et pur ceo ycy en cest case per son graunt il serra entend le nomination del vicarage quant devient voyde, quar auterment le graunt serra voyde.

Mez[2] semble a le contrarie. Et son reson fuit pur ceo que le graunt fayt del avoydaunz del rectorie est voyde (ratio patet), et issint mesme le ley est proximam advocationem ecclesie, quar ceo refer all rectorie et donquez per le reson avauntdit il serra voyde.

Et ilz disoyent que si home graunt proximam vacationem, rienz passera per cest graunt, quar rienz est emplie deinz cest graunt pur que le graunt serra bon. Mez si home graunt proximam advocationem ou nominationem, est assetz bon, quar per le graunt del nomination ou de prochein avoydanz le graunt est pris pro hac vice.

[27]

[*Fo. 22v*] Nota loppinion de *Wylloughby*, Justice, que si lez executourz recoveront en action de dett pur arrerages daccompt, ceo que est recover serra un assetz en lour maynez. Et issint mesme le ley est silz recoveront damagez en

---

[1] *Letter unclear.*
[2] *Followed by a deleted letter.*

25. ANON.

Common Pleas, 1528/29.

Note that it was held by FITZHERBERT in the Common Bench that the inquest is bound upon pain of attaint to take notice upon themselves of every feoffment or lease for term of life, even if it is not given to them in evidence. But is is otherwise of matters in writing or other private matters, because they are private matters between party and party.

26. ANON.[1]

Common Pleas, undated.

Note, concerning a parsonage which is appropriated, so that the abbot is parson imparsoné and the parsonage never becomes vacant. If the abbot in this case grants the nomination of the 'church', is this a good grant or not?

It seemed to [SHELLEY], Justice,[2] that it is a good grant, for if it were void the common principle (*ground*) would not hold place, namely that everyone's act shall be taken more strongly [against himself] etc. Therefore here in this case his grant shall be presumed to mean the nomination to the vicarage when it becomes vacant, for otherwise the grant would be void.

But [another judge] thought the contrary. His reason was that the grant made of the avoidance of the rectory is obviously void, and so by the same law is the next advowson of the church (*proximam advocationem ecclesiae*); for that refers to the rectory, and therefore it shall be void, for the reason aforesaid.

They said that if someone grants the next avoidance (*proximam vacationem*), nothing shall pass by this grant, for nothing is implied in this grant whereby the grant may be good. But if someone grants the next advowson[3] or nomination (*proximam advocationem [vel] nominationem*), it is good enough, for by the grant of the nomination or of the next [advowson] the grant is taken to mean for that time (*pro hac vice*).

27. ANON.

Common Pleas, in or after 1537 (when Willoughby became J.C.P.). Cf. Spelman, p. 130, pl. 4 (undated).

Note the opinion of WILLOUGHBY, Justice, that if executors recover in an action of debt for arrears of an account, that which is recovered shall be assets

---

[1] Between nos. 24 and 25 there is a Gray's Inn case ('casus in aula'). No. 26 itself is followed by a number of cases in Gray's Inn, in which Fitzherbert J. and Molyneux speak.
[2] 'I.' might alternatively denote Englefield.
[3] For a grant of the next 'advowson' see below, p. 340, no. 58; and Caryll, below, p. 408, no. 99.

brefe de trns. port per eux de bonis asportatis in vita testatoris. Et pur ceo en action de dett verz eux silz voy[l]ent pleder Pleynment administer et issint rienz enter maynez, le plaintife repl[i]era et monstre cest recoverie, le quell uncore remayne destre administer. Quere ouster.

[28]

Le case en le Comen Bank fuit tiel: le feffe alle use dun estate tayle est disseisi per un feme sole, verz que un brefe dentre sur disseisin est port, et el vouche celui que use en tayle. Que est fayt per ceo?

Et semble ryen, quar celui que fuit vouche navoyt ascun interest en lestat tayle neque en use neque en possession, quar il navoyt nascun ryen mez un droyt dun use, le quell ne poit estre recover per null mene. Mez sil fuit tenant en tayle en possession, donquez le ley serroit auterment: per Mons' *Baweldwyn*, Cheff Justice del Comen Banke.

[29]

Nota que *Conysby* dit que le ley est prise a cest jour que si un tient dun auter que est atteynt de hawet treason, que celui que fuit tenant ore tiendra del roy in capite.

[30]

Nota que fuit dit per le master del rollez et auterz que mon baylye ne poit fayer lessez ouster un an: et auxi ceo fuit agre en le Comen Banke.

in their hands. It is likewise the same in law if they recover damages in a writ of trespass brought by them for taking away goods in the testator's lifetime (*de bonis asportatis in vita testatoris*). Therefore in an action of debt against them, if they will plead 'Fully administered and so nothing in hand', the plaintiff may reply and show this recovery, which still remains to be administered. Query further.

28.

Common Pleas, in or after 1535 (when Baldwin became C.J.C.P.).

The case in the Common Bench was as follows: a feoffee to the use of an estate tail is disseised by a single woman, against whom a writ of entry sur disseisin is brought, and she vouches cestuy que use in tail. What is thereby effected?

Nothing, it seems; for the person who was vouched had no interest in the estate tail either in use or in possession, inasmuch as he had nothing but a right of a use, which cannot be recovered by any means. If, however, he was tenant in tail in possession, the law would be otherwise: by my lord BALDWIN, Chief Justice of the Common Bench.

29. NOTE

Note that CONYNGESBY[1] said that the law today is understood to be that if someone holds of another who is attainted of high treason, the person who was tenant shall now hold of the king in chief.

30. NOTE

Note that it was said by the master of the rolls[2] and others that my bailiff may not make leases for more than a year: and this was also agreed in the Common Bench.

---

[1] Probably Humphrey Conyngesby, J.K.B., who retired in 1532. His son William did not become a serjeant until 1540.

[2] Probably Sir Christopher Hales, bencher of Gray's Inn, master of the rolls 1536-41: *Readers and Readings*, p. 33.

[31]

Nota que fuit dit en le Comen Banke que home ne poit seer un gate en le hawte chemyn pur ceo [que] come il semble all *Balldwyne* que il fuit en maner dun nusaunz, et ceo per cest reson, pur ceo que il enstrayt le chymyn. Et auxi si ascun robberye ou murder soyt comyt sount pluiz communement fayt a tiel lew que est pluiz apte pur le purpose de eux queux entend de fayer tielx actes, et ceo est communement lou tielx gatez sont levez. Et auxi sil fueront ii. postez seez en le hawte chemyn, homez queux passeront sont enforcez de chivaucher so nere lez ditz postez que le growend est worne en tyel maner que le voye est empayre per reson de ceo. Et auxi si laronz pursont un home en le voy de luy robber, per reson del gate il est enforce de stoppe ou de stay, per reson de quell sovent foytz homez sont robbez. Et amyt que ne fuit ascun tyel mater, uncore per reson de tyelx gatez seez en le hawte chemyn homez sount steyez en lour journeys et ne passont cy spedement come ilz ferront si null tyels gatez ne fueront levez la. Et pur ceo si home chyvacha sur un sake, quant il vient a le gate il est enforce de lyghter de opener le gate, et per case en le mene temps le sake eschia[1] sur le terre. Issint le lever dez gatez en le haut chemyn est moulte a le nusaunz dez subjettz le roy.

[32]

Si home fayt son fytz son executour esteant dage de v. annez, ore fuit semble en cest case, entant que il faut discrescion pur ceo que il est deinz lage de discrescion, il ne poit occupier ne fayer ascun chose come executour ferra, mez lordinarie poit sequester ou comitt ladministration ouster a certen personz reservant quilz doyent accompter a le fytz quant il vient all age de xiiii. annez. Et si ascun tyel [que] soyt fayt un executour voyle graunter ascun home de prender ou de medeler ove lez bienz celui comaundement est voyde pur ceo que il mesme ne poit medeler ove eux, causa qua supra. Mez si un fayt son fytz son executour, esteant dage de xiiii. annez ou xv. annez, sil luy order auterment que le confidens est myse en luy, ceo serra deme le folye le testatour. Et quant home fayt son fitz son executour, ceo serra entend toutz foytz destre pur lavancement del fytz et que le pere pluiz tost voloyt que son fytz avera < la benefyte en le >[2] occupation de cez bienz que estraungez.

---

[1] *Reading unclear.*
[2] *Interlined.*

31. ANON.

Common Pleas, in or after 1535 (when Baldwin became C.J.C.P.). Perhaps a dictum from *Hikkys* v. *More* (1535) CP 40/1085(2), m. 442 (action on the case for erecting a hedge across a way; special imparlance); reported in YB Mich. 27 Hen. VIII, fo. 27, pl. 10.

Note that it was said in the Common Bench that one may not set a gate in the highway because, as it seemed to BALDWIN, it was in effect a nuisance; and the reason is because it narrows the way. Also if any robbery or murder is committed it is most commonly done at the kind of place which is most apt for the purpose of those who intend to do such acts, and that is commonly where such gates are erected. Also if there are two posts set in the highway, those who pass by are forced to ride so near the said posts that the ground is worn in such a manner that the way is impaired by reason thereof. Also if thieves pursue someone along the way to rob him, he is forced by reason of the gate to stop, or delay, and by reason thereof men are often robbed. Even if you do not admit these facts, still by reason of such gates set in the highway men are delayed in their journeys, and do not pass as quickly as they would if no such gates were erected there. For instance, if someone is riding on a sack, when he comes to the gate he is forced to alight to open the gate, and perhaps in the mean time the sack would fall on the ground. Therefore the erecting of gates in the highway is much to the nuisance of the king's subjects.

32. NOTE

Cf. above, p. 323, no. 24 (1529).

If someone makes his son his executor, being of the age of five years, it was thought in this case, inasmuch as he lacks discretion (because he is beneath the age of discretion), he may not occupy or do anything as an executor should; but the ordinary may sequester or commit the administration over to certain persons, with the reservation that they must account to the son when he comes to the age of fourteen years. And if any such infant who is made an executor will grant to anyone to take or meddle with the goods, this command is void, because he may not himself meddle with them, for the above reason. But if someone makes his son his executor, being of the age of fourteen or fifteen years, and he behaves otherwise than according to the trust which is put in him, this shall be deemed the foolishness of the testator. When someone makes his son his executor, this shall always be presumed to be for the advancement of the son, and that the father would rather have his son benefit from the occupation of his goods than strangers.

[33]

Nota que est tenuez pur ley que si jeo graunt mon revercion del mon tenant a terme de vie a un auter per fayt endent enroll, que ceo est en luy sufficientment per le ley saunz ascun attournement destre fayt a luy per le particular tenant.

[34]

Nota que fuit tenues en le Comen Banke que si feme sole graunt lez servicez de son tenant et devaunt attournement el prist all baron, ceo est un countermaunde de lattournement. Mez le ley varye lou le graunt est fayt per fyne.

[35]

[*Fo. 24v*] Lez est fayt a terme de vie, le remainder en tayle, le remainder en fee, le tenant a terme de vie enfeffe celuy en le remainder en tayle et sa feme, le tenant a terme de vie morust, celuy en le rermainder en le tayle morust saunz issue, celuy en le remainder en fee entre, et le feme port assise. Coment cesti feffment prendra effect, ceo fuit le mater.

Bawedwyn argue cest feffment destre bon, et de prender effect az ambydeux, scilicet a le baron et a sa feme, et autreforment ne poit. Et il agre bien que feffment fayt a celuy en le revercion per le tenant a terme de vie ou en tayle, ou lou home est seisi destate tayle en droit sa feme que en toutz ceux casez feffmentes faytes a celuy en le revercion nest ascun disseisin a luy ne forfaiture de son estat, entaunt que toutz foytz quant un prendera effect come discontinuans ou disseisin le feoffour doyt doner un fesimple et le feffe doyt prender un fesimple. Et si feffment soyt fayt per celuy que ad le particuler estate a celuy en le revercion serroit discontinuanz ou disseisin, donquez ensuera que serra ii. fesimplez dun mesme terre, que ne poit estre. Mez il dit que nient obstant quun lez soyt fayt ovesque le remainder pur terme de vie, le remainder en tayle, le remainder en fee, chescun estat est dependant sur auter, et si ascun de ceux en le remainder disagreont a lour remainder toutz lez remainders subsequentes sont voydez. Et ideo si en le case ut supra le primer lesse a terme de vie ust este un moygne issint que le lez a luy ust este voyde, donquez toutz lez remainders dependant sur mesme lestat sont voydez. Et si celuy en le remainder en tayle ust este un moygne professe, le remainder a luy nust este bon, et auxi le remainder en fee que depend sur mesme lestat. Mez uncore lez pur terme de vie et le

33. NOTE

Note that it is held as law that if I grant someone else my reversion upon my tenant for life, by an indented deed enrolled, this is sufficiently in him by the law without any attornment being made to him by the particular tenant.

34. ANON.

Note that it was held in the Common Bench that if a single woman grants the services of her tenant, and before attornment she marries, this is a countermand of the attornment. But the law is different where the grant is made by fine.

35. ANON.[1]

A lease is made for term of life, remainder in tail, remainder in fee; the tenant for term of life enfeoffs the remainderman in tail and his wife; the tenant for term of life dies; the rermainderman in tail dies without issue; the remainderman in fee enters; and the woman brings an assize. The matter was: how does this feoffment take effect?

BALDWIN argued that this feoffment was good, and takes effect to both of them, namely the husband and his wife; and it cannot be otherwise. And he quite agreed that a feoffment made to the reversioner by the tenant for term of life or in tail, or where someone is seised of an estate tail in right of his wife, in all these cases a feoffment made to the reversioner is no disseisin of him or a forfeiture of his estate, inasmuch as whenever a thing shall take effect as a discontinuance or disseisin the feoffor ought to give a fee simple and the feoffee ought to take a fee simple. If a feoffment made to the reversioner by the person who has the particular estate were to be a discontinuance or disseisin, then it would follow that there would be two fee simples of one same land, which cannot be. But he said nevertheless that if a lease is made with remainder for term of life, remainder in tail, remainder in fee, each estate is dependent on another, and if any of the remaindermen disagree to their remainders all the subsequent remainders are void. Therefore if in the case above the first lessee for term of life had been a monk, so that the lease to him had been void, then all the remainders dependent upon the same estate would have been void. And if the remainderman in tail had been a professed monk, the remainder to him would not have been good, and also the remainder in fee which depended upon the same estate. Nevertheless a lease for term of life, remainder *pur terme*

---

[1] Following more Gray's Inn cases, in which Yorke (d. 1536) and Hynde speak.

remainder a terme dauter vye sont ensuantz queux sont precedentes. Issint ycy, entaunt que le baron que est en le remainder ad prise estat en fee il ad per ceo disagre a son remainder, quar si son remainder demurrera en luy le feffment ne poit prender effect en luy, mez uncore, entaunt que il ad prise feffment il ad disagre a cel remainder. Donquez, sil disagree, le remainder a celuy en fee est voyde et de nul effect, entaunt que il est dependant sur lauter estat. Et issint lez remainders voyde, et lestat le feme loyall et indefesible verz chescun sinon enverz le lessour que ad cause dentre pur un forfeture. Et si issint, lassise per le feme mayntenable.

Mez cest arguement poit estre avoyde, quar admytt que nul disagrement poit estre per le baron per mater en fayt (ut credo que ne poit), uncore il ne poit disagreer pur le benefytt de le 3^{ce} person, scilicet pur le disavauntage celuy en le remainder en fee, ut patet en plusourz cases que pur lavauntage destraunge home ne serra en cest case que il serra sinon que fuissoyt pur le avauntage destraunge, ut patet per le case de wast ou le wast est dispunishablle pur le salvation del mesne remainder. Auxi celuy que ad forsque estat a terme de vie joyndera en wast ove son joynt graunte del revercion del fesimple, et ceo pur son avauntage auxi. Auxi le lyver est en un del xl^{mo} lou feme fuit remytt enconter son volunte pur lavauntage dun estraunge. Issint videtur pur le disavauntage que ensuera a celuy en le remainder en fee cest disagrement ne serra suffer. Donquez, admit (sicome croy videtur resonable) que nul prisell ne poit estre disagrement, ou que disagrement ne poit estre per luy, coment cest feffment prendra effect? Per feffment ne poit prender effect en le baron, causa qua supra, entaunt que il est en le revercion et il ne poit prender lun moyte per voye del surrender et le [fo. 25] lauter moyte per voye de feffment, sicome pereventure serra si ascun auter estraunge ussoyt estre joyne in le graunt ove le baron [. . .] feme, quar ilz puissoynt prende per moytez. Mez perenter le baron et sa feme nul moytez sont, et donquez per feffment ne serra prende estat, et surrender ne poit entaunt que la feme nest mye en le revercion. Et, sir, uncore ne serroit dit voyde mez prendra avauntage per voye del graunt del estate de ambydeux et nemi per surrender solement a le baron ne a le feffment solement per voye del feffment mez enurera all eux ambydeux per voye de graunt. Et, sir, semble a le case en vii^o H. vi^i ou tenant a terme de vie surrender ou grant tout son estate a celuy en le revercion et a un estraunge.

d'auter vie, are following [estates] which are precedent.[1] Likewise here, since the husband who is in the remainder has taken an estate in fee he has thereby disagreed to his remainder; for if his remainder stayed in him the feoffment could not take effect in him, but since he has taken a feoffment he has disagreed to this remainder. Therefore, if he disagrees, the remainder in fee is void and of no effect, inasmuch as it is dependent upon the other estate. Thus the remainders are void, and the woman's estate lawful and indefeasible against everyone except the lessor who has cause to enter for a forfeiture. If that is so, the assize by the woman is maintainable.

But this argument may be avoided, for [leaving aside the point] that there can be no disagreement by the husband by matter in fact (as I believe there cannot), still he may not disagree for[2] the benefit of a third person, namely for the disadvantage of the remainderman in fee. This appears in various cases where, [to protect] the advantage of a stranger, one shall not be in the same case as one would be but for the advantage of the stranger:[3] as appears by the case of waste, where the waste is unpunishable for the purpose of saving the mesne remainder. Also someone who has only an estate for term of life shall join in waste with his joint grantee of the reversion in fee simple, and that is for his advantage also. Also there is a book in one of the quadragesms[4] where a woman was remitted against her will for the advantage of a stranger. Thus it seems that this disagreement shall not be allowed, because of the disadvantage which would ensue to the remainderman in fee. Therefore, admit (as I believe seems reasonable) that no taking can be a disagreement, or that there cannot be a disagreement by itself, how shall this feoffment take effect? As a feoffment it cannot take effect in the husband, for the reason above, inasmuch as he is in the reversion and he cannot take one moiety by way of surrender and the other moiety by way of feoffment: as might perhaps be the case if some other stranger had been joined in the grant with the husband and wife, for they could have taken by moieties. Between a husband and his wife, however, there are no moieties, and therefore by feoffment it shall not be taken as an estate, and it cannot be a surrender inasmuch as the woman is not in the reversion. And, sir, it should nevertheless not be called void, but it shall take advantage by way of grant of the estate of both and not by surrender only to the husband or by feoffment only by way of feoffment, but it shall enure to both of them by way of grant. And, sir, it is like the case in 7 Hen. VI,[5] where tenant for term of life surrendered or granted all his estate to the reversioner and a stranger.

---

[1] Meaning obscure.
[2] Apparently meaning 'on account of'.
[3] This seems to be the gist of a very convoluted sentence.
[4] YB Mich. 41 Edw. III, fo. 17, pl. 2, at fo. 19; also cited by Caryll, below, p. 378, no. 19.
[5] *Re Gascoigne* (1428) YB Mich. 7 Hen. VI, fo. 2, pl. 7.

[36]

[*Fo. 26v*] Nota per *Shelley* que si le roy graunt per cez letterz patentes all mayre et cominalty de Lyncoll' quilz averont tielx libertes come le cyte del Lounderz ad, cest bon graunt et ilz per cest graunt averont semblable libertez. Mez si le roy voyle graunter a eux que ilz averont tielz customez come Lounderz ad, cest graunt ne vaut, pur ceo que custome ne poit estre mez per auncien continuanz, que ne poit commenser a cest jour per graunt. Et pur ceo si le roy graunt per cez letterz patentes a un home que son terre serra solonque le custome de gevelkynd ou del borowy Inglishe, ou que lez inhabitantz de tyel ville si ascun la fuit endett a auter que le creditour attachera lez bienz celui que est endett a son debtour come le custome de Londres [*fo. 27*] est, ceo ne voet estre (ratio satis constat), quar il disoyet que le custome de gavelkynd fuit devaunt le conquest.

[37]

[*Fo. 27v*] Un case fuit move per *Mountague*, que fuit tyel: autorite fuit done all viii. personz ou a ix. a founder un chantrie et de fayer constitutions et ordenauncez all tout temps pur lestablishement de mesme le chantrie. Et puis vii. de eux font le ust person le master de mesme le chauntrye. Ou ceo est bon ou nemi, ceo est le question. Et ii. questions sont en cest case: un est lou lauctorite fuit done all viii. ou a ix. et vii. fount lacte, ou ceo est bien fayt ou nemi, et lauter question est, quant vii. persons font le viii. person destre le master de mesme le chantrye.

Et pur le primer question, *Shelley* semble que lact que vii. personz fist ne fuit auctorized per le graunt a eux fayt. Et pur ceo il mytt le case de lobligation lou il fuit fayt per 3. ou 4. <jointment et severallment >¹ cy en cest case le suist doyt estre verz eux toutz joyntment ou verz un severallment. Et auxi il mytt le case lou un letter dattourney fuit fayt a 3. et ii. de eux font lyvere, ceo nest garrante.

Et pur lauter mater fuit semble a luy, et auxi all Seignior *Bawdwyn*, que quant lez vii. constitute le viii. persone en ceo ilz fount assetz bien, pur ceo que il fuit estrange a eux queux luy constat etc.

---

¹ *Reading unclear.*

36. ANON.

Common Pleas. Cf. Caryll's report of the case put in the Inner Temple concerning the city of York, below, p. 395, no. 62.

Note by SHELLEY that if the king by his letters patent grants to the mayor and commonalty of Lincoln that they should have such like liberties as the city of London, this is a good grant, and by this grant they shall have the like liberties.[1] But if the king grants them that they shall have such customs as London has, this grant is invalid, because there cannot be a custom except by ancient continuance, and that cannot begin at the present day by grant. Therefore if the king grants someone by his letters patent that his land shall be according to the custom of gavelkind or borough English, or grants to the inhabitants of such and such a vill that, if anyone there should be indebted to another, the creditor should attach the goods of the person who is indebted to his debtor (as the custom of London is), this will not be valid. The reason sufficiently appears. He said that the custom of gavelkind was before the conquest.

37. ANON.

Common Pleas, 1535/39.

A case was moved by *Mountague*, which was as follows: authority was given to eight or nine persons to found a chantry and to make constitutions and ordinances at any time for the establishment of the same chantry. Afterwards seven of them appointed the eighth person to be the master of the same chantry. Whether this is good or not is the question. There are two questions in this case: (1) where the authority was given to the eight or nine and seven did the act, whether this is well done or not; (2) the other question is, when seven persons make the eighth person the master of the same chantry, [is this good?].

As to the first question, SHELLEY thought that the act which the seven persons did was not authorised by the grant made to them. For this he put the case of the bond made by three or four jointly and severally: in that case the suit ought to be against all of them jointly, or against one of them severally.[2] He also put the case where a letter of attorney was made to three, and two of them made livery: that is not warranted.

As to the other matter, it was thought by him, and also my lord BALDWIN [C.J.], that when the seven constitute the eighth person [master] they do well enough, because he was a stranger to those who appointed him etc.

---

[1] YB Hil. 2 Hen. VII, fo. 13, pl. 16, *per* Rede sjt.
[2] Cf. YB Pas. 27 Hen. VIII, fo. 6, pl. 19.

[38]

[*Fo. 30*] Un case fuit move per *Knyghtley* all barre en le Comen Banke, que fuit tiel: un done en tayle est fayt reservaunt a luy xii. d. del rent pur toutz manerz de services salvo regali servicio. Le question depend sur cest paroll salvo regali servicio.

Et le Seignior *Bawdwyn* tenoyt le ley en cesti case destre en tyel maner: que a le comen ley devaunt lestatut de Quia emptores terrarum si home ust fayt feffment en fee et ust fayt nul reservation de null maner de tenure, donquez le ley ust creat un tenure, scilicet que le feffe tiendra del feffour per autielx servicez come le feffour tient ouster, mez sil ust reserve un tenure donquez le feffe tiendra del feffour per lez servicez issint reservez sur le tenure, et come le ley fuit donquez en sembleable maner est le ley aprez a cest jour sur un done en tayle. Donquez, coment cest paroll salvo serra prise: ou il serra prise que le feffe tiendra del donour per ascunz auterz servicez que per lez servicez issint expressez et reservez? Amytt que il tient per auterz servicez que per ceux queux fueront reservez, que sont milx parolx de fayer un tenure mez tenendum et reddendum? Mez salvo nest ascun paroll de fayer un tenure.

Et Seignior *Bawdwyn* [dit] que ceux parolx salvo regali servicio serront prisez que le done ferra autielx servicez come le donour fist devaunt le done, sil tenoyt per ascunz auterz servicez que per ceux queux sont reservez perenter le donour et le done. Et tielx servicez come le donour puissoyt faire per un debyte, toutz tielx servicez le done ferra per reason de ceux parolx salvo etc. ouster a cesti que le donour tyent, come de fayer sewt a son courte, ceo il poit fayer per un debyte, de payer rent, ceo il poit fayer per un debyte. Mez de fayer homage, cest service ne poit estre fayt mez en proper person, et pur ceo le done ne poit ceo fayer, causa qua supra. Et issint il entend ceux parolx salvo etc. Et il dit ouster que ceux parolx salvo regali servicio serra entend servicium militare.

Shelley tenoyt et dit que ceux parolx salvo etc. serront prise que le done per reson de ceo ferra ascunz auterz servicez que le donour fist ouster, a mesme le donour: quod quere.[1]

[39]

[*Fo. 30v*] Nota que fuit tenuez en le Comen Banke que tout soyt que proces dutlagarie gist en un capias ad satisfaciendum, en quell action gist que un capias et aprez un exigend, que ne serra ascun proclamation en le countie ou le

---

[1] *Four words follow, which resemble:* lesydes chose servic' reserved.

38. NOTE

Common Pleas, between 1535 (when Baldwin became C.J.) and *c.* 1538/9 (when Knightley retired from the bar).

A case was moved by *Knightley* at the bar in the Common Bench, which was as follows: a gift in tail is made reserving to the donor 12d. rent for all manner of services, 'saving royal service' (*salvo regali servicio*). The question depends upon these words *salvo regali servicio*.

And my lord BALDWIN [C.J.] held the law in this case to be in the following manner: at common law, before the statute *Quia emptores terrarum*,[1] if someone made a feoffment in fee and made no reservation of any kind of tenure, the law would have created a tenure, namely that the feoffee should hold of the feoffor by such services as those by which the feoffor held over; but if he reserved a tenure, then the feoffee would hold of the feoffor by the services thus reserved upon the tenure. And as the law was then, so in like manner is the law at the present day upon a gift in tail. Now, then, how shall this word *salvo* be taken? Shall it be taken to mean that the feoffee shall hold of the donor by some other services than the services thus expressed and reserved? And, admit that he holds by other services than those which were reserved, what better words are there to create a tenure than *tenendum* and *reddendum*? But *salvo* is no word to make a tenure.

And the lord BALDWIN said that these words *salvo regali servicio* shall be taken to mean that the donee shall do such services as the donor did before the gift, if he held by any services other than those which are reserved between the donor and the donee. And such services as the donor might perform by deputy—such as doing suit to his court, which he may do by a deputy, or paying rent, which he may do by a deputy—the donee shall perform all such services over, to the person of whom the donor holds, by reason of these words *salvo etc.* But doing homage is a service which cannot be done except in one's own person, and therefore the donee may not do it, for the above reason. And so he understood these words *salvo etc.* And he further said that these words *salvo regali servicio* shall be understood as knight-service (*servicium militare*).

SHELLEY held and said that these words *salvo etc.* shall be taken to mean that the donee by reason thereof shall do some other services to the same donor as the donor did over: but query this.

39. ANON.

Cf. *Lord Monteagle's Case* (undated) in Yorke, above, p. 241, no. 419.

Note that it was held in the Common Bench that although process of outlawry lies on a *capias ad satisfaciendum*, in which action there lies but one *capias* and afterwards an exigent, there shall be no proclamation in the county

---

[1] 18 Edw. I, *Quia emptores terrarum* (*SR* i. 106).

partie est demurrant. Et le reson est pur ceo que le proclamation ne fueront ordeynez mez all intent que le partie avera notice del sute ew envers luy, et ceo nest requisite en capias ad satisfaciendum entaunt que per le pleder et le condempnation le partie ad assetz sufficient notice del sute ewe envers luy, et pur ceo il est hors del mischeff del comen ley pur que lestatut fuit fayt.

[40]

Nota que *Mountagwe*, Cheff Justice, dit que si lappellaunt soyt nonsue en appelle que lez abbettourz ne serront enquerez, et silz sont il serra mez de bene esse, que ne serra appurpose, for it shall nowther do gud nor hurte. Et il dit ouster que ilz ne serra enqueres mez pur insufficiencye del lappellant, et le lew serra enquere lou labbettment fuit fayt.

[41]

[*Fo. 40v*] Nota que lorder est en le Starre Chamber que sur un manyfest perjurye commytte que il ou ilz serront agarde a le prison del Flete la de remayner quousque ilz ount fayt fyne pur lour mysdemeanour et auxi satisfye et recompence le partie que est dampnefye et greve per lour fauxe searment ou perjurye, et pur le weareng dez paperes ceo remayne ouster sur le discretion del seigniour chauncelour dengleterre etc.

Nota que un home que fuit appel Boune, que fuit demurrant en Darbyshyer et un manyfest perjurour[1] en le matter que fuit en controversye perenter John Vernon de mesme le payez et un Sharpe, fuit commytte al Flete et delonque a le pyllorye en le Palayz Yard ovesque un paper myse sur son test escrite en graundez letterz, pur wyllfyll perjurye etc.

[42]

Nota que experiens en Banke le Roy est que lou un home esteant en execution sur un condempnation port brefe derrour en mesme le banke que la il doyt trover suertyez a tyel entent et purpose que si le jugement soyt aferme lez

---

[1] perjurye.

where the party is living.[1] The reason is because the proclamations were only ordained with the intention that the party should have notice of the suit had against him, and this is not requisite in a *capias ad satisfaciendum* inasmuch as by the pleading and the condemnation the party has had sufficient enough notice of the suit against him, and therefore he is outside the mischief of the common law for which the statute was made.

40. NOTE

King's Bench, in or after 1539 (when Mountague became C.J.K.B.).

Note that MOUNTAGUE, Chief Justice, said that if the appellant is nonsuited in an appeal the abettors shall not be enquired into, and if they are it is only *de bene esse*, which is immaterial, 'for it shall neither do good nor hurt'.[2] And he said further that they shall not be enquired into except for insufficiency of the appellant, and the place shall be enquired into where the abetting occurred.

41. BOUNE'S CASE

Note that it is the procedure in the Star Chamber upon a manifest perjury committed that he or they shall be awarded to the prison of the Fleet, there to remain until they have made fine for their misdemeanour and also satisfied and compensated the party who is damaged and aggrieved by their false oath or perjury; and as to the wearing of papers, that is left over to the discretion of the lord chancellor of England etc.

Note that a man called Boune, who lived in Derbyshire and was a manifest perjuror in the matter which was in controversy between John Vernon of the same region and one Sharpe, was committed to the Fleet and from thence to the pillory in the Palace Yard, with a paper set upon his head inscribed in large letters 'For wilful perjury' etc.

42. NOTE

King's Bench.

Note that it is the experience in the King's Bench that where someone, being in execution upon a condemnation,[3] brings a writ of error in the same bench,

---

[1] I.e. in accordance with the statute of 6 Hen. VIII, c. 4 (*SR* iii. 126).
[2] Words in English.   [3] I.e. a judgment to pay money.

suertyez doyent satysfyer et payer le partie plaintife que primez recover, quar cesti que port le brefe derrour esteant une foytz horce del execution ne serra jammez en execution pur cest chose pur que il fuit primez en execution, et pur cest only reason lez suertyes [doyent][1] come devaunt etc.

[43]

[*Fo. 41*] Nota per Mr *Bromley*, justice dassysse, que en certenz casez pur le proffe dun chose [destre][2] voyer est requysyt que deux wittnessez et en certenz casez forsque solement un wittness. Il est requisite destre deus wyttnessez en tyelz casez lou un jugment est de proceder sur lour depositionz et declarationz. Mez en tyelx casez lou null jugment est de proceder sur ceo mez tauntsolement denformer un jure ou enquest accordant a son notyce, la nest requysyt daver plusourz wyttnessez que un etc.

[44]

Nota que fuit tenues en le Comen Banke que si un feme[3] soyt entytle destre endow, et communication est ewe enter leyre et le feme esteant sa mere que el avera un rent issuant hors de le dit terre[i] de quell el est endowablle, le quell doyt estre paye a deus jours, et devant le primer jour del payment le feme port son brefe de dower, le question est ore si tyel agrement ew enter le feme et leyre est sufficyent mater destopper le feme de porter son brefe de dower saunz acceptaunz del rent accordaunt a lour agrement <ou nemi>.[i] Mez si le feme ust accepte le rent, loppinion del tout le courte fuit que donquez le feme serra estoppe. Et ouster fuit agree per le court que si le rent soyt issuant del terre del quell el est endowablle, que cest graunt est assetz bon saunz fayt, mez si le rent soyt issuant horse dauter terre que tyel rent ne vaut saunz fayt.

---

[1] *Reading unclear.*
[2] *Conjectural: word lost in corner.*
[3] home *del.*

he ought to find sureties, to the intent and purpose that if the judgment is affirmed the sureties ought to satisfy and pay the plaintiff who first recovered; for the person who brought the writ of error, being once out of execution, shall never be in execution again for this thing for which he was first in execution, and, for this reason only, sureties ought to be found as above etc.

43. NOTE

Norfolk circuit, after 1542.

Note by Master BROMLEY, justice of assize,[1] that in certain cases for the proof of a thing to be true it is requisite that there be two witnesses, and in certain cases only one witness. It is requisite that there be two witnesses in those cases where a judgment is to proceed upon their depositions and declarations. But in cases where no judgment is to proceed thereon, but it is only to inform a jury or inquest according to his knowledge, there it is not requisite to have more than one witness etc.

44. ANON.

Common Pleas, 1535/45.

Note that it was held in the Common Bench[2] that if a woman is entitled to be endowed, and an informal agreement[3] is made between the heir and the woman (being his mother) that she should have a rent issuing out of the said land from which she is endowable, which ought to be paid at two days; and before the first day of payment the woman brings her writ of dower, the question now is whether this agreement between the woman and the heir is sufficient matter to estop the woman from bringing her writ of dower, without acceptance of rent in accordance with their agreement, or not. (If the woman had accepted the rent, the opinion of the whole court was that the woman would then be estopped.) It was further agreed by the court that if the rent is issuing out of the land from which she is endowable, this grant is good enough without a deed; but if the rent is issuing out of other land, such rent is invalid without a deed.

---

[1] Bromley went the Norfolk circuit from 1542 until his death. He was previously (for two years) on the Midland.
[2] The sentence so begins, but turns into a question.
[3] For the word 'communication' see 119 Selden Soc. 153, n. 1.

Et une divercite fuit prise per le Seigniour *Bawedwyn* perenter partition et eschange et cest case que est ore en question. Quar un partition fayt perenter coparsenerz, le ley eux compeller de issint fayer, et sur un partition fayt si le parte de lun coparsener soyt meynez que le parte de lauter coparsener < el avera >[i] en consideration de ceo cestui coparsener que ad le greynder parte graunt un rent a lauter coparsener, cest graunt est bon saunz fayt, et nient obstant que cestui coparsener a que il est graunt ne ceo accept, uncore est assetz bon. Et son reson fuit pur ceo que chescun deux fuit seisi del tout le terre devaunt le graunt en tyel maner come joyntenauntz sount etc. Et pur leschaunge nest bon quousque chescun deux ad enter en auter terre, quell entre est un perfection et execution de leschange. Quere ouster.

[45]

[*Fo. 41v*] Nota que le cource est en < le Comen >[1] Banke < le roy >[i] est lou home est prise sur legerment suspection la il serra maynprise corpz pur corpz. Mez lou il est prise ove le maynour ou auterment sur un graunde ou vehement suspection, la en cest case il est maynpernable pur certen summez dargent accordaunt a le discrescion del courte. Et issint nota le divercite.

[46]

Un question fuit move en le Comen Banke que fuit en tyel fourme, scilicet lou un home ust fayt devyse dez certen terrez sur condition que le lesse ne alyenera, resygnera ou all ferme dymyttera, et puis le lesse fyst trois homez sez executours et per son volunte devyse son terme a lun de cez executours: ou cest devyse fuit deinz le compas dez parolx avaundytz? Et semble fuit per lez justices que ne fuit. Quere ouster.

Et pur ceo il est destre remember pur lendenture del Jekelour pur le lez del mon[2] garrayne.

---

[1] *Del.*
[2] *Reading uncertain.*

And a distinction was taken by my lord BALDWIN between a partition and exchange and this case which is now in question. For a partition made between coparceners is something which the law compels them to make, and if when a partition is made the share of one of the coparceners is less than the share of the other, and in consideration thereof the coparcener who has the greater share grants a rent to the other coparcener, this grant is good without a deed; and it is perfectly good even if the coparcener to whom it is granted does not accept it. His reason was that each of them was seised of the whole land before the grant. in the same way as joint tenants are etc. In the case of an exchange, however, it is not good until each of them has entered in the other land, which entry is a perfection and execution of the exchange. Query further.

45. NOTE

King's Bench.

Note that it is the course in the King's Bench that where someone is taken upon light suspicion he shall be mainprised body for body. But where he is taken with the mainour, or otherwise upon great or vehement suspicion, in that case he is mainpernable for certain sums of money according to the court's discretion. Thus note the distinction.

46. ANON.

Common Pleas.

A question was moved in the Common Bench, which was in this form: where someone makes a devise[1] of certain lands upon condition that the lessee should not alien, resign or to farm let, and afterwards the lessee makes three men his executors and by his will devises his term to one of his executors: is this devise within the compass of the aforesaid words? It seemed to the justices that it was not. Query further.

This is to be remembered for Jekelour's indenture, for the lease of my warren.

---

[1] Perhaps 'demise'.

[47]

Un question fuit move en le Commen Banke per *Towneshend*, que lou home declare per son volunte que son terre serra vendue aprez le morte sa feme que en cest clause tout soyt que il nad done ascun chose a sa feme uncore sa feme per un resonable implication avera cest terre durant sa vye. Et issint fuit rule en Bank le Roy per le Seigniour *Fyneux*, Cheff Justyce Dengleterre. Le quell jugement et rwle fuit afferme per Justice *Shelley* destre bon ley etc.

Et un auter mater fuit move en cest case, ou cestui a que cest auctoryte fuit done a vender poet ceo vender meyntenant ou il doyt taryer tanque aprez le mort le feme? Et fuit semble per *Shelley* que nient obstant il poyt vender mayntenant, uncore cest bargayne et sale ne prendra ascun effect tanque aprez le mort le feme etc. Quere ouster.

[48]

Casus en le Comen Banke.

Deus joyntenantz dun terme dez annez, lun de eux graunt son interest a un auter sur condition, et puis le grauntor fayt cez executours et devye, et puis le condition est enfreynt, le executours del grauntor enter pur le condition enfreynt, ou en cest case le joyncture soyt revyve ou nemi, ou lez executors en cest case retayneront le terre a lour proper use et commodyte?

Et le melyour oppinion[i] dez justices en cest case fuit que lez executors averont le terre a lour proper oeps demesne. Et tout lour reson fuit pur ceo que le condition fuit enfreynt puis le morte del grauntor. Auterment le ley ust este si le condition ust este enfreynt [*fo. 42*] en le vye del grauntor et il donquez ust enter, donquez le joyncture ust este revyve, et sil aprez ceo morust son joynt graunte avera lestat per le survyvour.

[49]

Casus en le Comen Banke.

Home fayt lez a un auter dun mesuage ovesque lez appurtenaunces, le quell mesuage ad este del auncient temps continue destre occupye ove x. vel xx. acrez

47. ANON.

Common Pleas, 1540/48, perhaps 1542.[1]

A question was moved in the Common Bench by *Townshend*, that where someone declared by his will that his land should be sold after his wife's death, even though he has not [expressly] given anything to his wife, nevertheless his wife shall by reasonable implication have this land during her life. So it was ruled in the King's Bench by the lord FYNEUX, Chief Justice of England,[2] which judgment and rule was affirmed by Justice SHELLEY to be good law etc. Another matter was moved in this case: may the person to whom this authority was given to sell make the sale at once, or ought he to wait until after the wife's death? It was thought by SHELLEY that, even though he may sell at once, the bargain and sale shall nevertheless take no effect until after the wife's death etc. Query further.

48. ANON.

Common Pleas.

Two joint tenants of a term of years; one of them grants his interest to another upon condition; and afterwards the grantor appoints his executors and dies; then the condition is broken, and the grantor's executors enter for breach of the condition: is the jointure revived in this case, or not, or shall the executors in this case retain the land to their own use and benefit?

The better opinion of the justices in this case was that the executors should have the land to their own use. And the whole of their reason was that the condition was broken after the grantor's death. The law would have been otherwise if the condition had been broken in the grantor's lifetime, and then he had entered, for then the jointure would have been revived; and if he had died after that his joint grantee would have had the estate by survivorship.

49. ANON.

Common Pleas, 1545. Also reported by Gell, Pas. 36 [& 37] Hen. VIII, fo. 59. Cf. same point in Bro. Abr., *Feoffments*, pl. 53 (1531/32); *Leases*, pl. 55 (1539/40). Perhaps continued in no. 52.

Someone made a lease to another of a messuage with the appurtenances, which messuage had been continually occupied since old times with ten or

[1] Cf. *Anon.* (1542) Gell's reports, Mich. 33 [?*recte* 34] Hen. VIII, fo. 6v, where Shelley J. held that a devise to the testator's son and heir after the death of the testator's wife was effective to give the wife a life estate. Shelley J. there said that the point had been decided by the King's Bench the previous term. Cf. also Bro. Abr., *Devise*, pl. 48 (same point, 1537/38).   [2] I.e. between 1495 and 1525.

de terre, reservaunt xx. s. del rent, ou ycy en cest case lez x. ou xx. acrez del terre passera ou nemi, cest le question.

Et mon Seigniour Mountague, Cheff Justyce del Comen Banke, semble que le terre ne poit passer <ove le mesuage>[i] per ceux parolles cum pertinenciis, quar il dissoyt que il est un order et rwle en le ley en quell sorte home demandera ascun chose come appert per le register, et la appert quil demandera chescun chose in specie come il est, scilicet le maner, terre, pree, et sic de singulis, <a lentent que le tenant may well be asserte the t. what thynge he shall take answer,[1]>[i] mez un fyne ne poit estre leve dun tenement mez en le lewe de cest paroll tenementes mesuages serront myse eynz. Donquez en tyel sorte homez doyent departer per lour donez ou feffmentes per lour nosmez in specie come ilz sont appellez. Donques quant home fayt leez dun mesuage cum pertinenciis, tout sout que le x. ou xx. acrez ount este use toutz foytz daler ove le mesuage, uncore pur ceo que ilz ne sount parcell del mesuage ne fuit le messuage <ne conuez per le nosme del mesuage,>[i] ceux parolx cum pertinenciis ne sount aptez parolx de fayer le terre de passer, nient obstant [que] launcient rent soyt reserve, uncore le terre ne passera, nient obstant auxi que le meaneng dez parties soyt issint daver ceo. Uncore il voyt agreer que en un fyne lentent dez parties serra prise, come si home leve un fyne de xx. acrez de terre, xx. acrez de pree, xx. acrez de pasture, et cestui que leva cest fyne ad c. acrez de terre, c. acrez de pree, c. acrez de pasture, ore ycy en cest case le meaneng et lentent del conusor serra prise et entend, queux acrez et terrez passeront per cest fyne. Mez ceo est destre entend lou sount auterz terrez conuez per mesme le nosme come ceux terrez sount dez queux le fyne est leve, mez en le case lou home graunt ou lessa un chose que ne poit passer per mesme le nosme yt is graunted ou lett by ycy lentent ou le reservation del rent ne poit causer ceo de passer, mez tyellz chosez queux sont parcell ou appendant ou incident a lez chosez grauntez, come si home fayt feffment del maner cum pertinenciis nul auter chose passera mes solement avowesonz, comenz et auterz tielx. Et issint si un graunt un mesuage cum pertinenciis, nul auter chose passera mez tyelx chosez queux fount le mesuage, come lez bakhowsez, stablez, le petyt terre que est devaunt le huyse del mesuage, ou le garden, et nemi le close ou le terre, pur ceo que ilz ne poyent passer per le nosme del mesuage <ne sount conuez per tyel nosme>.[i]

Justyce S. in auter oppynion, et son reson fuit que lentent del lessour fuit daver ceo passer et auxi le rent <que fuit reserve,>[i] <quar le gretter>[2] in respect del terre et son acte serra prise etc.

---

[1] *Reading unclear.*
[2] *Reading uncertain.*

twenty acres of land, reserving 20s. rent. The question here in this case is: do the ten or twenty acres of land pass, or not?

And my lord MOUNTAGUE, Chief Justice of the Common Bench,[1] thought that the land could not pass with the messuage by these words *cum pertinenciis*.[2] He said that there is an order and rule in law in what sort one shall demand anything. This appears by the Register, and it appears there that one shall demand everything *in specie* as it is, namely the manor, land, meadow, and likewise everything else, to the intent that the tenant may well be ascertained what thing he has to answer for. However, a fine may not be levied of a tenement, but, instead of this word 'tenements', 'messuages' shall be put in.[3] Now, then, in the same way ought men to part with things in their gifts or feoffments, by their specific names that they are called by. Therefore, when someone makes a lease of a messuage *cum pertinenciis*, even though the ten or twenty acres have always been used to go with the messuage, yet because they are not parcel of the messuage, and were not the messuage, nor known by the name of the messuage, these words *cum pertinenciis* are not apt words to cause the land to pass. And even though the old rent is reserved, still the land shall not pass, notwithstanding also that the meaning of the parties was to have it so. Nevertheless he would agree that in a fine the intention of the parties shall be taken. For instance, if someone levies a fine of twenty acres of land, twenty acres of meadow, and twenty acres of pasture, and he who levied this fine has one hundred acres of land, one hundred acres of meadow, and one hundred acres of pasture, here in this case the meaning and intention of the conusor shall be taken and understood as to which acres and lands should pass by this fine. But that is to be understood where there are other lands known by the same name as these lands whereof the fine is levied, whereas in the case where someone grants or leases a thing which cannot pass by the same name that it is granted or let by, here the intention (or the reservation of the rent) cannot cause it to pass, but only such things as are parcel of or appendant or incident to the things granted. Thus if someone makes a feoffment of a manor *cum pertinenciis*, nothing else will pass but advowsons, commons and other such things. Likewise if someone grants a messuage *cum pertinenciis*, nothing else will pass but such things as make the messuage, such as the bakehouses, stables, the little piece of land which is in front of the door of the messuage, or the garden, and not the close or the land, because they cannot pass by the name of the messuage and are not known by such name.

S[HELLEY] J. was of another opinion; and his reason was that it was the lessor's intention to have it pass; Also the rent which was reserved was the greater in respect of the land, and his act shall be understood accordingly etc.

---

[1] The like opinion is attributed by Gell to Willoughby and Browne JJ., not mentioning Mountague C.J.

[2] Cf. *Partridge* v. *Straunge* (1553) Plowd. 77v at 85v, where Mountague C.J. said this was a 'grounde'.   [3] Cf. Caryll, below, p. 400, no. 70 (1528/29).

[50]

[*Fo. 43v*] Serjant Harryes en le Comen Banke demande de *Shelley*, Justyce, que si un home embleyer son terre et puis per son testament devyse le terre a un estraunge, le question fuit ou le devyse avera lez embleymentes ou <nemi semble>¹ lez executors le devisour.

Et semble fuit per le dit *Shelley* que lez executors le devysor averont lex embleymentz et nemi le devyse, et ne fuit semble a le case ou homeⁱ embleya son terre et puis fayt feffment de ceo, en cest case le feffe avera lez embleymentes pur ceo que il prent le terre ove toutz commodytes et advauntages etc. Quere ouster.

[51]

Nota que Seigniour *Mountague*, Cheff Justyce de le Comen Banke, dysoyt en le Sterre Chamber pur clere ley que si lez executors del ascun home trove un chyst en le meason lour testatour ove evydens lokyd que ilz ne poient medler ove cest chest, mez silz trovont le chest open donquez ilz poyent ceo prender. Et issint nota le divercite lou le chest est loked et lou il est open.

[52]

Nota que le dit seigniour en le Comen Banke tenoyt un divercite enter tenementum et mesuagium, quar tenementum est id quod tenetur, et ceo poit estre un meason et terre, mez mesuagium est un meson tantum saunz ascun terre. Quere ouster.

[53]

Nota pur experience en le Comen Banke que si un action de dett soyt port vers un auter sur un obligation pur performauns dez covenantes comprisez en un endenture, si le defendant voet pleder que le <condition>² obligation est endorse sur tyel condition come ut supra, et pleder ouster que il ad perfourme toutes lex covenantes comprisez en lendenture, et ne monstre <le>³ quell lez

¹ *Del.*
² *Del.*
³ *Del.*

50. ANON.

Common Pleas, 1540/48.

Serjeant *Harris* in the Common Bench asked SHELLEY J. this question: if someone sowed his land, and then by his testament devised the land to a stranger, shall the devisee have the emblements or the devisor's executors?

And it seemed to the said SHELLEY that the devisor's executors should have the emblements and not the devisee; and it was not like the case where someone sowed his land and then makes a feoffment thereof—in which case the feoffee shall have the emblements, because he takes the land with all commodities and advantages etc. Query further.

51. ANON.

Star Chamber, *c.* 1545/50.

Note that my lord MOUNTAGUE, Chief Justice of the Common Bench, said in the Star Chamber as clear law that if the executors of any man find a locked chest in their testator's house with evidence[1] they may not meddle with this chest; but if they find the chest open they make take it. Thus note the distinction: where the chest is locked and where it is open.

52. NOTE

Common Pleas, *c.* 1545/50. Related to no. 49.

Note that his said lordship, in the Common Bench, held there to be a distinction between *tenementum* and *mesuagium*; for a tenement is that which is held (*tenementum est id quod tenetur*), and that may be a house and land, whereas *mesuagium* is a house only without land. Query further.

53. NOTE

Common Pleas. Cf. *Anon.* (1541/42) Bro. Abr., *Conditions*, pl. 198; *Covenants*, pl. 35.[2]

Note for experience in the Common Bench that if an action of debt is brought against someone else upon a bond for performance of the covenants comprised in an indenture, and the defendant wishes to plead that the bond is

---

[1] I.e. muniments of title.
[2] A reversal of opinion since *Wellys* v. *Mompesson* (1528–29), above, p. 318, no. 13.

conditionz sont in specie, cest plee ne vawt ryenz, et si ple plaintife sur ceo demurre il recovera et le defendant serra condempne etc.

[54]

[*Fo. 44*] Nota que fuit agree en le Comen Banke que sur un action de dett port sur un contracte verz un auter, si le defendant tender son ley prist daffayer mayntenant, la en cest case le plaintife ne serra nonsue. Mez si le defendant tender son ley et ad jour done a luy de ceo fayer, la en cest case le plaintife poit estre nonsue. Et issint nota le divercite lou le defendant est prist de fayer son ley mayntenaunt et lou le defendant prent jour de fayer son ley.

[55]¹

Levesque del Wynchester disoyt apertement en le Chauncerye que le ley consyst en quater principall poyntes, and precipit, and prohibet, and permittit, and punit.

[56]

Casus en le Comen Banke termino Trinitatis anno primo E. vi^{ti}.

[*Fo. 45*] Home fayt un letter dattorney a un auter a delyver lyvere et seisin a luy et a cez heyres, ou ceo fuit un done del terre, ou auterment cest lyvere et seisin emply en luy mesme un done, ou nemi?

Et per mon seigniour *Mountegewe*, Cheff Justyce del mesme le banke, ceo ne fuit ascun done de le terre, quar ilz dysoyent que un lyvere de seisin ne poit estre fayt mez en respect dun done per matter en escripture ou auterment per paroll et en ceux cases le letter dattourney nest a ascun auter purpose mes de perfeter et dexecuter le done ou le feffment presydent. Semble a le case del graunt del revercion et lattournement del particuler tenaunt, que ne done ascun chose per son attournement mez de perfeter le graunt presydent. Et le Seigniour *Mountagwe* dyt ouster que si home scanne le perolx byen mentiones en le letter

---

¹ *Added to the foregoing in a different hand.*

endorsed with that condition, and to plead further that he has performed all
the covenants comprised in the indenture, but does not show in detail (*in
specie*) what the conditions are, this plea is invalid; and if the plaintiff demurs
upon it the defendant shall be condemned etc.

54. NOTE

Common Pleas.

Note that it was agreed in the Common Bench that if an action of debt is
brought upon a contract against another, and the defendant tenders his law and
is ready to do it forthwith, the plaintiff may not in this case be nonsuited. But if
the defendant tenders his law and has a day given him to do it, in this case the
plaintiff may be nonsuited. Thus note the distinction: where the defendant is
ready to do his law forthwith and where he takes a day to do his law.

55. NOTE

Chancery, undated.

The bishop of Winchester[1] said openly in the Chancery that the law consists
in four principal points: it prescribes, and prohibits, and permits, and punishes
(*praecipit, et prohibet, et permittit, et punit*).

56. ANON.

Common Pleas, Trin. 1547.

Someone makes a letter of attorney to another to deliver livery and seisin to
him and his heirs: is this a gift of the land, or does this livery and seisin imply in
itself a gift, or not?

According to my lord MOUNTAGUE, Chief Justice of the same bench,[2] [and
another judge],[3] this was no gift of the land; for they said that a livery of seisin
cannot be made except in respect of a gift by matter in writing or else by parol,
and in these cases the letter of attorney is to no other purpose than to perfect
and execute the preceding gift or feoffment. It is like the case of the grant of a
reversion and the attornment of the particular tenant, who does not give
anything by his attornment but perfects the preceding grant. And my lord

[1] Presumably Stephen Gardiner LL.D., bishop of Winchester 1531–51, 1553–55. The note is
added in a slightly later hand and might possibly refer to Gardiner's own chancellorship (1553–55).
[2] The Common Bench referred to in the headnote.
[3] There are two references below to the opinion being in the plural.

dattourney ne sount ascunz parolz deinz mesme le letter del done mez solement
ad deliberandum, le quell nest ascun paroll dell done. Et donquez en chescun
done il doyt aver un donour et un pernour, et en cest case nest ascun donour, et
pur ceo cest lyvere et seisin fayt per celuy a que letter dattourney ne done ascun
chose a luy a que le lyvere et seisin est fayt. Et auxi cestui que fayt le lyvere et
seisin nest my forsque un offycer solement dexecuter et de perfeter cest chose en
luy a que le feffment ou le done devaunt fuit fayte, et issint ilz ambydeux
concludont que per le lyvere et seisin null chose de le terre passera a cestui a
que le lyvere fuit fayt entaunt que ne fuit ascun done ou feffment presydent fayt
etc. Et en le case del letter dattourney celuy que ceo fayt poit ceo
countermaunder quant luy plerra etc. Quere ouster.

[57]

Poutrelles case.

Home vende son terre a un auter per fayt indent pur certen sommez dargent,
et est en le forme de le dit indenture en un proviso que si le vendor paya taunt
dargent a le vende devant tyel jour que donquez toutz estatez et conveyances
queux sount faytz serront a luse del vendor, et il y ad un auter covenant del
parte le vendor que sil vende mesme le terre a ascun auter que a le < feffe >¹
vende[i] et que donquez le feffe ou vende serra seisi a luse del dit vende, et puis il
ceo vende a un estraunge, que en cest case[i] per Justyce Halez cest matter soune
mez en covenaunt, quar il jamez navera le terre.

[58]

Casus en le Comen Banke termino Michaelis anno regni Regis Edwardi vi^{ti} primo.

Home fayt les dun acre de terre pur terme del xl. annes, le terme de comenser
mayntenant sur le les, et puis il fayt un auter les a un auter < pur terme de xxx.
annez >¹ de comenser le prochen jour apres, et puis le primer lesse purchas le
revercion de le lessour, ou per cest purchas le seconde < les est voyde ou
bon >² lesse avera son leas ou nemi, cest le question.
  Loppynion del Seigniour *Mountague*, Cheff Justyce del Comen Banke, fuit
que si le les ust este bon en le comencement que donquez le seconde lesse averoyt

---

¹ *Del.*
² *Del.*

MOUNTAGUE further said that if one scans well the words mentioned in the letter of attorney there are no words of gift in the same letter but only of livery (*ad deliberandum*), which is no word of gift. Now, then, in every gift there must be a donor and a taker, and in this case there is no donor, and therefore this livery and seisin made by the person to whom the letter of attorney was made does not give anything to him to whom the livery and seisin is made. Moreover, the person who makes the livery and seisin is only an officer to execute and perfect this thing in the person to whom the feoffment or gift was already made. And so they both concluded that by the livery and seisin nothing of the land shall pass to the person to whom the livery was made, inasmuch as there was no preceding gift or feoffment made etc. And in the case of the letter of attorney the person who made it may countermand it whenever he pleases etc. Query further.

57. POWTRELL'S CASE[1]

Common Pleas, *c.* 1549/50.

Someone sold his land to another by deed indented, for certain sums of money, and one of the terms of the said indenture (in a proviso) was that if the vendor should pay so much money to the vendee before such and such a day then all estates and conveyances which are made shall be to the use of the vendor; and there is another covenant on the side of the vendor that if he should sell the same land to anyone other than the vendee then the feoffee or vendee should be seised to the use of the said vendee; and afterwards he sold it to a stranger: in this case, according to HALES J.[2] this matter sounds only in covenant, for he shall never have the land.

58. ANON.

Common Pleas, Mich. 1547. Cf. *Anon.* (1550) BL MS. Hargrave 4, fo. 105, where the same points are laid down by Mountague C.J.

Someone makes a lease of an acre of land for a term of forty years, the term to commence forthwith upon the lease, and afterwards he makes another lease to another for a term of thirty years to commence the next day after, and then the first lessee purchases the reversion from the lessor. The question is: shall the second lessee have his lease, in view of this purchase, or not?

The opinion of my lord MOUNTAGUE, Chief Justice of the Common Bench, was that if the lease had been good at the commencement then the second lessee

---

[1] Perhaps Nicholas Powtrell of Gray's Inn (adm. 1531), who became a serjeant in 1559.
[2] Appointed 20 May 1549.

son les. Mez il dysoyt pur ceo que il appert sur le case que sur le fesanz del seconde les que mesme le les comensera a tyel temps que il ne poit prender effect, pur cest cause cest seconde les fuit merement voyde. Et il dysoyt que si home fayt les pur terme de x. annez et aprez il fayt un auter les a un auter pur terme de xx. annez a comenser aprez cest x. annez determine et expire, cest seconde les est bon. Mez si le seconde les soyt fayt de comenser a tyel jour que ne poit estoyer ovesque le ley, donquez toutz foytz le seconde lez est voyde. Et il mytt ceux cases. Si home fayt les pur terme dannez et ne expresse a quel temps le les comensera, et puis il fayt un auter les etc. in cest terre de quell le primer les fuit fayt, et ne expresse quant il comensera, ycy en cest case ambydeux ceux lesses sount bonz pur ceo que le ley avera un resonable construction ycy que ambydeux ceux lesses prenderont effect come ilz poyent < most best > [1] estoyer ove reason etc. Semble a cest case come si home esteant patron de lesglyse de Dale graunt proximam advocationem ecclesie de mesme lesglyse a un auter, et puis il graunte a un auter proximam advocationem de le dit esglyse a un estrange, ore en cest case le ley avera cest resonable contruction que le seconde graunte navera le prochen advoydans mez ill avera le prochen advoydans aprez le primer advoydans, et issint etc. Admytt ycy en cest case que le seconde lez ust este bon, donquez cest purchas nust este ascun impedyment mez que il serra bon, mez pur ceo que il fuit voyde le purchace del revercion per le primer lesse neque auget neque minuit. Et il dysoyt que per cest purchas del revercion toutz choses sount alez et determinez perenter le lessor et le lesse. Mez tyelz chosez a lez benefytes dez estraunges, come rent charges et tyelx semblablez ovesque [que] le terme est charge, ceux chosez remayne styll nient obstant tyel purchase. Quere ouster. Et[2] le dit Seignour *Mountague* mytt cest case. Si soyt seigniour, mesne et tenant, le mesne devie, son heyre deynz age, lou le tenant paravale ust purchasse le seigniorie, que fuit le mesnaltye devaunt le mort del mesne, que le seigiour paramount navera le garde del mesne pur ceo que ne fuit ascun tenancye a luy, quar le seigniorie paramont est joyne all tenancye paravale. Quere ouster etc.

[59]

Un auter mater fuit move en le dit Comen Banke que si un abbe ou pryour fayt feffment dez terrez del son monasterye nient esteant parcell dez terrez del foundation, ove lassent del convent, que cest bon feffment. Mez si le feffment soyt dez terrez parcell dell foundation, donquez le foundour avoydera cest feffment per brefe de contra formam collationis.

[1] *Reading unclear.*
[2] *Reading uncertain.*

should have his lease. But he said that because it appeared upon the case that, on making the second lease, the same lease was to commence at a time when it could not take effect, for that reason this second lease was absolutely void. And he said that if someone makes a lease for a term of ten years, and afterwards makes another lease to someone else for a term of twenty years to commence after these ten years determined and expired, this second lease is good. But if the second lease is made to commence at such a day as is inconsistent with the law, then the second lease is always void. And he put the following cases. If someone makes a lease for a term of years and does not express at what time the lease shall commence, and afterwards he makes another lease etc. of this land whereof the first lease was made, and does not express when it shall commence, here in this case both these leases are good, because the law shall have a reasonable construction that both these leases shall take effect in such a way as can best stand with reason etc. It is like this case: if someone being patron of the church of Dale grants the next advowson of the church (*proximam advocationem ecclesiae*) of the same church to someone else, and then he grants *proximam advocationem* of the said church to a stranger, in this case the law shall have this reasonable contruction that the second grantee shall not have the next avoidance but shall have the next avoidance after the first, and so etc. However, admit here in this case that the second lease was once good, and then this purchase would not have been any impediment to its validity; but because it was void the purchase of the reversion by the first lessee makes no difference (*neque auget neque minuit*). And he said that by this purchase of the reversion everything is gone and determined between the lessor and the lessee. But such things as benefit strangers, such as rent-charges and such like with which the term is charged, those things still remain despite such purchase. (Query further.) And my said lord MOUNTAGUE [C.J.] put this case: if there be a lord, a mesne and a tenant, and the mesne dies, his heir being under age, where the tenant paravail had purchased the lordship—which was the mesnalty before the death of the mesne—the lord paramount shall not have the wardship of the mesne because there was no tenancy to him, for the lordship paramount is joined to the tenancy paravail. Query further etc.

59. ANON.

Common Pleas, probably Mich. 1547. Continued in no. 60.

Another matter was moved in the said Common Bench: if an abbot or prior, with the assent of the convent, makes a feoffment of lands of his monastery which are not part of the foundation lands, this is a good feoffment. But if the feoffment is of lands which are part of the foundation, the founder may avoid this feoffment by writ of *contra formam collationis*.

[60]

[*Fo. 46*] Le Seigniour *Mountague* dysoyt en le case prochen avandyt que le lessor ne serra jamez suffer de pleder que il navoyt ryenz en lez tenementes all temps de le lez fayt, mez le[1] lesse pledera ceo assetz bien si ne soyt per fayt indent, quell matter luy estoppera de ceo pleder.

[61]

Nota que fuit tenuez a lez assyses tenuez all Thetford per *Edwarde Saunders*, serjeant le roye, et un dez justycez del assyssez et gaole delyvere, pur bon ley, que si faylent jurours queux sount empanellez en un enquest sur un enformation either for defaut of apparauns ou auterment per occasyon dez chalengez, que lenquest[i] ne serra prise de sircumstantibus to fyll up the jure, pur ceo que lestatute ne voet ceo porter. Et auxi fuit tenuez la que si un juroir soyt demurrant en foreyn countye il covient a luy daver ascun terre en cest countye ou il est empanelle ou auterment il est bon cause del chalenge. Quere et stude lestatut.

[62]

Casus en le Comen Banke.

[*Fo. 46v*] Pur un waste fayt en terrez deinz auncient demean, ou pur cest waste fayt action dell wast gist ou nemi?

Et semble all Seigniour *Mountague*, Cheff Justyce de mesme le lewe, que cest action ne gist la pur ceo que le proces de cest action est somons, attachement et distrez, et si le defendant ne vyent my a le distres brefe issera horce a le viconte, lez parolles del quell est quod accedat ad locum vastatum, et ills en auncien demeane ne poyent escryer a le viconte, nient pluis que en quare impedit port sur un disturbanz all un avoweson en auncient demesne cest brefe ne gist la pur ceo que ilz ne poyent agarder brefe all evesque.

Mez semble fuit all *Shelley*, Justyce, pur laction de wast, que le brefe denquerer del wast poit estre agarde a lez offycers come bayllyffes et auterz tyelx queux sont appoyntez dexecuter et server proces la.

---

[1] *Written twice.*

60. NOTE

Common Pleas, probably Mich. 1547; continued from no. 59.

My lord MOUNTAGUE [C.J.] said in the case next above that the lessor shall never be allowed to plead that he had nothing in the tenements at the time when the lease was made, though the lessee may plead it well enough so long as it is not by deed indented, which would estop him from pleading it.

61. ANON.

Norfolk assizes at Thetford, c. 1547/50.

Note that at the assizes held at Thetford it was held as good law by *Edward Saunders*, king's serjeant,[1] one of the justices of assize and gaol delivery, that if there is a failure of jurors who are impanelled in an inquest upon an information, either for default of appearance or otherwise by reason of challenges, the inquest shall not be taken from bystanders (*de circumstantibus*) to fill up the jury, because the statute will not bear it.[2] It was also held there that if a juror is living in another county he must have some land in this county where he is impanelled, or else it is a good cause of challenge. Query, and study the statute.

62. ANON.

Common Pleas, 1545/48.

Does an action of waste lie for waste committed in lands in ancient demesne, or not?

It seemed to my lord MOUNTAGUE, Chief Justice of the same place, that this action does not lie there, because the process in this action is by summons, attachment and distress, and if the defendant does not come at the distress a writ shall issue out to the sheriff, the words of which are that he should go to the place wasted (*quod accedat ad locum vastatum*), and they in ancient demesne cannot write to the sheriff, any more than in *quare impedit* brought upon a disturbance to an advowson in ancient demesne: that writ does not lie there, because they cannot award a writ to the bishop.

But it seemed to SHELLEY J., as to the action of waste, that the writ to enquire as to the waste may be awarded to the officers, such as bailiffs and others, who are appointed to execute and serve process there.

[1] King's serjeant 1547–53.
[2] 35 Hen. VIII, c. 6 (*SR* iii. 962).

Et ouster fuit move en le dit lewe si un formedon gist en Lounders, et semble fuit that it dyd. Mes formedon ne gist in le copyeholde. Et ouster fuit move que en replegiare, et action de accompt, auncien demesne fuit bon ple, mez en juris utrum auncient demesne nest pas ple. Quere le reason de ceo < quar semble destre diffuse et difficulte. Semble le reason destre que fourmedon ne gist del terre customary est pur ceo que customary terrez avoyent lour comencementes longe temps devaunt lestatut de W. ii. per quell le formedon est done. Quere ouster etc. > [1]

[63]

Casus en le Comen Banke.

Home declare son volunte and therby wyllethe que cez executors prenderont lez proffyttez del son terre quousque son fyle[2] vyent all age del xii. annes, fyndenge son dyt fyle convenyentment tanque all dyt age. Le fyle devie devaunt el ad accomplyshe lage avaundyt, ou lexecutors ou cestui a que cest volunte extend ou est fayt prenderont lez proffyttes < del surplusage > [i] del dit terre del quell le volunte fuit declare a son use demesne, ou nemi?

Et semble all Seigniour *Mountague*, Cheff Justyce del Comen Banke, et all *Shelley*, Justyce del mesme le banke, que cestui a que cest volunte est declare est quasi un amener del dit terre et issint que il trove[3] le fyle del testator convenyentment il poit assetz bien converter le surplusage dez proffyttes a son proper use pur ceo que il ad fayt tout ceo que il est lye ou oblyge de fayer per le volunte, et issint etc. Quere ouster. Et si el devie devaunt le dyt age, donquez cestui < a que etc. > [i] prendera lez proffyttes a son proper use demesne tanque al age devaunt mentionez. < Memorandum that the latter end of this case is the case of Lewys David[4] our other fealawe[5] etc. > [6]

[64]

Le Seignior *Montague*, Cheff Justyce del Comen Banke, mytt cest case. Si home fayt lez pur terme dannez rendaunt certen rent a tyell jour, et pur defaut del payment un reentre, et puis il fayt feffment en fee sur condition, le condition est enfreynt, pur que il entra, et puis son entre le rent arrere, ou il reentra ou

---

[1] *Added.*
[2] heyre *del.*
[3] *Reading unclear.*
[4] *Reading unclear.*
[5] *Reading unclear.*
[6] *Added.*

It was further moved in the said place whether a formedon lay in London: and it was thought that it did. However, formedon does not lie [for] copyhold. It was further moved that in replevin, and in an action of account, ancient demesne [is] a good plea, whereas in *juris utrum* ancient demesne is not a plea. Query the reason thereof, for it seems to be diffuse and difficult. The reason why formedon does not lie for customary land seems to be because customary lands had their origins long before the Statute of Westminster II, whereby the formedon is given.[1] Query further.

63. ANON.

Common Pleas, 1545/48.

Someone declared his will and thereby willed that his executors should take the profits of his land until his daughter came to the age of twelve years, finding his said daughter suitably until the said age. The daughter died before she accomplished the aforesaid age. Shall the executors, or the person to whom this will extends or is made, take the surplus profits of the said land whereof the will was declared to their own use, or not?

It seemed to my lord MOUNTAGUE, Chief Justice of the Common Bench, and to SHELLEY, Justice of the same bench, that he to whom this will is declared is like an almoner[2] of the said land and provided that he finds the testator's daughter suitably he may perfectly well convert the surplus profits to his own use, because he has done all that which he is tied or bound to do by the will, and so etc. Query further. And if she died before the said age, the person to whom etc. shall take the profits to his own use until the aforementioned age.

Memorandum that the latter end of this case is the case of Lewis David,[3] our other fellow[4] etc.

64. NOTE

Common Pleas, *c.* 1545/50.

My lord MOUNTAGUE, Chief Justice of the Common Bench, put this case: if someone makes a lease for a term of years, rendering certain rent at such and such a day, and for default of payment a re-entry, and afterwards he makes a feoffment in fee upon condition, and the condition is broken, by reason of

---

[1] Statute of Westminster II, c. 1, *De donis* (*SR* i. 71).
[2] Reading unclear.
[3] Reading unclear.
[4] Reading unclear.

nemi ceo fuit un question. Mez semble a le dit seignior que il entra. Et il prent divercite perenter cest case et lou le seignior enter sur un tenant et fayt feffment del son tenancye et le tenant reentre, le tenancye nest pas revyve etc. Quere ouster de cest mater.

[65]

[*Fo. 47*] Nota que en latteynt que fuit enter George Ogard, esquyer, et Edmund Knyvet, chivaler, defendant, la apparust del < enquest del >[1] graunde jure forsque nyen, et toutz lez auterz[1] fieront defaut, et pur le defendant fuit prie un xx[ti] tales ove un proviso. Et cest prier fuit denye per le courte, et ceo fuit le cause: pur ceo que null defaut fuit en le plaintife. Et donquez ceo fuit prise pur un grounde que venire facias ove proviso, ne tales ove un proviso, jamez ne serra graunt mez lou un defaut est ou poit estre assygne en le plaintife. Mez le non apparance del graunde jurye en cest atteynt fuit le[1] defaut dez jurourz mesmez, pur ceo etc.

[66]

Nota que le Seigniour *Mountague* dit en le Comen Banke que actez de parliament sount dez dyvers maners, scilicet ascunz actez sount generalles, ascunz actez sount speciallez, et ascunz actez sount generalles en un particularitye: sycome un acte est fayt que toutz evesquez ou toutz lez justices ferront ou averont tyel chose, cest un generall acte en un particularyte etc.

[67]

Casus en le Comen Banke.

[*Fo. 47v*] Home declare son volunte et per ceo wylled que lez proffyttes de son terre serront prises per cez executors et devydez enter lez chyldern tanque son eysgne fytz vyent all son pleyne age, le question fuit ou ceux parolx pur lez

---

[1] lez.

which he enters, and after his entry the rent is in arrear, shall he re-enter or not? That was the question. But it seemed to his lordship that he could enter. And he drew a distinction between this case and where the lord enters upon a tenant and makes a feoffment of his tenancy, and the tenant re-enters: there the tenancy is not revived etc. Query further concerning this matter.

65. OGARD v. KNYVET

Probably Common Pleas.

Note that in the attaint which was between George Ogard, esquire,[1] and Edmund Knyvet, knight, defendant,[2] only nine of the inquest of the grand jury appeared, and all the others made default; and on behalf of the defendant a twenty *tales* was prayed with a proviso. And this prayer was denied by the court. This was because there was no default in the plaintiff. For this purpose it was taken for a maxim (*grounde*) that a *venire facias* with proviso, or a *tales* with proviso, shall never be granted unless there is a default in, or a default may be attributed to, the plaintiff. But the non-appearance of the grand jury in this attaint was the default of the jurors themselves, and therefore etc.

66. NOTE

Common Pleas, *c.* 1545/50.

Note that my lord MOUNTAGUE [C.J.] said in the Common Bench that acts of parliament are of various kinds, namely some acts are general, some acts are special, and some acts are general in a particularity: for example, suppose an act is made that all bishops or all the justices shall do or have such and such a thing, this is a general act in a particularity etc.[3]

67. ANON.

Common Pleas, 1545/48.

Someone declared his will and thereby willed that the profits of his land should be taken by his executors and divided amongst the children until his eldest son came to his full age. The question was, whether these words should

---

[1] Of Emneth, Norfolk, and Gray's Inn (adm. 1539): *CPR 1553–54*, p. 436.
[2] Of Buckenham Castle, Norfolk; knighted 1538/39; J.P. for Norfolk since 1543; M.P. for Norfolk in 1547; died 1551: *HPHC 1509–58*, ii. 482.
[3] Cf. *Dyve* v. *Maningham* (1550) Plowd. 62 at 65, *per* Mountague C.J.

byenz serront prisez et weyez en le ley come ilz serront prises pur lez
< proffyttes de >[i] terrez?

Et tout le courte fuit en un mesme oppinion que pur lez proffytz ilz serront
devyde per lez executors enter lez chyldern et ilz averont eux a lour proper
oeps demesne tanque leysne fytz vyent a son pleyne age, et quant leysne fytz est
venuez a son pleyne age donquez il avera ceo et lez executors ne lez chylder ne
intromytteront ovesque [ceo] pluys avant. Donquez quant a lez byenz, ou lez
parolx avaundytz weyeront all un done < to their owne uses >[i] ou auterment
que lez profytz serra prisez mez solement a loepz leysne fytz, et donquez cest
done destre determyne come est devaunt pur lez profytz dez terrez?

Et semble all *Mountague*, Cheff Justyce, que lez chyldern averont les
proffyttes dez terrez mez solement a luse de leysne fytz. Et son reason fuit que
ceux parolx, tanque all pleyne age de laysne fytz, ceo purport et implye. Mez il
agrea, come Mr *Shelley* argue, que ceo fuit un bon done et lez chyldern lez
bienz prenderont a lour usez demesne. Come bonez sount donez a un pur terme
de xx. annez ou pur vye, ceo est bon done pur toutz jourz: et issint est en cest
case. Et si ceux parolx ount este omyttez, donquez nust este ascun question mes
que il serra un bon < question >[1] done.[i] Quere ouster de cest mater.

[68]

Nota un graunde mater en le quell quere que le ley voet. Le case est, le tenant
le roy, esteant seisi dez terrez en fesymple, sur un bon consideration dona cez
terrez a un home en tayle ou pur terme de vie et devie, le ley est uncore a cest
temps prise que le roy avera le terce parte del mesme le terre: que est verye
straunge, quar le ley, quell est come reason et equite, voet que chescun home
poit fayer ove son terre sicome son pleasure serra, si estoyt ove le ley. Donquez
cybien come il poit doner tout son terre del luy et cez heyrez all un auter sibien
il poit doner a un auter en tayle ou pur vye et cest done serra bone pur tout le
terre. Mez larguement que est fayt pur le parte del roy est que il avera le terce
part dez toutz ceux terrez dez queux il fuit sole possesse ou seisi all ascun temps
duraunt sa vye. < Mez loppinion dez ascunz sont arrermayne que le roy navera
son terce parte mez dez terrez descenduez. >[i] Quere ou lessez pur terme de
annez sount deinz le compas del estatut ou lexposityon del estatut ou nemy.
Quere ouster, quar est semble destre my Ladye Longes case.

---

[1] *Del.*

be taken and weighed in law in the same way with respect to the goods as they shall be taken for the profits of the land.

And the whole court was of one same opinion as to the profits, that they shall be divided by the executors amongst the children, and they shall have them to their own use until the eldest son comes to his full age, and when the eldest son has come to his full age then he shall have them, and neither the executors nor the children shall meddle with them any more thereafter. As to the goods, then, do the aforesaid words weigh as a gift to their own uses, or else that the profits shall be taken only to the use of the eldest son? And is this gift then to be determined as before in the case of the profits of the land?

It seemed to MOUNTAGUE, Chief Justice, that the children shall have the profits of the lands solely to the use of the eldest son. And his reason was that these words 'until the full age of the eldest son' purport and imply as much. But he agreed, as Mr [Justice] SHELLEY argued, that this was a good gift of the goods and that the children shall take them to their own uses. Similarly if goods are given to someone for a term of twenty years, or for life, this is a good gift for ever: and so it is in this case. If those words had been omitted, then there would have been no question but that it would be a good gift. Query further concerning this matter.

68. LADY LONG'S CASE

Probably c. 1546/50.

Note a great matter in which it is unclear what the law is. The case is this: the king's tenant, being seised of lands in fee simple, upon a good consideration gives these lands to someone in tail, or for term of life, and dies. The law is nevertheless understood at the present time that the king shall have the third part of the same land:[1] which is very strange, for the law—which is like unto reason and equity—wills that everyone may do with his own land as he pleases, so long as it is consistent with law. Therefore, just as he may give all his land away from him and his heirs to someone else, so he may give to someone else in tail, or for life, and this gift shall be good for the whole land. But the argument which is made on behalf of the king is that the king shall have the third part of all those lands whereof he was sole possessed or seised at any time during his life. However, the opinion of some is that the king shall not have his third part except of lands descended. Query whether lessees for a term of years are within the compass of the statute, or the exposition of the statute,[2] or not. Query further, for it is likely to be my Lady Long's case.[3]

---

[1] By virtue of the Statute of Wills, 32 Hen. VIII, c. 1 (*SR* iii. 745).
[2] Probably referring to the statute for exposition of the Statute of Wills, 34 & 35 Hen. VIII, c. 5 (*SR* iii. 901).
[3] Probably the widow of Sir Richard Long of Wilts., who died in 1546: P.C.C. 18 Alen; *HPHC 1558–1603*, ii. 486.

[69]

Nota que il est tenues pur ley que si tenant en tayle fayt lez pur iiii^{xx} annez, que ceo nest garrantyd per lestatut, quar lez parolx del estatut sount so that the lez < be made >^{1} above xxi. yerez, and these wordes < so that >^{i} be conditionall, and there be other wordes within the same statut^{i} that dothe make the leas to be voyde yf it be made above the number of xxi. yeres. And this oppinion was taken in the Starre Chamber before the lorde chauncelour and the lordes of the councell. Et issint le lez est voyde etc.

[70]

Casus in Chauncerye.

La fuit un byll exibyted pur evydence et especiallment declare dun fayt < en le >^{2} per le quell un done fuit fayt en tayle, et la fuit allege per le defendant que le party ne ces auncestors nont ryen en le possession dez ditz terrez lez queux le dit fayt conserne deynz le temps del lymytation, et pur le plaintife fuit replye que fuit un byll exibyte en le Chauncerye devant lestatut: et ou cest byll la exibyte fuit un suffycyent clayme ou nemi, ceo fuit le question la. Et semble per le master del rolles et tout le barre que ne fuit ascun clayme etc. Mez auterment est dun action all comen ley.

Donquez un auter question fuit move < ou >^{3} coment^{i} le temps del lymytation del brefe de droyt serra construe. Et semble fuit per tout le courte que il serra prise del lx. annez del brefe de droyt et del tytle del prescription. Et issint serra entend del un formedon en le discender, mez nemi dez formedon en le remainder ou en le reverter.

[71]

[*Fo. 49*] *James Halez*, le serjeant le roy, demande cest question del Seigniour *Mountague*, Cheff Justyce del Çomen Banke: que si home port brefe de droyt, coment le demandant gisera lez espleas et en le temps de quell roye, pur le case

---

^{1} *Reading uncertain.*
^{2} *Del.*
^{3} *Del.*

69. ANON.

Star Chamber.

Note that it is held as law that if tenant in tail makes a lease for four score years, this is not warranted by the statute,[1] for the words of the statute are 'so that the lease be made above twenty-one years', and these words 'so that' are conditional, and there are other words within the same statute which make the lease void if it is made above the number of twenty-one years.[2] And this opinion was taken in the Star Chamber before the lord chancellor and the lords of the council. Thus the lease is void etc.

70. ANON.

Chancery.

A bill was exhibited there for evidence, and it declared especially of a deed whereby a gift was made in tail; and it was alleged by the defendant that the party and his ancestors had nothing in possession of the said lands which the said deed concerned within the limitation period; and for the plaintiff it was replied that a bill was exhibited in the Chancery before the statute:[3] and the question there was whether this bill exhibited there was a sufficient 'claim' or not. And it was thought by the master of the rolls and all the bar that it was no claim etc. But it is otherwise of an action at common law.

Then another question was moved as to how the limitation period of the writ of right should be construed. And it was thought by the whole court that it should be understood as sixty years between the writ of right and the title of the prescription. So it shall be understood of a formedon in the descender, but not of formedon in the remainder or in the reverter.

71. ANON.

Common Pleas, 1545/49.

James Hales, the king's serjeant, asked this question of my lord MOUNTAGUE, Chief Justice of the Common Bench: if someone brings a writ of right, how shall the demandant lay the esplees, and in the time of what king, by reason of the new

---

[1] 32 Hen. VIII, c. 28 (*SR* iii. 784).

[2] The first section enabled tenants in tail to make leases, but the second section provided that this should not extend to 'any lease to be made above the number of twenty-one years'. The exception was in a 'provided always' clause, not a 'so that' clause.

[3] I.e. the Statute of Limitations, 32 Hen. VIII, c. 2 (*SR* iii. 747).

del novel estatute del lymytation del tytle del prescription et del brefe de droyt? Et le dit seigniour dysoyt que < il >[1] < le demandant >[i] gysera lez espleas que le demandant lez espleas prent etc. verz infra sexaginta annos jam elapsos en tyel maner come lez serjeantes usont de fayer en le comen recoverez en lez brefez dentres en le post etc. Et le tenant en le brefe de droyt tendera le demi marke pur oyerer[2] del pernancye dez dytz espleas etc.

[72]

Casus en le Comen Banke termino Trinitatis regni Regis Edwardi vi[ti] tercio.

[*Fo. 49v*] Le case que sourde sur levydence < done in mesme le banke >[i] fuit tyel: un home graunt < a un auter >[3] a trois homez un rent charge, et come il appert sur le case as it was agreed upon cest graunt fuit a luse del grauntour et dez cez heyres ou a luse del performauns del volunte del grauntour, quell fuit semble per le court destre tout de un effect, et puis le grauntour, esteant tenant del terre et owner del soyle, fist un feffment del dit terre horce del quell le dit rent fuit issuant az < lez >[4] deus dez dytz trois grauntez. Ceo est leffect del case come je remember. Et ceux sont lez questions del case: quant un rent est graunt ouster a un auter et nest expresse deinz le < fayt del >[i] graunt ascun use, donquez le graunte avera le rent a son use demesne, quar issint le ley implye ceo destre toutz foytz en un graunt, come appert en le serjauntes case en xii[mo] H. viii[vi]. Mez auterment le ley est dun feffment, quar si null use soyt expresse deinz le fayt dell feffment donquez le feffee serra seisi all use del feffour et nemi a [son] use demesne. Mez si ascun use soyt expresse deinz le fayt, donquez le use serra toutz foytz accordant come il est expresse deinz mesme[i] le fayt.

Un auter mater fuit move que fuit tiel: quant le tenant del terre fist son feffment, ou luse del rent passera per reason de cest feffment? Et semble all Justyce *Hales* que luse del rent passera enclude en le terre de quell le feffment fuit fayt. Et en proffe de cel il dit que si tenant en taile dun rent fuit que[i] purchase le terre horce de quell etc. et puis fayt feffment del terre, ore en cest case il dit que ceo fuit une discontinuanz del rent, quell provera que per le feffment del terre il done le rent enclude en le terre etc.

Et mon Seigniour *Mountague* dit que le < use del >[i] rent ne passera per reason del cest feffment. Uncore il voet agree que cestui que use del rent poit graunter cest rent ouster per reson de lestatut [*fo. 50*] del R. le terce, mez ceo covient estre per graunt et nemi come il fayt en cest case. Et en proffe de ceo il mytt ceux casez. Si home soyt seisi dez terrez en possession et auxi dez terrez en

---

[1] *Del.*
[2] *Reading unclear.*
[3] *Del.*   [4] *Del.*

statute[1] of limitation of the title of prescription and of the writ of right? And his lordship said that the demandant should lay the esplees as follows: that the demandant took the esplees etc. within sixty years now elapsed. That is the way in which the serjeants are accustomed to do it in common recoveries, in writs of entry in the *post* etc. And the tenant in the writ of right shall tender the demy-mark for oyer[2] of the pernancy of the said esplees etc.

72. ANON.

Common Pleas, Trin. 1549.

The case which arose upon evidence given in the same bench was this: someone granted a rent-charge to three men, and—as it appeared upon the case as it was agreed upon—this grant was to the use of the grantor and his heirs, or to the use of the performance of the grantor's will, which was thought by the court to be all one in effect; then the grantor, being tenant of the land and owner of the soil, made a feoffment of the said land out of which the said rent was issuing to two of the said three grantees. That is the effect of the case, as I recall. And these are the questions in the case: when a rent is granted over to another, and no use is expressed in the deed of grant, then the grantee shall have the rent to his own use, for the law implies this always to be so in a grant, as appears in the serjeants' case in 12 Hen. VIII.[3] But the law is otherwise of a feoffment, for if no use is expressed in the deed of feoffment the feoffee shall be seised to the use of the feoffor and not to his own use. However, if any use is expressed in the deed, the use shall always be according as it is expressed in the same deed.

Another matter was moved, which was this: when the tenant of the land made his feoffment, shall the use of the rent pass by reason of this feoffment? And it seemed to HALES J. that the use of the rent shall pass as included in the land whereof the feoffment was made. And in proof of this he said that if tenant in tail of a rent purchases the land out of which etc. and then makes a feoffment of the land, in this case he said that this was a discontinuance of the rent, which will prove that by the feoffment of the land he gives the rent as included in the land etc.

And my lord MOUNTAGUE [C.J.] said that the use of the rent shall not pass by reason of this feoffment. Nevertheless he would agree that cestuy que use of the rent may grant this rent over by reason of the statute of Richard III,[4] but

---

[1] 32 Hen. VIII, c. 2 (*SR* iii. 747).   [2] Reading unclear
[3] This is an error. The case intended is doubtless *Gervys* v. *Cooke* (1522) YB Mich. 14 Hen. VIII, fo. 4, pl. 5 (in which nine serjeants argued); 119 Selden Soc. 108 at p. 113. The serjeants' case was *Harcourt* v. *Spycer* (1521) YB Trin. 13 Hen. VIII, fo. 15, pl. 1 (a case which began in 12 Hen. VIII); 119 Selden Soc. 81.   [4] 1 Ric. III, c. 1 (*SR* ii. 477).

use, tout en un mesme vylle, et il fayt feffment de toutz cez terrez en mesme le vylle et fayt lyvere dez terrez en possession, en cest case ryenz passera dez terrez en use. Et issint il dit le ley destre que si home soyt seisi dez terrez en fee et auxi dez terrez pur annez ou pur vye, tout en un mesme vylle, et fayt feffment de toutz cez terrez en mesme le vylle, et fayt lyvere sur le terre que il ad en fee, ryenz de cez auterz terrez passera etc.

Et fuit ousterment dit en cest case que per reson del cest feffment del terre horce de quell le dit rent fuit issuant az deux grauntez que per reson de cest feffment deus partes del rent fuit extinguyshe et pur le terce parte il remayne pluis.

Et ilz dysoyent ouster que un use fuit ryen auter mez solement un confidence et truste etc.

[73]

Casus en le Comen Banke le terme avaundyt.

Home fayt lez a un auter pur terme de vye, le remainder ouster a lissue de corporibus del J. a D. et Alyce sa feme engendrez, ilz ount issue fytz et fyle, et puis le tenant pur vye devie, et le dit J. a D. et A. sa feme deviont. Cest le <case del>[1] question del case: ou le fytz avera le terre <si come leyre a leygne bar[2] >[i] ou le fytz et fyle averont le terre?

Et fuit semble al Justyce *Hales* et Seigniour *Mountague*, Cheff Justyce del Comen Banke, que auxi bien la fyle come le fytz averont le terre per le reason de cest paroll issue, le signification del quell paroll referre a tout lissue que est ew et enjender perenter le baron et sa feme. Et en reason il ne poit auterment estre[i] construe, quar le fyle est auxibien lissue enjender perenter son pere et son mere come est le fytz, et tout un.

Et le dit Seigniour *Mountagu* dit, admytt que le case ust este que le remainder ust este lemytt et assygne a lez chyldern del dit J. a D. et A. sa feme, uste este ascun question mez que le fyle avera le terre come bien come le fytz? (Quasi diceret que non.) Et issint il prent le ley destre si le remainder ust este tayle sanguini del dit J. a D. et A. sa feme, nust este question mez que le fyle avera le terre si bien come le fytz, pur ceo que le fyle est sybien del sanke etc. come est le fytz: ratio satis manifeste liquet. Et le dit seigniour dysoyt en son arguement que cest paroll heyre est sufficient paroll del purchase, et issint sont ceux parolles, sanguini, exitui, semini, et pueris. Et il dysoyt que si lez soyt fayt a un home pur vye, le remainder ouster <en fee>[i] a le fytz del J. a S., et le dit J. a S. nad ascun fytz mez il ad un bastard, cest remainder ne poit prender ascun effect

---

[1] *Del.*
[2] *Reading unclear.*

that must be by grant and not as he has done in this case. And in proof thereof he put the following cases. If someone is seised of lands in possession and also of lands in use, all in one same vill, and he makes a feoffment of 'all his lands in the same vill', and makes livery of the lands in possession, in this case nothing shall pass of the lands in use. And so he stated the law to be if someone is seised of lands in fee and also of lands for years or for life, all in one same vill, and makes a feoffment of 'all his lands in the same vill', and makes livery upon the land which he has in fee, nothing of these other lands shall pass etc.

It was further said in this case that by reason of this feoffment of the land out of which the said rent was issuing to two grantees, two-thirds of the rent was extinguished, and for the third part it remains still.

They further said that a use was nothing else but a confidence and trust etc.

73. ANON.

Common Pleas, Trin. 1549.

Someone made a lease to another for term of life, remainder over to the 'issue' begotten of the bodies of John at Down and Alys his wife; they have issue a son and a daughter; then the tenant for life dies, and the said John at Down and his wife die. This is the question in the case: shall the son have the land, as heir, or shall the son and daughter have the land?

And it seemed to HALES J. and my lord MOUNTAGUE, Chief Justice of the Common Bench, that the daughter as well as the son shall have the land by reason of this word 'issue', the signification of which word refers to the whole issue which is had and begotten between the husband and his wife. And in reason it cannot be otherwise construed, for the daughter is just as much the issue begotten between her father and mother as the son is, and there is no difference.

And the said lord MOUNTAGUE said: admit that the case had been that the remainder had been limited and assigned to the children of the said John at Down and Alys his wife, would there have been any question but that the daughter should have the land as well as the son? (As if to say, no.) And he took the law to be the same if the remainder had been entailed to the 'blood' (*sanguini*) of the said John at Down and Alys his wife; it would not have been a question but that the daughter should have the land as well as the son, because the daughter is as much of the blood etc. as the son is. The reason is quite apparent (*ratio satis manifeste liquet*). And his lordship said in his argument that this word 'heir' is a sufficient word of purchase, and so are these words: 'blood' (*sanguini*), 'issue' (*exitui*), 'seed' (*semini*), and 'children' (*pueris*).[1] And he said that if a lease is made to someone for life, remainder over in fee to the son of John at Style, and the said John at Style has no son, though he has

---

[1] Cf. *Anon.* (1533) in Pollard, above, p. 262, no. 37.

pur ceo que le dit J. a S. nad ascun fytz, quar un bastard ne poit estre un fytz, quar bastard est filius populi ou filius[i] nullius, whyche of them so ever you wull take it. Mez il relya quod fuit filius populi. Et auxi en proffe que le fyle avera le terre sybien come le fytz il mytt ceux casez: que si un feme est ravyshe et el consent al ravyshement, ore en cest case le statut est quod proximus de sanguine intrabit, si un feme soyt proximus de sanguine a cestui feme que consent a le ravyshment el avera le terre, nient obstant que un fytz soyt aprez nee etc. Et issint il disoyt le ley destre que si lez soyt fayt a un pur vye, le remainder ouster az droyt heyres del J. a S., et le dit J. a S. nad ascun auter issue mez un fyle all temps del remainder eschwe, cestui fyle avera le terre nient obstant que son mere est privement enseynt ove un fytz. Nota. Et semble bon reson. Quere ouster etc.

Justice *Hynde* et Justyce *Browne* fueront en contrarie oppynion, mez semble a moy que ilz prenderont le worst syde de le ley.

[74]

Casus en le Comen Banke termino Michaelis anno regni Regis E. vi[ti] tercio.

[*Fo. 50v*] Un home fuit oblige a deus en xx. li. solvendas as eux ambydeux et utrique eorum, et puis un deux morust, et cestui que survyve port un action de dett sur tout lobligation en son nosme demesne nient fesaunt ascun mention en son declaration del morte son compaynyon: cest le case. Deux questions apperont destre deyns cest case, queux sont ceux. Lun est, quant home est oblyge en un certen somme dargent solvendam as eux ambydeux et utrique eorum, ou ceux parolx utrique eorum sount bon ou voyde ou repugnant?

Et semble all Seigniour *Mountague*, Cheff Justyce de le Comen Banke, et *Halez*, un auter justyce del mesme le banke, que ceux parolles utrique eorum sont voyde et repugnant a le premisses de lobligation, quar en le commencement il est oblige as ceux deux et le fayt de lobligation est fayt as eux deux joyntment, donquez quant il expresse en le perclose de lobligation solvendas as eux ambydeux et eorum utrique, ceux parolx font un devysyon de le payement queux sont mere repugnant a lez primer parolx contenuex en mesme lobligation. Et donquez est semble a cest case, lou terrez sont donez a deux habendum a lun deux, ceux darren parolx pur le repugnancye et contraryetye sount voydez, quar primerment il fuit un joynt obligation ou un joynt done az eux ambydeyx, le quell ne poit estre abrigge ou restreyne per ascunz parolles subsequentes etc.

a bastard, this remainder cannot take any effect, because the said John at Style has no son: for a bastard cannot be a son, inasmuch as a bastard is *filius populi* or *filius nullius*, whichever of them you prefer. But he preferred to say that he was a son of the people (*quod fuit filius populi*).[1] And also in proof that the daughter should have the land as well as the son he put these cases: if a wife is ravished, and consents to the ravishment, in this case the statute says 'that the next of the blood shall enter' (*quod proximus de sanguine intrabit*), and if a woman is *proximus de sanguine* to the wife who consented to the ravishment she shall have the land, even if there is a son born afterwards etc.[2] And he stated the law to be thus, that if a lease is made to someone for life, remainder over to the right heirs of John at Style, and the said John at Style has no other issue but a daughter at the time when the remainder falls in, this daughter shall have the land, even if her mother is secretly pregnant with a son. Note. It seems a good reason. Query further etc.

HYNDE J. and BROWNE J., were of a contrary opinion, but it seems to me that they took the worst side of the law.

74. ANON.

Common Pleas, Mich. 1549.

Someone was bound to two in £20, payable to both of them 'and to each of them' (*et utrique eorum*), and then one of them died, and the one who survived brought an action of debt upon the whole bond in his own name, making no mention in his declaration of the death of his companion: that is the case. There appear to be two questions in this case, which are as follows. One is, when someone is bound in a certain sum of money to be paid to both of them *et utrique eorum*, are these words *utrique eorum* void or repugnant?

It seemed to my lord MOUNTAGUE, Chief Justice of the Common Bench, and HALES, another justice of the same bench, that these words *utrique eorum* are void and repugnant to the premisses of the bond; for in the commencement he is bound to these two, and the deed of the bond is made to the two of them jointly, and therefore when he expresses in the perclose of the bond 'to be paid to both of them *et eorum utrique*', those words make a division of the payment which is absolutely repugnant to the first words contained in the same bond. Therefore it is like this case, where lands are given to two, *habendum* to one of them, these last words are void for repugnancy; for at the outset there was a joint bond or a joint gift to both the two, which cannot be abridged or restrained by any subsequent words etc.

[1] Cf. *Anon.* (1542) Gell's reports, Mich. 33 [?*recte* 34] Hen. VIII, fo. 6v, *per* Shelley J., concerning a gift to A. and his firstborn son ('le bastarde ne fuit le *primogenitus filius* quar il fuit *filius populi*, et nemi son fitz').

[2] 6 Ric. II, stat. 1, c. 6 (*SR* ii. 27). Cf. Yorke, above, p. 182, no. 240; *Wymbysh* v. *Tailboys* (1547) Plowd. 38 at 42v–43, 56v–57v.

Donquez a lauter question: ou cestui que survyve de lez dytez oblygez que port son action de dett sur tout lobligation, ou il doyt alleger per mater en fayt en son declaration le morte son compaynyon ou autrement son declaration nest [pas][1] garante per lobligation. Quar quant lobligation est monstre en le courte, come il covient del necessyte de ceo fayer, come il appert per ceux parolles, et profert hic in curia scriptum predictum quod debitum predictum in forma predicta testatur, per ceo il appert que lobligation fuit fayt as deux, et quant il port action de dett sur cest obligation en son nosme solement lou il serra port en ambideux lour nosmez, cest declaration nest pas bone pur ceo que il nest garraunt per le obligation, per que il covient de necessyte de alleger en son declaration per mater en fayt le morte son compaynyon. Semble a ceo quant home port action dannuyte le quell il ad pur terme dauter vye, il doyt en son declaration dalleger per mater en fayt et daverrer le vye del cestui pur que vye.

Seigniour *Mountague* priste pur un ruele que a quecumque temps ascun home voyle porter son action il doyt luy enabler de porter son action ou autrement il navera pas action. Et ceo fuit son grounde. Et pur lexample de cest si un obligation soyt fayt a deus et lun deux est moygne professe, quant cestui que est person able port action en son nosme solement il doyt alleger en son declaration per mater en fayt que son compaynyon est moygne professe, et issint etc. Quere ouster.

Leffect de cest mater breffment est que si lun dez obligez est morte devaunt laction porte, donquez il monstra son morte ut supra, et si un deux morust pendant le brefe donquez le brefe abatera.

[75]

Casus en le Comen Banke termino Michaelis anno regni Regis E. vi[ti] tercio.

[*Fo. 51*] Serjant *Pollard* mytt cest case: que si un estatut soyt fayt que prohibyte que nul home ferra tyel chose < et sil fayt il serra >[2] sur un penaltye, et per mesme lestatut est done a chescun home que voet suer pur mesme le penaltye un action del dett, en le quell cestui que voet suer avera lun moyte et le roy avera lauter moyte. Le questyon fuit ou cestui que voet suer pur cest penaltye poit exibyter un enformation en lescheker, ou nemi?

Et semble fuit per *Mountague*, Cheyfe Justyce del Comen Banke, et Justyce *Halez*, que il ne puyssoyt, quar il nad ascun auter meane de recover le dit penaltye que per laction del dett quell est expresse deins le statut, pur ceo que nest ascun auter remedye done per letatut < pur le partye >[i] mez laction del dett. Mez le roy nient obstant prendera son recovere per ascun auter meane quell luy plerra, per action, enformation ou autrement, et en quell courte il luy plerra.

[1] p[ur].   [2] *Del.*

Now to the other question: where the survivor of the said obligees brings an action of debt upon the whole bond, he ought to allege by matter in fact in his declaration the death of his companion, or else his declaration is not warranted by the bond. For when the bond is shown in court—as must needs be done, as appears by these words, 'and he proffers here in court the aforesaid writing which witnesses the aforesaid debt in form aforesaid' (*et profert hic in curia scriptum praedictum quod debitum praedictum in forma praedicta testatur*)—it will appear thereby that the bond was made to two, and when he brings an action of debt upon this bond in his name only, where it should be brought in both their names, this declaration is not good, because it is not warranted by the bond; and therefore he must of necessity allege in his declaration by matter in fact the death of his companion. Similarly, when someone brings an action of annuity for an annuity which he has *pur terme d'auter vie*, he ought in his declaration to allege by matter in fact, and to aver, the life of cestuy que vie.

My lord MOUNTAGUE took it as a rule that, whenever someone wishes to bring his action, he ought to enable himself to bring his action or else he shall not have an action. That was his maxim (*grounde*). And for an example of this, if a bond is made to two, and one of them is a professed monk, when the one who is an able person brings an action in his name only he ought to allege in his declaration by matter in fact that his companion is a professed monk, and so etc. Query further.

The effect of this matter, briefly, is that if one of the obligees has died before the action is brought, the plaintiff must show his death (as above); and if one of them dies pending the writ, the writ shall abate.

75. ANON.

Common Pleas, Mich. 1549.

Serjeant *Pollard* put this case: if a statute is made which prohibits anyone from doing something under a penalty, and the same statute gives everyone who wishes to sue for the same penalty an action of debt, in which the party who wishes to sue shall have one moiety of the penalty and the king shall have the other moiety. The question was: may the party who wishes to sue for this penalty exhibit an information in the Exchequer, or not?

And it was thought by MOUNTAGUE, Chief Justice of the Common Bench, and HALES J. that he could not; for he has no other means to recover the said penalty than by the action of debt which is expressed in the statute, because no other remedy is given by the statute but the action of debt. The king, however, may nevertheless take his recovery by any other means which pleases him, by action, information or otherwise, and in whichever court he pleases.

Et Justyce *Hales* dyt que sont deus maners denformations en lescheker, lun pur le roy, quell est en tyel maner, R. Bradshaw[1] attornatus generallis domini regis qui pro domino rege sequitur [etc.], et lauter kynde del enformation que est pur le partye est[i] A. B. venit etc. et corporale prestitit sacramentum etc. Quere.

[76]

Nota per *Staunford* que lestatut que est fayt que home poit prender ten poundes in the hundred que mesme lestatut nether[2] makethe it usurye[i] nor yet no usurye, but that estatut weythe to this effect que nul home ne serra empeache per nostre ley syl ne prist pluis que est comprise deinz mesme lestatut, mez uncore il poit estre empeache per le spirituell ley. Mez nota que ceo est forsque bare remedye, mez le graunde mater est[i] pur loffence que est commytt enconter Dewe omnipotent etc.

[77]

Nota quun mater fuit rule en le Comen Banke per Serjant *Saunders*, que fuit tyel: feme sole port un action de dett, et all nisi prius fuit trove pur le plaintife, et meane perenter le verdytt et le jour en banke le feme que fuit le plaintife prent baron, coment le defendant aydera luy mesme en cest mater? Quar cest prisell all baron nabatera le brefe en fayt, mez le brefe est forsque abatable per le voye del ple, et ceo ne poit le defendant fayer, quar il nad jour en courte, nient pluis que sur un entre fayt per le demandant aprez verdytt. Mez cest mater is to be holpen per brefe derrour et nul auter remedy, per Justyce *Hales*.

[78]

[*Fo. 51v*] Un mater fuit rule en le Comen Banke que fuit tyel: le roy fayt lez pur terme de annez except tyelx measonz queux estoyent sur le terre whiche his pleasure shoulde be to sell or gyve awaye at eny tyme after the seid lez, et puis

---

[1] *Reading uncertain.*
[2] *Reading uncertain.*

HALES J. said that there are two kinds of information in the Exchequer: one is for the king, in the form, 'Henry Bradshaw, the lord king's attorney-general, who sues for the lord king etc.' (*Henricus Bradshaw attornatus generalis domini regis, qui pro domino rege sequitur etc.*), and the other kind of information—which is for the party—is in the form 'A. B. comes etc. and takes a corporal oath etc.' (*A. B. venit etc. et corporale praestitit sacramentum etc.*). Query.

76. NOTE

Probably in Gray's Inn, *c.* 1549.

Note, by *Staunford*, concerning the statute which has been made that one may take £10 in the hundred:[1] the same statute neither makes it usury or no usury, but the statute weighs to the effect that no one shall be impeached by our law if he takes no more than is comprised in the same statute. Nevertheless he may be impeached by the spiritual law; but note that that is but a bare remedy, for the great matter is the offence which is committed against almighty God etc.

77. ANON.

Common Pleas, *c.* 1549.

Note that a matter was [moved][2] in the Common Bench by Serjeant *Saunders*, which was as follows. A single woman brought an action of debt, and at nisi prius it was found for the plaintiff, and in between the verdict and day in banc the woman (who was plaintiff) married a husband: how shall the defendant help himself in this matter? For this taking of a husband does not abate the writ in fact,[3] but the writ is merely abatable by way of plea, and the defendant cannot do that because he has no day in court, any more than he can in the case of an entry made by the demandant after verdict. But this matter is to be helped by a writ of error; and there is no other remedy, according to HALES J.

78. ANON.

Common Pleas, *c.* 1549.

A matter was ruled in the Common Bench, which was as follows. The king made a lease for a term of years, excepting such houses as stood upon the land 'which his pleasure should be to sell or give away at any time after the said

---

[1] 37 Hen. VIII, c. 9 (*SR* iii. 996).   [2] Text says 'ruled', but it seems to be a question.
[3] I.e. automatically.

aprez le roy vende lez measonz queux sont sur mesme le terre all mesme le lessee, et aprez le roy graunta le revercion ouster a un estraunge, et aprez le vende que est le lesse pur annez abata lez dites measonz ou auterment eux permytta to fall doune, pur que le graunte del revercion port brefe de wast verz le vende, scilicet le lesse, que plede Nul wast fayt. Le question est, ou il pledra cest ple Nul wast fayt, que est le generall issue, ou lespeciall mater? Ceo fuit le mater.

Et *Edward Mountague*, Cheffe Justyce del Comen Banke, dit que le defendant pleadra Nul wast fayt, quar il dysoyt sur le mater la fuit nul wast fayt en fayt, quar il dysoyt quant le roy except lez measons sur son lez fayt donquez per reson del cest exception lez measonz ne unquez fueront parcell del dit lez, et primez per lexception dez measonz le terre ou le soyle sur le quell lez measonz estoyent sount auxi exceptez et reservez come bien lez measonz sount. Come si home fayt lez pur annez < except ou >[i] reservaunt le grosse boyes et subboyes, per cel exception ou reservation le terre ou le soyle sur le quell le dit boyez est cressaunt est auxi except ou reserve. Donquez, le ley weyant solonque cest sort que lez measonz ne sont ascun parcell de le chose lesse, quant il abate lez measonz ne poit estre wast en luy, pur ceo que fuit nul parcell de son lez, et donquez sur le mater quant laction de waste est port verz luy il poit savement pleder Nul wast fayt. Et si le graunte del revercion avera ascun remedie verz le lesse il serra per un action de trans. et nemi auterment. Quere ouster.

[79]

Casus en le Comen Banke termino Hilarii anno regni Regis E. vi[ti] tercio.

Serjant *Pollard* mytt cest case. Si un home fayt feffment a un auter a aver et tener a luy et a cez heirez et a cez assignes a luse del feffour et de cez heirez de son corps enjenders, et puis il fayt descontinuans et devie, son heyre port fourmedon, que[i] il supposera destre le donour en cest case? Cest le question.

Et le Seigniour *Mountagu* argue que le feffor mesme serra dit le donour, et lissue en tayle supposera luy destre eynz del son done. Et ceo fuit son reason, quar cy tost et eo instante cicome le feffment fuit[i] fayt et lyvere sur ceo fayt per loperation de lestatut et hoc instante fuit le possession del feffe transpose et conveyd a luse, et donquez nest ascun donour mez le feffour mesme, < que nul >[i] et nest ascun chose conveyd a le feffe pur ceo que le feffe nest intend mez

---

[i] *Del.*

lease'; then afterwards the king sold the houses which are upon the same land to the same lessee; and afterwards the king granted the reversion over to a stranger; and afterwards the vendee (who is the lessee for years) knocked down the said houses or otherwise permitted them to fall down, and so the grantee of the reversion brought a writ of waste against the vendee (that is, the lessee), who pleaded No waste done. The question is, may he plead this plea No waste done, which is the general issue, or should he plead the special facts? That was the matter.

And EDWARD MOUNTAGUE, Chief Justice of the Common Bench, said that the defendant may plead No waste done; for he said that upon the facts there was no waste done in fact. For he said that, when the king excepted the houses when his lease was made, the houses were by reason of that exception never part of the said lease, and by the exception of the houses the land or the soil whereon the houses stood was also excepted and reserved as well as the houses. Similarly, if someone makes a lease for years, excepting or reserving the timber and underwood, by this exception or reservation the land or the soil whereon the said wood is growing is also excepted or reserved.[1] Therefore the law, weighing after this sort that the houses are not part of the thing leased, when he knocks down the houses it cannot be waste in him, because they were not part of his lease, and therefore upon these facts when an action of waste is brought against him he may safely plead No waste done. And if the grantee of the reversion were to have any remedy against the lessee it should be by an action of trespass and not otherwise. Query further.

79. ANON.

Common Pleas, Hil. 1550.[2]

Serjeant *Pollard* put this case. If someone makes a feoffment to another to have and to hold unto him and his heirs and assigns to the use of the feoffor and his heirs of his body begotten, and then he makes a discontinuance and dies, and his heir brings formedon, whom shall he allege to be the donor in this case? That is the question.

And my lord MOUNTAGUE [C.J.] argued that the feoffor himself shall be called the donor, and the issue in tail shall allege himself to be in through his gift. And this was his reason: for as soon as and *eo instante* that the feoffment was made, and livery thereon made, by the operation of the statute[3] the feoffee's possession was in that instant (*hoc instante*) transposed and conveyed to the use, and therefore there is no donor but the feoffor himself; and there is

[1] Bro. Abr., *Reservations*, pl. 39 (1541/42). [2] Cf. *Anon.* (1543) Gell's reports, Hil. 34 Hen. VIII, fo. 14v, where the same point arose; Shelley J. held that the feoffor was the donor, but Browne J. was against him. [3] Statute of Uses, 27 Hen. VIII, c. 10 (*SR* iii. 539).

un instruement de vester le possession en le lewe ou luse fuit. Semble a le case del cestui a que use a le comen ley, lou il enter sur lez feffez et fist feffment, il ne fuit mez forque un instrument de fayer le chose de passer. Et en cest case le feme del cestui que use ne fuit pas endowable [...][1] is the wyffe of the feffe en le case all barr. [*Fo. 52*] Et ouster, de prover que nest ascun auter donour en le case ycy mez le feffour, il mytt cest case. Si le tenant le roy seisi en fee symple queux tyent del roy en capite et fayt feffment a luse del luy mesme et cez heyrez, ou en cest case le roy avera divers fynez pur alienation ou forque solement un fyne? Et il dysoyt pur clere ley que le roy en cest case navera mez solement un. Et cest case gothe so ner the princypall case that it resemblethe the <fyrst case>[i] fully.

Justyce *Hynde* fuit clerement[i] en oppynion que le feffe serra le donour, pur ceo que le feffment and the lyvere made <to hym>[i] was the foundation and the grounde sur le quell luse fuit create. Et ouster dysoyt que le feme del feffe serra endow. Et issint pur ceux reasonz il argue that the use was conveyd from the feyfe et que donquez le feffe serra le donour.

Justyce *Halez* argue que le feffour ne poit estre dit le donour, et fist son arguement pur ceo que cest mater fuit ambyguus et doutefull que de eux serra dit le donour, scilicet le feffour ou le feffe, et donquez quant cest mater vient en construction de le ley il ne jammez ferra tyell construction en ascun mater come ascun empertynencye shuld folow theruppon, et si ycy en cest case le feffour serra dit le donour, donquez il donera un chose a luy mesme, quell serra chose impertinent, et pur cest reason le feffour ne serra dit le donour. Quere ouster de cest mater.

[80]

Nota que loppynion dez toutz lez justyces del Comen Banke sont que lez grauntez dez revercionz del comen personz prenderont <tyel et semblable>[i] avauntage pur cez conditionz enfreynts et dez reentrez cy bien et cy amplement come le pattentez et grauntez le roy serront etc.

[81]

Nota per Serjeant *Saunders* que si home soyt prise pur petyte larcenye il ne serra myse all ascun punyshment devaunt que il soyt endyte, et aprez son endytement donquez il serra punishe per le discrescyon dez justices ou del justyce, scilicet by the setteng upon the pyllorye ou en lez stokes ou auterment

---

[1] *Some unintelligible words in English.*

nothing conveyed to the feoffee, because the feoffee is intended only as an instrument to vest the possession in the place where the use was. It is like the case of cestuy que use at common law, where he entered upon the feoffees and made a feoffment, he was only an instrument to cause the thing to pass. And in this case the wife of cestuy que use was not endowable, any more than the wife of the feoffee in the case at the bar. Moreover, to prove that there is no other donor in the case here but the feoffor, he put this case. If the king's tenant, being seised [of lands] in fee simple and holding them of the king in chief, makes a feoffment to the use of himself and his heirs, shall the king in this case have several fines for alienation or only one fine? And he stated as clear law that the king in this case shall have but one. And this case goes so near the first case that it resembles it fully.

HYNDE J. was clearly in opinion that the feoffee shall be the donor, because the feoffment and the livery made to him was the foundation and the ground whereon the use was created. He further said that the feoffee's wife shall be endowed. Therefore, for these reasons, he argued that the use was conveyed from the feoffee, and that therefore the feoffee shall be the donor.

HALES J. argued that the feoffor cannot be called the donor; and he made his argument because it was ambiguous and doubtful which of them shall be called the donor, namely the feoffor or the feoffee, and therefore when this matter comes to be construed by the law they will never make such a construction in any matter that any inconsistency should follow thereupon. And if here in this case the feoffor shall be called the donor, then he would give something to himself, which would be an inconsistent thing, and for this reason the feoffor shall not be called the donor. Query further concerning this matter.

80. ANON.

Common Pleas.

Note that it was the opinion of all the justices of the Common Bench that the grantees of reversions from common persons shall take such like advantage for breach of their conditions, by re-entries, as well and as amply as the king's patentees and grantees shall etc.

81. NOTE

Note by Serjeant *Saunders* that if someone is taken for petty larceny he shall not be put to any punishment before he is indicted, and after his indictment he shall be punished by the discretion of the justices or justice, namely by setting upon the pillory or in the stocks, or otherwise as the discretion of the justice

come le discrescion del justice [serra].[1] Et mesme lorder serra observe en cest case come en lez comen cases del endytmentes del trans., lez homez endytez fount lour fynez meyntenant sur lour endytementes sinon que ilz voylent traverser lour endytementes. Et issint meyntenaunt sur lendytement del petyte larcenye lendyte serra myse a son punyshement.

[82]

xxix° H. viii.

[*Fo. 53*] Fuit agree per toutz lez justicez del Comen Bank que si tenant en tayle en possession fayt feffment en fee que le feffe serra seisie a luse del feoffour et de sez heyres et il ne serra seisie a le use de le tayle.

[83]

[*Fo. 59*] Nota per Seigniour *Mowntague* et *Thomas Bromley*, justyces dassyse et gaole delyvere, que en toutz casez dendytementes[2] del burglarye que lez parolx de tyelx endytmentes ne doyent estre quare clausum fregit, mez quare domum mancionis sive domum et mansionem dun tyel, et sil soyt auterment frame lendytment est voyde et insuffycyent darrayner ascun home sur ascun tyel endytment etc. eyant ceux parolx quare clausum fregit.

[84]

Nota quun divercite fuit prise en le Comen Banke perenter un single obligation et un obligation endorsed ove un condition, quar en le case del single obligation si loblige port action de dett sur cest obligation devaunt le jour que le argent doyte estre paye, il serra barre, mez si loblige port action de dett sur lobligation endorse ove un condition devaunt le jour all quell largent doyt estre paye il ne serra barre. Quere le divercite del reason en ceux cases, quar semble all Seigniour *Mountague*, Cheff Justyce del Comen Banke, que le plaintife ne

---

[1] suer' *underlined*.
[2] dentyt[tes].

shall be. The same procedure shall be observed in this case as in the common cases of indictments for trespass: the men so indicted make their fines forthwith upon their indictments, unless they wish to traverse their indictments. Therefore, immediately upon the indictment of petty larceny, the indictee shall be put to his punishment.

82. ANON.

Common Pleas, 1537/38.

It was agreed by all the justices of the Common Bench that if a tenant in tail in possession makes a feoffment in fee the feoffee shall be seised to the use of the feoffor and his heirs and he shall not be seised to the use of the tail.

83. NOTE

Norfolk assizes, c. 1542/50.[1]

Note, by my lord MOUNTAGUE and *Thomas Bromley*, justices of assize and gaol delivery, that in all cases of indictments for burglary the wording of such indictments ought not to be for breaking a close (*quare clausum fregit*), but for breaking the dwelling house (*quare domum mansionis fregit*) or house and dwelling (*domum et mansionem*) of such and such, and if it is otherwise framed the indictment is void; and it is insufficient to arraign anyone upon such an indictment etc. having the words *quare clausum fregit*.

84. ANON.

Common Pleas, c. 1545/50.

Note that a distinction was taken in the Common Bench between a single bond and a bond endorsed with a condition, for in the case of the single bond if the obligee brings an action of debt upon this bond before the day when the money ought to be paid, he shall be barred, whereas if the obligee brings an action of debt upon the bond endorsed with a condition before the day at which the money ought to be paid, he shall not be barred. Query the distinction of reasoning in these cases, for it seemed to my lord MOUNTAGUE, Chief Justice of the Common

---

[1] This and the following case are entered in the manuscript between Southwell's reading, Lent 1538, and Moyle's reading, Lent 1539, but Bromley seems not to have become an assize justice until 1542, and no. 84 must date from after 1545.

serra barre whether[1] en lun case ne en lauter. Et en proofe del son reason il mist
cest case: si home en le vye del son pere ou cestui a que un remainder est en
tayle voyle porter un action consernant cest terre il ne serra barre mez aprez le
mort son pere ou aprez le morte del particuler tenant le fitz ou cestui en le
remainder avera son action. Quere ouster de ceo.

[85]

[*Fo. 61v*] Mon Seigniour *Mountague*, Cheff Justyce del Comen Banke, dysoyt
en le case dun rescous retourne que si un capias soyt agarde horse del Comen
Banke saunz ascun orygynall et un rescous soyt fayt all vyconte, ore cestui que
fayt cest rescous serra agard all Flete et fra fyne, nient obstant que cest proces
alera saunz garrante. Et le reason est pur ceo que le proces del roy doyt estre
obeyd en toutz casez.

[86]

Nota per Seigniour *Mountague*, < Cheyf Justyce del Comen Banke >,[i] que si
home voet graunter toutz cez terrez gysauntz en tyel vyle que ne sount
melyourz parolx de fayer toutz ceux de passer que de graunter toutz cez
tenementes demurrantz la, quar per ceux parolx toutz cez advowsonz,
revercionz et toutz manerz des chosez queux gysont en tenure passeront per
ceux parolx tenementes. Quere ouster. Mez de fayer feffment del maner de D.
cum pertinenciis, nothynge elles shall passe but the thynges that makethe the
maner or be parcell or incydent to the maner, come lez demeanez et services, le
courte baron, lavowsonz appendant, comenz appendant, vyllenz regardant, et
tyelz semblablez. Quere ouster.

[87]

Nota pur un comen experiens que sur un fyne leve si ascunz dez partyes < a
le fyne >[i] deviont devant lez deners le roy entre, tout le fyne est voyde et
frustrat, mez auterment est si lez deners le roy sont un foytz entre, nient obstant
ascunz dez parties deviont aprez uncore le fyne est assetz bon etc.

---

[1] *Reading unclear; perhaps* in nether.

Bench, that the plaintiff shall not be barred in either case. And in proof of his reasoning he put this case: if someone in the lifetime of his father, or the person to whom a remainder is entailed, will bring an action concerning this land, he shall not be barred, but after his father's death, or after the death of the particular tenant, the son or remainderman shall have his action. Query further of this.

85. NOTE

Common Pleas, 1546.[1] Also reported by Gell, Mich. 38 Hen. VIII, fo. 45.

My lord MOUNTAGUE, Chief Justice of the Common Bench, said in the case of a rescue returned that if a *capias* is awarded out of the Common Bench without any original, and a rescue is made against the sheriff, the person who made this rescue shall be awarded to the Fleet and make a fine, even though this process went out without warrant. The reason is because the king's process ought to be obeyed in all cases.

86. NOTE

Common Pleas, c. 1545/50.

Note, by my lord MOUNTAGUE, Chief Justice of the Common Bench, that if someone wishes to grant all his lands lying in such and such a vill, there are no better words to cause them all to pass than to grant 'all his tenements lying there', for by those words all his advowsons, reversions and all manner of things which lie in tenure will pass by the word 'tenements'. (Query further.) But if a feoffment is made of the manor of Dale 'with the appurtenances' (*cum pertinenciis*), nothing else shall pass but the things that make the manor or are parcel of or incident to the manor, such as the demesnes and services, the court baron, the advowsons appendant, commons appendant, villeins regardant, and such like. Query further.

87. NOTE

Note for a common experience that upon a fine levied if any of the parties to the fine die before the king's silver is entered, the whole fine is void and frustrated; but it is otherwise if the king's silver is already entered, for then even if any of the parties die afterwards the fine is still perfectly good etc.[2]

[1] This and the next two cases are entered in the manuscript between Moyle's reading, Lent 1539, and Hales's reading, Lent 1540, but must date from after 1545.
[2] Cf. *Anon.* (1551) BL MS. Hargrave 4, fo. 117, *per* Montague C.J. ('... si un conust un fine icy devant nous et morust devant le fine soit engrosse, jeo voile agreer que le fine est bon...').

[88]

[*Fo. 69v*] Loppinion del Seigniour *Bawldwyne* [fuit] que si home declare per son volunte son terre pur terme de vie, le remainder ouster a leyre male del mesme cestui tenant pur vye, le remainder ouster az dyverz auterz en tayle, et le tenant pur terme de vie nad ascun heyre male en esse, que le remainder prendera effect a lez auterz etc. < que sont en le seconde remainder >[i] nient obstant que nest ascun in esse que poit prender le primer remainder etc.

[89]

[*Fo. 71v*] Un question fuit move en le Comen Banke per *Mountague*, serjaunt, que si un convicte soyt committe a lordinarie et puis le prison en le quell lez convictes sont ove lez temporaltiez sont deveyne en lez maynez le roy, le question est an levesque procedera a le purgation de lez convictes saunz commission an nemi?

Et lez juges sembleront clerement que il ferra, pur ceo que lexecution de cest mater attient tauntsolement a le jurisdiction ordinarie et a null auter, et sil hapa destre un eschape del un dez convictes ceo serra a le jeopardie de lordinarie, et nemi materiall que le prison attient a le roy, quar en effect est le prison lordinarie pur le temps, scilicet si longe temps come lez convictes demurront en ceo. Quar le comen experiens est en divers countez en Engleterre lou lez vicontez loyent lour jealz dez auterz, uncore pur le temps est le jeal le viconte mesme. Quere ouster.

[90]

Un auter question per mesme le serjaunt, que sur un bergayn et sale fayt, si le vende vient devant lez justicez ove son parte del indenture dicendo ad instanciam le vendor et pria que il soyt enrolle accordant a le novell estatut de ceo provyde, et est enrolle, ou cest enrollement soyt bon ou nemi? Et sil nest bon, ou le covenant soyt bon et le[1] continuera ou nemi, nient obstant que le enrollement soyt voyde come il est?

---

[1] *Sic but otiose.*

88. NOTE

Common Pleas, c. 1535/45.

The opinion of my lord BALDWIN [C.J.] was that if someone declares his will of his land for term of life, remainder over to the heir male of the same tenant for life, remainder over to various others in tail, and the tenant for term of life has no heir male *in esse*, the remainder to the others in the second remainder shall take effect even though there is no one *in esse* who can take the first remainder etc.

89. ANON.

Common Pleas, c. 1538.[1]

A question was moved in the Common Bench by *Mountague*, serjeant: if a convict is committed to the ordinary, and afterwards the prison in which the convicts are held comes with the temporalities into the king's hands, shall the bishop proceed to the purgation of the convicts without a commission, or not?

And the judges thought clearly that he shall, because the execution of this matter belongs solely to the ordinary jurisdiction and to no other, and if there happens to be an escape of one of the convicts this shall be at the ordinary's risk, and it is immaterial that the prison belongs to the king, for in effect it is the ordinary's prison for the time being, that is, for as long as the convicts remain therein. For it is the common experience in various counties in England where the sheriffs hire their gaols from others, and yet for the time being it is the sheriff's own gaol. Query further.

90. ANON.

Common Pleas, c. 1538.[2]

Another question by the same serjeant: if, upon a bargain and sale made, the vendee comes before the justices with his part of the indenture, saying that he does so at the instance of the vendor, and prays that it may be enrolled in accordance with the new statute therefor provided,[3] and it is enrolled, is this enrolment good or not? And, if it is not good, is the covenant good and does it continue, or not, even though the enrolment is void as it is?

---

[1] Follows two cases in Gray's Inn hall dated Trin. 29 Hen. VIII.
[2] Evidently from the same date as no. 90.
[3] Statute of Enrolments, 27 Hen. VIII, c. 16 (*SR* iii. 549).

Et semble a lez justicez que covient de necessite destre a chescun enrollement ambideux lez partiez a le bergayne et sale, et all meynz le vendor ou bargaynour, pur le mischeff que ensuera a luy ou auterment il ensuera graunde enconveniencie, quar auterment un home poet vener a le justice de peas portant ove luy un indenture comprisaunt un bargayn et sale fayt a luy per un auter lou de verite il ne fuit unquez ascun tiel sale, et il serra per cest enrollement lye et conclude a toutz jourz si le ley serra que le enrollement serra bon. Mez lentent et le meanenge de ceux queux fieront lestatut fuit que ambideux lez partez a le bargayne et sale serront privez a le enrollement. Uncore, nient obstant que lenrollement soyt voyde, uncore le covenant continuera et serra bon daver un recovere sur ceo ou daver ceo enrolle en le Comen Banke ou en Banke le Roy. Et lez justicez preignont un graunde lake del discrescon en le [*fo. 72*] justice que prent cest enrollement. < Nota cestui case bene quar est bone destre consyderez. >[1]

[91]

Fitzherbert, Justice, semble que si un lez soyt fayt pur terme de vie, le remainder pur terme de vie, le remainder ouster en fee, que si le tenant pur terme de vie fayt wast que cestui en le remainder en fee avera action de wast. Et le cause pur que il serra enduce a cest oppinion est un brefe en le register grounde sur mesme cel cause. Uncore devaunt le reformation del [cest][2] oppinion le ley ad este toutz foytz prise a le contrarie. Et le divercite ad este comenment prise en le case devant expresse [que][3] lou lez ad este fayt pur anz, le remainder pur anz, le remainder en fee, ycy en cest case si le primer tenant pur anz fayt wast cestui en le remainder en fee avera action de wast, pur ceo que le primer remainder nest favour in le ley entaunt que est merment un chattell. < Nota le divercite, quar il semble destre bone ley. >[4]

[92]

Nota que est tenuez per Mr *Shelley*, Justice, que si home ad delyver a son botyller son plate ou a son horskeper cez shyvalles, que silz avoyent run a wey de lour masterz ove lour plate que ceo fuit felony a le comen ley et il ne regard le reason pur ceo que le plate ou le chyvallx toutz foytz continueront en le

---

[1] *Added in darker ink.*   [2] e[n].
[3] et.   [4] *Added in darker ink.*

It seemed to the justices that both the parties to the bargain and sale—and at least the vendor or bargainor—must of necessity be present at every enrolment, on account of the mischief which would ensue to him. There would otherwise follow a great inconvenience, for someone could come to a justice of the peace bringing with him an indenture comprising a bargain and sale made to him by another, whereas in truth there never was any such sale, and by this enrolment he would be bound and estopped for ever if the law were that the enrolment should be good. But the intent and meaning of those who made the statute was that both the parties to the bargain and sale must be privy to the enrolment. Nevertheless, even though the enrolment is void, the covenant shall still continue, and it will be good for having a recovery thereon or having it enrolled in the Common Bench or in the King's Bench. And the justices deemed it a great lack of discretion in the justice who took this enrolment. (Note this case well, for it is good to be considered.)

91. ANON.

Common Pleas, in or before 1538.

FITZHERBERT J. thought that if a lease is made for term of life, remainder for term of life, remainder over in fee, and the tenant for term of life commits waste, the remainderman in fee shall have an action of waste. And the reason for which he should be led to this opinion is a writ in the register based upon this same cause.[1] Nevertheless before the reform of this opinion the law has always been taken to the contrary. A distinction has commonly been taken in the case just set out that where a lease has been made for years, remainder for years, remainder in fee, here in this case if the first tenant for years commits waste the remainderman in fee shall have an action of waste, because the first remainder is not favoured in law, inasmuch as it is merely a chattel. (Note the distinction, for it seems to be good law.)

92. ANON.

Probably in the Common Pleas.

Note that it is held by Mr Justice SHELLEY that if some has delivered his plate to his butler, or his horses to his horsekeeper, and they run away from their masters with their plate [or horses], this was felony at common law; and he did not have regard to the reason [given to the contrary] that the plate or the horses

---

[1] *Registrum omnium brevium* (1634 ed.), fo. 75.

possession de lez ownerz ou que il poet aver action de detinew enverz eux a que le delyvere de ceux chosez fueront faytz.

[93]

[*Fo. 78v*] Nota quun chalenge fuit prise en le Comen Banke a une jurour pur ceo que il fuit dage de lx et x annez, le quell chalenge ne fuit allowe, quar le courte voet prender le jure en tyel maner come il est returne, et le jurour avera son remedy ouster verz le viconte. Nota que Justyce *Browne* dit que ceux estatutes queux sount faytez en le negattyff done toutz foytz un action. Tamen quere ouster.

[94]

Nota que Seigniour *Mountagwe*, Cheff Justyce del Comen Banke, dysoyt a un felone que fuit devaunt luy a le barre all assissez et gaole delyvere all cyte de Norwyche, le quell felone avoyt son cappe sur son teate, que il pluckera son cappe del son teate, quar il dysoyt que le ley del realme fuit que chescun felon que vyent a son triall estoyera [son] teate discover, ongyrded and barefooted.

[95]

[*Fo. 79*] Mon Seigniour *Mountegue* dit en le Comen Banke que declarationz et replicationz, pleez en abatement < del brefe >[i] et estopelles doyent estre toutz foytz plede certenment, et ceo pur ceux causez: [primerment] pur ceo que le courte ne serra trouble with manye matterz contenuez en un ple. Un auter mater que le defendant fuit[i] enforce a responder az dyverz materz. Et le terce cause[1] est pur ceo que le jure ne serra envaygle ovesque double mater.

Nota que le dit seigniour dysoyt en son arguement que estatutes serront

---

[1] *Written twice.*

continued throughout in the possession of the owners, or that he could have an action of detinue against those to whom the delivery of these things was made.

93. NOTE

Common Pleas, c. 1545/50.[1]

Note that a challenge was taken to a juror in the Common Bench because he was [over] three score and ten years of age,[2] which challenge was not allowed; for the court will take the jury in such manner as it is returned, and the juror may have his remedy over against the sheriff. Note that BROWNE J. said that those statutes which are made in the negative always give an action. Nevertheless query further.

94. NOTE

Norwich city assizes, c. 1545/50.

Note that my lord MOUNTAGUE, Chief Justice of the Common Bench, said to a felon who was before him at the bar at the assizes and gaol delivery for the city of Norwich, which felon had his cap on his head, that he should pluck his cap from his head; for he said that the law of the realm was that every felon who came to his trial should stand with his head uncovered, ungirt, and barefooted.

95. NOTE

Common Pleas, c. 1545/50.

My lord MOUNTAGUE [C.J.] said in the Common Bench that declarations and replications, pleas in abatement of the writ, and estoppels, ought always to be pleaded with certainty, and that for the following reasons: (1) because the court should not be troubled with many matters contained in one plea; (2) that the defendant is forced to answer to several matters; (3) and the third cause is so that the jury will not be enveigled with double matter.

Note that his lordship said in his argument that statutes shall be taken

[1] In a Gray's Inn note following this case, Hendley cites the case of 'Justyce Hynde' before the lord cardinal. Hynde was appointed a judge in 1545.
[2] See Statute of Westminster II, c. 38 (*SR* i. 89), that *senes ultra sexaginta et decem annos* should not be put in juries.

prisez accordant a lez meanenges et lez intentes dez fesourz dez ditz estatutes. Come, pur example de ceo, lestatut de Westm. seconde, In casu quando vir amisit per defaltam tenementum quod fuit jus uxoris sue, ceo covient estre entende lou le baron et le feme perdont per defaut. Auxi lestatut de West. seconde, capitulo 1°, De donis conditionalibus, en le quell chapter sont ceux parolx, quod finis ipsi juris sit nullus, uncore nient obstant ceux parolx si tenant en tayle leve un fyne ceo est un barre. Et auxi il remember lestatut de Gloucester, quell reherce lez discontinuances dez droytz dez femez dont nul fyne est leve, ceo serra entende dont null fyne est leve per le baron et le feme. Auxi lestatut del R. le terce reherce que leyre del cestui a que use serra en garde dont nul volunte soyt per luy declare, que volunte serra entende lou le fee symple et lenheritaunce est expresse et declare en cest volunte etc.

[96]

[*Fo. 79v*] Nota que *James Halez*, serjaunt, mova a le barre en le Comen Banke que si tenant en tayle en possession devaunt lestatut de xxvii. ust fayt feffment az certen personz a luse de luy et sa feme pur terme de lour ii. vyez et puis lour decessez a luse del mesme cestui feffor et de cez heirz, et puis lestatut le baron et le feme deviont, le question nest my auter mez ou leyre en tayle soyt remytt, ou nemi?

Et semble al *Shelley* que nest remytt, quar mesme lestatut fayt cest mater verye pleyne, quar le parolx de lestatut sont que en[i] le lewe ou luse fuit la serra le possession, issint que per le vesteng et execution del possession lou luse fuit luse est ale et confound, et lez parolx del estatut sount ouster que cestui que avoyt luse avera <tyel et>[i] semblable estate en possession come il avoyt en luse, donquez ycy devaunt il avoyt un fesimple en use et ore per loperation de lestatut il avera fesimple en possession. Et de prover ouster que le ley est issint, si luse devant lestatut fuit dependant sur condition, ore puis lestatut ad prise effect le possession serra en semblable cource dependant sur condition. Mez *Shelley* dysoyt aprez que si fuit ascun chose en lestatut de helper ceo toutz sount ceux parolles, savyng every mannez interest and right etc. Quere plus de ceo, quar videndum est.

according to the meanings and intents of the makers of the said statutes. As, for an example of this, the Statute of Westminster II, *In casu quando vir amisit per defaltam tenementum quod fuit jus uxoris suae*:[1] this must be understood where the husband and wife lose by default. Also the Statute of Westminster II, chapter 1, *De donis conditionalibus*,[2] in which chapter are these words, 'that the fine shall be void by operation of the law itself' (*quod finis ipso jure sit nullus*): nevertheless, despite these words, if a tenant in tail levies a fine it is a bar.[3] He also remembered the Statute of Gloucester, which recites the discontinuances of rights of women whereof no fine has been levied:[4] this shall be understood to mean, whereof no fine has been levied by the husband and wife. Also the statute of Richard III recites that the heir of cestuy que use shall be in ward where no will is by him declared:[5] this will shall be understood to be where the fee simple and the inheritance is expressed and declared in this will etc.

96. ANON.

Common Pleas, 1540/48.

Note that *James Hales*, serjeant, moved at the bar in the Comon Bench: if tenant in tail in possession made a feoffment before the statute of 27 [Hen. VIII][6] to certain persons to the use of him and his wife for term of their two lives, and after their deceases to the use of the same feoffor and his heirs, and the husband and wife die after the statute, the question is nothing else but whether the heir in tail is remitted, or not.

It seemed to SHELLEY that he is not remitted, for the same statute makes this matter very plain; for the words of the statute are that in the place where the use was there shall be the possession, so that by the vesting and execution of the possession, where the use was, the use is gone and confounded; and the words of the statute are further that he who had the use shall have such and such like estate in possession as he had in the use: therefore here he previously had a fee simple in use, and now by the operation of the statute he shall have a fee simple in possession. To prove further that the law is so, if the use before the statute was dependent upon a condition, now since the statute has taken effect the possession shall be in a similar course dependent on the condition. But SHELLEY said afterwards that if there was anything in the statute to help,[7] there are these words, 'saving every man's interest and right etc.'. Query more of this, for it is to be looked into.

---

[1] Westminster II, c. 3 (*SR* i. 73).   [2] Westminster II, c. 1 (*SR* i. 71).

[3] That, however, was by statute: 4 Hen. VII, c. 24 (*SR* ii. 547).

[4] Explanation of the Statute of Gloucester, *Eodem modo currat statutum de terris uxoris alienatis per virum ubi finis non est levatus* (*SR* i. 50).   [5] 1 Ric. III, c. 1 (*SR* i. 477).

[6] Statute of Uses, 27 Hen. VIII, c. 10 (*SR* iii. 539).

[7] The text here does not seem to make full sense.

[97]

Nota que Serjaunt *Towenshend* mova a le barre en le Comen Banke que si un parson fayt lez de son rectorye a un auter pur annez < et fayt indenture >[i] ove ceux parolx comprisez en mesme lendenture, with all the glebe londes, tythez, oblationz, obventionz and all other proffyttes and emolumentes to the same rectorye apperteyneng, ore le trowethe est en cest case que mesme le parson le lessor avoyt un portion of tythes en le parishe del auter parson, pur le quell sur un composition il fuit agree et finallment determine [. . .tz][1] tythez gysaunt en auter parishe il avoyt un annuite, ore le question nest [auter] mez ou cest annuite passera a le lesse per reson de cest lez, ou nemi?

Et semble fuit per *Shelley*, Justyce, et nest denye per auterz mez que le lesse del rectorye avera cest annuite per reson de [cest] lez, per lez parolx emolumentes et proffyttes. Mez pur ceo que cest annuite fuit en luy en recompence de son tythe, et fuit en luy come parson, et donques cestui que est parson ceo avera, et cestui que est lesse est parson pur son temps, scilicet durant son lez, et cest annuite est toutz foytz est[2] annexe all person del cestui que est parson.

Et Serjaunt *Saunders* mytta cest case: si home soyt seisi dun maner per reson de quell il ad comen en auter terre, cestui en que terre cest comen est grauntera a < luy un annuite >[3] cestui[i] que ad le comen un annuite, ore en cest case cestui que ad le maner fayt feffment de ceo cum pertinenciis, ou en cest case cest annuite passera ou nemi?

Et Mr *Shelley* disoyt que lez casez ne sont semblablez pur ceo que cest darren case de maner nest mez en un privite et singuler person, mez en le case del parson est auterment, quar la il avoyt en droyt de son rectorye et va en succession, et cestui que est parson ceo avera.

Et *Shelley* demanda per le voye ou cest composition fuit enter eux pur lour vyez ou nemi. And it was answeryd unto hyme that it was, pur que il dit que donquez le composition lyera etc.

Auxi il fuit tenuez en le Comen Banke que si un parson eschaunge son glebe terre < pur auter terre >[i] que per reson de ceo eschaunge cest terre est ore devenuez et fayt parcel del glebe terre etc.

---

[1] *Word or two lost.*
[2] *Sic.*
[3] *Del.*

97.

Common Pleas, 1540/48.

Note that Serjeant *Townshend* moved at the bar in the Common Bench [the following question]. If a parson makes a lease of his rectory to someone else for years, and makes an indenture with the following words comprised in the same indenture, 'with all the glebe lands, tithes, oblations, obventions, and all other profits and emoluments belonging to the same rectory', and the truth is in this case that the same parson (the lessor) had a portion of tithes in the parish of another parson, for which, upon a composition, it was agreed and finally determined that in return for the tithes lying in the other parish he should have an annuity, the question now is nothing other than whether this annuity shall pass to the lessee by reason of this lease, or not.

It was thought by SHELLEY J., and this was not denied by the others, that the lessee of the rectory should have this annuity by reason of this lease, by virtue of the words 'emoluments and profits'. [The reason is] because this annuity was in him in recompense for his tithe, and was in him as parson, and therefore he who is parson shall have it, and he who is lessee is parson for the time being, namely during his lease, and this annuity is always annexed to the person of him who is parson.[1]

And Serjeant *Saunders* put this case: if someone is seised of a manor, by reason whereof he has common in another's land, and he in whose land this common is grants an annuity to him who has the common, and in this case the person who has the manor makes a feoffment thereof with the appurtenances (*cum pertinenciis*), shall the annuity pass in this case, or not?

Mr [Justice] SHELLEY said that the cases are not alike, because in this last case of a manor there is a privity and a distinct person, whereas in the case of the parson it is otherwise, for there he had it in right of his rectory and it goes in succession, and he who is parson shall have it.

And SHELLEY asked by the way whether this composition between them was for their lives, or not. And it was answered unto him that it was; and so he said that therefore the composition will bind etc.

It was also held in the Common Bench that if a parson exchanges his glebe land for other land, by reason of this exchange this land has now become and is made part of the glebe land etc.

---

[1] Cf. *Anon.* (1544) Gell's reports, Pas. 36 Hen. VIII, fo. 54 ('... *Dyer* dit que SHELLEY fuit del oppinion en le Comen Place deinz petite temps que le parson icy en cest cas avera son tythe del glebe terre per luy lesse ou grante devaunt. PORTEMAN: Il fuit mez pur son plesure').

[98]

[*Fo. 81*] Mr *Bromley* dit que nul surrender poit estre mez all cestui en le remainder, et dit ouster [que si lez][1] soyt fayt a un pur vye, le remainder a un auter pur vye, le remainder az droyt heyrez [...] tenant pur vye que fayt lez pur xx. annez et puis devie deinz le terme, cest lez ne lyera [cestui en le] remainder, mez si cestui en le remainder devie cest lez lyera lez heirez del primer tenant pur vye, et [le case][2] fuit Rychard Fytzwilliamz.

[99]

Nota que fuit dit per Seigniour *Mountagwe*, Cheffe Justyce dengleterre, et *Bromley*, Justyce, quun fayt fuit assetz bon nient obstant that it laked a daie, quar il ne fuit [...] le fayt bon ou materiall issint que il avoyt escripture, seale, [...].

[100]

[*Fo. 81v*] [Nota][3] loppinion de *Mountagwe*, Seigniour Cheffe Justyce, que si un home soyt seisi dun maner il ne besoigne de prescryber daver un fraunke folde en cez terrez demesnez, mez daver un fraunke folde en lez terrez de cez fraunktenantes il devoyt prescriber. Et en le primer case son reson fuit pur taunt quun fraunkfold fuit incydent mez il nest my issint en lauter case. Quere ouster.

[101]

Nota que loppinion del *Shelley*, Justyce, fuit que si un dit a un auter que sil soyt come tyel et tyel report il fuit worthy to sytt upon the pyllory or elles to

---

[1] *Conjectural: words lost.*
[2] *Conjectural.*   [3] *Conjectural: word lost.*

98. FITZWILLIAM'S CASE

Probably King's Bench, 1544/45 (cf. no. 99).

Mr BROMLEY[1] said that no surrender may be made except to the remainderman. He further said that if a lease is made to someone for life, remainder to someone else for life, remainder to the right heirs [of the first][2] tenant for life, who makes a lease for twenty years and then dies within the term, this lease shall not bind the remainderman; but if the remainderman dies, this lease shall bind the heirs of the first tenant for life. [The case] was Richard Fitzwilliam's.

99. NOTE

King's Bench, 1544/45.

Note that it was said by my lord MOUNTAGUE, Chief Justice of England,[3] and BROMLEY J. that a deed was perfectly good even though it lacked a day, for it was not [the date which made][4] the deed formal or material, so long as it had writing, a seal, [and delivery].[5]

100.

Probably King's Bench, c. 1544/45.

Note the opinion of MOUNTAGUE, Lord Chief Justice, that if someone is seised of a manor he need not prescribe to have a frank-fold in his demesne lands; but to have a frank-fold in the lands of his free tenants he ought to prescribe. In the former case his reason was that a frank-fold is incident; but it is not so in the other case. Query further.

101. NOTE

Common Pleas, probably c. 1545.

Note that the opinion of SHELLEY J. was that if someone says to another that, if it be as such and such reports, he was worthy to sit upon the pillory or

---

[1] Appointed J.K.B. on 5 Nov. 1544.   [2] Conjectural: text lost through damage.
[3] I.e. of the King's Bench. Mountague was translated to the Common Pleas on 6 Nov. 1545.
[4] Conjectural: text lost through damage.   [5] Conjectural: text lost through damage.

have < [such] punyshement > [i] [que] un tyel avoyt, et ne fuit ascun tyel report come il ad dyt: ore en cest case il mesme est le cause et le grounde de cest infamy et slaunder, per que action sur le case gist verz luy.

[102][1]

Loppinionz del Seigniour *Baweldwyne* et *Henley*, attourney daugmentationz, en le case cestui que ad marye le fyle del Thomas Myller del Massyngham [fueront] que le fyle est seisi pur terme de sa vye a son use demesne, et nemi all use son [...], quar est entende toutes foytes quant home prist surrender ou feffment a luy et [...] a luy et a son fytz ou fyle que ilz sount de tyelz estates queux [...] seisiez a lour proper[i] usez accordant a lestates queux sont [...]

[Hen]ley dit ouster que home poit estre seisi dun particular estat [...] feffez habendum a eux toutz et a lez heirz le feffour [...].

[103]

xix H. viii.

[*Fo. 86v*] Home fayt feffment a certen personz a son use et declare son volunte a son cosen en tayle, et si il devie saunz heyre de son corps donquez il voet que cez executourz vendront le terre et distribueront lez denerz pur son alme, et puis devie, lun executour morust, lauter executour fyst cez executourz et devie, le done en tayle morust saunz issue, lez executourz del executour vend le terre, et leyre le donour entre.

Wylby. Semble que lez executourz ne poyent vender, quar le volounte per quell ilz ount auctorite voet que cez executourz vendront et lez executourz del executour ne sont mye cez executourz. Et ceo est prove quar a le comen ley devaunt lestatut de anno xxv[to] E. 3. ilz ne puyssont aver ascun action de < dett >,[2] trns. ou accompte dewe a le primer testatour. Auxi est prove per le user del action a cest jour, quar le brefe voet Precipe A. B. quod reddat etc. J.

[1] *Text lost at bottom corner of page.*
[2] *Interlined.*

else to have such punishment as such and such had, and there was no such report as he has said: in this case he himself is the cause and the ground of this infamy and slander, and so an action on the case lies against him.[1]

102. ANON.

Perhaps Court of Augmentations, 1540/45. Damaged text.

The opinions of my lord BALDWIN[2] and *Hendley*, attorney of the Augmentations,[3] in the case of the person who married the daughter of Thomas Miller of Massingham were that the daughter is seised for term of her life to her own use, and not to the use of her [husband],[4] for it is always presumed when someone takes a surrender or feoffment to him and [. . .] to him and his son or daughter that they are of such estates as [. . .] seised to their own uses according to the estates which are [. . .]

Hendley further said that one may be seised of a particular estate [. . .] feoffees, *habendum* to all of them and to the heirs of feoffor [. . .].

103. ANON.

Exchequer Chamber, 1527. Also reported in YB Trin. 19 Hen. VIII, fo. 9, pl. 4; anon. reports, above, vol. I, p. 60, no. 49 (also dated Trin. 1527); Pollard's reports, above, p. 260, no. 33 (dated 17 Hen. VIII).

Someone makes a feoffment to certain persons to his use and declares his will to his kinsman in tail, and then wills that if he should die without an heir of his body his executors should sell the land and distribute the money for his soul; then he dies; and one of the executors dies; the other executor appoints his executors and dies; the donee in tail dies without issue; the executors of the executor sell the land; and the donor's heir enters.

WILLOUGHBY. It seems that the executors may not sell, for the will through which they have authority wills that his executors should sell, and the executor's executors are not his executors. This is proved because at common law, before the statute of 25 Edw. III,[5] the executors of an executor could not have any action of debt, trespass or account due to the first testator. It is also proved by the use of the present action, for the writ says 'Command A. that he render etc. to J. C., executor of the testament of C. D., executor of the testament of W. M.' (*Praecipe A. B. quod reddat etc. J. C. executori testamenti*

---

[1] Cf. *Vaus* v. *Serle* (1540) KB 27/1116, m. 110 ('If it be true that is reported. . .').
[2] Chief Justice of the Common Pleas 1535–45.
[3] Walter Hendley, bencher of Gray's Inn, attorney-general of the Augmentations 1540–47.
[4] Conjectural: text lost through damage.   [5] 25 Edw. III, stat. 5, c. 5 (*SR* i. 321).

C. executori testamenti C. D. executori[s] testamenti W. M., issint est prove que ilz ne sont executourz. Et null poet vender sinon ceux executourz, et issint le sale per eux fayt est voyde. Et auxi ceo est un offyce de truste que est comyse a eux de fayer le sale, le quell ilz ne poynt commytter ouster as auterz: sicome jeo face lettre dattourney a un A. pur delyver season, il ne poet doner son auctorite ouster as auterz. Et issint il semble le sale voyde.

   Ro, Moore, Port et *Broke.* Semble le sale bon. Et a ceo que ad este dit que lez executourz ne sount mye executourz le primer testatour, pur ceo que ilz ne puysont aver action, ilz semble a le comen ley que ilz puyssont aver action de dett: et issint appert en dyverz lyverz. Et auxi appert que ilz avoyent sue execution del estatut merchaunt ou staple et elegit dewe all primer testatour. Issint ore ilz sont cez executourz. Donquez quant il voet per son voulounte que cez executourz vendront le terre, ceo fuit un generall commission a eux per cel nosme executourz, issint que per cel generall commission quaunt ilz fount lour executourz et deviont lour executourz averont mesme le auctorite et power le quell ilz avoyent adevaunt. Mez si il voet que J. a S. et J. B. ces executourz vendront cel terre, ore lour executourz ne poent vender cel terre, pur ceo que ilz ne ount auctorite per cel generall nosme executourz mez per lour nosmez especiall. Et lun [*fo. 87*] deux per luy ne poet fayer sale, mez covient a ambideux de joynder en sale, et si un devie lauter ne poyt fayer sale. Auxi le volount de chescun home est favour en le ley, issint que son entent apperera per lez parolx en le voulounte nient obstant que ne sont expresse tam pleynment sicome est requisite [in] auterz donz, unquore lez justicez construeront lez estatez fayt per tyel voulounte accordant a lentent de le devysour si ne soyt que lez parolx en le voulounte sont contrariantz a le ley. Sicome home devyse terre imperpetuum, ceo est bon fee et uncore per feffment forsque estate pur terme de vie. Donquez ycy est voulounte et entent que lez terrez serront venduez et ne poent estre venduez devant que le done en tayle morust sanz issue, le quell peraventure poet aver continuanz ii. c. anz ou imperpetuum, et donquez sez executourz ne poynt pas vender. Et chescun home resonable ad mesme le knowlege, issint quant il devysa que lez executourz aprez le mort le done en tayle vendront le terre, son entent amount ataunt sicome il dit que cez executourz vendront ou lez executourz del executourz [ou] auterment son entendment ne poet estre entenduez. Donquez ycy nest ascun lachez ou defaute en [...] lez primerz executourz quar ilz ne puyssont fayer sale devaunt le tayle determyne et devaunt cel [...] ambideux fueront mortez, issint null defaut est en [eux]: quar nest semble lou jeo devyse terre a mez executourz de fayer sale, la silz ne fount sale deynz convenient temps, scilicet ii. ou iii. anz, ou aprez un loyall profferr a eux, la leyre poet bien enter, quar la est un defaute en eux.

   Et toutz lez auterz justicez econtra, scilicet que lez executourz ne poent vender ou fayer sale, quar est graunde divercite perenter tyelx chosez queux

---

[1] *Reading unclear.*

C. D. executoris testamenti W. M.), and so it is proved that they are not themselves executors. No one may sell except [his] executors, and therefore the sale made by [their executors] is void. Moreover it is an office of trust which is committed to them to make the sale, which they may not commit over to others: as where I make a letter of attorney to one A. to deliver seisin, he may not give his authority over to others. Therefore he thought the sale void.

Roo, MORE, PORT and BROKE thought the sale good. As to what has been said that the executors are not executors of the first testator, because they could not have an action, they thought that at common law they could have an action of debt: and it appears so in several books. It also appears that they have sued execution upon statutes merchant or staple and *elegit* due to the first testator. Thus they are now his executors. Therefore when he wills by his will that his executors should sell the land, this was a general commission to them by this name 'executors', so that by this general commission when they appoint their own executors and die their executors shall have the same authority and power which they had before. But if he wills that John at Style and John Browne, his executors, should sell the land, their executors may not now sell this land, because they do not have authority by the general name of executors but only by their own special names. And one of them by himself may not make a sale, but both of them must join in the sale, and if one of them dies the other may not make a sale. Also, everyone's will is favoured in law, so that his intent shall appear from the words in the will even if they are not expressed as plainly as is requisite in other gifts, but the justices will construe the estates made by such a will according to the intent of the devisor, provided that the words in the will are not contrary to the law. For instance, if someone devises land 'for ever' (*imperpetuum*), this is a good fee, and yet by feoffment it would only be an estate for term of life.[1] Here, then, is a will and the intention is that the lands shall be sold; but they cannot be sold before the donee in tail dies without issue, which might perhaps have continuance for two hundred years or for ever, and then his executors cannot sell. Every reasonable man[2] has the same knowlege, so that when he devises that the executors should sell the land after the death of the donee in tail, his intent is tantamount to saying that his executors or his executors' executors should sell, or else his intention cannot be understood. Now, there is no laxity or default here in the first executors, for they could not have made a sale before the time when they were both dead, and so there is no default in them. It is not like the case where I devise land to my executors to make a sale, for there if they do not make a sale within a convenient time— namely, two or three years—or after a lawful proffer to them, the heir may well enter, for in that case there is a default in them.

All the other justices held the contrary, namely that the executors may not sell or make a sale, for there is a great difference between such things as are

---

[1] I.e. for want of the words 'and his heirs'.
[2] Note this early reference to the *home resonable*.

sont testamentori et queux nemi, quar toutz chatellx personallx et chattellx realx
sont testamentori et la executourz dez executourz averont lez chosez et mesme
lauctorite et power sicome lez primer executourz. Mez cel acte de fayer sale nest
testatmentori mez est un reall acte destre fayt per lez executourz, quar per le sale
un [estate]¹ de feesimple, scilicet le use, serra transmute en le vende. Issint cel
acte mere reall, quar il ne doyt prover le volounte devaunt lordinarye en cel
poynt, quar lordinarye nad ryenz a fayer forsque ovesque chosez personallx,
quar si jeo per mon volounte face ii. homez mez executourz et puis jeo voyle que
un auter prent lez profettes de ma terre pur iii. ans pur distributer en mariage de
mez fylez, ore il nest pas executour. Donquez ycy le auctorite est done a eux per
le volounte et nemi per le testament, et le nosmer del executourz nyent materiall
et nest a auter purpose forsque de monstre queux personz doyent fayer le sale.
Et auxi cest un office de trust le quell est comyse a eux, et ilz ne poent comytter
cel office as auterz, quar si jeo face un home mon seneschall de mez courtz ou
mon baylyffe de mon maner il ne poet commytter cel ouster a auter. Auxi ilz
doynt fayer solonque le trust que est comyse a eux, quar si jeo devyse que mez
executourz doynt vendre le terre il covient que ambideux doynt joynder en sale
quar issint le trust fuit commyse a eux et le sale per un est voyde.

Auxi fuit dit per le cheiffe justice et auterz que si home devyse que J. a D. et
J. N. vendront son terre et lun devie lauter ne poet fayer sale. Et mesme le ley
del executourz et null differens. Auxi fuit dit que si home voyle que sez feffez
doynt fayer estate a un tyel, ore, si lun feffe morust, lauterz poent executer²
estat. Ou si toutz devyont, leyre celuy que survesquist doyt executer estate,
quar cel fuit le confidens et trust le quell fuit comyse a eux sur le feffment,
scilicet que ilz doyent suffer et executer mon volounte. Et bon divercite fuit
prise per le cheiffe justice quaunt home devysera que sez feffez doyent fayer un
acte a ascun person certen, sicome le case devaunt, et ou lacte et le personz a
que le acte serra fayte est noun certeyn, sicome en cel case del sale, quar en le
primer case ilz doynt fayer et perfourmer lacte solonque lez parollx et lauctorite
a eyx comyse et nemi auterment. Et adire que un volounte est issint favouryd
en le ley que ilz doynt adjuger solonque son entent, ceo est voyer lou sont
parollx sufficient en le volunte a declarer son entent et auterment nemi, quar ilz
ne poynt adjuger son entent sinon que soyt expresse per parollx. Et en le case
lou home devyse terre imperpetuum, la son volounte apperte per parollx
expresse que il doyt aver fee, et solonque ceo ilz doynt adjuger. [fo. 87v] Mez en
le case ycy ne sont ascunz parollx que prove que son volounte est que lez
executourz del executour doynt fayer le sale, mez solement auctorite est don a
sez executourz. Donquez nouz ne poyamus auterment adjuger forsque
accordant a lez parollx. Et auxi nous ne doyemus juger toutz foytz
accordant a son entent, quar si home devyse terre a un home en fee et sil
devie saunz heyre que donquez le terre remayndera a un estraunge, ore cel
remaynder est voyde, et uncore son entent est que il doyt remaynder, mez ceo

¹ *Reading unclear.*
² *Altered from* fayer.

testamentary and those which are not; for all chattels personal and chattels real are testamentary and there the executors of the executors shall have the things and have the same authority and power as the first executors. But this act of making a sale [of land] is not testatmentary, but is a real act to be done by the executors, for by the sale an estate of fee simple—namely the use—shall be transmuted in the vendee. Therefore this act is purely real, for he ought not to prove the will before the ordinary in this point, for the ordinary has nothing to do except with things personal. If by my will I make two men my executors, and afterwards I will that someone else should take the profits of my land for three years to distribute towards the marriage of my daughters, [this is good and yet] he is not an executor. Here, then, the authority is given to them by the will and not by the testament, and the naming of the executors is immaterial and is for no other purpose than to show what persons ought to make the sale. Also, it is an office of trust which is committed to them, and they may not commit this office to others; for if I make someone my steward of my courts or my bailiff of my manor, he may not commit this over to someone else. Also they ought to act in accordance with the trust which is committed to them, for if I devise that my executors ought to sell the land, both must join in the sale, for that is how the trust was committed to them and a sale by one is void.

It was also said by the chief justice and others that if someone devises that John at Down and John at Noke should sell his land, and one of them dies, the other may not make the sale. The law is the same of executors, and there is no difference. It was also said that if someone wills that his feoffees should make an estate to such and such, and one of the feoffees dies, the others may execute an estate; of, if they all die, the heir of the survivor ought to execute an estate, for that was the confidence and trust which was committed to them by the feoffment, namely that they ought to suffer and execute my will. And a good distinction was taken by the chief justice as to when someone devises that his feoffees should do an act to some person certain, as the case is before, and where the act and the persons to whom the act is to be done are uncertain, as in this case of the sale; for in the first case they ought to do and perform the act according to the words and the authority committed to them and not otherwise. And to say that a will is so favoured in law that they ought to adjudge according to his intent, that is true where there are sufficient words in the will to clarify his intent, but otherwise not, for they cannot adjudge his intent unless it is expressed by words. In the case where someone devises land *imperpetuum*, his will appears from the express words that he ought to have fee, and they ought to adjudge in accordance with that. But in the case here there are no words which prove that his will was that the executors of the executors ought to make the sale, but authority is given solely to his executors. Therefore we may not adjudge otherwise than in accordance with the words. Moreover, we ought not always to judge in accordance with the intent, for if a man devises land to someone in fee and wills that if he dies without an heir the land should remain to a stranger, this remainder is void: and yet his intent is that it should

est contrariant a le ley que un remaynder doyt depender sur un fee simple et pur ceo est voyde. Mesme le ley est si home devyse terre a un home en fee et si il devie sanz heyre que donquez le terre ne doyt escheter mez doyt reverter, ceo est voyde, pur le cause avaundit.

Et issint toutz lez justicez fueront en oppinion que lez executourz del executour ne poent fayer sale. Auxi si home devyse que sez terrez serront venduez, et ne monstra per que, cel devyse est voyde pur le non certente, quar lez justicez ne poent construer son entent, pur ceo que il nad expresse son entent per parollx.

Fytzherbert a mesme lentent, quar devaunt lestatut R. iii[i] celuy que avoyt luse navoyt ryenz en le terre mez tout lenterest del terre fuit en lez feffez per le comen ley, quar si il ust declare son volunte de ceo ou devyse ou fayt bargayne si lez feffez ne voyllent executer estate accordant il navoyt remedie per le comen ley, mez ore per lestatut celuy que ad luse poet entre sur sez feffez et fayer feffment as auterz: issint le statut done auctorite et interest a eux a ore. Donquez quaunt il devyse que sez executourz doynt vender le terre, ore per ceux parollx le use est en lez executourz et taunt amount sicome il disoyt que il devyse sez terrez a sez executourz a fayer vende. Et ceo prove un case en le lyver dassises: un home devyse que sez executourz vendront son terre et aprez lexecutour entre en le terre et prist lez profettes per ii. anez, et puis vient un que fist un sufficient proferr de money pur le terre, et il refuse, et leyre entre, et adjuge loyall pur ceo que il nad fayt son sale deynz un resonable temps, le quell ley luy dona. Issint semble per lez parollx que lez executourz avera le terre, quar auterment lour sale serra voyde, quar si le use serroyt en le heyre donquez purroyt il fayer sale, pur ceo que le fee simplle de[1] use est discenduez a luy. Et auxi home ne poyt doner ceo le quell il nad, quar si ilz nont le use ilz ne poent vender, quar ceo serroit impertinent. Donquez si le use soyt en eux, cel use descendera apres son mort all heyre celuy que survyve et nemi a lez executourz del executour, et donquez ne poent ilz fayer sale de ceo.

Issint loppinion clere de toutz lez justicez que lez executourz del executour ne ownt power de fayer sale. Mez dyverz de lez justicez fueront enconter oppinion dell Fytzherbert que si home devyse que sez executourz doynt vender son terre per ceux parollx le use nest en [eux][2] ne ilz doynt prender lez profettz, mez le use discende a leyre, unquore ilz doent fayer sale. Quar nest impertinent que home poet doner ou vender en auter droyt chose le quell il nad: sicome jeo face lettre dattourney a un home a delyver lyvere et season, ore il poet fayer fraunktenement de[3] passer et unquore il nad ascun fraunktenement. Issint ycy. Auxi est comen argument en motes que home avera fyre hors del flynt et uncore nest ascun fyre en le flynte.

Finis de cel case.

---

[1] *Perhaps* le.
[2] use.
[3] *Interlined.*

remain, but it is contrary to law for a remainder to depend on a fee simple, and therefore it is void. The law is the same if a man devises land to someone in fee and wills that if he dies without an heir the land should not escheat but revert: that is void, for the aforesaid reason.

Thus all the justices were of opinion that the executors of the executor could not make a sale. Also, if someone devises that his lands shall be sold, and does not say by whom, this devise is void for uncertainty; for the justices cannot construe his intent, because he has not expressed his intent by words.

FITZHERBERT to the same purpose; for before the statute of Richard III[1] cestuy que use had nothing in the land, but all the interest of the land was in the feoffees by the common law; and so if he declared his will thereof, or devised or made a bargain, and the feoffees would not execute an estate accordingly, he had no remedy by the common law. Now, however, by the statute, cestuy que use may enter upon his feoffees and make a feoffment to others: and thus the statute now gives them an authority and an interest. Therefore when he devises that his executors should sell the land, by these words the use is in the executors and it is tantamount to saying that he devises his lands to his executors to make a sale. This is proved by a case in the book of assizes:[2] someone devised that his executors should sell his land, and afterwards the executor entered in the land and took the profits for two years, and then someone came who made a sufficient offer of money for the land, and he refused, and the heir entered, and it was adjudged lawful because he had not made his sale within the reasonable time which the law gave him. Thus it seems by the words that the executors should have the land, for otherwise their sale would be void; for if the use should be in the heir then he could make a sale, because the fee simple of the use has descended to him. Moreover one cannot give what he does not have; and so, if they to not have the use, they cannot sell, for it would be absurd. Therefore if the use is in them, this use shall descend after his death to the heir of the survivor and not to the executors of the executor, and therefore they cannot make a sale thereof.

Thus it was the clear opinion of all the justices that the executors of the executor have no power to make a sale. But several of the justices were against Fitzherbert's opinion that if someone devises that his executors should sell his land the use is not in them by these words, and they ought not to take the profits, but the use descends to the heir. Nevertheless they ought to make a sale. For it is not absurd for someone to give or sell in another right something which he does not have: as where I make a letter of attorney to someone to deliver livery and seisin, he may now cause a freehold to pass and yet he has no freehold. Likewise here. Also it is a common argument in moots that a man shall have fire out of a flint and yet there is no fire in the flint.[3]

End of this case.

[1] 1 Ric. III, c. 1 (*SR* ii. 477).   [2] Probably YB 39 Edw. III, Lib. Ass., pl. 17.
[3] *Faryngton* v. *Darell* (1431) YB Trin. 9 Hen. VI, fo. 23, pl. 19; Baker & Milsom, at p. 74, *per* Babington C.J.; cited by Brudenell C.J. in *Gervys* v. *Cooke* (1522) YB Mich. 14 Hen. VIII, fo. 10, pl. 5; 119 Selden Soc. 121.

[104]

Action de dett fuit port sur un obligation, le defendant dit que il delyver le obligation a loblige come un escrowe sur conditionz destre perfourme de parte loblige, et monstre que lez conditions ne sont perfourmez, et issint Nient son fayte. Et fuit adjuge null ple. Et divercite lou est issint delyver a le oblige et ou a un estraunge a delyver ouster a le oblige.

[105]

Home fist un fayt de feffment a certen personz all use et intent de performer son darren volounte accordant all fayte, videlicet ad usum B. C. pur terme de son vie, et aprez son deces volo quod il remayndra a un estraunge, et aprez cel feffment il fist lez pur anz a un auter. Si ore il poet aulter le use declare en le primer fayt ou nemi, ceo fuit le mater.

Shelley que il ne poet aulter le use, quar quant un use est expresse sur le lyvery en quell le terce person est de aver avauntage, donquez celuy que fist le feffment ne poet ceo aulter. Sicome home fayt feffment all use dun estraunge ou all use de luy mesme et sez heyrez de son corps engenderz, ore il ne...[1]

[106]

[*Fo. 88v, reversing*] Si home vouche luy mesme pur saver le tayle, cest voucher est toutz foytz pur le comodite del issue en le tayle et pur ceo il ne unquez suera execution mez son issue suera pur ceo que le voucher est pur le benefyte del issue. Cest le reason pur que il suera execution, per *Shelley*.

---

[1] *End of page. The following page is missing.*

104. ANON.

Undated, but the same point is reported in YB Pas. 19 Hen. VIII, fo. 8, pl. 12 (1527); and Gell, Mich. 36 Hen. VIII, fo. 23v (1544).

An action of debt was brought on a bond; the defendant said that he delivered the bond to the obligee as an escrow upon conditions to be performed on the part of the obligee, and showed that the conditions have not been performed, 'and so not his deed'. And it was adjudged no plea. There is a distinction between where it is so delivered to the obligee and where to a stranger to deliver over to the obligee.

105. BELE v. BENET

Common Pleas, 1527. Also reported in Spelman, p. 228, pl. 3 (Trin. 1527); YB Trin. 19 Hen. VIII, fo. 11, pl. 5, and fo. 13, pl. 11; and probably above, vol. I, p. 58, no. 46. Record: CP 40/1054, m. 316.

Someone made a deed of feoffment to certain persons to the use and intent of performing his last will in accordance with the deed, namely 'to the use of B. C. for term of his life, and after his decease I will that it should remain to a stranger'; and after this feoffment he made a lease for years to someone else. Whether he could thus alter the use declared in the first deed, or not, that was the matter.

SHELLEY said that he may not alter the use, for when a use is expressed upon the livery, in which a third person is to have advantage, then the person who made the feoffment may not alter it. For instance, if someone makes a feoffment to the use of a stranger or to the use of himself and his heirs of his body begotten, he may not...[1]

106. NOTE

Common Pleas, before 1549, perhaps c. 1527 (cf. nos. 103-105).

If someone vouches himself to save the tail, this voucher is always for the benefit of the issue in tail, and therefore he shall never sue execution, but his issue shall sue, because the voucher is for the benefit of the issue. That is the reason why he shall sue execution, according to SHELLEY.

[1] Rest missing.

9. REPORTS AND NOTES BY JOHN CARYLL, THE YOUNGER
(c. 1527–1537)
including some cases in the Inner Temple

(A)[1]

Hec habui ex libro Magistri Johannis Caryll
Attornati Ducatus Lancastrie
viri valde pii ac docti ac Interioris templi socii

[1]

Nota si deux coparceners soyent disseise et ount issue e devyont, lour issues averont severall actions pur ceo que le disseisin lun nest le disseisin lauter, issint les causez severall. Mes si deux coparceners soyent de terre en taylle et ilz fount feffmente joyntmente, uncore lour issues naveront deux formedons quar laction nest prise sur le feffmente ne cest le tytle einz le done.

[2]

25 H. 8.

Cest questyon fuit demande 25 H. 8. Un home fait lesse pur terme danz et le lesse fixe un furneys, al fyne del terme le lesse ceo pryst ove luy: si ceo soyt loyall?

Fitzherbert dit que cy, quar ceo nest myse forsque pur le ease del lessee quell il poit prender.

---

[1] From BL MS. Harley 1691, ff. 98–111, collated with IT MS. Petyt 511.13, ff. 1–6v (which lacks the first 24 cases).

9. Reports and Notes by John Caryll, the Younger
(c.1527–1537)
including some cases in the Inner Temple

(A)

I have taken these reports from the book of Master John Caryll
Attorney of the Duchy of Lancaster
an immensely pious and learned man
and a fellow of the Inner Temple

1. NOTE

Note that if two coparceners are disseised, have issue, and die, their issues shall have several actions, because the disseisin of one of them is not a disseisin of the other, and so the causes are several. But if there are two coparceners of land in tail, and they make a feoffment jointly, their issues shall not have two formedons; for the action is not taken upon the feoffment, nor is that the title, but the gift.

2. MASON v. WYTTON

Common Pleas, 1533. Record: CP 40/1080, m. 436.

This question was asked in 25 Hen. VIII: someone made a lease for term of years and the lessee affixed an oven, and at the end of the term the lessee took it with him; is this lawful?

FITZHERBERT said it was, for it was only put there for the ease of the lessee, and so he may take it.

Shelley. Si un home lesse son terre a un smythe et il face un anvelde et ceo fyxe en la terre, al fyne del terme il ceo prendra non obstante que soyt fyxe al fraunketenemente par cause queceo est de necessytye pur lexercyse de son faculte. Mesme la ley serra icy si cesti que fixe le furneys fuit un dyer ou bruer, causa qua supra.

Record

CP 40/1080, m. 436, Jenour.

Lincoln'. Ricardus Wytton nuper de Hornecastell in comitatu predicto, dyer, attachiatus fuit ad respondendum Willelmo Mason de placito quare vi et armis quoddam vas plumbeum vocatum a lede ponderans trescentas et sexaginta petras plumbi ipsius Willelmi precii viginti marcarum apud Horncastell nuper inventum cepit et asportavit et alia enormia ei intulit ad grave dampnum ipsius Willelmi et contra pacem domini regis nunc etc. Et unde idem Willelmus, per Antonium Irby attornatum suum, queritur quod predictus Ricardus, vicesimo tercio die Marcii anno regni domini regis nunc quartodecimo, vi et armis quoddam vas plumbeum vocatum a lede ponderans trescentas et sexaginta petras plumbi ipsius Willelmi precii etc. apud Horncastell nuper inventum cepit et asportavit et alia enormia etc. ad grave dampnum etc. et contra pacem etc. Unde dicit quod deterioratus est et dampnum habet ad valenciam viginti librarum. Et inde producit sectam etc.

Et predictus Ricardus, per Johannem Dyon attornatum suum, venit. Et defendit vim et injuriam quando etc. Et quoad venire vi et armis dicit quod ipse in nullo est inde culpabilis. Et de hoc ponit se super patriam. Et predictus Willelmus Mason similiter. Et quoad residuum transgressionis predicte superius fieri supposite idem Ricardus dicit quod predictus Willelmus Mason actionem suam predictam versus eum habere non debet, quia dicit quod loci in quibus supponitur transgressionem predictam fieri sunt et predicto tempore quo supponitur transgressionem predictam fieri fuerunt unum mesuagium cum pertinenciis in Horncastell predicta, de quoquidem mesuagio cum pertinenciis quidam Thomas Thymolby, clericus, ante predictum tempus quo etc. fuit seisitus in dominico suo ut de feodo, et sic inde seisitus ante predictum tempus quo etc., scilicet vicesimo octavo die Aprilis anno regni domini regis nunc duodecimo, apud Horncastell predictam in comitatu predicto, dimisit mesuagium illud cum pertinenciis cuidam Willelmo Wharfe habendum et occupandum sibi et assignatis suis a festo Sanctorum Philippi et Jacobi tunc proxime sequenti usque finem termini decem annorum extunc proxime sequentium et plenarie complendorum, virtute cujus dimissionis idem Willelmus Wharfe fuit inde possessionatus, et sic inde possessionatus ante predictum tempus quo etc. vas plumbeum predictum in quendam murum mesuagii predicti ut parcellam liberi tenementi ejusdem mesuagii affixit, posteaque et ante idem tempus quo etc., scilicet vicesimo die Marcii anno regni domini regis nunc terciodecimo, predictus Willelmus Wharfe apud Horncastell predictam concessit totum statum et interesse sua que ipse tunc habuit futura in mesuagio predicto cum pertinenciis eidem Ricardo, virtute cujus concessionis idem Ricardus in mesuagium predictum cum pertinenciis intravit et fuit inde possessionatus, predicto vase plumbeo tunc sic in murum mesuagii illius ut parcellam liberi tenementi ejusdem tunc affixo existente, posteaque et ante predictum tempus quo etc. predictus Ricardus vas plumbeum predictum extra murum mesuagii predicti surripuit et evulsit

SHELLEY. If someone leases his land to a smith and he makes an anvil and fixes it in the land, at the end of the term he may take it, even though it is fixed to the freehold, because it is necessary for the exercise of his trade (*faculté*). The law will be the same here if the person who fixed the oven was a dyer or brewer, for the above reason.

Translation of the record

De Banco roll, Hil. 25 Hen. VIII (1534).

Lincolnshire. Richard Wytton, late of Horncastle in the county aforesaid, dyer, was attached to answer William Mason concerning a plea why with force and arms he took and carried away a certain leaden vat called 'a lead', weighing 360 stone of lead, belonging to him the same William, price twenty marks, lately found at Horncastle, and inflicted other outrages upon him, to the grave damage of him the said William and against the peace of the present lord king etc. And thereupon the same William, by Anthony Irby his attorney, complains that the aforesaid Richard, on the twenty-third day of March [1523] in the twenty-third year of the reign of the present lord king, with force and arms took and carried away a certain leaden vat called 'a lead', weighing 360 stone of lead, belong to him the said William, price etc., lately found at Horncastle, and inflicted oither outrages etc. to the grave damage etc. and against the peace etc. Whereby he says he is the worse and has suffered damage to the extent of twenty pounds. And thereof he produces suit etc.

And the aforesaid Richard, by John Dyon his attorney, comes; and he denies the force and wrong when etc. As to the coming with force and arms he says that he is in no way guilty thereof, and thereof he puts himself upon the country; and the aforesaid William Mason likewise. As to the rest of the aforesaid trespass supposed above to have been committed, the same Richard says that the aforesaid William Mason ought not to have his aforesaid action against him, because he says that the places in which the aforesaid trespass is supposed to have been committed are, and at the aforesaid time when the aforesaid trespass is supposed to have been committed were, one messuage with the appurtenances in Horncastle aforesaid, of which messuage with the appurtenances a certain Thomas Thymolby, clerk, before the aforesaid time when etc., was seised in his demesne as of fee, and being so seised thereof before the aforesaid time when etc., namely on the twenty-eighth day of April [1520] in the twelfth year of the reign of the present lord king, at Horncastle aforesaid in the county aforesaid, he demised the messuage with the appurtenances to a certain William Wharfe to have and to occupy unto him and his assigns from the feast of SS Philip and James then next following until the end of the term of ten years then next following and fully to be completed, by virtue of which demise the same William Wharfe was thereof possessed, and being so possessed thereof, before the aforesaid time when etc., he fixed the aforesaid leaden vat into a certain wall of the aforesaid messuage as part of the freehold of the same tenement; and afterwards, before the same time when etc., namely on the twentieth day of March [1522] in the thirteenth year of the reign of the present lord king, the aforesaid William Wharfe at Horncastle aforesaid granted all his estate and interest which he then had to come in the aforesaid messuage with the appurtenances to the same Richard, by virtue of which grant the same Richard entered into the aforesaid messuage with the appurtenances and was thereof possessed, the aforesaid leaden vat being then so fixed in the wall of the messuage as part of the freehold of the same tenement; and afterwards, before the aforesaid time when etc., the aforesaid Richard removed and pulled the aforesaid leaden vat out of the wall of the aforesaid messuage

ac illud cuidam Johanni Johnson deliberavit salvo custodiendum et eidem Ricardo cum inde requisitus foret reliberandum, posteaque et ante predictum tempus quo etc. predictus Johannes Johnson vas plumbeum predictum deliberavit prefato Willelmo Mason salvo custodiendum, pretextu cujus deliberationis idem Willelmus fuit inde possessionatus quousque predictus Ricardus predicto vicesimo tercio die Marcii anno quartodecimo supradicto vas plumbeum predictum apud Horncastell predictam inventum extra possessionem ipsius Willelmi cepit et asportavit prout ei bene licuit. Et hoc paratus est verificare. Unde petit judicium si predictus Willelmus Mason actionem suam predictam versus eum habere debeat etc.

Et predictus Willelmus Mason dicit quod ipse per aliqua preallegata ab actione sua predicta habenda precludi non debet, quia dicit quod ante predictum tempus transgressionis predicte facte predictus Thomas Thymolby fuit seisitus de mesuagio predicto cum pertinenciis in dominico [suo] ut de feodo, et sic inde seisitus ante tempus illud, scilicet predicto vicesimo octavo die Aprilis anno duodecimo supradicto, apud Horncastell predictam in comitatu predicto, dimisit mesuagium illud cum pertinenciis prefato Willelmo Wharff et assignatis suis a predicto festo Sanctorum Philippi et Jacobi tunc proxime sequenti usque finem termini decem annorum extunc proxime sequentium et plenarie complendorum, virtute cujus dimissionis idem Willelmus Wharfe fuit inde possessionatus, ac de vase predicto ut de vase suo proprio possessionato existente dictum vas plumbeum in quandam fornacem ex lapidibus constructam in quadam domo exteriori mesuagii predicti juxta dorsum cujusdam camini infra dictam domum exteriorem mesuagii illius posuit et affixit, posteaque et antequam predictus Willelmus Wharfe concessit prefato Ricardo statum et interesse sua que ipse tunc habuit futura in mesuagio predicto et ante predictum tempus transgressionis predicte facte, idem Willelmus Wharfe apud Horncastell predictam vendidit predictum vas plumbeum eidem Willelmo Mason, per quod idem Willelmus Mason fornacem predictam fregit et vas illud prefato Willelmo Wharfe deliberavit salvo custodiendum et eidem Willelmo Wharfe cum inde requisitus fuisset reliberandum, posteaque et ante predictum tempus transgressionis predicte facte predictus Willelmus Wharfe concessit totum terminum et interesse sua que ipse tunc habuit futura in mesuagio predicto prefato Ricardo, per quod idem Ricardus ante predictum tempus transgressionis predicte facte in mesuagio predicto cum pertinenciis intravit et fuit inde possessionatus, ipso Willelmo Mason de dicto vase ut de vase suo proprio in dicta domo exteriori possessionato existente, quosque predictus Ricardus predicto tempore transgressionis predicte facte vi et armis vas plumbeum predictum apud Horncastell predictam inventum cepit et asportavit contra pacem domini regis nunc, prout idem Willelmus Mason superius versus eum queritur, absque hoc quod predictum vas plumbeum fuit affixum in murum mesuagii predicti prout predictus Ricardus superius allegavit. Et hoc paratus est verificare. Unde, ex quo predictus Ricardus captionem et asportationem vasis plumbei predicti superius cognovit, idem Willielmus Mason petit judicium et dampna sua ea occasione sibi adjudicari etc.

Et predictus Ricardus, protestando non cognoscit aliqua per prefatum Willelmum Mason superius allegata fore vera, pro placito idem Ricardus ut prius dicit quod predictum vas plumbeum fuit affixum in murum mesuagii predicti ut parcella liberi tenementi ejusdem mesuagii, prout idem Ricardus superius allegavit. Et de hoc ponit se super patriam. Et predictus Willelmus Mason similiter. Ideo preceptum est vicecomiti quod venire faciat hic a die Pasche in xv dies xii etc. per quos etc. et qui nec etc. ad recognoscendum etc. quia tam etc.

[*See opposite.*]

and delivered it to a certain John Johnson to be kept safely and returned to the same Richard upon request; and afterwards, before the aforesaid time when etc., the aforesaid John Johnson delivered the aforesaid leaden vat to the said William Mason to be kept safely, by virtue of which delivery the same William was thereof possessed until the aforesaid Richard on the aforesaid twenty-third day of March in the above-mentioned fourteenth year took the aforesaid leaden vat, found at Horncastle aforesaid, out of the possession of the selfsame William, and carried it away, as well he might. And this he is ready to verify. Whereupon he prays judgment whether the aforesaid William Mason ought to have his aforesaid action against him etc.

And the aforesaid William Mason says that he ought not by reason of anything previously alleged to be barred from having his aforesaid action, because he says that before the aforesaid time when the aforesaid trespass was committed the aforesaid Thomas Thymolby was seised of the aforesaid messuage with the appurtenances in his demesne as of fee, and being so seised, before that time, namely on the aforesaid twenty-eighth day of April [1520] in the abovesaid twelfth year, at Horncastle aforesaid in the county aforesaid, demised that messuage with the appurtenances to the said William Wharfe and his assigns from the aforesaid feast of SS Philip and James then next following until the end of the term of ten years then next following and fully to be completed, by virtue of which demise the same William Wharfe was thereof possessed, and, being possessed of the aforesaid leaden vat as his own vat, he placed and fixed the said leaden vat in a certain oven (*fornax*) built of stones in a certain outhouse of the aforesaid messuage, against the back of a certain chimney in the said outhouse of that messuage; and afterwards, before the aforesaid William Wharfe granted to the said Richard his estate and interest which he then had to come in the aforesaid messuage, and before the aforesaid time when the aforesaid trespass was committed, the same William Wharfe at Horncastle aforesaid sold the aforesaid leaden vat to the same William Mason, whereby the same William Mason broke the aforesaid oven and delivered the vat to the said William Wharfe to be kept safely and returned to the same William Wharfe on request; and afterwards, before the aforesaid time when the aforesaid trespass was committed, the aforesaid William Wharfe granted all his term and interest which he then had to come in the aforesaid messuage to the said Richard, whereby the same Richard, before the aforesaid time when the aforesaid trespass was committed, entered into the aforesaid messuage with the appurtenances and was thereof possessed, he the said William Mason being possessed of the said vat as his own vat in the said outhouse, until the aforesaid Richard at the aforesaid time when the aforesaid trespass was committed with force and arms took and carried away the aforesaid leaden vat, found at Horncastle aforesaid, against the peace of the present lord king, as the same William Mason above complains against him, without this that the aforesaid leaden vat was fixed in the wall of the aforesaid messuage as the aforesaid Richard has above alleged. And this he is ready to verify. Therefore, inasmuch as the aforesaid Richard has above confessed the taking and carrying away of the aforesaid leaden vat, the same William Mason prays judgment and his damages for this cause to be awarded to him etc.

And the aforesaid Richard, protesting that he does not confess anything alleged above by the said William Mason to be true, for a plea the same Richard says (as before) that the aforesaid leaden vat was fixed in the wall of the aforesaid messuage as part of the freehold of the same messuage, as the said Richard has alleged above. And of this he puts himself upon the country; and the aforesaid William Mason likewise. Therefore the sheriff is ordered to cause to come here in the quindene of Easter twelve etc. by whom etc. and who neither etc. to make recognition etc. because both etc.

[At the assizes held before Fitzherbert and Luke JJ. at Lincoln Castle on the Thursday (6 August 1534) before St Lawrence the Martyr a verdict is given for the plaintiff for £11. 6 s. 8d., and judgment is given accordingly the next term.]

[3]

25 H. 8.

Un home fait lesse pur terme danz, le lessor coupast un arbre, si le lesse poit ceo prendre?

Fitzherbert semble que le lessor ceo avera.

Shelley semble clerement que non, quar cest un casuell proffytt quell est don al lesse, sicome un wyndfall et his similia. Et quant le lessor ceo fait il fyst tort al lesse et ceo nest wast, pur ceo que le lessor mesme que duyst aver laction fyst le wast, et issint quaunt est severe del fraunketenement est maintenaunt en le lesse.

Fitzherbert dymurt en contrare opynyon mes ne fyst ascun reson.

Quere, quar semble per le comen ley le propertye del arbre fuit en le lesse et a cest jour ryens est restrayne per lestatute mes que le lesse ne ferra wast, mes uncore per ceo ryen del propertye est prise hors de luy, donques quaunt le lessor mesme ceo coupast il est excuse de wast et poit ceo prendre pur ceo que il mesme ad le property come il avoit al comen ley. Quere hoc, et nota lestatute De donis conditionalibus quaunt a cest purpose.

[4]

25 H. 8.

Fitzherbert tyent que pur heryott custome home poit dystrener pur ceo que est parcel del tenure, come relyef.

Shelley tyent clermente le contrary, et il dit que cest heryott covyent estre pryse des avers le mort et ceux sont a les executours, par que serroit enconvenyent a dystrener lheire.

[5]

25 H. 8.

Nota que un fyne fuit refuse quell fuit levye per le baron et feme et le tierce par cause que toutz garr[antont] en le fyne ou ilz doyent aver que le garrante lun, et ceo est de cestui de que lestate move. Quere en fyne levye per joyntenauntz ou coparceners si toutz ne poyent garranter.

3. ANON.

Common Pleas, 1533.

Someone makes a lease for term of years, and the lessor fells a tree: may the lessee take it?

FITZHERBERT thought the lessor should have it.

SHELLEY thought clearly not, for it is a casual profit which is given to the lessee, like a windfall and such like. When the lessor did this he did wrong to the lessee; and it is not waste, because the lessor (who ought to have any action of waste) committed the waste himself. Therefore when it is severed from the freehold it is immediately in the lessee.

FITZHERBERT remained of the contrary opinion, but did not give any reason.

Query, for it seems that by the common law the property in the tree was in the lessee, and at the present day nothing is restrained by the statute[1] but that the lessee shall not commit waste; nevertheless none of the property is thereby taken out of him, and therefore when the lessor himself cuts it down the lessee is excused of waste, and he may take it, because he himself has the property as he had at common law. Query this, and note the statute *De donis conditionalibus* as to this purpose.[2]

4. ANON.

Common Pleas, 1533.

FITZHERBERT held that one may distrain for heriot custom because it is part of the tenure, like relief.

SHELLEY held clearly the contrary, and he said that this heriot must be taken from the beasts of the deceased, which belong to the executors, and so it would be absurd to distrain the heir.

5. NOTE

Common Pleas, 1533.

Note that a fine was refused which was levied by a husband and wife and a third party, because all of them warranted in the fine whereas there ought to have been a warranty by one, and that is the person from whom the estate moves. Query: in a fine levied by joint tenants or coparceners, may not all of them warrant?

---

[1] Statute of Gloucester, c. 5 (*SR* i. 48).
[2] Westminster II, c. 1, *De donis conditionalibus* (*SR* i. 71). Relevance unclear.

[6]

Nota per *Bromle,* donques reder, que si home ad rent en fee issant hors de terre en divers countyes, la feme navera unques brefe de dower, quar ceo nest don in confinio comitatus. Mes si lheire voet de son gree ceo assigner el poit dystrener. [*fo. 98v*]

[7]

25 H. 8.

Browne, serjant, demande de les justyces si home devaunt lestatute de Quia emptores terrarum que tyent xx acres per servyce de chivaler et per entyer fee fait feffmente dun acre salvo forinseco servicio, coment tyendra le feffe?

Et fuit cleremente agre per servyce de chivaler, mes il payera relyef forsque pro rata, scilicet le vint part de fee chivaler.

Et *Shelley* reherce un jugement libro assisarum, mes il dit que nest reson que il payera soloncque le rate de entyer fee de chivaler pur cest acre non obstante que il dit salvo forinseco servicio, et que en mayne le feffor cest acre fuit charge al dystres pur lentyer fee, donques quaunt il fait feffmente salvo forinseco servicio ore poit estre dit que toutz les servyces serront saves al feffor queux purront estre demandes de cest acre devaunt, et ceo fuit tout le fee. Mes en droit la ne fuit issint que le xx. parte de fee hors de cest acre, ergo ore ne serra tenus per pluis, et ceo prove si le seignior avoit purchace un acre lapportyonmente serra accordant.

[8]

25 H. 8.

Un lesse fuit fait a un feme pur terme de vie, le remainder ouster en fee, el prist baron, el et son baron fezoyent un feffmente en fee a cesti en remainder et fezoyent lyverez, le baron devie: si la feme poit entrer?

Et semble al *Fitzherbert* que el poit, pur ceo que ceo nest que surrender, et ceo ne poit faire discontynuance, et auxi son estate ne poit estre dyscontynue mes ou le remainder est discontynue.

Mes *Shelley* tyent le contrary, et que cest lyverey del baron ne serra defait

6. NOTE FROM THOMAS BROMLEY'S READING

Inner Temple, August 1533.[1]

Note by *Bromley,* then reader, that if someone has a rent in fee issuing out of land in various counties, the wife shall never have a writ of dower, for that is not available *in confinio comitatus*. But if the heir will gratuitously assign it, she may distrain.

7. ANON.

Common Pleas, 1533/34.

Browne, serjeant, asked the justices this question: if someone before the statute *Quia emptores terrarum* held twenty acres by knight-service by an entire fee, and made a feoffment of one acre 'saving the forinsec service' (*salvo forinseco servicio*), how shall the feoffee hold?

And it was clearly agreed that it was by knight-service, but he should only pay relief *pro rata*, namely the twentieth part of a knight's fee.

SHELLEY recited a judgment in the book of assizes,[2] but he said that it is not right that he should pay according to the rate of an entire knight's fee for this acre, even though he said *salvo forinseco servicio*. In the feoffor's hands this acre was charged with distress for the entire fee, and therefore when he made a feoffment *salvo forinseco servicio* it could be said that all the services should be saved to the feoffor which could have been demanded from this acre before, and that was the whole fee. But in right there was nothing but the twentieth part of a fee out of this acre, and so it shall not now be held by more, and this is proved because if the lord had purchased an acre the apportionment would have been in accordance.

8. ANON.

Common Pleas, 1533/34.

A lease was made to a woman for term of life, remainder over in fee; she married, and she and her husband made a feoffment in fee to the remainderman and made livery; the husband died. May the woman enter?

It seemed to FITZHERBERT that she could, because this is only a surrender, and that cannot make a discontinuance, and also his estate cannot be discontinued unless the remainder is discontinued.

But SHELLEY held the contrary, and that this livery from the husband shall

---

[1] Bromley read on 11 Hen. VII, c. 20 (*SR* ii. 583): *Readers and Readings*, p. 79.
[2] Probably YB 30 Edw. III, Lib. Ass., pl. 30.

sauns accord la feme, non obstante que le remainder nest dyscontynue. Come si feme tenaunt en taylle prist baron que fait feffmente al donor, ceo serra discontynuance a luy et nemi a son yssue.

Et nota que John Caryll reherca loppinion de Frowyke 15 H. 7, en le reporte de Serjante Caryll son pere, estre accordant al oppinion Fitzherbert et myst mesme les casez. Et auxi il tyent si un home fait done en taylle, le remainder en taylle, le remainder en fee, le tenaunt en taylle enfeffe cestui en remainder en fee, cest nest dyscontynuance.

[9]

25 H. 8.

En accompt vers un que fuit son rescevor pur accompt render per ses mains demesne, il dit que il ceo resceva de payer a un B., a que il paya, jugement si action. Et le ple fuit tenus bon barre sauns ascun travers. [*fo. 99*]

[10]

25 H. 8.

En brefe de dower le tenaunt dit que le baron le demandant, de que seison el demande dower, fuit seisi dauter terre, et myst ceo en certeyn, et de ceo enfeffe J. et W. al use de luy mesme et le demandant sa feme et a les heirs de lour deux corps en pleyn recompence et satisfaction de tout sa dower et joynture que eedem petenti accidere seu per aliquem modum devenire poterit per sive post suam mortem vel aliquo alio modo, jugemente si action.

Et *Wylughby* demande dez justyces si ceo fuit bon ple ou non.

Fitzherbert semble null ple.

Shelley. Peraventure si tiell feffmente ust estre allege devaunt le coverture en recompence il serra bon ple. Mes come cest case est il est sauns doubte que nest ple, quar fuit fait durant les espouselles, en quell case la feme poit apres le mort le baron disagreer al use et luy prendre a sa dower.

not be defeated without the wife's agreement, notwithstanding that the remainder is not discontinued. Similarly, if a woman tenant in tail marries a husband, who makes a feoffment to the donor, this shall be a discontinuance to her and not to her issue.

And note that *John Caryll* recited the opinion of Frowyk in 15 Hen. VII, in the report of Serjeant Caryll his father,[1] to be in accordance with Fitzherbert's opinion, and he put the same cases. He also held that if someone makes a gift in tail, remainder in tail, remainder in fee, and the tenant in tail enfeoffs the remainderman in fee, this is not a discontinuance.

9. ANON.[2]

Common Pleas, 1533/34.

In account against someone who was his receiver by his own hands for the purpose of rendering an account, he said that he received it to pay to one B., and that he paid it, and prayed judgment whether the plaintiff should have the action. And the plea was held a good bar, without any traverse.

10. ANON.

Common Pleas, 1533/34.

In a writ of dower the tenant said that the demandant's husband, of whose seisin she demanded dower, was seised of other land, and set it out with certainty, and thereof enfeoffed J. and W. to the use of himself and the demandant (his wife), and the heirs of their two bodies, in full recompense and satisfaction of all her dower and jointure which might fall due or in any way come to the same demandant through or after his death or in any other way (*quae eaedem petenti accidere seu per aliquem modum devenire poterit per sive post suam mortem vel aliquo alio modo*), and prayed judgment whether the plaintiff should have her action.

Willoughby asked the justices whether this was a good plea or not.

FITZHERBERT thought it no plea.

SHELLEY. Perhaps if such a feoffment in recompense had been alleged before the coverture it would have been a good plea. As this case is, however, it is beyond doubt that it is no plea; for it was made during the espousals, in which case the woman may disagree to the use after the husband's death and betake herself to her dower.

---

[1] Not traced in surviving texts, but this citation is direct evidence that the reports passed to his son: 115 Selden Soc. xvii, n. 59.

[2] Cf. *May* v. *Anger* (1535) CP 40/1085(2), m. 412, which may be the same case.

Wylughby. Vous ditez voier, et semble que use ne poit estre recompence, quar nest choce en possession ne regarde en nostre ley, issint el nad quid pro quo.

Et *Fitzherbert* fuit de mesme lopynion.

Et puis il amend son ple per le pleder dagremente del feme al terre en use, et sur ceo fuit dymurre.

[11]

25 H. 8.

En replevin pur dyre que le terre est son fraunkenemente et avower pur damage fezant nest ple, mes covyent luy entytler especiallmente al fraunktenemente. Auterment est en trespas.

Et ceo est le cours, come *Fitzherbert* dit, mes il ne savoit le reson.

[12]

Casus argue in Interiori Templo.

Tenaunt en taylle, le revercyon al roy, graunt un rent charge en fee et suffer un recovere per voucher et ad jugemente de recover en value, et ad yssue et devie seisi sans execution sue: si lheir en taylle tiendra cest terre charge ou nemi?

Bromley semble que il tyendra discharge, quar prymermente a ceo que ad este move si lissue poit averrer continuance de possession, semble que en ascun case il poit et en ascun case nemi, quar le avermente de continuance de possession est suffre en avoydance de cyrcuite daction, quar lou le tenaunt en taylle suffre recovere per defaut ou per confessyon et devie seisi et ceo discende a son yssue, ore si lissue ad droit est pluis reson que quaunt le droit et le possession sont ambideux en luy per droyturell mesnez que il serra receu de monstre son droyt et de averrer contynuance de possession, esteant en possession, que a suffrer le demandant aver execution per entre ou suer de execution, et apres que lissue recoverast arere per formedon et la de fauxer le recovere, quar ceo nest que cyrcuist daction quell la ley ne favour lou null auter impediment est. Et ceo appyert 7 H. 4, quar la est tenus que lissue averrera contynuance de possession ou le recovere est feynt, et serra remytt. Mes icy est recovere ewe ove voucher issint que lissue en tayll est daver recompence, quell recompence serra un barre a luy del tayll, ergo ore nest reson que il doit averrer continuance de possession et estre remytte et issint davoyder le recovere lou

Willoughby. What you say is true; and it seems that a use cannot be recompense, for it is not a thing in possession and is not regarded in our law, and so she does not have *quid pro quo*.

FITZHERBERT was of the same opinion.

Then he amended his plea by pleading an agreement by the wife to the land in use, and thereupon it was demurred.

11. ANON.

Common Pleas, 1533/34.

In replevin it is no plea to say that the land is his freehold and avow for damage feasant, but he must entitle himself specially to the freehold. It is otherwise in trespass.

That is the course, as FITZHERBERT said; but he did not know the reason.

12. A MOOT

A case argued in the Inner Temple, *c.* 1533.

Tenant in tail, where the reversion is in the king, grants a rent-charge in fee, suffers a recovery by voucher, and has judgment to recover in value; and he has issue and dies seised without having sued execution: shall the heir in tail hold this land charged, or not?

Bromley thought that he should hold it discharged. Firstly, as to the point which has been moved whether the issue may aver continuance of possession, it seems that in some cases he may and in some cases not. The averment of continuance of possession is allowed in avoiding circuity of action, for where the tenant in tail suffers a recovery by default or by confession and dies seised, and it descends to his issue, if the issue has right it is more reasonable that when the right and the possession are both in him by lawful means he shall be received to show his right and aver continuance of possession, being in possession, than to allow the demandant to have execution by entry or suing execution, and then afterwards the issue should recover back by formedon and falsify the recovery there, for that is mere circuity of action, which the law does not favour where there is no other impediment. That appears in 7 Hen. IV,[1] for it is there held that the issue may aver continuance of possession where the recovery is feigned, and shall be remitted. But here there is a recovery had with voucher, so that the issue in tail is to have recompense, which recompense shall be a bar to him in the tail, and so it is not now reasonable for him to aver continuance of possession and to be remitted and in that way to avoid

---

[1] YB Trin. 7 Hen. IV, fo. 19, pl. 26.

appyert bon matter de luy barrer: nyent pluis que serra ou recovere est per bon tytle.

Quere del recovere per action trye ou lissue poit fauxer en auter poynt quell son pere poit aver plede, et ne fyst, si a ore apres le mort son pere, esteant seisi per dyscent, poit averrer contynuance de possession et fauxer cest recovere per cest matter en possession ou sil serra myse a son formedon? Come si lissue [*fo. 99v*] fuit sur le don a ore non obstante discent il serra myse a son atteynt, et si les jurors soyent mortz nad ascun remedie sil nad error en le record. Quere cest matter, quar ceo ne fuit touche.

Mes *Bromley* dit que cestui en revercyon poit averrer contynuance de possession encontre un recovere vers son tenaunt pur vye, mes cest entende lou le recovere est sur feynt tytle et null matter est de luy barrer. Et lissue en tayll poit averrer continuance de possession encontre un fyne sur graunt et rendre sil ne fuit execute per action ou entre en le vie le pere. Mes contrarie a fyne sur conusance de droit nemi, pur ceo que est privey en sanke a son pere, que est estoppe et est contrarie al supposell del fyne. Mes issint nest dun recovere, quar ceo estoit ove le recovere mesme que la fuit tiell recovere mes que null execution fuit sue, come en le fyne sur graunt et render. Donques icy, non obstante que soit matter de barre et que les recoverors poyent lexecuter, uncore le pere morust seisi destate taylle, quell est discende al yssue, et ryens de cest estate uncore prise de luy, ergo le rente determyne mayntenaunt per le mort de tenaunt en tayll. Mes si le tenaunt en tayll graunt rent charge et puis fait feffmente ou suffer un recovere sur feynt tytle, come icy, et le recovere est execute en son vye, ore est clere que le recoverer et le feffe tyendront charge, pur ceo que le tenaunt en tayll ne morust seisi destate taylle que discende a son yssue come icy. Mes icy lestate taylle est discende pur le temps non obstante le recovere, et ceo prove byen quar si fuit emplede per estraunge il avera son age. Et il est cleare en ma conceyt que si jeo enfeffe un home ove garrante et il est emplede et perde, et devaunt execution un auter luy emplede, il vouchera moy et jeo ne poye pleder cest matter en anyentismente de son lyen. Mes in 9°, 8° vel 10 E. 3. contrarie est tenus. Mes jeo teigne la ley issint come jeo aye dit que il avera voucher, ergo son estate nest chaunge per le recovere. Et pur ceo si un moy disseise et graunt rent charge et ieo aye jugemente de recover per lassise, uncore devaunt execution il tyendra charge pur ceo que lestate sur que le charge comenca contynue tanque execution suyt sue. Sic icy, ergo donques la terre discharge.

Et a ceo accordent *Latton*, *Hare* et *Brokysbye*.

Et *Bromley* dit que en cest case il recovera un fee simple dependant sur lestate taylle, et uncore il nest tyell fee simple de que il avera assise de mordauncestre mes especiall fee simple sur le matter, et le veray fee simple dymurt en le roy, quar ceo nest devest hors de son person sauns petytion a luy.

the recovery where there appears to be good matter to bar him: no more than there would be where there is a recovery by good title.

Query in the case of a recovery by action tried, whether the issue may falsify in another point which his father could have pleaded but did not, and may now after his father's death, being seised by descent, aver continuance of possession and falsify this recovery by this matter in possession where he should be driven to his formedon? Similarly if the issue now was upon the gift, notwithstanding the descent he shall be driven to his attaint, and if the jurors are dead he has no remedy unless there is an error in the record. (Query this matter, for it was not touched upon.)

But *Bromley* said that a reversioner may aver continuance of possession against a recovery against his tenant for life; but this is intended where the recovery is upon a feigned title and there is no other matter to bar him. And the issue in tail may aver continuance of possession against a fine *sur grant et render* if it was not executed by action or entry in the father's lifetime. But not against a fine *sur conusance de droit*, because he is privy in blood to his father, who is estopped, and it is contrary to the supposal of the fine. But this is not so of a recovery, for it is consistent with the recovery itself that there was such a recovery but that no execution was sued, as in the fine *sur grant et render*. Here, then, although it is a matter in bar and the recoverors may execute it, still the father died seised of an estate tail, which has descended to the issue, and nothing of this estate has yet been taken from him, and therefore the rent is determined immediately by the death of the tenant in tail. But if a tenant in tail grants a rent-charge and then makes a feoffment or suffers a recovery upon feigned title, as here, and the recovery is executed in his lifetime, it is clear that the recoveror and the feoffee shall hold charged, because the tenant in tail did not die seised of an estate tail which descended to his issue as here. Here, however, the estate tail has descended for the time being, despite the recovery, and this is fully proved because if he was impleaded by a stranger he could plead his age. And in my view it is clear that if I enfeoff someone with warranty and he is impleaded and loses, and before execution someone else impleads him, he may vouch me and I may not plead this matter in annulment of his lien. But in 8, 9 or 10 Edw. III,[1] the contrary is held. However I hold the law to be thus, as I have said, that he shall have a voucher, and therefore his estate is not changed by the recovery. Therefore if someone disseises me and grants a rent-charge and I have judgment to recover by the assize, nevertheless before execution he shall hold charged, because the estate whereon the charge began continues until execution is sued. Likewise here, and therefore he shall hold the land discharged.

With this agreed *Latton, Hare* and *Brokesby*.

Bromley said that in this case he should recover a fee simple dependent upon the estate tail, and yet it is not such a fee simple whereof he could have an assize of mort d'ancestor, but a special fee simple upon the matter; and the true fee simple remains in the king, for it is not divested out of his person without a petition

---

[1] Unidentified.

Et nest impertinent daver deux fee simples dun terre per severall mesnez. Come si mon villen purchace terre en taylle et jeo entre, jeo aye estate en fee dependent sur lissue del corps le vyllen, et uncore le fee simple dymurt en le donor, quar jeo ne pue per cest entre quell est don per la ley ryen prendre de luy, et si jeo navera tiell estate jeo navera cy graunt estate come mon villen ad, quell ne serra reson entant que la ley ceo moy don. Et estate taylle jeo ne pue aver, quar ceo null poit aver sinon le done ou ascun de ses yssues. Et pur ceo covyent daver fee simple al mynes, mes de cest fee simple null assise de mordancestre, quar nest pure fee simple mes especiall fee simple sur le matter. Et est semble a cest case ou feme port brefe de dower et le feffe vouche lheir le baron et chescun recover vers auter, et ount execution, en cest case le feffe ad fee simple a luy et a ses heirs pur le vye le feme, mes de ceo lheir navera assise de mordancestre. Et mesme la ley ou terre est lesse a un home et a ses heires pur le vye dun J. S. Et issint [*sic*]. [*fo. 100*]

[13]

Nota per *Hare* que si jeo enfeffe un home de ma terre sauns consideratyon que le feffe serra seisi a ma use. Uncore si un abbe moy enfeffe ove lassent de son covent sauns consyderacion, ceo est a mon use et nemi al use dabbe et ses successors.

Bromley. Pur que ne serra jeo seisi al use labbe et ses successors la, cybien come en lauter case? Quar ore quaunt le feffmente est per assent del covent ceo nest tort ne discontynuance. Mes si fuit discontinuance ascun choce serra. Come lou le tenant en tayll enfeffe un sans consyderatyon, le feffe est seisi al use le tenaunt en tayll et a ses heirs et nemi al use del primer tayll, pur ceo que le feffmente est discontynuance et destroy le tayll. Donques en le case labbe, sil avoit fait le feffmente sans lassent de covent et sauns consyderatyon, ore semble que le feffe serra seisi a son oeps demesne, quar il ne poit estre seisi al primer use pur ceo que lestate commence ove tort et discontynuance al meson et pur ceo mesme le feffmente ne serra prise a son opes et al opes del abbe mesme ne poit estre pur ceo que il nad auter capacyte que al use de meson, mes quaunt il est fait per assent de covent ceo nest ascun tort, per que etc.

Hare. Vostre casez sont bon ley, mes cest case varye. Et est clere que il ne serra seisi forsque a son use demesne et nemi al use del abbe ne del meson, et le cause est pur ceo que un use al comencemente fuit invente al entent de faire fraude al comen ley, scilicet de faire declaratyon dun volunte et issint a defrauder le droit heire et a ouster la feme de sa dower ou ouster tenaunce per

to him. And it is not absurd to have two fee simples of one land by separate means. For instance, if my villein purchases land in tail and I enter, I have an estate in fee dependent upon the issue of the villein's body, and yet the fee simple remains in the donor, for I may not by this entry which is given by the law take anything from him; and yet, if I did not have such an estate, I should not have as large an estate as my villein has, which would not be right, inasmuch as the law gives it to me; and I cannot have an estate tail, for no one can have that except the donee or any of his issue. Therefore I must have at least a fee simple; but for this fee simple no assize of mort d'ancestor lies, inasmuch as it is not a pure fee simple but a special fee simple upon the matter. It is like the case where a woman brings a writ of dower and the feoffee vouches the husband's heir, and each recovers against the other, and they have execution: in this case the feoffee has fee simple to him and his heirs for the life of the woman, but the heir shall not have an assize of mort d'ancestor for it. The law is the same where land is leased to someone and his heirs for the life of John Style. Likewise...

13. NOTE

Inner Temple, *c.* 1533.

Note by *Hare* that if I enfeoff someone of my land without consideration the feoffee shall be seised to my use. Nevertheless, if an abbot enfeoffs me with the assent of his convent, without consideration, this is to my use and not to the use of the abbot and his successors.

Bromley. Why shall I not be seised to the use of the abbot and his successors there, as well as in the other case? For when the feoffment is by assent of the convent it is no wrong or discontinuance. If it were a discontinuance, however, there would be something to argue.[1] For instance, where the tenant in tail enfeoffs someone without consideration, the feoffee is seised to the use of the tenant in tail and his heirs and not to the use of the first tail, because the feoffment is a discontinuance and destroys the tail. Therefore in the case of the abbot, if he made the feoffment without the assent of the convent and without consideration, it seems that the feoffee would be seised to his own use, for he may not be seised to the first use, because the estate commences by wrong and discontinuance as against the house, and therefore the same feoffment shall not be understood to his use; and it cannot be to the use of the abbot himself, because he has no other capacity but to the use of the house. But when it is done by assent of the convent there is no wrong, and so etc.

Hare. Your cases are good law, but this case differs. It is clear that he shall not be seised except to his own use and not to the use of the abbot or of the house, and the reason is because a use was invented in the beginning with the intention of making a fraud at common law, namely to make a declaration of a will and so to defraud the right heir and oust the wife of her dower or oust

---

[1] The figure of speech 'ascun chose serra' is obscure.

le curtesye, et si null tiell choce estre entend en cest case la ne poit ascun use surder sur tiell acte. Donques un abbe ne poit faire devyce ne purra dower ne purra tenance per curtesye ou eschete etc. ne poient estre entend etc. Et il dit que Audeley fuit de cest opynion en son redinge, et issint il teigne la ley. Et issint fuit tenus si le roy est seisi de terre en droit son corone et fait feffmente per ses lettres patentes.

[14]

Nota per *Bromley* que si le tenaunt pendant un brefe enfeffe un auter bona fide pur money payer, le feffe nyent sachant dascun action pendant vers luy, uncore cest champartye et le feffe ne dyrra que le feffmente fuit bona fide et luy nient sachant dascun brefe pendant vers luy sans ceo que il prist a champartye: ceo nest ple, quar sil confesse le feffmente pendant le brefe cest champartye en la ley. Et la ley ceo intende, a quell intendmente le partye navera travers. Et issint est si un disseisor fait feffmente as persons disconus ou as graund homes pur maynnenaunce, et il mesme pryst les proffyttes. Si le feffmente fuit fait soullmente pur declarer son volunte ou pur auter bon consyderatyon et le feffor prist les proffyttes ceo serra voyde vers le disseisor non obstante que fuit pur bon consyderatyon et nemi pur mayntenance. Et en assise sil plede non tenure et le plaintife monstre que il fuit seisi tanque etc. et que il fyst feffmente as persones disconus pur luy defrauder de son action ou pur mayntenance, et que il mesme prist les proffyttes, le disseisor ne dirra que il eux enfeffe pur declarer son volunte sauns ceo que il luy enfeffa pur defrauder etc., ceo nest ple quar covient responder al disseisin ou al pernance des proffyttes, quar si ceo soit confesse la ley entend le feffmente a cest entente. Sic en le case de champarte quaunt feffmente est fait pendant le brefe.

[15]

Casus in banco regis.

Un covenaunte de fair bon, suer et suffysent et loyall estate in la ley en fee simple de son maner de Dale devaunt tyell jour, be it by fyne or fynes, recovere or recoveres, dede or dedes with warantye or otherwyse as shalbe devysed by the said A. or his heirs or theire learned counsell, et A. pryast feffmente et fuit enfeffe, en cest case il ne ferra auter devyse pur ceo que son devyse fuit execute. Come si home covenante de fair un meson de tiell longure que J. S. devysera

tenancy by the curtesy, and if no such thing is to be presumed in this case no use may arise upon such an act. Now, then, an abbot cannot make a devise, and no dower or tenancy by the curtesy or escheat etc. can be presumed etc. And he said that *Audley* was of this opinion in his reading,[1] and so he held the law. And it was similarly held if the king is seised of land in right of his crown and makes a feoffment by his letters patent.

14. NOTE

Inner Temple, *c.* 1533.

Note, by *Bromley*, that if while a writ is pending the tenant enfeoffs someone else in good faith (*bona fide*) for money paid, the feoffee being unaware of any action pending against him, this is still champerty and the feoffee may not say that the feoffment was *bona fide* and without his knowing of any writ pending against him, without this that he took by champerty: that is no plea, for if he confesses the feoffment pending the writ that is champerty in law. The law presumes it, and this presumption the party may not traverse. So it is if a disseisor makes a feoffment to persons unknown or to great men by way of maintenance, and takes the profits himself. If the feoffment was made solely in order to declare his will or for some other good consideration, and the feoffor took the profits, that would be void as against the disseisor, notwithstanding that it was for good consideration and not for maintenance. In an assize if he pleads non-tenure and the plaintiff shows that he was seised until etc. and that he made a feoffment to persons unknown in order to defraud him of his action, or for maintenance, and that he himself took the profits, the disseisor shall not say that he enfeoffed them in order to declare his will, without this that he enfeoffed them to defraud etc.: that is no plea, for he must answer the disseisin or the taking of the profits, for if he confesses it the law presumes the feoffment to have been with that intent. Likewise in the case of champerty when a feoffment is made pending the writ.

15. ANON.

King's Bench, date uncertain (perhaps 1539/45).

Someone covenanted to make a good, sure and sufficient and lawful estate in the law, in fee simple, of his manor of Dale before such and such a day, 'be it by fine or fines, recovery or recoveries, deed or deeds with warranty or otherwise as shall be devised by the said A. or his heirs or their learned counsel',[2] and A. asked for a feoffment and was enfeoffed: in this case he shall not make another devise, because his devise was executed. Likewise if someone

---

[1] Inner Temple (August 1526), on 4 Hen. VII, c. 17 (*SR* ii. 540). See the passage excerpted in Baker & Milsom, pp. 103–105. For texts of the reading see *Readers and Readings*, p. 78.

[2] Words in English.

devaunt tyell jour, en cest case devaunt le jour il devysa que jeo ferra un meson de longure de xx. peez, il ne ferra auter devyse devaunt le jour.

Et ceo fuit opynion *Mountague* et *Spyllman*.

Et *Shelley* fuit de mesme loppinion, et que les parolx duissent estre when so ever and as often as ye shalbe requested. [*fo. 100v*]

[16]

Nota que fuit tenus per dyvers de les benchers que le roy poit graunt chartre a un destre exempte del jures ou que il serra exempte destre vicount, serjante, ou tiell semblable etc., nyent obstant que cest exemptyon va en prejudyce del comen welthe, quar per mesme le reson que il poet exempt un il poit exempt toutz issint que donques null serra jure enter partye et partye et donques null issue enter comen personez poit estre trye, null serjant de pleder pur le comynalte. Mes le reson que serra bon fuit touche pur ceo que a cest temps null private persone est intytle daver danger per ceo mes en generalte, et pur ceo est assetz suffrable. Mes si un fuit impanell enter moy et un auter, ore jeo aye interest daver luy jure, et pur ceo semble a eux ore si le roy voille graunter a luy que il serra exempte etc. cest voyde pur le perde que jeo doye aver. Et mon interest fuit certeyn en luy daver luy jure, et issint la un generall exemption ne voille server. Mes en auters matters il voet server queux sont incerten, quar le lyberte le roy ne poit estre restrayne a un poynt coment[1] que le roy ne luy ferra exemption par cause que poit estre que il serra retorne in un jure cest incerteyn et auxi poit estre que il ne serra et donques null ad lede la mes poit estre que ne serra regarde. Et a ceo que est dit que per mesme le reson le roy poit discharger toutz, a ceo la ley ne intende, quar la ley entende que le roy que est le teste de justyce et de comen welthe voet pluis toste avancer le comen welthe et le tryell de justyce que de ceo decresser, quar a ceo il est tenus per son seremente. Et auxi cest le choce que preserve luy en son estate. Mes si home que ad tyell patent dexemptyon est testmoigne en un fait le patent ne luy aydra par cause que le partye per le fait est intytle de luy aver jure. Et fuit dit que si soyt allege que per lexemptyon justyce ne poit estre fait, issint que le matter est reduce a tyell enconvenyence en fait, le chartre ne serra allowe: mes ceo ne poit estre disalowe par presumtyon mes per matter en fait, issint que si la verete soit conus destre issint donques le chartre serra disalowe.

---

[1] *Reading unclear.*

covenants to make a house of such length as John Style shall devise before such and such a day, and in this case he devises before the day that I shall make a house twenty feet long, he shall not make another devise before the day.

That was the opinion of MOUNTAGUE[1] and SPELMAN.

SHELLEY [J.C.P.] was of the same opinion, and that the words ought to have been 'when so ever and as often as ye shall be requested'.

16. NOTE

Inner Temple.

Note that it was held by divers of the benchers that the king may grant a charter to someone to be exempt from juries or from being a sheriff, serjeant at law,[2] or such like etc., even though this exemption goes in prejudice of the common wealth—for by the same reason that he may exempt one he might exempt everyone and then there would be no juries between party and party and then no issue between common persons could be tried, and there would be no serjeants at law to plead for the community. But the reason why it is good was well explained, because at the present time no private person is entitled so as to have any danger thereby, except in general terms, and therefore it is allowable. However, if someone has been impanelled between me and another, I now have an interest in having him sworn, and therefore it seemed to them that if the king now grants to him that he should be exempt etc. that is void, on account of the loss which I would have. My interest in having him sworn was certain, and therefore a general exemption would not serve there. But in other matters which are uncertain it will serve, for the king's freedom cannot be restrained to one point, even though the king shall not exempt him because it may be that he will be returned on a jury, which is uncertain, because it might also be that he will not be, and then no one has any harm; but it may be that it will not be regarded. As to what has been said that by the same reason the king might discharge everyone, the law does not presume that, for the law presumes that the king—who is the head of justice and of the common wealth—will rather advance the common wealth and the trial of justice than decrease it, for he is bound to that by his oath. Also it is the thing which preserves him in his estate. However, if someone who has such a patent of exemption is a witness in a deed, the patent will not help him, because the party is entitled by the deed to have him sworn. And it was said that if it is alleged that justice cannot be done because of the exemption, so that the matter is reduced to such an inconvenience in fact, the charter will not then be allowed: but it cannot be disallowed by presumption, but only by matter in fact, so that if the truth is known to be so, then the charter will be disallowed.[3]

[1] C.J.K.B. 1539–45.   [2] John Pakington, bencher of the Inner Temple, had a patent of exemption in 1529 from being knighted or made a baron of the Exchequer or serjeant at law: *Letters & Papers of Henry VIII*, iv. 2434; Baker, *Serjeants at Law*, p. 168.
[3] For these cases see the Provisions of Westminster, 43 Hen. III, c. 14 (*SR* i. 10).

[17]

Nota per *Bromley* que home en ple reall poit estre somon per son corps et pur ceo si un soit vouche nest counterple adyre que cestui que est vouche nad ryen de terre per quell il poit estre somon pur ceo que son persone poit estre somon et il poit purchacer terre apres quell serra fait en value.

[18]

Browne, serjant, vient al barre et dit al Fitzherbert: Sir, un brefe de faux jugemente est port icy dun jugemente en auncien demesne, et nous sumus a yssue sur troix severall poyntz, et jeo voille sacher vostre opynion de quell venue pays viendra.

Fitzherbert. Estes a yssue sur troix severall poyntz en brefe de faux jugemente? Verament aves byen fait pur vostre clyent, quar aves fait pluis pur luy que unques fuit view, quar jeo dye que en faux jugemente vous ne poyes aver forsque un yssue, et sur un poynt, et ceo trove destre faux jugemente revercera tout le record: ergo ne poyes aver forsque lun. Et pur ceo gardes byen. Et rideont. Et dit que mesme la ley est en brefe derror.

(Et *Bromley* in Templo dit que cest voyer derror sinon que soit apparant en le record, quar la il poit assigner tantz come il voille pur ceo que ils sont apparant en le record. Mes en faux jugemente il navera forsque un tantum pur ceo que null error est apparant mes averrable per paiz, et les errors sont tryable per pays. Mez il dit que faux seremente poit estre assigne en dyvers poyntz.)

Et donques *Browne* dit: De quell visne le pais viendra?

Fitzherbert. Del visne le court.

Browne. Ceo est auncien demesne.

Englefylde. Donques le pays serra del procheyn hundred. [*fo. 101*]

[19]

Tenant en taylle discontynue le taylle et reprist estate en fee simple, et ad yssue et devie, estraunger abate, et lissue port assise de mordancestre. Et tenus que il avera lassise ou formedon a son plesure, quar les poyntz del brefe sont voyer et lissue nest remytte forsque a son plesure, pur ceo que le remitter est pur lavantage de cestui que serra remytt toutz ditz et nemi pur son disavantage. Et null persone poit prendre avantage de cest remytter forsque cestui que serra

17. NOTE

Inner Temple.

Note, by *Bromley*, that in a plea real one may be summoned by one's body; and therefore if someone is vouched it is no counterplea to say that the person who is vouched has no land whereby he may be summoned, because his person may be summoned, and he might purchase land afterwards which shall be made up in value.

18. ANON.

Common Pleas, 1521/38.

Browne, serjeant, came to the bar and said to FITZHERBERT: Sir, a writ of false judgment has been brought here in respect of a judgment in ancient demesne, and we are at issue upon three separate points, and I would like to know your opinion from what venue the country shall come.

FITZHERBERT. Are you at issue upon three separate points in a writ of false judgment? Truly you have done well for your client, for you have done more for him than was ever seen; for I say that in false judgment you cannot have more than one issue, and upon one point, and if that is found to be a false judgment it will reverse the whole record: therefore you can only have one. So watch out. (And they smiled.) He said the law was the same in a writ of error.

(*Bromley* said in the Temple that this is true of error unless it is apparent in the record, for then he may assign as many errors as he wishes, because they are apparent in the record. But in false judgment he shall only have one, because no error is apparent but it is averrable by the country, and the errors are triable by the country. But he said that a false oath may be assigned in different points.)

Then *Browne* said:. From what venue shall the country come?

FITZHERBERT. From the venue of the court.

Browne. It is ancient demesne.

ENGLEFIELD. Then the country shall be from the next hundred.

19. ANON.

Common Pleas or Inner Temple.

Tenant in tail discontinues the tail and takes back an estate in fee simple, has issue, and dies, a stranger intrudes, and the issue brings an assize of mort d'ancestor. And it was held that he may have the assize or formedon at his pleasure, for the points of the writ are true and the issue is not remitted unless at his pleasure, because a remitter is always for the advantage of him who is to be remitted and not for his disadvantage. And no one may take advantage

remytte ou son heire et nemi estraunge, quar remytter est entende pur lour dysavantage. Mes un que ad mesne interest ou estate dependent prendra avantage de remytter. Et pur lour avantage il serra remytt maugre sa teste, come tenant en taylle, le remainder ouster en fee, en cest case icy ust estre il serra remytt maugre sa teste. Vide inde 19 H. 6, fo. 45. Et vide pur cestui que ad estate dependant 41 E. 3, fo. 19. 44 E. 3, fo. 14.

[20]

[A]

Nota si home soit endyte de felonye et puis arraigne sur mesme lenditemente et trove coupable et pria son lyver, a que est objecte que il navera le benefyt de son clerge pur ceo que il est bygamus, et il ceo denya, sur quell brefe issast al evesque de ceo certyfyer, et devaunt le jour de certyficat le roy luy pardone, et puis sur cest pardon plede il est dysmysse, en cest case il ne perdra ses bienz ne ses terres ne null ryens, non obstant cest verdit don encontre luy. Mes sil ust estre certyfye null bigamus, par que il ust ewe sa lyver, et ust estre save per cest voye, la ces bienz ussent estre forfaitz mes ses terres nemi, ne null sanke corrupte. Et fuit dit que ceo fuit dymurre en ley en le Comen Banke et argue et adjuge accordant 22 H. 8, termino Michaelis, en le case dun Wyse de Devonshyre que fuit fader in lawe al Whiddon. Le reson fuit fait pur ceo que le verdit nest ascun atteynder mes come un dyrection et wytnes a leder le juge pur doner son jugemente, et le jugemente est le choce quell lya les partyes, et sicome le wytnes a xii nest que lour instruction a doner lour verdit nyent pluis est le verdit de xii que instructyon al juge a doner son jugemente, issint que le jugemente est leffecte et le rest nest que conveyance. Et quant felon pria son lyver et ad son lyver en cest case il perdra ses bienz pur ceo que un jugemente tiell quell est done sur luy, scilicet committatur ordinario, quell est suffycient de perder ses chatellz entant que per ceo il est hors del laye power et en maner come un utlage en personell actyon que perdra ses chatellx mes nemi ses terres. Mes en le princypall case le partye avoit pardon le roy que luy excuse de chescun maner de jugemente et close les mainz les justyces de proceder pluys avaunt mes tout oustermente a luy dysmysser et discharger de toutz jugementes issint que il alera a Dyeu.

of this remitter except the person to be remitted and his heir, and not a stranger, for a remitter is presumed for his disadvantage. But someone who has an intermediate interest or dependent estate may take advantage of a remitter; and for their advantage he shall be remitted against his will: as where there is a tenant in tail, remainder over in fee, in this case case he shall be remitted against his will. For this see 19 Hen. VI, fo. 45.[1] And for the person who has a dependent estate see 41 Edw. III, fo. 19; 44 Edw. III, fo. 14.[2]

20. WYSE'S CASE

Common Pleas, Mich. 1530.

A

Note that if someone is indicted of felony and then arraigned upon the indictment and found guilty, and prays his book, to which it is objected that he should not have the benefit of his clergy because he is *bigamus*, and he denies it, whereupon a writ issues to the bishop to certify it, and before the day of the certificate the king pardons him, and then upon pleading this pardon he is discharged: in this case he shall not lose his goods or lands or anything else, despite this verdict given against him. But if he had been certified no *bigamus*, so that he had had his book, and had been saved in that way, his goods would have been forfeited—but not his land, nor would any blood be corrupted. And it was said that this was demurred in law in the Common Bench and argued and adjudged accordingly in Michaelmas term 22 Hen. VIII, in the case of one Wyse of Devonshire, who was Whiddon's father in law.[3] The reason given was that the verdict is no attainder but is a direction and witness to lead the judge in giving his judgment, and the judgment is the thing which binds the parties; and just as the witness before the dozen is but their instruction in giving their verdict, so the verdict of the dozen is no more than an instruction to the judge in giving his judgment, so that the judgment is the effect and the rest but introduction. When a felon prays his book, and has his book, in this case he shall lose his goods, because a judgment of a kind (*tiel quel*) is given upon him, namely 'let him be committed to the ordinary' (*committatur ordinario*), which is sufficient for losing his chattels inasmuch as he is thereby outside the lay power and in a way like an outlaw in a personal action, who shall lose his chattels but not his lands. In the principal case, however, the party had the king's pardon, which excuses him from every kind of judgment and closes the justices' hands from proceeding further, but utterly dismisses and discharges him from all judgments so that he may go quit (*alera a Dieu*).

[1] YB Mich. 19 Hen. VI, fo. 45, pl. 95.   [2] YB Mich. 41 Edw. III, fo. 17, pl. 2, at fo. 19 (also cited on this point by Yelverton, above, p. 329, no. 35); Trin. 44 Edw. III, fo. 17, pl. 7.

[3] According to Foss, John Whiddon (bencher of the Inner Temple since 1529) married (1) Anne Hollis, and (2) Elizabeth Shilston. He was later J.K.B. and died in 1576. He was seated at Chagford, Devon, where there is a funeral monument.

Et *Shelley*, Justice, fuit in opynion en ceo case de Wyse que apres purgatyon fait il duyst reaver ses bienz pur ceo que le purgatyon est come reversell del jugemente cybyen come brefe derror sur actyon personell.

Nota que est bon respons a bygamye a dyre que il fuit precontract a un auter a prover les spousellz nyent loyall, et issint de luy enabler a son clerge: et ceo fuit adjuge 22 H. 8. en le case dun Bromeham.

[B]

MS. Hargrave 30, fo. 71, collated with BL MS. Hargrave 373, fo. 196v.[1]

< Cest jeo ad de veiell reportes. >[2] Mr Carrell ad reporte en son lyver de reportes que il fuit agree in anno 22 H. 8. que un Wise fuit indite de felony et arreyne de ceo et trove culpable et priast son cleargie, et fuit dit que il[3] fuit bigamus, et les justices escrieront[4] al evesque pur[5] certifier sil fuit bigamus ou nemi, et avant que levesque certifie[6] riens Wise ad son pardon. Et sil forfetera ses biens ou nemi fuit le question. Et fuit tenus que il ne forfetera ses biens car quant il ad son pardon avant que il prist son cleargie issint que il nest entre en le recorde Tradatur ordinario, ne fuit ascun tiel conviction per que il forfetera ses biens.

[21]

Si home fait lesse pur vye rendant rent, pur le rent arere il ne poit aver brefe de det pur ceo que cest rent est fraunketenement. Mes si lestate le tenaunt soit determyne est devenus chatell et demandable per actyon de dett: mes cest a entender ou est determyne per acte de Dieu ou auter choce quell nest le fait cestui en revercyon. Et pur ceo semble que si apres le rent arere le tenaunt surrender, action de dett ne gyst, quar ceo ne poit estre sauns lacceptance de cestui en revercyon. Et est comen grownde que home ne donera a luy mesme cause daction, et pur ceo si mon tenaunt pur vye fait wast ore jeo sue entytle daver actyon de wast quas tenet et en quell case jeo recovera le liew waste, mes si mon tenaunt pur vye surrender a moy jeo navera ascun remedie pur le wast quar per mon acte demesne jeo aye change le nature de mon actyon et don a moy mesme auter cause dactyon, scilicet daver action de wast quas tenuit, pur ceo que le tenance est determyne, en quell action jeo ne recovera la lieu [*fo. 101v*] wast.

[1] MS. Hargrave 30 is inserted in some reports dated 1619 in the hand of Arthur Turnour. MS. Hargrave 373 contains the same text embedded in some late Elizabethan reports.
[2] *Margin of Hg 30 only.*   [3] *Om. Hg 373.*   [4] escryont *Hg 373.*   [5] a *Hg 373.*   [6] certifiast *Hg 373.*

SHELLEY, Justice, was of opinion in this case of Wyse that after making purgation he ought to have his goods back, because the purgation is like a reversal of the judgment, just like a writ of error upon a personal action.

Note that it is a good answer to bigamy to say that he was precontracted to another woman, so as to prove the espousals unlawful, and thus to enable him to his clergy: and that was adjudged in 22 Hen. VIII in the case of one Bromeham.

B

Abridged version from later reports (after 1576).

(This I have taken from some old reports.) Mr Caryll has reported in his book of reports that it was agreed in the year 22 Hen. VIII that one Wyse was indicted of felony and arraigned thereof and found guilty, and prayed his clergy, and it was said that he was *bigamus*, and the justices wrote to the bishop to certify whether he was *bigamus* or not, and before the bishop certified anything Wyse had his pardon. The question was whether he should forfeit his goods or not. And it was held that he should not forfeit his goods, for when he has his pardon before he takes his clergy, so that it is not entered in the record 'Let him be delivered to the ordinary' (*Tradatur ordinario*), there was no such conviction whereby he should forfeit his goods.[1]

21. NOTE

If someone makes a lease for life, rendering rent, he may not have a writ of debt for arrears of the rent because this rent is freehold. But if the estate of the tenant has ended, it has become a chattel and is demandable by action of debt: but this is to be understood where it is ended by act of God or something else which is not the act of the reversioner. Therefore it seems that if after the rent is in arrear the tenant surrenders, an action of debt does not lie, for this cannot be without the acceptance of the reversioner. And it is a common maxim (*grownde*) that one may not give oneself a cause of action. Therefore if my tenant for life commits waste I am entitled to have an action of waste *quas tenet*, in which case I shall recover the place wasted, whereas if my tenant for life surrenders to me I shall have no remedy for the waste, for by my own act I have changed the nature of my action and given myself another cause of action, namely to have an action of waste *quas tenuit*, because the tenancy is ended, in which action I shall not recover the place wasted. Similarly if in a writ of right

---

[1] There follows, in both manuscripts, a note on the statute 18 Eliz. I, c. 7 (*SR* iv. 617).

Come si en brefe de droit de garde lenfant vient a pleyn age pendant le brefe, mon brefe abatera, et uncore ceo nest mon acte mes le cause est la pur ceo que jeo ne purra aver leffecte de mon suyste, scilicet de recover le garde quell jeo demande toutz ditz en droit de garde. Mes en le case de wast si jeo face lesse pur terme dauter vye, le tenaunt fait wast, ore jeo sue entytle daver action de wast quas tenet, [mes] si cestui a que vye devie et jeo entra, ore jeo avera action quas tenuit, quar la nature de mon action ne fuit chaunge per mon fait demesne einz il fuit change per le mort de cestui a que vye. Mes en mesme le case si jeo avoy commence laction quas tenet en le vye de cestui a que vye et pendant le brefe il ust devie, ore mon brefe abatera, come semble, pur ceo que ore jeo ne poye aver leffect de mon suyst, scilicet le liew wasted, accordant al purporte de mon brefe de wast, que suppose quas tenet et le terme destre contynye, que est faux per le mort de cestui a que vye. Mes peraventure si jeo face un lesse pur terme de vye, et le tenaunt pur vye face wast, et jeo port mon brefe de wast quas tenet, et pendant le brefe il fait feffmente et jeo entre pur forfeyture, peraventure ceo nabatera mon brefe (mes cest bon questyon) quar non obstante que jeo aye fauxyfye mon brefe per mon entre en lauter terre, issint que jeo ne purra aver leffecte de mon suyste, uncore de ceo faire jeo fue compelle per le defendant mesme, quar per son alienation il poit estre que jeo nentra mes sue avaunt mon brefe que un collaterall auncestre de moy poit relesser ove garrante que discendra sur moy pendant le brefe et donques jeo ne purra unques entre pur lalienation et issint jeo serra a graund myschief. Et nyent obstante que jeo aye enter en avoydance de cest daunger, il nest reson que ceo abatera mon brefe, quar ceo fuit lacte le lesse de moy dryver a un de ceux myschiefes, scilicet de perder mon terre a toutz jours peraventure per un garrante ou autermente en avoydance de cest dentrer et abater mon brefe. Mes a ceo poit estre dit que labater de brefe nest que de comencer un novell brefe quas tenuit, quell serra pluis toste sufficient que daver un enconvenyence ensuer, scilicet que home avera brefe quas tenet et en ceo avera jugemente de recover le liewe waste lou le plaintife mesme ad ceo devaunt. Mes quere inde. Et si lesse soit fait pur vye, rendant rent, le rent est arere, le lesse fait wast, le lessor recover: semble que il poit aver brefe de dett. Et semble que cy, quar la jeo ne don a moy mesme cause dactyon quar la terre al comencemente est oblyge ove condytion in ley que si le tenaunt fait wast ou alyen en fee que lestate per ceo est determynable. Donques quaunt jeo entre ou recover en brefe de wast le cause del determynation est lacte del tenaunt et jeo ne don actyon a moy mesme mes preigne avantage de choce don a moy per la ley don.[1] Et mesme la ley est ou lesse pur vye est fait rendant rente et pur non paymente reentre, et le rent est arere et il entre.

Un home ad annuite a luy graunt tanque il soyt avance a un benefyce, il prist feme, per ceo il avera brefe de dett pur les arrerages incurrus adevaunt: quod vide 35 H. 6.

---

[1] *Sic.*

of ward the infant comes of age while the writ is pending, my writ shall abate, and yet this is not my act; but the reason there is because I cannot have the effect of my suit, namely to recover the ward, which I always demand in right of ward. But in the case of waste, if I make a lease pur terme d'auter vie, and the tenant commits waste, I am now entitled to have an action of waste *quas tenet*; whereas if cestuy que vie dies and I enter, I shall have an action *quas tenuit*, for the nature of my action was not changed by my own conduct but was changed by the death of cestuy que vie. In the same case, however, if I had commenced the action *quas tenet* in the lifetime of cestuy que vie and he had died while the writ was pending, my writ would abate, as it seems, because now I cannot have the effect of my suit, namely the place wasted, in accordance with the purport of my writ of waste, which supposes *quas tenet* and that the term continues, which is falsified by the death of cestuy que vie. But perhaps if I make a lease for term of life, and the tenant for life commits waste, and I bring my writ of waste *quas tenet*, and pending the writ he makes a feoffment and I enter for forfeiture, perhaps that would not abate my writ—though it is a good question—for even though I have falsified my writ by my entry in the other land, so that I cannot have the effect of my suit, nevertheless I was compelled to do this by the defendant himself, for by his alienation it may be that I shall not enter but sue forth my writ, which a collateral ancestor of mine might release with warranty, which would descend upon me pending the writ, and then I could never enter for the alienation and thus I should suffer a great mischief. And although I have entered to avoid this danger, it is not right that this should abate my writ, for it was the act of the lessee to drive me to one of these mischiefs, namely either to lose my land for ever (perhaps) by a warranty or else in avoiding that to enter and abate my writ. But to this it may be said that the consequence of abating the writ is only to commence a new writ *quas tenuit*, which would be preferable to having an inconvenience follow: namely, that one should have a writ *quas tenet* and have judgment therein to recover the place wasted, where the plaintiff himself already has it. (But query this.) And if a lease is made for life, rendering rent, the rent is in arrear, the lessee commits waste, and the lessor recovers, it seems that he may have a writ of debt. Likewise here, for I do not give myself a cause of action, inasmuch as the land is bound at the outset with a condition in law that if the tenant commits waste or aliens in fee the estate is thereby determinable. Therefore when I enter or recover in a writ of waste the cause of the determination is the act of the tenant and I do not give myself an action but take advantage of a thing given to me by the law. The law is the same where a lease for life is made, rendering rent, and for non-payment a re-entry, and the rent is in arrear, and he enters.

Someone has an annuity granted to him until he should be advanced to a benefice, and he marries a wife: he shall have a writ of debt for the arrears incurred earlier: see this in 35 Hen. VI.[1]

---

[1] YB Hil. 35 Hen. VI, fo. 50, pl. 14.

[22]

Memorandum que a Newgate 22 H. 8. devaunt Englefyld, Justyce, un fuit arraigne sur endytmente et lendytmente fuit pur ceo que il avoit imble deux chyvallx price de xl. s. des bienz et chateux un J. S., et sur ceo arraigne et le dit J. S. et un auter veignont a doner evydence, et sur levydence aparust que lun chyvall fuit a J. S. et lauter a cestui que vient pur doner evydence ove luy. Et sur ceo le prisoner fuit reprie, quar fuit tenus cleremente que le evydence ne garrante lendytemente issint que ore lendytmente ne vaut, quar appiert que un des chyvallx nappertyent al parte. Mes uncore si lendytmente ust estre polytykment fait il duyst aver estre arraigne pur lauter chyvall, come si lendytment ust de un chyvall pryce etc. et dauter chyvall pryce etc. Mes come est ore ambideux chyvallx sont value a un pryce, donques quaunt il est dyscharge de lun ne appyert que pryce lauter est, et endytmente ou null pryce est est voyd. [*fo. 102*]

[23]

Item, a mesme le temps, un auter fuit endyte pur ceo que il avoit debruse un esglise en tyell paroche et le pixe pryce de xx. li. en que le precious corps de nostre seigniour Jhesu Chryste fuit contenus, dez bienz et chateux des parochiens del dit paroche et del dit esglise en les mainz et custodye J. S. et J. M. gardeins del eglise avauntdit, feloniousmente prist et importe. Et ore il fuit arraigne sur mesme lendytmente et plede non coupable, et en verytye un des gardeyns avoit a nosme Thomas et nemi J.

Et cest matter fuit monstre a *Hales*, Baron del Excheker, un de les justyces del gaole deliverey de London, et il dit que lendytmente fuit assetz bon et ne pryst regarde a ceo, quar il dit que cest endytmente est de bonis parochianorum et issint assetz bon non obstante que lun des gardeinz soit misnosme. Mes il ne demanda le questyon dascun de ses compaignons ne ilz ne savoyent de ceo, ideo quere.

Et puis un doughtant de ceo matter monstre le cause a *Hare*, que dit que il fuit bon matter daver ceo destre respyte et daver reprye le prysoner, quar semble a luy que sur le matter monstre le jurye doyt luy trover de ryen coupable, quar lenditment est des bienz esteantz en le custodye de J. S. et J. M. joyntmente, et quaunt le matter appyert que le custodye est en J. S. et W. D. le jure nount ryens a fair mes primerment denquirer et donques sur le matter de luy acquiter de prise des bienz hors de custodye J. S. et J. M., quar en fait cest

22. ANON.

Newgate sessions, 1530/31.

Remember that at Newgate in 22 Hen. VIII, before ENGLEFIELD, Justice, someone was arraigned upon an indictment, and the indictment was for stealing two horses priced at 40s. of the goods and chattels of one John Style, and he was arraigned thereon, and the said John Style and another came to give evidence; and it appeared upon the evidence that only one of the horses belonged to John Style and the other belonged to the person who came to give evidence with him. Thereupon the prisoner was reprieved, for it was held clearly that the evidence did not warrant the indictment, so that now the indictment is invalid, inasmuch as it appears that one of the horses does not belong to the party. Nevertheless if the indictment had been politicly drawn he ought to have been arraigned for the other horse: as, if the indictment had been for one horse price etc. and another horse price etc. But, as it is, both horses are valued at one price, and therefore when he is discharged in respect of one it does not appear what price the other is, and an indictment with no price is void.

23. ANON.

Newgate sessions, 1530/31.

Someone else was indicted at the same time for breaking into a church in such and such a parish and feloniously taking and carrying away the pix, price £20, in which the precious body of our Lord Jesus Christ was contained, of the goods and chattels of the parishioners of the said parish and of the said church, being in the hands and custody of J. S. and J. M., wardens of the church aforesaid. And now he was arraigned upon the same indictment and pleaded Not guilty, and in truth one of the churchwards was called Thomas and not J.

This matter was shown to HALES, Baron of the Exchequer, one of the justices of the gaol delivery for London, and he said that the indictment was good enough, and did not pay regard to this point; for he said that the indictment says 'of the goods of the parishioners' (*de bonis parochianorum*) and is therefore good enough even if one of the churchwardens is misnamed. But he asked the question of some of his fellows, and they did not know, so query.

Afterwards someone, doubting this matter, showed the cause to *Hare*,[1] who said it was a good matter to have it respited and to reprieve the prisoner, for it seemed to him that upon the facts shown the jury ought to find him not guilty, for the indictment is for goods being in the custody of J. S. and J. M. jointly, and when the fact appears that the custody is in J. S. and W. D. the jury have nothing to do but firstly to enquire and then upon the facts to acquit him of taking goods out of the custody of J. S. and J. M., for in fact this indictment

---

[1] Nicholas Hare, barrister of the Inner Temple (reader in 1532; later M.R.).

endytmente est faux. Uncore il agrea que si lendytmente ust estre que il pryst hors del custodye des gardeins del dit paroche, et sauns monstrance de lour nosmes, ceo ust estre bon. Mes quaunt ils sont nosmez covyent estre nosmes per lour droit nosmes. Come si precipe soit port vers labbe de Westm., sans luy nosmer, ceo est bon. Mes si precipe soit port vers J., abbe de Westm., et il ad nosme W., le brefe abatera. Sic hic etc.

[24]

22 H. 8.

Un home avoit terres en execution sur un estatute merchant et la feme le conusor recover le terce parte pur sa dower, si le conuse retyendra les deux partz tanque il soit paye de tout le dett?

Englefeld semble que il ad perdu execution de cell parte et que il ne tyendra les deux partes tanque etc., quar cest case ad estre adjuge que lou parcell ad estre surrounde per le mere il ne retyendra le remainder pluis avaunt que le temps dextent. Sic hic.

Fitzherbert al contrarie. Et graunde diversite lou parcell est perdue per lacte de Dyeu et lou parcell est perdue per lacte del parte, quar lou parte est perdue per lacte de partye[1] semble que il retyendra le remainder tanque il soyt satysfye de tout. Come si home ad terres et mesons en execution, et le conusee enter et enrace les mesons. Mesme la ley si home ad execution des terres queux le conusor ad per disseisin, et queux il avoit droyturell tytle, et le disseisie enter, quar icy le conuse perde le possession per le conusor et son acte, scilicet le disseisin. Et issint icy le tytle de dower est per les espouselles et cest son acte demesne. Et dit que le cause fuit bon darguer.

Norwyche, serjante, dit que en le case que il mytta de raser des mesons il serra remedie per action de trespas. [*fo. 102v*]

[25]

Nota per *Audeley*, donques speker del parlyamente, que si home fait son testamente et en mesme le volunte declare son testamente de ses terres queux sont en use ou devysable, et devie, et lordynarie compell les executors de prover cest volunte, come le comen experience est, en cest case il est deinz le case de premunire, quar pur la terre son testament ne besoigne estre prove, quar le

---

[1] Dyeu *deleted.*

is false. Nevertheless he agreed that if the indictment had been that he took them out of the custody of the churchwardens of the said parish, without setting out their names, that would have been good. But once they are named they must be named by their correct names. Likewise if a *praecipe* is brought against the abbot of Westminster, without naming him, this is good; whereas if a *praecipe* is brought against John, abbot of Westmminster, and his name is William, the writ will abate. Likewise here etc.

24. ANON.

Common Pleas, 1530/31.

A man had lands in execution upon a statute merchant, and the conusor's wife recovered the third part for her dower: shall the conusee retain the two-thirds until he has been paid the whole debt?

ENGLEFIELD thought that he had lost execution of that part and that he should not hold the two-thirds until etc.; for this case has been adjudged, that where part of the land has been flooded by the sea he shall not retain the remainder beyond the time of the extent. Likewise here.

FITZHERBERT to the contrary. There is a great difference where part is lost by the act of God and where it is lost by the act of the party, for where part is lost by the act of a party it seems he shall retain the remainder until he has been satisfied for the whole: for instance, if someone has lands and houses in execution, and the conusee enters and pulls down the houses. The law is the same if someone has execution of lands which the conusor has by disseisin and of those whereof he has rightful title, and the disseisee enters, for here the conusee loses the possession through the conusor and his act, namely the disseisin. Likewise here, the title of dower is through the espousals and that is her own act. And he said that the cause was good to be argued.

Norwich, serjeant, said that in the case which he put of pulling down houses there shall be a remedy by action of trespass.

25. NOTE

Inner Temple, 1529/32. Cf. *Wales' Case* (1530) Spelman, p. 87.

Note by *Audley*, then speaker of the parliament,[1] that if someone makes his testament, and in the same [testament] declares his [will] of his lands which are in use or devisable, and dies, and the ordinary compels the executors to prove this will, as the common experience is, in this case he is within the case

---

[1] Audley served as speaker until May 1532, when he was appointed lord keeper of the great seal.

probatyon de ceo est choce temporall et attyent al court le roy destre prover la per proves a un jure la prise sur un issue del volunte quaunt les terres sont en debate, per que il ad prise sur luy de medler en son spirituall courte de choce temporall, quell est consernant jurisdiction del temporall court, et cest clerement en case de premunire.

Latton. Donqes vous voilles fair lordynarye de sacher a son perell quell choce est comprise deinz le volunte dun home devaunt que il agard proces, et ceo serra enconter reson.

Audeley. Non sir, quar le proces serra [1]de prover son volunte de ses bienz et chateux et auters choces probable deinz son court et donqes quaunt ilz appere et tyell volunte appyert il poit fair severance de ceo, come a dyer quaunt a son volunte de ses terres ilz ne voillont ovesque ceo medler mes pur le rest ilz ceo approvont.

[26]

Les feffees en use sont disseisiez et cestui que use declare son volunte et devie, les feffes entront, si ceo serra bon entant que le use fuit discontynue? Quere, quar per le rentre il serra adjuge toutz temps contynue.

[27]

Deux coparceners sont dun rent servyce de iiii. s. issant hors de deux acres de terre, lun coparcener purchace lun acre, quere coment la terre serra tenus? Et semble que le tenaunt tyendra cell acre quell il ad en son mayne de ambideux per deux sous, et le coparcener que purchace tyendra lacre de lauter per xii. d., et xii. d. est extynct.

[28]

Nota per *Baker*: si seignior et tenaunt sont, le tenaunt alyen en mortmayne, labbe enfeffe le roy, le seignior navera son petytion.

Pakynton. Cest voyer, quar le seignior nad ascun droyt dentre, mes tytle dentre et null droyt tanque il ad entre. Et son remedie vers comen persone serroit soullment per entre et nemi per voy de ascun maner daction, scilicet brefe de droit ne auter brefe, pur ceo que nad droyt. Donques quaunt labbe ad enfeffe le roy per fait inrolle, le seignior ne poit entrer sur le possession le roy, quar null poit entrer sur le roy. Donques petytyon ne poit aver, quar ceo est en lieu de son action, et action il nad en ceo case. Et auxi petytion est en lieu de

---

[1] *This is where the Petyt MS. begins.*

of *praemunire*, for his testament does not need to be proved for the land, for the proof thereof is a temporal thing and belongs to the king's court to be proved there by proofs to a jury taken there upon an issue concerning the will when the lands are in dispute. Thus he has taken upon himself to meddle in his spiritual court with a temporal thing concerning the jurisdiction of the temporal court, and that is clearly in the case of *praemunire*.

Latton. Then you would make the ordinary know at his peril what is contained in a man's will before he has awarded process, which would be against reason.

Audley. No sir, for the process shall be to prove his will of his goods and chattels and other things provable in his court, and therefore when they appear and such a will appears he may separate them, as by saying that they will not meddle with it as to his will of his lands but will prove it for the rest.

26. NOTE

Feoffees in use are disseised, cestuy que use declares his will and dies, and the feoffees enter: is this entry good, inasmuch as the use was discontinued? Query, for by the re-entry it shall be deemed to have continued throughout.

27. NOTE

There are two coparceners of a rent-service of four shillings issuing out of two acres of land; one of the coparceners purchases one of the acres: how shall the land be held? It seems that the tenant shall hold this acre which he still has in his hands of both of them by two shillings, and the coparcener who purchased shall hold the acre of the other by 12d., and 12d. is extinguished.

28. NOTE

Inner Temple.

Note by *Baker*: if there are a lord and a tenant, and the tenant aliens in mortmain, and the abbot enfeoffs the king, the lord shall not have his petition.

Pakington. That is true, for the lord has no right of entry. He has a title to enter, but no right until he has entered. His remedy against a common person should be solely by entry and not by way of any kind of action, namely a writ of right or any other writ, because he has no right. However, when the abbot has enfeoffed the king by deed enrolled, the lord may not enter upon the king's possession, for no one may enter upon the king. Therefore he cannot have a petition, for that is in lieu of his action, and he has no action in this case. Also a petition is in lieu of a writ of right, and here he has no right until he enters.

brefe de droit, et icy il nad null droit tanque il entre. Et pur rent charge home navera petytion pur ceo que est encontre comen droit, de quell null brefe de droit gyst enter comen personez.

Quere inde, quar *Bromley* tyent le contrarie et que brefe de droit gyst en Comen Banke, mes nemy en court dascun seigniour, pur ceo que ne gyst en tenure. Et dit que il ad view autoryte de ceo.

Hare dit que il ne unques veiast. [*fo. 103*]

[29]

Nota per *Pakynton* et *Baker* que le tenaunt le roy que tyent de luy in capite, soyt il en socage come il poit estre ou en servyce de chivaler, sil voet faire alyenation covyent toutz ditz aver lycence del roy ou autermente le roy seisera. Et cest tenure in capite est ou un tyent de roy per reson de coron ut antiquo de corona, scilicet ceux seigniories que le roy ad seignorie en eux come roy tantum. Mes home poit tener de roy en socage ou per servyce de chivaler et nemi in capite, come si le roy purchace un seigniorie de quell jeo teigne per servyce de chivaler ou en socage, cest terre est tenus ore de roy come de comen persone, et la jeo poye alyener sauns lycence, et auxi la le roy navera ascun auter prerogatyve pluys que comen persone averoit forsque soulmente en le corps de mon heir il serra preferr devaunt ascun auter seignior de que jeo teigne per servyce de chivaler, mes al terre il navera ascun prerogatyve einz chescun seignior avera le terre tenus de luy per servyce de chivaler et les terres tenus in socage serront hors de gard, et al pleyn age lheir ne suera ascun lyverey nyent pluis que sil avoit tenus del comen persone. Issint nota le diversite enter tenour in capite et auter tenure.

Et *Baker* dit que lou seigniorie dyscende al roy per reson dauter auncestre que les tenauntz que teignont de cest maner ne teignont in capite. Issint est en plusors auters cases que home poit remembre. Mes il dit lou un est attaynt de treson que ad terres, la les auters naveront unques lour seigniories et il ceo ad come roy, ergo ceux queux teignont dascun de ceux maners teignont de roy in capite, et la le roy avera son prerogatyve quar il est fait seignior come roy et ceux terres sont venus a luy come roy ratione corone. Quere inde, quar de ceo mult ensuast.

[30]

Le villen le roy et un estraunge sont enfeffes: semble que ilz sont joyntenantez, quar non obstante que le villen fait feffmente que le roy avera

And one may not have a petition for rent-charge, because it is against common right, and no writ of right lies for it between common persons.

Query this, for *Bromley* held the contrary and that a writ of right lies in the Common Bench, though not in any lord's court, because it does not lie in tenure. And he said he had seen authority for this.

Hare said he never had.

29. NOTE

Inner Temple. Cf. Yorke, vol. I, p. 163, no. 194.

Note, by *Pakington* and *Baker*, that the king's tenant who holds of him in chief, be it in socage (as it may be) or in knight-service, if he wishes to make an alienation, must always have a licence from the king or else the king may seize it. This tenure in chief is where someone holds of the king by reason of the crown *[ab] antiquo de corona*, namely those seignories where the king has the lordship in them as king alone. But one may hold of the king in socage or by knight-service and not in chief, as where the king purchases a lordship of which I hold by knight-service or in socage: this land is now held of the king as it was of the common person, and there I may alien without licence, and there also the king shall not have any other prerogative more than a common person would have, save only that in the body of my heir he shall be preferred before any other lord of whom I hold by knight-serivce. With respect to the land, however, he shall not have any prerogative but every lord shall have the land held of him by knight-service, and the lands held in socage shall be out of ward, and at full age the heir shall not sue any livery, any more than if he had held of a common person. Thus note the difference between tenure in chief and other tenures.

Baker said that where a lordship descends to the king by reason of another ancestor, the tenants who hold of this manor do not hold in chief. So it is in various other cases which one might remember. But he said that where someone who has lands is attainted of treason, the others shall not there have their lordships, and the king shall have the forfeiture as king; therefore those who hold land of any of these manors hold of the king in chief, and the king shall there have his prerogative, for he is made lord because he is king and these lands are come to him as king by reason of the crown (*ratione coronae*). Query of this, for much followed[1] from it.

30. NOTE

The king's villein and a stranger are enfeoffed: it seems they are joint tenants, for even if the villein makes a feoffment the king shall have it, because no time

---

[1] But perhaps intending the future tense.

quia nullum tempus occurrit regi. Uncore ceo ne prove mes que devaunt son entre le franketenemente dymurt en le villen.

Et ascuns teignont que ilz serront tenauntz en comen, pur ceo que lauter ne prendra avantage del survyvor et le roy serra respondu des proffyttes de temps le purchace. Et semble que un villen le roy et un alyen purchacant est tout un case.

[31]

Nota que ou feffmente est fait sauns consyderation et null tort est fait sur le feffmente, ceo serra al prymer use. Mes si ascun tort est fait serra prise toutz foitz al use le feffor.

[32]

Le roy ne poit per son charter dispenser ove choce quell fuit malum in se et prohybyte per le comen ley. Mes malum prohibitum, quell est per estatute punyshable, il poit: quod nota, per *Bromley*.

[33]

Si home suast en court baron ou auter court de choce le jurisdiction de quell appertyent al court le roy, et per quell suyt le roy est daver proffytt, cest en case de premunire, pur ceo que lestatute est in curia romana vel alibi: et ceo est loppinion de *Hare*.

Bromley tyent le contrarie, et que cest alibi serra intende in spirituall court. [*fo. 103v*]

[34]

Nota per *Bradshawe* et *Bromley* que home ne poit justyfyer le bater dun en defence de ses bienz pur ceo que il ad suffycient remedie per action. Et dit que Spylman, serjant, fuit de mesme loppinion.

runs against the king (*quia nullum tempus occurrit regi*). Yet this does not prove otherwise than that before his entry the freehold remains in the villein.

Some held that they shall be tenants in common, because the other shall not take advantage of survivorship and the king shall be answered for the profits from the time of the purchase. And it seems that a villein of the king's and an alien purchasing are all one case.

31. NOTE

Note that where a feoffment is made without consideration, and no wrong is done upon the feoffment, this shall be to the first use. But if any wrong is done it shall always be taken to the use of the feoffor.

32. NOTE

Probably in the Inner Temple.

The king may not by his charter dispense with something which [is] *malum in se* and prohibited by the common law. But he may dispense with *malum prohibitum*, which is punishable only by statute: note that, by *Bromley*.

33. NOTE

Inner Temple.

If someone sues in court baron or another court for something whereof the jurisdiction belongs to the king's court, and by which suit the king is to have profit, this is within the case of *praemunire*, because the statute says 'in the Roman Curia or elsewhere' (*in curia romana vel alibi*): and that is the opinion of *Hare*.

Bromley holds the contrary, and that this word 'elsewhere' (*alibi*) shall be understood to mean in a spiritual court.

34. NOTE

Inner Temple, probably before Trin. 1531.

Note, by *Bradshaw* and *Bromley*, that one may not justify beating someone in defence of his goods, because he has a sufficient remedy by action. And he said that Serjeant Spelman[1] was of the same opinion.

---

[1] Appointed J.K.B. in July 1531.

Hare tyent que il poit cybien come en defender son franketenemente.

Bromley. Cest don per estatute quaunt il ad ewe possession per troix anz, mez il ne poit ceo faire al comen ley. Mes en defence de son person auterment est, quar la il est de aver un corporall peyne et auxi poit estre que lauter luy voill tuer.

[35]

Nota per *Hare* que si le baron et feme purchace terre joyntmente a eux et a lour heirs, et le baron paye tout largent et devie, la feme avera tout per le survyvor a son use demesne. Mes si le baron et feme et le terce purchace joyntmente, et le baron paye tout, ore serra entende si null use soyt expresse que le feme et le terce ne sont nosmes einz come feffees, et ceo est quaunt null use est expresse sur le feffmente.

[36]

Nota per *Inglefylde* que le roy ne recovera damagez en ascun action. Et quere per quell cause. Et quere si le declaration ne serra as damagez come est en accompt coment que nulls serront recovers. Mes fuit dit si home soyt oblyge a un auter al use de roy laction serra prise en le nosme loblige et il recovera damagez az opes de roy.

[37]

Nota que en plusors casez le persone de villen poit estre privelege et uncore jeo seisera ses bienz et enter en son terre: come il est dymurrant en auncient demesne per le space dun an, jeo prendra ses bienz ou entra en son terre si soit hors del fraunchyce, quar ceo nest que privelege de seiser ratione loci, mes il dymurt vyllen et serra disable en chescun action sinon que soit en trespas ou faux imprisonment pur ceo que il luy pryst deinz le fraunchyce. Et mesme la ley est ou il est fait pryeste. Et mesme la ley si mon villen soyt fait chivaler, son corps ne serra sese de fair villen servyce quar cest abhorre en lordre de

Hare held that he could, just as he may in defence of his freehold.

Bromley. That is given by statute, when he has had possession for three years;[1] but he could not do it at common law. In defence of his person, however, it is otherwise; for there he is to have bodily harm and it may be that the other will kill him.

35. NOTE

Probably in the Inner Temple.

Note by *Hare* that if husband and wife purchase land jointly unto them and their heirs, and the husband pays all the money and dies, the woman shall have it all by survivorship to her own use. But if a husband and wife and a third party purchase jointly, and the husband pays everything, now it shall be presumed (if no use is expressed) that the woman and the third party are named only as feoffees; and that is when no use is expressed upon the feoffment.

36. NOTE

Note, by ENGLEFIELD, that the king shall not recover damages in any action.[2] Query what the reason is. And query whether the declaration should not be 'to the damage', as it is in account, even if no damages may be recovered. But it was said that if someone binds himself to another to the use of the king, the action shall be taken in the name of the obligee, and he shall recover damages to the king's use.

37. NOTE

Note that in various cases a villein's person may be privileged and yet I may seize his goods and enter in his land: for instance, if he lives in ancient demesne for the space of a year, I may take his goods or enter in his land if it is outside the franchise, for that is but a privilege from seizure by reason of the place (*ratione loci*), but he remains a villein and shall be disabled in every action except trespass or false imprisonment for taking him within the franchise. The law is the same where is made a priest. And the law is the same if my villein is knighted: his body shall not be seized in order to do villein services, for that

---

[1] Statute of Forcible Entry, 8 Hen. VI, c. 9 (*SR* ii. 244), final proviso (right to defend with force possessions continued for three years).
[2] Cf. Yorke, above, vol. I, p. 123, no. 90.

chivaler, mes ses bienz et terres etc. et son issue serra villens. Quere si le nyeff prist baron. Et quere si mon villen luy conust destre villen al roy sil est enfranchyce.

[38]

Un Doctor Peter, un phisycion, port un action de sa feme abduce ove ses bienz, et en le record el fuit nosme Anne et le transcripte de record quell vyent a les justyces de nisi prius fuit Alyce, et le jurye luy trove coupable de ses bienz prises et sa feme abduce mes ilz ne savoyont si el avera nosme Anne. Et les justyces dysont que le record del nisi prius poit estre amende et que il avera jugemente.

[39]

Nota diversite parenter disclaymer et nontenure, quar per ple de non tenure mon droit nest ale mes per le disclaymer est, coment que jeo ne sue tenaunt: mes semble que null prendra avantage mes cestui que est privey al disclaymer et il avera per voy de conclusyon.

[40]

Un home fait lesse pur ans rendant rente et si le rente soit arere que il poit rentrer et reteyner in pristino statu quousque ei de redditu predicto sit plenarie satisfactum: si le lesse paye le rent uncore il navera son terme arrere pur ceo que fuit cleremente extinct, et donques ne poit estre revyve per le paymente del money. Sed quere inde, quar home poit surrender son terme sur condition et uncore la est extincte. < 21 Ric. 2 accordant est adjuge. >[1] [fo. 104]

[1] I only.

is abhorrent to the order of knighthood, but his goods and lands etc. and his issue shall be villeins. What if a neif marries a husband? And what if my villein acknowledges himself to be the king's villein and he is enfranchised?

38. DR PETRE'S CASE

One Dr Petre, a physician,[1] brought an action for abducting his wife with his goods, and in the record she was named Anne and in the transcript of the record which came to the justices of nisi prius she was Alyce; and the jury found the defendant guilty of taking his goods and abducting his wife, but they did not know whether she was called Anne. The justices said that the record of the nisi prius could be amended, and that he should have judgment.

39. NOTE

Note a distinction between disclaimer and non-tenure; for by the plea of non-tenure my right is not gone, whereas by the disclaimer it is, even though I am not tenant: but it seems that no one may take advantage except a person who is privy to the disclaimer, and he shall have it by way of estoppel.

40. NOTE

Someone made a lease for years, rendering rent, and if the rent should be in arrear he could re-enter and retain the land in the original estate until he should be fully satisfied in respect of the aforesaid rent (*in pristino statu quousque ei de redditu praedicto sit plenarie satisfactum*): even if the lessee pays the rent he shall still not have his term back, because it is clearly extinguished, and therefore it cannot be revived by the payment of the money. But query this, for one may surrender one's term upon condition and nevertheless it is [not] extinguished. (21 Ric. II is adjudged accordingly.[2])

---

[1] I.e. not William Petre, the civil lawyer (DCL 1533) and future secretary of state.
[2] Year not in print, though some of its contents were abridged by Fitzherbert.

[41]

Nota per *Hare* que en toutz brefez queux sont dones per estatute lou null tiell brefe fuit al comen ley et per mesme lestatute nest ascun proces don en le dit brefe, la le plaintife avera somons, attachmente et dystres infynite, et per defaut de dystres capias infynite, come est en covenaunte ou action sur le case, quar le brefe est foundu sur lestatute accordant a son case. Come en champartye nest proces don per lestatute ne tyell brefe nest al comen ley, einz le brefe avoit son commensemente soullmente per estatute, et pur ceo dystres infynite gyst et capias infynite en defaut de dystres, et null proces de utlagarie gyst. Mes si ascun proces de utlagarie soit agarde cest voyde et nemi error. Mes si brefe soit don en especiall case ou ne gysoit avaunt mes tyell nature de brefe fuit avaunt, la home avera tyell proces come fuit en tyell brefe avaunt: quod nota.

[42]

Un home pryst feme seisi de certen terre, el esteant deinz lage de consente, le baron alyen en fee, el dysagre: si ore el poit entrer ou que ceo serra un discontynuance et el myse a son brefe de droit? Quar cui in vita ne gyst ne cui ante divorcium.

[43]

Equitas statuti.

Lestatute quell don action vers le pernor des proffyttes ne dit que il pledra come tenaunt, mes entant que action est don vers luy la ley luy donera respons a ceo. Mes il ne poit voucher, per cause que lauter ne poit luy garranter pur ceo que vers luy est come null estate. Mes en formedon voucher est don per estatute.

41. NOTE

Probably in the Inner Temple.

Note, by *Hare*, that in all writs which are given by statute, where there was no such writ at common law, and no process is given by the same statute for the said writ, the plaintiff shall have summons, attachment and distress infinite, and for default of distress a *capias* infinite, as in covenant or action on the case; for the writ is based on the statute according to his case. Thus in champerty there is no process given by the statute,[1] nor is there any such writ at common law, but the writ had its commencement solely by the statute, and therefore distress infinite lies, and *capias* infinite in default of distress, and no process of outlawry lies. But if any process of outlawry is awarded it is void and not error. However, if a writ is given in a special case where it did not lie before, though there was a writ of the same kind before, one may there have such process as was used in such writs before: note that.

42. NOTE

A man married a woman seised of certain land, while she was under the age of consent, the husband aliened in fee, and she disagreed: may she now enter, or shall it be considered a discontnuance so that she is driven to her writ of right? For a *cui in vita* does not lie; nor does *cui ante divorcium*.

43. NOTE

Equity of the statute.

The statute which gives an action against the pernor of the profits[2] does not say that he shall plead as tenant, but since an action is given against him the law will give him a [right to] answer it. But he may not vouch, because the other cannot warrant, for as against him it is as if it were no estate. But in formedon [against the pernor] a voucher is given by the statute.

---

[1] Statute of Berwick (*SR* i. 216).
[2] 1 Hen. VII, c. 1 (*SR* ii. 500).

[44]

En replevin le defendant avowast, le plaintife est a issue sur un poynt en le avowrie, quell est trove pur lavowant, per que il ad un brefe de retorno habendo, sur quell est retorne que les avers sont mort: quere quell remedie? Et quere si home ad un chyvall en gage pur certen deners appromptz et le chyvall morust, quell remedie il avera pur largent?

[45]

Nota que en toutz cases si home voill demander jugement si le roy nient counsell la coviente monstre que les terres sont en mainz le roy per reson de gardship, ideoce, ou pur seiser dascun fyne, et tiell semble. Mes sil voill pryer en ayd il coviente monstre revercion de fraunketenemente ou reall possessyon et que la terre est en mayne le roy et il come servant ou bayle, et issint prier en ayde. Et per ayde pryer en assise le paroll nest myse sauns jour einz les partyes averont jour al procheyn assise et en le mesne temps que suera al roy et enterpledera ove le roy en le Chauncery, et sil ne vient al procheyn assise donques est discontynue et le partye serra reattache. Mes quaunt il demande jugemente si le roy nient counsell et lexchetor est examyne, come oportet, et trove est que les terres sont en mayne le roy, tout est discontynue. Mes ascuns dyont que lentre en ambideux cases est que ilz attendront a tiell jour et interim loquitur cum rege. [fo. 104v]

[46]

Nota per *Hare* et *Bromley*: Si jeo vouche J. S. come fitz et heire W. S. jeo poye quaunt il vyent luy lyer per son garrante demesne pur ceo que fitz et heire nest addition de surnosme. Mes ilz fueront en doubt sil soit vouche come J. S. sauns tyell addycion sil poit estre lye come heire pur ceo que cest voucher est en liew daction per quell il est destre charge ove cell garrante. Come en case si jeo port un action de dett vers un, il covient estre nosme heire en le brefe ou autermente jeo ne luy chargera. < 30 H. 6, fo. 5, accordant. >[1] Et issint est en dett vers un gaoler ou vers executor. Et semble pur cest cause sil soit vouche come fitz et heire a un auncestre il ne poit estre lye per cause de garrante dauter auncestre.

---

[1] *Margin, both mss.*

44. NOTE

In replevin the defendant avows, the plaintiff is at issue upon a point in the avowry, which is found for the avowant, and so he has a writ *de retorno habendo*, whereupon it is returned that the beasts are dead: what remedy is there? And if someone has a horse in gage for certain money lent, and the horse dies, what remedy shall he have for the money?

45. NOTE

Note that in all cases if someone demands judgment *rege inconsulto*, it must be shown that the lands are in the king's hands by reason of wardship, idiocy, or by seizure for some fine, and such like. But if he prays in aid [of the king] he must show a freehold reversion or real possession and that the land is in the king's hands, and that he [acted] as servant or bailiff, and thus pray in aid. By an aid prayer in assize the suit is not put off without day but the parties shall have a day at the next assize, and in the mean time may sue to the king and interplead with the king in Chancery; and, if he does not come at the next assize, it is discontinued and the party shall be reattached. But when he demands judgment *rege inconsulto*, and the escheator is examined, as he ought to be, and it is found that the lands are in the king's hands, everything is discontinued. Some say, however, that the entry [on the roll] in both cases is that they should await such and such a day and in the meantime speak with the king (*et interim loquitur cum rege*).

46. NOTE

Inner Temple.

Note, by *Hare* and *Bromley*, that if I vouch John Style as son and heir of William Style, when he comes I may bind him by his own warranty inasmuch as 'son and heir' is not an addition to the surname. But they were in doubt, if he is vouched as John Style without such an addition, whether he may be bound as heir, because this voucher is in lieu of an action whereby he is to be charged with this warranty. It is like the case where I bring an action of debt against someone: he must be named heir in the writ or else I may not charge him. (30 Hen. VI, fo. 5, agrees.[1]) So it is in debt against a gaoler or against an executor. And it seems, for this reason, that if he is vouched as son and heir to one ancestor he cannot be bound by reason of a warranty by another ancestor.

---

[1] YB Trin. 30 Hen. VI, fo. 5, pl. 2. (Citation in margin.)

[47]

Quere si jeo ou mes auncestres avomus este en possession peaseablemente per troix anz et puis un voille entrer sur moy et jeo luy teigne hors ove force, come jeo poye per expresse parollx destatute de anno 8 H. 6, et le justyce de peace vyent de moy remover hors de possession et jeo luy teigne hors: quere si jeo poye justyfyer?

Et dicitur que cy. Et auxi dicitur que sil port posse comitatus et moy treit dehors jeo poye aver action de trespas vers luy, quar il nad garrante de ceo faire per lestatute, ergo sil ceo face il est mysfezor et serra puny come auter comen person. Et issint il est tenus non obstante que il veiast le force a conuster que jeo aye ewe le possession per le space de troix anz.

Ascuns dyont le contrarie, pur ceo que il est juge de cell acte et de ceo ad jurisdiction. Donques sil ceo fait come juge il est excuse de ceo faire, pur ceo que il ad coulor, et la misfezance de ceo nest que defaut de conusance. Come si un juge don jugemente que un serra pendu ou il ne serra.

[48]

Nota si home soit seisi de terre en droit sa feme et ad yssue, ore le avowrie est chaunge et covyent estre fait sur le baron. Mes semble que il ferra notyce al seignior del yssue. Et quere si soyent dyvers seigniors si notyce fait a lun soyt bon? Et si dyvers soyent enfeffes si un de eux poit faire notyce?

[49]

Nota per *Dacres* que a les assyses a Exestre in 20 H. 8. larray dun pannell fuit challenge pur ceo que le vicount que fyst larray est desouthe le dystres le plaintife, et monstre coment, ut oportet, scilicet que il est seisi de tyell acre de terre en tyell liew et ceo tyent del dit plaintife come de son maner de Dale per tielx servyces etc., et al darreyn en le conclusyon il pria que larray serroit

47. NOTE

Probably in the Inner Temple. The *dicitur . . . ascuns diont* formula was an ancient figure used in reporting exercises.

If I or my ancestors have been in possession peaceably for thee years, and then someone wishes to enter upon me, and I keep him out with force—as I may by the express words of the statute of 8 Hen. VI[1]—and a justice of the peace comes to remove me from possession, and I keep him out, may I justify this?

It is said that I may. It is also said that if he brings the power of the county (*posse comitatus*) and drags me out I may have an action of trespass against him, for he has no warrant to do that by the statute, and so if he does it he is a wrongdoer and shall be punished like any other common person. Thus, even if he saw the force, he is obliged to know that I have had the possession for a period of three years.

Others said the contrary, because he is a judge of that act and has jurisdiction thereof. Therefore, if he does it as judge, he is excused for doing it, inasmuch as he has a colour and the wrongdoing is merely a lack of knowledge. Likewise if a judge gives a judgment that someone shall be hanged where he ought not to be.[2]

48. NOTE

Note that if someone is seised of land in right of his wife, and has issue, the avowry is now changed and must be made upon the husband. But it seems that he ought to give notice to the lord of having had issue. If there are various lords, is notice given to one of them good? And if several people are enfeoffed, may one of them give notice?

49. NOTE

Inner Temple: relation of a case at Exeter assizes in 1528.

Note, by *Dacres*,[3] that at the assizes at Exeter in 20 Hen. VIII the array of a panel was challenged because the sheriff who made the array was under the plaintiff's distress, and it was shown in what way (as is needful), namely that he was seised of such and such an acre of land in such and such a place and held it of the said plaintiff as of his manor of Dale by such and such services etc., and

---

[1] Statute of Forcible Entry, 8 Hen. VI, c. 9 (*SR* ii. 244).
[2] Cf. Yorke, above, vol. I, p. 187, no. 258; Yelverton, above, p. 322, no. 21.
[3] Robert Dacres, of the Inner Temple, clerk of assize on the Western circuit 1527–29; died 1543. His reports are cited in vol. I, p. 88.

quasshe. Et le veryte del matter fuit que il tyent ceo del plaintife mes come dauter maner, scilicet de son maner de Sale, et pur ceo les tryors fueront jures et charges denquier sil tyent del plaintife mesme la terre come de son maner de Dale ou nemi, et de null auter choce, pur ceo que il avoit conclude soullmente sur le principall challenge. Mes sil avoit conclude et issint le dit array favorablement fait, donques ilz inquieront del favor del vycount en son retorne et lauter especiall matter nest que conveyance, et le favor est leffecte del challenge. Et pur ceo est graunde folly de concluder sur lespeciall matter. [*fo. 105*]

[50]

Nota per *Fitzherbert* en le Comen Banke cleremente que si leschetor trove un offyce de mon terre apres le mort mon pere, et trove est que cest tenus de roy come de son duche de Bukyngham, ou similia, per servyce de chivaler, et en fait ceo nest tenus de luy per ascun mesne einz dun comen person, cest offyce est de null value de moy lyer ne jeo ne serra unques compelle de ceo traverser, quar loffyce est clere voyde que un eschetor trovast toutz ditz sil ne soyt trove tenus de roy en chyef, quar leschetor nad auter autoryte denquier del tenure sinon soullmente de ceo, nyent pluis que le pluys estraunge de mounde.

Shelley semble le contrarye.

Et *Fitzherbert* cleremente tyent son opynion ley.

Et *Bromley* intend son opynion ley.

[51]

Nota per ascuns si jeo delyver bienz a un comen carryer pur carryer a tyell liewe, et de ceo delyverer a tyell liewe, et il prist sur luy de ceo faire, ore il est charge ove ceo et sil soyt robbe per le voy il ne serra discharge vers moy pur ceo que il ad emprise sur luy de ceo faire et cest a son perell ore. Mes sil fuit mon servant et jeo luy mitta ove tiell choce a delyverer a un tyell liew, et il ceo fait accordant a mon commandmente, ore sil soit robbe per le voy il serra dyscharge vers moy pur ceo que il ne fyst ceo mes per comaundemente et come mon servant et ne pryst ascun charge sur luy ne fuit accompant a moy. Mes si jeo baylle un hanape a un pur savemente garder et pur delyverer a moy quaunt jeo ceo require, et il emprist sur luy de ceo faire, ore sil est robbe dicitur que il nest discharge vers moy. Et si jeo face un mon rent gatherer ou rescevor et don

finally in the conclusion he prayed that the array be quashed. The truth of the matter was that he did hold it of the plaintiff but as of another manor, namely his manor of Sale, and therefore the triers were sworn and charged to enquire whether he held the same land of the plaintiff as of his manor of Dale, or not, and of no other thing, because he had concluded solely upon the principal challenge. But if he had concluded 'and so the said array was favourably made', then they should enquire into the favour of the sheriff in his return and the other special matter is but introduction and the favour is the substance of the challenge. Therefore it is great folly to conclude upon the special matter.

50. ANON.

Common Pleas; perhaps related in the Inner Temple.

Note, by FITZHERBERT in the Common Bench, clearly, that if the escheator finds an office of my land after my father's death, and it is found that it is held of the king as of his duchy of Buckingham, or such like, by knight-service, and in fact it is not held of him by any mesne but of a common person, this office is of no value to bind me and I shall never be compelled to traverse it, for an office found by an escheator is always clearly void if it is not found to be held of the king in chief, for the escheator has no other authority to enquire of the tenure, any more than the greatest stranger in the world, but only of [tenure in chief].
SHELLEY thought the contrary.
FITZHERBERT clearly held his opinion to be law.
(And *Bromley* thought his opinion to be law.)

51. NOTE

Note, by some, that if I deliver goods to a common carrier to carry to such and such a place, and to deliver at such and such a place, and he takes upon himself to do this, he is now charged with it, and if he is robbed on the way he shall not be discharged as against me, because he has undertaken to do it and it is now at his risk. But if he is my servant and I send him with such a thing to deliver at such and such a place, and he does this according to my command, and is robbed on the way, he shall be discharged as against me because he only did it by my command and as my servant and did not take any charge upon himself and was not accountable to me. If, however, I bail a cup to be kept safely and redelivered to me when I request it, and he undertakes to do this, it is said that if he is robbed he is not discharged as against me. And if I appoint someone my rent-gatherer or receiver, and give him a fee or a certain sum to do it, and to deliver [the money collected] to me at such and such a place, and he is

a luy un fee ou certeyn somme pur ceo faire, et pur ceo delyverer a moy a tyell liew, et il est robbe, ascuns dyont que il est discharge la pur ceo que il nest forsque mon servant et est tenus de vener a moy ove mon money quaunt jeo mitta pur luy. Tamen quere inde, quar il est accomptable a moy, pur ceo que il ad imprist de ceo faire et ad certeyn fee et salarye de ceo faire, ergo il nest solemente come un servant retenus. Et si jeo face un mon baylye de mon maner et il est robbe, dicitur per ascuns que il serra discharge, pur ceo que il nest forsque come mon servant. Sed quere de ceux cases bene, quia dubia.

Et vide 41 E. 3, que un factor fuit accomptant a son master pur choces achates et il monstra pur son discharge que il fuit en jeopardye sur le mere et pur saver son vye eux jetta en le mere. Issint semble reson serroit que il dyrroit que il fuit robbe deux et pur salvation de son vye il fuit coharte de suffre les larons eux prendre. Quere.

[52]

Nota si home ad les lettres lordynarie ad colligendum il ne serra sue come admynistrator ne come executor, et sil soyt il monstra lespeciall matter.

[53]

Nota per *Audeley* que forma predicta avera relation a semble estate ou semble choce come ceo est quell precede plus procheyn a les parollx de forma predicta. Come si home fait lesse pur vye a un, le remainder a un auter en taylle, le remainder a un auter pur vye, le remainder a un auter in forma predicta, ceo avera relation al darrein estate. Et il avera pur son vye demesne, quar autermente son estate serra voyde. [*fo. 105v*]

[54]

Nota per ascuns que si home fait lesse de certeyn terre pur terme de vye le lesse al use le lessor, en cell case si le lessor devie le lesse serra seisi a son use demesne et nemi al use lheir le lessor, pur ceo que nest issint expresse en le lesse, et sil navoit

robbed, some say that he is discharged there, because he is only my servant and is bound to come to me with my money when I send for him. Query thereof, nevertheless, for he is accountable to me, because he has undertaken to do it and has a certain fee and salary for doing it, and therefore he is not exactly like a retained servant. If I appoint someone my bailiff of my manor and he is robbed, it is said by some that he shall be discharged, because he is only like my servant. But query well of these cases, because they are doubted.

See 41 Edw. III,[1] that a factor was accountable to his master for things bought, and he showed for his discharge that he was in danger on the sea and to save his life he threw them in the sea. Likewise it seems reasonable that he should be able to say that he was robbed of them, and to save his life was forced to let the thieves take them. Query.

52. NOTE

Note that if someone has letters from the ordinary *ad colligendum* he shall not be sued as administrator or as executor, and if he is he may show the special facts.[2]

53. NOTE

Probably in the Inner Temple.

Note, by *Audley*, that 'in the form aforesaid' (*forma praedicta*) shall have relation to an estate or thing similar to that which immediately precedes the words *forma praedicta*.[3] Thus if someone makes a lease for life to someone, remainder to another in tail, remainder to another for life, remainder to another *in forma praedicta*, this shall have relation to the last estate mentioned; but he shall have it for his own life, otherwise his estate would be void.[4]

54. NOTE

Probably in the Inner Temple.

Note, by some, that if someone makes a lease of certain land for term of the lessee's life to the use of the lessor, in this case if the lessor dies the lessee shall be seised to his own use and not to the use of the lessor's heir, because it is not so

[1] *Tamworth's Case* (1367) YB Mich. 41 Edw. III, fo. 3, pl. 8.
[2] Cf. *Capell* v. *Executors of Duplege* (1506) Caryll's reports, 116 Selden Soc. 505; *Anon.* (1525) Rastell, *Entries*, s.v. Executours: Barre, pl. 6 (citing Trin. 17 Hen. VIII, m. 28, but not found in KB 27/1056).
[3] Cf. Pollard, above, p. 271, no. 60.   [4] Cf. below, p. 396, no. 62, *per* Bromley.

expresse ascun use en le fait il serroit seisi a son use demesne. Donques semble en toutz casez lou home fait ascun estate a un auter et cestui a que lestate est fait serroit seisi a son use demesne per la ley sinon que contrarie use soit expresse, la toutz ditz accordant come luse est expresse il ceo extendra et nemi autermente. Come si home fait don en taill al use de un pur terme de vye apres son deces il serra seisi a son use demesne. Auterment est si home [fait] feffmente al use de luy mesme, ou al use de auter pur terme de vye, quar per le fee ilz sont seisies al use le feffor, pur ceo que si null use ust estre expresse issint serroit.

[55]

Nota per *Bradshawe* que est comen experyence que si un rescous soyt retorne proces serra fait pur le roy per lattorney le roy a faire lour fyne et silz veignont einz ilz naveront travers al retorne de vycount mes serront myse a lour actyon sur le case vers le vycount.

[56]

Vide que est tenus en detynue si le pleintife doubta que le defendant voile gager sa ley que serra un bon polyce de nosmer luy ove un auter que serra dassent de faire defaut al jour que ilz ount de faire la ley.

[57]

Nota per *Hare* et *Chydley* que ilz poyent voucher pur customarye landes.
Mes *Bromley* rydendo dit que ceo ne poit estre, quar null transmutation de possession sur que per entendmente le garrante duyst surder poit estre sans surrendre al seigniour, donques le seigniour fait lestate et le partye est einz per luy et nemi per cestui que surrendre. Quere coment il duyst recover en value, quar il ne poit aver frauuketenemente en recompence. Et lenterest dun copyholder ne point alterer sinon per surrender, et pur ceo il ne poit aver execution en value de copyhold terre.

expressed in the lease, and if there is no express use in the deed he shall be seised to his own use. Therefore it seems in all cases where someone makes any estate to another, and by law the person to whom the estate is made should be seised to his own use unless a contrary use is expressed, he shall always have it according as the use is expressed and not otherwise. Thus if someone makes a gift in tail to the use of someone for term of life, after his decease he shall be seised to his own use. It is otherwise if someone makes a feoffment to the use of himself, or to the use of someone else for term of life, for by the fee they are seised to the use of the feoffor, because it would have been so even if no use had been expressed.

55. NOTE

Probably in the Inner Temple. Cf. above, p. 275, no. 69.

Note, by *Bradshaw*, that it is common experience if a rescue is returned for process to be made out on the king's behalf by the king's attorney to make their fine, and if they come in they shall not traverse the sheriff's return but shall be driven to their action on the case against the sheriff.

56. NOTE

Observe that it is held in detinue that, if the plaintiff fears that the defendant will wage his law, it is a good policy to name him with someone else who has agreed to make default at the day which they have to do the law.

57. NOTE

Inner Temple.

Note, by *Hare* and *Chidley*, that there may be a voucher for customary lands.

But *Bromley* (smiling) said that this cannot be, for there can be no transmutation of possession whereon by presumption a warranty may arise without a surrender to the lord, and then the lord makes the estate and the party is in through him and not through the person who surrendered. Query how he should recover in value; for he cannot have a freehold in recompense. The interest of a copyholder cannot be altered except by surrender, and therefore he cannot have execution in value of copyhold land.

[58]

Nota per *Hare* que si lesse pur vye soit fait sans impechmente de wast, [et] le lesse graunt ouster son estate, il avera mesme lavantage pur ceo que fuit choce annexte al estate et passera ove lestate. Auterment est si le graunt fuit fait puis le lesse, quar la est forsque covenante annexte al persone et nemi al terre et pur ceo il navera avantage. Mes ad este questyon si le lesse mesme poit ceo pleder en barre, et de darreyn temps ad este dit que cy, en avoydance de circuyte daction. Mes le graunte ne poit aver action et pur ceo il ne pledra.

[59]

Quere si deux[1] joyntenantes soyent en fee et lun relesse a [lauter][2] pur vye, le remainder ouster: si cest remainder poit estre fait sur cell reles? Et semble a *Hare* que cy, quar icy cell reles va per voy de fezance destate et le parte de cestui que relesse est a lauter pur vye per force del relesse. [*fo. 106*]

[60]

Nota quod anno 20 H. 8. un prisoner fuit arraigne a Newgate et fuit trove coupable et avoit jugemente destre pendu, et puis il eschapa et prist sentuarye a les Grey Freres. Et per advyse de *Baker*, recorder de London, *Whyte* et *Pakynton*,[3] south vycountz, et auters sages offycers del cytye, il fuit prise hors de sentuarye. Et fuit dit que les justyces fueront en opynion que fuit byen fait, et que il serroit pendu et ne serra suffer dabjure.

---

[1] 3 *I.*
[2] lun.
[3] Pakingeton *I.*

58.

Probably in the Inner Temple.

Note, by *Hare*, that if a lease for life is made without impeachment of waste, and the lessee grants over his estate, the grantee shall have the same advantage, because this was something annexed to the estate and shall pass with the estate. It is otherwise if the grant was made after the lease, for there it is only a covenant annexed to the person and not to the land, and therefore he shall not have advantage. But it has been a question whether the lessee himself may plead it in bar; and in recent times it has been said that he may, to avoid circuity of action. But the grantee cannot have an action, and therefore he shall not plead.

59. NOTE

Probably in the Inner Temple.

If there are two joint tenants in fee and one of them releases to the other for life, with remainder over: may this remainder be made upon this release? It seemed to *Hare* that it could, for here this release goes by way of making an estate and the share of the one who releases goes to the other for life by virtue of the release.

60. ANON.

Newgate sessions, 1528/29; probably related in the Inner Temple. Also reported in Spelman 46, pl. 8 (Pas. 20 Hen. VIII; but no decision reported).

Note that in the year 20 Hen. VIII a prisoner was arraigned at Newgate and was found guilty and had judgment to be hanged; and afterwards he escaped and took sanctuary in the Greyfriars. And by the advice of *Baker*, Recorder of London, *White* and *Pakington*, under-sheriffs,[1] and other wise officers of the city, he was taken out of sanctuary. And it was said that the justices were of opinion that this was well done, and that he should be hanged and not allowed to abjure.[2]

---

[1] John Baker, Henry White and John Pakington were all benchers of the Inner Temple: *Readers and Readings*, pp. 76–77.
[2] Cf. Bro. Abr., *Corone*, pl. 110, which says clergy was allowed at Newgate in such a case in 22 Hen. VIII.

[61]

Nota per *Shelley*, Justice, que si home face lesse pur vye et puis luy oblyge en estatute merchaunte et graunt le revercion ouster, cell terre serra myse en execution, quar ceo poit le lessor cybyen chargera lexecution come sil avoit fait un graunt de rent.

[62]

Le case fuit tyell. Le roy graunta al mayer de Yorke que il avera easdem libertates que le mayer de Londres ad.

Le reder semble que il avera semblable lybertes que le mayer de Londres avera.

Bromley semble le graunt voyde pur le contraryete des parolls. Quar per les parolls il averoit mesmes les lybertyes que London, quest impossible, quar per ceo ensueroit que le mayor de Yorke averoit les lybertees de London en le cytye de London lou il ad ryens de faire. Et, sir, donques serra semblable a le case que si jeo aye conusance de ple deinz mon maner de Dale et le roye graunt a un auter que il avera mesme le conusance deinz son maner de Sale, cest graunt semble voyde, quar per cest graunt lestraunger averoit conusance que jeo avoy devaunt, quell le roy ne poit prendre de moy per cest secunde graunte. Et, sir, le construction des lettres patentz le roy serra prise pluis benefyciall pur le roy lou les parollx sownent en doubte, et pur ceo jeo ne voille agreer le case quell le reder ad myst, scilicet si le roy graunt a un home terres ou lybertyes pur terme de vye et ne monstre pur terme de que vye, adyre que ceo serra prise pur terme de vye le roy ou pur terme de vye le graunte, ceo ne serra [prise],[1] mez jeo entende que serra prise pluis benefyciall pur le roy pur le incertente, scilicet que le graunte ceo avera durant le plesure, quar voyde ne poit estre pur ceo que appyert que le plesure le roy fuit que il ceo avera, mes pur le noncertente de temps serra prise tanque le roy ad determyne son plesure issint que le patente ne serra accomptable pur les mesne proffyttes prises tanque le roy ad determyne son plesure. Mes pur lestate jeo entende clere que nad auter estate forsque a volunte. Et mesme la ley est si le roy graunt terres a deux pur terme de lour deux vyes, si lun devie jeo entende cleremente que lauter navera pas per le survyvor sinon que le roy ad expresse que survyvera en son patent: come si le patent soyt et alteri eorum diutius viventis. Mes en le case de comen persone serra prise pluis benefyciall pur [fo. 106v] le graunte et pluys fort encontre le grauntor lou le graunt sowne en

---

[1] pre *in both mss, reading unclear.*

61. NOTE

Note, by SHELLEY, Justice, that if someone makes a lease for life and afterwards binds himself in a statute merchant, and grants the reversion over, this land shall be put in execution, for the lessor may just as well charge the execution as if he had made a grant of rent.

62. NOTE FROM A READING

Inner Temple. The case may have been prompted by the case of the city of Lincoln, reported by Yelverton, above, p. 330, no. 36.

The case was as follows: the king granted the mayor of York that he should have the same liberties (*easdem libertates*) as the mayor of London.

The reader thought he should he have the like (*semblables*) liberties as the mayor of London.

Bromley thought the grant void because of the self-contradiction in the words. For by the words he was to have the 'same' liberties as London, which is impossible, for it would follow from that that the mayor of York should have the liberties of London in the city of London, where he has nothing to do. And, sir, it would then be like the case where I have cognizance of pleas within my manor of Dale, and the king grants me and another that he shall have the same cognizance within his manor of Sale, this grant seems void, for by this grant the stranger would have the cognizance which I had before, which the king cannot take from me by this second grant. Sir, the construction of the king's letters patent shall be taken more beneficially for the king where the words sound in doubt, and therefore I would not agree the case which the reader has put, namely if the king grants someone lands or liberties for term of life, and does not set out for whose life, to say that this shall be taken to mean for term of the king's life or for term of the grantee's life, this cannot be so taken, but I think it shall be taken more beneficially for the king on account of the uncertainty, namely that the grantee shall have it during the king's pleasure; for it cannot be void, inasmuch as it appears to be the king's pleasure that he shall have it, but because of the uncertainty of time it shall be taken to mean until the king has determined his pleasure, so that the patentee shall not be accountable for the same profits taken until the king has determined his pleasure. As to the estate, however, I think it clear that he has no other estate but at will. The law is the same if the king grants lands to two people for term of their two lives, and one of them dies, I think clearly that the other shall not have it by survivorship unless the king has expressed in his patent that he shall, as where the patent says 'and to whichever of them lives the longer' (*et alteri eorum diutius viventis*). However, in the case of a common person it shall be taken more beneficially for the grantee and more

dowte. Mes en case le roy est tout auterment et serra semblable a cest case: home don terres a J. S. en taylle, le remainder a J. N. in forma predicta, cest remainder est clere voyde destre prise come state taylle a J. N., quar cest impossyble que poit remaynder a luy come fuit a lauter, quar donques ensuera que J. N. ceo avera a luy et a les heires de corps J. S. engendres, que ne poit estre: issint pur le contraryete ne poit aver en mesme le forme que lauter avoit. Mes peraventure lou home done terre a J. S. et a les heirs de son corps issantz et garrante mesme la terre in forma predicta, cest bon garrante pur ceo que le garrante alera a mesme le persone et a mesme les heirs, issint ceo nest contrariant etc. Mes en lauter case forma predicta est referre a estraunge sanke, que ne poit estre. Donques, si ceo ne poit estre en le case de comen person, a fortiori ceo ne poit estre bon lou il sounde in contraryete in graunt le roy. Et, sir, en le case de Quyntyn en le liver dassises un rent fuit graunt per le tenaunt pur vye et cestui en revercyon recyta mesme le graunt al graunte et confirma son estate en le rent et graunta que il et ses heires purront dystrener pur mesme le rent, [et] ceo fuit tenus la bon graunt per voy de confirmatyon de cestui en revercyon de charger son revercyon come novell graunt apres le mort le tenaunt, mes nemi de faire mesme le rent que fuit dependant sur estate pur vye destre fee simple: ceo ne poit estre, quar est impossyble que le graunte dystrenera pur cest rent apres le mort le tenaunt pur vye pur ceo que est determyne per son mort. Mes en le case de comen persone fuit tenus que serra prise come novell graunt. Mes si ceo ust este en le case le roy ne purra estre. Et, sir, si. deux homes soyent severallmente endettes al roy et le roy eux pardone toutz dettes, ceo en le case de comen person serra bon pur lour severall dettes mes en case le roy le pardon nest bon mes pur joynt dettes. Issint lou le patent de roy sounde en doubte le pluys benefyciall serra prise pur luy. Sic hic, quant le roy graunt easdem libertates cest repugnant come jeo aye dit adevaunt, ergo le patent voyde.

Hare al contrarye. Et dit que ou lentent le roy appyert en le patent serra prise soloncque son entent, et icy son entent est que le mayer de Yorke avera semblable lybertes que le mayer de London ad ou autermente le patent ne comprehent ascun entent ne meanynge. [*fo. 107*]

[63]

28 H. 8.

Nota que fuit tenus per toutz les justyces del Comen Banke que si lesse pur vye soit fait per endenture, rendant rent, et en lendenture sont plusors

strongly against the grantor, where the grant sounds in doubt. But in the king's case it is quite otherwise, and shall be like this case: someone gives lands to John Style in tail, remainder to John Noke *in forma praedicta*,[1] this remainder is clearly void if taken as an estate tail to John Noke, for it is impossible that it can remain to him as it was to the other, for then it would follow that John Noke would have it unto him and the heirs of the body of John Style begotten, which cannot be, and so because of the contradiction he cannot have it in the same form as the other did. But perhaps where someone gives land to John Style and the heirs of his body issuing, and warrants the same land *in forma praedicta*, this would be a good warranty, because the warranty will go to the same person and to the same heirs, and so it is not contradictory etc. But in the other case *forma praedicta* refers to a stranger's blood, which cannot be. Therefore, if this cannot be so in the case of a common person, a fortiori it cannot be so where it sounds in contradiction in the king's grant. Sir, in Quintin's case in the book of assizes,[2] a rent was granted by the tenant for life, and the reversioner recited the same grant to the grantee and confirmed his estate in the rent and granted that he and his heirs should be able to distrain for the same rent, and this was held a good grant by way of confirmation of the reversioner to charge his reversion as a new grant after the tenant's death, but not to cause the same rent—which was dependent upon an estate for life—to be a fee simple: that cannot be, for it is impossible that the grantee should distrain for this rent after the death of the tenant for life, because it is determined by his death. But in the case of a common person it was held that it should be taken as a new grant. However, if it had been in the king's case it could not be so. And, sir, if two men are separately indebted to the king, and the king pardons them all debts, in the case of a common person this would be good for their separate debts, but in the king's case the pardon is good only for joint debts. Thus where the king's patent sounds in doubt the most beneficial interpretation shall be taken for him. Likewise here, when the king grants *easdem libertates* that is repugnant, as I have already said, and so the patent is void.

Hare to the contrary. And he said that where the king's intention appears in the patent it shall be understood according to his intention; and here his intention is that the mayor of York shall have the like liberties as the mayor of London has, or else the patent does not contain any intention or meaning at all.

63. ANON.

Common Pleas, 1536/37. Cf. another version of this same text in Hare, above, vol. I, p. 85, no. 4.

Note that it was held by all the justices of the Common Bench that if a lease for life is made by indenture, rendering rent, and in the indenture there are

[1] Cf. above, p. 392, no. 53. [2] *Quintin's Case* (1352) YB 26 Edw. III, Lib. Ass., pl. 38.

covenauntz, et le lesse est oblige de performer les covenauntz en lendenture, et puis le rent est arere: ore il ad forfeyte son oblygation car cest un agremente enter eux sur le lease que il payera tant de rent, et il pryst la terre ove cest reservatyon, ergo son agremente, donques chescun agremente est un covenante, quar convenire nest auter choce mes de condiscendere ou agreer, queux parolls sont cy bon parolx de covenante come covenante et graunt. Et ilz dysont que ceo fuit argue et agree en temps Brudnell.

[64]

28 H. 8.

Un abbe en auncient temps avoit graunt a les auncestors de Sir Nicholas Carow, chivaler, de trover deux chappelleyns chantant en tyell chappell chescun jour, et graunta en quell temps que ilz faylont en chantant que il et ses successors payeront x. li. al dit auncestor et a ses heirs. Et fuit monstre al court que ilz ount fayle en trovant, et ore le questyon fuit quell action lheir averoit, scilicet brefe dannuitie ou brefe de dett, pur ceo que cest choce ad contynuance?

Et fuit dit que lheir avera brefe de dette, et fuit resemble al case dannuitie graunt et un peyne pur defaut de paymente, quar est choce casuell et nemi annuell, en quell case non obstante le contynuance il avera brefe de dett, come pur relyef.

Mes *Fitzherbert* doubta le case de relyef.

Shelley tyent ceo clere, et dit que il avoit un lyver issint adjudge. Et nota que il dit que lheir avera le penaltye et nemi ses executors, pur ceo que il ale ove [lenherytance],[1] come le brefe de covenante in 42 E. 3.[2]

[65]

28 H. 8.

Un home fyst lesse pur anz rendant rent per indenture, et les covenantes fueront en le fait, et al darrein le lesse covenante et graunta que sil grauntast ouster son estate in parte ou en tout que adonques byen lyrroit al lessor

[1] lhenerytance.
[2] E. 2. *I.*

various covenants, and the lessee is bound to perform the covenants in the indenture, and afterwards the rent is in arrear: he has now forfeited his bond, for this is an agreement between them upon the lease that he shall pay so much rent, and he took the land with this reservation, and so it is his agreement, and every agreement is a covenant, for *convenire* is nothing else but *condiscendere* (or agree), which words are just as good words of covenant as 'covenant and grant'. And they said that this was argued and agreed in the time of Brudenell.[1]

64. SIR NICHOLAS CAREW'S CASE

Common Pleas, 1536/37.

An abbot in ancient times granted to the ancestors of Sir Nicholas Carew, knight,[2] to find two chaplains singing in such and such a chapel every day, and granted that whenever they should fail in singing he and his successors would pay £10 to the said ancestor and his heirs. And it was shown to the court that they have failed in finding the chaplain, and the question now was what action the heir should have. Should it be a writ of annuity or a writ of debt, inasmuch as this is something which has continuance?

It was said that the heir should have a writ of debt, and it was likened to the case of an annuity granted with a penalty for default of payment, for it is something casual and not annual, in which case notwithstanding the continuance he shall have a writ of debt—as for relief.

FITZHERBERT doubted the case of relief.

SHELLEY held it clear, and said that there was a book so adjudged. And note that he said that the heir shall have the penalty and not his executors, because it goes with the inheritance, as in the writ of covenant in 42 Edw. III.[3]

65. HYNDE v. WHELER

Common Pleas, 1536/37. Also reported in Dyer, ff. 6a–7a (Pas. 1536); Dyer, ff. 13b–14a (Trin. 1536). Cf. below, p. 413, no. 110, which seems to be the same case. Record: CP 40/1089, m. 457 (demurrer, Pas. 1536; c.a.v. to Pas. 1537).

Someone made a lease for years by indenture, rendering rent, and there were covenants in the deed, and at the end the lessee covenanted and granted that if he granted over his estate in part or in whole it would be fully permissible for

---

[1] YB Pas. 14 Hen. VIII, fo. 25, pl. 4; 119 Selden Soc. 175.
[2] Of Beddington, Surrey, esquire of the household, knighted by 1520, J.P., M.P., died 1539: *HPHC 1509–58*, i. 575.   [3] *Pakenham's Case* (1368) YB Hil. 42 Edw. III, fo. 3, pl. 14.

dentrer. Le questyon fuit, si ceo serra un condition ou un covenante, pur ceo que le lesse nest sur condition einz absolute et cest un covenante per le lesse soullment.

Et les justyces, toutz save *Shelley*, semble que le lesse fuit condytyonell et que cest un condition, quar chescun clause en lendenture est le covenante, clause et parollx dambideux partyes, scilicet cybyen del lessor come del lesse, et toutz les parollx en lendenture sont come ilz fueront parles sur le lease per le lessor et annexe a lestate.

Et *Shelley* tyent fortemente que est un covenante et soullmente les parollx le lesse et son covenant de son parte. Mes il dit que per cest covenante le lessor poit entrer, quar cest lybertye il mesme ad don al lessor per son covenante. Uncore en pleder il covyent estre plede come un covenante le lesse, et non obstante que chescun endenture est le fait dambideux uncore les covenantz dun parte sont les covenantz de cestui soulmente. Et ceo prove le pleder: sur ascun covenante enfreynt il dyrra que il ad performe toutz les covenantz de son parte sauns medler ove les auters covenantz. [*fo. 107v*]

[66]

28 H. 8.

Nota que fuit tenus per toutz les justyces que si jeo vende a un home xx quarters de corne destre delyveres al bargane ou ses executors a tyell liew et tyell jour, et jeo amesne le corne a mesme le jour et a mesme le liew et le vende ne vyent de ceo rescever: en dett pur ceo jeo pledra cest matter sauns dyer uncore prist, pur ceo que corne est choce coruptyble et wastable et est charge en le custodye de ceo. Mes ove money auterment est. Et nota que en cest case le plaintife en dett avoit count que le delyverey serroit quaunt il ceo require, et pur ceo que cest auter contracte fuit adjuge que il poit dyre Ryen luy doit modo et forma, prist per sa ley. Et auxi fuit tenus en mesme le case que si un vende a moy xx. quarters de corne sauns parler quaunt ilz serront delyvers, jeo purra demander eux quaunt moy pleast, est cest le folly de parte mesme que il fait tyell bargayne. Et en mesme le case si jeo veigne a luy devaunt le delyvere et dye que jeo ne voille aver ascun corne, et que jeo luy discharge de mon bargeyne, et il est content per parollx, que la sil port action pur le corne apres il semble az justyces que il poit safement gager sa ley.

the lessor to enter. The question was, whether this shall be deemed a condition or a covenant, inasmuch as the lease is not upon condition but is absolute and this is a covenant by the lessee only.

All the justices except SHELLEY thought that the lease was conditional, and that this is a condition, for every clause in the indenture is the covenant, clause and words of both parties, namely both the lessor and the lessee, and all the words in the indenture are as if they were spoken upon the lease by the lessor and annexed to the estate.

SHELLEY held strongly that it is a covenant and only the words of the lessee, and his covenant on his side. But he said that by this covenant the lessor may enter, for he himself gives this liberty to the lessor by his covenant. Nevertheless in pleading it must be pleaded as the lessee's covenant, and even though every indenture is the deed of both nevertheless the covenants by one party are his covenants alone. That is proved by the pleading: for upon any covenant broken he shall say that he has performed all the covenants on his side, without meddling with the other covenants.

66. ANON.

Common Pleas, 1536/37. Cf. Dyer, fo. 24, pl. 154, where under Mich. 28 Hen. VIII Dyer cites a case of 1520 to the contrary, without reporting the principal case.[1]

Note that it was held by all the justices that if I sell someone twenty quarters of corn to be delivered to the bargainee or his executors at such and such a place and such and such a day, and I bring the corn at the same day and the vendee does not come to receive it, in debt for this corn I may plead these facts without saying I am still ready to deliver (uncore prist), because corn is a corruptible and wastable thing and there is a charge in keeping it. But it is otherwise with money. Note that in this case the plaintiff in debt had counted that the delivery should be when he requested it, and because that is another contract it was adjudged that he could say 'He owes him nothing in the manner and form as he has counted' (Rien luy doit modo et forma), and wage his law. It was also held in the same case that if someone sells me twenty quarters of corn without saying when they should be delivered, I may demand them when I please, and it is the foolishness of the party himself to make such a bargain. In the same case if I come to him before the delivery and say that I do not want any corn, and that I discharge him of my bargain, and he is content at these words, if he afterwards brings an action for the corn it seemed to the justices that he may safely wage his law.

[1] Cf. also Lewys v. Fanne (1529) CP 40/1061, m. 608; Spelman, p. 88 (decided the other way).

[67]

28 H. 8.

Nota que cest questyon fuit demande de les justyces sur le novell estatute quell don les primers fruytes al roy de toutz benefyces, que lou devaunt cest temps lordynare avera les primer fruytes dun prebende toutz ditz quaunt devyent voyde, et sur ceo devaunt cest estatute la fuit un composycion ewe parenter le prebendare et lordynare que le prebendare et ses successors payeront anuellmente al ordynare et ses successors xx. s. pur les primer fruytz, et ore per le novell estatute le roy ad lez prymer fruytz de toutz benefyces, et ore le questyon fuit si le prebendare serra discharge vers lordynare entant que est charge a chescun avoydance pur les primer fruytz vers le roy?

Fytzherbert semble que ne serra dyscharge, et resembla ceo al case que lou deux homes exchaunge terres et puis le parte dun est don a un home per parlyamente, il ne unques entra en les auters terres don per luy en exchaunge. Jeo dye que non. Et si home ad castle garde de son tenaunt et pur le castell garde il est agree per fait enter le seignior et tenaunt que le tenaunt payera xii. d. al seignior pur ceo, et puis le castell eschewast, serra le tenaunt ore dyscharge de cest xii. d.? Nemi, pur ceo que cest un rent ore et le nature de castell garde est ale.

Shelley et *Bawldwyn*[1] semble le contrarie, mes ne fyeront ascun reson. [*fo. 108*]

[68]

Nota per *Pakynton*[2] que cest bon polyce si un soit en doubt que son heir voille vender son terre pur graunter rent charge a un auter hors de celle terre al value del terre per an, le rent a commencer a celle temps que son heir vendra la terre ou ascun parcell: et cest bon graunt.

[69]

Nota que si un prist mon chyvall et le chyvall luy jetta et ove les pees luy occydyst, ceo serra un deodand et jeo nay remedie.

---

[1] Baldwin *I.*   [2] Pakingeton *I.*

67. ANON.

Common Pleas, 1536/37.

Note that the justices were asked this question upon the new statute which gives the first fruits of all benefices to the king:[1] whereas before this time the ordinary should always have the first fruits of a prebend when it became vacant, and thereupon (before this statute) there was a composition between the prebendary and the ordinary that the prebendary and his successors should pay annually to the ordinary and his successors 20s. for the first fruits, and now by the new statute the king has the first fruits of all benefices, the question now is whether the prebendary shall be discharged against the ordinary, inasmuch as he is charged on every vacancy with the first fruits against the king?

FITZHERBERT thought he should not be discharged, and likened this to the case where two men exchange lands and afterwards the share of one of them is given to someone by parliament: he shall never enter in the other lands given by him in exchange. I say not.[2] If someone has castle-guard from his tenant, and in return for the castle-guard it is agreed by deed between the lord and tenant that the tenant should pay 12d. to the lord for it, and then the castle falls down, shall the tenant now be discharged of this 12d.? No, because it is now a rent and the nature of castle-guard is gone.

SHELLEY and BALDWIN thought the contrary, but did not give any reason.

68. NOTE

Probably in the Inner Temple.

Note, by *Pakington*, that if someone is afraid that his heir will sell his land, it is a good policy to grant a rent-charge to someone else out of this land to the annual value of the land, the rent to commence at such time as his heir should sell the land or any part thereof: and that is a good grant.

69. NOTE

Note that if someone takes my horse, and the horse throws him and kicks him to death, it shall be deodand and I have no remedy.

---

[1] 26 Hen. VIII, c. 3 (*SR* iii. 493).
[2] Meaning uncertain.

[70]

20 H. 8. fuit adjuge que un precipe dun tenemente nest bon, mes coviente porter son precipe dun mesuage.

[71]

Nota per *Bromley* que chescun choce quell est fait per un enfant per matter en fait il covient estre execute mayntenant per son done accordant al done ou autermente est voyde et nemi voydable, nyent obstante que soit fait per lyverey: come si lenfant fait feffmente et lettre dattorney de faire lyverey, et ceo est fait, il avera assise. Mesme la ley ou il graunt seigniorie, quar le graunt nest execute mayntenaunt mes executory per attornemente.

[72]

Nota per *Bromley* que si un soit ideott et le roy ad seise ses terres, le roy ad fraunketenemente en la terre determynable sur le vye le ideott ou son ideoce: come si home seisi de terre en droit sa feme est attaynt, le roy ad un fraunketenemente determynable per les espousellx.

[73]

Nota per *Bromley* que si deux coparceners fount partytion et parte de purparte lun est destroy per entre, tout le partytion serra anyent. Mes si soit per action, autermeut est, quar la el priera en ayde de lauter parcener et recovera pro rata.

70. ANON.

1528/29.

In 20 Hen. VIII it was adjudged that a *praecipe* for a 'tenement' is not good, but he must bring his *praecipe* for a messuage.[1]

71. NOTE

Probably in the Inner Temple.

Note, by *Bromley*, that everything which is done by an infant by matter in fact must be executed immediately by his gift according to the gift or else it is void and not voidable, even though it is done by livery: as where the infant makes a feoffment and a letter of attorney to make livery, and this is done, he shall have an assize. The law is the same where he grants a lordship, for the grant is not executed at once but is executory until attornment.

72. NOTE

Probably in the Inner Temple.

Note, by *Bromley*, that if someone is an idiot and the king has seized his lands, the king has a freehold in the land determinable upon the life of the idiot or the end of his idiocy. Likewise if a man seised of land in right of his wife is attainted, the king has a freehold determinable by the espousals.

73. NOTE

Probably in the Inner Temple.

Note, by *Bromley*, that if two coparceners make partition, and part of one share is destroyed by entry, the whole partition shall be annulled. But if it is destroyed by action it is otherwise, for then she shall pray in aid of the other parcener and recover *pro rata*.

---

[1] Cf. *Anon.* (1545) in Yelverton, above, p. 336, no. 49.

[74]

[Nota bene.[1]] Nota, si jeo covenante ove un auter per endenture que sil maryast ma fyle que adonques jeo donera a luy le maner de Dale en taylle ou en fee, sil marye ma fyle jeo sue seisi mayntenaunt a son use: issint le performance del suffycient consyderation, coment que le covenante ne fuit forsque dexecuter estate, change le use. Mes auterment est de un nude covenante, quar la le parte est myse a son action de covenante.

[75]

Nota, si terre en taylle soyt myse en execution sur un voucher, ceo nest discontinuans. Mesme la ley de terre la feme. Et le terre de tenaunt pur vye serra myse en execution pur terres en fee et nest forfeyture.

[76]

Nota que en action de dett sur oblygation le defendant en les premysses de brefe serra nosme per son verey nosme, mester et degree quell il est en fait al temps del action comence, et de le ville quell il est, et donques il avera alias dictus pur faire lobligation et le brefe accordant. [*fo. 108v*]

[77]

Nota, si tenaunt en taylle fait feffmente en fee sauns consyderatyon, les feffees serront seisyes al use de feffor et ses heirs et nemi al primer use.

Et *Mounteford* dit que ceo fuit loppinion des justyces pur ceo que cest feffmente disprove lestate taylle et est repugnante in reson que cestui que disprove et est einz en disprovant lestate taylle serroit seisi a mesme le use. Mesme la ley de recovere ewe vers tenaunt en taylle. Et issint est quaunt home seisi de terre en droit sa feme fait feffmente, cest al use le feffor.

---

[1] *I only.*

74. NOTE

Note that if I covenant with another by indenture that if he will marry my daughter I will give him the manor of Dale in tail, or in fee, and he marries my daughter, I am forthwith seised to his use. Thus the performance of the sufficient consideration changes the use, even though the covenant was only to execute an estate. But it is otherwise of a naked covenant, for there the party is driven to his action of covenant.

75. NOTE

Note that if land in tail is put in execution upon a voucher, this is not a discontinuance. The law is the same of a wife's land. And the land of a tenant for life may be put in execution for lands in fee, and it is not a forfeiture.

76. NOTE

Cf. *Bradmore's Case* (1525/26) in Yorke, above. p. 196, no. 279.

Note that in an action of debt upon a bond the defendant shall be named in the premisses of the writ by his true name, mystery and degree, as it is in fact at the time when the action is commenced, and by the vill of which he is, and then there shall be an *alias dictus* to make the bond and the writ agree.[1]

77. NOTE

Probably in the Inner Temple.

Note that if a tenant in tail makes a feoffment in fee without consideration, the feoffees shall be seised to the use of the feoffor and his heirs and not to the first use.

Mountford said that this was the opinion of the justices,[2] because this feoffment disproves the estate tail and it is repugnant in reason that someone who disproves and is in by disproving the estate tail should be seised to the same use. The law is the same of a recovery had against tenant in tail. And so it is when someone seised of land in right of his wife makes a feoffment, this is to the use of the feoffor.

[1] I.e. by giving the name in the *alias* exactly as it is in the bond.   [2] Cf. below, p. 448, no. 26.

[78]

Casus bonus.

Pollstede[1] myst le case al boordes ende. Seignior et tenaunt sont per servyce de chivaler et rent de x. s., le tenaunt devie, son heire deinz age, le seignior seise le garde de corps et entre en la terre et graunt ceo a un estraunger, que tender marryage al enfant, et il luy marye deinz age, le graunte al pleyne age lheir tyent la terre tanque il ad levye le duble value, le grauntor de que la terre est tenus distrene pur le rent: sil ceo ferra?

Et fuit dit per ascuns que non, entant que le graunte ad ceo en ses maynes per le grauntor et serra issint come sil avoit contynue son possession. Mes fuit dit que le seigniorie est revyve quaunt lheir vyent a pleyn age. Et le cause de forfeyture est per lacte lenfaunt puis le graunt fait per le seignior, et auxi les servyces le seignior serra recoupes en mayne le graunte. Et issint serra si le seignior ust ceo graunt, il averoit le duble value ouster les servyces et rent, quar ceo serra recoupe. Et ceo prove byen que le seigniorie est revyve, quar autermente le seignior mesme ne serroit alow pur ceo si ust este en ses mainz. Et si seignior et tenaunt soit, le seignior ad le garde, et devie, ses executors averont le garde et lheire le seigniorie, uncore semble que nest revyve mes que serra suspende durant le temps etc.

[79]

Home ne serra disable per villinage en action quell il port pur ceo dysprover: come en attaynt ou error sur jugemente ou il fuit trove villen. Mesme la ley si home port brefe derror pur defaire ut utlagarye.

[80]

Home ad issue deux fitz dun nosme, John, et devyse terre a John son fitz, ceo serra entende al puisne fitz pur ceo que sil avoit entende que leigne ceo avera ne besoigne de faire ascun devyse pur ceo que il duissoit ceo aver per cours de ley. [*fo. 109*]

---

[1] Polsted *I.*

78. NOTE

Inner Temple.

A good case

Polsted[1] put this case at the board's end.[2] There are a lord and a tenant by knight-service and a rent of 10s.; the tenant dies, his heir being under age; the lord seizes the wardship of the body and enters in the land, and grants it to a stranger, who tenders a marriage to the infant, and he marries her while under age; when the heir is of full age the grantee holds the land until he has raised the double value; and the grantor of whom the land is held distrains for the rent. May he do that?

It was said by some that he could not, inasmuch as the grantee has it in his hands through the grantor and it shall be as if he had continued his possession. But it was said that the lordship is revived when the heir comes to full age. And the cause of forfeiture is by the act of the infant after the grant made by the lord, and also the lord's services shall be recouped in the grantee's hands. So it would be if the lord had granted it: he would have had the double value beyond the services and rent, for that would be recouped. This well proves that the lordship is revived, for otherwise the lord himself would not be allowed this if it had been in his hands. If there are a lord and a tenant, and the lord has the wardship, and dies, his executors shall have the wardship and the heir shall have the lordship, and yet it seems that it is not revived but that it shall be suspended during the time etc.

79. NOTE

One shall not be disabled by villeinage in an action which he brings to disprove it: as in an attaint or error upon a judgment where he was found a villein. The law is the same if someone brings a writ of error to undo an outlawry.

80. NOTE

A man has issue two sons of the same name, John, and devises land 'to John, [my] son': this shall be understood as the younger son, because if he had intended the elder to have it there would have been no need to make any devise, inasmuch as he would have had it by course of law.

---

[1] Thomas Polsted, reader-elect of the Inner Temple in 1537. [2] For this expression see also below, p. 409, no. 101. Cf. 'at the end of the table' below, p. 403, no. 81.

[81]

Casus myse per *Bromley* al fyne del table. Le baron et feme purchace terres joyntmente et levyont un fyne, le feme esteant deinz age: quere si la feme avera brefe derror?

Ascuns dyont que cy, pur reverser pur tout, pur ceo que la feme ad droit daver error et el ne poit ceo aver sauns son baron, et si el taryera tanque apres le mort son baron per case el serra de pleyn age per ceo temps et donques el navera son brefe derror. Et pur lentyerte covient pur ceo que null moytes sont enter eux, et son droit curge per tout. Et le baron, pur ceo que il clayme en auter droyt, poit joyner contrarie a son fyne. Come si home disseise un abbe et fait feffmente ouster, et puis est fait abbe de mesme le liew, il entra encontre son feffmente demesne.

Et ascuns dyont que la feme serra sauns remedie durant le coverture per cause que le baron contrarie a son fyne ne poit aver brefe derror pur ceo que quaunt a luy le fyne est bon et sauns luy le feme ne poit ryens faire.

Et ascuns dyont que ilz averont brefe derror et le fyne serra reverse quaunt al feme et ses heirs et estoiera pur le baron.

[82]

Vide que *Chydley* reherce que les justyces de Banke le Roy en appell port per le feme dun Vahan, alderman de Brystowe, de son mort, el fuit admytt de faire attorney.

[83]

Si jeo soy disseise et le disseisor graunt a moy un rent hors del terre quell il ad per disseisin et hors dauter terre, et puis jeo entre en la terre dount il moy disseisist, mon rent est tout extinct. Uncore jeo entra per la ley, mes cest mon acte demesne que jeo veigne al parcell del terre charge, et la ley ne jette le terre sur moy puis le graunt le rent mes jeo avoy tytle dentre devaunt le graunt. Mesme la ley semble ou mon feffe sur condition graunt a moy un rent hors de cest terre et auter, et jeo entre pur le condition enfreynt etc.

81. NOTE

Inner Temple.

A case put by *Bromley* at the end of the table.[1] A husband and wife purchase lands jointly and levy a fine, the wife being under age: shall the wife have a writ of error?

Some say yes, to reverse everything, because the wife has right to have error and she cannot have it without her husband, and if she delays until after her husband's death perhaps she will be of full age by that time and then she shall not have her writ of error. And it must be for the whole, because there are no moieties between them, and her right runs throughout. And the husband, because he claims in another right, may join [issue] contrary to his fine. Likewise if someone disseises an abbot and makes a feoffment over, and he is afterwards made abbot of the same place, he may enter contrary to his own feoffment.

Some say that the wife shall be without remedy during the coverture because the husband cannot have a writ of error contrary to his fine, since the fine is good with respect to him and without him the wife cannot do anything.

And some say that they shall have a writ of error and the fine shall be reversed as to the wife and her heirs but shall stand in force for the husband.

82. VAUGHAN'S CASE

King's Bench; related in the Inner Temple.

Observe that *Chidley* told us that the justices of the King's Bench, in an appeal brought by the wife of one Vaughan, alderman of Bristol, for his death, admitted her to make attorney.

83. NOTE

If I am disseised and the disseisor grants me a rent out of the land which he has by disseisin and also out of other land, and afterwards I enter in the land whereof he disseised me, my rent is completely extinguished. Yet I entered by the law; but it was my own act that I came to that part of the land charged, and the law does not cast the land upon me after the grant of the rent, but I had a title of entry before the grant. The law seems to be the same where my feoffee upon condition grants me a rent out of this land and other land, and I enter for breach of condition etc.

---

[1] Cf. 'at the board's end' in no. 78.

[84]

Nota per *Hare* que en toutz cases lou home voille pleder un recorde, et son ple nest que dylatorye ou en abatemente de brefe, la covyent de monstre le record, quar ne serra reson de prendre yssue sur cest recorde et quaunt trove est pur le demandant le tenaunt nest ascun perde, quar de ceo ensuera que chescun serra delaye sauns cause. Et pur ceo en trespas home ne pledra utlagarye sauns monstrans le record, pur ceo que nest que dylatorye entant que il ne poit forfeyter cest actyon. Mes en dett sur oblygation il avera le ple sauns monstrance del record, quar la il va en barre entant que le roy ceo duyst aver. Et si le recorde soyt en court pluys bas, les justyces escryeront pur ceo. Si soyt en court pluys haut, a son perell il avera jour de ceo amener.

[85]

En toutz cases lou le defendant plede matter quell lye le plaintife, soyt medyate ou imedyate, et convey luy interest en le choce, la le plaintife covyent responder al especiall matter et ne dyrra De son tort: come ou il plede en trespas le lesse le plaintife a luy mesme ou a un auter que graunta a luy. [*fo. 109v*]

[86]

21 H. 8.

Nota que en Comen Banke un arbytremente fuit plede en barre, quell fuit que le defendant payera al plaintife x. s., et plede le payment de ceo, le plaintife dyt que le ilz agarderont ceo et auxi que il viendra en leglise parochyell lou le plaintife dymurt et la luy cryera mercye, quell il nad fait. Ore le questyon est, si ceo soyt bon sauns travers, scilicet sauns ceo que ilz agarderont come le defendant ad allege ou nemi?

Inglefylde semble le ple bon, pur ceo que il ad luy confesse et avoyde, ergo ne besoigne luy traverser.

Shelley. Il covyent traverser, quar auterment il ne responde son ple, quar cest arbytremente de quell le plaintife ad parle nest larbytremente de quell le defendant plede einz sont dyvers arbytrementz.

Spyllman. Chescun arbytremente est un jugemente et choce entyer et ne poit estre plede per parcells, pur ceo que est cy entyer come un recorde. Donques

84. NOTE

Probably in the Inner Temple.

Note, by *Hare*, that in all cases where someone wishes to plead a record, and his plea is only dilatory or in abatement of the writ, the record must be shown, for it would not be right to take issue on this record and when it is found for the demandant the tenant has no loss, for it would follow from thence that everyone could be delayed without cause. Therefore in trespass one may not plead outlawry without showing the record, because it is only dilatory inasmuch as he may not forfeit this action. But in debt on a bond he shall have the plea [of outlawry] without showing the record, for there it goes in bar inasmuch as the king ought to have it. And if the record is in a lower court, the justices shall write for it. If it is in a higher court, he shall have a day to bring it in at his peril.

85. NOTE

In all cases where the defendant pleads a matter which binds the plaintiff, be it mediate or immediate, and traces to him an interest in the thing, the plaintiff must answer the special matter and shall not say 'Of his own wrong' (*De son tort*): as where in trespass he pleads a lease from the plaintiff himself to him or to someone who granted to him.

86. ANON.

Common Pleas, 1529/30.

Note that in the Common Bench an arbitration was pleaded in bar, which was that the defendant should pay the plaintiff 10s., and he pleaded the payment thereof; the plaintiff said that they had awarded that and also that he should come into the parochial church where the plaintiff lived and there cry mercy, which he had not done. Now the question is: is this good without a traverse, namely 'without this, that they awarded as the defendant has alleged', or not?

ENGLEFIELD thought the plea good, because he has confessed and avoided, and so there is no need to traverse him.

SHELLEY. He must traverse, for otherwise he does not answer his plea, inasmuch as this arbitration whereof the plaintiff has spoken is not the arbitration whereof he pleads, but they are different arbitrations.

Spelman. Every arbitration is a judgment, and an entire thing, and cannot be pleaded in bits, because it is as entire as a record. Therefore when he pleads an

quaunt il plede un arbytremente de payer x. s., ore cest entende tout cell arbytremente. Donques le plaintife plede que fuit un arbytremente fait que il payera x. s. et un choce ouster, quell nest performe, ore cest entende auter arbitremente. Donques si ceux deux plees sont de dyvers arbytrementz, ergo il nad my confesse et avoyde, quar il ne medle ove son ple, ergo coviente luy traverser. Et est semble si home voille pleder un simple contract, ceo covyent estre plede entyer, pur ceo que chescun contract est tout entyer et ne poit estre plede per parcells.

Row. Il y ad un lyver come Spyllman dit.

Shelley. Oyell certes, et ceo semble ley. Est semble al case de contracte.

[87]

Nota que ascuns dyont que en toutz actyons foundus sur recorde, si per mon actyon jeo sue a executer le recorde la coviente a moy en mon declaration de monstre tout le substance del recorde alarge, mes nemi le proces. Come en scire facias dexecuter un fyne, covyent a moy de monstre le fyne et coment il per le fyne conust tout son droit que il avoit en la terre estre le droit un tyell, et pur cell conusance etc. Issint est en error ou attaynt, queux sont adefeter le recorde. Mes en mayntenaunce ou tiell semblable auterment est.

[88]

Nota per *Hare*: si un home plede un recovere vers estraunger per defaut ou reddycion lestate le plaintife mesne parenter le tytle del actyon et le recovere, il coviente ouster aver le tytle de son brefe, quar ceo est le choce quell fait son barr bon, quar si soyt feynt ou faux lauter nest lye.

[89]

Nota, si home en pleder voille dyre que un tyell fuit seisi et fyst un lesse pur vye, anz, ou don en taylle, le ple nest bon sauns monstre de quell estate il fuit seisi. [*fo. 110*]

arbitration to pay 10s., that is now understood to be the whole of this arbitration. Now, the plaintiff pleads that there was an arbitration made that he should pay 10s. and do something further, which has not been performed, and this shall be understood to be another arbitration. If, then, these two pleas refer to different arbitrations, he has not confessed and avoided, for he does not meddle with his plea, ergo he must traverse. It is like where someone wants to plead a simple contract, it must be pleaded in its entirety, because every contract is wholly entire and cannot be pleaded in bits.

Roo. There is a book as Spelman says.

SHELLEY. Yes, certainly, and it seems to be law. It is like the case of a contract.

87. NOTE

Note that some say that in all actions founded upon a record, if by my action I am to execute the record, I must in my declaration show the whole substance of the record at large, but not the process. For instance, in *scire facias* to execute a fine, I must show the fine and how by the fine he acknowledged all his right that he had in the land to be the right of such and such, and for this acknowledgment etc. So it is in error or attaint, which are to defeat the record. But in maintenance or such like it is otherwise.

88.

Probably in the Inner Temple.

Note, by *Hare*: if someone pleads a recovery against a stranger by default or surrender, the plaintiff's estate being between the title of the action and the recovery, he must further aver the title of his writ, for that is the thing which makes his bar good; for if it is feigned or false the other is not bound.

89. NOTE

Note that if someone wishes to say in pleading that such and such was seised and made a lease for life, or years, or a gift in tail, the plea is not good without showing of what estate he was seised.

[90]

Si un home plede matter de recorde devaunt temps de memorye, come un fyne, recovere, etc., cest matter de recorde est answerable non obstante que soyt devaunt temps de memorye. Mes un matter en fait, come un graunt de rent charge, comen, etc., per fait devaunt temps de memorye, nest a purpose ne serra respondu. Et le reson est pur ceo que tiellx choces queux serront trye per pays covent estre pledes puis temps de memorye, et puis temps de lymytatyon, quar home ne poit tryer choce de que null poit aver memorye. Mes matter de recorde serra trye per recorde, quell poit estre assetz trye non obstante que fuit devaunt memorye, pur ceo que appyert per le recorde: per *Horwood*, et *Hare* concessit. Et pur ceo fuit dit per eux que si jeo plede un graunt de roy per lettres patentes devaunt temps de memorye, et prescribe que jeo et toutz mes auncestors etc. avomus use de temps dount etc. cest lyberte accordant as lettres patentes, est duble, quar les lettres patentes est un tytle et respoignable et le prescription auter tytle. Mes graunt per estraunger comen person devaunt temps de memorye de comen ou rent a mon auncestor, et prescription puis, nest duble pur ceo que le graunt nest respoignable, quar nest que conveyance al prescription. Mes les lettres patentes sont matters de recorde et tryable per le recorde. Et pur ceo *Hare* dit la il coviente prescriber soullmente et doner les lettres patentes en evydence.

[91]

Nota per *Shelley*: si J. S., evesque de Wynch., ou J. S., parson de Dale, soyent vouches, le counterple serra duble, scilicet a son possession et de ses auncestors et a son possession et le possession de ses predecessors, par cause que il ad deux capacytes et ne appyert per cause de quell il est vouche.

[92]

Si le baron, tenaunt en taylle, et sa feme que nest tenaunt soyent impledez en brefe dentre en le post, et ilz voucheront a garrante un estraunge, que entre et parde, et execution est ewe accordant, le baron tenaunt en taylle morust, et son

90. NOTE

If someone pleads a matter of record before time of memory, such as a fine, recovery, and so forth, this matter of record is answerable even though it is before time of memory. But a matter in fact, such as a grant of rent-charge, common, and so forth, by deed made before time of memory, is immaterial and shall not be answered. The reason is because such things as are to be tried by the country must be pleaded since time immemorial, and since the time of limitation, for one cannot try something of which no one can have any memory. But a matter of record shall be tried by record, which may be tried well enough even if it was before memory, because it appears by the record: by *Whorwood*,[1] and *Hare* agreed. Therefore it was said by them that if I plead a grant from the king by letters patent before time of memory, and prescribe that I and all my ancestors etc. have from time immemorial used this liberty in accordance with the letters patent, this is double, for the letters patent are one title and answerable and the prescription is another. But a grant of common or rent to my ancestor by a common person before time of memory, and prescription after, is not double, because the grant is not answerable and it is only introductory to the prescription, whereas letters patent are matters of record and triable by the record. Therefore *Hare* said there that he must prescribe only and give the letters patent in evidence.

91. ANON.

Probably in the Common Pleas.

Note, by SHELLEY: if 'John Style, bishop of Winchester', or 'John Style, parson of Dale', are vouched [in that manner], the counterplea shall be double, namely as to his possession and that of his ancestors and also as to his possession and that of his predecessors, because he has two capacities and it does not appear by reason which of them he is vouched.

92. ANON.

Probably in the Common Pleas.

If a husband, tenant in tail, and his wife who is not tenant, are impleaded in a writ of entry in the *post*, and they vouch to warrant a stranger, who enters in the warranty and loses, and execution is had accordingly, the husband tenant

---

[1] William Whorwood, solicitor-general 1536–40. Since he was a bencher of the Middle Temple, this cannot have been an exchange in the Inner Temple.

yssue port formedon: cest recovere ovesque recompence nest barre, quar le reson quell done que ceo serra barr al yssue est per cause de son recompence quell per intendmente discendra al yssue. Donques quaunt ilz deux voucheront icy il est entende per cause de garrante fait al feme devaunt le coverture ou as auncestors la feme et pur ceo le recompence per entendmente est a eux durant le coverture, et apres a les heirs la feme, et donques faut recompence al yssue, et pur ceo null barr. Et ceo fuit loppinion de *Shelley*, Justice.

[93]

Nota que fuit tenus per *Barons*, lectorem, que si le tenaunt le roy alyen sauns lycence et devie, son heir deinz age, et trove est per offyce que il devie seisie, le feffe ne poit traverser loffyce tanque il ad pardon del alienatyon. [*fo. 110v*]

[94]

Nota per *Shelley*, Justice, et agree per toutz, que en chescun case lou le roy ad tytle a ascun terre et si ceo tytle ust este en comen persone il puissoit entrer, le roy sur cest tytle trove per offyce seisera sauns scire facias sue vers le partye que ad possession. Mes si comen persone ayant mesme le tytle ne poit entre mes serra myse a son actyon, la apres offyce trove covyent al roy de suer scire facias. Come si le tenaunt de roy fait wast ou cesse, ou auncestor le roy tenaunt en taylle fait discontynuance, quar la comen persone serroit myse a son actyon. Auterment est si tytle de mortmayne est trove pur le roy, la il ne serra chace de suer scire facias, et sic in case soen.[1]

[95]

Vide que lheir ne serra sue pur dett sur un oblygation si les executors ount assetz. Mes si le dett fuit per matter de recorde, come per jugemente en personell action, estatute merchant, ou reconusance, la auterment est, pur ceo que les terres fueront lyes mayntenaunt. Mes nest issint per lobligation.

---

[1] *Last word unclear.*

in tail dies, and his issue brings formedon: this recovery with recompense is no bar, for the reason which provides that it should bar the issue is because of his recompense, which by presumption will descend to the issue. Therefore when the two of them vouch here it is presumed to be because of a warranty made to the woman before the coverture or to the woman's ancestors, and therefore the recompense by presumption is to them during the coverture, and afterwards to the woman's heirs, and therefore there lacks recompense to the issue, and therefore it is no bar. This was the opinion of SHELLEY, Justice.

93. NOTE FROM A READING

Inner Temple, August 1527.

Note that it was held by *Barons*, reader,[1] that if the king's tenant aliens without licence and dies, his heir being under age, and it is found by office that he died seised, the feoffee may not traverse the office until he has a pardon for the alienation.

94. ANON.

Probably in the Common Pleas.

Note, by SHELLEY, Justice, and agreed by all, that in every case where the king has title to some land, and if this title had been in a common person he could have entered, and this title is found by office, the king may seize without a *scire facias* sued against the party who has possession. But if a common person, having the same title, could not enter but would be driven to his action, there after the office is found the king must sue a *scire facias*. This is so if the king's tenant commits waste or ceases to perform services, or the king's ancestor as tenant in tail makes discontinuance, for there a common person would be driven to his action. It is otherwise if a title of mortmain is found for the king, he shall not there be driven to sue a *scire facias*.

95. NOTE

Observe that the heir shall not be sued for debt upon a bond if the executors have assets. But if the debt was by matter of record, as by a judgment in a personal action, statute merchant, or recognizance, it would be otherwise, because the lands were bound forthwith. But it is not so by a bond.

---

[1] Peter Barons: *Readers and Readings*, p. 78.

[96]

Nota, si home recover dett deinz un fraunchyce, si le defendant ryen ad deinz le fraunchyce pur faire execution est bon pollyce de porter brefe derror et remover le recorde et quaunt le jugemente est afferme donques il poit aver execution ou il voet. Semble que est assetz bon remedie de porter brefe de dett en le Comen Banke.

[97]

Nota que le tenaunt apres conusance demande en un precipe poit toller le court del jurisdiction a son plesure, come per forreyn voucher, et il poit eslyer en banke de voucher luy un auter ou de pleder en barr et le ple ne serra unques remaunde.

[98]

Nota si deux soyent enfeffes et lyverey fait a un, cestui devie, et vers lauter un estraunger port precipe, et il disclayme, ceo vestera en lheir lauter. Quere si cest disclaymer ferra un morant seisi pur toller un entre?

[99]

Un graunt a moy proximam advocationem cum ecclesia de Dale, que ad illius spectat donationem, vacare contigerit: semble tyell graunt ne vault, quar jeo graunt a luy proximam advocationem sauns dyer a quell esglise. Mes si ust este proximam advocationem de ecclesia de S. cum ecclesia de B. vacare contigerit, cest bon: mes si lesglise de S. devyent voyde, leglise de B. esteant pleyn, il ne presentera. [*fo. 111*]

96. NOTE

Note that if someone recovers a debt within a franchise, and the defendant has nothing within the franchise to make execution, it is a good policy to bring a writ of error and remove the record, and when the judgment is affirmed he may have execution where he wishes. It seems that it is a perfectly good remedy to bring a writ of debt in the Common Bench.

97. NOTE

Note that after cognizance is demanded in a *praecipe* the tenant may deprive the court of jurisdiction at his pleasure, as by foreign voucher, and he may choose in banc to vouch [himself or] someone else or plead in bar and the plea shall never be sent back.

98. NOTE

Note that if two are enfeoffed and livery is made to one, who dies, and against the other a stranger brings a *praecipe*, and he disclaims, this shall vest in the other's heir. Shall this disclaimer work a dying seised for the purpose of tolling an entry?

99. NOTE

Someone grants to me 'the next advowson[1] when the church of Dale, which belongs to his gift, should chance to become vacant' (*proximam advocationem cum ecclesia de Dale, quae ad illius spectat donationem, vacare contigerit*): it seems that such a grant is invalid, for [he has granted to me] *proximam advocationem* without saying to which church. However, if it had been 'the next advowson of the church of Sale when the church of B. should chance to become vacant' (*proximam advocationem de ecclesia de S. cum ecclesia de B. vacare contigerit*), that would be good, though if the church of Sale became vacant while the church of B. was filled he should not present.

[1] For this phrase cf. Yelverton, above, p. 325, no. 26; and p. 340, no. 58.

[100]

Si home soyt oblige a moy et mon servant rehercant coment il est servant a
moy, et coment il per mon comaundment et come servant a moy et a mon use
ad receu de lobligor le somme contenus en lobligation, et acquite luy per le dit
acquitance en son propre nosme, ceo est voyde: come fuit adjuge en dett port
per Thomas Caryll, merchaunt, vers un Wylliam Coldwell.

[101]

Hare myst cell case al boordes ende. Home fait feffmente en fee sur
condition, le fitz del feffor disseise le feffe et fait feffmente ouster, le condition
est enfreynt, le pere devie devaunt ascun entre, le fitz entre, et le darren feffe
port assise.

[102]

Troix choces fount felonye, scilicet il covyent prendre rem alienam, et animo
felonico, et invito domino.

[103]

Nota per *Fytzherbert* que null home conveyera a luy que estate per voy de
tytle, replycation, ou come actor, sauns monstrer coment.

[104]

Un seigniorie est graunt sur condition, le tenance eschete, le tenaunce est
charge ove le condition.

100. CARYLL v. COLDWELL

If someone is bound to me, and my servant, reciting that he is servant to me, and that he by my command and as servant to me and to my use has received from the obligor the sum contained in the bond, then acquits him by the said acquittance in his own name, this is void: as was adjudged in debt brought by Thomas Caryll, merchant, against one William Coldwell.

101. NOTE

Inner Temple.

Hare put this case at the board's end.[1] Someone makes a feoffment in fee upon condition; the feoffor's son disseises the feoffee and makes a feoffment over; the condition is broken; the father dies before any entry; the son enters; and the latter feoffee brings an assize.

102. NOTE

Three things make felony: namely he must take [1] the property of another, [2] with a felonious mind, [3] against the will of the owner (*rem alienam, et animo felonico, et invito domino*).[2]

103. ANON.

Probably in the Common Pleas.

Note, by FITZHERBERT, that no one shall trace title to himself by *que estate* by way of title, replication, or as actor, without showing how.

104. NOTE

A lordship is granted upon condition, the tenancy escheats: the tenancy is charged with the condition.

[1] For this expression see also above, p. 402, no. 78.
[2] Presumably from *Bracton*, fo. 150b (ii. 425). Francis Mountford expressly cited this in his Inner Temple reading of 1527: CUL MS. El. 5.19, fo. 113.

(B) Addenda from other sources

[105]

Keil. 202v–203v, pl. 1 ('Anno xxj. Henrici octaui').

Un action sur lestatute pur chaser en parkes, le defendant dit que le plaintife
navoit park la.

Shelley, Justice. Ceo nest mie plee, et si le defendant ust dit que le plaintife
nad mie parke la et traverse le parke, ceo ne [ferroit]¹ issue.

Brudnell. Semble bon plee pur ceo que si le plaintife nad parke la, donques il
ne poit aver cest action sur lestatute, car nest mie reason que le defendant serra
punishe accordant a lestatute et le plaintife nad mie parke, et lestatute ne parle
forsque lou le defendant enchase en un parke, ergo si le plaintife nad parke il ne
poit aver action sur cest estatute, per que etc.

Shelley. En briefe de trespas quare servientem suam verberavit, est bone plee
adire que il ne fuit le servant le plaintife; et auxy en briefe de trespas pur baterie
de mon villein, est bon plee adire que il ne fuit vostre villein. Mes [*fo. 203*] en le
case al barre nest mie plee que le plaintife nad mie parke, pur ceo que ceo ne
poit faire issue, car tiel issue ne poit estre trie enter le plaintife et le defendant
mes est destre trie enter le roy et le plaintife. Car si jeo imparke certeyne terre
sans licence, nul avera avantage de ceo sinon le roy, et ceo est chose triable
perenter le roy et moy. Et in Hillarii 34 Hen. 6. placito 8, quare liberam
warrennam suam intravit, le defendant voilet aver le ple que le defendant ad
plede icy, mes il ne fuit suffer, mes fuit chase per le court de pleader de rien
culpable. Issint semble que il ferra icy.

Brooke. Pur pleader de rien culpable il serroit perilous issint pur mitter en le
bouche des layes gentes, car si le veritie soit que le plaintife nad mie parke la
mes un close ovesque savages, et le defendant inchasast eux in fait, et ceo
matter appiert en evidence, les layes gents ne voilent regarder sil ad parke la ou
nemy petit ou nient, mes ils voilent regarder lenchasement, et ils ne sachent le
ley si le plaintife pur ceo que il nad parke ad misconceive son action ou nemy,
et issint pur ceo que il inchasa la en fayt il serroit graund colour a eux pur
trover luy culpable, per que etc.

¹ serroit.

(B) Addenda from other sources

105. ANON.[1]

Common Pleas, dated 1529/30. Also reported in YB Trin. 19 Hen. VIII, fo. 9, pl. 2 (dated Trin. 1527); and in BL MS Harley 1691, fo. 143v, below, p. 434, no. 8 (wrongly dated Mich. 1534).

In an action on the statute for hunting in parks,[2] the defendant said that the plaintiff had no park there.

SHELLEY, Justice.[3] That is no plea. If the defendant had said that the plaintiff had no park there and traversed the park, that would not make an issue.

BRUDENELL.[4] It seems a good plea, because if the plaintiff has no park there he cannot have this action upon the statute, for it is not right that the defendant should be punished in accordance with the statute if the plaintiff has no park, and the statute speaks only where the defendant hunts in a park, ergo if the plaintiff has no park he cannot have an action on this statute, and so etc.

SHELLEY. In a writ of trespass for beating one's servant (*quare servientem suam verberavit*), it is a good plea to say that he was not the plaintiff's servant; and also in a writ of trespass for battery of my villein, it is a good plea to say that he was not [my] villein. But in the case at bar it is no plea that the plaintiff has no park, because that cannot make an issue, for such an issue cannot be tried between the plaintiff and the defendant but is to be tried between the king and the plaintiff. For if I impark certain land without licence, no one shall have advantage of that but the king, and that is something triable between the king and me. And in Hil. 34 Hen. VI, pl. 8,[5] [in trespass] for entering a free warren (*quare liberam warrennam suam intravit*), the defendant wanted to plead as the defendant has pleaded here, but he was not allowed to do so, but was driven by the court to plead Not guilty. So it seems he should here.

BROKE.[6] It would be dangerous, by pleading Not guilty, to put it in the mouths of the laymen, for if it be the truth that the plaintiff has no park there but has a close with wild animals, and the defendant hunted them in fact, and this matter appears in evidence, the laymen will not pay heed to whether he has a park there, or only a small one, or none at all, but will pay heed to the hunting, and they do not know the law whether the plaintiff has misconceived his action, in that he does not have a park, or not, and therefore because he hunted in fact there would be much colour to find him guilty; and so etc.

---

[1] Cf. *Bishop of Bangor* v. *Rokeley* (Trin. 1529) CP 40/1062, m. 451 (action on statute *De malefactoribus in parcis*; pleads Not guilty).

[2] 21 Edw. I, stat. 1, *De malefactoribus in parcis* (*SR* i. 111).   [3] Appointed Mich. 1526.

[4] C.J.C.P. 1520–30; last sat in Mich. 1530.   [5] YB Hil. 34 Hen. VI, fo. 28, pl. 9.

[6] His presence is difficult to explain. He was J.C.P. until 1526, then C.B. Exch. It is more likely one of the serjeants: perhaps Browne.

Inglefield. Semble que lun ple ou lauter est asses bone.

Shelley. Non certes, il covient de necessitie pleder de rien culpable, ou auterment son plee ne vaut a ma entent clerement.

Spilman. Si nous pledomus de rien culpable, il covient le plaintife de prover en evidence que nous sumus culpable de lenchasement en son parke, ou auterment nous poiomus demurrer sur son evidence: quod Shelley concessit.

Brudnell. Pleades a vostre perill.

Et adjornatur.

Et puis *Willoughby*, serjeant, demaunde des justices si le plaintife doyt recover damages pur le tuant de les savages ou nemy.

Shelley. Non verament, pur le tuant solement il ne recovera damages.

Et *Brudnell* negavit.

Shelley. 3 Hen. 6 le brief fuit abatus pur ceo que il dit quare cuniculos suos cepit, que prove bien sil ne poit dire suos, pur ceo que il nad propertie en eux, il ne poit aver damages pur le tuant de eux. Mes pur tuant de columbes deins mon columbarie, ou pur heronshewes prises horse de lour nides, javera damages.

Brooke. Si home ad dames il est un graund pleasure a luy sil soyt home de abilitie, et est necessarie pur chescun home de habilitie daver pleasures. Donques quant cest pleasure est destroy nest il reason que il avera dammages [*fo. 203v*] pur ceo? (Quasi diceret sic etc.)

Shelley intend precise que il ne recovera damages pur les savages en ceo case.

Tota curia contra.

< Vide 18 H. 6. 21, [parco][1] fracto, et 3 H. 6, fol. 51, trespas, et 12 H. 6, fol. 3, et 43 E. 3, pl. 2, trespas. >[2]

[106]

Keil. 203v, pl. 2 ('Anno xxj. Henrici octaui').

In trespas le defendant plead de rien culpable et le plaintife monstra en evidence que ses beasts fueront prises sur le terre, a que le defendant dit que il ad un close adjoynant just al terre le plaintife et que le plaintife ad use touts foits de faire le closure parenter les terres le plaintife et le defendant, et pur default del closure le plaintife mesme ses beastes que il mitta en son close

---

[1] pacto.   [2] *References perhaps added.*

ENGLEFIELD.[1] It seems that either plea is good enough.

SHELLEY. Surely not. It is my view clearly that he must needs plead Not guilty, or else his plea is inavlid.

Spelman. If we plead Not guilty, the plaintiff must prove with evidence that we are guilty of hunting in his park, or else we may demur upon his evidence. (SHELLEY granted that.)

BRUDENELL. Plead at your peril.

It was adjourned.

Afterwards *Willoughby*, serjeant, asked the justices whether the plaintiff ought to recover damages for the killing of the wild beasts or not.

SHELLEY. No, indeed; he shall not recover damages for the killing alone.

But BRUDENELL denied this.

SHELLEY. In 3 Hen. VI,[2] the writ was abated because he said that he took his rabbits (*quare cuniculos suos cepit*), which proves well that if he cannot say 'his' (*suos*)—because he has no property in them—he cannot have damages for killing them. But I shall have damages for killing the doves in my dovecote, or for herons taken out of their nests.[3]

BROKE. If someone has deer it is a great pleasure for him, if he is man of ability, and it is necessary for every man of ability to have pleasures. Therefore, when this pleasure is destroyed, is it not right that he should have damages for it? (As if to say that it is etc.)

SHELLEY meant precisely that he shall not recover damages for the wild beasts in this case.

The whole court was against him.

(See 18 Hen. VI, fo. 21, *de parco fracto*; 3 Hen. VI, fo. 51, trespass; 12 Hen. VI, fo. 3; 43 Edw. III, pl. 2, trespass.[4])

106. ANON.

Common Pleas, dated 1529/30. Briefly reported in YB Pas. 19 Hen. VIII, fo. 6, pl. 2 (dated Pas. 1527). The first paragraph recurs below, p. 438, no. 20.

In trespass the defendant pleaded Not guilty and the plaintiff showed in evidence that his beasts were taken on the land, to which the defendant said that he had a close next adjoining the plaintiff's land and that the plaintiff had always been used to make the enclosure between the lands of the plaintiff and the defendant, and because of the plaintiff's own default in making the

---

[1] Appointed J.C.P. in Mich. 1526.

[2] *Archbishop of Canterbury's Case* (1425) YB Trin. 3 Hen. VI, fo. 55, pl. 34.

[3] *Bishop of London v. Nevell* (1522) YB Mich. 14 Hen. VIII, fo. 1, pl. 1; CP 40/1029, m. 535; 119 Selden Soc. 88 (damages recovered for taking herons out of their nests).

[4] YB Mich. 18 Hen. VI, fo. 21, pl. 6; the other references are incorrect. Cf. YB Trin. 3 Hen. VI, fo. 55, pl. 34 (last note); Hil. 43 Edw. III, fo. 8, pl. 23.

aleront en le terre le plaintif et la fieront le trespas.

A que *Shelley*, Justice, dit: Pur que ne pledastes ceo matter especial, car ore vous estes passe lavantage de ceo matter? Car vous aves mise le contrary en issue quant distes que nestes culpable, et ore per vostre evidence distes que estes culpable, et ceo voiles avoider et excuser per cause del default del plaintif mesme, que ne poit estre.

A que *Willoughby*, le serjeant, disoit que il ne fuit de counsel ove le pleding, mes jeo voile monstre ceo ore al jurie pur enducer eux de assesser le meinder damages pur le trespas, entant que fuit fait en son default.

Shelley. Ceo ne voet vous serve, car peraventure ils per ceo poient encurrer le daunger de attaint. Quaere inde etc.

< Semble matter 12 H. 8, fo. 1, waste. >[1]

[107]

BL MS. Lansdowne 1084, fo. 3.

Per *Shelley*, si cesti in reversion de tenaunt pur vie graunt son reversion per fine et le fine est engros sans quid juris clamat sue, et puis le grauntee ceo grant oustre per fine, son grauntee avera quid juris clamat nient obstant que son grauntour ne poet ceo aver. Mes *Fitzherbert* econtra etc. rule oustrement clerement 24 H. 8.

[108]

BL MS. Lansdowne 1133, fo. 140v (*c.* 1568).

Si tenant en taile, le remainder al roy, face lease pur vie et devy, son issue prist feme et devye sans issue, si ell serra endowe? Et *Plowden* semble quel ne serra endowe, car coment que le leasse ne fait aschun discontinuance [uncore][2] le lesse nest defeat ne le franktenemente hors de luy: et issint fuit rule en 24 H. 8. come appiert par un report que Carrell monstre a Plowden et Phetiplace . . .

---

[1] *Reference perhaps added.*   [2] encore.

enclosure the beasts which he put in his close went into the plaintiff's land and there committed the trespass.

To which SHELLEY, Justice, said: Why did you not plead these facts specially, for you are too late now to take advantage of them? For you put in issue the contrary when you said you were not guilty, and now by your evidence you say you are guilty but wish to avoid and excuse it because of the default of the plaintiff himself, which cannot be.

To which *Willoughby*, serjeant, said he was not of counsel with the pleading. But I want to show this to the jury now in order to persuade them to assess lesser damages for the trespass, since it was done in his default.

SHELLEY. That will not serve you, for perhaps they would thereby incur the danger of an attaint. (Query this etc.)

(Similar matter in 12 Hen. VIII, fo. 1, in waste.[1])

107. ANON.[2]

Common Pleas, after 1532/33.

By SHELLEY, if the reversioner of a tenant for life grants his reversion by fine, and the fine is engrossed without a *quid juris clamat* being sued, and afterwards the grantee grants it over by fine, his grantee shall have *quid juris clamat* even though his grantor cannot have it. But FITZHERBERT ruled it clearly to the contrary etc. in 24 Hen. VIII.

108. ANON.

Probably in the Common Pleas, 1532/33; cited *c.* 1568.

If tenant in tail, remainder to the king, makes a lease for life and dies, and his issue marries and dies without issue, shall she be endowed? *Plowden* thought she should not be endowed, for although the lessee did not make any discontinuance the lease is not defeated and the freehold is not out of him: and so it was ruled in 24 Hen. VIII, as appears by a report which *Caryll* showed to Plowden and Fetiplace . . .

---

[1] *Browne* v. *Elmer* (1520) YB Trin. 12 Hen. VIII, fo. 1, pl. 1; 119 Selden Soc. 2. Reference perhaps added.

[2] This is not attributed to Caryll, but see the note to no. 109, which it follows on the page.

[109]

BL MS. Lansdowne 1084, fo. 3; also in HLS MS. 1058, fo. 1

Si jeo face leas pur ans a un et le lessee covenant pur lui et son assignes de repaier les mess[uages] ou de edifier un mease sur le terre, si le lessee graunt oustre son estate jeo avera action de covenant vers assignee pur non performer de ceux covenantes pur ceo que sont annex al terre. 26 H. 8. per toutz les justices.

[110]

BL MS. Lansdowne 1084, fo. 3.

Per *Fitzherbert* et *Baldwin* si lees soit fait sur condition que ne serra loiall al lessee, son executours ou assignes de ceo graunt ouster, et le lessee fait son feme executrix et morust, et el prist baron que ceo graunt oustre, per ceo le condition est enfreint. Et per *Fitzherbert* si le condition ust estre que ne licet a lessee de ceo graunt sans parlar de son executour, donques lexecutour serra hors del compas del condition. 27 H. 8. lib. Carell.

(C)[1] Autograph annotations
to manuscript Year Books of Henry V

[111]

Fo. 150: marginal note to YB Mich. 3 Hen. VI, fo. 9, pl. 9.

[*Martyn. Jeo die que il yad graund diversite lou un recovere est tout solement sur le proces et lou un recovere est sur un verdit . . .*]

Nota que ceo fuit tenus bon diversite in Bank le Roy anno 26 H. 8. termino H. Mez per Fitzjames chyf jusice la fuit tenus que si le originall soit malement

---

[1] From BL MS. Harley 5158.

109. ANON.[1]

Common Pleas or Exchequer Chamber, 1534/35. Cf. 25 Hen. VIII, Bro. Abr., *Covenant*, pl. 32.

If I make a lease for years to someone, and the lessee covenants for himself and his assigns to repair the messuages or to build a house on the land, and the lessee grants over his estate, I shall have an action of covenant against the assignee for not performing these covenants because they are annexed to the land. 26 Hen. VIII, by all the justices.[2]

110. HYNDE v. WHELER

Common Pleas, 1535/36. CP 40/1089, m. 457. Cf. above, p. 397, no. 65, which seems to be another version of the case (dated 28 Hen. VIII).

By FITZHERBERT and BALDWIN, if a lease is made upon condition that it shall not be lawful for the lessee, his executors or assigns to grant it over, and the lessee makes his wife his executrix and dies, and she marries a husband who grants it over, the condition is thereby broken. And, by FITZHERBERT, if the condition had been that it should not be lawful for the lessee to grant it over, without speaking of his executors, the executor would be outside the compass of the condition. 27 Hen. VIII, in Caryll's book.

(C) Autograph annotations
to manuscript Year Books of Henry V

111. NOTE

King's Bench, Hil. 1535.

[YB Mich. 3 Hen. VI, fo. 9, pl. 9: . . . *Martin. I say that there is a great difference between where a recovery is solely upon the process and where a recovery is upon a verdict* . . .]

Note that this was held a good distinction in the King's Bench in Hilary term, 26 Hen. VIII. But, by FITZJAMES C.J., it was there held that if the original writ is

---

[1] This is not attributed to Caryll but this case and the next are on similar points, and no. 110 is so attributed. They are followed by a case 'de libro de report de Serjant Carell' (i.e. Caryll's father).
[2] Cf. vol. I, p. 201, no. 294; *Thirkill* v. *Gore* (1529) Spelman 75.

returne ou nient duement servy et ceo apiert, donquez soit il que le party recover sur defaut ou aprez aparans in lun cas et in lauter est errour.

[112]

Fo. 178v: marginal note to YB Pas. 4 Hen. VI, fo. 19, pl. 5.

Et nota que les justices a cest jour, scilicet 19 H. 8., sont en opinion que si un comon laborar covenant ove moy de moy server en husbondry per ii. ans et jeo done a luy plus gages qest lymyt per lestatut, sil port action vers moy a fyn de son terme pur son salary jeo poy gager ma ley, et si jeo devie il navera action vers mez executours pur ceo que le reteyner ne fuit accordant a lestatut et pur ceo hors de cas destatut.

[113]

Fo. 212: marginal note to YB Mich. 9 Hen. VI, fo. 55, pl. 41. [. . . *quaunt home plede un feffement en barre et dit que ceo fuit saunz ascun condition, ceux parols saunz ascun condition sont voidez* . . .]

Cest est tenus pur ley a cest jour, xvii° H. viii°.

[114]

Fo. 251: marginal note to YB Trin. 18 Hen. VI, fo. 11, pl. 1, at fo. 13.

[*Yelverton a Fortescue: . . . en un lete sont plusours que ne sount en un sherifstourne, ergo le sherifstourne nest lete. . .*]

Nota que Moomford disoit que il ny ad diversite perenter un lete et le sheryfstorne quar le shryfstorne est le lete le roy, et lete est dun comen person, et issint nul auter diversite. Et disoit que cest lyver ne fuit ley en cest poynt. Et disoit auxi que le court de county jours nest forsque le corte baron le roy, et nul auter diversite mez lun fuit al comen person et lauter al roy. Ideo quere.

badly returned or not duly served, and this appears, then in either case it is error whether the party recovers upon a default or after appearance.

112. NOTE

Probably Common Pleas, 1527/28.

Note that the justices at the present day, namely 19 Hen. VIII, are of opinion that if a common labourer covenants with me to serve me in husbandry for two years, and I give him more wages than are apppointed by the statute,[1] and he brings an action against me at the end of his term for his salary, I may wage my law; and if I die he shall not have an action against my executors, because the retainer was not in accordance with the statute and therefore outside the scope of the statute.

113. NOTE

1525/26.

[YB Mich. 9 Hen. VI, fo. 55, pl. 41: *when someone pleads a feoffment in bar and says it was without any condition, these words 'without any condition' are void.*]

This is held to be law at the present day, 17 Hen. VIII.

114. NOTE

Inner Temple, perhaps Lent 1527 (at the time of Francis Mountford's reading).

[YB Trin. 18 Hen. VI, fo. 11, pl. 1, at fo. 13: *Yelverton to Fortescue: . . . there are several articles in the leet which are not in the sheriff's tourn, ergo the sheriff's tourn is not a leet . . .*]

Note that *Mountford* said that there is no difference between a leet and the sheriff's tourn, for the sheriff's tourn is the king's leet, and a leet is a common person's [tourn], and there is no other difference. And he said that this book was not law on this point. He also said that the county court is only the king's court baron, and there is no other difference but that the one belongs to a common person and the other to the king. Therefore query.

[1] 23 Edw. III, Ordinance of Labourers, cc. 3–5 (SR i. 307), and 25 Edw. III, stat. 1, Statute of Labourers (SR i. 311).

(D)[1]

Larraignment del Segnior Dacre et Greystock de hault treason reported by Serjant Gawdy que morust en le temps le Roigne Mary.

Nota[2] que le Joves[3] jour apres le feast del translation de Saint Thomas anno 26 H. 8. William, Seignour Dacre et Grist:, fuit arreigne de haute treson pur ceo que [il][4] fuit adherent et aydant a les Scotts enemies le roy en temps de guerre. Et al primes per grand temps il ne voile responder al treson mes pria respite etc. Et fuit agree per toutes les justices Dengleterre la adonques esteant que sil ne voile responder directment a le treson et auxi de mitte lui sur ses peeres destre trie sur cell, que il avera judgment destre trahe et pende cybien sicome il fuit trove culpable. Car lestatute de W. 1, ca. 12, des felons escries que estoient mutes etc., est solement intend de[5] fellony et nemi de treson. Et auxi fuit agree per mesme les justices que il covient estre trie per ses peeres et nemi per auters persons, coment que le prisoner ceo voit prier, car lestatute de Magna Carta est un prohibition in le negative, Nec super eum ibimus nec super eum etc. Et auxi lestatute de 25 E. 3, ca. 2, de proditionibus, voit que tiels persons que offend in tiel manner et de ceo [sont provablement][6] atteinte de overt [fait][7] per gentes de son condition, per que apiert que [il][8] covient estre trie per ses peeres et nemi auterment. Et fuit tenus per plusors[9] des justices que il navera ascun challendge a les seignours pur ceo que ills ne sont come jurors, car ils ne serront jures mes sont plus proprement come judges, coment que ils ne doner[ont] le judgment mes le graund seneschall Dengleterre doner[a] le judgment, mes serra per lour verditt monstre a lui que chescun de eux done severallment per lui mesme al seneschall, car chescun deux est tenus de monstre et declarer son intent et conscience in ceo.[10] Et donques fuit move per les

---

[1] From BL MS. Hargrave 373, ff. 134–135 (*A*), collated with MS. Add. 35953, fo. 52 (*B*). There are also texts in IT MS. Petyt 511.13, fo. 58v; Herts. Record Office, Verulam MS. XII. A. 44.
[2] Memorandum *B*.
[3] *Om. B*.
[4] *B. Om. A*.
[5] *B.* de[str]e *A*.
[6] *B.* stat. *A*.
[7] *B.* fuit *A*.
[8] *B. Om. A*.
[9] ascuns *B*.
[10] icell *B*.

(D)

R. v. LORD DACRE AND GREYSTOCK

Before the lord high steward of England, and his peers, 9 July 1534. Also reported in Spelman, pp. 54–55; and by Edward Halle (reprinted in 1 St. Tr. 407). Record: KB 8/6 (abstracted in *Third Report of the Deputy Keeper of Public Records*, app. II, pp. 234–236).

The arraignment of the Lord Dacre and Greystock for high treason, reported by Serjeant Gawdy who died in the time of Queen Mary.[1]

Note that on the Thursday after the feast of the translation of St Thomas [9 July 1534] in the twenty-sixth year of Henry VIII, William, Lord Dacre and Greystock,[2] was arraigned of high treason for that he was an adherent and gave aid to the Scots enemies of the king in time of war. At first for a long time he would not answer to the treason but prayed a respite etc. And it was agreed by all the justices of England, who were then there, that if he would not answer directly to the treason and also put himself upon his peers to be tried thereon, he should have judgment to be drawn and hanged just as if he had been found guilty. For the Statute of Westminster I, c. 12,[3] concerning accused felons who stand mute etc., is intended only of felony and not of treason. It was also agreed by the same justices that he must be tried by his peers and not by other persons, even if the prisoner prays [the lattter], for the statute of Magna Carta is a prohibition in the negative, 'We will not proceed against him . . . [except by the judgment of his peers] (*Nec super eum ibimus nec super eum etc.*).[4] Also the statute of 25 Edw. III, c. 2, concerning treasons,[5] speaks of persons who offend in such manner and are thereof probably attainted of an overt act 'by people of their condition', whereby it appears that he must be tried by his peers and not otherwise. And it was held by several of the justices that he shall not have any challenge to the lords, because they are not like jurors; for they are not sworn, but are more properly like judges, even though they do not give the judgment— the high steward of England shall give the judgment—but it shall be by their verdict shown to him, which each of them gives separately by himself to the same steward, inasmuch as each of them is bound to show and declare his

---

[1] I.e. Thomas Gawdy of the Inner Temple (admitted *c.* 1527/29, reader 1548), later a serjeant at law (1552), died 1556: *Readers and Readings*, p. 82. As to whether this is a correct attribution see the introduction, above, vol. I, p. xli.

[2] William Dacre, summoned to parliament in 1529 as Lord Dacre and Greystock (the barony of Greystock having descended to him through his mother), but also styled Lord Dacre of Gillesland. He was commonly known as Lord Dacre of the North, to distinguish him from Thomas Fiennes, Lord Dacre of the South.

[3] Westminster I, c. 12 (*SR* i. 29), concerning the *prisone forte et dure*.

[4] Magna Carta 1225, c. 29.

[5] Treason Act, 25 Edw. III, stat. 5, c. 2 (*SR* i. 319).

segniors daver jour ouster destre advise de doner et monstre lour severall
verdittes et intentes sur ceo matter. Et fuit responde per les justices que ceo ne
fuit unques view avant ceux heures, pur ceo que ilz ne sont jures, et ils ont oye[1]
lenditement et evidence done a prover ceo, et le respons del prisoner al evidence
et linditement, et ore le matter est recent et prompt in lour remembraunces et ils
ne sont lies mes que chescun de les segniors [devoyent][2] parler et monstre ceo
que il pense sur le matter come a lui et a son conscience semble bon. Et puis[3]
pur ceo que les segniors avoient plus longement enterparle ensemble enter eux
mesmes, et ne puissoient[4] agreer in doner lour severall verdittes ceo jour, < fuit
demande >[5] sils serront garde insemble sans departure un del auter tanque ils
ont doner lour severall verdittes [fuit auxy move a les justices].[6] Et il semble
adonque a les justices que ils ne doiont[7] depart mesque ils sera gard insemble
tanque ils ont doner lour verditt et que ils aver maunger et boier etc. Et
donques fuit move a les justices sils doner lour verditt et x. deux[8] trove lui
culpable et x. deux trove lui nient culpable, les queux sont toutes les segniors
que passe sur ceo matter, que serra fait].[9] Et les justices pense que ceo ne fuit
perfitt ne plein verditt a doner judgment de vie et de membre sinon que xii. de
les segniors al meins trove lui culpable. Car le ley del terre est pur le tryall de
chescun home et de chescun matter in variance que le triall serra per xii.
probable[10] homes. Et donques coment que le segnior serra trie per ses peeres il
covient que il soit trove culpable per xii. de ses peeres al meins, auterment il
serra in plus pejor case que [ascun][11] auter comen person. Et ceo[12] tryall per ses
peeres est done a lui pur son advantage per lestatutes suisdites, per que il
covient que xii. segniors agree de trove lui culpable, auterment il ne serra
atteint per ceo verditt. Mes si fueront 26 segniors et 30 ou plusors que devoient
done lour verditt sur le matter, et si xii. ou xiiii. segniors trove lui nient
culpable, et xv. ou xvi. trove lui < nient >[13] culpable del treason, [si ore le
segnior seneschall donera judgment dattaynder? Et ceo fuit move a les justices.
Et en ceo case les justices respond que le segnior seneschall Dengleterre devoit
doner judgment solonque ceo que le greinder nombre accord et agree. Et fuit
move si apres le verdict des segniors done][14] le segnior seneschall poit adjorne
les sessions a auter jour destre advise de son judgment in le mesne temps. Et a
ceo les justices disont que ils pense que il poit ceo faire, car son comission hac
vice est fait [etc.][15] come le comission de les justices de gaole deliverye le comen
course est dadjorne lour sessions al auter jour. Et puis les segniors veigne
mesme le jour et done lour verditt severallment, chescun < per lui mesme >[16]
que le Segnior Dacre < del Greystocke >[17] ne fuit [culpable][18] de ceux treasons
[des][19] queux il fuit indite, per que le segnior seneschall done [sur luy][20] son
judgment que le court luy discharge de ceux treasons, payant ses fees etc.

---

[1] ewe B.   [2] B. Om. A.   [3] Om. B.   [4] poyent B.   [5] Om. B.   [6] B only.
[7] deveront B.   [8] Om. B.   [9] B. Om. A.   [10] prodeables B.   [11] B. Om. A.
[12] Om. B.   [13] A only, clearly an error.   [14] B. ore si A, by haplography.   [15] B. Om. A.
[16] aperluy B.   [17] Om. B.   [18] B. Om. A.   [19] B. Om. A.   [20] B. Om. A.

intent and conscience therein. Then it was moved by the lords that they might have a further day to be advised in giving and showing their separate verdicts and intents upon this matter. And it was answered by the justices that that was never seen before these days, because they are not sworn, and they have heard the indictment and the evidence given to prove it, and the prisoner's answer to the evidence and to the indictment, and now the matter is recent and prompt in their memories, and they are not under restraint, but each of the lords ought to speak and show what he thinks upon the matter as to him and his conscience seems good. Afterwards, because the lords had been in conference so long amongst themselves, and could not agree in giving their separate verdicts on this day, it was also moved to the justices whether they should be kept together without departing from one another until they should have given in their separate verdicts. And it then seemed to the justices that they ought not to leave but should be kept together until they had given in their verdicts, and that they should have food and drink etc. Then it was moved to the justices what should be done if they gave their verdicts and ten of them found him guilty and ten of them found him not guilty, and those were all the lords who passed upon this matter. And the justices thought that it would not be a perfect or plain verdict for giving judgment of life and limb unless at least twelve of the lords found him guilty. For the law of the land for the trial of everyone, and of every matter in variance, is that the trial shall be by twelve reliable men. Therefore, even though the lord shall be tried by his peers, he must be found guilty by at least twelve of his peers, or else he would be in a worse case than any other common person. And this trial by his peers is given to him for his advantage by the above-mentioned statutes, and so there must be twelve lords in agreement to find him guilty, otherwise he shall not be attainted by this verdict. But if there were twenty-six lords—[or] thirty or more—who ought to give their verdict upon the matter, and twelve or fourteen lords find him not guilty, and fifteen or sixteen find him guilty of the treason, shall the lord steward now give judgment of attainder? This was moved to the justices. And in this case the justices answered that the lord steward of England ought to give judgment according to what the majority have accorded and agreed. And it was moved whether, after the verdict of the lords had been given, the lord steward might adjourn the sessions to another day so as to be advised of his judgment in the mean time. To this the justices said they thought he could do that, for his commission is made *hac vice*, like the commission of the justices of gaol delivery, where the common course is to adjourn their sessions to another day. Afterwards the lords came back on the same day and gave in their verdicts separately, each by himself, that the Lord Dacre and Greystock was not guilty of these treasons whereof he was indicted. Therefore the lord steward gave judgment upon him that the court discharged him of those treasons, paying his fees etc.

10. ANONYMOUS FRAGMENTS

[1]

[A]

BL MS. Hargrave 5, fo. 106 (17th century copy).

H. 21 H. 8.

Dett sur obligation port per un come executour, le defendant dit que le plaintife per son fait monstre avant avoit release a luy touts manners dactions personalls queux il fuit entitle daver ratione executionis testamenti defuncti, judgment si action. A que le plaintife dit que il fuit deins age al temps de cest releas fait et sur cell plee le defendant demurrer in ley.

Inglefielde semble ceo bon barre quar cest releas il est tenus de faire per ley et pur ceo il ne ceo avoidra. Come sil present al esglise ou chappell donative ou deliver biens et legacyes accordant al volunt le testatour, il ne unquez ceux avoidra per son nonage quar fuit tenus deux faire. Et icy le testator ad done a luy power de faire toutz tielx choses queux il mesme ferroit sil ust este in vie, et ad luy enable nient obstant son nonage, quar le ley intende que le testator fuit bien apprise de son discretion: et donques, quant le testator ad luy enable dadministration et de prender sur luy loffice dun executour, nest in nous a luy diasabler mes covient a nous luy accepter ore come home de pleine age. Est agree que sil ust paye le money le releas est bon, quar donquez il nest devastavit del biens le testatour. Et moy semble que ceo nest diversitye, quar le payment nest issuable mes le fait est le chose que est pledable enconter loblige, et in nostre ley si fait soit un foits seale et deliver come perfecte escripte il nest unques inquirable si le matter comprise deins le fait soit execute ou nemy mes le fait est le chose issuable. Come si home soit oblige de paye 20. li. que il apprompte de moy, nest issuable ou mater[ial] si largent fuit apprompte ou

417

10. ANONYMOUS FRAGMENTS

1. ANON.

Common Pleas, Hil. 1530. Also reported in Spelman, p. 133, pl. 5 (Mich. 1529); Pollard, above, p. 265, no. 44 (Hil. 1530); and Yelverton, above, p. 323, no. 24.

A

Dated Hil. 1530.

Debt on a bond brought by an executor; the defendant said that the plaintiff by his deed (which was shown forth) had released to him all manner of personal actions which he was entitled to have by reason of the execution of the testament of the deceased (*ratione executionis testamenti defuncti*), and prayed judgment whether the plaintiff ought to have his action. To this the plaintiff said that he was under age at the time of making this release; and upon this plea the defendant demurred in law.

ENGLEFIELD thought it a good bar, for he is bound by law to make this release and therefore he may not avoid it. Likewise if he presents to a church or chapel donative, or delivers goods and legacies according to the testator's will, he shall never avoid these things by reason of being under age, for he was bound to do them. Here the testator has given him power to do all those things which he could have done himself if he had been alive, and has enabled him despite being under age, for the law presumes that the testator was fully apprised of his discretion: therefore, since the testator has enabled him to the administration, and to take upon him the office of an executor, it is not in us to disable him, but we must accept him now as if he were a man of full age. It is agreed that if he had paid the money the release would be good, for then it is not a *devastavit* of the testator's goods. It seems to me that this is no distinction, for the payment is not issuable, but the deed is the thing which is pleadable against the obligee; and in our law if a deed is once sealed and delivered as a perfect writing it is never enquirable whether the matter comprised in the deed is executed or not, but the deed is the issuable thing. Likewise if someone makes a bond to pay £20 which he has borrowed from me, it is not issuable or material whether the money was

417

nemy. Issint icy, sil fuit alledge per le pleder que il receve le money et pur ceo fist le releas, le party ne poit dire que il ne unquez receve le money mes covient responder al releas. Et sil expende les biens le testatour il serra charge pur ceo de ses biens propers come chescun person de pleine age. Et in mults cases jugement ou authorite a luy done serra ouste de avoider son acte per nonage: come si jeo authorise infant de lesse mes terres ou densealer un fait, il ne unquez eux avoydera, et sil est enable destre executour il [avera][1] touts choses incident a ceo, scilicet a rescever dettes et faire sufficient acquittances etc. Et jeo pose que si apres dettes et legacyes payes il done parte del surplusage pur le alme del testatour, ceo est bon et nient avoidable, et mittomus que auter port dett vers luy apres sur obligation et recover, et devastavit est trove, uncore cest done loyalment fait estoyera et ne serra defeate. Et si le done ne soit [defesible], per mesme le reson ne serra le releas auxi, coment que soit devastavit. Issint icy, le ley doit luy enabler que le testatour ad enable. Issint semble le plaintife serra barre.

Fitzherbert econtra. Et quaunt adire que il est enable per le testatour a releas action, faire acquittance et devaster les biens le testatour, ceo nest issint: quar il nest enable forsque come le ley voit et accordant al office de trust in que il est depute. Quar loffice del executour est de resceiver et payer les dettes le testatour in le plus hastye temps que il poit, et de veyer les biens dispose accordant al volunt le testatour, et a disposer le surplusage pur lalme le mourt. Donquez, quant il releas le dett le testatour cest un devastavit et in manner come un tort fait al testator. Est ceo donquez son office de vaster les biens le mourt et de prejudicer le alme le testatour? Certes non, quar cest merement encounter loffice del executour. Donquez le ley ne le testatour ne luy enable a pluis forsque a choses faire concernant loffice dun executour. Et le ley ne luy enable forsque de resceiver et nemi a discharge sans receit en defraude del testatour. Donquez voiles vous luy enabler a plus que le ley luy enable? Vous ne poyes, quar null[y] per son testament poit change le ley del terre. Quar infant ne unquez suera ou appearer per attorney. Serroit il ore admitt dappere per atturney pur ceo que il est executour et admitt per le testatour come person de pleine age? Certes nemi. Ne infant ne unquez serra receu de confesser action, quar prejudice poit ensuer a luy per ceo. Et en cest cas serra lenfant receu a confesser action sil poit appere a nous que il est deins age? Jeo dye que non, nient obstant que le testatour ad luy enable, quar il ne poit luẏ enable a tiel chose que chaungera le ley del terre. Auxi per ley infant ne sera atturne dascun. Ore si un voil enabler infant destre atturne pur luy, serra il ore receu per nous pur ceo que le partye ad luy enable pur le discretion que per case il ad view in luy? Jeo dye que non, quar cest contrarye al ley, a que le partye ne poit luy enabler. Donques cest releas, esteant un devastavit et chose que nest fait come executour, donquez son office come executour ne serve riens de faire son releas bon. Et jeo ne agree le case del

---

[1] avoidra. *Conjectural emendation.*

borrowed or not. Likewise here, if it was alleged in pleading that he received the money and made the release for it, the party could not say that he never received the money but must answer the release. And if he spends the testator's goods he shall be charged for it out of his own goods, like every person of full age. In many cases where a judgment or authority is given to him he shall be prevented from avoiding his act by his infancy: for instance, if I authorise an infant to lease my lands or to seal a deed, he shall never avoid these things; and if he is enabled to be executor he may do everything incident thereto, namely receive debts and make sufficient acquittances etc. Suppose that if, after the debts and legacies have been paid, he gives part of the surplus for the testator's soul: this is good and not avoidable. And suppose someone else brings debt against him afterwards upon a bond and recovers, and a *devastavit* is found: nevertheless this gift which was lawfully made shall stand and shall not be undone. And, if the gift is not defeasible, by the same reason also the release shall not be, even if it is a *devastavit*. Likewise here, the law ought to enable what the testator has enabled. So it seems the plaintiff shall be barred.

FITZHERBERT to the contrary. As to the assertion that he is enabled by the testator to release actions, make acquittances and waste the testator's goods, this is not so: for he is only enabled as the law wills and in accordance with the office of trust in which he is deputed. For the office of an executor is to receive and pay the testator's debts as promptly as he can, and to see the goods disposed of according to the testator's will, and to dispose of the surplus for the soul of the deceased. Therefore, when he releases the testator's debt, that is a *devastavit* and in effect a wrong done to the testator. Is it then his office to waste the goods of the deceased and to prejudice the testator's soul? Surely not, for it is absolutely contrary to the office of an executor. Therefore neither the law nor the testator enable him to do more than those things which concern the office of an executor. And the law only enables him to receive, not to discharge without receipt in fraud of the testator. Will you therefore enable him to do more than the law will enable him to do? You cannot, for no one by his testament can change the law of the land. An infant shall never sue or appear by attorney. Should he now be admitted to appear by attorney because he is an executor, and admitted by the testator as a person of full age? Surely not. Nor shall an infant ever be received to confess an action, for prejudice might thereby ensue to him. Shall the infant in the present case be received to confess an action if it can appear to us that he is under age? I say not, even though the testator has enabled him, for he cannot enable him to do something which would change the law of the land. Moreover, by law an infant shall never be anyone's attorney. If, then, someone will enable an infant to be attorney for him, shall he now be received by us, because the party has enabled him on account of the discretion which perhaps he has seen in him? I say no, for that is contrary to the law, and the party cannot enable him to that. Therefore, this release being a *devastavit* and something which is not done as executor, his office as executor serves as nothing to make his release good. And I do not

acquittance, que cest bon, quar il demurre deins age et pur ceo son fait ne
<poit estre >[i] prist mes come le fait dun infant, et cest voidable. Mes il poit
receve money et deliver lobligation al party ou ceo cancelle, mes nemi de faire
escripte que serra de force: nient plus que moigne sil soit fait executour que est
mort home et pur ceo son fait ne vault. Et jeo teigne clere que si infant done
biens le testatour ceo nest bon, mes il avera action de detinewe deux recover,
quar le ley ne voit luy suffer de faire done que turnera luy in prejudice pur le
devastinge del biens. Et touts agree que il ne forfetra eux sil soit utlage pur
felonye, donquez a fortiori il ne poit eux done al auter, et sil ne poit done lez
biens al auter pur cause de devastavit a fortiori il ne poit releas les dettes que est
auxi haut devastavit del biens come done deux. Et quant adire que in ceo que il
est executour que il est per ceo enable come de home de pleine age, ceo nest
issint, quar sil expende touts les biens le mort et nad riens de ses proper biens
uncore jeo dye que capias ne serra agarde vers ly de prender son corps, pur ceo
que est deins age, quel priviledge de son nonage nest ale per le fesant de luy
executour. Et si infant soit attaint de forcible entre sur 8. H. 6. capias ne serra
agarde vers luy, quar esteant deins age le ley luy priviledge. Et mesme le
priviledge est a luy quant il est fait executour, et que il ne ferra ascun escripte de
luy lier nient obstant que il est enable al office come person de pleine age. Per
que [etc.].

Brudnell al contrarye. Et a ceo que est dit que il nest enable per le testatour a
riens faire mes tantsolement a resceiver debtes et legacyes accordant al
testament, sir, ceo nest issint: quar le testatour ad luy enable destre executour.
Donquez attient al executour de medler ove les biens le mourt et eux imployer
a son plesure, quar le testatour ad mise son trust in luy, et pur ceo le ley
intende que il avoit sufficient conusance de son discretion et conversation et
pur ceo le ley done a luy le plus greinder authorite in les biens, et pur ceo sil
eux destroie et wast null remedye pur ceo redresser[i] mes in le spiritual ley pur le
non performance del testatmemt. Mes si le testatour fuit indebt in obligation et
action est port sur lobligation, la si lexecutour ad done les biens le remedye in
nostre ley est done a luy de charger luy de ses biens propers. Donquez si infant
est fait executour il ad cy grande authorite done a luy come [si] home de pleine
age ust este executour, et tout un in ley. Donquez si le ley luy ajudge <come
person>[i] de pleine age a cest intent, donquez il est reason que le ley luy
ajudgera auxibien able de faire touts choses incidents a son office come ascun
person de pleine age. Come si terres in socage descende a un al age de 14. ans,
le ley luy ajudge de pleine age pur aver son terre. Et quant il ad son terre ne
ferra il leases de ceo come person de pleine age? Oyle certes, si rent soit reserve
et ceo ne soit que pur reasonable number dans, come 7. ou 8. ans, et nemi pur
40. ans ou pluis, ceo liera luy come home de pleine age. Et in mults cases infant

agree the case of the acquittance—that it is good—for he remains under age, and therefore his deed cannot be taken but as the deed of an infant, and that is voidable. He may receive money, and deliver the bond to the party or cancel it, but may not make a writing which shall have any force: any more than a monk may, if made an executor, since he is a dead man and therefore his deed is invalid. I hold it clear that if an infant makes a gift of the testator's goods it is not good, but he shall have an action of detinue to recover them back, for the law will not allow him to make a gift which shall prejudice him by wasting the goods. Everyone agrees that he shall not forfeit them if he is outlawed for felony, and therefore a fortiori he may not give them to someone else; and if he may not give the goods to someone else because it would be a *devastavit*, a fortiori he may not release the debts, which is as high a *devastavit* of the goods as a gift of them. As to the assertion that inasmuch as he is an executor, he is thereby enabled as a man of full age, that is not so; for if he spends all the goods of the deceased and has nothing of his own goods, I still say that a *capias* shall not be awarded against him to take his body, because he is under age, which privilege of his infancy does not go away by making him an executor. And if an infant is attainted of forcible entry upon 8 Hen. VI,[1] a *capias* shall not be awarded against him, for, being under age, the law privileges him. The same privilege exists for him when he is made an executor, so that he may not make any writing to bind himself, even though he is enabled to the office as a person of full age. And so etc.

BRUDENELL [C.J.] to the contrary. As to the assertion that he is not enabled by the testator to do anything but receive debts and legacies according to the testament: sir, that is not so, for the testator has enabled him to be executor. It belongs to the executor to meddle with the goods of the deceased and to employ them at his pleasure, for the testator has put his trust in him, and therefore the law presumes that he had sufficient knowledge of his discretion and conversation, and therefore the law gives him greater authority in the goods, and therefore if he destroys and wastes them there is no remedy to redress this but in the spiritual law for the non-performance of the testatment. But if the testator was indebted in a bond, and an action is brought on the bond, and the executor has given the goods away, the remedy provided in our law is to charge him out of his own goods. If an infant is made executor he has as much authority given to him as if a man of full age had been executor, and they are all one in law. Now, if the law adjudges him to be like a person of full age for this purpose, it is right that the law should adjudge him just as able to do everything incident to his office as any person of full age. Similarly if lands in socage descend to someone of the age of fourteen years, the law adjudges him of full age for the purpose of having his land. And when he has his land, may he not make leases thereof like a person of full age? Yes, of course, if rent is reserved and it is only for a reasonable number of years—such as seven or eight years, though not for forty or more—that shall bind him like a man of

---

[1] 8 Hen. VI, c. 9 (*SR* ii. 244).

<ad power de >[i] faire contractes, come sil soit apprentice et garde le shop son master et vende ses biens, ou si husbondman mist butter, egges et chese per ses infants al markett et vende per eux, est bon. Si abbot soit deins age, come il poit estre a ceo enable per le covent, et il fait leases [et] contractes et releas dettes del meason, ceo est bon ratione officii. Uncore la poit estre dit que il ne fuit enable a faire prejudice a son meason, mes quant il ad loffice dun abbot il per ceo ad le power come auter person ad. Si roy soit deins age il poit faire actes come home de pleine age ratione officii. Mesme le ley lou home done office per inheritance: come les cryours de cest place sont fait per Billeney, que ad linheritance, sil face un cryour icy esteant deins age il ne serra remove quant il vient al pleine age, quar cest place covient estre serve et pur ceo le ley luy ajudge de pleine age touts foits que donera ceux offices, et sil tary tanque il vient de pleine age serra enconter le comen wealth, et pur ceo le ley luy admitt person de pleine age. Sic hic, cest infant quant il est fait executour est admitt able de faire loffice dun executour, et si ore le testament ne serra execute tanque al pleine age ceo serra perillous al alme le mort, quar le plus sone que lexecutour poit il est tenus de performe le volunt, et pur ceo le ley luy covient doner power ratione officii, esteant deins age, a faire touts choses queux executour de pleine age faira. Mes per case, come ad este dit, le ley ne voit que riens luy admitteremus come atturney que est deins age ne de confesser action dascun person, nient obstant que le partye[1] mesme luy enable, quar si nous purramus admitter un atturney deins age per mesme le reason purramus admitter auters. Mes atturney est common servant as lieges le roy et son office est de tiel hautnes que il purroit pur le frailetye de son age faire mult prejudice as lieges le roy, et pur ceo que il est sicome common servant infant ne poit estre admytt pur atturney, et sil soit est errour. Mes executour que est infant poit confesser action port vers luy come executour, quar il est admitte come person de pleine age. Quere inde. Et sil wast <les biens >[i] touts ount agree que il serra charge de ses biens propres, quar est tort fait per luy. Donquez sil nad biens, moy semble que capias issera vers luy, quar lacte est chose fait de son tort demesne. Mes per case sil fuit attaint de forcible entre capias ne issera vers luy, quar cest statute ley et null infant est intende punishable, per que ne serra imprison. Et per comen ley lou infant fait tort il serra punye et esteme come home de pleine age, come sil disseise moy il serra mist a responder. Issint sil committ felonie et murder il serra pende, si ascun discretion poit estre ajudge in luy. Issint de lunaticke, sil poit appere que il avoit conusance ou memorye quant il fist lacte, il serra pende. Issint divers foits le disablement per discretion poit estre avoid et le partye esteme come auter person. Sic hic, le disablement de cest infant de faire le releas effectuall est avoid entant que per entendment le testatour ad ajudge discretion in luy destre son executour, a que office il

---

[1] *Altered from* person.

full age. And in many cases an infant has power to make contracts. For instance, if he is an apprentice and keeps his master's shop and sells his goods, or if a husbandman sends butter, eggs and cheese to market by his infants and sells through them, it is good. If an abbot is under age—as he may be if enabled thereto by the convent—and he makes leases and contracts, and releases the debts of the house, this is good by reason of office (*ratione officii*). Even there it could be said that he was not enabled in order to prejudice his house; but when he has the office of an abbot he thereby has the same power as another person has. If a king is under age he may do things like a man of full age, *ratione officii*. The law is the same where someone gives an office by inheritance: for instance, the criers of this place are made by Bilney, who has the inheritance, and if he appoints a crier here the crier shall not be removed when he comes of age, for this place must be served, and therefore the law adjudges him of full age who gives these offices, and if he waited until he came of age it would be against the common wealth, and therefore the law admits him as a person of full age. Likewise here, when this infant is made executor he is admitted able to perform the office of an executor, and if now the testament shall not be executed until his full age this would be perilous to the soul of the deceased, for as soon as the executor may he is bound to perform the will, and therefore the law must give him power *ratione officii*, while he is under age, to do everything which an executor of full age may do. Perhaps, however, as has been said, the law will not allow us to admit anyone as an attorney who is under age, nor to confess an action for any person, even though the party himself has enabled him; for if we could admit one attorney under age, we could (by the same reason) admit others. But an attorney is a common servant to the king's lieges and his office is of such highness that he might, on account of the frailty of his age, do much prejudice to the king's lieges, and because he is like a common servant an infant cannot be admitted as an attorney, and if he is it is error. But an executor who is an infant may confess an action brought against him as executor, for he is admitted as a person of full age. (Query this.) And if he wasted the goods, everyone has agreed that he shall be charged out of his own goods, for it is a wrong done by him. Therefore, if he has no goods, it seems to me that a *capias* shall issue against him, for the act is something done of his own wrong. But if perhaps he was attainted of forcible entry, a *capias* would not issue against him, for that is statute law and no infant is presumed punishable, and so he shall not be imprisoned. And by common law where an infant does wrong he shall be punished and treated like a man of full age: for instance, if he disseises me, he shall be driven to answer. Likewise if he commits felony and murder he shall be hanged, provided some discretion can be adjudged in him. Likewise of a lunatic: if it may appear that he had knowledge or memory when he did the act, he shall be hanged. Thus at various times the disablement may by discretion be avoided and the party treated like another person. So here, the disablement of this infant from making the release effectual is avoided, inasmuch as the testator is presumed to have adjudged discretion in him to be

appent de charger les dettors le testatour et discharge eux cibien per releas come acquittance. Et issint il [est] ajudge come person de pleine age, en quel case son releas serra bon barre. Et il tient que donquez le done des biens est bon per luy.

Fitzherbert. Non certes, quar il nad cy graunde power en auters biens come il ad in ses proper biens, et uncore il ne poit doner ses biens propers.

Norwich. Est agree que il ne poit eux forfeter, ex quo ne poit eux doner: ad quod non fuit responsum.

[B]

BL MS Harley 1691, fo. 141v.

Det fuit port per B. come executour, le defendant plede que le plaintife relessa etc., le plaintife dit que il fuit deinz age al temps del relez fait.

Brudnell, Inglefild et *Shelley.* Ceo est bone relez, quar il ad son power de executorshipe per le confidence quel le testatour avoit in luy, et quaunt le testatour fait le enfant son executour il done a luy power pur distributer lez biens per son discretion, et pur ceo sil done lez biens son testatour in almez pur le alme son testatour durant son nonage il navera aprez action de detinewe, nient obstant que son testatour fuit in dett in xx. li. per obligation de quel il navoit ascun conusanz devaunt, quar quaunt enfant fait chos per reason dun office ou power que est done a luy ceo luy liera. Quar si un fait un infant son bailyff et done a luy power et authorite pur faire leases pur terme dez ans et il fait accordaunt, ceo luy liera et son master auxi. Ou si le darren volunte soit que un B. vendera sa terre, et B. vende sa terre esteant deins age, ceo est bon. Issint si un infaunt per reason dun letter de attorney delyver possession in lew dun auter, ceo est bone, quar ceux chosez il fait per reason de son office et in auter droit. Auxi chescun voille agreer sil receava le dett et fait de ceo acquitance que ceo est bone, uncore in debt sur obligation un payment saunz acquittaunce nest ple, et quant acquitaunce serra monstre issewe ne poit estre prise sur le payment, mez si cell acquitaunce soit son fait ou nemi, et auter melior discharge dun obligation home ne poit aver forsque acquitaunce ou relez, et cestui que ad power come executour a distributer lez bienz son testatour ad auxi bone power pur relesser le dewty son testatour. Peradventure serra bone cause in conscienz, ou pur ceo que est cy bone ou melior a luy pur

his executor, to which office it belongs to charge the testator's debtors and discharge them both by release and acquittance. So he is adjudged as a person of full age, in which case his release shall be a good bar. And he therefore held that the gift of the goods by him is good.

FITZHERBERT. Surely not, for he has not so great a power in another's goods as he has in own goods, and yet he may not give his own goods.

Norwich. It is agreed that he cannot forfeit them; and hence he cannot give them. (To this there was no answer given.)

B

Undated.[1]

Debt was brought by B. as executor; the defendant pleaded that the plaintiff released etc.; the plaintiff said he was under age at the time when the release was made.

BRUDENELL [C.J.], ENGLEFIELD and SHELLEY. This is a good release, for he has his power of executorship through the confidence which the testator had in him, and when the testator made the infant his executor he gave him power to distribute the goods by his discretion, and therefore if during his infancy he gives his testator's goods in alms for his testator's soul he shall not afterwards have an action of detinue, even though his testator was indebted in £20 by a bond whereof he had no previous knowledge; for when an infant does something by reason of an office or power which is given him, this will bind him. For if someone makes an infant his bailiff and gives him power and authority to make leases for term of years, and he does so accordingly, this will bind him and his master also. Or if the last will is that B. shall sell his land, and B. sells his land while under age, this is good. Likewise if an infant by reason of a letter of attorney delivers possession instead of someone else, this is good; for he does these things by reason of his office and in another's right. Also, everyone will agree that if he receives a debt and makes an acquittance for it, this is good, and yet in debt on a bond a payment without acquittance is no plea, and when an acquittance is to be shown issue may not be joined upon the payment, but only as to whether this acquittance is his deed or not; and one cannot have a better discharge from a bond than an acquittance or release, and he who has power as executor to distribute his testator's goods also has good power to release his testator's due. Perhaps it would be a good case in conscience, whether it is not as good (if not better) for him to discharge

[1] The text follows immediately after the Exchequer Chamber case of 1527 printed as YB Trin. 19 Hen. VIII, fo. 9, pl. 4. There is then a blank at the foot of the page, and on fo. 142 begins a series of cases dated Mich. 26 Hen. VIII (1534), printed below, pp. 431–436, nos. 6–11.

discharger le dett que pur ceo prendre, et pur ceo le relez semble bone. Issint dun feme covert ou moygne professe que sont executourz.

Fitzharbart fuit al contrary.

[2]

BL MS Harley 1691, fo. 132v.

En formedon le tenant voche, le voche fuit essone, al jour de lessoyne le voche fait defaut, et le tenant auxi, et ajuge que petit cape serra agarde vers le tenaunt, quar per son defaut il ad perdew son vocher et issint le voche dismise a toutz jours: et ceo en le Comen Place circa xxiiii. H. 8.

[3]

BL MS Harley 1691, fo. 123.

De termino Michaelis anno regni Regis Henrici 8. xxv^{to}.

Un H. vende all auter xx. arbres et covenant ovesque luy per indenture que il avera et caria eux hors de sa terre saunz interruption de ascun home, per [que le] vende eux succida et voille eux importare, et le parson clayme de luy dismez pur lez arbres et sua citation en le court christien vers [le] vende pur eux, et le vende port brefe de covenant verz H.

Norwiche, Juge, et *Shelley*, que laction ne gist, quar ceux sont dues de comen droit. Et ceo est charge que accruist aprez le vende, et donques il nest oblige pur discharger de ascun charge mez de tielx queux sont claymes dun title que commensa avaunt le vende. Et semble al case que si jeo enfeffe un ovesque garrante, le feoffe devie, et le feme le feoffe port brefe de dower, le heire le feoffe ne vouchera le feoffor en ceo brefe pur ceo que le title de dower accrua aprez le garrante. Et semble al case 3 H. 7. fo. [*blank*] lou un fuit oblige pur faire done in taile dun acre discharge, unquore un seignorie serra perenter le donour et le done, et lobligation ne serra forfett, quar ceo fuit chos que accruist per operation del ley.

Mez *Fitzharbart* fuit de contrary oppinion, quar il dit que le dit H. duist perimpleshe son covenant accordaunt a son indenture.

the debt as to take it, and therefore the release seems good. Similarly of a married woman or professed monk who are executors.

FITZHERBERT to the contrary.

2. ANON.

Common Pleas, c. 1532/33.

In formedon the tenant vouched; the vouchee was essoined; at the essoin day the vouchee made default, and the tenant also; and it was adjudged that a petit *cape* should be awarded against the tenant, for by his default he has lost his voucher and so the vouchee is dismissed for ever. This was in the Common Place around 24 Hen. VIII.

3. ANON.

Common Pleas, Mich. 1533.

One H. sold twenty trees to someone else and covenanted with him by indenture that he should have them and carry them away from his land without interruption by anyone, and so the vendee felled them and wanted to carry them away, and the parson claimed tithes from him for the trees and sued a citation in the court christian against the vendee for them; and the vendee brought a writ of covenant against H.

NORWICH [C.J.] and SHELLEY, held that the action did not lie, for these are due by common right. This is a charge which accrued after the sale, and therefore he is not bound to discharge him in respect of any charges other than those which are claimed under a title which commenced before the sale. It is like the case where I enfeoff someone with warranty, and the feoffee dies, and the feoffee's wife brings a writ of dower: the feoffee's heir shall not vouch the feoffor in this writ, because the title of dower accrued after the warranty. It is like the case in 3 Hen. VII, fo. [4],[1] where someone was bound to make a gift in tail of an acre discharged, and yet there was a lordship between the donor and the donee, and the bond was not forfeited, for that was something which accrued by operation of law.

But FITZHERBERT was of a contrary opinion, for he said that the said H. should perform his covenant in accordance with his indenture.

---

[1] YB Trin. 3 Hen. VII, fo. 4, pl. 14, *arguendo*.

[4]

BL MS Harley 1691, ff. 123v–124 (dated Mich. 1533).

Un J. fuit oblige a un G. en un obligation sur tiel condition, que si le dit J. delivera al dit G. toutz charterz et munimentz et toutz auterz biens queux il ou ascun a son use ad in possession queux fueront al un B., testatour lavantdit G., que adonques etc. Et le dit G. port action de det sur le obligation, et le dit J. dit quil ne null a son use ad ascun charterz, munimentz ou biens lavantdit B. son testatour. Ore le question: sil avera ceo ple enconter ceo condition, ou sil serra estoppe per le dit condition adire que il nad ascunz?

Et fuit dit per *Shelley* que ceo nest ascun estoppell, quar chescun estoppell est propement per operation del ley, et le operation del ley reducera chescun choce a un perfection, et chescun perfection fait un certente, et donques en ceo case nest ascun certen chose per le quel il serra estoppe, et donques un ne serra estoppe mez pur reason dun chose certeyne. Et en ceo case le condition est cest, que il delivera toutz muniment[z] et charterx etc., issint que ceo paroll toutz ne comprehenda ascun certente. Et pur ceo si le condition soit que sil enfeoffa le oblige de toutz sez terrs deinz le counte de M. que adonques etc., ore en action de det il dirra que il navoit ascun terre deinz mesme le counte, causa qua supra. Issint serra si per indenture home bargaine sa terre et le vendour covenaunt per mesme le fait pur enfeoffer le vende per tiel jour del terre discharge de toutz executions, joyntures ou dowerz et auterz tielx incombrances, ore sil ne purroit pleder in brefe de covenaunt que il ne fuit ascun execution, joyntures ou dowers issauntes dez dits terres il serra a graunde mischefe, quar poit estre que il ne fuit ascun tiel charge et donques sil ne ceo pleder il serra a graunde mischeyf, quar donques chescun sur tiel indenture purroit aver action de covenaunt lou lauter ne enfrenda ascun covenaunt. Mez si le condition soit que si lobligour enfeoffa le plaintife de son maner de D. avaunt tiel jour que adonques etc., ore en action de dett il ne dira que il navoit ascun tiel maner, quar la il luy estoppa per le condition, quar le condition est reduse sur certen poynt, scilicet sil luy enfeoffe de son maner etc., issint que ceo paroll maner est certen. Issint en semblable casez etc. Et il dit que nient obstant que ceo paroll toutz en plusors cases est dun substaunce ou dun chose nest uncore si le dit paroll toutz ad relation a un nichill, la tout serra nichill. Sicome jeo done a vouz toutz lez denerz en ma burse, ou toutz mez terres deins Engleterre, ore si jeo navoit ascun denerz deinz ma burse ou si jeo navoy ascun terres deinz Engleterre ore le dit paroll toutz serra nichil, pur ceo quil ad relation a lez denerz ou terrez lou ne sont ascun tielz. Et il prist diversite lou condition serra dit impossible et ou nemi. Quar il ne serra dit james impossible mez lou il [*fo. 124*] appiert per lez parolx del

4. SAYNTPOLL v. CONYERS

Common Pleas, Mich. 1533. Also reported by Pollard, above, p. 259, no. 30.
Record: CP 40/1079, m. 612 (noted above, p. 259).

One J. was bound to one G. in a bond upon this condition, that if the said J. should deliver to the said G. all charters and muniments and all other goods which he (or anyone to his use) had in possession which belonged to one B., testator of the aforesaid G., then [the bond would be void]. And the said G. brought an action of debt upon the bond, and the said J. said that neither he nor anyone to his use had any charters, muniments or goods of the aforesaid B. his testator. The question now is: shall he have this plea, contrary to the condition, or shall he be estopped by the said condition from saying that he has none?

It was said by SHELLEY that this is no estoppel, for every estoppel is properly by operation of law, and the operation of the law reduces everything to a perfection, and every perfection makes a certainty. However, in this case there is no certain thing whereby he could be estopped, and one shall not be estopped except by reason of something certain. And in this case the condition is that he should deliver all muniments and charters etc., so that this word 'all' does not comprehend any certainty. If the condition were to enfeoff the obligee of all his lands in the county of M., in an action of debt he could say that he had no land within the same county, for the above reason. So shall it be if someone bargains his land by indenture, and the vendor covenants by the same deed to enfeoff the vendee by such and such a day of the land discharged of all executions, jointures, dowers and other such encumbrances, he would be at a great mischief if he could not plead in a writ of covenant that there were no executions, jointures or dowers issuing from the said lands, for it may be that there was no such charge and therefore if he could not plead it he would be at a great mischief, for then everyone could have an action of covenant upon such an indenture where the other party had not broken any covenant. But if the condition is that the obligor should enfeoff the plaintiff of his manor of de Dale before such and such a day, in an action of debt he may not say that there is no such manor, for there he has estopped himself by the condition, inasmuch as the condition is reduced to a certain point, namely if he should enfeoff him of his manor etc., so that this word 'manor' is certain. Likewise in similar cases etc. And he said that even though this word 'all' is in many cases of one substance or of one thing, it is nevertheless not so if the said word 'all' has relation to a nothing, for there everything shall be nothing. For instance if I give you all the coins in my purse, or all my lands in England, and I have no coins in my purse, or I have no lands in England, the said word 'all' means 'nothing', because it refers to the coins or lands where there are no such things. And he took a distinction where the condition shall be called impossible and where not. For it shall never be called impossible except where it appears

condition que est chos impossible. Sicome le condition soit que jeo fra un meason en le aire ou que jeo alera de ycy a Rome in un jour, quar ceux appieront impossible pur faire. Mez si le condition soit que jeo granta al oblige xx. s. de rent dont estrange est seisi, ceo nest impossible condition, uncore prima facie appiert que jeo ne purra granter un rent dont auter est seisi, mez <poit issint estre >[1] jeo puisse purchaser ceo rent et donques a luy graunter, et issint la est un possibilite. Et issint est diversite.

Inglefeld a mesme lentente. Et dit que lentente et le meaning dez parties serra construe en chescun case [de] condition, et donques lentent dez parties ycy ne fuit auter mez que lobligour duist deliver al oblige lez ditz chartres etc. sil avoit ascunz. Et a prover que lintent serra construe le liver est que si un ad 3. feoffees de son terre et est oblige en un obligation sur condition que si sez feoffes graunteront al oblige xx. s. de rent que adonques etc., ore si deux de lez feoffes graunteront un rent a luy uncore le condition nest performe, et uncore lez parolx del condition sont performes, quar sez feoffes ount graunt a luy un rent. Mesme le ley si le condition soit que le obligour enffefera le plaintife del son maner de D. et il fait feoffment del parcell del maner et puis luy enfeoffa del remenant, uncore le condition nest performe, et uncore il avoit luy enfeoffe del maner, quar il est maner nient obstant le feoffment del parcell. Et ceo <ne purra >[2] estre estoppel, quar <il nad confesse que il ad ascun chartres etc. mez implicative, et donques un implication ne serra estoppel >[3] mez lou il puissoit aver plede le chos imply en le primer action. Come en brefe de measne le defendant plede Nient distrayne in son defaut, ore le acquitall est confesse per implication. Issint en brefe de garrante de charters, il dit que le plaintife nest implede, ore le garrante est confesse per implication. Et pur ceo donques il serra conclude adire que il ne duit luy acquitare ou que il ne doit a luy garranter per lez ditz implications pur ceo que il poit eux aver plede en le primer action. Mez sil ne poit aver eux plede en le primer action, donques ne serra estoppel. Sicome le defendant en brefe de detinew pria garnishement et le garnishe dit que lez conditions sont performes de son parte, et ceo trove vers le garnishe, per que le plaintife ad lyverie del fait et port action de det verz le garnishe, il pledera Nient son fait, uncore per implication fuit confesse per son ple en le brefe de detinewe que ceo fuit son fait, mez pur ceo que il ne poit ceo aver plede en le brefe de detinew ceo ne serra estoppel.

---

[1] *Del.*
[2] *Altered from* serra.
[3] *Written twice, and partly a third time, but del.*

by the words of the condition that it is an impossible thing. For instance, if the condition is that I should build a house in the air, or that I should go from here to Rome in one day; for these are evidently impossible to do. But if the condition is that I should grant the obligee 20s. of rent whereof a stranger is seised, this is not an impossible condition, even though *prima facie* it appears that I cannot grant a rent whereof another is seised; but it may be so if I purchase this rent and then grant it to him, and thus there is a possibility. Thus there is a distinction.

ENGLEFIELD to the same purpose. And he said that the intention and meaning of the parties shall be construed in every case of a condition, and the intention of the parties here was nothing other than that the obligor should deliver the said charters etc. to the obligee if he had any. To prove that the intention shall be construed, the book says that if someone has three feoffees of his land and is bound in a bond upon condition that if his feoffees should grant to the obligee 20s. of rent then [the bond would be void], and two of the feoffees grant a rent to him, the condition is nevertheless not performed: and yet the words of the condition are performed, for his feoffees have granted him a rent. The law is the same if the condition is that the obligor should enfeoff the plaintiff of his manor of Dale, and he makes a feoffment of part of the manor and later enfeoffs him of the rest, the condition is nevertheless not performed, and yet he has enfeoffed him of the manor, for it is a manor despite the feoffment of the part. This cannot be an estoppel, for he has not confessed that he has any charters etc. except by implication (*implicativè*), and an implication shall not be an estoppel except where he could have pleaded the implied thing in the first action. Thus in a writ of mesne, if the defendant pleads 'Not distrained in his default', the acquittal is confessed by implication. Likewise in a writ of warranty of charters, if he says that the plaintiff has not been impleaded, the warranty is confessed by implication. Therefore he shall be concluded by the said implications from saying that he ought not to acquit him or to warrant him, because he could have pleaded these things in the first action. But if he could not have pleaded them in the first action it shall not be an estoppel. Thus if the defendant in a writ of detinue prays garnishment, and the garnishee says that the conditions have been performed on his side, and this is found against the garnishee, so that the plaintiff has livery of the deed and brings his action of debt against the garnishee, he may plead *Non est factum*, and yet by implication it was confessed by his plea in the writ of detinue that it was his deed; but because he could not have pleaded it in the writ of detinue it shall not be an estoppel.

[5]

[A]

BL MS Harley 1691, ff. 124v–126 (Mich. 1533).

Un executour port brefe de accompte dez arrerages dues a son testatour, le defendant plede Nient son recevour etc., et trove encontra luy, scilicet le defendant, per que il est agarde pur accompter, et trove en arrerages et mis en execution, et puis le testament del executour revoke et adnull avant le ordynary pur ceo que le testatour fuit un ideott et fole naterall, issint que il navoit ascun reason ou jugement pur faire testament, et cestui que fuit en execution sua audita querela sur son matter. Nota que il fuit argue en ceo cas que il ne soit forsque deux natures dun audita querela dones per le Regester, lun sur matter en fait ou escript, lauter sur un surmise: scilicet sur matter en fait ou escript come sur release et tiel sembleable faitz, sur un surmise come lou le conusor en estatute marchant ou estatute staple fait feoffement as diverz et le conusee sua execution vers lun dez feoffes, il avera audita querela pur charger chescun pur sa portion. Mesme la ley lou un recover sur un vocher ou lou le tenaunt vochera un D., garde dun H., en brefe de dower et recovera. Issint serra lou le conuse delyvera al conusour le reconusanz en lew dacquitaunce, et puis happa le possession del reconusanz arere et suit execution, le conusour avera audita querela. Issint si le reconise purchas lez terres le reconisour puis le reconusans fait, et fait feoffement, et puis le jour incure et le reconuse sua execution vers le feoffe et ad execution, le feoffe avera audita querela: 20 E. 3. Mez en chescun cas lou un ad jour in court pur pleder tiel defesaunz et ne ceo plede, il navera jamez audita querela. Sicome cestui que recovera sua execution apres le anne et jour per scire facias, et le vicount luy retourne somone, et il fait defaut, per que execution est agarde sur son defaut, audita querela ne gist, causa qua supra. Mez nota si le reconusor fait feoffement as dyverz et retient parcell de sa terre en sa mayne, le reconuse suera execution de ceo que remayne en son mayne solement sil voylle <et il navera audita querela >[1] pur faire chescun dez feoffez contributory al charge pur ceo que le charge fuit fait per luy mesme. Mez cell audita querela est foundu sur un acte que fuit fait en le spirituall ley, scilicet le disanulment et disproving del testament, issint que nest ascun audita querela sur tyel matter purvew per le Regester, issint que en ceo cas le brefe fayla.

---

[1] *Written twice.*

5. CARVANELL v. MOWER

Common Pleas and Exchequer Chamber, Mich. 1533. Also reported in Port, p. 74 (see headnote there). Record of the account: KB 27/1061, m. 74 (noted below); Rast. Ent. 16v.

A

An executor brought a writ of account for arrears due to his testator; the defendant pleaded 'Not his receiver etc.'; and it was found against him, namely the defendant, whereby he was awarded to account; and he was found in arrear and put in execution. Aferwards the executor's testament was revoked and annulled before the ordinary because the testator was an idiot and a natural fool, so that he had no reason or judgment to make a testament, and the person who was in execution sued an *audita querela* upon his matter. Note that it was argued in this case that there are only two kinds of *audita querela* given by the Register, one upon matter in fact or writing, and the other upon a surmise: namely upon matter in fact or writing, as upon a release and such like deeds, or upon a surmise, as where the conusor in a statute merchant or statute staple makes a feoffment to various persons and the conusee sues execution against one of the feoffees, he shall have *audita querela* to charge each of the others for his share. The law is the same where someone recovers upon a voucher or where the tenant vouches one D., ward of one H., in a writ of dower, and recovers. So it is where the conusee delivers the recognizance to the conusor in lieu of an acquittance, and afterwards gets possession of the recognizance again and sues execution, the conusor shall have *audita querela*. Likewise if the reconusee purchases the reconusor's lands after making the recognizance, and makes a feoffment, and afterwards the day arrives and the reconusee sues execution against the feoffee and has execution, the feoffee shall have *audita querela*: 20 Edw. III.[1] But in every case where one has a day in court to plead such defeasance and does not plead it, he shall never have *audita querela*. Similarly if he who recovered sues execution by *scire facias* after the year and day, and the sheriff returns him summoned, and he makes default, so that execution is awarded upon his default, *audita querela* does not lie, for the above reason. But note that if the reconusor makes a feoffment to various persons and retains part of his land in his hands, the reconusee may sue execution only of that which remains in his hands, if he wishes, and may not have an *audita querela* to make each of the feoffees contributory to the charge, because the charge was made by himself. But this *audita querela* is founded on an act which was done in the spiritual law, namely the annulment and disproving of the testament, and there is no *audita querela* provided upon such facts in the Register, and so in this case the writ fails.

[1] Perhaps Mich. 20 Edw. III, Fitz. Abr., *Audita querela*, pl. 30.

Mez a ceo fuit respondew que le chaunceler per lestatute W. 2. purroit framer un brefe sur le cas lou tiel matter nad estre view avaunt.

Et auxi fuit dit que ceo audita querela est ore pur defetter le jugement done in ceo court, et lestatute est quod judicia reddita in curia domini regis non adnihillentur nisi per errorem vel attinctam, et issint le brefe ne gist.

Mez a ceo fuit respondew que le nature de ceo brefe nest pur defeter le primer jugement mez il est pur defeter le execution, et affirme per le suite del dit[1] le primer jugement. Mez le nature dun brefe [*fo. 125*] de errour, atteynte, et brefe de disceyte, est pur defeter le primer jugement. Et auxi le dit estatute que dit quod judicia reddita in curia domini regis etc. est en lestatute de W. 2, ca. 5, de advocationibus ecclesiarum, et est entendu solement lou un recovera un advowson verz particuler tenauntes, quar jugement[s] serront defetz saunce ascun de lez dites breffes in plusours cases, come per fauxifier et auterment.

Et fuit dit que le testament dun ideotte est voyde et nemi voydeable, quar un ideotte nad ascun volunte per reason. Mez il ad un volunte de nature, come il ad volunte pur manger et boyer et pur deviner,[2] et pur eschew tielx choses queux sont a lui prejudiciall, et issint ad chescun brute beaste, quar ceux sont voluntes dones a eux per nature mez nemi de ascun reason. Et chescun testament et darren volunte est ordeyne solement pur le salvation et weale del alme le testatour, et donques un ideott natura nad ascun reason ou conusaunce quel chos serra benefycyall pur sa alme et quel nemi, et pur ceo il ne purra faire testament nient plus que un home de non compos mentis. Mez enfaunt al age reasonable, ou feme covert per licence de son baron, poit faire testamentes quar ilz ount le use de reason.

Per *Shelley*, *Fitzharbarte* et *Norwiche* le brefe gist, quar primerment le brefe daccompt fuit fowndew sur deux causez, lun temporall, lauter espirituall, scilicet le fesaunce del executor et le probate del testament. Et donques quant le testament est disprove lun cause quel meyntena son action est defete, issint que parcell del foundation de son action faylla, et issint tout laction est perryche, issint que cestuy que fuit executour ne purra ore aver execution, quar son authorite est disprove et defete per le adnullment del testament. Et semble al case lou un fait deux testamentes, et le primer testament est prove et lexecutour port action et recover, et ad le parte in execution, et puis lauter est prove, ore cestui que est in execution avera audita querela. Et issint en chescun sembleable case. Mez si cestui que fuit condemne ust pay lez arrerages et puis le testament ust este disprove, cestui que paya lez denerz navera ascun remedy pur lez denerz que il avoit pay. Mez cestui a que lordynary aprez avoit committe le administration avera brefe daccompt vers cestui que fuit executour

---

[1] *Apparently* d̄ *but evidently a slip.*
[2] *Reading unclear.*

However, to this it was answered that, by the Statute of Westminster II,[1] the chancellor may frame a writ upon the case where the matter in question has not been seen before.

It was also said that this *audita querela* here is to undo a judgment given in this court, and the statute says that 'judgments given in the court of the lord king shall not be annulled save by error or attaint' (*quod judicia reddita in curia domini regis non adnihillentur nisi per errorem vel attinctam*),[2] and therefore the writ does not lie.

However, to this it was answered that the nature of this writ is not to undo the first judgment but to undo the execution, and by suing it the first judgment is affirmed, whereas the nature of a writ of error, attaint, and deceit, is to undo the first judgment. Also the said statute which says *quod judicia reddita in curia domini regis etc.* is in the statute of Westminster II, c. 5, *de advocationibus ecclesiarum*, and is only to be understood where someone recovers an advowson against particular tenants, for judgments may be undone without any of the said writs in various cases, as by falsifying and in other ways.

It was said that the testament of an idiot is void and not voidable, for an idiot has no will by reason, though he has a will of nature, for instance a will to eat and drink and [marry],[3] and to eschew such things as are prejudicial to him: and so has every brute beast, for these are wills given to them by nature but not by any reason. But every testament and last will is ordained solely for the salvation and weal of the testator's soul, and therefore an idiot by nature has no reason or knowledge of what shall be beneficial for his soul and what not, and therefore he cannot make a testament, any more than a man of unsound mind (*non compos mentis*). But an infant at a reasonable age, or a married woman with her husband's permission, may make testaments, for they have the use of reason.

According to SHELLEY, FITZHERBERT and NORWICH [C.J.], the writ lies; for the writ of account was at first based upon two causes, one temporal and the other spiritual, namely the appointment of the executor and the probate of the testament. Therefore when the testament is disproved one of the causes which supported his action is defeated, so that part of the foundation of his action fails, and therefore the whole action has perished, so that the person who was executor cannot now have execution, for his authority is disproved and undone by the annnulment of the testament. It is like the case where someone makes two testaments, and the first testament is proved and the executor brings an action and recovers, and has the party in execution, and afterwards the other is proved: now the person who is in execution may have *audita querela*. Likewise in every simiar case. But if the person who was condemned had paid the arrears and then the testament had been disproved, the person who paid the money would have no remedy for the money which he had paid. But the person to whom the ordinary had afterwards committed the administration may have

---

[1] Westminster II, c. 24, *In consimili casu* (*SR* i. 83).   [2] Westminster II, c. 5 (*SR* i. 75).
[3] Reading unclear. But cf. similar passage in Port, p. 131, pl. 89.

et receva lez denerz. Mez en ceo case lexecution de son corps est auxi forte si come il ust pay lez denerz, quar le corps nest pris in satisfaction mez est pris ad satisfaciendum. Et accordant a ceo vide 33 H.6, fo. [*blank*] en brefe de det. Et si un soit seisi de terre in droit sa feme et fait feoffement, et puis devorce est ewe enter eux, et le feme port cui ante devorcium et recovera, et puis le baron suit appell et le matrymoney est affirme, et le baron enter en la terre, ore fuit dit que le feoffe serra restore a le terre arrere durant le vie le baron, quar le feoffe estoppe le baron durant son vie per son feoffement. Si un soit en execution sur un condempnation et puis purchase un maner a que le plaintife que recovera est villen regardaunt, ore le court dischargera le partie dexecution. Issint serra si le plaintife que recovera fait cestui que est en execution son executour, et devie, quar en ceux cases nest ascun partie que puit aver le execution et serra encontra reason in ceo case que il demurra [*fo. 125v*] en prison: quar admitt que cestui que est en execution voille payer lez denerz, est nul home que purra eux recever, quar lexecutour ne purra quar ore il nest executour, et lordynary ne purra quar il est estraunge al jugement, et pur ceo serra reason que il serra discharge.

Inglefyld dit que le audita querela ne gist, quar il dit que en chescun cas lou home puissoit aver plede le matter sur quel son audita querela est grounde et aver jour en court pur aver ceo plede, et nad ceo plede, il navera jamez audita querela pur ceo qil serra arrecte son folly que il ne ceo plede. Issint vide 21 E.3. Et pur ceo si action de trespas soit port vers un et le plaintife relessa all defendant pendant le brefe et puis le defendant plede ovesque le plaintife et ne prist advantage de ceo al prochein contynuaunce mez soit trove pur le plaintife, le defendant navera james audita querela sur son releez, causa qua supra. Et issint en auterz tielx sembleable cases. Issint en ceo case le plaintife ycy puissoit aver plede en le brefe daccompt que le testatour non constituit eum executorem, nient obstant le probate avaunt lordinary, auxi bien que il dira que il murrust intestate nient obstant le probate avaunt le lordynary. Mez il navera directe traverz al testament, quar ceo serra trye per le certificate lordynary, et donques lordynary ne voile certyfyer contrary a ceo que il ad admitte avaunte. Issint que il puissoit aver plede en le dit brefe de accompt que le testatour fuit un ideotte nient obstant le probate avaunt lordynary. Mez il ne ceo pleda, mez pleda que il ne fuit son recevour pur accountant, admittaunt que le plaintife in le brefe de accompt fuit loyalment executour, issint que en apres il serra estoppe adire que il ne fuit executour. Et auxi graunde mischyfe insuera sil serra dismise, quar puit

a writ of account against the person who was executor and received the money. In this case, however, the execution of his body is as strong as if he had paid the money, for the body is not taken in satisfaction but is taken in order to make satisfaction (*ad satisfaciendum*). In accordance with this see 33 Hen. VI, fo. [47],[1] in a writ of debt. And if someone is seised of land in right of his wife, and makes a feoffment, and then a divorce is had between them, and the wife brings *cui ante divorcium* and recovers, and then the husband sues an appeal and the matrimony is affirmed, and the husband enters in the land, it was said that the feoffee shall be restored to the land again during the husband's lifetime, for the feoffee shall estop the husband during his lifetime by his feoffment. If someone is in execution upon a condemnation, and then I purchase a manor to which the plaintiff who recovered is a villein regardant, the court shall discharge the party from execution. So shall it be if the plaintiff who recovers makes the person who is in execution his executor, and dies, for in these cases there is no party who can have the execution, and it would be against reason in this case that he should remain in prison. For, admit that the person who is in execution is willing to pay the money, there is no one who can receive it: the executor cannot, for he is not now executor, and the ordinary cannot, for he is a stranger to the judgment: and therefore it is right that he should be discharged.

ENGLEFIELD said that the *audita querela* did not lie, for he said that in every case where someone could have pleaded the matter whereon his *audita querela* is grounded, and had a day in court when he could have pleaded it, and he has not pleaded it, he shall never have *audita querela*, because it shall be reckoned his foolishness that he did not plead it. Similarly see 21 Edw. III.[2] Therefore if an action of trespass is brought against someone and the plaintiff releases to the defendant while the writ is pending, and then the defendant pleads with the plaintiff and does not take advantage of the release at the next continuance, but it is found for the plaintiff, the defendant shall never have *audita querela* upon his release, for the above reason. Likwise in other similar cases. Thus in this case the plaintiff here could have pleaded in the writ of account that the testator did not appoint him executor (*non constituit eum executorem*), notwithstanding the probate before the ordinary, just as he could say that he died intestate notwithstanding the probate before the ordinary. But he may not have a direct traverse to the testament, for that shall be tried by the ordinary's certificate, and the ordinary will not certify contrary to what he has already admitted. Thus he could have pleaded in the said writ of account that the testator was an idiot, notwithstanding the probate before the ordinary. He did not plead that, however, but pleaded that he was not his receiver in an accountable way, thus admitting that the plaintiff in the writ of account was lawfully executor, and so he shall be estopped afterwards from saying that he was not executor. Also great mischief would ensue if he should be dismissed,

---

[1] *Blakeman* v. *Halman* (1454) YB Mich. 33 Hen. VI, fo. 47, pl. 32.
[2] YB Hil. 21 Edw. III, fo. 13, pl. 14.

estre que lexecutour voille suer appell et affirme le testament arere, et donques sil serra ore dismisse et le testament soit auterfoytes affirme il navera jamez auter brefe daccompte.

Fitzharbart, Chefe Justice, a mesme lentente. Et il prist diversite lou lez espiritualx juges certyfiont un chos per reason dun certificat[1] a eux per lez temporalx juges et lou ilz certifiont choce saunce ascun certyficat directe a eux, quar en le primer case si tyell certificat soit fait ceo liera en ceo court, mez en lauter case nemi. Come si basterde soit certyfy per levesque lou le temporall [court] escrye a eux, ceo estoppe chescun. Mez si le baron et feme sont devorsez, le baron devie, et le feme port brefe de dower, ore lauter ne purra luy estopper per tiel devorce mez pleda le devorce et demande [*fo. 126*] jugement si dower duist aver. Et auxi il dit que audita querela la nest meyntenable sur ascun matter mez lou tiel matter purporta en luy ascun matter de discharge, come sur releez ou defesanz. Et pur ceo le liver est 28 E. 3, lou un executour sua execution hors dun estatute fait a son testatour, et cestui verz que lexecution fuit sue porta audita querela pur ceo que il sua execution come executour lou il ne fuit fait unques executour, et ajuge que le brefe ne gist, quar cel matter ne purporta ascun cause de discharge. Et si un garrante ovesque assetz soit plede in barre en un formedone, le plaintife dit que riens per discent et ceo trove encontra luy, il ne serra aprez [oye][2] pur dedire le fait son auncestor per que le garrante commensa. Mez auterment serra si son ple ust este trove pur luy, scilicet que il navoit riens per discent. Issint serra si executourz pledont Pleinment administre et ceo trove encontra eux, scilicet que ilz ount assetz, ore ilz serront estoppes pur pleder auterfoitz Nient executourz. Mez sil ust este trove pur eux que ilz ount pleynement adminster, donques en auter action ilz serront receu adire Nient executourz. Et issint il dit que en cell case, intant que son primer ple quel il plede en le dit brefe de accompt, scilicet Ne unques son recevour etc., fuit trove encontra luy, que ore il ne serra receu adire que il fuit ideot. Mez si le issue ust este trove pur luy, il ne serra per cel estoppe.

Auxi fuit dit per *Shelley* que si le baron et sa feme sount devorz que lissewe ewe enter eux serra dit bastard, et si apres le devorce soit repelle ou adnulle il serra mulier. Auxi si tenaunt in tayle discontinue le tayle et ad issue fyle, et devie, sa feme privyment enseynt ovesque fitz, et auncestor collaterall relessa ovesque garrante, et le garrante discende sur le file, et puis le fitz est nee, il confessera le garrante et ceo avoydera. Et auxi il [dit] que le temporall ley et lespirituall ley concurre, et lun nest contrariant a lauter, mez lun [ayde][3]

---

[1] *Altered from* certification.
[2] *Apparently written* ore.
[3] avoyd.

for it may be that the executor will sue an appeal and affirm the testament again, and if he were now dismissed and the testament were again affirmed he would never have another writ of account.

[FITZJAMES],[1] Chief Justice, to the same purpose. And he took a distinction where the spiritual judges certify something by reason of a certificate[2] to them by the temporal judges and where they certify something without any certificate directed to them; for in the former case if such a certificate is made it shall bind in this court, whereas in the other case it shall not. Thus if bastardy is certified by the bishop, where the temporal court has written to him, that estops everyone. But if a husband and wife are divorced, and the husband dies, and the wife brings a writ of dower, the other shall not estop her by such a divorce but may plead the divorce and demand judgment whether she ought to have dower. He also said that *audita querela* is not maintainable upon any matter except where the matter purports in itself some matter of discharge, as upon a release or defeasance. To this effect is the book in 28 Edw. III:[3] an executor sued execution out of a statute made to his testator, and the person against whom the execution was sued brought *audita querela* because he sued execution as executor whereas he was never made executor, it was adjudged that the writ did not lie, for this matter did not purport any cause of discharge. If a warranty with assets is pleaded in bar in a formedon, and the plaintiff says 'Nothing by descent', and it is found against him, he shall not afterwards be heard to deny the deed of his ancestor whereby the warranty commenced. But it would be otherwise if his plea had been found for him, namely that he had nothing by descent. So it would be if executors plead 'Fully administered' and this is found against them, namely that they have assets, they shall now be estopped from pleading on another occasion 'Not executors'. But if it had been found for them that they had fully administered, then in another action they would be received to say 'Not executors'. And so in this case he said that, since his first plea which he pleaded in the said writ of account, namely 'Never his receiver etc.', was found against him, he shall not now be received to say that he was an idiot. But if the issue had been found for him, he would not have been estopped by it.

It was also said by SHELLEY that if a husband and wife are divorced, the issue between them shall be called bastard, and if afterwards the divorce is repealed or annulled he shall be legitimate (*mulier*). Also if a tenant in tail discontinues the tail and has issue a daughter, and dies, his wife being secretly pregnant with a son, and a collateral ancestor releases with warranty, and the warranty descends upon the daughter, and then the son is born, he may confess the warrant and avoid it. He also said that the temporal law and the spiritual law concur, and the one is not opposed to the other, but each of them helps

[1] Wrongly described as Fitzherbert in the report. Since the report says above that Fitzherbert J. and Norwich C.J.C.P. were both in favour of the writ, it seems likely that this is Fitzjames C.J. Text C shows that there was a hearing in the Exchequer Chamber.

[2] Here meaning a writ directing them to make a certificate, i.e. a *certiorari*.

[3] YB Mich. 28 Edw. III, fo. 23, pl. 31.

lauter. Et pur ceo quant un [est] excommenge en spirituall ley et ne voylle obeyer, ilz certifierount ceo per significavit in le Chauncery et sur ceo issera un brefe de excommunicato capiendo. Issint serra si un soit atteynt de herisy, il ne purront faire execution de luy, mez luy mitter all roy et sur ceo issera brefe de heretico comburendo. Issint que en ceux cases le temporall ley ayda le espirituall ley. Issint de lauter parte, si bastardy soit allege in un le court temporall escriera all espirituall court pur ceo certifier. Issint ilz certifieront profession voyde et nient voyde etc. Issint que appiert per ceux casez que lun ley aydera lauter.

[B]

CUL MS. Ee. 6. 15, fo. 113 (Gilbert Gerrard's commonplace).

Ou un jugement serra defett per acte subsequent.

Come si home seisi en droit sa feme fist feofement de sa terre et aprez devorse est ewe perenter le baron et la feme et la feme port cui ante devorcium et recover, et devaunt execution le devorse est repelle, ore le jugement est avoyde per cest mater subsequent. Issint si le baron et feme port assise et recovere, et devaunt execution devorse est ewe, ore le jugement est avoyde. Issint est si home avoit yssue fyle et devie, sa feme privement ensaint ove fitz, et estrange abbate, et le fyle port assise de mortdancestor et recover, et devaunt execution fitz est nee, ore le jugement est avoyde per cest mater subsequent etc. Mesme la ley si tenant en taille especiall prist action de wast et recover, et devaunt execution il est tenant en taylle aprez possibilite etc., ore le jugement est avoyde. Quar ore est null en ceux cases que poit prie execution accordant all recovere etc.

Et le princypall case fuit anno 25. H. 8. en le Comen Banke lou executour port action daccompt et le defendant fuit ajuge daccompter, et auditours assignes, et trove en arrerages et fuit comytt al Flete, et remaine en execution, et aprez le testament fuit dysprove devant lordinare, et sur cest mater le defendant sue audita querela et avoit certiorare all ordynare hors del Chauncery, et ceo certyffie la et mys en le Comen Banke per mittimus etc. Quere si audita querela gist sur cest matter? Fuit bien argue la etc., et loppinion de *Shelley* [fuit] que gist assetz bien, et que per le mater subsequent, scilicet quant le testament est dysprow, que le jugement est avoyde. Et ceux cases devaunt fueront mys a prover ceo etc.

the other. Therefore when someone is excommunicated in the spiritual law and will not obey, they certify this by *significavit* in the Chancery and thereupon a writ *de excommunicato capiendo* shall issue. So shall it be if someone is attainted of heresy: they cannot make execution upon him, but they shall send him to the king and thereupon a writ *de haeretico comburendo* shall issue. So in these cases the temporal law helps the spiritual law. Likewise on the other side, if bastardy is alleged in someone the temporal court shall write to the spiritual court to certify it. Similarly they may certify whether a profession is void or not void etc. Thus it appears by these cases that each law helps the other.

B[1]

Where a judgment shall be undone by a subsequent act.

For instance, if someone seised in right of his wife makes a feoffment of her land and afterwards a divorce takes place between the husband and wife, and the woman brings *cui ante divorcium* and recovers, and before execution the divorce is repealed: the judgment is now avoided by this subsequent matter. Likewise if the husband and wife bring an assize and recover, and before execution a divorce takes place, the judgment is now avoided. So it is if someone has issue a daughter and dies, his wife secretly pregnant with a son, and a stranger intrudes, and the daughter brings an assize of mort d'ancestor and recovers, and before execution a son is born, the judgment is now avoided by this subsequent matter etc. The law is the same if tenant in tail special takes an action of waste and recovers, and before execution he becomes tenant in tail after possibility etc., the judgment is now avoided. For there is no one in these cases who can pray execution in accordance with the recovery etc.

The principal case was in the year 25 Hen. VIII in the Common Bench, where an executor brought an action of account and the defendant was adjudged to account, and auditors assigned, and he was found in arrear and was committed to the Fleet, and remained in execution, and afterwards the testament was disproved before the ordinary, and upon this matter the defendant sued an *audita querela* and had a *certiorari* to the ordinary out of the Chancery, and certified it there, and it was sent into the Common Bench by a *mittimus* etc. Does an *audita querela* lie upon such matter? It was well argued there etc., and the opinion of SHELLEY was that it lay well enough, and that the judgment is avoided by the subsequent matter, namely when the testament is disproved. The cases above were put to prove this etc.

---

[1] From Gilbert Gerrard's notebook. The first two cases are those put by Shelley J. in the last passage of the preceding text.

[C]

BL MS. Harley 1691, fo. 57v.

In Lexcheker Chamber devaunt toutz les justyces en le tearme de Sainct Michaell lan du raigne le Roy Henry le viii. 25, *Shelley*, Justice, reherce le case en le forme ensuant. Auterfoitz un More come executour a un Guysors port byll daccompt en Banke le Roy vers un Karavennell, clerke, et vers luy declare la in custodia mariscalli coment le defendant fuit rescevour son testator come de certen terres et par plusours mainz, et monstra par queux (come oportet), a que le defendant plede que ne fuit unques recevour le testator pur accompt render en le maner etc. Et sur ceo fueront a yssue, quell fuit trove vers le defendant, et jugemente sur ceo que il accomptera. Et auditors fueront assigne, devaunt queux il fuit trove en arrerages de viii.^{xx} li., pur queux il fuit committe al marshall ad satisfaciendum les deners. Et fuit en execution par le space de iiii anz, deinz quell temps le testamente le pleintife fuit adnulle en le spirituall court <et>[1] pur ceo que le dit Guysors, le testator, fuit un ideott nee. Et tout cest matter desouthe le sealle lordinare fuit certyfye en le Chauncerye, et sur ceo le defendant avoit un audita querela as justyces del dit banke ove un mittimus del dit certyficat. Et si laudita querela gysoit sur cest matter, ceo fuit le questyon.

Note from the record of the action of account

KB 27/1061, m. 74, Rooper.

On 11 October 1526 Thomas Mower of London, skinner, executor of John Gysours, citizen and skinner of London, prefers a bill of account against John Carvanell, clerk, as the testator's receiver from 24 June 1513 to 24 June 1523 in the parish of St Andrew Hubbard, Billingsgate ward. The defendant pleaded that various sums were received in performance of the last will of John Gysours, father of the plaintiff's testator, under which he was appointed guardian of the younger John Gysours, and traversed that he received the money *ad compotum reddendum*. The issue was tried before Fitzjames C.J. at the Guildhall on 28 May 1527 and found for the plaintiff, who was adjudged to account. The court appointed John Palmer and Edmund Page as auditors, though Page was subsequently replaced by Henry See. After several adjournments, Palmer and See took the account at Westminster on 28 January 1530. The account is set out in detail, and includes numerous allowances, such as £66. 17s. 4d. paid to Anne Gysours, widow

---

[1] *Sic but otiose.*

C

In the Exchequer Chamber before all the justices in Michaelmas term in the twenty-fifth year of the reign of King Henry VIII, SHELLEY, Justice, recited the case in the following manner. One Mower, as executor to one Gysours, previously brought a bill of account in the King's Bench against one Carvanell, clerk, and declared against him there in the custody of the marshal (*in custodia mariscalli*) that the defendant was his testator's receiver by various hands, as of certain lands, and showed by whose hands (as is needful); to which the defendant pleaded that he was never the testator's receiver for the purpose of rendering account in the manner alleged etc. Thereupon they were at issue, and it was found against the defendant, and judgment was thereupon given that he should account. Auditors were assigned, before whom he was found in arrears of eight score pounds, for which he was committed to the marshal in order to make satisfaction for the money. And he was in execution for the space of four years, within which time the plaintiff's testament was annulled in the spiritual court because the said Gysours, the testator, was a born idiot. All this matter was certified under the ordinary's seal into the Chancery, and thereupon the defendant had an *audita querela* to the justices of the said bench with a *mittimus* of the said certificate. And the question was: did the *audita querela* lie upon this matter?

Note from the record of the action of account

Coram rege roll, Mich. 18 Hen. VIII (1526).

[Continued from opposite page]

of John Gysours the elder, for maintenance. The auditors disallowed, as insufficient in law, 13s. 4d. given for bringing the letters notifying the defendant of Gysours' death and 20s. given to Anne Gysours because she was poor and had bestowed care on her husband. Final judgment was given for the plaintiff to recover £178. 10s. 4d. and for the defendant to remain in prison until the plaintiff was satisfied.

[6]

BL MS Harley 1691, ff. 142–143.

Ceo fuit argue per les justicez de Comen Banke M. 26. H. 8.

Le roy dona un advowson a un home et a sez heires males.

Ore *Shelley* dit que le done avera estate pur terme de sa vie et nemi estate in fe simple ne in taile, et prist diversite lou un voile luy conveyer estre heir a un estate tayle et lou a un estate in fee simple. Quar in le primer cas il covient conveier luy heir al donee et auxi all cestui que darren tenda estate, mez lou un voile luy conveyer estre heire al terre in fee simple sufficit sil luy conveya [estre][1] heire a cestui que darren morust seisi et ne fra ascun mention in son conveyaunce del primer purchaser. Et dit ouster que le graunt le roy serra pris pluis beneficiall pur le roy pur ceo que le roy est un corps pollityk et est le test de tout le comen wealle et pur ceo serra reason que in toutz chosez il ad un prerogatiffe. Et donques lentente le roy ne puit estre construe in ceo cas quele graunte avera fee simple, quar donques il ne voyle aver mis eux parolx males in le graunt, quar si serroit un fee simple donques le grauntee ceo avera auterment que le roy ceo a luy done, quar lez heires femalez ceo avera, quel est mere contrary al meninge le roy, et pur ceo il navera fe simple intant que le roy fuit deseave in son graunt et pur ceo le graunt serra dit voyde. Et pur ceo le graunt le roy in toutz casez serra construe pluis beneficiallement pur le roy. Come si le roy per le premisses dun fait done terre a un et a sez heires, et puis in le habendum il est a aver et tener pur terme de sa vie, ore le graunte navera estate forsque pur terme de sa vie, uncore si un comen persone fait tiel fait le feoffe avera fee simple. Issint si le roy infeoffa un ovesque garrante, le feoffe ne recovera in valewe sinon que parrolx de recompensation soit in le fait. Issint si le roy enfeoffa son villen, il nest my per cel infranchise, mez le roy nient obstant puit luy seiser come son villeyne. Et ou le roy est disceyve in son graunt le graunt est voyde. Come si un sua al roy per petition pur luy enfeoffer del maner de D., et dit in le petition que le maner ne valt forsque x. li. ou le maner valt xx. li., ore nient obstant que le roy luy done le dit maner accordant a son petition, si aprez soit trove per office que le maner vaut xx. li. le roy ceo resesera. Si le roy fait done in frankemariage ou done terres en frankealmoygne ou done terres as deux et a les heires de lour deux corps, tielx dones sont bone mez il ne voit ceo admitter. Mes il dit que, admitte que tielx dones sont bones, uncore ceux ne provera cel case, quar en toutz ceux casez est tiel maner de estat de enheritaunce in sa ley, et est conus que estate passa per tielz parrolx, mez nemi issint in cel case. Mez il dit que le graunte ceo avera pur terme de sa vie, quar icy appiert que le roy done a luy deux estatez, [*fo. 142v*] lùn pur terme de sa vie,

---

[1] *Seems to read* f.

6. ANON.

Common Pleas, Mich. 1534. Also reported by Pollard, above, p. 261, no. 36.

The king gave an advowson to a man and his heirs male.

SHELLEY said that the donee should have an estate for term of his life and not in fee simple or in tail, and he drew a distinction between where someone wishes to make himself out to be heir to an estate tail and where to an estate in fee simple. For in the former case he must make himself out to be heir to the donee and also to the person who last held the estate, whereas where someone wishes to make himself out to be heir to land in fee simple it suffices if he makes himself out to be heir to the person who last died seised and he need not mention the first purchaser in his tracing of title. He further said that the king's grant shall be taken more beneficially for the king, because the king is a body politic and is the head of all the common weal, and therefore it is right that he has a prerogative in all things. Now, then, the king's intention cannot be construed in this case to be that the grantee should have fee simple, for then he would not have put the word 'male' in the grant; for if it should be a fee simple the grantee would have it otherwise than as the king gave it to him, for the heirs female would have it, which is absolutely contrary to the king's meaning, and therefore he shall not have fee simple inasmuch as the king was deceived in his grant and therefore the grant shall be deemed void. Therefore the king's grant in all cases shall be construed more beneficially for the king. For instance, if the king by the premisses of a deed gives land to someone and his heirs, and then in the *habendum* it says 'to have and to hold for term of his life', the grantee shall only have an estate for term of his life, and yet if a common person made such a deed the feoffee would have fee simple. Similarly if the king enfeoffs someone with warranty, the feoffee shall not recover in value unless there are words of recompense in the deed. Likewise if the king enfeoffs his villein, he is not thereby enfranchised, but the king may nevertheless seize him as his villein. And where the king is deceived in his grant the grant is void. For instance, if someone sues to the king by petition to enfeoff him of the manor of Dale, and says in the petition that the manor is only worth £10, whereas the manor is worth £20, even though the king gives him the said manor in accordance with his petition, if it is afterwards found by office that the manor is worth £20 the king may seize it back. If the king makes a gift in frankmarriage, or gives lands in frankalmoign, or gives lands to two and the heirs of their two bodies, such gifts are good: though he would not admit it. But he said that, admit that such gifts are good, still that will not prove this case, for in all these case there is an inheritance of that kind in the law, and it is known that an estate passes by such words, whereas that is not so in this case. But he said that the grantee should have it for term of his life, for here it appears that the king has given him two estates, one

lauter a ses heires, et donques nient obstant que le graunt est voyde ayant regarde a ses heires, uncore pur luy pur terme de sa vie ceo est bone, quar ne fuit ascun collusion ou desceyt in cell estate, quar il fuit toutz foytz le menynge le roy que il avera ceo pur terme de sa vie. Et semble al cas 20 H. 6. lou terrez fueront dones a un home et heredibus, enterlessant suis, ceo fuit voyde pur ses heires mes bon pur le feoffe pur terme de sa vie. Mez si le roy done terrez ou avowson a un saunce plus parler, ore il nad estate forsque a volunte, quar la nappiert que per ascun parroll que il ceo avera pur terme de sa vie. Mes icy est auterment.

Norwiche, Chif Justice, et *Fitzharbart*, all contrary, quar ills diont que en nul cas le graunt le roy serra voyde ou il puit aver ascun resonable construction accordaunt all meninge le roy et dell partie auxi a que le graunt ceo fist. Et pur ceo in ceo cas le graunt serra construe accordaunt al meninge del parties, et ceo est que le graunte ceo avera a luy et a cez heires de son corpus loyalment engendres, quar fuit lentente le roy que le graunte ceo avera a luy et a sez heires de son corpus loialment engendres, quar fuit lentent le roy que le graunte ceo avera issint, quar auterment il ne voile aver mis ceux parolx males en le fait. Et pur ceo lestatute de W. 2. dit que ou terres sont dones sur condition que le volunte le donour serra observe, et ne parla ou terrez sont dones in taile. Et en ceo cas ceo est done sur condition, et pur ceo le volunte le donour serra observe. Et pur ceo in plusours cases home avera estate taile et uncore il ne parlera de ascun corpus engendres. Et pur ceo si home fait feoffement reservaunt le revertion a luy et a sez heirez, ore le feoffe avera estate taile: et issint est le cas 5 H.5 in formedone. [*fo. 143*]

Fitzharbart dit que si un done terrez a un et garrante mesme le terre a luy et a sez heires de son corpus, ore il avera estate taile. Et si terrez sont dones a un et a sez heires auxi longement que J. S. ad issue de son corpus, ore le feoffee ad fee simple sur condition. Et auxi il dit que si le roy avaunt lestatute de W. 2. cap.1. ust done certen terrez a un home et a sez heires de son corpus loyalment engendres, ore post prolem suscitatem il avoit fee simple issint que il puit aliener, et son heir collaterall enheretra, et uncore ceo est contrary all menynge le roy. Mez le roy est tenus de prender notice de sa ley. Et pur ceo in ceo cas il diont que le graunt le roy serra construe accordaunt a un devise fait per testament, que en toutz cases serra construe accordaunt ell entent cestuy que ceo fist. Et pur ceo il dit si un devise a un certen terre a luy et a sez heires malez il avera estate taile et nemi fee simple. Et fuit dit per luy que si terrez sont dones a un ovesque sa cosyn que est heire de iiii. degrez, le entent del donour serra construe.

Norwiche dit que si le roy ad un revercion en un ville et est seisi de diverz auterz terrez deins mesme le ville, et done a un per ses lettres patentz omnia

for term of his life and the other to his heirs, and therefore even if the grant is void with respect to the heirs, it is still good for him for term of his life, for there was no collusion or deceit in that estate, for it was always the king's meaning that he should have it for term of his life. It is like the case in 20 Hen. VI,[1] where lands were given to a man 'and the heirs' (*et haeredibus*), leaving out 'his' (*suis*), and this was void for his heirs but good for the feoffee for term of his life. However, if the king gives land (or an advowson) to someone without saying more, he has but an estate at will, for there it does not appear by any word that he should have it for term of his life. But here it is otherwise.

NORWICH, Chief Justice, and FITZHERBERT to the contrary; for they said that the king's grant shall in no case be void where it may have some reasonable construction according to the meaning of the king and also of the party to whom the grant was made. Therefore in this case the grant shall be construed according to the meaning of the parties, and that is that the grantee should have it to him and to his heirs of his body lawfully begotten; for it was the king's intention that the grantee should so have it, for otherwise he would not have put the word 'male' in the deed. The Statute of Westminster II[2] says that where lands are given upon condition the will of the donor shall be observed, and does not say 'where lands are given in tail'. And in this case it is given upon condition, and therefore the will of the donor shall be observed. Therefore in several cases one shall have an estate tail without speaking of any bodies begotten. Thus if someone makes a feoffment reserving the reversion to himself and his heirs, the feoffee shall have an estate tail: and so is the case in 5 Hen. V, in formedon.[3]

FITZHERBERT said that if a man gives land to someone and warrants the same land to him and his heirs of his body, he shall have an estate tail. And if lands are given to someone and his heirs as long as John Style has issue of his body, the feoffee has a fee simple upon condition. He also said that if the king, before the Statute of Westminster II, c. 1, had given certain lands to a man and his heirs of his body lawfully begotten, after the birth of issue (*post prolem suscitatem*) he had a fee simple so that he could alien and his collateral heir inherit, and yet it was contrary to the king's meaning. But the king is held to take notice of his law. Therefore in this case the king's grant shall be construed in the same way as a devise made by testament, which in all cases shall be construed according to the intention of the person who made it. Therefore he said that if one devises to someone certain land, to him and his heirs male, he shall have an estate tail and not fee simple.[4] And it was said by him that if lands are given to someone with his kinswoman, who is heir within four degrees, the donor's intention shall be construed.

NORWICH said that if the king has a reversion in a vill and is seised of various other lands in the same vill, and gives someone by his letters patent

[1] *Otterworth* v. *Godsalve* (1443) YB Mich. 22 Hen. VI, fo. 15, pl. 28.
[2] Statute of Westminster II, c. 1, *De donis* (*SR* i. 71).
[3] YB Hil. 5 Hen. V, fo. 6, pl. 13.
[4] Cf. YB Mich. 27 Hen. VIII, fo. 27, pl. 11, *per* Fitzherbert and Shelley JJ.

terras [et] tenementa sua, per cell graunt le revertion ne passa. Uncore si un comen persone fait feoffement per tielx parrolx le revertion passa.

Fitzharbart dit que si done soit fait al baron et sa feme en frankemariage, le revertion a un estranger en fee, ceo est especiall estate taile, et issint est le cas 45 E. 3.

Nota que *Shelley* dit en le case avauntdit que si le roy done terrez a un evesque et a ses successours et sez heires, que ore levesque nad auter estate forsque pur terme de sa vie, pur le incertenty del graunt, quar ambideux, scilicet sez successours et ces heires, ne purront ceo aver, et pur ceo la done est incerteyne.

[7]

BL MS Harley 1691, fo. 143v (Mich. 26 Hen. VIII).

Un abbe fuit oblige en un obligation enseale ovesque son seale demesne pur certen denerz quex viendront all use del meason. Il morust [et] le oblige port action de dett vers le successour, que dit que riens luy doit, prist a faire per sa ley. Sil gager ley sur ceo mater?

Knightley, serjant, dit quil ne gagera sa ley, quar ceo action est foundu sur deux choses, lun sur lobligation que est matter en fait, et lauter sur laverment que lez deners viendront al use del meson, et pur ceux deux causes il ne gagera sa ley: lun pur ceo que laction est grounde sur matter en fait et lauter pur ceo quil est dauter contracte, quar sanz lobligation laction ne gist et sanz laverment que lez biens viendront al use del meson laction fail auxi, quar nient obstant que le contracte fait al use de meson est parcel de cause de son action, pur quell contracte le ley gissoit, uncore quant un obligation est joine ove un contracte lobligation est de pluis haut nature que le contracte, et pur ceo lobligation faire le contracte de mesme le nature que lobligation est, quar omne magis dignum trahit ad se omne minus dignum. Et pur ceo si un lesse certen barbitz pur terme danz reservant certen rent, le lesse ne gagera sa ley, causa qua supra. Issint si un port brefe de detinue dun boxe de certen chartres, ore si le plaintife dit en son counte que lez chartres consernont certen terre, le [defendant][1] navera sa ley

---

[1] pl.

'all his lands and tenements' (*omnia terras et tenementa sua*), by this grant the reversion does not pass. Yet if a common person made a feoffment in such words the reversion would pass.

FITZHERBERT said that if a gift is made to a husband and his wife in frankmarriage, the reversion to a stranger in fee, this is a special estate tail; and there is a case to this effect in 45 Edw. III.[1]

Note that SHELLEY said in the aforesaid case that if the king gives lands to a bishop and his successors and his heirs, the bishop has no other estate than for term of his life, on account of the uncertainty of the grant; for both—that is, to his successors and his heirs—they cannot have, and therefore the gift is uncertain.

7. ANON.[2]

Common Pleas, Mich. 1534. Also briefly noted in Spelman, p. 95, pl. 5, and p. 160, pl. 2.

An abbot was bound in a bond sealed with his own seal for certain moneys which came to the use of the house; he died, and the obligee brought an action of debt against the successor, who said 'Nothing owed him' and was ready to make his law. May he wage law upon these facts?

Knightley, serjeant, said that he should not wage his law, for this action is founded upon two things, (1) the bond, which is a matter in deed, and (2) the averment that the moneys came to the use of the house; and for these two causes he shall not wage his law: in one case because the action is grounded upon a matter in deed and in the other because it is another's contract. For the action does not lie without the bond; and without the averment that the goods came to the use of the house the action fails also, for even if the contract made to the use of the house is part of the cause of his action, for which contract the wager of law should lie, nevertheless when a bond is joined with a contract the bond is of a higher nature than the contract, and therefore the bond makes the contract of the same nature as the bond is, for everything of greater worth draws to itself everything of lesser worth (*Omne magis dignum trahit ad se omne minus dignum*). Therefore if someone leases certain rabbits for a term of years, reserving certain rent, the lessee shall not wage his law, for the above reason. Likewise if someone brings a writ of detinue for a box of certain charters, if the plaintiff says in his count that the charters concern certain land, the defendant shall not have his law for the box for it is but accessory to the

---

[1] YB Trin. 45 Edw. III, fo. 19, pl. 22.

[2] Cf. *Nunny* v. *Abbot of St Albans* (Mich. 1534) CP 40/1083, mm. 150, 156 (debt on numerous contracts made by predecessor for fish, which came to use of house—but no mention of bond; pleads Nil debet); and m. 145 (similar action, without mention that the fish came to the use of the house).

pur le boxe quar nest que accessorie a lez chartres. Et lou mon frere Chamley avoit miz diverz cases lou home avera sa ley dauter contracte, come lou le servant fait contracte al use de son master, que en action de det port vers son master il avera sa ley, jeo agre cest cas, quar le contracte del servant est le contracte del master, quar qui per alium facit per seipsum facere videtur, quar le servant est en vie et poit enformer son master assez bien sil en consciens il purra faire sa ley que riens a luy doit. Et auxi jeo agre que le baron et sa feme per un contracte fait per le [feme][1] avant le coverture ferront lour ley jointement, pur ceo que le feme puit enformer son baron sil puit faire sa ley in consienz. Mez in nostre cas icy, admitte que ne fuit ascun obligation, uncore le successour navera sa ley, pur ceo que cestui que le contracte fist est mort issint que le successour ne puit aver conusaunce del contract: nient pluis que si un action de accompt soit port per executourz verz le recevour lour testatour, ilz ne serront james examines.

Et puis fuit adjuge que le defendant navera sa ley, mez le plaintife recovera son det et sur ceo avoit brefe de execution.

Nota que fuit ajuge circa 7 H. 8. que lou un port action de det verz le successour pur contract fait per le predecesour, que avient al use del meason, le successour ne fuit reseve pur faire sa ley.

[8]

BL MS Harley 1691, fo. 143v (Mich. 26 Hen. VIII).

En action sur lestatute de parco fracto le defendant dit que le plaintife navoit ascun parke la etc.

Shelley. Ceo nest ple, quar serra in triall perenter le roy et le partie sil ad parke in quo warranto et nemi enter lez parties. Come en trespas pur enter en son garren, nest ple adire que il nad warren, mez covient dire Rien culpable et donera en evidence que il nad <warren. Issint icy. Mez si >[2] un port action pur batery de son servant est bon ple adire que il ne fuit son servaunt etc.

Englefield. Lun et lauter est bone ple, quar est tout a un effecte adire que nul tiel parke ou warren et a dire Rien culpable et done en evidence nul tiel parke ou warren.

---

[1] baron.
[2] park. Et nient semble ou *YB*.

charters. And whereas my brother Cholmeley has put various cases where a man shall have his law in respect of another's contract, as where a servant makes a contract to the use of his master, in an action of debt brought against his master he shall have his law: I agree that case, for the servant's contract is the master's contract, for whoever does something through another is deemed to do it himself (*Qui per alium facit per seipsum facere videtur*), for the servant is alive and may inform his master well enough whether in conscience he may make his law that he owes him nothing. Also I agree that a husband and his wife, shall make their law jointly for a contract made by the wife before the coverture, because the wife may inform her husband whether in conscience he may make his law. In our case here, however, admit that there was no such bond, and still the successor would not have his law, because the person who made the contract is dead, and so his successor cannot have knowledge of the contract. No more shall executors ever be examined where they bring an action of account against their testator's receiver.

Afterwards it was adjudged that the defendant should not have his law, but the plaintiff should recover his debt, and thereupon he had a writ of execution.

Note that it was adjudged around 7 Hen. VIII that where someone brought an action of debt against the successor for a contract made by the predecessor, which came to the use of the house, the successor was not received to make his law.[1]

8. ANON.

Common Pleas, Mich. 1534. The same text is printed in YB Trin. 19 Hen. VIII, fo. 9, pl. 2. Also reported Keil. 202v; above, p. 410, no. 105 (where it is dated 1529/30).

In an action upon the statute *de parco fracto*[2] the defendant said that the plaintiff had no park there etc.

SHELLEY. That is no plea, for whether he has a park shall be put in trial between the king and the party in a *quo warranto* and not between the parties. Similarly in trespass for entering in his warren, it is no plea to say that he has no warren, but he must say Not guilty and give in evidence that he has no warren. Likewise here. But if someone brings an action for battery of his servant it is a good plea to say that he was not his servant etc.

ENGLEFIELD. Either is a good plea, for it is all to one effect to say that there is no such park or warren and to say Not guilty and give in evidence that there is no such park or warren.

---

[1] *Cowplond* v. *Abbot of Wymondham* (1515) CP 40/1010, m. 404; Caryll's reports, 116 Selden Soc. 679-681.

[2] Meaning 21 Edw. I, *De malefactoribus in parcis* (*SR* i. 111); above, p. 410.

[9]

BL MS Harley 1691, fo. 144 (Mich. 26 Hen. VIII).

Un vient en court ovesque le oryginall dun formedon insealed et delivera ceo in mesme le court al viscount de recorde, per que le bref fuit enfreint et entra <de recorde>[1] de verbo in verbum et deliver all viscount. Et le brefe fuit retourne le prochin terme aprez. Et le demandant surmitte <que le tenant ad fait>[2] wast et estrepament et praya brefe de estrepament.

Englefield. Le brefe ne gist, quar lestatute de Glouc' [cap. 13][3] est que si le tenaunt fait wast ou distruction pendaunt le ple etc., et ceo formedon nest pendant en cell court tanque al jour <de retourne de cell>,[4] quar si a cell jour le viscount retourne nul brefe cell court nad power <pur tener ple sanz sicut alias, pur ceo que est nul brefe en court sur que le ple serra tenus[5].>[6]

[10]

BL MS Harley 1691, fo. 144 (Mich. 26 Hen. VIII).

Terres fueront dones as deux et a lez heires de corps lun, cestui que avoit lenheritaunce fait feoffement, et morust, et puis lauter morust, et le heire del tenaunt en le taile port formedon in le discender et alleage coment son pier fuit seisi in taile: et ceo fuit tenus bone seisin del estate taylle pur carier le formedon, nient obstant le joynt possession.

[11]

BL MS Harley 1691, fo. 144 (Mich. 26 Hen. VIII).

Home seisi de deux acres de terre tient lun del roy in capite et lauter dun comen person per service de chivaler, et morust, son heire deins age. Le roy seisit le garde del corps le heire et ambideux acres, et quant le heire vient a son pleine age lauter seignior distraine pur lez arrerages de son seigniorye queux fueront dew durant le noneage, et auxi pur reliffe.

---

[1] *Om. YB.*   [2] *Om. YB.*   [3] *YB.*   [4] del brefe rec' [*probably for* retorne] *YB.*   [5] *Written twice.*
[6] de tener ple sans brefe, et le demandant est mis a son novel original hors del Chancerie *YB.*

9. ANON.

Common Pleas, Mich. 1534. The same text (with a variant ending) is printed in YB Mich. 19 Hen. VIII, fo. 5, pl. 18.

Someone came into court with the original of a formedon, sealed, and delivered it in the same court of record to the sheriff, and the writ was broken open and entered of record word for word (*de verbo in verbum*) and delivered to the sheriff. And the writ was returned the next term after. And the demandant then alleged that the tenant had committed waste and estrepement and prayed a writ of estrepement.

ENGLEFIELD. The writ does not lie, for the Statute of Gloucester[1] says 'if the tenant commits waste or destruction while the plea is pending etc.', and this formedon is not 'pending' in this court until the return-day thereof; for if at that day the sheriff returns no writ this court has no power to hold plea without a *sicut alias*, because there is no writ in court whereon the plea may be held.

10. ANON.

Common Pleas, Mich. 1534.

Lands were given to two persons and to the heirs of the body of one of them; the one who had the inheritance made a feoffment, and died; and then the other one died; and the heir of the tenant in tail brought formedon in the descender and alleged that his father was seised in tail: and this was held a good seisin of the estate tail for the purpose of carrying the formedon, notwithstanding the joint possession.

11. ANON.

Common Pleas, Mich. 1534. Also reported in YB Mich. 26 Hen. VIII, fo. 8, pl. 5.

Someone seised of two acres of land held one of them of the king in chief and the other of a common person by knight-service, and died, his heir under age. The king seized the wardship of the heir's body and both acres, and when the heir came of age the other lord distrained for the arrears of his lordship which were due during the infancy, and also for relief.

---

[1] Statute of Gloucester, c. 13 (*SR* i. 50).

Et tenus per *Norwiche*, Chif Justice, *Inglefield* et *Shelley* que il ne purra distrayner pur lez arrerages, quar duraunt le noneage le seigniorye del comen person fuit en suspence per le possession le roy. Et nient semble all[1] case que si le tenaunt dun comen person lessa le tenancy all roy pur ans, ore le seignior ne purra distrayner pur cell rent durant le possession le roy, mez apres le terme finie il distraynera son tenant pur toutz lez arrerages incurre durant le possession le roy: quar en cell cas le tenant per son acte demesne ad suspendewe le segnorye, mez en cell cas le seignorye est suspende per le acte del ley, scilicet per le nonage et nemi per lacte del tenaunt.

[12]

BL MS Harley 1691, fo. 133.

Tenaunt in taile fait lees a un pur terme de vie, et devie, son heire graunt le revercion a un auter pur annes ou pur vie: ore leire navera formedon duraunt sa vie, coment que le graunte del revertion morust, ou aprez lez anns expire, quar per le graunt del revertion apres le mort le tenant in taile per le pier il ad agre all lease fait per son pier et encontre son agrement il ne purra apres ceo defeter: et ceo fuit agre in le Chancerye in le case de Geele.

[13]

BL MS Harley 1691, fo. 133.

Nota que fuit ajuge en Banke le Roy que si un prist mes biens hors de mon possesion et jeo done ceux biens a luy per paroll, que ceo est voyde done, quar per le prisell il[s] sont hors de mon possession et jeo nay forsque un droit a eux, et donques un droit ne purra passer [per parroll][2] nient plus que si jeo soy disseisi et done le terre al disseisor per par parroll. Mez auterment serra si le done soit fait per fait.

---

[1] *Altered unnecessarily to* a cell.
[2] p[er] cell.

And it was held by NORWICH, Chief Justice, ENGLEFIELD and SHELLEY that he may not distrain for the arrears, for during the infancy the lordship of the common person was in suspense by the king's possession. It is not like the case where the tenant of a common person leases the tenancy to the king for years: the lord cannot distrain for this rent during the king's possession. But after the term has ended he may distrain his tenant for all the arrears incurred during the king's possession: for in that case the tenant has suspended the lordship by his own act, whereas in this case the lordship is suspended by the act of the law, namely by the infancy, and not by the tenant's act.

12. GEELE'S CASE

Chancery, 1530s.

Tenant in tail makes a lease to someone for term of life, and dies; his heir grants the reversion to another for years or for life: the heir shall not now have formedon during his lifetime, even if the grantee of the reversion dies, or after the years have expired, for by the grant of the reversion after the death of the tenant in tail's father he has agreed to the lease made by his father and he may not afterwards defeat it contrary to his agreement. This was agreed in the Chancery in the case of Geele.

13. ANON.

King's Bench, 1530s.

Note that it was adjudged in the King's Bench that if someone takes my goods out of my possesion and I give these goods to him by parol, this is a void gift, for by the taking they are out of my possession and I have nothing but a right to them, and a right cannot pass by parol, any more than where I am disseised and give the land to the disseisor by parol. But it would be otherwise if the gift was made by deed.

[14]

BL MS Harley 1691, fo. 133 (dated Hil. 28 Hen. VIII).

Home fuit arreste per capias et fuit oblige all viscount pur son apparaunce, et puis avoit supersedeas a mesme le viscount: et ceo nient obstaunt fuit tenus que il duist apperer pur salver son obligation.

[15]

BL MS Harley 1691, fo. 133 (follows no. 14).

Un enquest fuit, et un juror fuit jure, et puis le defendant challenge toutz paravaile: ore cestui que est [jure][1] esliera un de eux a luy pur trier les auterz. Mes si le defendant avaunt ascun soit jure challenga toutz paravaylle donques lez justices duissent eslier deux triors.

[16]

BL MS Harley 1691, fo. 133 (follows no. 15).

Un enquest remayne pur defaut dez hundredourz, et sur ceo le cownsell le plaintife monstra al court que ne sont ascun franktenauntes deins mesme le hundred mez toutz tient per copy de court roll ou auncyen demesne, et pur ceo ilz preyont procez as prochin hundryd. Et fuit dit per le court que ceo duist estre retorne per le viscount, et donques il avera son prayer, mez il ne duist done credence a lour dit.

[17]

BL MS Harley 1691, fo. 133 (follows no. 16).

Un home covenaunt per endenture pur paier certen money et sur ceo il port action de dett, le defendant plede payment saunz ascun acquitaunce ou

---

[1] jo[ur].

14. ANON.

Common Pleas, Hil. 1537, seemingly a paraphrase of the report printed in Dyer, fo. 25, §157.

Someone was arrested by *capias* and was bound to the sheriff for his appearance, and afterwards he had a *supersedeas* to the same sheriff: despite this, it was held that he ought to appear to save his bond.

15. ANON.

Common Pleas, Hil. 1537, seemingly a paraphrase of the report printed in Dyer, fo. 25, §156.

There was an inquest, and one juror was sworn, and then the defendant challenged all those below: now the one who has been sworn shall choose one of them to try the others with him. But if the defendant challenged all those below before anyone was sworn, then the justices ought to have chosen two triers.

16. ANON.

Probably 1537.

An inquest remained for default of the hundredors, and thereupon the plaintiff's counsel showed the court that there were no freeholders in the same hundred, but all held by copy of court roll or in ancient demesne, and therefore they prayed process to the next hundred. And it was said by the court that this ought to be returned by the sheriff, and then he would have his prayer, but they ought not to give credence to their word.

17. ANON.

Common Pleas, 1537. Differently reported in Dyer, fo. 25, §160 (Hil. 1537), where a similar opinion is attributed to Mountague sjt.[1]

Someone covenanted by indenture to pay certain money and thereupon he brought an action of debt; the defendant pleaded payment without any

[1] Cf. *Palmer* v. *Byllyngton* (Trin. 1537) KB 27/1104, m. 74 (covenant on a promise to pay £60 in a marriage agreement; pleads bill of receipt; undetermined demurrer; c.a.v. to Trin. 1538). See also *Anon.* (Mich. 1534) Dyer, fo. 6, pl. 3.

especialte, et adjuge nul ple sans monstre acquitaunce, nient plus que en det sur lobligation, pur ceo que en ambideux cases le action est fownde sur lespecialte.

[18]

BL MS Harley 1691, fo. 133 (follows no. 17).

Trespas fuit port vers Jo. at S. de Dale, chyvaler, et trove fuit culpable, et sur ceo il port attainte per le nosme J. at S., chyvaler, enterlessant de Dale: et le brefe tenus bone, nient obstant le variaunce, per *Fitzharbart* et *Shelley*.

[19]

BL MS Harley 1691, fo. 133 (follows no. 18).

Nota que fuit tenus per toutz lez justicez que si un home ad un chien que tua barbitz, son master ne serra charge pur cell sinon que il scia et avoit notice avaunt que son chien solat issint faire.

[20]

BL MS Harley 1691, fo. 133 (follows no. 19).

Nota en trespas le defendant plede Rien culpable, et done en evidence al jure que il avoit un close adjoynant all close le plaintife en que le trespas est suppose, et dit que le plaintife et cez auncestorz de temps dont memorie ne court duist closer et repayre lez hegges perenter lour terrez, et dit que pur defaut de [*fo. 133v*] bon clausure sez bestez eschapent inz[1] et issint in le defaut le plaintife: et tenus per toutz lez justicez que il ne purra doner cell matter in evidence, quar ceo est contrariant a son ple avaunt plede.

---

[1] *Reading unclear.*

acquittance or specialty, and it was adjudged no plea without showing an acquittance, any more than in debt on a bond, because in both cases the action is founded on the specialty.[1]

18. ANON.

Common Pleas, Hil. 1537, seemingly a paraphrase of the report printed in Dyer, fo. 25, §161.

Trespass was brought against John at Style of Dale, knight, and he was found guilty, and thereupon he brought attaint by the name of John at Style, knight, leaving out Dale: and the writ was held good, despite the variance, by FITZHERBERT and SHELLEY.

19. ANON.

Common Pleas, Hil. 1537, seemingly a paraphrase of the report printed in Dyer, fo. 25, §162.

Note that it was held by all the justices that if someone has a dog which killed sheep, its master shall not be charged for this unless he knew and had previous notice that his dog was accustomed to do this.

20. ANON.

Note, c. 1530. This may be an abridgment of the case in Caryll's reports, above, p. 411, no. 106.

Note that in trespass the defendant pleaded Not guilty, and gave in evidence to the jury that he had a close adjoining the plaintiff's close in which the trespass is supposed, and said that the plaintiff and his ancestors from time immemorial ought to enclose and repair the hedges between their lands, and said that for default of good enclosure his beasts escaped, and so this was in default of the plaintiff. And it was held by all the justices that he could not give this matter in evidence, for it is contrary to his plea as previously pleaded.

[1] However, the fact of payment does not contradict the wording of a covenant to pay money, whereas it does contradict the wording of a money bond acknowledging that the money is owed.

[21]

BL MS Harley 1691, fo. 133v (follows no. 20).

Si un home challenge un pur ceo quil est cosin all plaintife ou defendant, il covient a luy monstre coment cosyn et auxi conclude Et issint favorable, quar coment que il soit son cosyn uncore sil ne soit favorable il serra ceo nient obstant jures.

[22]

[A]

BL MS Harley 1691, ff. 113–115 (dated 31 H. 8).

En quare impedit port per Sir William Hawles, chivaler, vers levesque de Lychefelde, Sir Godfrey Fowljam, chivaler, et John Waule, clerk, le dit Sir Wylliam Hawles, chivaler, fyst son tytle al avowzon per reson que un Sir Rafe Longford, chivaler, fuit seisi del maner de D. en le com. de N., a que cest avowzon est appendant, en son demesne come de fee, et issint seisi presenta un H. Whyte, <et conveya luy per fyne al maner >[i], per que al dit plaintife apent a presenter, et les ditz defendants luy ount disturbe. A que veigne einz les defendants et levesque plede que il est ordynary et demande jugemente si sauns especiall dysturbance en son persone assigne cest action doit le plaintife mayntener. Et le dit Sir Godfrey Foljamb, auter des defendants, plede que il disturba pas. Et le dit John Waule, encumbent, dit que byen et veryte est que le dit Rafe Langfoord fuit seisi del dit maner a que cest avowzon est <et donques fuit appendant >[i] et issint seisi presenta ut supra, et puis le dit Sir Rafe Longford per son fait que cy est portant date etc. graunta le procheyn avoydance del dit esglise al dit Sir Godfrey Foljam, chivaler, John Folljam, esquier, Richard Folljam et John Waule, clerke, et uni eorum conjunctim vel

21. ANON.

Note, perhaps c. 1537.

If one challenges someone because he is kinsman to the plaintiff or defendant, he must show how he is kinsman and also conclude 'And thus favourable', for although he is his kinsman he may nevertheless be sworn if he is not favourable.

22. HOLLYS v. FOLJIAMBE and WALTHAM

Common Pleas, 1539. Also briefly reported by Bendlowes, below, p. 444. Record: CP 40/1102, m. 420 (*quare impedit* for Barlborough, Derbs.; judgment for defendant on demurrer, Mich. 1539); record summarised in Benl. 24-25; abridged in Moo. K.B. 4, pl. 14; 1 And. 2, pl. 2.

A

In *quare impedit* brought by Sir William Hollys,[1] knight, against the bishop of Lichfield, Sir Godfrey Foljambe, knight,[2] and John Waltham,[3] clerk, the said Sir William Hollys, knight, made his title to the advowson by reason that one Sir Ralph Longford, knight,[4] was seised of the manor of [Barlborough] in the county of [Derby], to which this advowson is appendant, in his demesne as of fee, and, being so seised, presented one H. Whyte; and he traced his title to the manor by fine, so that it belongs to the said plaintiff to present, and the said defendants have disturbed him. To which the defendants came in and the bishop pleaded that he is ordinary and demanded judgment whether the plaintiff ought to maintain this action [against him] without a special disturbance assigned in his person. And the said Sir Godfrey Foljambe, another of the defendants, pleaded that he did not disturb. And the said John Waltham, incumbent, said that it is well and true that the said Ralph Longford was seised of the said manor to which this advowson is and then was appendant, and, being so seised, presented as above, and afterwards the said Sir Ralph Longford—by his deed, which is here, bearing date etc.—granted the next avoidance of the said church to the said Sir Godfrey Foljambe, knight, John Foljambe, esquire, Richard Foljambe and John Waltham, clerk, and one

[1] 'Hawles' in the manuscript; adjusted throughout to correspond with record. Sir William Hollys or Holles (died 1542) was a wealthy mercer and sometime lord mayor of London.
[2] Died 1541: P.C.C. 2 Spert; brass in armour and tabard, with inscription, at Chesterfield, Derbs.
[3] 'Waule' in the manuscript; adjusted throughout to correspond with record.
[4] Probably Sir Ralph Longford or Langford (died 1543), who married Dorothy, daughter of Fitzherbert J.; but possibly his grandfather of the same name. See Spelman, p. 212; Port, p. 136; 102 Selden Soc. xxii.

devisim, et puis leva le fyne al dit plaintife, et puis lesglise devient voyde per morte le dit White, per que le dit John Foljam, esquier, luy presenta, ove ceo que il voet averrer que cest le procheyn avoydance apres le graunt, et demaunde jugemente si action. A que le plaintife dit que cestui John Waule ore un de les defendants et le dit John Waule un de les grauntees sont tout un persone et nemi dyvers, sur que le defendant dymurre en ley. Et sur cell case fueront ceux poyntes move: scilicet, si cest graunt soyt bon ou nemi, et si serra joynt ou severall ou coment enurera, et de quell effect ceux parollx et eorum uni conjunctim vel devisim serra, et donques si cest ple gyst en le bouche dencumbent.

Et primermente le graunt fuit tenus bon per toutz. Et fuit tenus per toutz les justyces que le plaintife serra barr sur le matter mesme.

Mes pur le force del graunt *Jenney*, *Wyllughbye* et *Baldwyn* tyendront le graunt joynt a toutz et que ceux darreyn parols et eorum uni conjunctim et devisim fueront voydes pur le contraryete, quar primermente il graunta ceo a eux toutz, donques quaunt il dit apres et eorum uni et ne monstre que serra le dit un que ceo avera, ergo uncerteyn. Come si home fait lesse pur vye, le remainder uni eorum que viendra a Powles lendemayne ou uni filiorum J. S. et ne monstre que deux et J. S. ad dyvers fitz, cest voyde pur le noncertente. Auxi ceux parollx conjunctim et devisim sont voydes, quar cest paroll conjunctim est voyde et nugacyon, quar per les premysses ilz ount ceo joyntment sauns cest paroll, ergo frustrat [*fo. 113v*] et especiallment ove cest paroll et uni eorum, quar adyre que eux toutz ceo averont conjunctim et un de eux per soy ne poit estre. Donques del devisim, ne poit faire lour interest severall que est joynt per les premysses, quar ne poit estoier ensemble que ilz serront joyntenauntez et auxi tenauntz en comen a un mesme temps, mes deux poyent estre joyntenauntez pur le fraunketenemente et aver [lenheritance][1] en comen: come terres donez a deux et a lour heirs de lour corps engendres.

Baldwyn, Chyefe Justyce, dit que si home done deux acres de terre a deux, habendum lun acre (et monstre quell acre) a lun de eux, et lauter acre a lauter, que icy cest lymytation nest bon ne fait eux tenauntz en comen, quar per les premysses le graunt est joynt et ambideux acres sont dones a eux ambideux, issint que chescun de eux ad interest ove lauter, et ceo en chescun acre, et donques per le habendum il voille restrayner lour joynt power del premysses.

Al auter poynt, fuit semble a eux excepte *Shelley* et *Baldwyn* que le presentment ne fuit bon per voy de presentment mes serra come un pryer destre admyt et come un collation, que ne mittera ascun persone hors de possession. Come si un que est priest purchace un maner a que avowzon est appendant, ou si tiell maner discende a un pryest, leglise devient voyde et le patron mesme

---

[1] lheneritance.

of them jointly or severally (*et uni eorum conjunctim vel divisim*), and afterwards levied a fine to the said plaintiff, and then the church became vacant by death of the said White, and so the said John Foljambe, esquire, presented him, with this, that he would aver that this is the next avoidance after the grant; and demanded judgment whether the plaintiff ought to have his action. To which the plaintiff said that this John Waltham, now one of the defendants, and the said John Waltham, one of the grantees, are all one person and not different, whereupon the defendant demurred in law. And upon this case these points were moved: [1] whether this grant is good, or not; [2] whether it shall be joint or several, or how it shall enure; [3] what is the effect of these words *et eorum uni conjunctim vel divisim*, and [4] whether this plea lies in the mouth of an incumbent.

As to the first, the grant was held good by everyone. And it was held by all the justices that the plaintiff shall be barred upon the matter itself.

As to the force of the grant, however, JENNEY, WILLOUGHBY and BALDWIN held the grant to be a joint grant to them all and that the latter words *et eorum uni conjunctim et divisim* were void on account of self-contradiction; for firstly he granted it to them all, and when he said afterwards *et eorum uni* and did not show which one should be the said one who should have it, it was therefore uncertain. Similarly, if someone makes a lease for life, remainder to one of those (*uni eorum*) who shall come to St Paul's tomorrow, or to one of the sons of John Style, and does not show which of them, and John Style has several sons, this is void for uncertainty. Moreover these words *conjunctim et divisim* are void, for this word *conjunctim* is void and superfluous, for by the premises they have it jointly without that word, and so it is in vain, and especially with the words *et uni eorum*, for to say that they should all have it jointly and one of them by himself cannot be. Then, as to *divisim*, he cannot make their interest several when it is joint by the premises, for it cannot stand together that they shall be joint tenants and also tenants in common at one same time, though two may be joint tenants of the freehold and have the inheritance in common: as where lands are given to them and to their heirs of their bodies begotten.

BALDWIN, Chief Justice, said that if someone gives two acres of land to two, *habendum* as to one acre (showing which acre) to one of them, and as to the other acre to the other, here this limitation is not good to make them tenants in common, for by the premises the grant is joint and both acres are given to them both, so that each of them has an interest with the other, and that is in each acre, and then by the *habendum* he wishes to restrain their joint power in the premises.

As to the other point, it seemed to them [all] except SHELLEY and BALDWIN that the presentation was not good by way of presentation, but it is like a prayer to be admitted and a collation, which shall not put any person out of possession. For instance, if someone who is a priest purchases a manor to which an advowson is appendant, or if such a manor descends to a priest, the church becomes vacant, and the patron himself comes to the ordinary and

vyent al ordynare et luy pria destre admytte al benefyce, cest bon et ore il est parsone et patron, mes ceo nest per voy de presentmente, quar est impossyble que il ceo dona a luy mesme, nyent pluis que home poit enfeffer luy mesme nyent pluis poit il presenter luy mesme et doner le benefyce a luy mesme. Issint cest presentment de cest patron de un de ses joynt grauntees ne poit estre come un presentmente mes quaunt il est einz un foitz et levesque ad luy admytt cest bon encontre toutz estraungers. Mes semble que en ceux cases lordynare poit refuser le partye que issint vient a luy destre admytt, quar nest presentmente en ley: et si le patron mesme que est pryest voille prier levesque de admytter soy, si lordynare ne voille ceo faire et puis levesque pur laps fyst collation, lauter nad remedie pur cest refusell, quar en quare impedit covyent alleger que il presenta son covenable clerke et que levesque luy refusa ou disturbe de presenter, quell nest voyer. Mes si levesque luy admytt[1] et il est einz il est loyallmente parsone per ceo. Et si deux joyntenauntes sont e lun soull present, lordinare nest tenus de rescever son clerke, mes sil ceo fait est bone et le presentmente ne mittera lauter hors de possession. Mesme la ley semble de tenauntz en comen. Mes de coparceners la ley est auter, quar silz ne poyent accorder en presentment leigne presentera prymes, et si el soyt disturbe el avera quare impedit en son nosme soulle. Mes icy cest clerke est einz lou il mesme est un des patrons, et ceo per voy de son prier destre admytt, come en le case lou un est patron et priest, ergo entant que il est einz il ad droit vers le plaintife et toutz auters. Et semble come la case est icy il poit pleder cest ple per le comen ley et nemi per lestatute de anno 25 E. 3, quar cest estatute don power al encumbent de pleder vers le roy ou le patron ne voet, et per lequitye de mesme lestatute est prise que [*fo. 114*] lencumbent poit pleder vers comen persone, quar estatute quell lye le roy et done remedie sur tyell comen myschief per comen reson a fortiori covyent doner remedie vers comen persone en semble myschief. Mes cest case est hors de case destatute, quar cestui encumbent come appyert per son ple et le replycation le plaintife est patron, que poit pleder en barre per le comen ley, per que semble que il serra barre.

Shelley semble a mesme lentente, et que le plaintife ne recovera sur lentyer matter pur ceo que per son replycation il ad abate son brefe demesne. Mes sil avoit dymurre sur le barre, semble a luy que il duissoit recover. Et quaunt al graunt il semble le graunt bon, et que les grauntees ceo averont ove toutz les parollx destre use joyntmente ou severallmente per eux toutz ou per lun de eux a lour plesure. Et semble a luy que poit byen estoier ove reson que per ceo liberte soyt graunt a eux de user ceo joynt ou severall a lour plesure. Come en case dun letter de attorney fait a deux conjunctim et devisim, et est bon, et ore est liberte don a eux jonymente destre use ou severallmente a lour plesure, et uncore per les premysses il don a eux autoryte ensemble et cest

---

[1] *Altered from* refusa.

prays him to be admitted to the benefice, this is good, and now he is parson and patron, but this is not by way of presentment, for it is impossible that he should give it to himself; and, just as a man may not enfeoff himself, no more may he present himself and give the benefice to himself. Therefore this presentation by this patron of one of his joint grantees cannot take effect as a presentation, but when he is once in and the bishop has admitted him, it is good against all strangers. But it seems that in these cases the ordinary may refuse the party who so comes to him to be admitted, for it is no presentation in law: and if the patron himself, who is a priest, prays the bishop to admit him, and the ordinary will not do it, and afterwards the ordinary makes a collation on account of lapse, the other has no remedy for this refusal, for in a *quare impedit* he must allege that he presented his suitable clerk and that the bishop refused him or hindered him from presenting, which is untrue. If, however, the bishop admits him and he is in, he is thereby lawfully parson. And if there are two joint tenants and one of them alone presents, the ordinary is not bound to receive his clerk, but if he does so it is good and the presentation shall not put the other out of possession. The law seems to be the same of tenants in common. But of coparceners the law is different, for if they cannot agree in a presentation the elder shall present first, and if she is hindered she shall have *quare impedit* in her sole name. But here this clerk is in where he is himself one of the patrons, and that is by way of his own prayer to be admitted, as in the case where someone is patron and priest, and therefore since he is in he has right against the plaintiff and all others. And as the case is here, it seems he may plead this plea by the common law, and not by the statute of the year 25 Edw. III,[1] for that statute gives power to the incumbent to plead against the king where the patron will not, and by the equity of the same statute it is taken that the incumbent may plead against a common person, for the statute which binds the king, and gives a remedy upon such common mischief, by common reason must a fortiori give a remedy against a common person in a similar mischief. But this case is outside the case of the statute, for this incumbent (as appears by his plea—and the plaintiff's replication) is patron, who may plead in bar by the common law; and so it seems that he shall be barred.

SHELLEY thought to the same purpose, and that the plaintiff should not recover upon the whole matter because by his replication he has abated his own writ. But if he had demurred upon the bar, as it seemed to him, he ought to have recovered. As to the grant, he thought the grant good, and that the grantees should have it with all the words to be used jointly or severally by them all or by one of them, at their pleasure. And it seemed to him that it may well stand with reason that liberty is thereby granted to them to use it jointly or severally at their pleasure. As in the case of a letter of attorney made to two *conjunctim et divisim*, it is good, and it is a liberty given to them to be used jointly or severally at their pleasure, and yet by the premisses he gives them

---

[1] 25 Edw. III, stat. 6, c. 3 (*SR* i. 325). This is stat. 3 in *Statutes at Large*.

paroll conjunctim per se la ne serra deffecte, quar est issint sauns expresse,
mes quaunt il ad adde a ceo vel devisim ceo fait les parollx devaunt, scilicet et
eorum uni conjunctim vel devisim, daver perfytt intendmente et destre
materyall de fair lentent le grauntor et le graunte dapperer et de faire le
sentence full soloncque nostre comen parlance. Issint le meninge dez partyes
est pluis pleyne sett furthe per ceux parollx ensemble, et cest que les grauntes
ceo averont quaunt est temps de presentmente per eux toutz ou autermente
forsque per un de eux soullmente. Mes jeo voille agreer que toutz ou un
covyent de present, et deux ne poyent, pur ceo que ne accorde al graunt.
Issint ilz ount liberte de user ceo joyntmente ou severallmente. Come ou un
annuite de x. s. ou un robe est graunt a moy, cest al liberte del grauntor.
Issint est si jeo graunt a dyvers homes <et a chescun de eux >[i] de carryer et
recarrier ouster ma terre, ceo est bon destre use per toutz ou ascun de eux.
Donques appyert icy que ilz ount use ceo severallment, scilicet un de eux que
nest nosme en le brefe, scilicet John Folljam, esquier, ad present soullmente,
ergo ore nest auter mes sicome le graunt ust estre fait soullmente a luy et
toutz les auters ount relinquishe lour joynt patronage et il est devenus soull
patron. Mes admytt pur largumente de lauter poynt que fueront joynt
grauntees toutz et que les parollx vel uni eorum devisim fueront voyde,
donques moy semble que un de les joynt grauntees ne point present son
compaignyon come ad este dit, quar est impossible que un de eux donera a
lauter ceo que il mesme ad. Mes jeo ne voille agreer que le presentmente la
serra voyde, mes semble que, lordynare acceptant luy et admyttant, ad gaigne
le patronage luy mesme per ceo, et pur ceo moy semble en le case quell ad
este myse que si un que est patron mesme et priest vyent al ordynarye destre
admytt a son advowzon demesne que le ordynare come est dit poit luy
refuser, quar ceo nest presentmente. Mes sil luy admytt, moy semble que il
mesme serra hors de possession de son avowzon per ceo, et que lordynarye
ad per ceo gaigne le patronage vers luy. Quere hoc. Et *Shelley* semble que per
le presentmente J. Folljam il est devenus full patron [*fo.114v*] per reson de les
parollx de graunt. Donques est a voyer si lencumbent avera cest ple. Et moy
semble que nemi, quar al comen ley lencumbent ne poit pleder en barre ne al
tytle le plaintife en un quare impedit, quar le quare impedit est action reall et
ceo prove byen quar al comen ley null damagez fueront en quare impedit:
issint ne sont a cest jour en ascuns cases, ut patet 9. H. 6. Donques ceo prove
que fuit reall, quar il recoverast per le comen ley le presentmente et patronage
et null auter choce tanque lestatute vyent quell luy don damagez. Et apres
tytle fait al avowzon garrante est bon ple, issint laction de son nature est
reall. Donques si laction soyt reall, covyent de necessyte daver un nosme que
ad le choce reall que serra recover a lentent que il serra defende per cestui que
ceo ad ou render, et cest le patron, quar il ad tout lavowzon et le

authority together and this word *conjunctim* by itself shall not be of any effect there, for it is so without being expressed, but when he has added to it *vel divisim* that causes the previous words—namely, *et eorum uni conjunctim vel divisim*—to be perfectly understood, and to be material in causing the intention of the grantor and the grantee to appear, and to make the sentence complete according to our common parlance. Thus the meaning of the parties is more fully set forth by these words together, and it is that the grantees shall have it when the time comes for presentation by them all or else just by one of them alone. I would agree, however, that all or one must present, and two cannot, because it would not accord with the grant. Thus they have liberty to use it jointly or severally. Similarly if an annuity of 10s. or a robe is granted to me, this is at the grantor's liberty. Likewise if I grant to various men and to each of them to carry and recarry over my land, this is good to be used by them all or by any of them. Now, then, it appears here that they have used it severally, namely one of those who is named in the writ, namely John Foljambe, esquire, has presented alone, and therefore now it is nothing other than as if the grant had been made solely to him and all the others had relinquished their joint patronage and he had become sole patron. Admit, however, for the sake of argument of the other point, that they were all joint grantees and that the words *vel uni eorum divisim* were void, and it then seems to me that one of the joint grantees cannot present his fellow (as has been said), for it is impossible that one of them should give to the other what he himself has. However, I would not agree that the presentation there is void; but it seems that, when the ordinary accepts and admits him, he has thereby gained the patronage himself. Therefore it seems to me in the case which has been put—if someone who is himself patron and a priest comes to the ordinary to be admitted to his own advowson—that the ordinary may refuse him (as has been said), for it is not a presentation. If he admits him, however, it seems to me that he shall thereby himself be out of possession of his advowson, and that the ordinary has thereby gained the patronage as against him. (Query this.) And SHELLEY thought that by the presentation of John Foljambe he has become full patron by reason of the words of grant. Now it is to be seen whether the incumbent may have this plea. It seems to me that he may not, for at common law the incumbent could not plead in bar or plead to the plaintiff's title in a *quare impedit*, for *quare impedit* is a real action, and this is well proved because at common law there were no damages in *quare impedit*: and that is still so at the present day in some cases, as appears in 9 Hen. VI.[1] This, then, proves that it was real, for by the common law one recovered the presentation and patronage and nothing else, until the statute came which gave him damages.[2] After title has been made to the advowson, a warranty is a good plea, and so the action is real in its nature. If, then, the action is real, it behoves of necessity to have someone named who has the real thing which is to be recovered, to the intent he shall be defended by the person who has it, and that is the patron, for he has

[1] YB Mich. 9 Hen. VI, fo. 32, pl. 1. [2] Statute of Westminster II, c. 5 (*SR* i. 75).

presentmente, et lencumbent ne lordynare nount ryens en le patronage, ergo
ilz ne poyent pleder en barre per reson per le comen ley, nyent pluys que le
disseisor en assise. Et sicome en assise est bon ple de monstre que nest ascun
tenaunt nosme en le brefe, issint est en quare impedit de monstre que nest
ascun patron. Et nyent pluys que le disseisor en asise ne poit pleder en barre,
pur ceo que il nad le tenaunce, ne le tenaunt del terre en assise de rent ou un
pernor est nosme, entant que il nest tenaunt del choce destre recover, scilicet
le rent, quell le pernor ad, nyent pluys poit lencumbent per le comen ley
pleder en barre en defence del patronage, de que choce il ryen ad. Mez ore
per lequite del estatute de anno 25 E. 3. il poit pleder come moy semble, mes
ceo covyent estre accordant a lentente dez fezors destatute, et ceo est toutz
ditz lou le patron est nosme, quar lestatute parle expressemente ou le suyte
est prise vers le patron et il ne voet defender que donques lencumbent serra
receu de defender et traverser le tytle le plaintife, et issint est del ordynarye:
donques lentent dez fezors ne fuit que lencumbent averoit power de pleder en
barre lou le patron ne fuit nosme, quar donques myschefe ensuera per lour
provysion az patrons, quar chescun home voille suer son quare impedit vers
lencumbent soullmente et il per son covyn perdra le avowzon lou il nad ryens
en ceo, et le patron ne poit ceo ayder quar il ne poit ceo defender quaunt il
nest nosme, mes quaunt est nosme reson fuit a doner ple al encumbent
quaunt le patron ne voille ceo defender, et la est le defaut le patron que etc.
Donques icy est null patron nosme en le brefe, quar lencumbent ad monstre
que J. Folejam, esquier, luy presenta, quell J. Folejam nest nosme, et sil
solemente luy presenta il est le patron et le dit Godfrey Folejam nemi, quar il
ne fyst ascun presentmente. Donques quaunt lencumbent plede cest matter
supra in barre et null patron nosme, le plaintife poit aver demurre sur son
ple. Mes quaunt il prist lavermente que le dit encumbent est un des grauntees,
per ceo il confessa tout le ple lencumbent destre voyer, et sur ceo per son
conusance demesne appyert que nest ascun patron nosme en le brefe, quar
ore il ad confesse que lencumbent que il nest einz de presentmente lordynare
ne del presentmente de Godfrey Folljam mes de presentmente dun estraunger
que nest nosme, ergo null patron nosme en le brefe, pur quell le brefe
abatera. [*fo. 115*]

Mes fuit agree per les justyces que en quare impedit est bon ple pur
lencumbent de monstre que il est einz de presentmente dun estraunge que est en
pleyn vye, nyent nosme en le brefe, jugement de brefe. Quere tamen. Et vide
Lorkyns case 22 E. 4.

the whole advowson and the presentation, and neither the incumbent nor the ordinary have anything in the patronage, and therefore they may not in reason plead in bar by the common law, any more than the disseisor may in an assize. And just as in an assize it is a good plea to show that there is no tenant named in the writ, so it is in a *quare impedit* to show that there is no patron. And just as the disseisor may not plead in bar in an assize, because he does not have the tenancy, no more may the tenant of the land in an assize for rent where a pernor is named, since he is not tenant of thing to be recovered, namely the rent, which the pernor has; and no more may the incumbent at common law plead in bar in defence of the patronage, in which he has nothing. But now, by the equity of the statute of the year 25 Edw. III,[1] he may plead, as it seems to me; but this must be in accordance with the intention of the makers of the statute, and that is always where the patron is named, for the statute says expressly that where the suit is taken against the patron, and he will not defend, the incumbent shall be received to defend and to traverse the plaintiff's title. And so it is of the ordinary. Therefore the intention of the makers was not that the incumbent should have power to plead in bar where the patron was not named, for then mischief would ensue to the patrons by their enactment, for everyone would sue his *quare impedit* against the incumbent alone, and by his covin he would lose the advowson, whereas he had nothing in it, and the patron could not help it, for he cannot defend when he is not named, though when he is named it was right to give a plea to the incumbent when the patron would not defend it, and there it is the patron's default etc. Here, then, there is no patron named in the writ, for the incumbent has shown that John Foljambe, esquire, presented him, which John Foljambe is not named, and if he alone presented him he is the patron and the said Godfrey Foljambe is not, for he did not make any presentation. When, therefore, the incumbent pleads this matter above in bar, and no patron is named, the plaintiff could have demurred upon his plea. But when he took the averment that the said incumbent is one of the grantees, he thereby confessed all of the incumbent's plea to be true, and thereupon by his own acknowledgment it appears that there is no patron named in the writ, for now he has confessed that the incumbent is not in by the presentation of the ordinary, nor by the presentation of Godfrey Foljambe, but by the presentation of a stranger who is not named, and therefore no patron is named in the writ, and so the writ shall abate.

But it was agreed by the justices that in *quare impedit* it is a good plea for the incumbent to show that he is in by the presentation of a stranger, who is alive and not named in the writ, and pray judgment of the writ. (Nevertheless, query. And see Lorkin's case, 22 Edw. IV.[2])

[1] 25 Edw. III, stat. 6, c. 3 (*SR* i. 325). This is stat. 3 in *Statutes at Large.*
[2] *Lorkin's Case* (1482) YB Hil. 22 Edw. IV, fo. 44, pl. 7.

[B]

Benl. 25–26, pl. 40; whence Moo. 4, pl. 14; 4 Leon. 119, pl. 240; 1 And. 2, pl. 2.

Le dit [Sir][1] Raffe Longforde esteant seise del dit manner de Barleboroughe ove les appurtenances a quel le dit advowson fuit appendant in fee presenta a mesme le esglise, esteant voide, le dit John White son clarke, le quel fuit admitt et institute, et apres le dit Rauffe per son dit fait graunt le procheine avoidance de mesme le esglise as ditz [Sir][2] Godfrey Follyambe, James Follyambe, George Follyambe et Waltham et eorum uni conjunctim vel divisim, et apres ceo graunt le dit [Sir][3] Rauffe Longford levie un fyne de mesme le mannor etc. al quel etc. al dit [Sir][4] William Hollis in fee, et apres le dit esglise devient voide per le mort le dit John White. Et le dit [Sir][5] Godfrey Follyambe solement present le dit William Waltham son clarke etc., le quel fuit admitte et institute etc.

Et cest case fuit argue per les serjeants et justicez de mesme le Bank en Michaelmas terme procheine apres. Et fuit la adjuge que le brefe abatera, [quar][6] ils adjudger[ont] que cest presentment del dit [Sir][7] Godfrey solement fuit bon del dit William Waltham, nient obstant que le dit William fuit un de lez grauntees del dit advowson. Le author de cest liver fuit present et [oya][8] mesmes les arguments et judgement.

[23]

BL MS Harley 1691, fo. 115 (dated '33 H. 8').

Cest case fuit demande de les justyces de Comen Banke: si lesse pur anz devyse per son testamente que la feme avera les terres en lesse pur terme de sa vye, le remainder a un J. S. et a les heirs de son corps, et pur defaut de tyell yssue le remainder a ses enfantz et a lour heirs de lour corps, le testatour devie, et la feme avoit le lesse et devie. Le questyon fuit, si les executours averont le resydue de les anz ou cestui en remainder?

Baldwyn semble que alera accordant a lentent del devyse.

---

[1] seignior.
[2] Sñr.
[3] Sñr.
[4] Sñr.
[5] Sñr.   [6] quel.
[7] Sñr.   [8] oyer.

B[1]

The said[2] Sir Ralph Longford, being seised of the said manor of Barlborough with the appurtenances, to which the said advowson was appendant, in fee, presented to the same church when it was vacant the said John White, his clerk, who was admitted and instituted, and afterwards the said Ralph by his said deed granted the next avoidance of the same church to the said Sir Godfrey Foljambe, James Foljambe, George Foljambe and Waltham, 'and one of them jointly or severally' (*et eorum uni conjunctim vel divisim*), and after this grant the said Sir Ralph Longford levied a fine of the same manor etc. to which etc. to the said Sir William Hollys in fee, and afterwards the said church became vacant by the death of the said John White. And the said Sir Godfrey Foljambe alone presented the said William Waltham, his clerk etc., who was admitted and instituted etc.

This case was argued by the serjeants and justices of the same Bench in Michaelmas term next after. And it was there adjudged that the writ should abate, for they adjudged that this presentment of the said William Waltham by the said Sir Godfrey alone was good, notwithstanding that the said William was one of the grantees of the said advowson. The author of this book was present and heard the same arguments and judgment.

23. ANON.

Common Pleas, 1541. Probably the same case as Brooke Abr., *Done*, pl. 57; *Chattelles*, pl. 23 (dated Mich. 1541).

This case was demanded of the justices of the Common Bench. A lessee for years devises by his testament that his wife should have the lands in lease for term of her life, remainder to one John Style and the heirs of [his body], and for default of such issue remainder to his children and the heirs of their bodies; the testator dies; and the woman has the lease and dies. The question was: shall the executors or the remainderman have the rest of the years?

BALDWIN thought it should ago according to the intention of the devise.

[1] Bendlowes' report.
[2] The report is preceded by a copy of the record.

[24]

BL MS Harley 1691, fo. 115r–v (dated '33 H. 8').

Nota que le vycar de Stamford Mountfychett en le countye Dessex suyst en court christyan pur dismez de coppye woodes que fuit ouster xx. anz cress[ance],[1] et prohybityon fuit sue sur ceo, surmysant que lou per lestatute de anno 45 E. 3. est ordeyne que des arbres ouster xx. anz cress[ance] dismes ne serra paye, la ad le dit vycar eux trahe en court christyan pur dismes de arbres ouster xx. anz cress[ance]. Et le prohibition ala hors del Banke le Roy as jugges del court [de] Arches levesque de Canterbury. Sur que vyent le vycar per son counsell en le dit banke et monstre cest matter de surmyse del prohybytyon, et dit que le veryte de son case est que il et ses predecessors ount use de temps dount memorye ne court daver les dismes des arbres queux ount estre destre scies pur coppyes, non obstante que soyent de xxi. ans ou pluys, et entant que le veryte de mon case est issint jeo entende de pleder cest prescription a cest surmyse, et si trove soit pur moy donques daver consultatyon.

Mountague, Chief Justyce. Coment voilles vous prescriber encontre estatute? Quar lestatute est que dez arbres ouster xx. anz cress[ance] tythes ne serra dones, et home ne poit prescriber encontre un estatute.

Le counsell del vycar. Lestatute de religiosis voet que terres et tenementz ne serra don a mortmayne, et uncore ceux de Lond' prescribe a doner terres en mortmayne.

Lewke, Justyce. Le cause de ceo est pur ceo que lour lybertyes sont preserves per estatute.

Le counsell le vycar. Sir, lestatute voet que prohybytion serra graunt, et sur ceo attachmente, come ad este use. Donques cest estatute nest meremente que prohybition girra en toutz cases mes est que serra graunt ou ad este use, et cest a entender lou null prescription fuit avaunt lestatute daver dismes de arbors de cress[ance] ouster xx. anz, que la le prohybition fuit grauntable devaunt lestatute et issint serra ore.

Mountagew lya lestatute et <dit que>[i] il entende lestatute lou [*fo. 115v*] home est implede pur dismes dez arbres ouster xx. anz cress[ance] que la prohybytion serra graunt, et sur ceo attachmente, come ad este use, issint que en chescun case fuit use de ceo graunter lou tiellx tythes fueront demandes devaunt lestatute, scilicet si fuit dez arbres ouster xx. anz, quar de comen droit home ne doit tythes de eux per comen ley pur ceo que ne sont uses destre coupes per entendmente et pur ceo la prohybytion est toutz ditz grauntable.

---

[1] *Or* cress[er].

24. CASE OF THE VICAR OF STANSTED

King's Bench and Common Pleas, 1541. Cf. Bro. Abr., *Prohibition*, pl. 17
(1539/40).

Note that the vicar of Stansted Mountfitchet in the county of Essex sued in
court christian for tithes of coppice woods which were over twenty years'
growth, and a prohibition was thereupon sued, alleging that whereas by the
statute of the year 45 Edw. III it was ordained that tithes should not be paid
from trees above twenty years' growth,[1] the said vicar had drawn them into
court christian for tithes of trees above twenty years' growth. And the
prohibition went out of the King's Bench to the judges of the Arches court of
the archbishop of Canterbury. Whereupon the vicar came into the said bench,
by his counsel, and showed this matter of surmise for the prohibition, and said
that the truth of his case was that he and his predecessors have been
accustomed since time immemorial to have the tithes of the trees which have
been felled for coppice, notwithstanding that they are of twenty-one years or
more, and since that is the truth of my case I intend to plead this prescription
against this surmise, and if it is found for me to have a consultation.

MOUNTAGUE, Chief Justice. How will you prescribe against a statute? For
the statute says that no tithes shall be given of trees above twenty years'
growth; and one cannot prescribe against a statute.

The vicar's counsel. The statute *De religiosis* says that lands and tenements
shall not be given in mortmain,[2] and yet Londoners prescribe to give lands in
mortmain.

LUKE, Justice. The reason for that is because their liberties have been
preserved by statute.[3]

The vicar's counsel. Sir, the statute says that a prohibition shall be granted,
and thereupon an attachment, as had been the usage; therefore this statute is
not merely that a prohibition will lie in all cases, but that it shall be granted
where it had been used, and that means where there was no prescription before
the statute to have tithes of trees above twenty years' growth, for there the
prohibition was grantable before the statute and so it shall be now.

MOUNTAGUE read the statute and said that he understood the statute to
mean that where someone is impleaded for tithes of trees above twenty years'
growth a prohibition shall be granted, and thereupon an attachment, as had
been the usage, so that it was the usage to grant it in every case where such
tithes were demanded before the statute, namely if it was for trees over twenty
years, for of common right one does not owe tithes thereof at common law
because by presumption they are not used to be felled; and therefore the
prohibition is always grantable.

[1] 45 Edw. III, c. 3, *De sylva caedua* (*SR* i. 393).
[2] 7 Edw. I, *De viris religiosis* (*SR* i. 51).
[3] Magna Carta 1225, c. 9.

Er issint fuit loppinion del court.

Et nota que puis le counsell le vycar mova le case en le Comen Banke, scilicet si home ad coppice woodes que ad use destre fell ascun foitz al xix anz, ascun foitz meindre, come happera destre growen, sil succide eux quaunt sont de cress[ance] ouster xx. anz sil payera tythes ou nemi?

Et la toutz les justyces, scilicet *Baldwyn*, *Shelley* et *Wylughbye*, semble que il payera tythes pur tyell boys.

Browne dit que les justyces de Bank le Roy sont de contrare opynion.

Shelley. Pur que?

Browne. Pur ceo que lestatute est al contrare.

Shelley et toutz. Lestatute nest al contrare, quar lestatute fist mesne que pur grosse arbres queux ne sont uses destre vendus et coupes pur coppye wood mes sont succide pur tymbre que la null tythes serra paye, et si tyell tymbre soit succide et le parson voille demander tythes de ceo per nosme de silva cedua lou est silva cedua en fait, scilicet wood quell est use destre felles, si soyt de xl. anz il tythera pur ceo que lentent dez fezors destatute ne[i] fuit douster ascun parson dez dismes de silva cedua mes de ouster eux de dismes de graund arbres queux sont coupes pur tymbre et byldinge de mesons et shypps.

Quere, et vide 50 E.3: et la en attachment pur suer pur dismes de grosse arbres in court christyn lissue fuit prise que il suast pur dismes de silva cedua sauns ceo quill semble que dez grosse arbres il ne tythera mes per silva cedua il voet.

Quere que serra dit grosse arbres: et semble que arbres uses pur tymber queux nount estre use destre coupes pur coppye woodes et fyar woodes et destre garde de recresser.

Quere tamen quell fyne le matter prist, quar les justyces del Banke le Roy ne voillont assenter a ceo.

Et puis le vycar suast attachmente sur le prohybytion vers luy mesme al entent de vener einz et <avoit jour de>[i] pleder, et la donques de tender un issue ut supra, ut en le dit lyver de 50 E. 3, quar fuit tenus que il ne poit prender ascun yssue sil ne vyent einz sur lattachmente.

That was the opinion of the court.

And note that afterwards the vicar's counsel moved the case in the Common Bench, namely: if someone has coppice woods which have been used to be felled sometimes at nineteen years, sometimes less if they happen to have grown, and he fells them when they are above twenty years' growth, shall he pay tithes or not?

And all the justices, namely BALDWIN [C.J.], SHELLEY and WILLOUGHBY, thought that he should pay tithes for such wood.

BROWNE said that the justices of the King's Bench were of a contrary opinion.

SHELLEY. Why?

BROWNE. Because the statute is to the contrary.

SHELLEY and all the others. The statute is not to the contrary, for the statute creates a means whereby no tithes should be paid of great trees which are not used to be sold and felled for coppice wood but are felled as timber; and if such timber is felled and the parson demands tithes thereof by the name of *sylva caedua* where it is *sylva caedua* in fact, namely wood which is used to be felled, [even if] it is of forty years' growth, he shall tithe, because the intention of the makers of the statute was not to oust any parson from tithes of *sylva caedua* but to oust them from tithes of great trees which are felled as timber for building houses and ships.

Query, and see 50 Edw. III,[1] where in an attachment for suing in court christian for tithes of great trees the issue taken was that he sued for tithes of *sylva caedua*, without this [that he sued for other wood]: whereby it seems that he would not tithe for great trees though he would for *sylva caedua*.

What shall be called great trees? It seems that they are trees used for timber which have not been used to be felled for coppice wood and firewood and kept to grow back again.

Query nevertheless how the matter ended, for the justices of the King's Bench would not assent to it.

Afterwards the vicar sued an attachment upon the prohibition against himself with the purpose of coming in and having a day to plead, and then to tender an issue there as above—as in the said book of 50 Edw. III—for it was held that he could not take any issue if he did not come in upon the attachment.

---

[1] *Frankley* v. *Heyning* (1376) YB Hil. 50 Edw. III, fo. 10, pl. 21.

[25]

BL MS Harley 1691, fo. 144v.

Cell case argue T. 33 H.8.

Un J. delivera certen som de money a un G. pur deliver ouster a un feme a son use et profitt quaunt il serra marrye, et mesme le jour, puis delivere fait, est accorde enter le baillour et le dit G. que si le dit baillour mista son lettre ensealle al dit G. pur lez denerz que adonques il redelyvera eux a le bailour. Et puis le baillour per son testament voille que le dit G. eux delivera a un estraunger, et il issint fait. Et puis le feme est marye, et ell ovesque son baron port brefe de accompte vers le dit G.

Fuit dit per *Shelley* et *Baldewyn*, Chif Justice, que J. le bailour purra bien revoker cell don fait al feme. Et ceo diversite pris per *Shelley*: lou est un done perfett, scilicet donatio perfecta, et lou il est forsque un done commence, scilicet donatio incepta. Quar est done perfet quaunt delyvery est fait, et le done a ceo agre: come lou jeo done a vous esteant present un chos, et vous a ceo agrea et ceo accepta, ceo est done perfett ou execute, et la le donour ne purra recover ceo. Issint dun feoffement fait et livery execute all feoffe. Mez lou il est forsque don commence ou executorye, la le donour purra bien ceo revocare: come feoffement fait et lettre de attorney fait pur faire livery et seisin, la le feoffour purra ceo revoker et commaunde a luy a que le [lettre]¹ est fait que il ne fesoit livery. Issint si jeo aye iiii. chyvalles et jeo dye, Jeo don cell chivall a R., que nest donques present, et issint de chescun dez auterz chivalles, et puis devaunt lyvery fait pur diverz consyderations jeo revoca ceo done, ceo est bon. Mesme le ley si home appoynta dyverz newares gyftes a sez amites, et delivera eux a son servant et commaunda a luy pur eux deliver, et puis il remember luy mesme et en alaunt a sez amies il mista et countermaunde son servaunt, ceo est bon. Issint si jeo delivera biens al [bailer]² ouster a un estrange, le bailour poit ceo countermaunde, quar en toutz ceux cases lez dones ne sont perfectes mez incepta. Mez sil fuit ascun consideration per le done expresse, pur que le done duist estre fait, la le baillour ne purra ceo revoker. Come si J. enfeoffe moy dun acre et jeo dye a un A. en tiell forme, scilicet, A. preignes ycy de moy ceux xx. li. et pur ceo [que] J. ad moy enfeoffe dun acre de terre jeo voile que vous luy delivera ceux denerz, la le baillour ne purra ceo revoker pur ceo que la est un bone consideration expres pur que le dit [J.]³ avera eux. Mez en toutz ceux cases si avaunt le countermaundement le baile ad execute le done, donques le revocation ou contermaundement fait est voyde. Et issint en ceo cas, le done ne

---

¹ liv[er]y.
² bailo[u]r.
³ *Blank.*

25. LYTE v. PENY

Common Pleas, Trin. 1541. Also reported in Dyer, ff. 48b-49b (Pas. 1541). Record: CP 40/1099, m. 340d.

This case was argued in Trinity term, 33 Hen. VIII.

One J. delivered a certain sum of money to one G. to deliver over to a woman to her use and profit when she married, and on the same day, after the delivery was made, it was agreed between the bailor and the said G. that if the said bailor sent his sealed letter to the said G. for the money he would then redeliver it to the bailor. Afterwards the bailor by his testament willed that the said G. should deliver the money to a stranger, and so he did. Afterwards the woman married, and she with her husband brought a writ of account against the said G.

It was said by SHELLEY and BALDWIN, Chief Justice, that J. (the bailor) could well revoke this gift made to the woman. And this distinction was taken by SHELLEY: where it is a perfect gift, namely *donatio perfecta*, and where it is only a gift commenced, namely *donatio incepta*.[1] For it is a perfect gift when delivery is made and the donee agrees to it: as where I give something to you, being present, and you agree to it and accept it, this is a perfect and executed gift, and there the donor cannot recover it back. Likewise of a feoffment made and livery executed to the feoffee. But where it is only a commenced or executory gift, the donor may well revoke it: for instance, a feoffment made with a letter of attorney to make livery and seisin, the feoffor may revoke this and command the person to whom the letter was made that he should not make livery. Likewise if I have four horses and I say, 'I give this horse to R.', who is not then present, and similarly with each of the other horses, and then before delivery is made I revoke this gift for various considerations, that is good. The law is the same if someone appoints various new-year's gifts to his friends, and delivers them to his servant and commands him to deliver them, and then he remembers himself and sends for and countermands his servant while he is going to his friends, this is good. Likewise if I deliver goods to be bailed over to a stranger, the bailor may countermand this, for in all these cases the gifts are not *perfecta* but *incepta*. If, however, there was any consideration expressed on the gift, explaining why the gift was made, the bailor could not revoke it. For instance, if J. enfeoffs me of an acre and I say to one A. in this manner, 'A., take here from me this £20, and forasmuch as J. has enfeoffed me of an acre of land I wish you to deliver this money to him', there the bailor cannot revoke it because there is a good consideration expressed why the said J. should have the money. But, in all these cases, if the bailee has executed the gift before the countermand, the revocation or countermand is void. Likewise

---

[1] This learning is from *Bracton*: see Dyer, fo. 49a, §8.

duit estre execute tanque le mariage, et auxi nest ascun consideration recite in le ple pur que le done eux avera, et avaunt le mariage le bailour ceo revoca, per que il est bone: quar, admitte que le baile ne unques maria ou que il disagre a cell done et ne voille prender lez denerz, ou morust avaunt mariage, donques est clere que le bailour reavera lez denerz arrere. Issint que toutz ceux cases prove que le done ne fuit execute mez que le revocation est bone.

[26]

BL MS. Harley 1691, fo. 57 (Anno '34 H. 8').

Portmayne vient al barre en le Comen Banke termino Pasche et demande des justices si tenant en tayle en possession devant estatute de anno 27 quell execute possession al use ust suffre un recovere sauns ascun consyderation, si cesti que recover serra seisi a son use en taylle ou en fee?

Willughbye, Justyce, dit quil fuit byen remembre que cell question fuit debate en temps de Fitzherbert, et donques cell diversite fuit pryse: quant il fait feffmente sauns consyderation et quaunt il suffre un recovere. Quar en le prymer case il serra seisi al use en taylle pur ceo que le possession nest disafferme par le feffmente. Mes en le case de recovere auterment est.

Shelley semble null diversite et que en ambideux cases il serra seisi a son use en taylle quar le feffment disprove lestate auxibyen come le recoverye. Quar il dyscontynue le taylle et ascuns foitz barre ceo par garrante et donques est impertinent que sur tiell choce le taylle serra save en use quell ceo dyscontynue et ascuns foitz defete.

Mes a ceo fuit dit que ceo poit estre auxibien. Come tenant en fee simple don son fee simple, uncore ceo serra luy save en use.

Fuit dit per *Browne* que si home fait feffmente sauns consyderation de terre dount il est seisi de part le mere, le use serra a mesme lheir et ensuera le tenaunce. Mesme la ley de feffmente des terres en gavelkynde.

Bawdwyn dit que nest ascun reson que sur feffmente ou recovere serra ascun use mes pur le contynuance de ceo est devenus un ley.

in this case, the gift is not to be executed until the marriage, and also there is no consideration recited in the plea why the donee should have the money, and the bailor revoked it before the marriage, and so it is good: for, admit that the bailee never married, or that she disagreed to this gift and would not take the money, or died before marriage, then it would be clear that the bailor should have the money back. Thus all these cases prove that the gift was not executed but that the revocation is good.

26. ANON.

Common Pleas, Pas. 1542.

Portman came to the bar in the Common Bench in Easter term and asked the justices: if a tenant in tail in possession before the statute of the twenty-seventh year, which executes possession to the use,[1] had suffered a recovery without any consideration, would the person who recovered be seised to his use in tail or in fee?

WILLOUGHBY, Justice, said he well remembered this question being debated in the time of Fitzherbert,[2] and at that time a distinction was made between when he makes a feoffment without consideration and when he suffers a recovery. For in the first case he shall be seised to the use in tail, because the possession is not disaffirmed by the feoffment, whereas in the case of a recovery it is otherwise.

SHELLEY thought it no distinction, and that in both cases he should be seised to his use in tail, for a feoffment disproves the estate just as a recovery does.[3] For it discontinues the tail, and sometimes bars it by warranty; and it would be absurd if something which discontinues (and sometimes defeats) the tail should save it in use.

But as to this it was said that it could do so well enough. For instance, if a tenant in fee simple gives his fee simple, this shall nevertheless be saved for him in use.

It was said by BROWNE that if someone makes a feoffment without consideration of land whereof he is seised from his mother's side, the use shall be to the same heir and shall follow the tenancy. The law is the same of a feoffment of lands in gavelkind.[4]

BALDWIN [C.J.] said there was no reason why there should be any use upon a feoffment or recovery, but by the continuance thereof it has become law.

---

[1] Statute of Uses, 27 Hen. VIII, c. 10 (*SR* iii. 539).
[2] J.C.P. 1522–38.
[3] Cf. the note in Caryll's reports, above, p. 401, no. 77.
[4] Cf. the next case (no. 27), which Browne argued as a serjeant seven years earlier.

[27]

Gell's MS., Library of Congress, part 1, fo. 40.[1]

Devaunt le statute de usez home fuit seisi del terre que vient a luy per discent a son meere, et il fait feffement en fee a son use demesne. Le question est, le quel ceo terre serra discende a lez droit heirs de parte son pere ou a lez heyrs de parte son meere?

Et *Wyllowby* dit que il covient discend a lez heirs de parte son miere.

Bromley. Moy semble le contrarie, quar quaunt il ad fait un feffement a son use il est eins come per un novell estate, quar il est come un purchase, que est un novell estate, et pur ceo que il est eins per un novell estate la terre doit discender a lez droit heirs de part son piere.

Browne all contrarie, quar mittomus que une home est seisi del terre en gavelkynde ou en borowght Englische et il fait feffement en fee a un autre, la terre serra discend a lez droit heirs per le custome et nemi a lez heirs per le comen ley: quod fuit concessum per tout la court.

Et une dez serjantes reherse le case et dit que il ad voie un liver en quel il est adjudge que la terre covient discender a lez heirs de parte son pier. Ideo nota.

[28]

Gell's MS., Library of Congress, part 1, fo. 40.

Un move al barre si home recover envers tenaunt en tayle et ad un brefe de habere facias seisinam et le tenaunt en tayle entre arere sur le recoverer et le recoverer morust, loppinion de tout la court fuit que lissue le recoverer poit bien enter.

---

[1] *Among cases printed as Trin. 27 Hen. VIII.*

27. ANON.

Common Pleas, Trin. 1535.

Before the Statute of Uses[1] someone was seised of land which came to him by descent from his mother, and he made a feoffment in fee to his own use. The question is, whether this land shall descend to the right heirs on his father's side or to the heirs on his mother's side?

Willoughby said that it must descend to the heirs on his mother's side.

Bromley. I think the contrary; for when he has made a feoffment to his use he is in as by a new estate; for it is like a purchase, which is a new estate. Since he is in by a new estate, the land ought to descend to the right heirs on his father's side.

Browne to the contrary. Suppose someone is seised of land in gavelkind or borough English, and makes a feoffment in fee to another: the land shall descend to the right heirs by the custom and not to the heirs by the common law. (This was agreed by the whole court.[2])

One of the serjeants recited the case, and said he had seen a book in which it is adjudged that the land ought to descend to the heirs on his father's side. Therefore take note.

28. ANON.

Common Pleas, Trin. 1535.

Someone moved at the bar: if a man recovers against a tenant in tail and has a writ of *habere facias seisinam*, and the tenant in tail re-enters upon the recoveror, and the recoveror dies, [what then?]. The opinion of the whole court was that the recoveror's issue might well enter.

[1] 27 Hen. VIII, c. 10 (*SR* iii. 539).
[2] Cf. the previous case (no. 26).

11. Reports by Randle Cholmeley (1544)[1]

[1]

Detnewe dun escript[2] indent de un lesse <fait per un R. all plaintife etc. >[i] fuit port en le Gyldhall de Loundres et count sur un trover. Le deffendant dit que longe temps devaunt que il riens avoit que le plaintife mesme fuit possesse de ceo, et ceo perde, et J. Stokysley, evesque de Loundres, ceo trova, <en que possession >[3] a que mesme le plaintife relles toutes maners dactions, variances[i], sutes et demaundes per son fait que cy est, et que le evesque ceo dona all deffendant, le quel ceo perda, et un John Downe ceo trova et dona all plaintife, et apres ceo le plaintife ceo perda et il devient en possession le defendant,[4] per que il ceo garde come bien a luy lyst. Et nota que le barre fuit certenment plede. Sur quel fuit demurre en ley. Et fuit argue devaunt *Crafford*, donques southviconte la.

Curson reherce le case, et sur ceo il move iii. poyntes. Primerment quel est fait per le relles ut supra, scilicet si laction del partie est ale solement et nemi son interest del choce issint que il poit seiser, ou si tout lenterest est ale. Et donques, admitte que riens est ale forsque laction, si per le darren possession launcient droit que le partie avoit all choce est restore <en possession >[i]. Et donques, si cestui ore defendant prendra advantage de cest relles fait al evesque, pur ceo que ill est mere estraunge a ceo ou nemi. Et primerment, quant all relles, moy semble que il nad dispence forsque ovesque son action tantsolement, quar le ley ad limitte le meane coment chescun fait serra prise et construe. Come si home dona terres a moy et a mes assignes, jeo nay fee per ceo. Sur lauter part, si home fait lesse a moy pur vie saunz parler de mes assignes, jeo puis faire assigne durant mon terme pur vie. Et si jeo relles actions personals, actions reals ne sount dispence per ceo. Et si home prist ma toge jay 4. remedyes, scilicet per brefe de trans., ou detnewe, ou replegiare, et

---

[1] Lincoln's Inn, MS. Hale 189, ff. 249–256.
[2] *Written over* fait, *del.*
[3] *Del.*
[4] *Altered from* pl.

450

11. REPORTS BY RANDLE CHOLMELEY (1544)

1. ANON.

Sheriffs' Court, Guildhall, London, *c.* 1544. Cf. very similar facts in *Anon.* (1542) Bro. Abr., *Releases*, pl. 90; Gell's reports, Mich. 33 [?recte 34] Hen. VIII, fo. 2.

Detinue for an indented writing of a lease made by one R. to the plaintiff etc. was brought in the Guildhall of London; and he counted on a trover. The defendant said that long before he had anything the plaintiff himself was possessed thereof, and lost it, and John Stokesley, bishop of London,[1] found it, and the plaintiff released to him all manner of actions, variances, suits and demands, by his deed which is here; and the bishop gave [the deed of lease] to the defendant, who lost it; and one John Downe found it and gave it to the plaintiff; afterwards the plaintiff lost it, and it came into the possession of the defendant, and so he kept it as well he might. Note that the bar was pleaded with certainty. Whereupon it was demurred in law; and it was argued before *Crafford*, then under-sheriff there.[2]

Curson[3] recited the case, and thereupon he moved three points. First, what is effected by the release as above? That is to say, is it only the party's action which is gone, and not his interest in the thing, so that he can still seize it, or is the whole interest gone? Then, assuming that nothing is gone but the action, is the old right, which the party had to the thing, restored in possession by the last possession? And then, may the present defendant take advantage of this release made to the bishop, given that he is an absolute stranger to it, or not? Firstly, as to the release, it seems to me that he has not dispensed with anything except his action; for the law has limited the means whereby every deed shall be understood and construed. Thus if someone gives lands to me and my assigns, I have no fee thereby. On the other hand, if someone makes a lease to me for life without speaking of my assigns, I may make an assignment during my term of life. And if I release actions personal, actions real are not thereby dispensed with. If someone takes my gown I have four remedies, namely by writ of

---

[1] Bishop of London 1530–39.
[2] Guy Crafford, bencher of Lincoln's Inn (1532), one of the under-sheriffs of London.
[3] Robert Curson, bencher of Lincoln's Inn (1529), common pleader in the city of London 1532–47: *Readers and Readings*, p. 119.

auxi per voy de seiser, et en cest case[i] si jeo relles toutz actions unquore jeo puy seiser. Et si jeo sue disseisi et apres relles alle disseiser toutz maners de actions et damaundes, unquore jeo puy enter, et le reyson est pur ceo que jay divers remedyes. Et ceux parolx demaundes va forsque pur user de action et nemi a auter purpose. Issint moy semble que le partie nest conclude a seiser, et donques quaunt il vient a le possession apres ceo perfite le droit <et interest>[i] que il avoit all choce, et donques quaunt le defendant ceo detient ore ceo est novell tort et issint punyshable per son action. Et all darren moy semble que il ne prendra avantage de cest rellesse pur ceo que il est estraunge a ceo, quar si home prist mes bienz et jeo relles a luy <ut supra>[i] ore sil dona eux a un estraunge et jeo port action il ne pledra cest reles quar est estraunge. Et null prendra avantage de tiel fait si non cestui a que il est fait ou sez executours, que sount privey en ley. Et si home moy disseise et jeo relles a luy ut supra, ore si un estraunge luy disseise et jeo port assise et il plede le relles fait all lauter, ceo nest plee, pur ceo que il est estraunge. Et pur cest cause principalment moy semble que cest action per le maner est bien maintenable et que le ple en barre nest bon, per que nous devomus recover le dit escript etc. [fo. 249v]

Rastell. Moy semble que le plee est bon. Et reherce lez poyntes move per Curson, et dit que le primer poynt enclude le second en luy mesme: et ceo fuit deny de nulluy. Et quant a ceo <il dit>[1] moy semble que per le relles de toutz demaundes le interest del choce est determyne, quar demaunde est per iii. voyes, scilicet per matter de recorde, come action, per nude parol, come a demaunder delivery, et auxi per entre ou seiser. Et pur ceo 21 libro assisarum est ajuge que en assise de rent tiel relles est bon plee. Et si home ad rent charge et relles toutz demaundez il ne poit distreiner quar ceo est demande en ley. Vide 6 H. 7. <40. E. 3. relles de toutes demandez forsque fe tout pas.>[2] Et si cestui que ad comen relles ut supra il ne poit occupyer ovesque sez bestes, quar ceo est demaunde en ley. Et jeo luy conclude de ceo per son fait demesne. Auxi 19. H. 6, home ne suera execution contrary a tiel relles, quell prove que il est plus fort que relles de toutz actions. Et auxi en launcient liver de Lit. il est clere que home ne entra contrary a tiell relles. Unquore en lez novels livers il est mis un quere, et ceo fuit pur lopynyon de mon seigniour Fitzjamez, per que etc. Et all darren poynt moy semble que il pledra le ple assetz bien, quar si un moy disseise et jeo relles a luy, et puis enfeoffe un auter, le feoffe prendra avantage de cest relles. Et issint est que le lesse pledra fait fait a son lessour, et tenant en dower pledra fait fait a son baron. Et issint le ple est bon.

---

[1] *Del.*
[2] *Added in margin.*

trespass, or detinue, or replevin, and also by way of seizure; and in this case even if I release all actions I may still seize. And if I am disseised, and afterwards release to the disseisor all manner of actions and demands, I may still enter; and the reason is because I have various remedies. The word 'demands' goes only to the using of an action and not to any other purpose. Thus it seems to me that the party is not barred from seizing, and therefore when he comes to the possession afterwards this perfects the right and interest which he had in the thing, and therefore when the defendant detains it this is a new wrong and so punishable by his action. As to the last point, it seems to me that he shall not take advantage of this release, because he is a stranger to it; for if someone takes my goods and I release to him as above, and he gives them to a stranger, and I bring an action, he shall not plead this release, because he is a stranger. And no one shall take advantage of such a deed but the person to whom it is made, or his executors, who are privy in law. If someone disseises me, and I release to him as above, and then a stranger disseises him, and I bring an assize, and he pleads the release made to the other person, this is no plea, because he is a stranger. And for that cause principally it seems to me that this action is well maintainable in the way it is brought, and that the plea in bar is not good; and so we ought to recover the said writing etc.

Rastell.[1] It seems to me that the plea is good. (He recited the points moved by Curson, and said that the first point included the second in itself: which nobody denied. As to that, he said:) It seems to me that by the release of all demands the interest in the thing is determined, for a 'demand' may be made in three ways, namely [1] by matter of record, such as an action; [2] by bare word, as by asking for delivery; and [3] by entry or seizure. Therefore it is adjudged in 21 Lib. Ass. that in an assize for rent such a release is a good plea.[2] And if someone has a rent-charge and releases all demands, he may not distrain; for that is a demand in law. See 6 Hen. VII.[3] 40 Edw. III, a release of all demands except fee: everything passes.[4] If someone who has a common releases as above, he may not occupy it with his beasts, for that is a demand in law. And I will estop him from it by his own deed. Also 19 Hen. VI, one may not sue execution contrary to such a release,[5] which proves that it is stronger than a release of all actions. Also in the old book of Littleton it is clear that one may not enter contrary to such a release.[6] Nevertheless in the newer books it is put as a query, on account of the opinion of my lord Fitzjames,[7] and so etc. As to the last point, it seems to me that he may perfectly well plead the plea; for if someone disseises me and I release to him, and then enfeoff another, the feoffee shall take advantage of this release. Similarly the lessee may plead a deed made to his lessor, and a tenant in dower may plead a deed made to her husband. Thus the plea is good.

---

[1] William Rastell, barrister of Lincoln's Inn (called 1539).
[2] YB 20 Edw. III, Lib. Ass., pl. 5.   [3] YB Hil. 6 Hen. VII, fo. 15, pl. 6, *ad finem.*
[4] *Lord Percy v. Earl of Angus* (1366) YB Pas. 40 Edw. III, fo. 22, pl. 21; Mich. 40 Edw. III, fo. 47, pl. 32.   [5] YB Mich. 19 Hen. VI, fo. 3, pl. 7.
[6] Littleton, *Tenures*, ss. 508–509.   [7] Chief Justice of the King's Bench 1526–39.

Cholmeley. Moy semble que le case mult consyst en le primer poynt, come
ad este move, scilicet quel est fait per cest relles. Et moy semble que le
propertie est alter per ceo, et cest relles est plus fort que ascun auter, quar per
relles de toutz actions reals et personals ceux actions et auxi actions mixt sont
ale mes nemi un appelle. Mes si home relles toutz demaundez ut supra apelle
est ale. Auxi il apiert in Lit. en continuall clayme que sur un contynuall clayme
fait si le partie occupy apres ceo cestui que fait le clayme avera pur chescun
entre action de trans. ou sur lestatut de R., quel est forsque demaunde en fait,
et en cest case sil relles toutz demaundez il ne poit faire tiel clayme. Et auxi il
dit que le fayt de chescun serra pris fort[ment] vers luy, quar 2 E. 4. apiert que
si jeo face lesse a un et puis face mention que lou il tient del feffement J. S. etc.
que ceo relles a luy, le relles est bon, unquore il ne tient del feffement J. S.
causa qua supra. Et reherce lez cases de Rastell et eux affirme. Issint il semble
que per le relles le interest est ale auxibien come laction. Et il dit que sil
admittera que lenterest nest ale, donques largument de Curson ne poit estre
deny. Et all darren moy [semble] <de estre bien >[1] que il prendra avantage de
cest relles nient obstant que il est estraunge, quar il convey de luy a que le
relles est fait. Come si le seigniour conferme lestate son tenant a tener per
maynder services, si le tenant enfeoffe estraunge le feoffe pledra cest
confirmation assetz bien, quar va en discharge del terre. Et sic est le ley en
personal action, quar si ii. fount tns. lun pledra relles fait al auter ou laction
est port jointment vers eux. Issint moy semble que le ple per le maner est assetz
bon [*fo. 250*]

Broke, Comen Serjant, a mesme lentent. Primerment quel est fait per le
relles de demaundez? Et moy semble que le partie ad done per ceo tout son
interest al evesque. Sil avoit relles tout son title ou tout son interest null
dowtera forsque fuit bon et son interest determyne. Et jeo agree bien que est
un maner de demaunde a demaunder per action en court del roy. Mes a dire
que est nul auter demaunde ceo serra trop dure <en ley >,[2] quar divers bon
demaundez en ley ount este reherce, come entre ou distres pur rent. Et quant le
relles est generall toutz demaundez quecumque sount alle, scilicet demaundez
en fait et demaundez en ley. Et en ascuns cases un fait en ley serra auxi fort
come matter en fait. Come si home ad issue ii. filz, bastarde et mulier, et il
disseise R. et devie, le bastarde entre en tout, le disseisi ou son heire port
action, le mulier poit pleder nontenure si el voiet et luy discharge de damages.
Mes si elle voile faire partition, ore per cest fait el ad fait luy mesme tenant,
unquore le partition nest direct entre et seisin mes il amount a taunt. Auxi si

---

[1] *Appears to read* de eē bre.
[2] *Del.*

Cholmeley.[1] It seems to me that the case largely consists in the first point, as it has been moved, namely what is the effect of this release? And it seems to me that the property is thereby altered, and this release is stronger than any other, for by a release of 'all actions real and personal' those actions and also mixed actions are gone, but not an appeal, whereas if someone releases 'all demands' (as above) an appeal is gone.[2] Also it appears in Littleton, in 'Continual Claim',[3] that upon a continual claim made, if the party occupies afterwards, the person who made the claim shall have an action of trespass or [forcible entry] upon the statute of Richard[4] for each entry, which is only a demand in fact, and in this case if he releases 'all demands' he may not make such a claim. (He also said that everyone's deed shall be taken strongly against him; for in 2 Edw. IV it appears that if I make a lease to someone, and then mention that whereas he holds by the feoffment of John Style etc. I release to him, the release is good even if he does not hold by the feoffment of John Style, for the above reason. And he repeated Rastell's cases and affirmed them.) Thus it seems that by the release the interest is gone as well as the action. (And he said that if one were to admit that the interest is not gone, then Curson's argument could not be denied.) As to the last point, it seems to me to be for him to take advantage of this release even though he is a stranger, for he traces title from the person to whom the release was made. Likewise if a lord confirms the estate of his tenant to hold by lesser services, and the tenant enfeoffs a stranger, the feoffee may perfectly well plead this confirmation, for it goes in discharge of the land. And that is the law in a personal action; for if two commit a trespass, one of them may plead a release made to the other, where the action is brought jointly against them. Thus it seems to me that the plea as pleaded is perfectly good.

Brooke, Common Serjeant,[5] to the same effect. First, what is effected by the release of 'demands'? It seems to me that the party has thereby given his whole interest to the bishop. Had he released all his title or all his interest, no one would doubt that it was good and his interest determined. And I fully agree that it is a kind of demand to demand by action in the king's court. But to say that there is no other demand would be too harsh in law, for various good demands in law have been mentioned, such as an entry or distress for rent. And when the release is general for 'all demands' all kinds are gone, that is, demands in fact and demands in law. In some cases an act in law shall be as strong as a matter of fact. For instance, if someone has issue two daughters, one a bastard and one legitimate, and he disseises R. and dies, the bastard enters in the whole, and the disseisee or his heir brings an action, the legitimate daughter may plead Nontenure if she will and discharge herself from damages. But if she will make partition, by this act she has made herself tenant, and yet the partition is not

---

[1] Randle Cholmeley, barrister of Lincoln's Inn (called 1543), the reporter.
[2] Littleton, *Tenures*, s. 508.
[3] Ibid., ss. 430–431.
[4] 5 Ric. II, stat. 1, c. 7 (*SR* ii. 20).
[5] Robert Brooke, bencher of the Middle Temple (1542), common serjeant of London 1536–45.

jeo face lesse pur vie, et action est port vers moy, jeo puis abate le brefe. Mes si jeo pendant le brefe accept surrender <de tenant pur vie >[i] jay fait le brefe bon sur matter en ley, et sic matter en ley et matter en fait sount tout un. Et auxi en ascun case un choce passera per auter nosme et circumstance que il est comenment conus, come si jay tenant pur vie et jeo grant totum statum, tenant pur vie attornera, le revercion pas per ceo, unquore jeo ne parle de ascun revercion. Et simile est 50. E. 3. Et en tiel case si jeo grant toutz mes terres, le tenant attorne, le revercion pas, et unquore le franktenement del terre ne fuit en moy a ascun entent: et sic est 38. E. 3. Auxi si home ad comen en le terre dun auter, et il ad chymyn ouster ma terre, sil relles a moy le chymyn per ceo le comen est ale, quar quaunt il dispence ovesque le measne per que il avenera all choce il dispence ovesque le choce auxi. Issint moy semble que son interest del choce est clerement ale et determyn per le relles avandit. Auxi pur ceo que ad este move que cest relles ne serra barre pur ceo que fuit fait devaunt son darren possession, et pur ceo il nest plee, jay prise le ley contrary, quar quant mon interest va devaunt son title jeo serra bien resceu de pleder ceo. Et un brefe ou un pleynt sount forsque supposell. Et pur ceo en assise de mordancestor supposant que son pere morust, jeo pledra feffment per son ayell et est bon, unquore est contrary all supposell de son brefe. Mes quant jeo face title precedent ceo covient estre responde. Et en assise de novel disseisin le brefe est suppose sur son possession demesne, mes unquore feffement del pere ou ayell est bon plee, quar le matter de mon plee est devaunt le supposell de son brefe. Et en chescun tiel case javera le pleder assetz bien. Et all darren, sil pledra pur ceo que il nest privey. Et moy semble petit dowt de ceo, come en le case de tns. que ad este mys, et en lez cases que va ovesque le terre. Et sic cest interest va ovesque lescript. Et si jeo port action de wast vers luy, il pledra le <fait del >[i] graunt de le revercion et que il attorne, et unquore il fuit ousterment estraunge a ceo. Issint moy semble primerment que tout son interest est ale per le relles et que le defendant[i] prendra avantage per pleder de ceo assetz bien, per que le barre est bon. Et ouster pur ceo que avomus demurre en ley nous avomus demurre de tout que est deins le recorde. Et moy semble que le count nest bon pur ii. causes. Lun pur ceo que il dit scriptum indentatum <de un lesse >[i] et ne dit factum, quar un lesse ne poit estre per scriptum si non que soit factum, et unquore est bon per nude parol. Et en verite brefe de detinw est en le Register de un escript, mes covient estre factum per que lesse pas. Et auter exception fuit pris pur ceo que il ne ad monstre le lew ou le lesse fuit fait, et ceo ne besoigne en cest case, come semble, nient plus que de obligation [*fo. 250v*]

a direct entry and seisin, but it is tantamount. Also, if I make a lease for life, and an action is brought against me, I may abate the writ; but if, pending the writ, I accept a surrender from the tenant for life, I have made the writ good upon a matter in law, and thus matter in law and matter in fact are all one. Also in some cases a thing shall pass by another name and circumstance than that by which it is commonly known, as where I have a tenant for life and I grant the 'whole estate' (*totum statum*), and the tenant for life attorns, the reversion thereby passes, and yet I did not speak of any reversion. There is a similar case in 50 Edw. III. And in such a case if I grant all my lands, and the tenant attorns, the reversion passes, and yet the freehold of the land was not in me for any purpose: and that is in 38 Edw. III. Also if someone has common in the land of another, and he has a way across my land, and he releases the way to me, the common is thereby gone, for when he dispenses with the means whereby he was to come to the thing he dispenses with the thing as well. So it seems to me that his interest in the thing is clearly gone and determined by the aforesaid release. Also, inasmuch as it has been moved that this release shall not bar because it was made before his last possession, and therefore it is no plea, I have taken the law the other way; for when my interest goes before his title I shall be received to plead it well enough. A writ or a plaint is only a supposal. Therefore in an assize of mort d'ancestor, supposing that his father died, I may plead a feoffment by his grandfather, and it is good, and yet it is contrary to the supposal of his writ. But when I make a title precedent it must be answered. In an assize of novel disseisin the writ is supposed to be upon his own possession, and yet a feoffment from the father or grandfather is a good plea, for the matter of my plea is before the supposal of his writ. And in every such case I may have the pleading perfectly well. As to the last point—whether he may plead, in that he is not privy—it seems to me there is little doubt of this: as in the case of trespass which has been put, and in the cases which go with the land. Therefore this interest goes with the writing. If I bring an action of waste against him, he may plead the deed of grant of the reversion and that he attorned, and yet he was a complete stranger to it. Thus it seems to me, firstly, that all his interest is gone by the release, and that the defendant may perfectly well take advantage thereof by pleading, and so the bar is good. Moreover, because we have demurred in law, we have demurred in respect of everything which is in the record. And it seems to me that the count is not good, for two reasons. One is because he says 'an indented writing' (*scriptum indentatum*) of lease, and does not say 'deed' (*factum*); for a lease may not be made by *scriptum* if it is not *factum*, though it is good by bare word. There is indeed a writ of detinue in the Register for a writing, but it must be a deed whereby a lease passes. (Another exception was taken because he has not shown the place where the lease was made; but that is not needed in this case, as it seems, any more than in the case of a bond.)

[2]

In termino Sancti Michaelis anno tricesimo sexto Henrici octavi cest matter subsequent touchant un especial assise arrayne per Elisabethe Penyngton vers un Hunte de terres en Sevenocke in comitatu Kantie, fuit argue en leschecker chamber devant mon seignour *Baldewyn*, Cheff Justice del Comen Banke, et *Richard Lyster*, Cheff Baron dell Eschecker, justices de assise deins mesme le countie.

1. Primerment exception fuit prise all returne dell brefe, quar le viconte de Kent returne le brefe et escribe son nosme sur le dorce dell brefe hoc modo, Humfredus Style armyger vicecomes. Et exception fuit prise que covient estre Humfridus, et auxi armiger ovesque un y est faux Laten, et issint le returne insufficient.

2. Manucaptores summonitorum <recogn. >[1] juratorum fuit enterlesse en le returne.

3. Auxi exception fuit prise pur ceo que le plaintife sue especiall assise et especial patent en quel patent ill avoit ceux parolz, una cum hiis quos vobis associaverimus, que ilz nount authorite de prender cest assise sanz brefe de association.

4. Donques pur ceo que ilz navoient fait garrante all viconte de faire vener le assise devaunt eux per force de cest especiall assise pur ceo que les parolx del brefe sount, ad certum locum quem idem J. B. et R. L. tibi scire faciant.

5. Si per le especial patent le authoritie dell generall patent est determine ou nemi?

6. Ouster pur ceo que le brefe fuit ad certum locum etc. ut supra, ou ilz pretende que il serra ad certum diem et locum.

7. Pur ceo que ceux parolx en le brefe, quod tunc facias tenementum illud reseisiri[2] de catallis que in ipso capta fuerunt, ou ill serra fuerint, come fuit pretende sur lexception.

8. Si ceux defautes en le brefe et returne serront amendes ou nemi?

Et devaunt lez justices avaunditz, *William Rastell*, un dez utterbarresters de Lyncolnes Inne, prise lez exceptions en order come ilz sount mis ycy avaunt. Et all primer exception, pur le nosme dell viconte, ill semble que [le] returne est come nulle returne en le ley, quar cest paroll Humfredus nest pas le nosme de Humfrey, mes serra Humfridus. Quar si un nosme nest escry dument et en perfite Laten ill ne poit estre entende un mesme person. Quar si un que ad a

---

[1] *Del.*
[2] reseisire.

2. PENYNGTON v. HUNTE

Exchequer Chamber and Serjeants' Inn (adjourned assize), Mich. 1544. Also reported by Gell, Mich. 36 Hen. VIII, fo. 23.

In Michaelmas term in the thirty-sixth year of Henry VIII this matter following, touching a special assize arraigned by Elizabeth Penyngton against one Hunte, for lands in Sevenoaks in the county of Kent, was argued in the Exchequer Chamber before my lord BALDWIN, Chief Justice of the Common Bench, and RICHARD LYSTER, Chief Baron of the Exchequer, justices of assize in the same county.

1. First, exception was taken to the return of the writ in that the sheriff of Kent returned the writ and wrote his name on the dorse of the writ in this way, 'Humfredus Style, armyger, vicecomes' (Humphrey Style, esquire,[1] sheriff). And exception was taken that it ought to be *Humfridus*; and also *armyger* with a *y* is false Latin; and so the return is insufficient.

2. 'Mainpernors of the summoners of the jurors' was left out in the return.

3. Exception was also taken because the plaintiff sued a special assize and a special patent, in which patent there were these words, 'together with those whom we shall associate with you' (*una cum hiis quos vobis associaverimus*), so that they have no authority to take this assize without a writ of association.

4. Again, in that they have not made a warrant to the sheriff to cause the assize to come before them by virtue of this special assize, the words of the writ being, 'at a certain place which the same John Baldwin and Richard Lyster shall cause you to know' (*ad certum locum quem idem J. B. et R. L. tibi scire faciant*).

5. Is the authority of the general patent determined by the special patent, or not?

6. Further, in that the writ said 'at a certain place etc.' (*ad certum locum etc.*), as above, whereas they suppose it ought to be at a certain day and place (*ad certum diem et locum*).

7. In that the words in the writ were, 'that then you should cause the tenement to be reseised of the chattels which were taken therein' (*quod tunc facias tenementum illud reseisiri de catallis quae in ipso capta fuerunt*), whereas it should have been 'should be taken' (*fuerint*), as they supposed upon the exception.

8. May these faults in the writ and return be amended, or not?

And, before the justices aforesaid, *William Rastell*, one of the utter-barristers of Lincoln's Inn, took the exceptions in order as they are put here before. As to the first exception, for the sheriff's name, he thought the return was as no return in law; for this word *Humfredus* is not the name of Humphrey, but it should be *Humfridus*. If a name is not written duly and in perfect Latin it

[1] Of Beckenham, Kent, and Lincoln's Inn (specially adm. 1523), esquire of the body, sheriff of Kent 1543–44; knighted 1544; died 1552; brass in armorial tabard at Beckenham.

nosme Mattheus luy escrie per le nosme de Matthias, ceo ne poit estre entende un mesme person. Issint est lou un que ad nosme de Ranulph [et] son nosme est escry per nosme de Radulphus ou il serra Ranulphus, ceo alter tout le nosme: et unquore ill est forsque le alteration de un lettre, quel est mult materiall en tiell case. Et ouster il semble que armyger, come il est escry, nest bon Laten, per que le returne en cest poynt est insufficient. Et auxi pur ceo que ill est ordeyne per lestatut de Eborum que le nosme del viconte serra mis all brefe <sur le returne>[i], et ycy ill ne poit estre entende son nosme pur lez causes avaunditz, et issint le brefe nest dument returne, per que ill abatera. <Et auxi ill ne serra amende come jeo voile apres touche.[1] >[i] Et ouster pur ceo que manucaptores summonitorum juratorum sount enterlesse en le returne il semble que nest bon.

Et donques *le cheff baron* luy disturbe et dit que ill nest dowte mes que ceo covient estre returne, come il entende. Mes ill dit que lez brefez fuere escries la, et a ore ilz sount obscures, per que ill dit que il serra en lour jugement de determyne si cest parte dell returne fault ou nemi. Et lou ill apiert un [*fo. 251*] parcell de tiell m[esme],[2] per que ilz agarderont quod hoc habeatur pro scripto.

Hares pur le plaintife prie que soit amende.

Bawdwyn dit que nest materiall en son opinion si cest parte dell returne, scilicet manucaptores summonitorum juratorum, <ouste este omitte>[i] quar null tiell matter est conteyne en le brefe et ill suffist al viconte de perimplishe lez parolx dell brefe. Et donques il comaund Rastell de proceder.

Et il dit que manucaptores etc. covient estre returne ou auterment ill nest bon. Et ill dit que low lez jourours covient de appearer en court la ill covient de returner manucaptores etc. come en brefe de habeas corpora ou en un tales sur [ceo] la lez parolx dell brefe sount quod habeas corpora A. B. et C. juratores in curia etc. Mes sill soit en un venire facias la il nest requisite de returner manucaptores etc. quar la il nest tenus de eux aver en court, quar lez parolx dell brefe nextende a ceo.

Et mon seignour [Lister][3] en mesme le ple dit que en assise ill covient returner manucaptores. Et pur ceux cases de manucaptores etc. 22. E. 4. est agree.

Issint ill semble pur cest cause que le returne nest bon. Et all 3. poynt moy semble que pur ceo que le plaintife nad sue brefe de association que vous naves power pur determyne cest assise, quar lez parolx dell patent sount, una cum hiis quos vobis associaverimus, quell est un copulative, et quant authorite est done a ii. jointment lun ne poit performer ceo saunz lauter[i], come si le patent oust

---

[1] *Reading unclear.*
[2] *Unclear.*
[3] Lit.

cannot be supposed to be one same person.[1] For if someone named Matthew writes himself by the name of *Matthias*, this cannot be supposed one same person. So it is where someone is named Ranulph and his name is written as *Radulphus*, where it should be *Ranulphus*, this alters the whole name: and yet it is but the alteration of one letter, which is most material in such a case. Further it seems that *armyger*, as it is written, is not good Latin; and so the return in this point is insufficient. Moreover, since it is ordained by the Statute of York that the sheriff's name shall be put to the writ upon the return,[2] and here it cannot be supposed to be his name, for the reasons aforesaid, the writ is therefore not duly returned, and so it should abate. Also it shall not be amended, as I will touch upon later. Moreover, because the mainpernors of the summoners of the jurors (*manucaptores summonitorum juratorum*) are left out in the return it seems that it is not good.

Then THE CHIEF BARON interrupted him and said that there is no doubt but that this must be returned, as he thought. But he said that the writs were so written, and now they are obscure, and so he said that it should be in their judgment to determine whether this part of the return is wanting or not ... and so they awarded that this should be taken as read (*quod hoc habeatur pro scripto*).[3]

Hare, for the plaintiff, prayed that it might be amended.

BALDWIN said that in his opinion it was immaterial whether this part of the return—namely *manucaptores summonitorum juratorum*—was omitted, for no such matter is contained in the writ, and it suffices for the sheriff to fulfil the words of the writ. Then he commanded Rastell to proceed.

And [*Rastell*] said that *manucaptores etc.* must be returned or else it is not good. And he said that wherever the jurors must appear in court, he must return *manucaptores etc.*; as in a writ of *habeas corpora* or in a *tales* thereon, the words of the writ are 'that you have the bodies of A., B. and C., jurors, in court ...' (*quod habeas corpora A. B. et C. juratores in curia etc.*).[4] If, however, it is in a *venire facias*, it is not requisite to return *manucaptores etc.*, for there he is not bound to have them in court, for the words of the writ do not extend to that.

My lord LYSTER said in the same plea that in an assize it is necessary to return *manucaptores*. For these cases of *manucaptores etc.* 22 Edw. IV is agreed.[5]

[*Rastell.*] Thus it seems, for this reason, that the return is not good. As to the third point, it seems to me that because the plaintiff has not sued a writ of association you have no power to determine this assize; for the words of the patent are, 'together with those whom we shall associate with you' (*una cum hiis quos vobis associaverimus*), which is a copulative, and when authority is given to two jointly, one of them may not perform it without the other. Thus if the patent

[1] Cf. *Fenton* v. *Choppyn* (1544) CP 40/1122, m. 303d (writ of debt abated because defendant named *Rogerum* in writ and *Rohertum* in bond).   [2] Statute of York, 12 Edw. II, c. 5 (*SR* i. 178).
[3] Translation uncertain.   [4] See YB Trin. 9 Edw. IV, fo. 13, pl. 7.
[5] Unidentified. Cf. YB Trin. 9 Edw. IV, fo. 13, pl. 7; Mich. 3 Hen. VII, fo. 14, pl. 23.

este fait a lez ii. justices et a un auter ill est saunz dowte que ilz nount power de
proceder saunz lauter pur ceo que lour authorite est joint come est avaundit.
Sicome lettre de attorney est fait a ii. de faire livery et seisin, lun de eux ne poit
faire lyvery saunz lauter pur le cause avaundit. <Et Fitzh[erbert] dit que
association serra en special assise ou il ad ceux parolx avaundits. >[i] Auxi moy
semble que le authorite que ilz ount per un generall patent est determyne per
cest especiall patent, quar lour primer authorite est deryvy del roy et donques
per le darren patent le force dell primer patent ayent regarde a cest assise est
merement determene. Et null dowte est mes si le roy oust graunt cest especiall
patent a ii. auters nient nosme en le generall patent, ore ilz <per lour generall
patent >[i] ne poient entermedle en cest assise. Et come le case est ycy ill est tout
un. Issint moy semble que ilz ne poient proceder per reson de lour generall
patent. Donques pur ceo que ilz ne fesont ascun garrante all viconte de faire
vener le jury, moy semble que ilz appere saunz garrante, et donques nest
warrant per le ley. Et le warrant dell generall assise ne poit ayder cest matter
pur ceo que ilz ne determen cest assise pur cause dell generall patent. <Et mon
seigniour Fitzherbert >[1] Et donques si lez justices procede sur ceo ill est coram
non judice pur ceo que le jury appere saunz garrante. Donques pur ceo que le
brefe est ad certum locum ill semble que ill serra ad certum diem et locum, quar
le jour covient estre mis en certen auxi bien come le lewe. Mes jeo ne voile tarier
sur ceo. Donques pur ceo que ceux parolx en le brefe sount, de catallis que in
ipso capta fuerint, moy semble que ill serra fuerint, quar fuerunt est en le
preter temps et ill est impossible de reseiser de lez catell queux fuere, quar ceux
referre a temps passe. Mes covient estre fuerint, quel est le future temps et le
subjunctive mode. Et jay peruse lez auncient regesters que sount fuerint. Issint
pur cest cause moy semble que le brefe nest bon. Auxi moy semble que le brefe
ne serra amende, ne le returne de ceo, per lestatut de anno 8. H. 6. ca° 12 ne per
lestatut de 14. E. 3. ca° 3, pur le forme dell brefe ne serra amende. Quar lou
originall fault forme ill nest amendable per ascuns des ditez estatutes. Come si
brefe de dette vers executours soit debet et detinet ou il serra detinet tantum, ill
ne serra amende. Et auxi si le brefe soit precipe quod solvat lou il serra precipe
quod reddat, ou en brefe de garranty de chartres si le brefe soit unde pactum
habet lou ill serra unde cartam habet, en toutz ceux cases pur ceo que ilz faunt
forme, le quel est de cours en le Chauncery, ilz ne serra amende. Et en 27. H. 6.
19. le brefe fuit quod sit ibi ou il serra quod tunc sit ibi, et tenus la clerement
per opinion que le brefe abatera et que ill ne serra amende, pur ceo que ill est
vicious per default de cours. Issint moy semble pur toutz ceux causes que le
brefe abatera. [fo. 251v]

---

[1] Del.

had been made to the two justices and another, it is without doubt that they would not have had power to proceed without the other, because their authority is joint (as aforesaid). Likewise if a letter of attorney is made to two to make livery and seisin, one of them may not make livery without the other, for the reason aforesaid. And Fitzherbert says that there shall be association in a special assize where the aforesaid words are used.[1] Also, it seems to me that the authority which they have by a general patent is determined by this special patent, for their first authority is derived from the king, and then by the latter patent the force of the first patent with respect to this assize is absolutely determined. There is no doubt that if the king had granted this special patent to two others not named in the general patent, they could not now have meddled with this assize by virtue of their general patent. And, as the case is here, it is all one. Thus it seems to me that they may not proceed by reason of their general patent. Then again, since they have not made any warrant to the sheriff to cause the jury to come, it seems to me that they appeared without warrant, and therefore it is not warranted by law. And the warrant of the general assize cannot help this matter, because they are not to determine this assize by reason of the general patent. Therefore, if the justices proceed thereon it is *coram non judice*, inasmuch as the jury appear without warrant. Then there is the point that the writ says 'at a certain place' (*ad certum locum*). It seems that it ought to say 'at a certain day and place' (*ad certum diem et locum*), for the day must be specified as well as the place. But I will not dwell on that. Next, inasmuch as the words of the writ are, 'of the chattels which were taken therein' (*de catallis quae in ipso capta fuerunt*), it seems to me that it should be *fuerint*, for *fuerunt* is in the preter tense and it is impossible to reseise him of the chattels which were there, for those refer to a time past. But it must be *fuerint*, which is in the future tense and the subjunctive mood. I have perused the old registers, and they say *fuerint*. Therefore, for this reason, it seems to me that the writ is not good. Also it seems to me that the writ shall not be amended, nor the return thereof, by the statute of 8 Hen. VI, c. 12, nor by the statute of 14 Edw. III, c. [6],[2] for the form of a writ may not be amended; for where an original lacks form it is not amendable by any of the said statutes. Thus if a writ of debt against executors says *debet et detinet* where it ought to be *detinet* only, it shall not be amended. Also, if the writ says *praecipe quod solvat* where it should be *praecipe quod reddat*, or in a writ of warranty of charters if the writ says *unde pactum habet* where it ought to be *unde cartam habet*, in all these cases, because they want form—which is the course in the Chancery—they shall not be amended. And in 27 Hen. VI, pl. 19,[3] the writ was *quod sit ibi* where it ought to have been *quod tunc sit ibi*, and it was clearly held there by opinion that the writ should abate and that it should not be amended, because it is defective for want of course. So it seems to me for all these reasons that the writ should abate.

[1] F.N.B. 186v, citing YB Mich. 32 Hen. VI, fo. 10, pl. 7; 51 Selden Soc. 101.
[2] 8 Hen. VI, c. 12 (*SR* ii. 248); 14 Edw. III, stat. 1, c. 6 (*SR* i. 282).
[3] YB Mich. 27 Hen. VI, fo. 2, pl. 19.

Bradshawe, sollicitor le roy. Moy semble le contrary. Quant all primer exception, pur ceo que le nosme dell viconte sur le returne est escry Humfredus, moy semble que il est bon et accordant all Laten erudition. Et nest semble al case de Mattheus et Matthias que ad este mis, quar la ilz sont deux severall nosmes, mes Humfredus et Humfridus est tout un nosme et lun ou lauter est assetz bon. Et sil soit faux Laten ill poit amender assets bien, quar le defaut de sillabille ou tiell semble serra amende. Et sic est pur armyger, nient obstaunt est escrie ovesque un y, unquore come moy semble il serra amende. Et pur ceux exceptions le brefe est assetz bon. Et pur le manucaptores summonitorum etc. jeo ne voile parler, pur ceo que le court ad ceo admitte de estre en le returne. Donques a ceo que ad este dit que per lespeciall patent le aucthorite de lez justices a eux done per le generall patent est restreyne, ceo nest issint come jeo entende, quar quant le roy ad graunt a eux authorite per le generall patent de prender assisas, certificationes et juratas arramiatas tam tempore regis Henrici septimi quam tempore domini regis nunc, ore per le especial patent ceo authorite nest my abbridge, quar apres tiell generall patent si le roy voile graunt a eux un auter patent a mesme leffect unquore moy semble que ceo ne diminishe le force dell primer patent pur ceo que ilz ount authorite done a eux per ii. patentes et donques ilz poient executer lour authorite sur lun ou lauter a lour ellection. Et jeo agree le case que ad este mise que si lespeciall patent oust este fait a ii. estraunges donques mon seigniours Baldwyn et Lyster ne poient proceder, quar le especiall authorite de cest assise donques fuit done a auters persons. Mes ne sumus en le case ycy pur le reyson que jay dit devaunt. Et si lour authorite ne serra prise per le generall patent de proceder sur assises nient arrayme devaunt le generall patent fait, donques lez justices de gaole delivery nount my power de arrayner ascuns[i] auters felons que sount en le prisone all temps dell patent a eux fait, quel est faux, quar silz ne poient proceder vers eux per lour generall patent eins il covient de eux aver un especiall patent per chescun laron que ne fuit en le prison all temps dell patent fait, donques lez justices serra en graunde daunger: quel nest issint, quar le experience en ceo poynt est playne et saunz ascun dowte en ley. Et issint moy semble ycy que per lespeciall patent le force del generall patent nest determyne mes que ilz poient bien proceder en cest assise. Donques pur le association, moy semble que ilz ne besoigne daver association, quar lez parolz sount una cum hiis[i] quos vobis associaverimus, queux sont parolx de futuro queux a ceo temps ne done ascun authorite a ascun auter forsque[i] a eux que sount expressment nosme en le patent.

Bromley dit tacite que ill ne voile mult tarier sur ceo poynt, et unquore il fuit sur lauter party. Et ill dit: passe ouster ceo poynt.

Et *Bradshawe*, per mesme lez reysons quell prove que lez justices poient proceder per force de lour generall patent, per mesme le reyson ill semble que il ne besoigne daver ascun especiall garrant all viconte de faire vener lez jurours,

Bradshaw, the king's Solicitor[-General]. I think the contrary. As to the first exception, because the sheriff's name on the return is written *Humfredus*, it seems to me that it is good according to the Latin learning. It is not like the case of *Mattheus* and *Matthias* which has been put, for those are two separate names, whereas *Humfredus* and *Humfridus* are all one name, and either of them is good enough. And if it is false Latin it may perfectly well be amended, for the want of a syllable or such like shall be amended. So it is for *armyger*, even though it is written with a *y*, still I think it may be amended. With respect to these exceptions the writ is perfectly good. As to the *manucaptores summonitorum etc.* I will not speak, because the court has admitted this to be in the return. Now, then, as to what has been said that by the special patent the authority of the justices given to them by the general patent is restricted, that is not so, as I think, for when the king has granted them authority by the general patent to take 'assizes, certificates and juries arraigned both in the time of King Henry VII and in the time of the present lord king' (*assisas, certificationes et juratas arramiatas tam tempore regis Henrici septimi quam tempore domini regis nunc*), now by the special patent this authority is not abridged; for if, after such general patent, the king will grant them another patent to the same effect it seems to me that this nevertheless does not diminish the force of the first patent, because they have authority given to them by two patents and therefore they may execute their authority upon either of them at their election. I agree the case which has been put that if the special patent had been made to two strangers then my lords Baldwin and Lyster could not proceed, for the special authority of this assize was then given to other persons. But we are not in that case here, for the reason which I have already stated. If their authority shall not be taken by the general patent to proceed upon assizes not arraigned before the general patent was made, then justices of gaol delivery have no power to arraign any felons other than those who are in the prison at the time when the patent is made to them, which is false, for if they cannot proceed against them by their general patent but must have a special patent for every thief who was not in the prison at the time when the patent was made, then the justices would be in great danger: but it is not so, for the experience in this point is plain, and without any doubt in law. Thus it seems to me here that by the special patent the force of the general patent is not determined but that they may well proceed in this assize. Now for the association: it seems to me that they do not need to have an association, for the words are 'together with those whom we shall associate with you' (*una cum hiis quos vobis associaverimus*), which are future words which at that time give no authority to anyone other than those who are expressly named in the patent.

Bromley said under his breath (*tacitè*) that he would not dwell much on that point—though he was on the other side. And he said: pass over that point.

Bradshaw. By the same reasons which prove that the justices may proceed by virtue of their general patent, by the same reasons (he thought) there was no need to have any special warrant to the sheriff to cause the jurors to come. It is

quar ill nest requisite entaunt que lour authorite extende auxi bien all triell de cest assise come de chescun auter, et donques le generall <garrante et >[i] somons est sufficient.[1] [*fo. 252*] Ouster ou lez parolx del brefe sount ad certum locum et nemi ad certum diem et locum, moy semble que ill est accordant all register, quel est nostre presedent, et issint le brefe bon ut supra. Donques, ou le brefe est de catallis que in ipso capta fuerunt, moy semble que ill est assetz bon. Et unquore jeo ne puis denier mes que divers auncient registers sount fuerint, mes fuerunt come jeo entende est melliour Laten que fuerint, quar ycy nest ascun reyson que ill serra fuerint en le subjunctive mode. Et auxi le livere de mon seigniour Fitzherbert est fuerunt, et ill fuit un home discrete et erudite, et dowtelesse devaunt le fesans de son liver ill avoit peruse plousours de lez registers et sur le plus perfite de eux il founde son forme de brefe en son liver. Issint pur ascun choce que ad este dit moy semble que nous devomus aver lassise.

Hales, serjant. Moy semble le contrary et que le brefe abatera. All primer matter, ou le returne est Humfredus Style armyger, moy semble que le returne nest bon, quar son proper nosme en Laten est Humfridus et auxi en cest case le viconte covient de luy nosmer accordant a lez lettres patentes de son office, et per tiell nosme que ill resceu le office per tiell nosme ill execute le authorite de ceo. Et sill soit fait chivaler, quel est nosme de dignite, unquore ill mittera son nosme accordant a lez lettres patentes, scilicet H[umfridus] S[tyle] miles nuper armiger, pur ceo que ill ne doit varier dell patent. Auxi armyger ovesque y est faux Laten. Et pur lun cause et lauter ill ne poit estre entende mesme le person que est viconte. Issint le brefe nient returne, per que ill abatera. Auxi pur ceo que le plaintife ad sue especial assise, et especial patent conteynant ceux parolx una cum hiis quos vobis associaverimus, que ilz nount authorite de prender cest assise saunz brefe de association pur ceo que le authorite est joint et ill covient estre exercise accordant ou auterment nest bon. Quar si jeo face lettre de attorney a ii. jointment de deliver possession, un de eux aperluy ne poit ceo faire, quar ill nest garrante per lescripte que done a eux le authorite, per que lez justices ne poient proceder saunz association. Donques pur ceo que ilz navoient fait garrante al viconte de faire vener le assise devaunt eux per cause dell especiall assise, quar quant lez justices seont per speciall assise il covient que le viconte ad garrante accordant a ceo, quar auterment le court ne poit proceder en ceo. Et donques si ilz poient proceder en cest assise per lour generall patent ou nemi? Et moy semble que nemi, quar le generall patent done a eux authorite de prender assisas, certificationes et juratas arramiatas etc., queux parolx ount rellation forsque all assises queux sount ore arraigne et nemi a ceux queux serront arrayne, quar lez parolx ne sount arramiatas et arramiandas, et nest semble all case que ad este mise del justices de gaole delivere ou lez parolx sount ad gaolam et prisonarios in eo detentos deliberandos, quar la ilz ount

---

[1] perfet *del.* generallment *del.*

not requisite, inasmuch as their authority extends as well to the trial of this assize as to every other, and therefore the general warrant and summons is sufficient. Further, where the words of the writ are *ad certum locum* and not *ad certum diem et locum*, it seems to me that it is in accordance with the Register, which is our precedent, and therefore the writ is good (as above). Then, where the writ says *catallis quae in ipso capta fuerunt*, it seems to me that it is perfectly good. Yet I cannot deny that various old registers say *fuerint*; but *fuerunt* (as I think) is better Latin than *fuerint*, for there is no reason here why it should be *fuerint* in the subjunctive mood. Also my lord Fitzherbert's book says *fuerunt*,[1] and he was a learned and discreet man, and doubtless before making his book he had perused many of the registers and based the form of writ in his book on the most perfect of them. Thus, for anything that has been said, it seems to me that we ought to have the assize.

Hales, serjeant. I think the contrary and that the writ should abate. As to the first matter, where the return is 'Humfredus Style, armyger', it seems to me that the return is not good; for his proper name in Latin is *Humfridus*. Also in this case the sheriff must name himself in accordance with the letters patent of his office; and by such name as he received the office, by that name shall he execute the authority thereof. If he is made a knight, which is a name of dignity, he shall still put his name in accordance with the letters patent, namely 'Humphrey Style, knight, lately esquire' (*Humfridus Style, miles, nuper armiger*), because he ought not to vary from the patent. Also *armyger* with a *y* is false Latin. And for the one reason and the other he cannot be understood to be the same person who is sheriff. Thus the writ is not returned, and so it shall abate. Also, because the plaintiff has sued a special assize, and a special patent containing the words 'together with those whom we shall associate with you' (*una cum hiis quos vobis associaverimus*), they have no authority to take this assize without a writ of association, because the authority is joint and must be exercised accordingly or else it is not good. If I make a letter of attorney to two jointly to deliver possession, one of them by himself cannot do it, for it is not warranted by the writing which gives them the authority; and so the justices may not proceed without association. The next point is because they have not made a warrant to the sheriff to cause the assize to come before them by reason of the special assize; for when the justices sit by special assize the sheriff must have a warrant according therewith, for otherwise the court cannot proceed therein. Next, may they proceed in this assize by their general patent, or not? It seems to me they may not, for the general patent gives them authority to take 'assizes, certificates and juries arraigned etc.' (*assisas, certificationes et juratas arramiatas etc.*), which words bear relation only to the assizes which are already arraigned and not to those which are to be arraigned, for the words are not 'arraigned and to be arraigned' (*arramiatas et arramiandas*), and it is not like the case which has been put of the justices of gaol delivery, where the words are 'to deliver the gaol and the prisoners therein detained' (*ad gaolam et prisonarios in eo detentos*

---

[1] F.N.B. 177v (*fuer'* in 1634 ed.).

authorite de arrayne toutz felons queux sount prise adonques ou apres, quar
lez parolx dell patent ceo warant. Et auxi per le especial patent le authorite del
generall patent est determene, et semble all case dell commission del peace,
quar la per le 2. patent le force del primer patent est determine. Et sic est si le
roy fait un auter commission a lez justices de assise et joine un auter ove eux,
ore per ceo le force dell primer commission est determen. Et semble all case si
un fist lesse a moy pur terme de ans et puis il fist a moy un auter lesse de mesme
le terre, ceo est un surrender dell primer lesse. Et issint ycy, per le especiall
patent lour authorite de proceder sur le generall patent est determen. Auxi ill
semble que le brefe serra ad certum diem et locum, pur ceo que il covient estre
consonant al brefe. Auxi ou le brefe est de catallis que in ipso capta fuerunt,
ceo ne poit estre bon quar il fault sentence, quar fuerunt est en le preter temps
et il est impossible de faire un choce ou le temps est passe <en que ceo doit
estre fait >[i] mes il serra fuerint, quel est en le future temps, et issint sount lez
plus auncient regesters et ilz sound de estoier plus ove reyson. Issint pur toutz
ceux causes moy semble que le brefe abatera.

Harrys, serjant. Moy semble le contrary. Primerment pur le nosme del
viconte Humfredus ou Humfridus, lun ou lauter est assetz bon, quar il ad
sufficient entendement en ceo. Come lez nosmes en lenglishe tonge John et
Jynkyn toutz sount un. Et sil soit faux Laten unquore le brefe ne abatera pur
ceo cause, quar lestatut de Everwicke que done que le nosme dell viconte serra
mis all brefe nest prise que pur defaut de ceo le brefe abatera, eins que le
viconte serra [amerce].[1] Et sic est de armiger ove y. Issint il semble que ceux
exceptions ne sont material. [*fo. 252v*] Ouster all association. Ill <vouche 32.
H. 6. que il ne besoigne de aver association et ouster >[i] fist mesme le argument
en effect que le sollicitour fist. Donques pur le garrante de cest fait all viconte,
moy semble que ore ilz sount passe lavantage de ceo, quar quant le viconte
avoit returne le brefe servy, et le court ceo resseyve, donques sil soit per
garrante ou nemi tout est un, quar quant lez justices a que le roy ad graunt
authorite ount resceu cest matter de recorde, ore il nest de disputer per quel
garrante le viconte ad execute ceo que appent son office, quar le partie ad
surcesse son temps quar ceo covient estre plede devaunt le brefe returne en
court. Et pur le proceder sur le auncient patent ill mist en effect mesme lez cases
queux fuere mise per le sollicitour de lez justices de gaole delivery. Et mista le
case de 13. H. 4. 1, assise, que lez justices de gaole delivery hac vice si un appelle
soit commence devaunt eux ilz ount power de agarde proces sur ceo vers lez
appelles de faire eux vener a auter jour tanque le appelle soit termene, quar
auterment lour commission ne serra de effecte. Issint ycy, per le novell patent le
force del primer patent nest en ascun part determen entaunt que est fait a

---

[1] *Word unclear.*

deliberandos), for there they have authority to arraign all felons who are taken, whether before or afterwards, for the words of the patent warrant that. Also by the special patent the authority of the general patent is determined. It is like the case of the commission of the peace, for there by a second patent the force of the former patent is determined. Likewise here, if the king made another commission to the justices of assize and joined another with them, the force of the [first] commission would be thereby determined. It is like the case where someone makes a lease to me for a term of years, and afterwards makes another lease to me of the same land, this is a surrender of the first lease. Likewise here, by the special patent their authority to proceed upon the general patent is determined. Also it seems that the writ should be *ad certum diem et locum*, because it must be consonant with the writ. Also, where the writ says *de catallis quae in ipso capta fuerunt*, that cannot be good, for it lacks sense,[1] for *fuerunt* is in the preter tense and it is impossible to do something where the time has passed in which it ought to be done; but it should be *fuerint*, which is in the future tense, and so are the oldest registers, and it stands better with reason. So, for all these reasons, it seems to me that the writ should abate.

Harris, serjeant. I think the contrary. Firstly, as to the sheriff's name, *Humfredus* or *Humfridus*, the one or the other is perfectly good, for there is sufficient understanding therein: just as the names in the English tongue John and Jenkin are all one. Even if it is false Latin, still the writ shall not abate for that reason; for the Statute of York, which provides that the sheriff's name shall be put to the writ, is not understood to mean that in default of this the writ shall abate, but only that the sheriff shall be amerced.[2] So it is of *armyger* with a *y*. So it seems that these exceptions are immaterial. Moving on to the association, he vouched 32 Hen. VI,[3] that there is no need to have an association; and further made the same argument in effect as the solicitor-general. Next, as to the warrant thereof made to the sheriff, it seems to me that they are out of time to take that point,[4] for once the sheriff has returned the writ served, and the court has received it, then it is all one whether it was by warrant or without, for when the justices to whom the king has granted authority have received this matter of record, it is not to be disputed by what warrant the sheriff has executed that which belongs to his office, for the party has overrun his time, in that it must be pleaded before the writ is returned in court. As to the proceeding upon the old patent, he put in effect the same cases which were put by the solicitor-general concerning the justices of gaol delivery. And he put the case of 13 Hen. IV, fo. 1,[5] assize, that the justices of gaol delivery *hac vice* have power, if an appeal is commenced before them, to award process thereon against the appellees to make them come at another day, until the appeal is determined, for otherwise their commission would be of no effect. Likewise here, by the new patent the force of the first patent is not in any part determined, inasmuch as it is made to

---

[1] The text says 'sentence'.   [2] Statute of York, 12 Edw. II, c. 5 (*SR* i. 178).
[3] YB Mich. 32 Hen. VI, fo. 10, pl. 7; 51 Selden Soc. 101.   [4] The text says 'they have passed the advantage of that'.   [5] Cf. YB Mich. 9 Hen. IV, fo. 1, pl. 7.

mesme lez justices a que le primer generall patent est fait. Et pur lez auters exceptions il luy referre al forme del register.

A auter jour, *Lyster*, le Cheff Baron, argue mesme lez poyntes a Serjauntes Inne, quel argument jeo ne poy certenment reporter.

Et a mesme le temps *Baldwyn*, le Cheff Justice, peruse lez pointes en order et dit: Primerment all nosme dell viconte, sil soit Humfredus ou Humfridus ceo nest materiall, quar null auter ycy devaunt nous poit pleder que son nosme est auter que il mesme returne. Mes sil fuit en court ou son patent est de recorde, come en <le Bank le Roy ou >[1] le Comen Banke la home avera avantage de ceo per un meane, mez ceo nest per voy de plee eins per brefe de errour. Come si a ore lez novels vicontes sount eslus, admitte que le auncient viconte voile returne un brefe, le partie navera respons per plee adire que il nest viconte, eins il serra mis a son brefe de errour, et le partie est mere estraunge all viconte et null poit prender plus precise notice del nosme dell viconte que le viconte mesme, quar si action soit port vers moy et un auter jeo navera avantage a pleder misnomer de mon compaignon, quar jeo sue estraunge a ceo et le ley entende que ill ad le plus perfite notice de son nosme demesne. Et issint ycy, per que per ceo cause moy semble que le brefe est assetz bon. Mez *Bawdwyn* dit que si brefe de dower soit port, le tenant pledra un fyne leve per le baron devaunt le coverture, elle poit bien averrer continuans de [possession] quar elle est estraunge all fyne. Mes ycy nest tiell mischeff, quar le plaintife poit aver son remedy per brefe de errour et nemi per plee pur le cause que jay monstre avaunt. Auxi pur monstre mon conseyte pur erudition, si en le returne il covient aver manucaptores summonitorum juratorum ou nemi? Et semble a moy que ill nest de necessite de aver ceux parolx en le returne, quar tout que est compris deins le brefe est perimplishe, quel est quod habeas ibi sommonitores, nomina plegiorum et hoc breve. Quar per le auncient ley lez somoners covient estre prest en court, et si lenquest fuit prist de passer si lez somoners sur lour examination disont que le partie ne fuit somone, lenquest ne[i] serra prise, mes est mise a son action vers le viconte, issint que le viconte quant il perimplish tout que est a luy commaunde deins le brefe ill ad fait sufficientment. Mes pur ceo que il est[i] comenment use de faire tiell returne jeo ne voile repugner ceo. [*fo. 253*] Mes il nad ascun necessite de faire tiell returne, pur ceo que il nest conteigne deins le brefe per ascuns parolx <del brefe >.[2] Et issint mon opinion apiert a ceo purpose. Donques pur le association. Moy semble que il covient de aver association, quar autrement il nest bon, quar lez parolx sount una cum hiis quos vobis associaverimus, quel prove que le roy voile associate a nous auters persons queux avera joint authorite ove nous. Et ceo association covient estre date apres le date dell patent, quar associaverimus est en le future temps, quar lez parolx prove que ilz serront associate et ne sount il ore associate, per que le auncient association quel fuit fait sur le generall patent, scilicet le

---

[1] *Del.*
[2] en ceo *del.*

the same justices to whom the first general patent was made. As to the other exceptions, he referred to the form in the Register.

At another day, Lyster, Chief Baron, argued the same points at Serjeants' Inn, which argument I cannot report with certainty.

On the same occasion BALDWIN C. J. went through the points in order and said: Firstly, as to the sheriff's name, whether it is *Humfredus* or *Humfridus* is immaterial, for no one else may plead here before us that his name is other than he himself has returned. If, however, it was in a court where his patent is of record, as in the Common Bench, one could have advantage of it by a means; however, the means is not by way of plea, but by writ of error. Likewise if new sheriffs have now been elected, and suppose the old sheriff returns a writ: the party shall not have an answer by plea to say that he is not sheriff, but shall be driven to his writ of error, for the party is an absolute stranger to the sheriff. And no one may take more precise notice of the sheriff's name than the sheriff himself; for if an action is brought against me and another, I may not have advantage by pleading misnomer of my fellow defendant, for I am a stranger to that and the law presumes that he has the most perfect notice of his own name. Likewise here, and so for that reason it seems to me that the writ is perfectly good. But BALDWIN said that if a writ of dower is brought, and the tenant pleads a fine levied by the husband during the coverture, she may well aver continuance of possession, for she is a stranger to the fine. But here there is no such mischief, for the plaintiff may have his remedy by writ of error and not by plea, for the reason which I have already shown. Also, to show my thinking for the sake of learning,[1] must there be *manucaptores summonitorum juratorum* in the return, or not? It seems to me that it is not of necessity to have those words in the return, for everything comprised in the writ is accomplished, which is 'that you have there the summoners, the names of the pledges, and this writ' (*quod habeas ibi summonitores, nomina plegiorum et hoc breve*). By the old law the summoners had to be ready in court, and if the inquest was ready to pass and the summoners upon their examination said that the party was not summoned, the inquest could not be taken, but the plaintiff was driven to his action against the sheriff. Thus when the sheriff has fulfilled all that he is commanded to do in the writ he has done enough. Since it is commonly used to make such a return I will not impugn it; but there is no necessity to make such a return, because it is not contained in the writ by any words of the writ. Thus my opinion appears to this purpose. Now for the association. It seems to me that there must be an association, for otherwise it is not good, for the words are 'together with those whom we shall associate with you' (*una cum hiis quos vobis associaverimus*), which prove that the king wishes to associate other persons with us who will have joint authority with us. And this association must be dated after the date of the patent, for *associaverimus* is in the future tense; for the words prove that they are to be associated and not already associated, and so the old association which was made upon the general patent—namely

---

[1] I.e. this is *obiter*.

association dell clerkes[1] de assise, ne poit server pur proceder sur cest especial patent, pur ceo que le teste de son association est devaunt le teste dell novell patent. Et apres tiell association fait il est use de faire a eux un patent quel est appell si non omnes, quel est fait auxi bien a lez justices de assise come a eux queux sount associate, que silz toutz ne poient vener a un temps de prendre ceux assises que ceux de eux queux viendront prendront le assise, quel patent de si non omnes fait mention del primer patent et auxi dell association et dit ouster que si vos omnes captionem [assisarum predictarum][2] commode interesse non possitis tunc tres vel duo vestrum, quorum alterum vestrum vos prefati Johannes Baldwyn et Ricardus Lyster unum esse volumus, ad captionem eorundem assisarum etc. procedatis etc., issint que quant le roy ad maunde son authorite certen per sez lettres patentes ceo covient estre pursue accordant. Et issint moy semble que il covient de aver brefe de association sur cest especial patent. Mes si nous poiemus proceder en cest assise per le generall patent? Moy semble que cy, quar le darren patent ne abbridge ascun parte del generall patent, quar quant le roy done severall patentes a nous ill est en nostre ellection de executer lun de eux ou le auter et nest semble all case mise per Hales que si un fait a moy un lesse pur ans et jeo prist un auter lesse de luy, ceo est un surrender del primer lesse, mes ycy le acceptans del speciall patent ne poit estre dit per ascun reyson de deminisher le authorite dell generall patent. Il vary mult del case de justices de pexe que ad este mis, quar la le entent del roy est que lour authorite per le primer patent surcessera, pur ceo que ovell authorite est done a eux et a auters per novell patent. Et issint moy semble que sur le auncient patent et sur le auncient association nous poimus bien proceder. Donques pur le garrante al viconte. Moy semble que <le generall garrante>[i] est assetz bon saunz auter especiall garrante sur lespeciall patent, quar si jeo esteant en mon circute die all viconte que tiell jour jeo voile seer all Dartfford pur lez assises de Kent, et luy commaunde de estre prest la ove sez besoignes, ceo suffist saunz plus, quar il nest necessary que ill eite garrante en escripte. Ou sil soit la attendaunt devaunt nous, <saunz>[3] eiant notice de nostre venue, ceo est assetz bon saunz auter garrante. Issint ceo exception nest mult materiall etc. Donques pur ceo que il ad ceux parolx en le brefe, de catallis que in ipso capta fuerunt, sil soit bon? Et moy semble que cy, quar fuerunt ad relation all temps del disseisin fait, quel est melliour en mon opinion que sil oust este fuerint en le future temps, pur le consideration avaundit. Et issint moy semble que sur tout le matter le assise est maintenable.

Harrys prie que le assise soit agarde.

Browne, clerke dez assises, dit que ilz pristeront lez exceptions <ut supra>[i] en pais, et monstre que le plaintife avoit fait son title en son pleint, et que le

[1] *Perhaps a slip for the singular.*
[2] ass. pdcē.
[3] *Del.*

the association of the clerk of assize—cannot serve for proceeding upon this special patent, because the date (*teste*) of his association is before the *teste* of the new patent. After such an association has been made it is usual to make them a patent which is called *si non omnes*, which is made both to the justices of assize and to those who are associated, that if they cannot all come at one time to take these assizes then those of them who do come shall take the assize, which patent of *si non omnes* mentions the first patent and also the association and further says that 'if you cannot all conveniently be present at the taking of the aforesaid assizes then three or two of you, of whom we wish either of you the said John Baldwin and Richard Lyster to be one, should proceed to the taking of the same assizes etc.' (*si vos omnes captionem assisarum praedictarum commode interesse non possitis tunc tres vel duo vestrum, quorum alterum vestrum vos praefati Johannes Baldwin et Ricardus Lyster unum esse volumus, ad captionem eorundem assisarum etc. procedatis etc.*), so that when the king has sent his certain authority by his letters patent this must be pursued accordingly. So it seems to me that here there must be a writ of association upon this special patent. But may we proceed in this assize by the general patent? It seems to me that we may, for the last patent does not abridge any part of the general patent; for when the king gives several patents to us it is in our election to execute one or other of them. And it is not like the case put by Hales where someone makes me a lease for years and then I take another lease from him, that is a surrender of the first lease, whereas here the acceptance of the special patent cannot be said by any reason to diminsh the authority of the general patent. It differs much from the case of justices of the peace which has been put, for there the king's intention is that their authority by the first patent shall cease, because equal authority is given to them and to others by the new patent. So it seems to me that we may well proceed upon the old patent and upon the old association. Next for the sheriff's warrant. It seems to me that the general warrant is perfectly good without another special warrant upon the special patent; for if I, being in my circuit, say to the sheriff that on such a day I will sit at Dartford for the Kent assizes, and command him to be ready there with his business, this suffices without more, for it is unnecessary that he have a warrant in writing. Or if he is in attendance before us, without having notice of our coming, this is perfectly good without any other warrant. Therefore this exception is not very material etc. Then, is it good, inasmuch as there are these words in the writ, *de catallis quae in ipso capta fuerunt*? It seems to me that it is, for *fuerunt* has relation to the time when the disseisin was made, which is better in my opinion than if it had been *fuerint* in the future tense, for the consideration aforesaid. Thus it seems to me that, upon the whole matter, the assize is maintainable.

Harris prayed that the assize be awarded.

Browne,[1] clerk of the assizes, said that they had taken the above exceptions in the country, and showed that the plaintiff had made his title in his plaint,

---

[1] Anthony Browne, barrister of the Middle Temple; clerk of assize on the Home circuit since 1538; later chief justice of the Common Pleas; died 1567.

tenant apres lez exceptions ut supra prise avoit dit, Veigne lassise sur le title.

Harrys. Il ne dirra issint saunz pleder en barre devaunt.

Baldewyn. Si le assise soit port vers un solement, il dirra generalment Veigne le assise, mes sil soit vers ii. il que voile dire Veigne le assise etc. covient prendre le tenancy sur luy de luy enable a dire Veigne le assise etc. Et auxi il dit que lou le plaintife ne travers le barre le tenant la ill dirra Veigne le assise etc. Mes sil travers le barre donques il ne dirra Veigne le assise etc. eins il covient a luy de maintener son barre: quod nota. Mes soies avise. [*fo. 253v*]

[3]

36 H. 8.

Willelmus Manley de Manneley en le county de Chester, esquier, fuit oblige a Peter Dutton de Dutton en mesme le county, chivaler, en le somme de ducentis millenis libris, per statut merchant devaunt le maire del cyty de Chester, a quel estatute le seale del partie fuit mis et auxi le seale dell roy, quell seale ne fuit devide en ii. severall pecys, scilicet parte sur lun syde dell sere et parte sur lauter, eins tout un seale saunz ascun tiell devision issint que il apiert evidentment que le seale que fuit mis a ceo ne fuit en deux peces accordant al limitation dell statute de mercatoribus. Ore si cest estatute est bon pur extender lez terres ou nemi? Et sill soit sufficient sur lestatut de Acton Burnell ou sur lestatut De marcatoribus, ou coment ceo serra prise en le ley, ill fuit argue devaunt toutz lez justices dell ambideux bankes all Serjantes Inne en Fletestrete. Et nota que en lestatut ill avoit ceux parolx, Et nisi fecerim volo et concedo quod currant super me, heredibus et assignatos meos, districtiones et pena provise in statuto domini regis apud Acton Burnell pro marcatoribus edito et postmodum apud Westmonasterium recitato, In cujus rei testimonium etc.

Forster, le prentice, reherce lez parolx dell statute avaundit. Et moy semble le dit estatute est voide a toutz ententes de prender ascun force come statute merchant, quar le primer consideration del fesans dell statute de Acton Burnell fuit all entent que marchauntes ne serra defraude de lour deuties eins serront

and that the tenant after the above exceptions had been taken had said, 'Let the assize come on the title'.

Harris. He shall not say that without pleading in bar beforehand.

BALDWIN. If the assize is brought against one only, he may say generally 'Let the assize come'; but if it is against two, the one who wishes to say 'Let the assize come etc.' must take upon himself the tenancy to enable him to say 'Let the assize come etc.'. He also said that where the plaintiff does not traverse the tenant's bar, he may say 'Let the assize come etc.'. But if he traverses the bar, then he may not say 'Let the assize come etc.', but must mainatin his bar: note that. But be advised.

3. DUTTON v. MANLEY

Serjeants' Inn, Fleet Street, Mich. 1544. Also fully reported by Gell, Mich. 36 Hen. VIII, ff. 33-37.

William Manley of Manley in the county of Chester, esquire, was bound to Piers Dutton of Dutton in the same county, knight,[1] in the sum of £200,000,[2] by a statute merchant, before the mayor of the city of Chester, to which statute the seal of the party was put and also the king's seal, which seal was not divided into two separate pieces—that is, part on on side of the wax and part on the other—but all one seal without any such division, so that it appears evidently that the seal which was put to it was not in two pieces in accordance with the terms of the Statute *De mercatoribus*.[3] Is this statute good for extending the lands or not? And whether it is sufficient upon the Statute of Acton Burnell,[4] or upon the Statute *De mercatoribus*, or how it should be understood in law, was argued before all the justices of both benches at Serjeants' Inn in Fleet Street. Note that there are these words in the statute: 'And, unless I do this, I will and grant that the distresses and the penalty provided in the lord king's statute at Acton Burnell, enacted for merchants, and afterwards repeated at Westminster, shall run upon me, my heirs and assigns, In witness whereof etc.' (*Et nisi fecerim, volo et concedo quod currant super me, haeredibus et assignatos meos, districtiones et poena provisae in statuto domini regis apud Acton Burnell pro marcatoribus edito, et postmodum apud Westmonasterium recitato, In cujus rei testimonium etc.*).

Forster, apprentice,[5] recited the words of the aforesaid statute. It seems to me that the said statute is void to all intents for taking any effect as a statute merchant; for the first consideration at the making of the Statute of Acton Burnell was the intention that merchants should not be defrauded of their debts

---

[1] Sheriff of Cheshire 1542–43; pedigree in Benolt's visitation, BL MS. Harley 2076, fo. 18v.
[2] *Sic*, but perhaps an error.   [3] 13 Edw. I, *Statutum mercatorum* (*SR* i. 98).
[4] 11 Edw. I, Statute of Acton Burnell (*SR* i. 53).
[5] William Forster, bencher of Lincoln's Inn (1541).

satisfye et pay per lour dettours, quell estatute est declare apres per un auter estatute quel est lestatute De mercatoribus, et ceux deux estatutes ensemble create un perfite statute merchaunt. Quar lestatute de Acton Burnell est limitte forsque a certen villes especials, scilicet London, Everwicke ou Bristoll, et en ceo estatute il est limitte que le seale dell roy serra mis, mes il ne monstre en quel sort le seale serra mis. Donques vient lestatute De mercatoribus fait anno 13° E. 1. que expounde lestatute de Acton Burnell et limitte en certen coment le marchant ferra son dettour de vener devaunt le maire de Loundres ou auter garden de cell ou de auter bon ville et devaunt le clerke ordeyne per le roy et face reconiser le dette, et quel temps[i] le dettour mittera son seale all estatute et soit le seale le roy a ceo mis, que serra en ii. peces dont lun, scilicet le greinder pece, demurrera ove le meyre ou garden et le auter ove le clerke. Issint per ceux parolx de ceo estatute lestatute de Acton Burnell est declare especialment, quar lou cest estatut dit que le seale dell roy serra mis, ore cest estatut determen le forme et circumstance de ceo <et en ascun pointes>[i] tolle et abbridge ascun parte dell statute de Acton Burnell <come ou le viconte malenterpreta lestatute ceo est remedy>[i] <et en divers pointes>[ii] ceo explaine, come jay dit devaunt. Et multfoitz nous avomus erudite que un estatute expounde et declare un estatute precedent, et mist ceo en plus certenty que il fuit devaunt, come lestatut de 32. H. 8. que done que home poit deviser sez terres tenus en socage et le 3. parte de sez terres tenus en chivalry, quel estatut est generall, mes per un auter estatut fait anno 34. mesme le roy ill est limitte et declare que lestatut de 32. ne serra pris que terres en tail serront devise per reyson de ceo estatute eins terres en fee simple tantum, [fo. 254] per que si un voile faire devise de sez terres per son volunte et en ceo conteigne que il eux devise accordant all statute de 32. & 34. H. 8. ore sill soit de terres en taile le devise est voide, unquore lez parolx del statut de 32. sount generall, mez ilz sount declare et mis en certen apres per lauter estatut subsequent, accordant a quel declaration le estatut serra construe et nemi auterment. Et sic est del lestatut de Magna Carta, que dit que heredes maritentur absque disparagatione, la ceo estatut est generall, mes apres vient lestatut de Merton, ca° 6, que ditte que si le garden ne[i] mary leire villanis et burgensibus etc. et mist le disparagement en certen, et adde un penalty a ceo, et expounde et mist en certen lestatut que fuit en generall parolx devaunt. Et issint mon conceyte apiert, que le dit estatut de Acton Burnell est declare et mis en certenty per lestatut De mercatoribus, quel estatut limitte que le seale serra en ii. peces, ut supra, all entent que le choce serra fait saunz fraude

---

[i] eins del.

but should be satisfied and paid by their debtors, which statute was clarified afterwards by another statute—which is the Statute *De mercatoribus*—and these two statutes together create one perfect statute merchant. For the Statute of Acton Burnell is limited only to certain special towns, namely London, York or Bristol; and in that statute it is limited that the king's seal shall be applied, but it does not show what sort of seal shall be applied. Then comes the Statute *De mercatoribus*, made in the thirteenth year of Edward I,[1] which expounds the Statute of Acton Burnell and lays down in detail how a merchant should make his debtor come before the mayor of London, or other warden of that or other good town, and make a recognizance of the debt before the clerk ordained by the king, and at the time when the debtor should put his seal to the statute the king's should also be applied thereto, which should be in two pieces, whereof one, namely the larger piece, should remain with the mayor or warden and the other with the clerk. Thus, by these words of this statute, the Statute of Acton Burnell is specifically clarified; for whereas that statute said that the king's seal should be applied, this statute now determines the form and circumstance thereof, and in some points takes away and abridges some parts of the Statute of Acton Burnell—as where sheriffs had misinterpreted the statute, that is remedied—and in various points explains it (as I have already said). We have often learned of a statute which expounds and declares a preceding statute, and puts it in more certainty than it was before: for instance, the statute of 32 Hen. VIII, which provides that a man may devise his lands held in socage and the third part[2] of his lands held in chivalry,[3] which statute is general, but by another statute made in the thiry-fourth year of the same king it is limited and declared that the statute of 32 Hen. VIII shall not be taken to mean that lands in tail should be devised by reason of that statute but lands in fee simple only,[4] so that if someone wishes to make a devise of his lands by his will and therein states that he devises them in accordance with the statute of 32 and 34 Hen. VIII, and they are lands in tail, the devise is void: and yet the words of the statute of 32 Hen. VIII are general, but they are clarified and put in certain afterwards by the other subsequent statute, and the statute shall be construed in accordance with this declaration and not otherwise. So it is of the statute of Magna Carta, which says that heirs shall be married without disparagement (*Haeredes maritentur absque disparagatione*):[5] this statute is general, but then comes the Statute of Merton, c. 6, which says that 'if the guardian marries the heir to villeins and burgesses etc.', and thus puts the disparagement in certain, and adds a penalty to it, and expounds and puts in certain the statute which was previously in general words.[6] Thus my thinking appears, that the said Statute of Acton Burnell is clarified and put in certainty by the Statute *De mercatoribus*, which statute directs that the seal shall be in two pieces (as above), to the intent

---

[1] 13 Edw. I, stat. 3, *Statutum mercatorum* (*SR* i. 98).   [2] *Recte* two-thirds.
[3] Statute of Wills, 32 Hen. VIII, c. 1 (*SR* iii. 745).
[4] Statute of Explanation of the Statute of Wills, 34 & 35 Hen. VIII, c. 5 (*SR* iii. 901).
[5] Magna Carta 1225, c. 6.   [6] Statute of Merton, c. 6 (*SR* i. 3).

ou collusion, quar est melliour de mitter confidence en deux homez de aver le custody dell seale que de committer ceo all governance de un home. Et issint moy semble que pur ceo que ill apiert ycy a vous que le seall nest devide en deux peces accordant al dit estatut, moy semble que le statute est voide. Et admitte que il serra bon sur lestatut de Acton Burnell, unquore lez terres ne serront pas extende per cest estatut, quar lestatut de Acton Burnell est precise que burgages serront mis en execution sur ceo et ne parle de ascun auters terres. Quar si lestatut De mercatoribus ne eust este fait nul auters terres forsque burgage serroit mis en execution, quar ne fuit deins le purvew del statut de Acton Burnell. Et issint, pur toutz lez reysons et causes, moy semble que lestatut est voide de estre use come un statut. Mes il poit ceo user come un obligation, et donques le partie poit dire Nient son fait, et lauter ne poit luy estopper per son conusans fait devaunt le maire entaunt que ceo nad obteyne le force de un statute. Ou sil fit perfite statute, et le party ne use ceo come statute eins come un obligation, lauter poit pleder Nient son fait. Et sic est le melliour opinion 3. E. 4. Et issint, sur tout le matter disclose, moy semble que lestatute est voide et que nous devomus estre discharge de ceo.

Carrell. Moy semble le contrary, et que le estatut est assetz bon, quar le fesans dell statute de Acton Burnell come jeo entend fuit principallment pur le benefite de lez merchauntes, pur eux encorager de porter lour merchaundise en cest realme pur le proffette et commoditie de mesme le realme, quel estatute pur ceo que il fuit fait pur bon et reysonable consideration est favorablement construe en nostre livers. Quar lou en mesme lestatute il est purvewe que si lez extendours extende lez bienz trope haute que ilz serra deliver a lez extendours, le statute ne parle que terres silz sount extende trope haute serra issint deliver a lez extendours, mes unquore le ley est prise clerement que terres serront deliver a lez extendours sur ceo estatut auxi bien come bienz. Et sic est le liver 44. E. 3., et auxi in 40. mesme le roy. Et ceo est pur le favour de lez merchauntes et pur eux satisfier de lour duties, de eux encorager de faire lour dever en merchaundize pur le utilite dell realme come jeo aye dit devaunt. Et auxi lestatut ne parle de terres que le conusour purchace apres et unquore le ley est clere que ilz serront mis en execution auxi bien come lez terres queux il avoit all temps [del] statut reconise. [*fo. 254v*] Et jeo entende, come ad este touche[1] devaunt moy, que lestatute de Acton Burnell nest abbrogate per lestatute De mercatoribus, mes fuit augment per cest estatute. Et ill vary dell case que ad este mise sur lestatut de 32. le roy que ore est pur deviser de terres, quar ceo statute est alter per lestatut de mesme le roy que dit que terre taile ne serra devise, quar ceo va en le negative mes il nad ascuns parolx en lestatut De mercatoribus que ferra lestatut de Acton Burnell de estre voide pur ceo que mesme lestatute fuit fait pur bon consideration ut supra. Et si un estatute oust este fait meane parenter Acton Burnell et le auter statut De mercatoribus serra

---

[1] confesse *del.*

that the thing shall be done without fraud or collusion, for it is better to put confidence in two men having custody of the seal than to commit it to the control of one man. So it seems to me that, because it appears to you here that the seal is not divided in two pieces according to the said statute, it seems to me that the statute is void. Even if we admit that it is good upon the Statute of Acton Burnell, nevertheless the lands shall not be extended by that statute, for the Statute of Acton Burnell says specifically that burgages shall be put in execution thereon and does not speak of any other land. If the Statute *De mercatoribus* had not been made, no other lands but burgage could have been put in execution, for they were not within the purview of the Statute of Acton Burnell. Therefore, for all the reasons and causes, it seems to me that the statute is void with respect to being used as a statute. But he may use it as a bond, and then the party may say *Non est factum*, and the other cannot estop him by his acknowledgment made before the mayor, inasmuch as this has not obtained the force of a statute. Had it been a perfect statute, and the party did not use it as a statute but as a bond, the other could plead *Non est factum*. That is the better opinion in 3 Edw. IV.[1] Therefore, upon all the matter disclosed, it seems to me that the statute is void and that we ought to be discharged therefrom.

Caryll.[2] I think the contrary, and that the statute is perfectly good; for the making of the Statute of Acton Burnell, as I think, was principally for the benefit of merchants, to encourage them to bring their merchandise into this realm, for the profit and commodity of the same realm, which statute—because it was made upon good and reasonable consideration—is favourably construed in our books. For whereas it is provided in the same statute that if the valuers extend the goods too high they shall be delivered to the extenders, the statute does not speak of lands which are extended too high, and say that they shall be likewise delivered to the extenders, and yet the law is taken clearly to be that lands shall be delivered to the extenders upon this statute as well as goods. So is the book 44 Edw. III, and also in 40 Edw. III.[3] This is for favour to merchants and to satisfy them of their debts, to encourage them to carry on their trade for the utility of the realm, as I have already said. Also the statute does not speak of lands which the conusor purchases afterwards, and yet the law is clear that they shall be put in execution as well as the lands which he had at the time when the statute was acknowledged. And I think, as has been touched upon before me, that the Statute of Acton Burnell is not abrogated by the Statute *De mercatoribus*, but was augmented by that statute. (And he differed from the case which has been put upon the statute of 32 Hen. VIII for devising lands, for that statute is altered by the statute of the same king which says that entailed land shall not be devised, for that goes in the negative, but there are no words in the Statute *De mercatoribus* which make the Statute of Acton Burnell void, because the same statute was made for good consideration, as above). If a statute had been made between Acton Burnell and the other Statute *De*

---

[1] YB Mich. 3 Edw. IV, fo. 27, pl. 24.   [2] John Caryll, bencher of the Inner Temple (1537), att.-gen. of the duchy.   [3] YB Hil. 44 Edw. III, fo. 2, pl. 5; Trin. 40 Edw. III, fo. 27, pl. 2.

ceo entende de estre voide? Jeo entende clerement que nemi, quar lentent dez fesourz de ceo ne fuit de faire estatute que serra voide pur certen temps, quar parenter le fesans dell lun statut et lauter est le space de ii. ans. Et pur ceo que il est dit que le seale doit estre de deux peces, pur riens que apiert a vous ycy il poit estre de ii. pecys, quar jay vewe un seale divers foitz de ii. peces que ad este joyne en tiell sort que ill est fort de perseyver si ceo soit de ii. peces ou de un tantum. Et auxi pur ceo que le maire ad certefy ceo come un estatut, cest court covient doner credence a ceo, et que ceo est un perfite statute. En mesme le maner come si le evesque certefy bastardy avera le partie averment enconter ceo, a dire que il nest bastarde? Jeo die clerement que nemi, pur ceo que le court covient doner foy et credence a son certeficat ou auterment un choce dependera en triall infinite. Et si jeo recover vers un en Bancke le Roy ou en Comen Banke et il dit que ill navoit ascuns justices en court all temps que le recovere est suppose, avera il cest plee? Jeo die clerement que nemi, pur ceo que le contrary apiert de recorde. Et si home sue brefe de errour per que un recorde est remove, avera le auter partie averment a dire que il nad ascun tiel recorde? Certes nemi, quar le court donera credence a ceo que est certefy en un recorde saunz ascun dowte, <quar le court doit credite le choce que vient devaunt eux de recorde >[1] et pur ceo le liver est en 2. R. 3, en Dupleges case, que si le maire certefy un mesme statute a deux ou iii. temps, le partie avera son severall execution sur ceo, et le court entendra que ceo est severall statutes et nemi tout un, quar le certeficacion del maire que vient devaunt lez justices de recorde covient[2] estre credit come le evaungelist, et null entendement ne presumption serra prise ou preferre contrary a ceo que est certefy. Et nient obstant que le seale nest de ii. severall peces, quel ycy ne appiert de estre issint, unquore le seale dell roy assigne a mesme le purpose poit estre mis a ceo et issint lestatute sufficient, quar come le liver est 27. H. 6. si divers fount un fait que nad que un seale, unquore ceo poit estre le seale de toutz, quar si toutz sealont ove un mesme seale et en un mesme lewe ceo est le seale de eux toutz. Et issint il apiert in 8. H. 4. en brefe de wast, ou un fait fuit plede et le partie suppose ceo de estre fait per divers et quant [fo. 255] ceo monstre devaunt all court il avoit forsque un sealle, et tenus la que assetz bon, quar serra entende que ceo un seale est le seale de toutz, quel nest inconvenient. Et issint moy semble ycy que, entaunt que il ne apiert contrary ycy mes que le seale est de ii. peces, et sil soit aliter de un pece unquore est bon. Et jeo agree que si le partie perde lestatut ill perde son avauntage, scilicet son dette, auxi, come apiert anno 27. H. 6, mes nous ne sumus en ceo case ycy quar ore ill est certefy devaunt eux per le maire que est officer a mesme

---

[1] *Del.*
[2] covēt.

mercatoribus would that be understood to be void? I think clearly not, for the intention of the makers thereof was not to make a statute which would be void for a certain time, for there is an interval of two years between the making of the one statute and the other. And inasmuch as it is said that the seal ought to be of two pieces, for anything that appears to you it may have been of two pieces; for I have several times seen a seal of two pieces which has been joined in such sort as it is hard to perceive whether it is of two pieces or only one. Also, because the mayor has certified this as a statute, this court ought to give credence thereto, and that this is a perfect statute. In the same way, if the bishop certifies bastardy, shall the party have an averment against that, to say that he is not a bastard? I say that clearly he shall not, because the court must give faith and credence to his certificate or else one thing would depend on infinite trial. If I recover against someone in the King's Bench, or the Common Bench, and he says that there were no justices in court at the time when the recovery is supposed, shall he have that plea? I say that clearly he shall not, because the contrary appears of record. If someone sues a writ of error whereby a record is removed, shall the other party have an averment to say that there is no such record? Surely not, for the court shall give credence to that which is certified in a record, without any doubting, for the court ought to credit a thing which comes before them of record. For this there is the book in 2 Ric. III, in Duplege's case, that if the mayor certifies one same statute at two or three times, the party shall have his separate executions thereon, and the court will presume that there are several statutes and not all one, for the mayor's certificate which comes before the justices of record must be credited like the evangelist, and no intendment or presumption shall be taken or preferred contrary to that which is certified. Even if the seal is not of two separate pieces, which here does not appear to be so, still the king's seal assigned for the same purpose may be applied to it, and therefore the statute sufficient: for, as the book is in 27 Hen. VI,[1] if several people make one deed, and they only have one seal, this may still be the seal of them all, for if they all seal with one same seal and in one same place this is the seal of them all. And so it appears in 8 Hen. IV,[2] in a writ of waste, where a deed was pleaded and the party supposed it to have been made by several, and when it was shown forth to the court it had only one seal, and it was there held to be perfectly good, for it shall be presumed that this one seal is the seal of them all, which is not absurd. Likewise it seems to me here that, since it does not appear contrary but that the seal is of two pieces, then even if it is otherwise of one piece, it is still good. I agree that if the party loses the statute he loses his advantage also, namely his debt, as appears in the year 27 Hen. VI,[3] but we are not in that case here, for it has now been certified before us by the mayor, who is an officer for

---

[1] Hil. 27 Hen. VI, Fitz. Abr., *Feffements et faits*, pl. 105. Cf. YB Mich. 22 Hen. VI, fo. 4, pl. 6, *per* Portington J.

[2] Probably YB Mich. 8 Hen. IV, fo. 8, pl. 12, though this was in an assize of novel disseisin by the duke of York and not in a writ of waste.

[3] Probably intending YB Mich. 37 Hen. VI, fo. 6, pl. 11. But cf., as to the loss of a tally, Trin. 27 Hen. VI, fo. 9, pl. 1.

le purpose, per que moy semble que le court doit ceo prender pur un bon et perfite statute, et que sur ceo lez terres etc. covient estre mis en execution.

Hales, serjant. Moy semble le contrary et que lestatute est clerement voide, quar lestatut de Acton Burnell est declare per lestatut De mercatoribus, et auxi augmente per mesme lestatut, come ad este bien move per Mr Forster devaunt moy, quar lestatut de Acton Burnell per le precise parolx de mesme lestatut ne serra prise sinon en lez villes de London, Everwick ou Bristoll accordant come il est limitte deins mesme le estatut. Issint clerement come jeo entende le cyty de Chester navoit ascun authorite per ceo estatut de prender lestatut merchaunt, nient plus que lou ill est ordeigne per le parliament que lez measons en Bristowe serront repaire ou lez stretes pave, clerement ceo ne va a auters villes nient nosme en le statute, quar donques un statute servera pur tout le realme, quel nest issint clerement. Donques si le cytye de Chester ne avoit authorite per Acton Burnell, donques de necessite ilz covient aver lour authorite per lestatute De mercatoribus, quel statute reherce Acton Burnell et limitte le maner et forme de conuser del statut merchant, quel forme covient estre observe stricte accordant all dit estatute ou auterment ill nest bon. Et de ceo jeo voile mitter forsque un case, quel est 14. E. 4., ou un acte de parliament fuit que le chauncelor dangliterre pur le temps, appellant a luy lez justices dell lun banke et de lauter, averont power de agarder subpena vers un all sute de un auter, et sur ceo acte le partie que fuit plaintife sua subpena vers lauter de estre devaunt le chauncelour a certen jour, et le brefe fuit un comen subpena, et pur ceo que ne fuit recorde que lez justices fueront ovesque le chauncelour accordant all limitation dell acte de parliament fuit tenus que le subpena esteant comen subpena nest bon, quar lour authorite fuit done a eux jointment per lestatut, quel covient estre pursue accordant ou auterment nest bon. Issint ycy, lestatut De mercatoribus reherce que le viconte devaunt ceo estatute malement enterpreta lestatut de Acton Burnell, quel ore est remedy, et pur le plus just execution de tiels estatutes et pur le creation de eux ceo estatute limitte que le seale serra en ii. peces, le consideration de quel fuit pur avoider fauxite, quar plus credence est de estre done a deux homez que a un home tantum, et est graund presumption que ilz ambideux ne voile forger ascun estatute tortiousment vers ascun home. Et issint moy semble que sill faute tiell seale que est limitte per lestatut que il nest bon pur le consideration avaundit. Et vary mult del case que ad este mise lou un fait aiant forsque un seale poit estre le fait de divers, quar ceo servera pur toutes lour seales ovesque lour assentes, mes ycy le seale limitte per lestatute et auxi assigne per le roy a mesme le purpose ne poit estre chaunge ne alter per le assent ne agrement de ascun home, quar sill soit lestatute seale ovesque tiell seale est merement voide de prender ascun effecte come statute merchant. [*fo. 255v*] Et ou il est dit que le court donera credence a cest statut merchant, et que ceo serra prise pur bon et perfite pur ceo que est certefy per le maire, ceo nest pas issint: quar il vary mult de lez

the same purpose, and so it seems to me that the court ought to take it as a good and perfect statute, and that thereupon the lands etc. must be put in execution.

Hales, serjeant. I think the contrary, and that the statute is clearly void, for the Statute of Acton Burnell is clarified by the Statute *De mercatoribus*, and also augmented by the same statute, as has been well moved by Mr Forster before me; for the Statute of Acton Burnell, by the precise words of the same statute, shall not be taken to apply except in the towns of London, York or Bristol, according to the terms of the same statute. Thus clearly, as I think, the city of Chester had no authority by that statute to take the statute merchant, any more than where it is ordained by parliament that the houses in Bristol should be repaired, or the streets paved, clearly that would not extend to other towns not named in the statute, for then a [local] statute would serve for the whole realm, which is clearly not so. If, then, the city of Chester had no authority by Acton Burnell, then of necessity they must have their authority through the Statute *De mercatoribus*, which statute recites Acton Burnell and directs the manner and form of acknowledging a statute merchant, which form must be observed strictly according to the said statute or else it is not good. As to this, I will put but one case, which is 14 Edw. IV,[1] where an act of parliament was made that the chancellor of England for the time being, calling to him the justices of either bench, should have power to award a subpoena against someone at the suit of another, and upon this act the party who was plaintiff sued a subpoena against the other to be before the chancellor at a certain day, and the writ was a common subpoena, and because it was not recorded that the justices were with the chancellor according to the terms of the act of parliament it was held that the subpoena, being a common subpoena, was not good, for their authority was given to them jointly by the statute, which must be pursued accordingly or else it is not good. Likewise here, the Statute *De mercatoribus* recites that sheriffs before this statute had misinterpreted the Statute of Acton Burnell, which is now remedied, and for the juster execution of such statutes and for the making thereof this statute directed that the seal should be in two pieces, the consideration whereof was to avoid falsity, for more credence is to be given to two men than to one alone, and there is a strong presumption that both of them will not forge any statute wrongfully against anyone. And so it seems to me that, if such seal as is specified by the statute is lacking, it is not good, for the consideration aforesaid. And it differs greatly from the case which has been put where a deed having only one seal may be the deed of several, for that seal may serve for all their seals with their consents, but here the seal specified by the statute and also assigned by the king for the same purpose cannot be changed or altered by the consent or agreement of anyone, for, if it is, the statute sealed with such a seal is absolutely void for the purpose of taking any effect as a statute merchant. And where it is said that the court should give credence to this statute merchant, and that it shall be taken as good and perfect because it is certified by the mayor, that is not so: for it differs much from

---

[1] YB Mich. 14 Edw IV, fo. 1, pl. 1.

cases que ount este mise de recordes remove per brefe de errour etc. Jeo confesse que le partie ne dirra contrary a ceo que ill ne avoit unques ascun tiell recorde contrary a ceo que est certefy, mes ycy cest seale est apparant all court et ilz sount ore a determiner si ceo soit perfite statute a toutz ententes ou nemi, et per le inspection de ceo lez justices determineront cest matter. Come jeo mitta le case que un home plede lez lettres patentes dell roy southe le graunde seale de Angliterre et monstre eux avaunt, et ill apiert evidentment all court per vewe dell seale que ceo nest le graunde seale eins un auter seale fait all similitude de ceo, ne ajugera le court ceux lettres patentes de estre ousterment voide? Jeo die clerment que cy. Et issint ycy, pur ceo que ill est ore apparant all court que cest statute nest seale ovesque le ordinary seale esepcialment ordeyne a mesme le purpose, moy semble que lestatute est voide et que nous ne devomus estre mise en execution per mesme lestatute ne per ascun choce en ceo conteyne.

Saunders, serjant. Moy semble le contrary, et que le statut est bon. Et come le case est ill est reyson que nostre parte avera la favour que loyalment poit estre done, quar cest estatute fuit fait en consideration de un mariage enter le file de Sir Piers Dutton et le dit Manley, et pur le performans de <promises et >[i] covenauntes concernantes mesme le mariage, et il dit que fides inter homines precipue est observanda, scilicet quod verbi et facta concord[ant]. Et auxi pur le ley en cest matter moy semble que cest statute est bon, pur ceo que le cytye de Chester est un auncient cyty dell realme, en quel cyty merchaundise est mult occupy, et graund recours de merchantes est a mesme le cyty, quel est mult commodious et proffitable all realme, et statutes merchantes en tiel forme enseale come ceo statute est, ount este la toutz temps use, et ount este enforce come auters statutes prise en auters lewes de cest realme ount este. Et saunz dowte le seale ad este deliver a eux per le roy, quar ilz ne voile unques forge un seale de lour tettes demesne, et donques moy semble per reyson de user de ceo per cy long temps que un estatut prise la serra bon. Et nest empertinent que ilz avera un sort de statut merchant deins un particuler vill que nest use en auter lewes dell realme, quar ill ad ascuns customez que sount directment encontre le comen ley ou statut ley et unquore ilz sount bon, [*fo. 256*] quar ill apiert en 30. E. 3. que en Surrey ill ad un custome que leire avera heir loumes apres le mort de son auncestor, scilicet le melliour lete en le meason, et similibus, et unquore leire per le comen ley ne poit claymer ascun tiell choce. Auxi en le ville de Nottingham le puisne fitz enheritera, et unquore en auters lewes de mesme le cytie tiell custome nest. Et auxi il reherce auter custome de Norhamptonshyre, et dit que pur le continuans de temps ceux customez sount bon et unquore sount merement contrary all comen ley. Donques pur que serra lestatute ley favour plus per le comen [ley][1]? Issint moy semble que per reyson dell usage cest statute est bon. Auxi moy semble que lestatut de Acton Burnell nest fait frustrate per le fesans dell lauter statut apres, quar il nad ascuns parolx en le

[1] *Conjectural.*

the cases which have been put of records removed by writ of error etc. I confess that the party may not say, contrary thereto, that there is no such record, contrary to that which is certified, but here this seal is apparant to the court and they are now to determine whether it is a perfect statute for all purposes, or not, and the justices shall determine this matter by the inspection thereof. For instance, I put the case where someone pleads the king's letters patent under the great seal of England, and shows them forth, and it appears evidently to the court by looking at the seal that this is not the great seal but another seal made in its likeness, shall not the court adjudge these letters patent to be utterly void? I say clearly that it shall. Likewise here, because it is now apparant to the court that this statute is not sealed with the ordinary seal specifically ordained for the same purpose, it seems to me that the statute is void and that we ought not to be put in execution by the same statute nor for anything contained therein.

Saunders, serjeant. I think the contrary, and that the statute is good. As the case is, it is right that our side should have the favour which may lawfully be given, for this statute was made in consideration of a marriage between the daughter of Sir Piers Dutton and the said Manley, and for the performance of promises and covenants concerning the same marriage. (And he said that trust between men is especially to be observed (*Fides inter homines praecipue est observanda*), namely that actions should agree with words (*Verbi et facta concordant*).) As to the law in this matter, it seems to me that this statute is good, because the city of Chester is an ancient city of the realm, in which city trade is much occupied, and there is great recourse of merchants to the same city, which is most commodious and profitable to the realm; and statutes merchant sealed in this form (as this statute is), have always been used there, and have been enforced in the same way as other statutes taken in other places of this realm have been. And without doubt the seal has been delivered to them by the king, for they would never forge a seal of their own heads. Therefore it seems to me that, by reason of such long usage, a statute taken there should be good. It is not absurd that they should have a sort of statute merchant within a particular town which is not used in other places of the realm; for there are some customs which are directly against the common law or statute law and yet they are good. Thus it appears in 30 Edw. III[1] that in Surrey there is a custom that the heir should have heirlooms after his ancestor's death, namely the best bed in the house, and the like, and yet by the common law the heir cannot claim any such thing. Also in [parts of] the town of Nottingham the youngest son shall inherit, and yet in other places in the same city there is no such custom. (He also recited another custom, of Northamptonshire,[2] and said that by the continuance of time these customs are good, and yet they are absolutely contrary to the common law.) Why, then, should statute law be favoured more than the common law? So it seems to me that by reason of the usage this statute is good. It also seems to me that the Statute of Acton Burnell is not frustrated by the making of the other

[1] YB Hil. 30 Edw. III, fo. 2.
[2] This was the serjeant's own county. The reference may be to YB Mich. 30 Edw. III, fo. 23.

darren statute que fait lestatut de Acton Burnell voide, per que, come Mr
Carrell ad [dit] il nest de estre resemble all case dell statut de[1] 32. le roy que ore
est, quar la le darren statute distroy le primer statute all purpose que ad este
declare per Mr Forster. <Et ascuns foitz lez parolx de un estatut sount voide,
come lestatut de Magna Carta, ca° 3, antequam homagium ejus acceperit
nullus habeat custodiam alicujus heredis, >[i] mes ycy ill est semble all case que
est 1. libro assisarum, lou un rent de xx. s. fuit graunt a un home de un acre de
terre quel un tiel tenant tient dell grauntour, a percever le rent per le mayne del
dit tenant, et sil avient que le terre soit alien ou si ceo eschete que donques le
graunte poit distreigne pur le dit rent en le maner de D., si le <grauntor >[i]
aliene le terre apres, et le graunte port assise, ambideux lez terres serront mis en
vewe, scilicet le acre que fuit charge et auxi le maner de D., quar le acre nest pas
discharge, quar le charger dell maner de D. ove le rent nest ascun discharge pur
le primer acre, quar ill nad ascun parolx en le fait que poient enure a ceo
discharger. Et sic est le liver 8. E. 3. libro assisarum, lou un rent <de x.
markes >[i] fuit graunt all baron et feme, et si le baron devie devaunt le feme que
le feme avera 40. s. et si le feme devie devaunt le baron que ill avera x. markes,
le baron devie, et la feme port assise, et sur le matter ell recovera le somme de x.
markes, quar quant le grauntor fist le graunt all commencement ut supra il ne
avoit ascuns parolx en le fait que si le baron devie que la feme avera xl. s. et
nemi x. markes, issint il nad ascun parolx de repeller ascun parte dell principall
graunt, per que ill est bon en tout. Issint ycy, pur ceo que ill appiert ycy que
lestatut De mercatoribus enlarge lestatut de Acton Burnell et ne determen ceo,
ill ne poit estre dit en ley ne reyson mes que le dit estatut de Acton Burnell
estoit unquore en sa force. Et ceo, come jeo entende, est expressement prove
per le register, quar le register est extendi facias etc. terras et tenementa etc.
secundum formam statuti de Acton Burnell, et va ouster secundum formam
statuti predicti, issint que tout ceux parolx referre solement all statut de Acton
Burnell et a null auter. Et il ad un case que prove fortement ovesque nous, quel
est 25. E. 3. [17],[2] quar la vient en question si terres et tenementes serront mise
en execution sur un statute merchant per lestatut de Acton Burnell ou per
lestatut De mercatoribus: et la ajuge que ilz serront mis en execution
per lestatute de Acton Burnell, et donques ceo prove que nostre estatute est
bon en ley et il covient estre favour pur [lez] considerations avaunt reherce: per
que moy semble que nous devomus aver nostre execution.

---

[1] *Written twice.*
[2] *Margin.*

statute afterwards, for there are no words in the latter statute to make the Statute of Acton Burnell void; and so, as Mr Caryll has said, it is not to be likened to the case of the statute of 32 Hen. VIII, for there the later statute destroyed the first statute for the purpose which has been declared by Mr Forster. Sometimes the words of a statute are void: for instance, the statute of Magna Carta, c. 3, 'no one shall have the wardship of any heir before he has taken his homage' (*antequam homagium ejus acceperit nullus habeat custodiam alicujus haeredis*). But here it is like the case which is in 1 Lib. Ass.,[1] where a rent of 20s. was granted to someone from an acre of land which such and such a tenant held of the grantor, the rent to be taken by the hands of the said tenant, and if it should happen that the land be aliened or that it should escheat, then the grantee might distrain for the said rent in the manor of Dale: if the grantor aliens the land afterwards, and the grantee brings an assize, both the lands shall be put in view, namely the acre which was charged and also the manor of Dale, for the acre is not discharged, inasmuch as charging the manor of Dale with the rent is no discharge for the first acre, for there are no words in the deed which may enure to discharge it. So is the book in 8 Edw. III, Lib. Ass.,[2] where a rent of ten marks was granted to a husband and wife, and if the husband should die before the wife then the wife should have 40s., and if the wife should die before the husband he should have ten marks; the husband died, and the woman brought an assize, and upon these facts she recovered the sum of ten marks: for when the grantor made the grant at the commencement (as above) there were no words in the deed that if the husband died the woman should have 40s. and not ten marks, and so there were no words to repeal any part of the principal grant, and so it is good for the whole. Likewise here, because it appears here that the Statute *De mercatoribus* enlarged the Statute of Acton Burnell and did not determine it, it cannot be denied in law or in reason that the said Statute of Acton Burnell still stands in its force. And that, as I think, is expressly proved by the Register, for the Register says 'cause the lands and tenements etc. to be extended etc., according to the form of the Statute of Acton Burnell' (*extendi facias etc. terras et tenementa etc. secundum formam statuti de Acton Burnell*), and goes on further to say 'in accordance with the form of the aforesaid statute' (*secundum formam statuti praedicti*), so that all these words refer solely to the Statute of Acton Burnell and no other. There is a case which proves strongly with us, which is 25 Edw. III, fo. 17,[3] for there it came in question whether lands and tenements should be put in execution upon a statute merchant by the Statute of Acton Burnell or by the Statute *De mercatoribus*; and it was there adjudged that they should be put in execution by the Statute of Acton Burnell, and therefore this proves that our statute is good in law, and it must be favoured, for the considerations recited above: and so it seems to me that we ought to have our execution.

[1] YB 1 Edw. III, Lib. Ass., pl. 9.   [2] YB 8 Edw. III, Lib. Ass., pl. 10.
[3] YB Mich. 25 Edw. III, fo. 96, pl. 17.

12. Midland Circuit Assize Cases (1544–45)[1]

[1]

Nota que fuit dyt per *Luke*, Justice de gaole delyvere a Warwick in xl^{ma} anno 35. H. 8, que si un home soit clerk convict et puis il est endite de auter felony fait devaunt le dit conviction, que le partie serra discharge de [le] dit enditment.

[2]

[*fo. 37v*] Nota que home fuit endite de felony al Northt' in xl^{ma} anno 36. H. 8, et sur ceo arraigne et trove culpable, sur que le prisoner pria son lyver et dit que il est clark, et sur ceo le clerk del assise averr' pur le roy que il fuit clerk convict a Warwyck adevaunt et monstra le record de son conviction et de son delyveraunce al ordynary. Et le prisoner dit que il nest le mesme person que fuit adevaunt convicte. Et sur ceo per *Shelley* et *Whorwood*, tunc Justices del gayle delyvery ibidem, fuit un enquest prise ad inquirendum si fuist le mesme person que fuit clerk convict adevaunt ou nemy. Et linquest disount que il est mesme le person que fuit adevaunt clarke[i] convict, et sur ceo judgment fuit done que serra pendue: que fuit fait al Northt' eodem tempore.

---

[1] Newberry Library, Chicago, Case MS. fK 545.33575, fo. 37r-v.

12. MIDLAND CIRCUIT ASSIZE CASES (1544–45)

1.

Warwick assizes, Lent 1544.

Note that it was said by LUKE,[1] justice of gaol delivery at Warwick in Lent [1544] in the year 35 Hen. VIII, that if someone is a clerk convict and is afterwards indicted of another felony committed before the said conviction, the party shall be discharged from the said indictment.

2.

Northampton assizes, Lent 1545.

Note that a man was indicted of felony at Northampton in Lent [1545] in the year 36 Hen. VIII, and thereupon arraigned and found guilty, whereupon the prisoner prayed his book and said that he was a clerk; and thereupon the clerk of assize averred for the king that he was previously a clerk convict at Warwick, and showed the record of his conviction and of his delivery to the ordinary. And the prisoner said that he was not the same person who was previously convicted. Thereupon an inquest was taken by SHELLEY and WHORWOOD,[2] then justices of the gaol delivery there, to enquire whether he was the same person who was previously a clerk convict or not. And the inquest said he was the same person who was previously a clerk convict; and thereupon judgment was given that he be hanged: which was done at Northampton at the same time.

[1] Walter Luke, J.K.B., died 21 July 1544.
[2] William Whorwood, bencher of the Middle Temple, att.-gen. 1540–45, died 28 May 1545.

[3]

Nota que a Leic' tempore xlme anno 36. H. 8. home fuit endite de felony et sur ceo arraigne devaunt *Shelley* et *Whorwood* adonques Justices, que disount[1] que devaunt cest temps il fuit endite de mesme le felonye in le countie del Staff', et sur ceo illonque acquite. Et demaunde judgment sil serra myse auter foitz a responder al dit felonye. Et sur ceo lez justices doneront jour a le prisoner a averr' son recorde al procheyn generall gaole delivere a son perill.

---

[1] Sic.

3.

Northampton assizes, Lent 1545.

Note that at Leicester in time of Lent [1545] in the year 36 Hen. VIII, a man was indicted of felony and thereupon arraigned before SHELLEY and WHORWOOD, then justices, who said[1] that before the present time he was indicted of the same felony in the county of Stafford, and acquitted of it there, and demanded judgment whether he should be driven to answer the said felony again. Thereupon the justices gave day to the prisoner to verify[2] his record at the next general gaol delivery, at his peril.

---

[1] Plural in text, but this evidently refers to the prisoner.
[2] Or perhaps 'have'.

13. ADDENDA (1544–46)

From the notebook of Gilbert Gerrard[1]

[1]

Fo. i, verso.

Item fuit agree per toutz lez justicez termino Trinitatis anno 36 H. 8. en le Common Banke que si home ad lesse pur anz de certen terre et est oblige en un estatut etc. et aprez alien le leasse all estrange, que aprez cest lesse ne serra mys en execution, nient obstant que ceo fuit un foitz liable all execution, pur ceo que est frosque[2] un chatelle et null bienz ou chatelles sont chargable frosque ceux que il ad all temps dexecution sue. Mez auterment est de terre etc., quar lestatut parle frosque de terre.

[2]

Fo. i, verso.

Nota que action sur le case est maintenable vers executors sur un symple contract fait per lour testatour en Bank le Roy, mez en le Comen Bank nemi. Anno. 36 H. 8. termino Hillarii.

[3]

Fo. x.

Anno 37 H. 8. termino Hillarii. Nota que si home soit utlage et est appelle de D. en le com. de Midd. ou London, cest utlagarie est bon saunz ascun

---

[1] CUL MS. Ee.6.15.
[2] *Gerrard consistently used this spelling of* forsque.

471

13. ADDENDA (1544–46)

From the notebook of Gilbert Gerrard[1]

1.

Common Pleas, Trin. 1544.

It was agreed by all the justices in Trinity term 36 Hen. VIII, in the Common Bench, that if someone has a lease for years of certain land and is bound in a statute etc., and afterwards aliens the lease to a stranger, this lease shall not afterwards be put in execution, even though it was once liable to the execution, because it is only a chattel and no goods or chattels are chargeable except for those which he has at the time when the execution is sued. It is otherwise, however, of land etc., for the statute speaks only of land.

2.

Hil. 1545.

Note that an action on the case is maintainable against executors in the King's Bench upon a simple contract made by their testator, but not in the Common Bench. Hilary term, 36 Hen. VIII.

3.

Probably King's Bench, Hil. 1546.

Hilary term, 37 Hen. VIII. Note that if someone is outlawed and is described as being 'of Dale in the county of Middlesex (or in London)', this outlawry is

---

[1] Gerrard (d. 1953) was admitted to Gray's Inn in 1537 and became a bencher in 1553; he was later attorney-general and master of the rolls. For another case from this notebook see above, p. 429, no. 5B.

proclamation etc. Mez si il soit appelle nuper de D. in comitatu etc. donquez proclamation doit estre agarde en le com. lou il est demurrant ou auterment nest bon: et ceo lestatut de anno 6 de cest roy.

[4]

Fo. x.

Si home bargayne et sell sa terre a un home et aprez fist auter bargayne all estrange, lestrange enrolle cest fait devant le primer bargaynee deinz 6 moys, ore il avera le terre per lestatut, quar luse nest change devaunt enrollement etc.

[5]

Fo. xi.

Item lestatut de 27 H. 8. est que si le terre fuit don all baron et feme pur vie ou en taille etc. que le feme navera sa dower et auxi sa joyntture. Et issint lestatut parle del baron et feme, quel est tout temps aprez le coverture, et uncore si terre soit don a un home et feme devaunt le coverture pur le joynture le feme, le feme navera dower. Et uncore ceux casez ne sont deinz lez parolles del estatut, mez sont prisez per lequitie accordant all meanyng del makers de ceo etc.: per *Bromley,* anno xxxvi^{to} Regis Henrici viii, termino Michaelis etc.

[6]

Fo. 26v.

Nota per *Bromeley,* cheff justice, que per lestatut de anno 25 E. 3. nontenure de parcell nabatera le brefe, mez uncore si home port un precipe dun manour et le tenant plede nontenure de parcell tout le brefe abatra, quar laction doit estre port del manour ovesque froprise[1] etc. et le dit estatut est entende lou laction est port del terre ou auter chose que est severable et nemi lou laction est port del chose entier que nest severable.

---

[1] *I.e.* forprise.

good without any proclamation etc. But if he is described as 'late of Dale in the county of etc.', then a proclamation must be awarded in the county where he is living or else it is not good: and this is by the statute of the sixth year of this king.[1]

4.

Undated, *c.*1546.

If someone bargains and sells his land to one man, and afterwards makes another bargain to a stranger, and the stranger enrols this deed before the first bargainee, within six months, he shall now have the land by the statute,[2] for the use is not changed before enrolment etc.

5.

King's Bench, Mich. 1544.

The statute of 27 Hen. VIII[3] says that if the land was given to the husband and wife for life or in tail etc. the wife shall not have her dower as well as her jointure. Thus the statute speaks of husband and wife, which is always understood to mean after the coverture; and yet if land is given to a man and woman before the coverture for the woman's jointure, the woman shall not have dower. Although these cases are not within the words of the statute, they are nevertheless taken by the equity according to the meaning of the makers thereof etc.: by BROMLEY, in Michaelmas term 36 Hen. VIII etc.

6.

Undated, *c.*1545.

Note, by BROMLEY C.J., that by the statute of 25 Edw. III[4] nontenure of part shall not abate the writ; and yet if someone brings a *praecipe* for a manor and the tenant pleads nontenure of part the whole writ shall abate, for the action ought to be brought for the manor with an exception etc. and the said statute is understood to mean where the action is brought for land or something else which is severable and not where the action is brought for an entire thing which is not severable.

[1] 6 Hen. VIII, c. 4 (*SR* iii. 126).
[2] 27 Hen. VIII, c. 16 (*SR* iii. 549).
[3] Statute of Uses, 27 Hen. VIII, c. 10 (*SR* iii. 539).
[4] 25 Edw. III, stat. 5, c. 16 (*SR* i. 322).

ANNOTATIONS AND CORRIGENDA
TO REPORTS IN PRINT

APPENDIX

ANNOTATIONS AND CORRIGENDA
TO REPORTS IN PRINT

(1) *The Reports of John Caryll* (Selden Soc., vols. 115–116).

p. 4, pl. 8   *Note* (1486/87), headnote: *for* Mich. 8 Hen. VII *read* Mich. 9 Hen. VII. Cf. p. 265, pl. 184. Note 3: Sedgwick was not a bencher at the time of this note, but a student admitted in 1482.

p. 12, pl. 18   *Lord Ormonde* v. *The King* (1488), headnote: *for* YB Hil. *read* YB Pas.

p. 91, pl. 102   *Anon.* (1492) is perhaps part of *Waller* v. *Debenham*, which returns at p. 125.

p. 122, pl. 120   *Anon.* (1492), line 8: *for* and entered *read* and he (the defendant) entered

p. 122, pl. 121   *Anon.* (1492) is perhaps also part of *Waller* v. *Debenham*, which returns at p. 125.

p. 125, pl. 123   *Waller* v. *Debenham* (1493). Perhaps continued from p. 91, pl. 102, and p. 122, pl. 121.

p. 142, pl. 128   *Hulcote* v. *Ingleton* (1493), para. 2, line 14: *for* suscitatem *read* suscitatam

p. 321, pl. 210   *Lord Willoughby* v. *Lord Latimer* (1497), lines 6 and 8: *for* acknowledgment *read* recognizance.

p. 388, pl. 249   *Anon.* (1501), headnote. Cf. also YB Mich. 14 Hen. VII, fo. 7, pl. 19.

p. 424, pl. 292   *Kebell* v. *Vernon* (1504), headnote. *Vernon* v. *Gell* is reported in YB Mich. 20 Hen. VII, fo. 2, pl. 4; Hil. 21 Hen. VII, fo. 13, pl. 17.

p. 440, pl. 310   *Langstone* v. *Dyne* (1505) = also cited in Plowd. 186 from 'un especial report de ceo', which may be the report copied in Dyer, fo. 2.

p. 616, pl. 448   *Millys* v. *Guldeford* (1511) = also (probably) in Chaloner's reports, above, p. 281, no. 8.

(2) *The Reports of Sir John Spelman* (Selden Soc., vol. 93).

3, pl. 2   *Ewer* v. *Elys* (1522) is cited by Yorke, above, vol. I, p. 241, no. 415. Cf. another complaint about Elys in *Cade* v. *Clarke* (1531) 25 Selden Soc. 184 (Star Chamber).

4, pl. 4   *Warton* v. *Ashepole* (1524) should be dated Trin. 1524, as in the text.

7, pl. 8   *Holygrave* v. *Knyghtysbrygge* (1535). Cf. *Holygrave* v. *Tateham* (1543) KB 27/1127, m. 20d (recovers £16. 13s. 4d. in *assumpsit* for the price of cloth). Tateham was the principal debtor in the 1535 case.

8, pl. 10   = (probably) *Anon.* (Pas. 1508) reported by Caryll senior, 116 Selden Soc. 579, pl. 422.

10, pl. 2   *Canon* v. *Crowe* (1530). Cf. CP 40/1073, m. 319 (attaint on same verdict; nonsuit).

12, pl. 1   *Abbot of Croyland* v. *Higdon* (1521). This is misdated as 1516, perhaps because 'xiii' in the autograph was misread as 'viii'. The record is CP 40/1032B, m. 346 (Mich. 1521; judgment to answer without aid; traverses seisin).

13, *Aide de roy*, pl. 2   *Anon.* (1487) = *Croftes* v. *Hemperden*, KB 27/901, m. 30.

15, pl. 1   *Parkhurst* v. *Prior of Lewes* (1523/38). Cf. similar action by John White as vicar (1514) CP 40/1008, m. 759.

16, pl. 1   *Ryshton* v. *Cripce* (1531) = also reported by Dyer, fo. 4; Yorke, above, vol. I, p. 193, no. 267; Pollard, above, p. 248, no. 6; Yelverton, above, p. 290, no. 1.

19, pl. 4   *Anon.* (1522). This should be dated Trin. 1522, as in the text.

21, pl. 6   *Lovel* v. *Dagworth* (1333) = also printed in YB 7 Edw. III, Lib. Ass., pl. 12.

22, *Atturneis*, pl. 1   *Gresley* v. *Saunders* (1522) = also reported in YB Pas. 14 Hen. VIII, fo. 24, pl. 2 (119 Selden Soc. 170). The record is printed in 119 Selden Soc. 171.

28, pl. 1   *Boynton* v. *Gascoigne* (1520/22) = CP 40/1031, m. 359.

29, pl. 4   *Shilston* v. *Coffyn* (1528). The demurrer is to the replication.

32, pl. 5   *Browne* v. *Abbot of Waltham* (1523). The imparlance roll is CP 40/1036, m. 470. John Saperton is Robert in the record.

33, pl. 8   *Magdalen College, Oxford* v. *Heron* (1528). The college is now spelt 'Magdalen'.

36, pl. 5   *Feoffees of Colt* v. *Heigham* (1529) = the King's Bench action mentioned above, vol. I, p. 76, no. 58.

36, pl. 7   *Heigham* v. *Colt* (1529) = also reported above, p. 76, no. 58.

36, pl. 8   *Anon.* (1529) = also reported in Port, p. 56.

39, pl. 1   *Re Sir Richard Rich* (1536). The autograph text was cited by Dyer C.J. in 1566: 109 Selden Soc. 123.

41, pl. 3   *Anon.* (1529), line 1: *for* obligator *read* obligor.

44, pl. 2   *Anon.* (1488) = also reported by Caryll senior, 115 Selden Soc. 8.

44, pl. 3   *R.* v. *Preston* (1491): *for* Add. 35168 *read* Add. 25168. Miles Sandys' MS. is now KB 15/42.

46, pl. 8   *R.* v. *Anon.* (1529) = also reported by Caryll, above, p. 394, no. 60 (where, however, abjuration was not allowed).

47, pl. 12   *R.* v. *Rice ap Griffith* (1531). The indictment was copied by Sir Robert Catlyn in Alnwick Castle MS. 475, fo. 224.

49, pl. 15   *Anon.* (1532) = also reported by Yorke, above, vol. I, p. 90, no. 5.

54, pl. 26   *R.* v. *Lord Dacre and Greystock* (1534) = also reported by Caryll, above, p. 415. On p. 55, line 4, 'Maxy' should read Max[well].

61, pl. 43   *R.* v. *Marquess of Exeter* (1538). There are notes on the indictment by Sir Robert Catlyn in Alnwick Castle MS. 475, fo. 236.

66, pl. 60   *Anon.* (before 1539) = probably the case noted by Yorke, above, vol. I, p. 90, no. 6, in which case it is before 1535.

69, pl. 69   *Coronation of Queen Anne* (1533). In line 3, *for* Westminster Abbey *read* the refectory of Westminster. This was the room in which the House of Commons used to meet. In line 21, Sir John Shelley (the name given in the text) should be Sir William (cf. pp. 80, 94).

71, pl. 69   *Attainder of Queen Anne* (1536). The warrant for execution, also in the disjunctive, was copied by Sir Robert Catlyn in Alnwick Castle MS. 475, fo. 175v.

72, pl. 72   This should be *R.* v. *Feron and Hale* (1535). There is a copy of the record in CUL MS. Ee.3.1.

72, pl. 73   *R.* v. *Parker* [1520?]. This was cited in *Maiden's Case* (1671) as 12 Hen. VIII: Rylands Lib., MS. Eng. 288, p. 18. However, Fitzherbert J. was not then a judge; so perhaps he 'showed' an old indictment.

74, *Covenant*, pl. 1   *Westacre's Case* (1511) = *Prioress of Dartford* v. *Prior of Westacre*, CP 40/994, m. 330 (demurrer to declaration; c.a.v. to Pas. 1511; judgment for plaintiff).

74, *Covenant*, pl. 2   *Prior of St Neots* v. *Wolley* (1523). Cf. an earlier suit between the same parties, CP 40/1029, m. 540 (debt for amercements in a leet; demurrer).

75, pl. 3   *Thirkill* v. *Gore* (1529). This seems not to be the same case as that reported by Yorke, above, p. 413.

75, pl. 1   *Bishop of Rochester* v. *Mayor etc. of Rochester* (1502/05). The Common Pleas record is CP 40/953, m. 342, which notes the writ of error received on 6 Jan. 1502.

76, pl. 2   *Fitzherbert's Reading* (1510), line 1: this refers to Marlborough, c. 11.

80, pl. 1   *Creation of serjeants* (1531), line 7: Sir John Shelley (the name given in the text) should in fact be Sir William (cf. pp. 69, 94).

81, pl. 2   One of these cases may be *Abell* v. *Heron* (1528), CP 40/1059, m. 506.

81, pl. 3   *Wadham* v. *Rogers* (1528/29) = also reported in the King's Bench, above, vol. I, p. 78, no. 60 (Trin. 1529, not Pas. 1530).

82, pl. 5   The case reported by Yorke is probably *More* v. *Fowler* (1532): see above, p. 197.

84, pl. 2   = *Polhill* v. *Tayller*, CP 40/1031, m. 413 (judgment for plaintiff, after verdict, Trin. 1521). Another instance is *Melton* v. *Bever* (1535) CP 40/1084, m. 630d (imparlance).

84, pl. 3   *Speke* v. *Flemyng* (1523). The records are: (first action) CP 40/1032B, m. 306 (demurrer; printed in 119 Selden Soc. 189); (second action) CP 40/1038, m. 439d (imparlance, Hil. 1523); CP 40/1039, m. 539 (issue; printed 94 Selden Soc. 284). The report is of the first action, and not that represented by the record printed in 94 Selden Soc. 284. Also reported in Port, p. 80; YB Pas. 14 Hen. VIII, fo. 25, pl. 7 (119 Selden Soc. 180).

87, pl. 11   *Anon.* (1524), line 1: *for* corn *read* wheat

88, pl. 12   *Anon.* (1528), line 1: *for* corn *read* wheat

94, pl. 4   *Ryshton* v. *Cripce* (1531), line 9: Sir John Shelley (the name given in the text) should in fact be Sir William (cf. pp. 69, 80).

95, pl. 5   *Anon.* (1534) = also reported above, p. 433, pl. 7.

105, pl. 29   = *R.* v. *Osbern* (1506) KB 27/980, Rex m. 5 (printed 116 Selden Soc. 536). Also reported by Caryll senior, 116 Selden Soc. 535.

106, pl. 2   *Fortescue* v. *Stonor* (1532). Cf. *Stonor's Case* (undated) in Port, p. 79.

123, *Estopellez*, pl. 1   = *Gorge and others* v. *Atwell*, CP 40/1000, m. 403 (demurrer, Trin. 1512; c.a.v. to Mich. 1512; judgment for plaintiff).

127, *Excommengement*, pl. 1   This is perhaps connected with *Re Lawles* (1529) Port, p. 66.

132, pl. 2   *Core* v. *May* (1536). The reference in the headnote to Dyer 20, §14, should be deleted.

133, pl. 5   *A. P.* v. *E. S.* (Mich. 1529) = also reported by Pollard, above, p. 265, no. 44 (Hil. 1530); Yelverton, above, p. 323, no. 24; and above, p. 417, no. 1 (Hil. 1530).

133, pl. 7   *Monoux* v. *Fairfax* (Trin. 1531) = probably the case reported by Yorke, above, vol. I, p. 198, no. 283.

134, pl. 9   Cf. *Fortescue* v. *Nevell* (1531) CP 40/1070, m. 319 ('In witness whereof I have put my seal sign manual'; demurrer).

135, *Feffementz*, pl. 1   = *Scrope* v. *Hyk* (1511), CP 40/995, m. 429 (printed 116 Selden Soc. 619). Also reported by Caryll senior, 116 Selden Soc. 618.

136, pl. 2   *Southwall* v. *Huddelston* (1522) = also reported in YB Hil. 14 Hen. VIII, fo. 17, pl. 6, 7 (119 Selden Soc. 150); and by Pollard, above, p. 252, no. 15.

136, pl. 3   *Burgh* v. *Potkyn* (1522) = also reported in YB Mich. 14 Hen. VIII, fo. 10, pl. 6 (119 Selden Soc. 125). In the headnote, *for* Brit. Lib., MS. Harg. 253 *read* Harvard Law School, MS. 47. The record is printed in 119 Selden Soc. 136.

137, pl. 5   *Bishop of London* v. *Kellett* (1533). Cf. two actions of trespass between the same parties in CP 40/1084, m. 328 (Hil. 1535; verdicts for plaintiff in both).

152, pl. 19   = (probably) *Rector of Edington's Case*, YB Pas. 19 Hen. VI, fo. 62, pl. 1.

154, pl. 2   *Dean and Canons of St Stephen's Case*: much more likely it is St Stephen's, Westminster.

159, pl. 2   *Wolsey's speech to Fitzherbert J.* (1522), line 9: the allusion is probably to the book of *Ecclesiasticus* (or *Sirach*), in the Apocrypha, c. 4, v. 9.

160, *Lete*, pl. 3   = also reported by Caryll senior, 116 Selden Soc. 460, pl. 323.

163, pl. 1   = *Arundell qui tam etc.* v. *Mylle*, CP 40/1011, m. 526 (demurrer, Trin. 1515; c.a.v. to Mich. 1515; judgment for plaintiff). The Serjeant Broke mentioned in the text is Richard.

165, pl. 1   *Case of the Haberdashers* (1522) is similar to the case reported by Yorke, above, vol. I, p. 134, no. 120.

167, *Obligacion*, pl. 1   *Millys* v. *Guldeford* (1512) = also reported by Caryll senior, 116 Selden Soc. 616, 625; anon. (1532) Keil. 165, pl. 7 (printed 116 Selden Soc. 627); YB Hil. 26 Hen. VIII, fo. 10, pl. 4 (printed 116 Selden Soc. 627); noted by Yorke, above, vol. I, p. 205, no. 301.

170, pl. 1   *Wadham* v. *Rogers* (1528), line 2: *for* Edward *read* Nicholas. This is also reported by Yorke, above, vol. I, p. 78, no. 60.

176, pl. 7   It is probably not necessary to treat the second paragraph as an interpolation. The words 'until lately' presumably refer to Fyneux C.J.'s decision.

183, pl. 32   *Serjeant Browne's Case* is misdated. The reference is to Browne's dismissal in 1532, and not to the 1540 incident recorded in the Star Chamber register.

184, pl. 1   *Case of the Earl of Northumberland's Servant* (1532). This text was cited in parliament by Christopher Yelverton in 1566: 109 Selden Soc. 4.

186, pl. 7   *Entwysell* v. *Gudman* (1534) = also reported by Port, p. 73.

187, pl. 4   *Marsshe* v. *Bele* (1530) could perhaps be the same as *Anon.* (1529/30) on p. 238, pl. 10

189, pl. 2   *Lady E. S.'s Case* = also reported by Yelverton, above, p. 292, pl. 2 (1530/35).

190, pl. 1   *Att.-Gen.* v. *Wolsey* (1529) = also reported by Port, p. 57. The record is printed in 102 Selden Soc. 58.

192, pl. 3   *Att.-Gen.* v. *Bishop of Norwich* (1534) = also reported by Port, p. 75.

193, pl. 4   *Torbervile's Case* (1501/02). In the manuscript version of Coke's reports in CUL MS. Ll.4.9, fo. 63, it is dated 17 Hen. VII as in Spelman.

193, pl. 1   *King's College, Cambridge* v. *Hekker* (1521) = also reported
                    in YB Pas. 13 Hen. VIII, fo. 12, pl. 2 (119 Selden Soc. 68)
                    (in Common Pleas); Mich. 14 Hen. VIII, fo. 2, pl. 2 (119
                    Selden Soc. 98) (in King's Bench). The Common Pleas
                    record is printed in 119 Selden Soc. 76. Cf. an earlier action
                    of *quare impedit* by King's College for Coltishall in CP 40/
                    911, m. 147 (1490).

195, pl. 3   *R.* v. *Benson and Cornwall* (1527). The principal record is CP
                    40/1056, m. 457 (the omission of the word *inductus* is
                    recorded in the margin; demurrer; c.a.v. to Hil. 1528; judg-
                    ment for the king).

196, pl. 5   *Owen* v. *Stradlyng* (1531). There is a later record in CP 40/
                    1068, m. 530. Cf. *R.* v. *Stradlyng* (1532) CP 40/1074, m. 416
                    (*quare impedit* by the king; special imparlance).

199, pl. 1   *Att.-Gen.* v. *Bishop of Norwich* (1521). The date should be
                    19–20 Aug. 1521.

199, pl. 1   *Att.-Gen.* v. *Bedell* (1521). The date should be 31 March-1
                    April 1521. *For* Add. 35168 *read* Add. 25168.

205, pl. 2   *R.* v. *Sparke and Thixstill* (1534). Cf. *Thixstill v. Sparke*, CP
                    40/1025, m. 460.

205, pl. 3   *Anon.* (1534) = also reported by Yorke, above, vol. I, p. 277,
                    no. 375.

207, *Sanz ceo*, pl. 1   *Zouche* v. *Cornwall* (1522). Cf. Chancery proceedings
                    between same parties, C261/9/71 (injunction to stay execu-
                    tion in an assize of novel disseisin, 1528).

212, pl. 2   *Re Langforth* (1523). See also Port, p. 136.

215, pl. 4   *Pope* v. *See* (1534) = also reported by Port, p. 22.

216, pl. 5   *Anon.* (1534) = also reported by Yorke, above, vol. I, p. 94,
                    no. 18.

223, *Vidue*, pl. 1   The verses are glossed in a late fifteenth-century reading, per-
                    haps from the Middle Temple, in BL MS. Add. 14030, fo. 17.

227, *Vouchers*, pl. 1   Line 3: the correct word is presumably *devoluper*, to
                    release (literally to unwrap). Cf. *Manual of Law French*
                    (2nd edn), p. 89, s.v. *desavlouper*.

228, pl. 3   *Anon.* (1527) = (probably) *Bele v. Benet*, CP 40/1054, m. 316
                    (demurrer; c.a.v. to Trin. 1527; judgment for plaintiff). Also
                    reported above, vol. I, p. 58, no. 46; and by Yelverton,
                    above, p. 365, no. 105.

232, pl. 9   *Throgmorton's Case*, line 2: *for* himself *read* him (i.e. Lord Grey).

233, pl. 1   Text, line 1: *for* an *read* en.

234, pl. 3   *Sandys* v. *Bray* (1510) = also reported by Caryll senior, 116 Selden Soc. 610 (Pas. 1511); anon., above, vol. I, p. 4, no. 7; and p. 24, no. 16. The record is printed in 116 Selden Soc. 611.

238, pl. 10   *Anon.* (1529/30) could perhaps the same as *Marsshe* v. *Bele* (Mich. 1530) on p. 187. Cf. 1 Rolle Rep. 217.

Addendum   CUL MS. Pell Papers 7(10): 'Le case de 11 H. 8. report per Spilman que si pier ad fites et file per un venter et fites per auter venter...' Related in a Gray's Inn moot, *c.* 1612.

(3) *The Notebook of Sir John Port* (Selden Soc., vol. 102).

10, pl. 6   *Cleymond* v. *Vyncent* (1521) = also reported in YB Mich. 12 Hen. VIII, fo. 11, pl. 3 (119 Selden Soc. 46).

10, note 3   *for* Pynson *read* Vyncent

13, pl. 7   *Anon.* (1497) = (probably) *Lord Willoughby de Broke* v. *Lord Latimer*, also reported by Caryll senior, 115 Selden Soc. 304; and in Port, p. 26.

15, pl. 12   *Anon.* (1495) = (probably) also reported by Caryll senior, 115 Selden Soc. 289, pl. 198.

26, pl. 26   *Lord Willoughby de Broke* v. *Lord Latimer* (1497) = also reported (on a different point) by Caryll senior, 115 Selden Soc. 304; and probably in Port, p. 13.

28, pl. 30   This is perhaps a dictum from *Lord Willoughby de Broke* v. *Lord Latimer* (see p. 26).

31, pl. 35   *Rollesley* v. *Toft* (1495) = also reported by Caryll senior, 115 Selden Soc. 285 (and see 116 Selden Soc. 712).

37, pl. 38   *R.* v. *Boswell* (1513) = also reported by Caryll senior, 116 Selden Soc. 709.

41, pl. 40   *Pauncefote* v. *Savage* (1519) = also reported by Caryll senior, 116 Selden Soc. 704. See also vol. I, p. 191.

69, pl. 12   *Tusser* v. *Walgrave* (1529). Cf. the note in Yorke's reports, above, vol. I, p. 217, no. 344.

71, pl. 14   *Staverton* v. *Logan* (1530). The Common Pleas record is CP 40/1044, m. 140 (1524).

74, pl. 19	*Carvanell* v. *Mower* (1533) = also reported above, p. 425, no. 5.
78, pl. 2	Also in *Moots*, p. 245, pl. 60.
80, pl. 7	The note is probably derived from *Wellys* v. *Robynson* (1484) YB Mich. 2 Ric. III, fo. 14, pl. 39; CP 40/890, m. 128. The query is at the end of the report.
80, pl. 8	*Speke* v. *Flemyng* (1522) = also reported in YB Pas. 14 Hen. VIII, fo. 25, pl. 7 (119 Selden Soc. 180). The record is printed in 119 Selden Soc. 189.
81, pl. 3	Also in *Moots*, 105 Selden Soc. 261, pl. 81.
82, pl. 10	Also in *Moots*, p. 262, pl. 82.
86, pl. 22	Line 2: the word *jueys* (apparently derived from *judicium*) is used in Littleton's reading (1493) to mean the *peine forte et dure*: CUL MS. Hh.3.6, fo. 4. That is probably the sense here.
87, pl. 24	*Hulcote* v. *Ingleton* (1493) = also reported by Caryll senior, 115 Selden Soc. 138.
90, pl. 25	*Southwall* v. *Huddelston* (1524) = also reported (in the Common Pleas) in YB Hil. 14 Hen. VIII, fo. 17, pl. 6 (119 Selden Soc. 150); and by Pollard, above, p. 252, no. 15. On p. 92, lines 4 and 10, *for* Sewall *read* Southwall.
96, pl. 27	*Ernley* v. *Garth* (1490) = also reported by Caryll senior, 115 Selden Soc. 65 (Mich. 1491). Cf. *Moots*, 105 Selden Soc. 261, pl. 78.
99, pl. 28	*Anon.* (1493) = fuller text of same report in the reports of Caryll senior, 115 Selden Soc. 193, pl. 150.
103, pl. 34	Also in *Moots*, 105 Selden Soc. 134, pl. 21.
104, pl. 36	*For* 1495 *read* 1492. Also in *Moots*, 105 Selden Soc. 257, pl. 74.
117, pl. 64	Also in *Moots*, 105 Selden Soc. 291, pl. 136
119, pl. 67	Also in *Moots*, 105 Selden Soc. 278, pl. 109.
123, pl. 73	This is perhaps the case of 1516 cited in 3 Co. Inst. 10.
123, pl. 74	*R.* v. *Lincoln* (1517). This case was moved in the Star Chamber by Wolsey in the king's presence (Port being also then present): Huntington Lib., MS. EL 2654, fo. 23v.
124, pl. 75	*R.* v. *Duke of Buckingham* (1521). The indictment was copied by Sir Robert Catlyn in Alnwick Castle MS. 475, fo. 226; and is noted in BL MS. Add. 17514, fo. 243v. The trial is noted in YB Pas. 13 Hen. VIII, fo. 11, pl. 1 (119 Selden Soc. 56). The record is printed in 119 Selden Soc. 59.

125, pl. 77a   *Perkin Warbeck's Case* (1499) = further versions in Dyer's notebooks, 109 Selden Soc. 205; and (twice) in Sir Robert Catlyn's notebook, Alnwick Castle MS. 475, ff. 178, 236. Dyer and Catlyn were collecting materials relating to the position of Mary, queen of Scots.

129, pl. 82   *For 1053 read* 1503.

133, pl. 94.   Also in *Moots*, 105 Selden Soc. 120, pl. 5. The case in *Moots*, p. 118, pl. 3, is abridged in BL MS. Lansdowne 1084, fo. 1, as 'de libro de reportes de Serjant Carell', which suggests that these unattributed cases in MS. Harley 1691 also derive from Caryll's manuscripts.

148, pl. 23   Cf. 105 Selden Soc. 208, pl. 17 (Grene's reading, 1490/91).

151, pl. 37   Also in 105 Selden Soc. 261, pl. 81 (Grevill's reading, 1492).

151, pl. 38   Also in 105 Selden Soc. 258, pl. 76 (Grevill's reading, 1492).

152, pl. 39   Cf. 105 Selden Soc. 282, pl. 115 (Littleton's reading, 1493).

163, pl. 65   Also in 105 Selden Soc. 300, pl. 155.

(4) *Reports of Cases by Sir James Dyer*, ed. J. Vaillant (1794).

1a, §1   *Anon.* (Pas. 1512) = *Bedell's Case* (Pas. 1514) reported by Spelman, p. 84.

1b, §8   *Battaile* v. *Cooke* (Pas. 1512) = *Bataille* v. *Cooke*, CP 40/990, m. 514 (special verdict; c.a.v. to Trin. 1512; judgment for plaintiff). The church in question was Magdalen Laver, Essex. Cf. an earlier action of formedon between the same parties, CP 40/958, m. 586.

1b, §1   *Oliver* v. *Emsonne* (Mich. 1514) = *Glover* v. *Empson*, CP 40/1006, m. 553 (demurrer to replication; c.a.v. to Mich. 1514; judgment for defendant). Also reported above, vol. I, p. 2, pl. 4. 'O. T.' in the report is Oliver Turnour, deputy lieutenant of the Tower.

2b, §8   The date of this case must be between Mich. 1526 and Mich. 1532. 'Fitzj.' is an error for Fitzherbert.

3a, §1   *Anon.* (Pas. 1527) = This is substantially the same text as YB Pas. 19 Hen. VIII, fo. 6, pl. 5.

3b, §7   *Anon.* (Trin. 1527) = This is substantially the same text as YB Trin. 19 Hen. VIII, fo. 8, pl. 1.

4b, §1   *Rushden's Case* (Trin. 1532) = *Ryshton* v. *Cripce*, KB 27/1076, m. 33 (printed 94 Selden Soc. 290). Also reported

in Spelman, p. 16; Pollard, above, p. 248, no. 6; Yelverton, above, p. 290, no. 1.

6a, §4   *Clotworthy* v. *Kingsland* (Mich. 1534) = *Clotworthy* v. *Kyngislond and Estchurche*, CP 40/1086, m. 511 (*ve. fac.*, Trin. 1535).

7b, §11   *Abbot of Bury* v. *Bokenham* (Trin. 1536) = CP 40/1088, m. 420 (demurrer to count; c.a.v. to Hil. 1537).

11a, §42   *Lord Roos's Case* (cited) = *Earl of Rutland* v. *Constable* (1528-29), CP 40/1059, m. 556d (printed 94 Selden Soc. 337). Also reported in Spelman, p. 143. Error thereon: KB 27/1076, m. 25.

13b, §65   *Hynde* v. *Wheeler* (1536) = CP 40/1089, m. 457; also reported by Caryll jun., above, p. 397, no. 65.

14a, §70   *Goddale's Case* (Trin. 1536) = *Brigges* v. *Goodale*, CP 40/1085(2), m. 313 (demurrer to plea; c.a.v. to Trin. 1536). John Goodale was an attorney.

14b, §72   *Bold* v. *Molineux* (Trin. 1536) = *Bolde* v. *Molyneux*, CP 40/1085(1), m. 331 (demurrer to replication; c.a.v. to Pas. 1537; judgment for defendant); printed in Benl. 13.

20a, §118   *Core's Case* (Trin. 1536) = *Core* v. *May*, KB 27/1097, m. 33 (abstract in 94 Selden Soc. 327). Also reported in Spelman, p. 132. Partial translation in Baker & Milsom, pp. 244-245.

22a, §135   The case of a bailment to give away in alms may be *Duchess of Norfolk* v. *Aleyn* (1497) Port, p. 3.

23a, §145   *May* v. *Core* (in Chancery) = C1/856/32 (abstract in 94 Selden Soc. 328).

24a, §150   *Englefielde's Case* (cited) = *Englefield* v. *Abbot of Missenden* (1525) CP 40/1048A, m. 520 (imparlance roll).

24b, §153   *Danvers* v. *Bishop of Worcester and others* (1509/10) = CP 40/989, m. 537 (judgment for plaintiff, Trin. 1510). The church in question was Lapworth, Warw.

25a, §156   Paraphrased above, p. 437, no. 15.

25a, §157   Paraphrased above, p. 437, no. 14.

25b, §160   Also reported above, p. 437, no. 17.

25b, §161   Paraphrased above, p. 438, no. 18.

25b, §162   Paraphrased above, p. 438, no. 19.

25b, §164   *Holmes's Case* (Hil. 1537) = *Frauncys* v. *Holmes*, CP 40/1090, m. 435 (demurrer to bar; c.a.v. to Trin. 1537); CP 40/1092, m. 421 (*venire facias*); printed in Benl. 17.

26b, §172   *Abbot of Westminster* v. *Executors of Clerke* (Hil. 1537) = *Abbot of Westminster* v. *Stephynson and others*, CP 40/1089, m. 524 (pleads performance of indenture of lease of rectory of Swaffham Market, Norfolk; demurrer, Pas. 1536; c.a.v. to Hil. 1537; judgment for plaintiff).

31b, §219   *Anon.* (Hil. 1537) = *Pope* v. *See*, KB 27/1089, m. 33 (printed 94 Selden Soc. 357). Also reported in Spelman, p. 215; Port, p. 22.

32a, §2   *Anon.* (Pas. 1537) = *Core* v. *Whalley*, CP 40/1087, m. 147 (demurrer to evidence at York assizes before Jenney J.; c.a.v.; judgment for plaintiff, Pas. 1536).

32b, §5   *Anon.* (Pas. 1537) = *Cokkys and Argall* v. *Playfote*, CP 40/1079, m. 515 (demurrer to plea; c.a.v. to Pas. 1537; judgment for plaintiff). Proceedings in error: KB 27/1089, m. 38.

35b, §32   *Maleverer* v. *Spinke* (Trin. 1537) = *Malyverer* v. *Spynke*, CP 40/1089, m. 345 (c.a.v.).

37b, §45   *Anon.* (1515) = *Wodmancye* v. *Gyrton*, CP 40/1009, m. 356.

37b, §46   *Marshall* v. *Eure* (Mich. 1537) = CP 40/1090, m. 402 (array affirmed).

38a, §50   *Gawen* v. *Hussee and Gibbes* (Mich. 1537) = *Gawen* v. *Hussey and Gybbys*, KB 27/1094, m. 40 (judgment for appellees, Hil. 1538). Also reported (at earlier stages) in Spelman, p. 53.

40b, §1   *Chafyn de Meere's Case* (Hil. 1538) = *Chaffin's Case, of Mere, Wilts*. Cf. vol. I, p. 238, no. 409.

42a, §9   *Executors of Grenelife* v. *W—* (Mich. 1538) = *Greneleff* v. *Annott*, CP 40/1096, m. 413 (c.a.v. to Trin. 1538).

46a, §8   *Anon.* (Mich. 1539) = (probably) *Sympson* v. *Brysto*, KB 27/1111, m. 71; also copied in BL MS. Harley 664, fo. 8v. Also reported in Spelman, p. 218.

46a, §8   *Anon.* (Middlesex case cited) = (probably) *Ley* v. *Froston*, KB 27/1089, m. 1d; also reported in Spelman, p. 56.

46b, §2   *Guier's Case* (Pas. 1540) = KB 27/1109, Rex m. 10 (pleads Not guilty, Mich. 1538). Discussed in 'Male and Married Spinsters' (1977) 21 A.J.L.H. 255-259.

49a, §7   *Lyte* v. *Peny* (Pas. 1541) = CP 40/1099, m. 340d. Also reported above, p. 447, no. 25.

50a, §4   *Saccombe's Case* (Mich. 1541) = *Saccombe* v. *Saccombe and Waren*, KB 27/1121, m. 117 (demurrer by appellees; nonsuit; arraigned at king's suit and discharged because indictment void).

53b, §11	*Rolfe* v. *Hampden* (Trin. 1542) = *Rolf* v. *Hampden and Smyth*, CP 40/1112, m. 416 (formal nonsuit).
54b, §22	*Sawyer* v. *Slifield* (Mich. 1542) = *Sawyer* v. *Slyffeld*, CP 40/1116, m. 501 (demurrer to replication; c.a.v. to Pas. 1543).
54b, §23	*Simons* v. *Chapman* (cited) = *Symondys* v. *Chapman*, CP 40/1111, m. 804 (demurrer to replication, Mich. 1541; c.a.v. to Hil. 1542; judgment for defendant).
55b, §8	*Trewennarde* v. *Skewys* (Pas. 1543) = (in court below) *Skewes* v. *Trewynnard*, CP 40/1104, m. 406 (judgment for plaintiff after trial at Cornwall assizes).
56a, §12	*Yong* v. *Sant* (Trin. 1543) = CP 40/1117, m. 555 (demurrer to replication; c.a.v. to Trin. 1543).
59b, §17	*Executors of Skewys* v. *Chamond* (Pas. 1545) = *Courtenay and Tomyewe* v. *Chamond*, KB 27/1134, m. 39 (writ of privilege pleaded; demurrer; c.a.v. to Mich. 1546).
197b, §47	*R.* v. *Blage* (1524) = also reported by Spelman, p. 150.
224b, §31	*Quilter's Case* = *Quylter* v. *Thornherst and Knell* (1537), KB 27/1100, m. 67 (judgment affirmed); copied by Sir Robert Catlyn in Alnwick Castle MS. 475, fo. 65v. Also reported by Spelman, p. 139.
275a, §47	The case mentioned at the end is *Ferrer's Case* (1542), but the roll reference is incorrect. For this case see also Moo. 57, pl. 163, and Dal. 58, pl. 7, *per* Dyer C.J. (1564); *HPHC 1509–58*, ii. 130; G. R. Elton, *The Tudor Constitution* (2nd edn), pp. 261–262, 275–277.

(5) *Year Books of Henry VIII*

YB 12-14 Hen. VIII	See new edition of all three years, with translation, in 119 Selden Soc. (2002).

YB Mich. 18 Hen. VIII

fo. 1, pl. 4	= *Swetenham* v. *Warde*, CP 40/1051, m. 311.
fo. 1, pl. 5	= (probably) *Stele* v. *Newton*, CP 40/1054, m. 524 (nonsuit after demurrer); also reported vol. I, by Yorke, p. 232, no. 392.
fo. 2, pl. 13	= *Earl of Northumberland* v. *Wedell*, CP 40/1039, m. 109 (abstracted in 94 Selden Soc. 262), also reported in Spelman, p. 9. The name 'Stoobs' is more correctly spelt 'Stubbez' (i.e. Edward Stubbe or Stubbes) in Gell MS.

fo. 3, pl. 15   = translated in Baker & Milsom, p. 272.

fo. 5, pl. 18   = same text above, p. 435, no. 9 (where it is dated Mich. 26 Hen. VIII).

YB Pas. 19 Hen. VIII

fo. 6, pl. 2   = also reported by Caryll, above, p. 411, no. 106 (where it is dated 21 Hen. VIII).

fo. 7, pl. 9   = *Tatton* v. *Faukner*, CP 40/1054, m. 348.

fo. 8, pl. 10   = *President etc. of Magdalen College, Oxford* v. *Heron*, CP 40/1061, m. 614, also reported in Spelman, p. 33, pl. 8.

fo. 8, pl. 11   = (probably) *Abell* v. *Heron*, CP 40/1059, m. 506; also reported below, fo. 11, pl. 7; and in Spelman, p. 81, pl. 2.

fo. 8, pl. 12   = (probably) *Anon.*, in Yelverton, above, p. 365, no. 48.

YB Trin. 19 Hen. VIII

fo. 9, pl. 2   = also reported by Caryll, above, p. 410, no. 105 (where it is dated 21 Hen. VIII); and at p. 434, above, no. 8 (where it is dated Mich. 26 Hen. VIII).

fo. 9, pl. 4   = also reported in vol. I, p. 60, no. 49; and by Pollard, above, p. 260, no. 33; and Yelverton, above, p. 361, no. 103.

fo. 11, pl. 5   = *Bele* v. *Benet*, CP 40/1054, m. 316; also reported below, fo. 13, pl. 11; and by Spelman, p. 228; and above, vol. I, p. 58, no. 46, and by Yelverton, above, p. 365, no. 105.

fo. 11, pl.7   = (probably) *Abell* v. *Heron*, CP 40/1059, m. 506; also reported above, fo. 8, pl. 11; and by Spelman, p. 81, pl. 2.

fo. 13, pl. 11   = *Bele* v. *Benet*, CP 40/1054, m. 316; also reported above, fo. 11, pl. 5; and by Spelman, p. 228; above, vol. I, p. 58, no. 46, and by Yelverton, above, p. 365, no. 105. Cf. Pollard, above, p. 276, no. 73.

YB Pas. 26 Hen. VIII

fo. 1, pl. 2   = *Prior of Healaugh* v. *Fulberne*, KB 27/1085, m. 22 (printed 94 Selden Soc. 314), also reported by Spelman, p. 116. This identification is confirmed by the Gell MS., which begins: 'En brefe de entre port per le prior de Holey vers un Fulbert...'. In the Gell MS. the text following 'Quod Nota' (i.e. 'En le brefe dentre avandit...') is a continuation on another page, from Trinity term. The same case is cited in Trin. 26 Hen. VIII, fo. 7, pl. 33, as 'Prior de Holls vers Fulstari' (or, in Gell, 'Prior de Holley vers Fulbert').

fo. 1, pl. 3   The words 'in Cambridge' are omitted in Gell MS. Cf. *Master of Peterhouse, Cambridge* v. *Tayler*, CP 40/1081, m. 551.

YB Trin. 26 Hen. VIII

fo. 3, pl. 14   = *Cosyn* v. *Serlys*, KB 27/1086, m. 38; also reported (on a different point) by Spelman, p. 222.

fo. 4, pl. 15   'Hals' is 'Hales' in Gell MS.

fo. 4, pl. 17   In the Gell MS. the plaintiff is 'John Grene'. Cf. *Marten* v. *Grene*, YB Pas. 27 Hen. VIII, fo. 12, pl. 31.

fo. 5, pl. 21   = *R.* v. *Worme*, KB 27/1092 (Rex), m. 15, also reported by Spelman, p. 170, pl. 5. 'Porter' is more correctly 'Port' in Gell MS.

fo. 5, pl. 25   = *Huntley and Colynryge* v. *Fulke*, CP 40/1078, m. 437. The defendant is spelt 'Fulke' in Gell MS.

fo. 5, pl. 26   The word *corrouce* in the vulgate is *irate* in Gell MS.

fo. 6, pl. 29   'Dirtelby' is more correctly 'Thirtleby' (Yorks.) in Gell MS.

fo. 6, pl. 30   = *Heighton* v. *Miles*, CP 40/1084, m. 347.

fo. 7, pl. 32   Cf. YB Trin. 27 Hen. VIII, fo. 22, pl. 18 (prior).

fo. 7, pl. 33   = Benl. 18, pl. 24 (dated Hil. 1537). The note at the end referring to *Prior of Healaugh* v. *Fulberne* has no relation to the principal case and is a separate entry in Gell MS. For that case see YB Pas. 26 Hen. VIII, fo. 1, pl. 2.

YB Mich. 26 Hen. VIII

fo. 7, pl. 1   = also reported by Spelman, p. 216, pl. 5; and Yorke, above, vol. I, p. 94, no. 18.

fo. 7, pl. 3   = same text as YB Pas. 27 Hen. VIII, fo. 11, pl. 26.

fo. 8, pl. 4   = (perhaps) *Foljambe* v. *Leke*, CP 40/1080, m. 460.

fo. 8, pl. 5   = also reported above, p. 435, no. 11.

YB Hil. 26 Hen. VIII

fo. 9, pl. 1   = *Maunder* v. *Ware*, CP 40/1083, m. 409d.

fo. 9, pl. 2   = *Dawney* v. *Lepton*, CP 40/1080, m. 134.

fo. 10, pl. 4, *ad finem* (case of 4 Hen. VIII)   = *Millys* v. *Guldeford*, translated 116 Selden Soc. 627; also reported by Caryll senior, 116 Selden Soc. 616, 625; *Anon.* (1532) Keil. 165, pl. 7 (translated 116 Selden Soc. 627); and noted by Yorke, above, vol. I, p. 205, no. 307; and probably by Chaloner, above, p. 285, no. 8.

YB Pas. 27 Hen. VIII

fo. 1, pl. 2   The plaintiff is 'J. Gryff' in Gell MS.

fo. 1, pl. 3   = *Gedney* v. *Burbanke*, CP 40/1083, m. 514. The puzzling
                  passage at the end ('Montague dit, que il ad veu auters
                  matieres quand il fuit Student a le University': vulgate) is
                  more correctly rendered in Gell MS.: 'Mountague dit que
                  il voilloit pleder auter matter, que il fuit student a un [*sic*]
                  universite de Oxford'.

fo. 3, pl. 11   = *Colepeper* v. *Lucas*, CP 40/1084, m. 511. The defendant is
                  named 'Lucas' in Gell MS.

fo. 4, pl. 12   'Holdstone' is 'Hodleston' (i.e. Huddleston) in Gell MS. 'T.
                  S.' is 'Thomas Smyth' in Gell MS.

fo. 4, pl. 13   = (probably) *Byngham* v. *Horsey*, CP 40/1084, m. 322.

fo. 5, pl. 14   = *Prior of Folkestone* v. *Wye College*, CP 40/1085(1), m. 129.
                  The college ('Wyer' in vulgate) is correctly spelt 'Wye' in
                  Gell MS.

fo. 5, pl. 14   'Hals' is 'Hales' in Gell MS.

fo. 6, pl. 17   'Barber' is 'Baker' (i.e. John Baker) in Gell MS.

fo. 7, pl. 20   = *Symondys* v. *Pekyt*, CP 40/1086, m. 550.

fo. 7, pl. 21   = (perhaps) *Tyrell* v. *Wyseman*, CP 40/1085(2), m. 102
                  (protesting that places are the same, pleads freehold).

fo. 7, pl. 22   = *Re Lord Dacre of the South*, also reported by Spelman,
                  p. 228; partly translated in Baker & Milsom, p. 106. 'Hore-
                  wood' (fo. 8) is spelt 'Whorwood' in Gell MS.

fo. 11, pl. 26   = same text as YB Mich. 26 Hen. VIII, fo. 7, pl. 3.

fo. 11, pl. 28   = *Capell* v. *Pygot*, CP 40/1086, m. 537. The defendant is
                  named 'Pygotte' in Gell MS.

fo. 11, pl. 29   = *Cowper* v. *Walpole*, CP 40/1085(1), m. 131.

fo. 11, pl. 30   = *Hudleston* v. *Falter*, CP 40/1084, m. 122.

fo. 12, pl. 31   = *Marten* v. *Grene*, CP 40/1085(1), m. 177. The defendant is
                  named 'G. Grene' in Gell MS.; but her name was Elizabeth
                  (record). Cf. YB Trin. 26 Hen. VIII, fo. 4, pl. 17.

fo. 12, pl. 32   = probably the same case noted in Yorke, above, vol. I,
                  p. 226, no. 371 (Mich. 1535).

fo. 12, pl. 34   The defendant is named 'Twissard' (i.e. probably Tussard, or
                  Tusser) in Gell MS.

fo. 13, pl. 35   = translated in Baker & Milsom, p. 272.

YB Trin. 27 Hen. VIII

fo. 14, pl. 2   = *Lord Fitzwaryn* v. *Swayne*, CP 40/1087, m. 517 (grand assize; abated because plaintiff created an earl *puis darrein continuance*). In the Gell MS. the plaintiff is less correctly 'le Senior Warren'.

fo. 14, pl. 4   = translated in Baker & Milsom, p. 626. Cf. *Elyot* v. *Mersshe*, CP 40/1086, m. 192d ('Thow art an erytyke...').

fo. 14, pl. 6   The defendant is spelt 'Docwrey' in Gell MS.

fo. 20, pl. 10, at fo. 21   'Montague Apprentice' at the end is more correctly 'Mollenex apprentice' (i.e. Edmund Molyneux) in Gell MS. Montague was at this date a serjeant.

fo. 21, pl. 14   = *Broune and Leason* v. *Umpton*, CP 40/1086, m. 121.

fo. 22, pl. 17   = *Pylfold* v. *Derrant*, CP 40/1086, m. 349.

fo. 22, pl. 18   = also reported in YB Trin. 26 Hen. VIII, fo. 7, pl. 32.

fo. 23, pl. 21   = translated in Baker & Milsom, p. 447.

fo. 23, pl. 22   = (probably) *Ap Evan* v. *Davys*, CP 40/1086, m. 527 (cf. five similar actions on mm. 528, 532, 535).

YB Mich. 27 Hen. VIII

fo. 24, pl. 2   = *Melton* v. *Earl of Northumberland*, CP 40/1089, m. 438; for which see Baker, 'Sir John Melton's Case' in *The Common Law Tradition*, ch. 20.

fo. 24, pl. 3   = *Holygrave* v. *Knyghtysbrygge*, KB 27/1094, m. 30d (printed 94 Selden Soc. 256); part translated in Baker & Milsom, p. 413; also reported by Spelman, p. 7. The 'Jordan' of the report is not mentioned in the record and is a mystery, unless it was the name of the defendant's wife. The bill of exceptions discussed in the year book is not in the record. 'Brook' (fo. 24) is more correctly 'Luke' in Gell MS.

fo. 26, pl. 6   The Gell MS. has the additional words at the end: 'per tout le court, quod nota'.

fo. 26, pl. 8   = *Goderd* v. *Dervy*, CP 40/1086, m. 668.

fo. 26, pl. 9   Cf. *Dormer* v. *Oliver Boner*, CP 45/8, m. 8d (*quare impedit* for Great Hampden).

fo. 27, pl. 10   = *Hikkys* v. *More*, CP 40/1085(2), m. 442. See also above, p. 327, no. 31.

fo. 28, pl. 14   = *Dean of Salisbury* v. *Martyn*, CP 40/1087, m. 156d.

fo. 29, pl. 19   = *Holgyll* v. *Barnard*, CP 40/1086, m. 538. The place 'E.' is identified in Gell MS. as 'Edmulton' (Edmonton).

INDEXES

INDEX OF NAMES

INDEX OF SUBJECTS

bastardy:

> bastard is filius populi or filius nullius, 348
>
> illegitimacy by reason of divorce, 428
>
> triable only in ecclesiastical court, 79

battery:

> in defence of property, 385–6
>
> in self-defence, 386
>
> of juror, 63; of servant, 410, 434
>
> writ must say 'verberavit', 228

benefice:

> appropriation of, 249, 325
>
> consolidation of benefices, 249
>
> deprivation, 248
>
> first fruits of, given to king, 399
>
> glebe land, exchanged, 359
>
> lease of rectory, lessee is parson, 359
>
> notice of vacancy, 217
>
> plurality, cession by reason of, 248–9
>
> provision to, 249
>
> resignation of, 248; effect on lease, 217
>
> vacated by creation of parson as bishop, 248
>
> vicarage, where church appropriated, 325
>
> *see also* advowson; tithes

benefit of clergy:

> after judgment of peine forte et dure, 93
>
> bigamus, 378–9
>
> burning in hand, 90; brand not a record, 91
>
> clerk convict: distinguished from clerk attaint, 91; escape of, 56; imprisonment by ordinary, 355; indicted for new offence, 469
>
> makes felon a new man, 90, 469
>
> not available: for murder of malice aforethought, 95; for high treason, 90; for women, 91
>
> position of real priests, 91, 92, 93, 279
>
> proof of clergy:
>
>> by letters of ordination, 93
>>
>> reading test, 93
>
> purgation, 91
>
> where felony confessed without indictment, 56

bill of exceptions, 126

binding over *see* surety of peace

birds *see under* animals

bishop:

> benefices vacant on creation, 248
>
> consent for annexation of hospital to college, 44
>
> grant to bishop and heirs, 433
>
> temporalities, in king's hands, 355
>
> writ to, 6–7, 24, 27, 78, 243, 244, 250, 257
>
> *see also* ordinary

blacksmith *see* smith

bond:

> condition of: added after delivery, 205, 281–2; discharged by accord, 160; frustrated by death, 165; impossibility, 81
>
> conditions:
>
>> to appear in court, 8
>>
>> to deliver all writings, 259, 423–4
>>
>> to make conveyance devised by counsel, 75, 204
>>
>> to make feoffment, 165
>>
>> to pay lesser sum, 160
>>
>> to perform award, 19, 59, 77
>>
>> to perform covenants, 244, 337; meaning of covenant, 85
>>
>> to permit occupation without interruption, 214
>>
>> to save harmless, 20, 23, 214
>
> erased in date, 198
>
> joint, 348–9
>
> may not be sued upon in inferior court, 158
>
> misread to illiterate obligor, 277
>
> payable by executors before contracts and legacies, 107
>
> repugnancy in, 348
>
> to use of king, 386
>
> void statute merchant effective as, 464
>
> when it binds executors, 107
>
> when it binds heir, 107, 185, 407

borough English, 298, 300, 330, 449, 467

boundary, marked by watercourse which dries up, 84

bread, assize of, 283, 284

bridge, duty to repair, 79

conversion, by executors, 108
coparcenary:
    of advowson, 225
    effect of disseisin, 366; of re-entry by
        one coparcener, 86
    final concord by coparceners, 369
    partition annulled by partial entry,
        400
    of rent, coparcener purchases part of
        land, 383
copyhold:
    conveyance of:
        admittance of husband and wife,
            58
        admittance is 'to use of' a
            person, 299, 309
        delivery by the virge, 297
        form of copy, 157
        lord 'but an instrument' to cause
            land to pass, 298, 309
        only by surrender, 393
    customs judicially noticed, 157
    fealty owed, 299
    forfeiture of, 157
    formedon for, 342
    heir may not enter without
        admittance, 158, 321
    land seized by bailiff, 46
    not a qualification for juror, 437
    proclamations, for heir to make
        claim, 157
    remedies for tenant: plaint in lord's
        court, 156, 158; subpoena, 299;
        trespass, 274–5
    voucher for, 393
    whether lord may oust copyholder,
        294–309
coroner:
    coroner's book, 167
    fees of, 111, 286
    finable by justices of the peace,
        111
    inquest super visum corporis, 111,
        289
    venire facias to, 43
corporation:
    annexation of old corporation to
        new, 44
    annuity granted to guild, 4

incorporation before time of
    memory, 43–4
name:
    change of, does not affect
        prescription, 306–7
    misnomer, 197
    see also religious houses
corpus cum causa ('habeas corpus'), 74
corrody, forfeiture of, 195–6
costs:
    for defendant, 109–10
    not recoverable by king, 123
    release of, upon confession, 21
council, lords of, 345
counsel:
    annuity for, effect of imprisonment, 3
    in an assize, 245; at trial, 437
    in pleading, 412
    to devise conveyance, 75, 204, 375
counterfeiting coin, 90
county, posse comitatus, 390
county (court):
    debt on bond in, 158
    'the king's court baron', 414
    not a court of record, 50
county palatine, 242
    land in, 63
court baron:
    amercement in: lord may bring debt
        for, 158; prescription for, 158
    appurtenant to manor, 354
    debt on bond in, 158
    false judgment from, 156, 219
    same jurisdiction as county court, 414
    when suitors are judges, 158
    whether praemunire lies for suit in,
        385
court leet see leet
covenant:
    compared with condition, 398
    distinguished from bargain, 138
    distinguished from 'dedi and
        concessi', 200–1
    informal, enforced by assumpsit,
        313–14
    meaning of, 85, 398
    naked, does not alter use, 401
    process in, 388
    reservation of rent as, 85

covenant, *contd*

  particular covenants:

    not to assign, 397–8, 413

    to allow buyer of trees to carry them away, 422

    to have wardship, 173

    to leave land to descend, 135, 146, 276

    to levy fine of wife's land, 229

    to make estate, can only be performed once, 375

    to pay money, 437–8

    to serve in husbandry, when outside the statute, 414

    to stand seised to uses, 138

  use altered by, 58–9, 135, 146, 276, 339, 401

  when it runs with land, 201, 394, 413

  whom it binds, 185, 199, 233

    assigns, 201

    heir with assets, 185, 199

covenant (action of):

  against apprentice, 315–17

  against lessor, 200–1

  on indentures made by friar, 1

  on naked covenant, 401

criminal procedure:

  arraignment, prisoner must be bareheaded, 357

  confession without trial, 352–3

  effect of pleading Not guilty, 92, 96

  mute of malice, 293, 415

  party must take single plea at his peril, 92

  penance (peine forte et dure), 93, 293

  process against defendants, 203

  reprieve for doubt in law, 381

  special verdict, 95, 96

  verdict not an attainder, 378

  see also abjuration; appeal; auterfoitz acquit (and) attaint; benefit of clergy; forfeiture; indictment; punishments; sanctuary

cui in vita *see under* entry, writs of

curia claudenda, 84

curtesy, tenancy by, 117, 118, 161, 184, 210

  issue need not be heard to cry, 87

  tenant holds of lord paramount, 164

tenant liable for fire, 239

tenant not bound by use, 137

customs (local):

  against common law, 298, 467

  against statute, 467

  allowance of, 62, 64, 67, 68

  cannot be changed by king or parliament, 69

  cannot be granted by king, 330

  invalidity, 64, 66

  must have reasonable beginning, 301, 308

  particular customs:

    as to heirlooms, 467

    executors liable upon a tally, 303

    foreign attachment, 330

    to convey freehold by surrender and admittance, 302, 308

    to devise freehold, 308

    to give lands in mortmain, 445

    to keep gages against true owner, 301

  see also prescription; *and index of names under* London

customs and services, writ of, 215

damages:

  direction as to, 313

  increased by court, 197

  king may not recover, 123, 386

  release of, upon confession, 21

  in what actions: dower, 200; quare impedit, 78; waste, 46

  for wild animals, 411

  treble damages, 46

  writ of inquiry, 30, 34; precedent of, 35–6

darrein presentment, writ to bishop, 244

de ejectione firmae *see* ejectment

de excommunicato capiendo, 429

de haeretico comburendo, 429

de homine replegiando, 40, 64

de retorno habendo, 389

de son tort demesne (de injuria) *see under* pleading

de valore maritagii, 22, 174, 177

death:

  effect on forfeiture, 263

  frustration by, 165, 354

husband and wife, *contd*
    wager of law on wife's contract, 434
    what actions widow may bring after
        husband's death, 229
    when seised to wife's use, 361
    wife as executrix, 107
    wife may make will, 426
    wife seised to use of stranger, 136
    see also divorce; marriage

idiocy:
    land in king's hands, 389
    testament annulled for, 425–30
imparlance, 17
    estoppel by, 257, 258
    special ('salvis advantagiis'), 257
impossibility:
    of award, 59
    of condition, 81, 423–4
imprisonment *see* false imprisonment;
    gaol
indictment:
    confession without, 56
    contra pacem, 97
    evidence must warrant, 381
    how it might be politicly drawn, 381
    no need for mainour, 222
    place of death required, 96
    vi et armis, 97
    particular forms:
        for burglary, 353
        for misdemeanour, confession
          without trial, 352–3
        for murder, 57
        for theft of horse, 264
        for trespass, 113
infangthief, claimed in quo warranto, 283,
    284
infant:
    acts of: valid, voidable or void, 323–4,
      400, 418–19
    as agent, 520
    ages:
        age of discretion, 327, 420
        reasonable age to make
          testament, 426
        apprentice must be twelve, 315
        socage tenant comes of age at
          fourteen, 419

as attorney, 418, 420, 421
capias against, 419, 420
contract made by, 107, 420
disseisin by, 420
estopped by acts on coming of
    age, 251
feoffment by, 230, 400
hanged for felony, 420
king not incapacitated by infancy, 420
lease or feoffment by, 265, 400,
    419–20
no laches in, 186
release by infant executor, 265, 323–
    4, 417–22
warrant of attorney from, 265, 400
information qui tam:
    challenges, 125
    death of party, 97–8
    nonsuit, 98, 238
    release by king, 220
    in what courts, 349–50
    tried at assizes, 96
    see also popular action
inheritance *see* heir
innkeeper, liability for refusing
    accommodation, 310
inns of court:
    benchers, 376
    case at board's end, 402, 403, 409
    learning: 'bon lerninge', 204;
      'enconter tout lernyng', 301
    learning exercises, xxxv, xxxvii, xxxix,
      xl, xli
    moots, 372; common argument in, 364
    reading cited in argument, 375
    utter-barrister named, 454
    see also the index of names for
      particular inns
inquisition post mortem:
    jurors do not know what services, 162
    mistake corrected by second office,
      167
    must find tenure in chief, 391
    retrospective as to profits, 148
    traverse to, 59–60, 407; by feoffees to
      uses, 149
    when it is void and needs no traverse,
      391
interrogatories, in ecclesiastical court, 79

quale jus, 3
quare ejecit infra terminum, 256
quare impedit, 202
  abatement of, 99
  against ordinary alone, 320
  by cestuy que use, 4
  by king, 224
  damages in, 78, 243
  inquisition as to the six months, 7
  judgment after six months, 250, 257
  judgment at nisi prius, 181
  pleading in, 24–9, 439–44
  record of (specimen), 4–7
  title in, 166, 439
quarter sessions, 110
  certification of bail to, 112–13
  see also justices of the peace
qui tam *see* information; popular action
quid juris clamat, 412
quid pro quo, use as, 372
  see also consideration
quo jure, 284
quo warranto:
  allowance, 66
  claims in the eyre of Middlesex
    (1519–20), 43, 282–8
  for park, 434
  when unavailable:
    against a justice, 282
    for land, 288

ravishment, consent to, 182, 348
ravishment of ward, 177
  before seizure by plaintiff, 122
reattachment, 49
recognizance:
  for appearance:
    bail, degree of suspicion
     relevant, 334
    bail, granted by justices of peace,
     112–13
    effect of supersedeas, 437
    sureties discharged where
     process void, 8
    where party not replevisable, 41
  for peace *see* surety of peace
  mainprise, in appeal of murder, 39;
    when it is body for body, 334
  release of, 110–11

removed by certiorari, 112
record:
  amendment of, 387
  conviction for felony, 91, 92, 278,
    469, 470
    branding of clerk convict not a
     record, 91
  enrolment of bargain and sale,
    355–6
  estoppel by, 197, 356
  exemplifications:
    of enrolled deed, 197, 201, 201–2
    of eyre, 283
    of lost patent, 197
    transcript, 254
  incontrovertible, 465
  letters patent pleaded, 40
  made before time of memory, 406
  monstrance of, 404, 405
  nisi prius, 3
  plea of nul tiel record, 23, 301
  removal into Chancery, 1
  sent to lower court when cognizance
    granted, 254
  see also under county
recordari facias, 3
recovery:
  collusive:
    against cestuy que use, 140,
     144–5
    to bar dower, 200, 322
    to evade mortmain, 118
    falsification of, 373
  feigned, 372–3, 405
  with recompense, whom it will bind,
    406–7
  stronger after verdict, 413
  see also common recovery
rege inconsulto, 213, 389
Register of Writs, 336, 356, 425, 453, 458,
  460, 468
  old registers, 456, 458
relation:
  acts of parliament relate to first day,
    117
  between attainder and felony, 271
  between fatal blow and death, 230
  of words, to last antecedent, 298, 299,
    301, 303, 305

release:
- of action of detinue, whether it destroys property, 450–3
- by infant executor, 265, 323–4, 417–22
- by one of two plaintiffs, 219
- may enure as bargain, 150
- of right, to person without possession, 150
- when it makes an estate, 394
- who may take advantage of, 450–3

religious houses:
- alienation of foundation lands, 340
- benefice appropriated to, 249, 325
- debt for money coming to use of, 433–4
- dissolution of, land returns to donor, 215–16
- feoffment to use of, 134, 141
- feoffment to uses by, 374
- head of:
    - action without baptismal name, 216
    - deposal of, 217
    - devise by, 375
    - disseisor of abbot becomes successor, 403
    - feoffment to uses without assent of convent, 374
    - infancy of, 420
    - outlawry of abbot, 214
    - presentations laid in abbots, 5
    - resignation of, effect on lease, 217
    - translation of, 216
    - wager of law on contract by predecessor, 264, 433–4
    - misnomer of, 197
- recovery by default, enquiry as to collusion, 117–18
- seised to use, 136
- *see also* mortmain

religious persons:
- Benedictine friar, 1
- bond made to monk and secular person, 349
- may be executors, 324, 419
- remainder after estate granted to monk is void, 328

remainder:
- after fee simple, 363–4
- ambiguous, 440
- in chattel, 228, 272
- contingent remainder, to heir of living person, 84–5, 355
- dependent on precedent estate, 328, 355
- disagreement to, 328, 329
- discontinuance of, 86, 103
- effect of final concord, 145, 146
- grant to three life tenants successively, 98
- limitations:
    - 'in forma praedicta', 271–2, 392, 396
    - to 'heir', 347, 355
    - to 'issue', 347
    - to king, 412
- remitter to, 103
- surrender to remainderman, 360, 370
- in use, 139
- vested before birth of son, 182, 348
- waste by remainderman in fee, 356

remembrance rolls, of filazer, 8

remitter, 102–5, 119, 121, 195, 358
- against one's will, 329
- of disseised tenant, 99
- presumed, where disseisee re-enters, 100
- to fee tail, 51–2, 86, 372, 377–8
- to part, 102, 105
- supposes earlier right, 103
- to remainder, 103

rent:
- apportionment of, 191–3, 247, 290–2
- appurtenant to house, 286, 287
- arrears, extinguished by re-entry, 179–80
- arrears, in father's lifetime, avowry for, 220
- becomes chattel when tenant's estate ends, 379
- collector, charged with what he could have collected, 199
- escheat of, 195
- extinguished:
    - by death of lessor for years, 209
    - by entry, 403